Good schools for young children

Sarah Hammond Leeper

University of Maryland

Dora Sikes Skipper

Florida State University

Ralph L. Witherspoon

University of South Carolina

# of Children

Self Development

AGES 3-4	AGES 5-7

1 Emotions

Self control beginning to be developed; can tolerate some frustration
Becoming more flexible and accepting of alternatives
Likes surprises and unusual stimuli
Sense of humor developing
Developing autonomy requires adult support
Giving and receiving overt affection important for developing emotional health
Fears the dark, being left alone, and strange situations

Expresses feelings freely, often in extreme form (fear, joy, affection, anger, shyness, jealousy)
Inhibition of aggression developing
More accepting and comfortable with separation from parents
Adult reassurance of competence and basic worth essential
Frequent assurance of being loved is important
Sense of humor expressed in riddles, practical jokes, nonsense words

2 Values

Learning values and roles from available adult models
Learning to distinguish between right and wrong
Learning to separate from parents and function independently

Has sense of duty and accomplishment
Developing conscience is in evidence; resulting behavior may be rigid and expressed in extremes, e.g., all right or all wrong
Beginning to accept that there are rules, but does not understand the principles behind them

3 Self

Aware of self as a separate person, and contrasts self with others
Has strong preferences
Shows pride in achievement
Beginning to understand concept of ownership
Aware of sex differences
Desires independence and is capable of some independent activity
Explores: each new experience is a challenge

Clarifies differences between adult and children's world
Achieving independence in physical self care
Gaining practical knowledge necessary for everyday living
Exploration is becoming more goal directed
Learning to forego immediate reward for delayed gratification

Thinking, Language Development

AGES 3-4	AGES 5-7

1 Thinking

Little differentiation of fantasy from reality
Attention span is short; easily distracted, moves from task to task
Many objects can be named. Beginning of categorization: groups objects which look alike or have similar functions
May use numbers without understanding concept of quantity
Judgments made hastily, with many mistakes
Can make a choice between two alternatives
Relates recent experiences with some understanding of sequence
Can follow instructions if not more than two ideas involved
Recall may be limited because what is seen and heard is not categorized or classified
Emotionally significant events are more likely to be remembered

Differentiates more clearly between fantasy and reality
Attention span by age seven shows dramatic lengthening; has ability to shift attention
Concepts largely functional; two things are alike because they occur together or serve the same purpose, e.g., spoon and fork alike because you eat with them
Can order objects on dimensions of size and quantity
Memory good for concrete sequences (numbers, letters), can remember more than two ideas for a short time. By age seven, spontaneous categorization of sights and sounds facilitates remembering. Memory for information enhanced when information presented in a meaningful context
Is able to give more thought to judgments and decisions

2 Language

May differ from others in language usage; is more fluent if accepted
Uses some functional abstract words such as up, down, now
Vocabulary increasing at rapid pace, enjoys talking, can say full name
Advancing sentence structure; uses 4–6 word sentences
Beginning to use words to express feelings
Repetitions of sounds and words are frequent

Learning that words and pictures represent real objects
Relates tales of present and past events
Vocabulary comprehension mostly concrete, e.g., words that represent objects and activities
Understanding of language greater than ability to use language
May use language aggressively
Adults should be aware of language difficulties which impede communication and may require remediation
Can verbalize similarities and analogies

Adapted from "Developmental Characteristics of Children and Youth." © 1975 by The Association for Supervision and Curriculum Development. Used with permission.

Good schools for young children

fourth edition

Macmillan Publishing Co., Inc.
New York
Collier Macmillan Publishers
London

Macmillan Publishing Co., Inc.
866 Third Avenue, New York, New York 10022

Collier Macmillan Canada, Ltd.

Library of Congress Cataloging in Publication Data

Leeper, Sarah Hammond, (date)
Good schools for young children.

   Includes bibliographies and index.
   1.   Education, Preschool—United States—Curricula.
2.   Child development.   3.   Day care centers—United
States.   I.   Skipper, Dora Sikes, joint author.
II.   Witherspoon, Ralph Leo, (date) joint author.
III.   Title.
LB1205.L35 1979   372.21   78-1332
ISBN 0—2-369260-X

Printing: 1 2 3 4 5 6 7 8   Year: 9 0 1 2 3 4 5

preface

Early childhood education during the 1960s and 1970s has been changed and shaped by powerful forces from within and outside the profession. Changing concerns in the society and economy, in theories of learning and child development, and subject matter content have all had their influence.

This fourth edition of *Good Schools for Young Children* includes an examination of these changes and their effect on both content and methods of teaching. Pervading the text of this edition is the consideration of such changes as concern for the culturally different child, children who need uniquely different services and the need for day care and related services, and the continuing need for effective teaching techniques and strategies based on new insights into the development of children. There are helpful suggestions for involving the family in the responsibility for the education of its children.

No longer are all centers planned alike. Instead they are planned according to the needs of the children who are attending the center and their parents. There are infant centers, day care centers, nursery schools, Head Start, kindergartens, cooperatives, and many other types of centers. There are teachers, aides, caregivers, volunteers, nurses, social workers, and psychologists who provide a team approach. Basic values and principles are retained and utilized but the operational procedures vary in different communities and even in centers in the same community.

All persons who guide the development of young children need an understanding of the child, the world, and the forces that influence him/her as well as the basic principles on which decisions are made regarding instruction and practice. This fourth edition has been prepared to fulfill the need of the undergraduate students in early childhood education and teachers who are inexperienced or who have little training in working with young children. The graduate student should also find this book valuable for study and reference in regard to research and practice. Parents, volunteers, and aides who are interested in the development and education of young children will likewise find this book a helpful guide.

The interdisciplinary approach in this volume draws upon the documented research of many disciplines as they affect the educational development of young children. The interrelationship of the culture, the research relating to children, the goals sought, and the practices employed is emphasized. As a basis for planning the program for young children, the findings of research in biological, sociological, and psychological areas are utilized. Factors in the social scene that influence children, their homes, and their family life, along with their implications for programs for young children, are included. Examples of activities and procedures are emphasized.

Extensive lists of related readings and of suggested activities are to be found at the end of each chapter. The photographs, illustrations, and case records are of real persons in actual situations and activities. They are used to clarify and extend concepts.

The book is divided into three parts:

Part I, "Why Centers for Young Children?," considers the young child as a person and the importance of the early years of life. The impact of changes in living styles, child abuse, housing, TV, mobility of population, mothers in gainful employment, changing roles of women, and conflicting philosophies of education is interpreted in the light of program needs. The goals of education for young children in a democracy and the guidance and discipline the child receives are discussed. Current developments in providing qualified personnel and the development and maintenance of adequate standards for children's programs are described. Each major component of early childhood education is placed in historical perspective to show the development of current trends.

Part II, "The Curriculum: Planning and Teaching," develops the school/center program within the framework of the concepts presented in Part I. Each subject area is planned to take these factors into account. Suggested teaching strategies, activities, and learning encounters are discussed and examples presented for each subject area. Plans for developing key concepts (units) are included. In planning and teaching, however, the subject areas are not isolated; they are interrelated in treating the concerns that young children have and wish to pursue.

Part III, "Organizing Centers for Young Children," concentrates on details essential to the organization of a good program for children, records and reports, physical facilities and equipment, working with children who have uniquely different needs, parental involvement, and transition to the first grade.

The fourth edition has many new photographs. The reference list has been

updated and expanded. The number of "Suggested Activities" has been increased and titles of films included. A listing of organizations and agencies
providing educational and related services to young children is also included.

   Much of the material of earlier editions has been rewritten However, a conscious effort has been made to preserve the qualities that have made the book
distinctive. *Good Schools for Young Children* continues to be a comprehensive and practical guide for those working with young children.

S. H. L.
D. S. S.
R. L. W.

acknowledgments

In the development of each edition of *Good Schools for Young Children,* the authors are deeply indebted to their families, friends, and professional associates at the Florida State University, the University of Maryland, and the University of South Carolina: Sarah Blackford, Nancy Douglas, Margaret Casson, Geraldine Edwards, Julia Fussell, Harriet Harlan, Lucy Harrison, Anna Lane, LaMattice Pearson, and Susie Whitener at the Florida State University, assisted with the first edition.

The following persons helped with the second edition: at the Florida State University, Myles Ritchie, Phyllis C. Smith, and Donald W. Rapp; at the University of Maryland, Glenn O. Blough, Jo Graham, Joan E. Moyer, Miriam E. Quigley, and Tupper D. Webster.

In the development of the third edition the following persons were most helpful: Robert R. Leeper, Colin K. Ducolon, Jean C. Findley, Arlene Friedland, April Garrard, Nancy Goldsmith, Cynthia Jones, Elizabeth T. King, Helen Rubin, Tupper Webster; the faculty of the Department of Early Childhood-Elementary Education and the Center for Young Children, University of Maryland; and Dean John C. Otts and the Early Childhood faculty of the College of Education, University of South Carolina.

Grateful appreciation is expressed to all those who helped in developing the fourth edition: Robert R. Leeper for guidance, inspiration, and editorial assistance; Kathleen Witherspoon for patience and encouragement; Lloyd C. Chilton, Jr. for continuing guidance and counsel; Jim Nolting, Virginia State College, and Charlene Rothkopf, ASCD, for photography; Mrs. Alexander's School, Beverly, MS., Jimmie L. Battle, Jean C. Findley, Mary and J. B. Hawkes, Nancy Goldsmith, Gail Linville, Nancy Mallory, Frances Midkiff,

J. E. Pflum, Jane Smart, Margaret G. Weiser, and Davis L. Williams for photographs and illustrative material: Henry Sublett and the faculty of the Early Childhood-Elementary Department and Marilyn Church and the faculty and staff of the Center for Young Children, College of Education, University of Maryland; and R. Eleanor Duff, Martha Heinz, Mary Leslie Hudson, Charlene Husband, Jeannie James, Sara Lovingwood, and Kevin T. Swick of the University of South Carolina Early Childhood Education Program; Sally Mullins of Richland County, S.C. School District 2; and Elizabeth A. Evans and Ross L. Witherspoon of the Leon County Public Schools, Tallahassee, Florida, and Mabel Jean Morrison of the Okaloosa County Schools, Crestview, Florida.

Permission to use selected portions of the chart "Developmental Characteristics of Children and Youth" was granted by the Association for Supervision and Curriculum Development and is gratefully acknowledged.

Credits for photographs follow: Center for Young Children, University of Maryland (Charles Bohn) 10, 11, 15C, D, 20D, 29A, B, 32, 36A, 37, 41, 42, 45A, B, 46A, B, C, 50, 52, 60A, 62A, B, C, 64, 68, 75, 77, (Charlene Rothkopf) 1B, 2, 6A, B, 7, 8, 14A, 16, 21A, B, C, 27A, 31A, 36B, 38, 45C, 54, 55, 58B, C, 59A, 61, 69B, 70A, B, C, 71B, 72D; Early Childhood Education Center, University of Iowa 13, 30B, 60C, 69A, 73A, B, 81; Fred Dickson 15A; Rita Eisenberg 39, 72A, B, C; Elizabeth Jenkins School, Millersville State College (Amos Hess) 1A, 3, 19, 20B, C, 51B, 60B, 63A, 76; April Garrard 24, 34, 43, 67; Mimi D. Harrington 5A, B, C, 29C, 65; J. B. Hawkes 20A, 31B, 49B, 51A, 58A, 63C, 71A, Picture Part I; Head Start 14B, 15B, 23, (James Foote) 25, 40, 47, 53, 56, 79, Picture Part III; Robert R. Leeper 4B; Helen Rubin 80; Center for Young Children, Virginia State College (Jim Nolting) 4, 17A, B, 18, 22A, B, 26, 28, 29D, 30A, C, 44, 49A, 57, 59B, 63B, 66, 74, Picture Part II.

contents

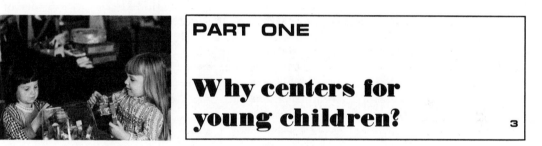

PART ONE

Why centers for young children?

3

3 The young child as a person 46

4 The young child and research 70

PART TWO
The curriculum: planning and teaching   **179**

PART THREE

Organizing centers for young children **463**

Good
schools
for
young
children

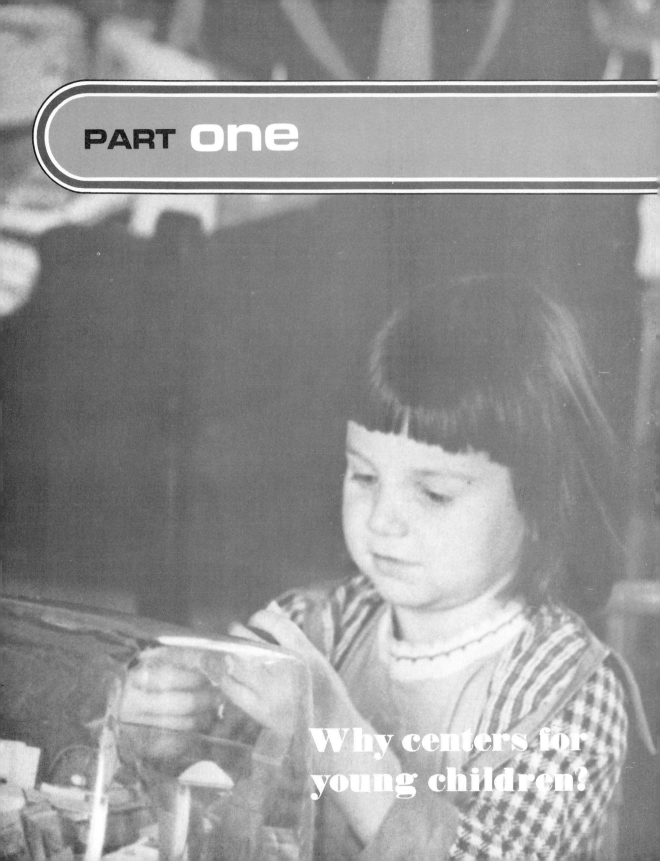

PART **one**

Why centers for young children?

Photo on previous page courtesy of Head Start.

chapter 1

The early years: their importance

Historically, young children below public school age have been primarily the responsibility of their parents, as far as nurturance and personal guidance are concerned. Consequently, there was no hectic rush to have Junior "parked" for the day at an early morning hour so mom and dad could arrive at work on time. However, as of this writing, various authorities estimate that approximately half of all children too young to enter public school have mothers who are gainfully employed, most of them full time. This means that provision for minimal "safe" care must be available for large numbers of very young children.

Currently there is no firm public commitment to provide such care for all children. While there has been growing acceptance of such provision for children of low-income families, public opinion has not convinced lawmakers to make programs suitable for the optimum development of young children generally available for all children prior to the age required for admission to the public schools. Since there is much interest in public support of these programs, it is possible that, as you read this book, your community may have provided funds for educational and day care programs for all preschool children whose parents desire such services.

IMPORTANCE OF EARLY EDUCATION

Safe care, health, and social services—these are the concerns that have dominated most efforts on behalf of young children, with education placed among the lower priorities. This has occurred despite rather convincing evidence that the early years represent the time in one's life when educational efforts are most promising. This is, in fact, the thrust of Early Childhood Education.

Growth of kindergartens

Since the first publication of this text in 1963, many exciting advances have been made in the field of Early Childhood Education. Breathtaking developments have occurred so rapidly that revisions were necessary in 1968 and again in 1974. Public school kindergartens have become a reality in most states. Many of the states have passed legislation that permits the funding and operation of comprehensive developmental programs for select four- and five-year-olds. The trend has been to make the implementation permissive, rather than mandatory, except for kindergarten and for children with handicapping conditions. Yet at this writing most three- and four-year-old children in group programs outside the home are under the funding and direction of public and private agencies and/or individuals other than the public schools. Most of the programs for prekindergarten children that are supported by public funds are limited to groups with special needs. These include children from low-income families, children whose mothers work outside the home, and children from families with culturally or linguistically different backgrounds. Children from these groups may also attend programs supported by government or foundations which serve as pilot, research, or experimental programs. Nevertheless, prekindergarten enrollments increased rapidly during the 1960s and early 1970s: 0.7 million prekindergarten children enrolled in 1967 as compared to 1.6 million by 1974. Of the latter number, 422,000 were enrolled in

A

B

Figure 1
The early years of a child's life may well be the most crucial as far as opportunities for effective educational experiences are concerned.

public facilities against 1,182,000 in nonpublic centers.[1] This burgeoning increase grew primarily out of the belief in the importance of the programs as compensation for early social and economic disadvantages. Emphasis was also placed on acceleration of cognitive development, especially in research and so-called model programs.

Social and educational trends

The 1970s witnessed larger public expenditures for Early Childhood Education than were made in this field prior to the mid-1960s. By the mid-1970s, in keeping with other economic trends, funding for Early Childhood Education had stabilized, and in some cases it had decreased. Evaluation and accountability had become important components of the process as those in charge of the purse strings attempted to find ways to assure taxpayers of the best possible results for each dollar spent. The result was that academic achievement became a major objective, and more structured activities began to take shape in the daily schedules. Combination care and educational programs with more flexible hours to meet the time schedules of the families involved became commonplace. Because parents were still recognized as the prime child-rearing agents in society, they were forced to become involved in every activity of the educational process. Such involvement included a decision-making role regarding what their children were to be taught, under what conditions, and by whom.

Continuing inflationary trends, an ever-increasing national debt, and unstable economic conditions in the sixties and seventies all had increased the need for assistance in many areas of life. More than half the mothers of young children were gainfully employed outside the home. In almost all cases, the father in intact families was employed as well. These conditions called for alternate means of providing for the health, safety, education, and nurturance of very young children, often infants less than a year old. By 1977, widely publicized government findings indicated that more than half the households consisted of one or two persons only. Elementary and middle schools were feeling the impact of these population trends toward fewer or no children in young families. Birthrate patterns and population statistics were changing so rapidly in the direction of fewer children that conflicting statements regarding family size, divorce rates, number of gainfully employed mothers of young children, and family structure were constantly appearing in the news media, college texts, popular books, and magazine articles intended for lay consumption.

[1] *1976 Databook the Status of Education Research and Development in the United States* (Washington, D.C.: The National Institute of Education, U.S. Department of Health, Education and Welfare, 1976), *p.* 6.

Although a change of direction is anticipated as the population majority shifts to those over the age of fifty, as indeed it has at the time of this writing, the economic need for children will once again be felt by younger families as they find themselves among a minority that must provide for a larger segment of the population, the aged. The provision of services and assistance to the aging majority population will make evident the need for a larger workforce. Consequently, larger families may be expected.

During the time span covered by this text in its previous three editions, many trends affecting young children have emerged. Changing lifestyles brought about by the rise of an industrialized and business-oriented society have created new family needs and activities. Divorce has become common and accepted by most groups. Large numbers of children are raised in one-parent (either male or female) families. While the increased divorce rate has accentuated this trend, many unmarried mothers have, by choice or by need, elected to raise their children without a male lifetime partner. Communal and multiple mothering arrangements flourished during the 1960s. However, recent years have seen a lessening of this trend. Even the much heralded Israeli Kibbutz as a child-rearing mode has given way to the more traditional family structure and child-rearing patterns.[2] According to a news item in *Extra*, September 1977, only 7 percent of American families are now typical. The "typical" family was defined as having a breadwinner husband, a homemaker wife, and two children. These findings were from a Department of Labor survey. The same source reports that a childless couple with both members working appears to be more typical than any other family structure. However, more than 46 percent of women with children under 18 years of age were then employed.[3] Obviously, although fewer children are being born, the number needing some nurturance outside the home has greatly increased.

Publicly funded innovation

The increasing need for day-care centers and other types of services for children below first-grade age has been recognized and backed by government at both the state and federal levels, with funds granted for ongoing experimental, research, and pilot programs for preschool-age children. All these programs share an understanding of the importance of parent involvement for the best possible development of their children. It is likely that the need for care services for young children will continue to increase to become an established and accepted part of American life. The value of early education is becoming increasingly appreciated by the public schools; they will most proba-

[2] Benjamin Beit-Hallahmi and A. L. Rabin, "The Kibbutz as a Social Experiment and as a Child-Rearing Laboratory," *Am. Psychol.*, 32:7 (1977), pp. 532–541.

[3] Sara Fritz, "Only 7 Per Cent of U.S. Families Now Typical," *Extra* (September 1977).

bly participate more in the future in such programs. The population trend has freed space in elementary school buildings, and a surplus of elementary—and in many instances early childhood—education teachers is beginning to develop. It has been demonstrated that, with proper in-service techniques, teachers of elementary school-age children can rather quickly and efficiently be taught to work competently with younger children.[4]

Integrated schools and centers for young children have been established in most sections of the country. In many instances, this has meant busing children away from their residential neighborhoods, often eliminating within-walking-distance neighborhood schools and other neighborhood community facilities. In those communities in which mixed racial housing is now a fact, the opportunity for a return to neighborhood children's programs and to neighborhood schools is becoming possible.

PROGRAMS FOR DIFFERING NEEDS

The time period under consideration has seen continuing improvement in opportunities for culturally different groups. Integrated housing and schools, innovative and adequately funded educational programs, better health and other human need delivery systems, guaranteed equal opportunity employment, equal rights in other areas, and the women's liberation movement have all enabled hitherto denied provisions for decision making. Such provisions have resulted in more creative participation of the many culturally different groups in the mainstream of American life and society.

Public acceptance of altered lifestyles brought about by these changes has brought about a need for adequate care and improved educational opportunities for large numbers of America's young below the traditional public school-age children. Public schools for older children have felt the impact of change; they have made, and continue to make, significant strides in creating innovative experiences to better meet the needs of all children. One such innovation is the creation of prekindergarten experiences in preparation for later cognitive achievement. It should be pointed out that a research effort of considerable magnitude has been launched in order to find ways to help children who might not be able to cope with the demands of public school when they become eligible to attend. In fact, the early years have enjoyed the efforts of researchers and funding agencies on a scale never anticipated before the mid-1960s.

[4] Minnie P. Berson and C. E. Sherman, "Divergent Views on Prekindergarten Teacher Education," *Educ. Leadership*, 34:2 (1976), pp. 142–149.

Interest, need, and research findings have translated into a great deal of expense and effort for the development of new materials, new methods, and model curricula for use with infants and preschool-age children. Delivery systems in operation range from computer-assisted individualized instruction in the home to elaborate and highly structured school or center arrangements. Perhaps this diversity represents one of the greatest strengths of Early Childhood Education, whether found in public schools or in private-for-profit offerings or as a service to employees of business or factory. Almost every community in the country has children's preschool child care centers operated by private individuals. In some cases, business firms provide child care programs for children of employees. It is significant that the private sector of society, including business and industry is involved along with public agencies and the public schools.

Professional responsibility

A tremendous responsibility is placed upon the care centers and schools and their caregivers and teachers, for everyone believes that children are the hope of the future. Schools and other provisions for care and education cannot afford to ignore either the mistakes of the past or the gains. Today's world is far more complicated than ever before, and there is a growing feeling that the demands on every life, if not properly met, can be disastrous. But what about the first half-decade of life? How prepared are today's young children for the demands of school? Does it matter, educationally, what has gone before? Until recently, in America, there has been little concern for the education of the very young child. This responsibility has been assumed to be that of the child's parents and immediate family.

Although parents today are better educated, our educational system has given little attention to preparation for marriage, to studies of home and family life, to a consideration of child-rearing practices, or to the values and needs of those who are culturally different. Most information of this type is left to their own experience, to certain professional personnel such as the pediatrician or family doctor, and to the flood of conflicting views found in all types of popular books, magazines, and newspapers. Consequently, many children approach their first group experience away from home with fear and trepidation. Some come with severe unavoidable physical, mental, and/or emotional handicaps as well. Fortunately, this latter group constitutes a small minority of the total child population. Nevertheless, their needs are real and must be provided for. Federal Public Law 94-142, enacted November 29, 1975, is designed to assure that all handicapped children between the ages of 3 and 18 will have available to them a free appropriate public education.

Salable skills

During the 1960s, the ever-increasing affluence of American economic life and of the demands of a complex technological society made it apparent that those who lacked special skills and advanced education were at a great disadvantage. The public school, with its relatively late entrance age, had become less and less able to cope with the two or three years' learning retardation present at school entrance in children from low-income homes and from some culturally different homes. Researchers had found that young children lacking the opportunity to experience a learning environment common to middle-class children had great difficulty in bridging the gap. They often became early school dropouts, later joining the ranks of the unemployed.

In an effort to break the poverty cycle thus engendered, the federal government beginning in the mid-1960s has set up unprecedented funds for the education of children from such homes—especially for preschool-age children. Thus the value of early education quickly became popular and the young child was "rediscovered" by educators, the public, and the parents. While slow to accept the responsibility, the public schools must accept the challenge and be prepared to meet the unique needs of these children as well as those of the great majority for whom the conditions of nature and nurture have been more favorable.

Bridging the gap

During the 1960s, the realization that one fourth of the children entering first grade were academically retarded by one to three years called for a reevaluation of the educational system. The public schools in the United States came under severe attack. Costs continued to rise, citizens revolted at rising taxes, and bonds issues were repeatedly voted down in many communities. Crime and delinquency were on the rise and high school dropouts increased. The federal government was called on to provide more funds to bolster the school system. Children primarily from low-income families had been denied the early experiential opportunities so necessary for normal cognitive growth enjoyed by their counterparts from middle- and upper-income families. Early (preschool) education for the first time in the history of the nation became the priority educational concern of educators, communities, and government.

Recently, the mother of a five-year-old started a conversation in the following manner: "Is it true that the first few years of a child's life are the most important?" Without waiting for a reply, she added, "I feel so helpless now that Mary is five years old. I'm afraid I have made too many mistakes and that there is nothing I can do about them now!" Such concepts often stem from only partially understanding what is written in popular articles about the young child, and far too often from the rather perfunctory treatment given child psychology in many introductory textbooks on psychology and child development. Emphasis on the futility of aiding the child's personality after the age of five could easily arise as a result of reading some of the popular interpretations of Freudian psychology. On the other hand, until the impact of Freud's theories began to be felt in the early part of the present century, it was all too commonly believed that the early years were unimportant as long as the physical needs of the child were met.

The questions asked by Mary's mother and by many young mothers today reveal the fears mothers have of frustrating their children by disciplining them, or of developing overdependent children by not giving them enough attention. Many have developed guilt feelings about not being "good mothers." It is generally agreed that the present generation of parents is more concerned about the personality development of their children than was shown by any previous generation of parents. Parents' misconceptions of how personality is influenced, and the lack of understanding on the part of adults in general as to what to expect developmentally from children, point dramatically to the need for study and planning by all persons who teach or work with young children.

To some, education of young children means very little other than what the child happens to learn before starting school, usually at the age of six. To many, education begins with the entrance to a public school. Others realize that there are nursery schools and kindergartens for younger children, but to many it is not necessary that they be "real" schools. Most parents, however, are unaware that play schools, day care and child development centers, nursery schools, and kindergartens are not just different names for the same services. They tend to think of them all as "schools." The importance of understanding these differences will be considered in detail in later chapters.

In recent years, many parents have come to feel that a good nursery school or child development center is a "must" for their children because they believe that what happens to a child's personality and attitudes during the preschool years is very important to later development. They also recognize that the teacher or caregiver has had, or they expect that he or she has had, special training for the work, a competency that most parents of young children feel they themselves sadly lack. Yet others feel that a child under six is "still a baby" and needs to be treated as one. These persons think that mothers can provide, at home, all the education that is necessary.

Research conducted during the late 1950s and the early 1960s (to be discussed in Chapter 4) had clearly demonstrated that at a very early age a child can master rather complex learnings, such as the abilities to read and to master complex mathematical concepts. Concurrently, emphasis on the necessity of a college education was increasing, and the demands for more and better education caused parents to become greatly concerned about the adequacy of their children's education. It was logical to assume that the more a child learned as early as possible, the better his or her chances would be to meet college entrance requirements. The proponents of a child-centered philosophy for nursery and kindergarten programs found themselves widely criticized by a new influx of researchers and scholars who held that the mastery of knowledge was not only possible and desirable at an early age, but necessary to later school success. It is small wonder that parents were worried if their children were not taught to read in kindergarten. (Throughout this text, the authors have carefully evaluated research and implemented the findings in terms of programs of instruction without losing sight of the values inherent in earlier programs with their heavy emphasis on the needs of children at various maturation and developmental levels.)

HISTORICAL PERSPECTIVE

Interest in schools for young children is not a modern innovation. In 1657 Comenius, in *The Great Didactic*,[5] advocated the Mother's School for the first six years of life. There was to be a Mother's School in every home for every child. He also advocated prenatal education for mothers. The course of study prescribed in his *School of Infancy*, first published in German in 1633, contained "Simple lessons in objects, taught to know stones, plants, and animals; the names and uses of the members of the body; to distinguish light and darkness and colors; the Geography of the cradle, the room, the farm, the street, and the field; trained in moderation, purity and obedience, and taught to say the Lord's Prayer,"[6] Comenius wrote the first picture book for children in 1658, the famous *Orbis Pictus*.[7] This book has been widely used and translated into every major language in the world.

Published in 1762, Rousseau's *Emile* gave great impetus to the importance of beginning education early.[8] Rousseau felt education should commence at birth and be continued until twenty-five years of age. He stressed the need for allowing natural development rather than preparation for later life—"the first of all blessings is not authority, but liberty. This is my fundamental maxim. We have but to apply it to childhood, and all the rules of education will flow from it." Rousseau's fundamental concept was that sense perception is the only true foundation of human knowledge.

During the early years of the nineteenth century, Frederick Froebel, influenced by the earlier work of Pestalozzi, became convinced that the most

[5] J. A. Comenius (Komensky), *The Great Didactic*, de Geer Family, Amsterdam, 1657.

[6] W. S. Monroe (ed.), *Comenius' School of Infancy* (Boston: D. C. Heath, 1908), p. ix.

[7] J. A. Comenius (Komensky), *Orbis Pictus*, Nuremberg, 1658. (Syracuse, N.Y.: C. W. Bardeen, 1887).

[8] J. J. Rousseau, *Emile*, trans. Barbara Foxley (London: J. M. Dent, 1911), p. 48.

needed educational reform concerned the early childhood years.[9] He considered carefully planned play materials essential to the proper education of the young. His gifts and occupations were not mere materials used in play for the sake of play. Rather, proper use of the gifts or material objects and the occupations or play activities expressed spiritual principles of deep philosophic significance essential to the child's proper development. Society is indebted to Froebel for the kindergarten idea, which recognized the educational value of play. The first kindergarten was established in Blackenberg in 1842, and the first kindergarten training college was founded by Baroness Bertha von Marenholtz Bülow-Wendhausen, a disciple of Froebel, in 1870 at Dresden. Mrs. Carl Schurz, a pupil of Froebel, established the first kindergarten in the United States at Watertown, Wisconsin, in 1855. This was a German-speaking kindergarten. The first English-speaking kindergarten in the United States was privately operated by Miss Elizabeth Peabody in Boston in 1860. A significant event in the history of education in the United States occurred in 1873 when Susan E. Blow (with William T. Harris) established the first public school kindergarten in St. Louis, Missouri. The following decade witnessed rapid developments in kindergarten education. Since the 1880s the kindergarten movement has had its ups and downs, often giving way to the pressures of the times for public education at other levels. Recent emphasis on quality education, higher education, and the sciences tended to de-emphasize the importance of kindergarten and nursery school education.

In the United States the early 1960s witnessed a revival of Early Childhood Education for exactly the same reason that early education had been advocated so often in the past by such leaders as Froebel, Montessori, the McMillan sisters, and many others. Conditions of the times had created slum cultures that produced serious social problems. In each case it was recognized that the lack of experience in early cognitive manipulations resulted in later incompetence and lack of self-esteem which proved difficult to overcome. Children from better homes seemed to escape these problems; it was therefore thought that early education in the slum home was inadequate. Projects such as Head Start had the same goals as those sponsored by the followers of Froebel, by Montessori, and by the McMillans.

Between periods of social crises, nursery and kindergarten education continued in a limited way, usually without public support but for quite different reasons. Middle- and upper-class parents believed that early education was essential to later school success, or at least necessary to maintaining family status in the community. Although there is evidence that Early Childhood Education found an acceptable place in the academic world during the 1960s, only time will tell the outcome.

In the search for panaceas and quick results, the Montessori approach

---

[9] F. Froebel, *The Education of Man* (New York: Appleton-Century-Crofts, 1903).

promised an answer. Montessori schools quickly became popular and were glamorized by magazines, television, and the news media. Maria Montessori began her work with slum children in Rome in 1907. A medical doctor by profession, she developed methods and accompanying materials that are used in today's schools exactly as she prescribed in the early 1900s. Her principal contributions lie in the emphasis on learning and the importance of the environment in the learning process. However, today's teacher of young children should be familiar enough with the total field of Early Childhood Education to choose which of the Montessori concepts, materials, and procedures will best serve children in the context of today's individual and cultural needs. The pros and cons of Montessori are objectively set forth in *Montessori in Perspective*.[10] Students of Early Childhood Education should become familiar with the history of education in the United States in order to understand thoroughly how the needs of society affect educational programs.

TODAY'S NEED

Analysis of the U.S. Census data reveals statistics vital to those involved in planning programs for young children. In 1970, of the 55 million children under fourteen years of age in the United States 18,013,000 were under five years of age. The next four years witnessed a dramatic change: The number of children under the age of fourteen had dropped to 50,386,000, and the number under the age of five was down to 16,304,000, representing decrements of 8.4 percent and 9.5 percent, respectively. This trend is reflected through 1974 in the falling birthrate.

Nevertheless, the Census Bureau anticipates a reversal in the birth statistics some time in the late seventies to the year 2000. According to this projection, by the turn of the century there will be 70,577,000 children under the age of fourteen (up 40.1 percent) and 24,654,000 under the age of five (up 51.2 percent).[11] At the time of this writing (March 1978) there had been several news reports that the trend in the number of births had started upward as predicted, with the largest increase in number of live births in 25 years occurring during 1977. This does not necessarily mean that the birthrate has changed. The increase in the number of births was likely due to the fact that there were a larger number of women of child-bearing age who were born during or toward the end of the baby boom years. The average number of children in the family remains small compared to earlier years in America's history.

When mothers of young children work outside the home, a need for alter-

---

[10] Evelyn Beyer et al. (eds.), *Montessori in Perspective* (Washington, D.C.: NAEYC, 1971).

[11] *Statistical Abstracts of the United States 1976* (Washington, D.C.: U.S. Department of Commerce, Bureau of the Census, 1976), p. 6.

Figure 2
Many young children have mothers who work outside the home. The increasing need for daytime care and other types of services for children is being recognized today.

nate forms of child rearing is created. It is interesting to note that the female labor force as percent of the total female population increased from 27.4 percent in 1940 to 45.9 percent in 1975. During the same time period the number of employed married women rose from 16.7 percent to 45 percent, and the number of widowed or divorced women rose from 32 percent to 37.8 percent of the total number of women employed.[12] By 1975, 21 percent of the mothers of children under 6 years of age, married with husband present, were counted in the labor force.[13] What effect does the fact that so many working mothers who are married, widowed, or divorced, have on this generation of preschool children? With their mothers working outside the home, most of these children receive little or no education other than that provided by maids, relatives, or the numerous day care centers and babysitting services, many of which are inadequate and, in some instances, are actually harmful to the normal development of the children involved.[14] The situation remained much the same in 1977, for large numbers of families still needed educational, as well as care, opportunities for their children.

In 1975, the average weekly earnings for white women were $138 and for black women $130, with black women earning 92.4 percent as much as white women. The same percentage differential in 1970 was 85.3 percent, indicating a relative economic gain for black women during the 1970–1975 time span.[15]

Few people are aware that in 1974 children under five years of age accounted for 7.6 percent of the population in the United States. The important 10-year span from 25 through 34 only amounted to 14 percent, while 19.4 percent were 55 years of age and older, and 10.3 percent were 65 and older. Only

[12] Ibid., p. 358.
[13] Ibid., p. 359.
[14] *Profiles*, White House Conference on Children, 1970 (Washington, D.C.: Superintendent of Documents, U.S. Government Printing Office, 1970), p. 85.
[15] *Statistical Abstracts of the United States 1976*, op. cit., p. 377.

8 percent of the total population were in the adolescent years 14 through 17. This latter group included the senior high school and lower college-age group where proportionately more dollars are spent for educational purposes.[16] It should be noted that as the more dependent over-65 age group continues to increase, there will be a need for more children to replace the labor force to balance the scale. On the basis of previous patterns, it is predicted that the birthrate will increase and that children will be more valued by society than they were at the time of this writing.

Despite the above conditions and trends, the provision for the care and education of young children outside the home by other than family members is far from adequate, and the need will increase in the years ahead. Next to the growing number of two-parent working families, the second strongest force in the increasing demand for making available supplemental child care and education to all citizens grows out of recent discoveries concerning the importance of early experience on human growth and development. Psychologists, pediatricians, psychiatrists, educators, nutritionists, anthropologists, and other investigators continue to document the critical significance of the first years of life.[17] Despite this interdisciplinary approach and the increasing recognition of the importance of the early years of life to laying the groundwork for effective education, prevailing conditions make the adequate provision of programs for young children difficult at best.

Education and the early years

While the nation was experiencing a severe case of jitters during the late 1950s after its "late start" in the Space Age race, practically nothing was being spent on the education of preschool-age children. Despite that major preoccupation, the twentieth century has witnessed a shift to intensive research in Early Childhood Education because of the many theoretical points of view concerning the importance of the early years to the later development and behavior of the individual. In view of transformed socioeconomic patterns and family environment in the United States and the rapidly expanding body of scientific knowledge relative to the importance of the education of the young child, could it be that lack of public concern for education for children under the age of six is another unfortunate "late start"? A detailed discussion of these factors is presented in the materials prepared for the deliberations of the 1960 White House Conference on Children and Youth.[18]

[16] Ibid., p. 6.

[17] *Report to the President,* White House Conference on Children, 1970 (Washington, D.C.: Superintendent of Documents, U.S. Government Printing Office, 1970), p. 276.

[18] E. Ginzberg (ed.), *The Nation's Children,* 3 vols., and *Children and Youth in the 1960's, Survey Papers* (Washington D.C.: The Golden Anniversary White House Conference on Children and Youth, Inc., 1960).

Figure 3
When one considers the importance of language throughout life, education during the foundation years becomes increasingly important.

Noting the needs of young children in the world in which they found themselves, delegates to the 1960 White House Conference on Children and Youth stressed that nursery schools, kindergartens, day care centers, and other children's groups be open to children of all socioeconomic levels, creeds, and national origins. They further recommended that every group of young children away from home be under the supervision of at least one person qualified in the field of Early Childhood Education.[19] It is of significance to note that the *Report to the President* issued by the 1970 White House Conference on Children made virtually the same recommendations.[20]

Much has been written and a great deal of research has been done about the early years of life. For example, one of the preschool child's greatest achievements is the basic mastery of a spoken language. While there are great individual differences, first-grade children have an average vocabulary of 23,700 words, and some first graders may know 48,800 words.[21] Typically a child ac-

---

[19] *Conference Proceedings* (Washington, D.C.: The Golden Anniversary White House Conference on Children and Youth, Inc., 1960).

[20] *Report to the President,* op. cit.

[21] Mary K. Smith, "Measurement of the Size of General English Vocabulary Through the Elementary Grades and High School," *Genet. Psychol. Monogr., 24*:2(1941), pp. 311–345.

quires a reasonable mastery of the spoken language between the ages of one and five.[22]

When one considers the importance of language throughout life, education during the foundation years becomes increasingly important. Many fields of research and knowledge are required to correctly interpret the needs of this period of development. The science of child development attempts an integration of these various aspects of knowledge in an effort to understand the factors at work in the development of the whole child. Although a young science, great strides have been made that point to the importance of education in the early childhood years. While their suggested procedures are not always applicable to today's child, much that the early educational philosophers believed to be true of the nature of childhood has been reaffirmed by present scientific research.

With the rediscovery of the importance of the early years to later development, research productivity using infants and young children as subjects reached a new high during the late 1950s and 1960s. For this reason, selected research as related to Early Childhood Education is presented in Chapter 4 of this text.

In Chapter 2 the young child is discussed in relationship to today's world and to our present concept of the child as a person. It should help you develop an awareness and knowledge of the growth of children as a factor to be considered in planning for young children and as a basis for planning and evaluating educational practice.

Suggested Activities

1. Using the most recent census data, determine how many children in your home (or college) community are three through six years of age. Find out how many are in some kind of nursery school or kindergarten. What proportion of the children in the three-to-eighteen age group fall in the three-to-six-year age group? In what proportion of homes in your community does a need exist for nursery schools, kindergartens, or all-day care centers? Plan a discussion on the need for nursery schools, or kindergartens, or both. Include members of the community other than teachers in this discussion.
2. It has been said that most communities cannot afford education for children of nursery school and kindergarten age because the need is so great for better education for children in grades 1 through 12. Gather facts and present arguments for or against this statement.
3. Contact your state department of education for statistics concerning the number of new kindergartens and other preschool programs established during the past five years. Chart or plot your findings. Explain the change.

[22] Dorothea McCarthy, "Language Development in Children," in *Manual of Child Psychology*, 2nd ed., edited by L. Carmichael (New York: John Wiley and Sons, 1954), p. 494.

4. Because of changing social and fiscal conditions, parents and those responsible for education are crying for results and "accountability." Check with several programs in the community and report what each is doing about this concern.

Related Readings

Aties, Phillippe. *Centuries of Childhood.* New York: Vintage Books, 1965.

Baylor, Ruth M. *Elizabeth Palmer Peabody.* Philadelphia, Pa.: University of Pennsylvania Press, 1965.

Castaneda, Alfreda, et al. *The Educational Needs of Minority Groups.* Lincoln, Nebraska: Professional Educator's Publications, 1974.

Church, J. (ed.). *Three Babies.* New York: Random House, 1966.

Cowen, E. L. *New Ways in School Mental Health.* New York: Human Sciences Press, 1975.

Davis, G. *Childhood and History in America.* New York: The Psychohistory Press, 1976.

Demause, L. *The History of Childhood.* New York: The Psychohistory Press, 1974.

Frank, L. K. *On the Importance of Infancy.* New York: Random House, 1966.

Gardner, J. E. *Paraprofessionals Work with Troubled Children.* New York: John Wiley and Sons, 1975.

Gartner, A., et al. (eds.). *Paraprofessionals in Education.* New York: Human Sciences Press, 1976.

Growing Free: Ways to Help Children Overcome Sex-Role Stereotypes. Washington, D.C.: ACEI, 1976.

Hildebrand, Verna. *Introduction to Early Childhood Education.* New York: Macmillan Publishing Co., 1976.

Hymes, J. L. *Early Childhood Education: The Year in Review.* Carmel, Calif.: Hacienda Press, annually since 1975.

Katz, Lillian G. (ed.). *Current Topics in Early Childhood Education*, Vol. 1. Hillsdale, N.J.: Lawrence Erlbaum Assoc., 1977.

Leidermann, H. P., et al. (eds.). *Culture and Infancy.* New York: Academic Press, 1977.

Marbach, Ellen S. *A Creative Kindergarten.* Provo, Utah: Brigham Young University Press, 1977.

Rasmussen, Margaret (ed.). *Readings from Childhood Education.* Washington, D.C.: ACEI, 1966.

Verma, Gajendra, and C. Bagley. *Race and Education Across Cultures.* Stamford, Conn.: Graylock Publishers, 1976.

chapter 2

The young child's world

During their lifetime, the adults responsible for the young child's care and guidance have seen many changes in society, but they may not recognize that the present is the only world known to the young child. It is difficult for older adults, who so vividly remember their own childhood, to appreciate that young children, even young adults, cannot even relate to the recent past agrarian and village and small-city cultural society which was America when they were growing up. If children are to understand and connect with their rich heritage, the daily curricular offerings will have to provide opportunities for experiencing some of the activities in which their forebears engaged in the process of living. Visiting farms, forests, and blacksmith shops, making butter, and learning how to grow vegetables will give today's youngsters a taste of what life was like in days gone by. It will also bring them closer to older people who were brought up in that quite different world.

THE CHANGING CHILD

Improvements in the means of travel and mobility associated with career opportunities have been such that many young children, long before their entrance to first grade, have traveled a great deal and have lived in many different and varied communities. Their eyes have thus been opened to a wider variety of experiences than that of many of the significant adults in their lives at the time of their entrance into preschool programs of whatever kind.

Although today the young child's world clearly offers more opportunities, it has a two-pronged effect, for it can equally be both confining and restricting, as well as frustrating and anxiety producing. Today's child is influenced by many forces outside the home and family, some of which are social, some economic, some political, and others philosophical. The child's individual personality is molded by the pressures and decrees of society. In addition, the child's development is shaped by others in the life space—by parents, other adults, peers, and siblings. The behavior of those who bring up and instruct

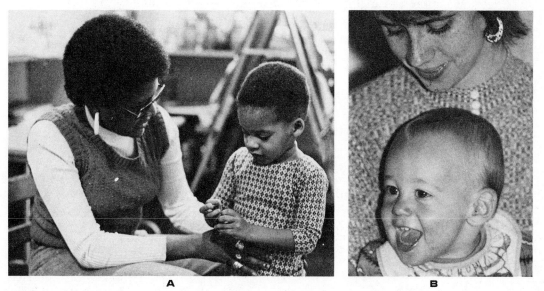

A   B

Figure 4
Young children are influenced by many forces, especially by persons around them—
parents, other adults, peers, and siblings.

the child is also affected by the influences of society, and this enters the total equation in the way it is reflected in the child's development.

INFLUENCE OF TELEVISION

A prime example of an all-pervasive and taken-for-granted influence on childrens' lives is television. Most significant has been the universal availability of television from birth on. Estimates vary, but most authorities agree that, in terms of time involved, television eclipses all other categories of influences when time engaged is a major criterion. It is likely that TV is a contributing factor in how children learn to solve personal conflicts and problems. Force and violence, because they are necessary to produce "action" are the most commonly used means to find solutions.

Television has become a popular means of dissemination of research findings concerning children and families. Often such findings are reported somewhat informally on talk shows, the news, or documentaries long before they appear in print in professional and scientific journals. Children and family concerns have become as much a part of daily newspaper and family-oriented magazines as the familiar weather report. William Glasser[1] points out that the "affluent television world" has created a new breed of children who feel self-important, have a need to be entertained, and are all too often passive recipients of the world around them. It should be noted, however, that despite certain handicaps, TV is a super vehicle for disseminating information for both children and adults. How children view their world is certainly strongly influenced by what they have seen on their TV sets.

THE CHANGING FAMILY

Parents have traditionally worked in the fields, in the home, in the business "downstairs" beneath the family living quarters, or at a nearby place of employment. A major difference today is that the parents work where the children cannot see or contact them. Today's parents are dealing with temporary and frequent or regular periods of separation from their children. Consequently, much of the daily socialization that was formerly a natural part of family life is now provided by others.

The extended family, once the primary source of alternate caregivers, is virtually nonexistent. Only about 5 percent of children with gainfully employed mothers have a "spare" adult in the family or household to care for them while

[1] William Glasser quoted in B. F. Feingold, "Are Today's Kids Different Than Yesterday's?" *Instructor* 87:2 (September 1977), *Special Report*.

their parents work. A rapidly growing phenomenon in America is the one-parent family. It is estimated that two out of five children born in the 1970s will spend a part of their lives in a single-parent family. Even today one of every six children under eighteen years of age is a member of such a family and the number is increasing. Another viable alternative is seen in the growing number of unmarried mothers, as society respects the rights of mothers to keep their children. In addition, nearly one out of two marriages ends in divorce, enabling the United States to claim the highest divorce rate in the world. Continuing inflation and the women's liberation movement are two strong factors that have encouraged acceptance of gainful employment and career aspirations for mothers, whether single or married.[2]

Each family unit, of necessity, arranges for the care of its children while the parent(s) work(s), usually involving a frequent change of caregivers. Will the lack of consistency of experiences rob children of the building blocks of self-esteem and personal security, as well as long-range attitudes, values, and orientation to others and to life in general? The need for continuity of caregivers with values compatible with those of the parent(s) of the young children in their care cannot be stressed too much if the children are to continue as participants in their own rightful cultural and ethnic heritage.

Because of longevity there are more grandparents in the child's world today. Some grandparents are in their early forties or fifties, hence more people are assuming grandparental roles than ever before. The role tends to be warm and indulgent with grandchildren, since less direct responsibility is assumed.[3] A grandparent may give the children more possessions and more affection, which may be both important and meaningful to them, as well as detrimental.

The elderly population (65 and older) has increased from 4.1 percent of the nation's total population in 1900 to 9.6 percent in 1970 and is projected to 10.1 percent by 1980. This means that there were nearly 20 million people in the United States aged 65 and over in 1970. Those aged 45 through 64 increased from 13.8 percent in 1900 to 20.4 percent in 1970. On the other hand, those in the high productive ages 25 through 44 decreased from 28.1 percent to 23.6 percent during the same period of time. These shifts in proportions by age groups have important implications for planning for housing, schools, and social services. For example, experts predict that elementary school enrollments will continue to decrease through the mid-1980s, and high school enrollments will continue to fall by as much as 25 percent until 1990–1991.[4]

In spite of the recent decline in births to women of child-bearing age, en-

[2] "Family Affairs," *Instructor* 87:2 (September 1977), *Special Report.*
[3] B. L. Neugarten and K. Weinstein, "The Changing American Grandparents," *Marr. Fam. Liv.,* *16* (May 1964).
[4] "House EL/SEC Panel Hears How Population Trends Affect Education," *Education Daily* (May 11, 1977), p. 3.

rollments in preschools have increased in 1976 to 5 million children, representing a 91 percent increase since 1964.[5]

During the 1969 school year, 6,934,000 or slightly over half of the 12,964,000 children aged three to six were enrolled in school. Of the total, 15.1 percent of the three- and four-year-olds and 89.2 percent of the five- and six-year-olds were in school.[6] Public school kindergarten enrollment increased 14.2 percent from 1964 to 1969, and many states, especially in the South, had passed legislation to have public school kindergartens for all children desiring to attend by the early 1970s.

Because of the disparity among income levels, most innovations in the schools have occurred in programs for children of low-income families. Best known are the Title I programs under the Elementary and Secondary Education Act of 1965, Head Start, Follow Through, the Parent Child Centers, whose target children are under three years of age, and the Pilot Parent and Child Advocacy Center programs, Home Start, and Title XX, SSA. These new programs will be discussed in Chapter 8, "Emerging School Programs for Young Children."

CHILD ABUSE

The incidence of child abuse is of great concern. In 1968, of the 6,617 abused children surveyed, 53.37 percent were six years of age or under.[7] So serious has the problem of child abuse become that "The Child Abuse and Treatment Act" (P.L. 93-247) was signed into law January 31, 1974. This Act established the National Center on Child Abuse and Neglect in the Children's Bureau within the Office of Child Development, now a part of the Administration of Children Youth and Families (ACYF), HEW. Historically,

> Up to the twentieth century, children were considered the property of their parents in most cultures. Aristotle wrote that "the justice of a master or a father is a different thing from that of a citizen, for a son or slave is property. . . . In ancient Rome, a man could sell, abandon, or kill his child if he pleased. . . ."
> Infanticide has been practiced throughout history, often for economic reasons: to limit family size, to relieve the financial burden of the unwed mother, to assure crop growth by human sacrifice to the appropriate god or gods. Children have been slain, abandoned, and sold into slavery by parents unable to support them, by mid-wives and wet-nurses greedy for money, and by rulers fearing loss of their

[5] Ibid., p. 3.

[6] U.S. Bureau of the Census, *Statistical Abstracts of the United States* (Washington, D.C.: U.S. Government Printing Office, 1970), p. 118.

[7] Ibid., p. 112 (From the U.S. HEW survey funded by the Children's Bureau study, *Physical Abuse of Children in the United States*, Dr. David Gil, Brandeis University, 1968).

power. Other children, perhaps more fortunate than those murdered or exposed, were mutilated to increase their appeal as beggars or freak performers.

Parents and schoolmasters, from the ancient philosophers to the American colonists, believed that sparing rods led to the spoiling of children. Whippings and floggings have been acceptable means of disciplining children in many cultures.

The Massachusetts Stubborn Child Law, enacted in 1654, was reaffirmed in 1971 by the state's highest court, which ruled that children have no right of dissent against the reasonable and lawful commands of the parents or legal guardians. The law was finally repealed in 1973.

Since the 1960's, all 50 states, the District of Columbia, the Virgin Islands, and Guam have enacted laws to protect children whose parents fail to meet minimal standards of care.[8]

While estimates vary, it is believed that there are from 2.5 to 4 million incidents of child abuse annually.[9] As would be expected, abused children have learning, behavior, and habit disorders, and they themselves grow up to be abusers of their own children. Excellent and helpful material on this topic is available from the National Center on Child Abuse and Neglect referred to previously.

POPULATION TRENDS

An important factor to consider is the effect of population trends on the child's environment. Chapter 1 reports on pertinent changes in terms of their significance to Early Childhood Education. These same population statistics will help you understand the child's world in relation to the people in their life space, particularly family size, family patterns, and alternatives to family care. If the prediction of larger families materializes, it will have a significant impact on the way in which the child develops.

CHANGES IN LIVING STYLES

Today's children live in a "push-button age" surrounded by new gadgets and inventions represented to them as intricate plastic toys. Through the increasing influence of advertising, adults strive to make more money to purchase more goods to increase the ease of living and to have more leisure time. One can only surmise what effect this continuous circle of striving will have on the growing child. Consideration is also given to the type of value system the

[8] *Child Abuse and Neglect—The Problem and Its Management*, Vol. 1 (first of 3 vols.), DHEW Publication No. (OHD) 75-30073 (Washington, D.C.: Superintendent of Documents. U.S. Government Printing Office, 1975), pp. 2, 3.
[9] Ibid., p. 10.

child is developing in this fast-changing world. Easy acquisition of toys and other possessions may tend to develop irresponsibility for their care and use. With the increased emphasis on new commodities, we need to be aware of the effect of the adult's constantly shifting values on those of the child. This problem is accentuated as children move from place to place. What is acceptable to children in one region may only seem cheap or unacceptable to children in another area.

The fast-paced lifestyle of most modern families has meant drastic changes in their eating habits. There is no longer time to prepare and then leisurely enjoy good meals at home. The food industry has gone all out to meet this challenge and to make food preparation and serving as quick and as painless as possible. Fast-food restaurant chains are everywhere, even providing school lunches and hospital food. In order to make these modern miracles possible, natural foods have been greatly altered with huge quantities of additives, including preservatives, artificial colors and flavors, and excessive amounts of sugar. Many believe these additives have a profound influence on behavior patterns, including scholastic performance, especially of children. Even vandalism, truancy, and violence have been attributed to food alteration and nutritional problems.[10]

Affluence and an expanding economy have made it possible for just about everyone to have almost endless material possessions. The discipline and psychological rewards derived from planning for the future and from the conservation of material things were almost unheard of until recently for large numbers of young children. At the time of this writing children are participating more in concern for the environment.

RESOURCES FOR PARENTS

A listing on page 150 gives some of the pertinent publications that are available from organizations. Some of these groups disseminate material as a function of their organization because of the heavy demand for information by the public. Parents and teachers are requesting up-to-date material; those working in the child-development field have recognized the need to convey such knowledge; child-development courses at the college and junior college level have continued to expand; and there is an increasing demand to incorporate more knowledge about children into the high school curriculum.

With the increasing use of television as a medium of communication, children as well as parents have been affected by changing attitudes and concepts. Studies seem to conclude that the cognitive effects are disappointing.

[10] B. F. Feingold, "Are Today's Kids Different than Yesterday's?" *Instructor* 87:2 (September 1977), *Special Report*.

Although children may be better informed, television has not been used as fully as it might as a result of commercialism. However, this medium has great potential in widening children's horizons.[11] There are many television programs designed especially for preschool children on both commercial and educational TV. Best known is "Sesame Street," which was developed to test the effectiveness of television as an instructional medium for preschool children, especially children living in the inner cities. "Sesame Street" is discussed in considerable detail on pages 165 and 166.

MOBILITY OF POPULATION

Another important social change that is exerting pressure on the child is the increased mobility of our present population.

> Of the 190.2 million persons 1 year old and over living in the United States in March 1966, 36.7 million, or 19.3 percent, had been living at a different address in March 1965, according to estimates from the Current Population Survey conducted by the Bureau of the Census. . . . In the 19 annual surveys conducted since 1948, the proportion of movers has ranged from 18.6 to 21.0 percent.[12]

The overall mobility rate has continued to be high. There is greater local mobility of nonwhites and higher mobility in general of the white population. Young adults aged 18 to 34 had a higher mobility rate (34 percent) than persons 35 years old and over (12 percent), and also a higher rate than children under 18 (21 percent).[13] This mobility factor causes persons interested in the child to ask, what does shifting from one place to another do to the children? Do children need the security that comes through establishing roots in one place, or are they able to adjust to continual change? Is it more advantageous for them to know more of the outside world than to have prolonged contacts with one neighborhood?

More divisions within the family have arisen as families move about; all family members develop their own friends thus increasing the contacts they acquire as they shift from place to place. Widening and broadening of acquaintances may shift both the adult's and the child's perspective as individuals in society. The concern is this: Does the individual thus acquire greater understanding of human relations or broader knowledge of regional differences? Does the family remain intact? What are the effects of shifting population upon the family with growing children? To date, the specific answers are

[11] Wilbur Schramm, J. Lyle, and E. B. Parker, *Television in the Lives of Our Children* (Stanford, Calif.: Stanford University Press, 1961), p. 173.
[12] U.S. Bureau of the Census, *Population Characteristics*, Series P-20, No. 156 (Washington, D.C.: U.S. Government Printing Office, December, 1966).
[13] Ibid.

not known. It is only surmised that personalities do undergo change the more contacts people make.

Both mobility and travel tend to separate family members, at least for varying, and often irregular, periods of time. In view of "critical periods and attachment" research, the possible effects on children of such separations would depend on such factors as the age of the child and the length of time involved in the separation. For example, "attachment" research would tend to discourage total separations from known caregivers with whom the child has developed a feeling of security for more than 24 hours before the age of at least one year.[14]

EASE OF TRAVEL

Along with increased mobility and expanded means of communication, the world is known more easily and readily to children and adults through ease of travel, whether to nearby state parks or to far-away vacation spots. Families tend to take vacations; thus mobility in leisure-time activities has increased. Advertising has tended to lure families to see the parts of the world known only in earlier times through a geography book. There has been an increased desire to become acquainted firsthand with other localities. State parks and camping facilities have expanded, and campers of all types are available for families. "Package" family trips are advertised to entice parents at any season of the year. Young children travel with their families by plane great distances in brief spaces of time. Thus the world is better known to children today than it was to a previous generation.

MOTHERS IN GAINFUL EMPLOYMENT

There has been a steady rise in the number of working mothers. In April 1948, 43.5 percent of mothers of children under 18 were in the labor force, in 1960 the percentage was 62.7, and in March 1969 the figure had risen to 81.1 percent. For the same years the percentage of mothers with children under six were 12.8, 20.2, and 30.4, respectively. Obviously the need for parent surrogates, day care, or both, has steadily increased since 1949. In 1975, 21 percent of the mothers of children under six, married with husbands present were gainfully employed.[15]

In 1965, husband–wife families with one or more children under eighteen

---

[14] J. Gewirtz (ed.), *Attachment and Dependency* (Washington D.C.: Winston, 1972).
[15] *Statistical Abstracts of the United States, 1976* (Washington, D.C.: Department of Commerce, Bureau of the Census, 1976), p. 359.

years of age accounted for 84.7 percent of all families with children. Although the remaining 15.3 percent consisting of mothers or fathers raising children without the other parent was proportionately small, it was large in actual numbers of children growing up with only one parent. In 1977 the number of children living in one-parent families was double what it was twenty-five years ago.[16] Problems faced by the one-parent family are many, with varying degrees of concern for the children.[17] Economic need has been the primary reason why mothers work. However, with more education, women tend to work for other reasons, to achieve career goals, or for personal satisfaction and freedom from being dependent on someone else. Whatever the effect on children when their mothers work (research is not at all definitive on this issue at this time), their days will be very different from those of children whose mothers are not gainfully employed outside the home.

THE ADULTS IN THE CHILD'S WORLD

Traditionally, young children have been reared in the warmth and security of parental care. Most would agree that parents should, with a high degree of responsibility, administer care that is very personal and designed to produce an intense relationship that is mutually responsive and emotionally involved. This type of care is what Katz[18] calls "particularistic" relationships as opposed to "universalistic" relationships encouraged by teachers and caregivers. Both types of relationship involve warmth and affection, but in the latter case there is personal "distance," which desirably prevents intense personal involvement on the part of the adult as well as the children.[19]

If you are familiar with previous editions of this text you will notice that there is considerably less use of the word teacher. This in no way downgrades the value of teachers in the world of young children. Rather, it acknowledges that recognition is now given to the importance of health, nutrition, and physical care in the early years and that there is a need for many adults in the program whose training and expertise differ from that of teachers. They form a significant part of the team of adults necessary for good Early Childhood Education programs. This does not depreciate the importance of the teacher, as learning is always taking place in the lives of children, regardless of the purpose or type of program involved. Indeed, highly skilled and adequately prepared teachers are essential to all programs, all of which should include a carefully planned education component. Other adults, with the same poten-

---

[16] "Family Affairs," op. cit.

[17] Ibid., p. 141.

[18] Lillian G. Katz, "Teachers in Preschools: Problems and Prospects," *Internatl. J. Early Childhood*, 9:1 (1977), pp. 111–123.

[19] Ibid., p. 119.

tial for educational influence, may include caregivers, Child Development Associates, parents, parent liaison workers, volunteers, students, maintenance personnel, and others. Obviously, the young child's "school" world influences are very different from the former young child's teacher–child nursery "school" relationship. In keeping with these developments, the term "nursery school" is fast disappearing in the Early Childhood Education literature.

HOUSING

Housing is an important area to consider in relation to the activity of a child and available play space. The home may be crowded, small, and have poor sanitation or safety hazards. It may be too large, overly clean, and have no playmates accessible. There may be good sleeping arrangements and storage space for the child, or there may be noise, confusion, clutter, and no place the children can call their own for their possessions. Outdoor play areas may be adequate on a roof or in a yard, or they may be nonexistent.

Lemkau feels that "the house does not have a constant relationship to the household which lives in it, but that the relationship changes according to economic ideals and philosophic ideals." As a psychiatrist he feels that a house must offer a place in which children can lead a satisfactory existence. Crowded conditions and too many adults lead to lack of independence and poor control in guiding children.[20]

Little research has been conducted on the effect of housing in rearing children, and yet recommendations have been made as to how children should be housed. Concern has been expressed that families have adequate housing, and building programs have been expanded. In 1965, more than 1.5 million housing units were started in the building process in the United Ststes, and in late 1977, the number was estimated to be 1.8 million for that year. During the twelve years involved, only 1968, 1971, 1972, and 1973 had more units started. The largest number built was in 1972 when there were 2,361,000 starts.[21]

During the same interval, condominiums and apartments mushroomed throughout the nation. In most cases, this type of home ownership is not the most appropriate housing for children, but these developments reflected attitudes toward children and the low birthrate of the times. In addition, inflationary trends continued to price the average family with children out of home ownership. "Proper balance between housing and income-supplementing

[20] P. V. Lemkau, "A Psychiatrist's View of Housing," *Proceedings of Housing Conference*, Publication 180 (Philadelphia: Pennsylvania State University, College of Home Economics), p. 27. (Unpublished paper) n.d.
[21] These figures are based on September 1977 news reports citing the Federal Home Loan Bank and the Department of Commerce as sources.

programs will be important in achieving the goal of decent housing for every family. . . . The Department of Housing and Urban Development is intensifying its efforts to formulate and develop a balanced relationship between housing and income-supplementing programs."[22]

It seems clear that adequate housing for families is a prerequisite to adequate family life and learning experiences for young children. Schools and universities bulged with children and students during the 1950s and 1960s as a result of the World War II baby boom. The 1970s found these same babies, then young adults, forming families of their own. Housing was the neglected industry during the 1960s, the same period in which rot and neglect, especially in the large inner cities, created acute housing problems for young families. Mobile homes, apartments, and government-subsidized low-cost housing mushroomed because of the rapidly rising cost of new housing. This trend is indicated by the fact that "44 percent of today's housing (1971) is multi-family row houses and apartments, vs. only 26 percent back in 1961."[23] The same source indicated that mobile homes increased fourfold during the past decade. Even so, inadequate as these types of housing are for families with young children, most of the new housing was not built where the need was the greatest.[24] What importance housing plays in the life of a child is an area that needs, and will continue to need, increased and intensive exploration.

PARENTS TODAY

The young child today may be reared in a home by parents who are both working or attending school. Young parents may be continuing their education, either in vocational school or college. These parents are likely to be in their early twenties. The present world in which they live with their offspring is very different from that known by many of the earlier child-development writers, researchers, or so called "experts." Many of these earlier writings are still used today either in the originals or by means of extensive quotes in some of the most recent materials. Much can be learned from these sources, and many of the findings are as true today as they were then. Nevertheless, many of the child-rearing practices prescribed as suitable for that day may, because of social and personal changes, be questionable for the world in which today's children find themselves. Heavy emphasis on longitudinal family and child research in the 1920s and 1930s highlighted an approach to early education based on the maturational and developmental needs. While this is certainly a valid approach and one approved by the authors of this text, children mature

---

[22] U.S. Department of Agriculture, *Family Economics Review*, ARS 62-5 (Washington, D.C., December 1966), p. 12.

[23] "Home Building: Is the Boom Hollow?" *Forbes*, *108*:9 (1971), pp. 28–36.

[24] Ibid., pp. 30–33.

earlier today as a result of better nutrition, health, and general lifestyles. In addition, the emphasis on infant and early childhood education as well as patterns of living documented elsewhere has produced children way ahead in their cognitive and personal–social development of children reared in the 1920s and 1930s. A high quality of longitudinal research on children and their families in today's world is needed. The emphasis on early intervention education and the needs for immediate answers demanded by current accountability practices, have made longitudinal research less appealing to those doing the research.

One out of three young children is likely to live, for at least some time, in a one-parent family due to divorce, death, desertion, or the option on the part of a growing number of single mothers to keep their babies. Contrary to tradition, the courts in divorce cases are increasingly awarding the custody of children to their fathers. Thus, the young child may be reared in a household without the presence of a mother, indeed without the presence of a regular female caregiver.

Children's clothing, games, and play equipment have become big business. Unfortunately, with the push for early academic achievement as documented throughout this text, educational materials, equipment, and systems of teaching have become highly commercialized. It becomes difficult for busy parents, teachers, and caregivers to know which of the magic formulas to invest in. A goal of parenting in terms of individual family needs should be established as a guide for decision making.

Parents today have a vast array of information and advice regarding children. So great is the amount of printed material, the frequency of radio and TV talk shows, and documentaries that it is easy to become confused by contradictory or conflicting points of view. Guidance is needed in distinguishing between advice based on sound research and theory and that proposed by biased persons or groups. Much advice and many valuable aids supplied by recognized and experienced professionals are available, a good example of which can be found in Mary B. Lane's work on education for parenting.[25]

VARIATIONS IN CHILD REARING

The child is an important factor in the continuation of the culture, being the connecting link between the cultures of succeeding generations. How a parent rears a child is primarily dependent on the culture, the trends of the decade in which the parent is presently living, and the past experiences of the adult. While psychologists, educators, and others have made much of the influences on children of culture and class differences, it seems apparent from

---

[25] Mary B. Lane, *Education for Parenting* (Washington, D.C.: NAEYC, 1975).

recent research and thought on the subject that in the United States "the great power of the middle class has rendered differences into deficits because middle-class behavior is the yardstick of success,"[26] hence the term "culturally disadvantaged." Pointing out that "cultural differences reside more in the situations to which cultural groups apply their skills than to differences in the skills possessed," Bruner casts doubt on the concept of "deficits" in minority and poverty groups."[27]

More than three decades ago, Sears, Maccoby, and Levin conducted research in the area of child rearing with 379 mothers of five-year-old children, pretty much a classic work in the field. These workers found wide variations in the different methods measured—from mothers who never under any circumstances permitted certain forms of behavior to others who felt that specific behavior should be ignored. Some mothers were quite uncertain in the strength of their convictions. Some of the child-rearing practices reported placed emphasis on training children, others on caretaking only, and others on reactions of love, annoyance, pride, or concern. One of the most pervasive qualities measured was the warmth of the mother's feeling for her child.[28]

The present emphasis on Early Childhood Education and day care is clearly an indication that today there is a change from the traditional socializing influences of the family and school. Emphasis on the disadvantaged child has dominated the field of Early Childhood Education since the early 1960s, and most research since then has been concerned with that group of children and families. Studying the teaching styles of mothers from different social classes, Hess and Shipman found that mothers of one culturally different group controlled the child's behavior by imperatives. This method did not provide an opportunity for mediation of behavior by verbal cues nor the use of language to bring meaning to the experience encountered.[29]

Such a cognitive environment, they conclude, "produces a child who related to authority rather than to rationale . . . and for whom the consequences of an act are largely considered in terms of immediate punishment or reward rather than future effects and long-range goals."[30] This, of course, is in *direct contrast to the future-oriented long-range planning goals of middle-class American families.* As a consequence, schools of middle-class value orientation have not provided for the needs of children from lower-income families in such a way as to enable them to cope with the schools' expectations and demands.

[26] J. S. Bruner, *Beyond the Information Given* (New York: W. W. Norton, 1973), p. 464.
[27] Ibid., pp. 453, 464.
[28] R. Sears, E. Maccoby, and H. Levin, *Patterns of Child Rearing* (Evanston, Ill.: Row Peterson, 1957), p. 482.
[29] R. D. Hess and Virginia C. Shipman, "Maternal Influences upon Early Learning," in *Early Education,* edited by R. D. Hess and Roberta M. Bear (Chicago: Aldine Publishing Co., 1968) p. 103.
[30] Ibid., p. 103.

A   B   C

Figure 5

The need for parent surrogates and/or day care has increased as the number of mothers working outside the home has grown. These children attend a fully licensed family day care center. The mother (director) is a college graduate with a major in Early Childhood Education.

Because of the time it takes to conduct research and to have it published and later interpreted for public consumption, there is a lag in adapting it to practice. Thus, if research finds it is "all right or better" to be less permissive in dealing with children, this concept may not be put into practice for seven or eight years. Therefore, we are likely to find some older parents still being very permissive in rearing children because of something they read in the late 1940s, while other parents who have attended a study group and discussed various ways of raising children may be recognizing individual differences and comparing these differences of their own children to new research findings.

SOCIAL CLASS

Regional and class differences are apparent in the literature and in research on ways in which parents rear their children. Attitudes and values of families in lower, middle, and upper classes differ in regard to customs and aspirations; these differences are revealed in most communities.

Some researchers classify the social groups in American urban society as upper, upper-middle, lower-middle, working, and lower class. Classification of variables that characterize these classes is made on the basis of value orientations as they form, integrate, and symbolize a certain way of life.[31] There is a tendency for modern writers in the field of Early Childhood Education to ignore some of the potent forces that have a strong influence on the orientation

[31] J. A. Kahl, *The American Class Structure* (New York: Holt, Rinehart and Winston, 1959).

to life of the young child, such as social class. They feel that there should be no "such distinctions" when the life of young children is concerned. We agree that there "should not" be such distinctions, but the cold facts of reality are that social classes do exist in America and membership in certain classes either paves the way, or strongly inhibits, the opportunities to achieve power and enjoy a role in important decision-making processes. Teachers and caregivers of young children "should" be aware of the insidious influence of social class on how children are reared if they are to work effectively with children and parents of different social classes, whatever their ethnic origins.

There is need to carefully analyze class influences that young children acquire from parents, teachers, and other adults. In the study by Sears, Maccoby, and Levin, the authors analyzed their data by socioeconomic status. Their cases were analyzed and divided into two groups, namely, "middle class" and "working class." There were marked differences in the practices and attitudes of these two classes of mothers. Working-class mothers were more punitive and restrictive. They were less permissive with respect to sex behavior, aggression, and dependency, and they placed high restrictions and demands on their children in all major respects. Many other findings with respect to differences in child rearing can be found in these research studies.[32]

Studies to date are limited with regard to subcultures of the very poor; however, Chilman has presented research findings that show differences in child-rearing patterns. These summarize studies on various aspects of child rearing according to middle-class versus very-low-income families. Since schools are basically middle-class institutions, lower-class children have trouble achieving in such centers. For example, some of the studies revealed that low-income families use inconsistent, harsh discipline and ridicule; the discipline is based on whether the child's behavior does or does not annoy the parent. Middle-class parents on the other hand, used verbal, mild, reasoning and consistent discipline with more emphasis on rewarding good behavior.[33]

Such studies, while helpful, merely describe differences and seldom produce an understanding of the differences and why they exist. The following quotations from the 1970 White House Conference on Children report will help bridge the gap:

> Many children, effectively isolated from their cultural heritage by poverty, home environment, racial discrimination, and geography, do not develop pride in their heritages, and their feelings of identity remain vague and confused. These children need help in finding out who they are and where they came from.[34]

---

[32] Sears, Maccoby, and Levin, op. cit., p. 480.

[33] Catherine Chilman, "Child-Rearing and Family Relationship Patterns of the Very Poor," *Welfare in Review* (Washington, D.C.: U.S. Department of Health, Education, and Welfare, January 1965).

[34] *Report to the President.* White House Conference on Children 1970 (Washington D.C.: Superintendent of Documents, U.S. Government Printing Office) p. 48.

Forum 6 reported,

> The Forum on Creativity and the Learning Process states that it has been jolted by the realization that the Child of America is growing up in captivity. His prison is his communication.[35]

On the role of culture, the same Forum reported,

> Cultural forces, like the forces of nature, are never fully under control. They are massive in comparison with the very limited power that man can exert through rational planning and design. Creativity depends upon the culture's emotional climate in its major institutions: the home, the church, the school, the mass media, and other forms of public communication, the town or city, the state or nation, and international relations.[36]

It would thus appear that social class and the influence of culture are powerful determinants of young children's behavior and must be taken into account when planning teaching and instructional strategies.

CHANGING SEX ROLES

There is a growing awareness by those interested in child development of the importance of the child's sex role. How the parents think of the feminine or masculine role plays an important part in how they rear the child. Questions relative to this include: Are the father's and mother's concepts the same or does each parent have a different way of looking at masculinity or femininity? Is the child's time spent mainly with the mother; if so, does the child have more awareness of the feminine role than the masculine? If the child is only seen and cared for by the father at brief intervals daily, is that enough for the child to identify with a masculine figure?

Changing roles of women

The recent emphasis on equal opportunity for women in education, the labor market, and the professions, along with public acceptance of one-parent (male or female) families and equality of the sexes has brought about a need for a new look at the concept of sex roles. The women's liberation movement, too, has had its impact creating the need for alternative forms of child rearing. As the sexes become less distinguishable from each other in these areas, it is reasonable to assume that sex-role differences will likewise tend to be less stereotyped or even eliminated.

[35] Ibid., p. 89.
[36] Ibid., pp. 90–91.

At the time of this revision, we could find no tangible evidence that today's young children are learning "equality" of sex roles, despite the fact that mothers engage in far fewer "feminine" activities at home and at work and fathers or other males in the household engage in far more "feminine" activities than formerly. Perhaps it is as Margolin[37] points out, "This [learning sex-linked traits] is a complicated issue. Whether they will begin to emulate certain males and accept their traits as their own will depend on how much they want to identify themselves with them." Today efforts are being made to eliminate sexism in children's (and adults') reading matter, illustrations, and everyday activities so that sex differences are becoming less clear cut. It will take many years to feel the full impact of these social changes.

A child learns early in life that boys and girls are treated differently, are dressed differently, and are expected to behave differently. Each culture defines the meaning of *male* or *female,* usually in terms of its social and economic needs. As these needs change so do the roles of each sex change. Nevertheless, early in life all children must find their own sex role at home and in the ethnic group to which they belong if they are to be accepted members.

FAMILY RELATIONSHIPS

The number of brothers and sisters as well as the ordinal position of each sibling should be taken into account in each individual family. Another factor is the effect of the parents' newness to the situation with the first child versus the parent becoming more sure of themselves with each successive child. Parents who rear only boys or only girls within their families have different ways of bringing up children. Some children may find themselves reared in a family in which they are more than wanted because their parents may be physically incapable of having other children; others may be unwanted. Still others are among the large number of exceptional children who are physically or mentally handicapped, or who are superior or gifted.

Many families are not aware that children identify closely with parents and others in the home. How the parents act with each other, how they treat those within the family group, constitute attitudes and values passed on to and acquired by the young child. Parents' reactions to various happenings locally or in the world and to the daily routines within the home are all part of how children accept and begin to acquire their own ways of conduct with others. Since today's world for the young child is brought into the home by many media, children in turn are influenced by how parents verbalize their reactions to this information. Early impressions of adults' concerns over the constantly chang-

---

[37] Edythe Margolin, *Sociocultural Elements in Early Childhood Education* (New York: Macmillan Publishing Co., 1974), p. 62.

ing world will continue to play an important part in their own attitudes as the world affairs shift or change.

CONFLICTING EDUCATIONAL THEORIES

Another factor in the child's world is the conflict of theories relative to educating the child. Parents have been advised to have the child ready for school at age six, "ready for school" meaning to them ability to read, write one's name, to know certain facts. Others have advised the parent to leave the child alone, that the school's job is to teach the child everything he or she should know. Some children therefore arrive in first grade with certain taught skills, others with none.

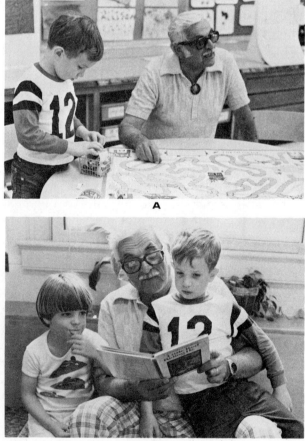

A

Figure 6
Many children have little contact with older persons. This grandfather serves as a volunteer in the center. He reads to the children and plays games with them.

B

The push to educate very young children has had growing impetus since the Atomic Age intensified the need for further education in all lines of endeavor. Parents may pressure young children to "know certain facts" where other parents have a "let well enough alone" attitude. Those working with or teaching young children in organized groups also may feel they should prepare the five-year-old to read and write in order that the child be equipped to meet the standards of first grade. Pressure from society that all five- or six-year-olds should be able to measure up to certain prescribed standards may find school and parents in conflict.

Along with conflicting theories of child rearing and education, there are conflicting beliefs regarding the responsibilities of the home. Many young parents depend mainly on outside agencies—welfare organizations, family services, clinics, state and local societies—to handle their problems. One has yet to determine whether or not the agencies are so numerous that young parents are over-aided and do not develop necessary self-sufficiency. Are there too many day care groups so that mothers may go to work, feeling secure that children are cared for properly?

The recognition of the importance of the early years has given impetus to research in early learning. As a result, many different theories, methods, and types of instructional materials exist and have a direct impact on the type of educational opportunities available in the young child's world.

In an effort to note trends in any area of our rapidly changing life today, it appears significant to identify landmarks by which the degree of change can be measured. In identifying trends in education for the young child, the following landmarks will indicate the changes that have developed both in beliefs and practice:

1. *The acceptance of the Froebelian philosophy and program for kindergartens.* For a time, the European philosophy of the kindergarten was transplanted with little change in relation to the needs of American life. The emphasis was on following Froebel and using his program and gifts for all children. Froebel's philosophy, rather than the child, was the center of study.

2. *The beginning of the child study movement.* Dewey and Hall found leaders in the kindergarten field eager to apply their findings and philosophy to the education of young children. But it was not easy. For, only a century ago, the study of children was frowned upon by many. G. Stanley Hall has told how difficult it was in the middle of the last century to measure the height and weight of schoolchildren because parents objected to the invasion of the child's rights.[38]

Studies today are far reaching and have great implications for what hap-

[38] J. E. Anderson, "Principles of Child Development," in *Early Education* (Washington, D.C.: NEA, 1956), p. 14.

pens to young children. For example, in the recent survey of "400 Famous People and How Their Childhood Affected Them," it was found that none of them had an easy time in their home but that certain common elements were in the backgrounds of these leaders. As children, these famous people had had more opportunity for traveling, reading, thinking, and initiating and conducting original experiments. Many children do not have these opportunities at home; therefore, they need to have experiences provided under guidance to assist them in developing qualities of leadership and creativity. Such studies substantiate the value of, and give direction to, the content of desirable programs in Early Childhood Education.[39]

3. *Expansion of interest in child development and research to include children under six, soon after World War I.* The research during this period was concerned with establishing the value of the kindergarten in relation to later school adjustment and progress. In the 1930s and early 1940s there was concern for establishing tests and norms of development. In light of these research findings, kindergarten teachers have tried to better understand and meet the needs of individuals in their groups—to relate findings of child development to practice.

4. *Progressive Education.* Although the era of the Progressive Education Movement is usually associated with the years between 1896 and the late 1930s, extensions of the movement are found today in many programs, such as the British Infant Schools and other examples of open education for children, as well as in various alternative forms of schooling.

   The common principles that Dewey felt existed in progressive schools included the following: expression and cultivation of individuality; free activity; learning through experience; acquiring meaningful and needed skills; making the most of each day of school because school is life; developing acquaintances with the social and physical world. Progressive education combined the psychological principles of child growth with the moral principles of democracy.[40]

5. *Federal interest in early childhood centers.* The federal government has not only appropriated money for childhood centers, but it has developed materials, established supervisory programs, and assisted parents and entire communities in developing a changed concept of early education. Many types of experimental programs have been established.

6. *The influence of Montessori.* The influence of Montessori may be found in special Montessori schools and to some extent in many preschools in the United States. The Montessori method provides for a personal space for each child, allowing them freedom to learn at a comfortable rate, but super-

[39] Mildred G. Goertzel and V. Goertzel, *Cradles of Eminence* (New York: Little, Brown & Co., 1962).
[40] James M. Squire (ed.), *A New Look at Progressive Education*, 1972 Yearbook (Washington, D.C.: ASCD, 1972), pp. 1–13.

vised by a teacher as they move about and talk. However, the first move-ment for exploration must come from the child. Each task is broken down into a series of smaller tasks. All the learning tasks, guided by the teacher, lead the child into the mastery of reading, writing, and mathematics as well as related skills. This program provides a variety of models for imitation as well as for older children to help and to teach younger children. The ma-terials have been modernized, the use of equipment is more permissive, and the methods are used to insure greater academic achievement.[41]

7. *The influence of Piaget.* Piaget's theory is concerned with the development of thinking or intelligence from infancy to adulthood. The theory consists of three interdependent aspects, namely structural, stage, and functional aspects.[42] Although Piaget's work has identified four major stages, two are especially important in early childhood: the sensorimotor period and the preoperational period. One of the preschool's basic functions is to facilitate the transition from one stage to another. By consolidating knowledge of ob-jects, time, and space, the child builds a foundation upon which at a later date he/she can build other structures.

SOME AREAS NEEDING SPECIAL CONSIDERATION IN THE 1980s

The rapid expansion of early education evident in the 1960's was even more apparent in the 1970's. With this expansion came some significant changes in points of emphasis. Among these are the following:

1. *Changes in philosophy and practice.* The confusion in early childhood education today "is as though a bombshell exploded with the pieces going in every direction."[43] In this period changes of points of view or of greater emphasis are significant in the areas of interrelated learnings and learning by inference; the place and importance of expectancy in the learning proc-ess; greater emphasis on the child's learning from the peer group, espe-cially in terms of hobbies and interests; the child's need for love from the teacher and his/her peers; the application of science to the child's develop-ment; and the positive interrelation between preschool attendance and be-havior in adolescent years.

2. *Environmental influences.* The environment exerts a powerful influence on the preschool child. Children need space to play in large and small

[41] Evelyn Beyer et al. (eds.), *Montessori in Perspective.* Washington, D.C.: NAEYC (1971), pp. 25–35.
[42] James M. Squire, op. cit., pp. 88–114.
[43] Edythe Margolin, "Critical Issues in Contemporary Childhood Education," *Child. Educ.,* 45:8 (1969), p. 503.

groups, to work, to discuss, to be alone, to listen, to think, and to create. They do need clean air, freedom from excessive noise, and a well-planned attractive environment indoors and outdoors that has adequate space. The emotional climate should provide security, develop positive self-image, and encourage good health.

3. *Acceptance of individuals who are culturally or racially different.* To meet the objective of accepting into our society individuals who are culturally or racially different, teachers and caregivers must be sensitive to all children. Although they may place little emphasis on direct teaching, they place great emphasis on the daily living within the center. Each child, rich, poor, or handicapped, racially or culturally different, makes his or her own contribution. Children need to learn other children for their own worth.

4. *The need for day care services.* Whether they are to serve the children of working mothers or the children of culturally different families, day-care services for the preschool child should provide adequate care and educational guidance. Not all children needing preschool care are from indigent families; many families can provide financially for the care of their children. In well-established day care centers, at least two adults are available at all times. In addition, they have professional help and volunteer workers to assist as scheduled. In one study, the mothers of young children expressed dissatisfaction with the care their children were receiving as follows: not being with their child, 18 percent; behavior, 27 percent; and general dissatisfaction, 20 percent. But on the whole, the working mothers believed that it was better for children to attend a full-time or part-time preschool than to remain at home with relatives or maids.[44]

Because there are many new pressures and continuing forces that bear on each child growing up in today's world, the teacher or caregiver needs to consider what adults can do to help this growing individual. These adults need to consider the effects upon the child of such factors as mass media, family relationships, social patterns, and other forces discussed in this chapter. Adults must be aware that children will be continually changing individuals because of these many forces acting upon them. Human relations will become a greater force as today's children become adults. The teacher will need to recognize the importance of such factors as the child's mother working outside the home; whether the child is the oldest, middle, or youngest child; the community or region from which the child has come; the age of the child's parents; whether the child has had a wide range of experiences; what attitudes or values the parents have in their rearing of this child. It is a challenge for a teacher or caregiver of young children to keep constantly in focus all the new

[44] Seth Low and Pearl G. Spindler, *Child Care Arrangements in the United States.* Washington, D.C.: U.S. Department of Health, Education and Welfare and U.S. Department of Labor, Women's Bureau (1968), pp. 6–12.

literature, research, and materials that appear as she or he attempts to assimilate these in connection with each new youngster she or he teaches.

Suggested Activities

1. Note the variety of nursery schools, kindergartens, day care centers, and other programs for young children in your community. Determine their sponsorship. Visit one and determine the goals of such a school.
2. Make a list of values or attitudes you feel you have acquired from your own family. Analyze one of these in detail in terms of how it originated.
3. Study two preschool children, one who has been given every advantage and one who has had very few. Contrast the two types of environment and predict what types of children they are likely to become.
4. Discuss the pros and cons of sending "your" child to a nursery school or kindergarten.
5. Watch and evaluate a preselected children's program on television. What changes would you recommend to the producers in the best interest of the children who view it? Why?

Related Readings

Chilman, C. *Growing Up Poor*, Publication 13. Washington, D.C.: U.S. DHEW, May 1966.

———(ed.). "Poverty in the United States in the Mid Sixties," *Marr. Fam. Liv.*, 26:4 (1964).

Kremer, J., and S. Day. *Indoor Play Areas for Preschool Children in the Homes of Farm Owners*, Bulletin 410. Raleigh, N.C.: Agricultural Experiment Station, February 1959.

Moore, Shirley G. "The Effect of Television on the Prosocial Behavior of Young Children," *Young Children*, 32:5 (July 1977), pp. 60–65.

Papalia, Diane, and Shirley Wendkes. *A Child's World*. New York: McGraw-Hill Book Co., 1975.

Polloway, Anne-Marie. *The Urban Nest*. Stroudsburg, Pa.: Dowden, Hutchison, and Ross, Inc., 1977.

Prall, R. C. "Child Development and the Dwelling Unit," *Forum on Neighborhoods Today and Tomorrow*, No. 2 Philadelphia Housing Association, March 1958.

Steiner, G. Y. *The Children's Cause*. Washington, D.C.: The Brookings Institution, 1976.

Winn, Marie. *The Plug-in Drug: Television, Children, and the Family*. New York: Viking Press, 1977.

chapter 3

The young child as a person

Young children's experiences from birth on have been influential in determining felt expectations of the adults who are meaningful in their lives. For example, the result of pressures to communicate the importance of being able to read or write is often firmly present at three or four years of age. Likewise, children of these ages may show fear of not being able to "measure up" to such expectations. Teachers and caregivers of young children are in a position to observe self-value, whether positive or negative, and to do something about it. How young children become self-confident and eagerly tackle new tasks, or become "crippled with anxiety and fear of failure" may well be the most important question asked by adults who work with young children.[1]

[1] Helen F. Robison, *Exploring Teaching in Early Childhood Education* (Boston: Allyn and Bacon, 1977), p. 93.

Current literature in child development tends to stress the importance of the way in which children view themselves.[2] Because of their own physical and mental characteristics, what adults do and say to them, their view of others, and their own inner feelings, children develop a self-image or self-concept early. The way each child views himself or herself may not be the way others see them, or may even be far from objective reality. Nevertheless, the view each child holds is how they feel about themselves and is all-important in determining what they say, do, and think.

This is in contrast to most child development writings of a decade or two ago which tended to be detailed descriptions of what the average child was like for a particular chronological age. These averages or norms had been obtained from observations of many children at each age level and were unrelated to the effects of particular teaching strategies, intervention techniques, or other than normal health care and family life patterns. It should not be inferred that information about normal growth and development is unnecessary for teachers (and parents). On the contrary, it is the base from which slow or fast, normal or deviate, behavior can be detected and is an invaluable aid in planning learning strategies for any group of children.

IMPORTANCE OF THE SELF-IMAGE

Although a child's awareness of differences because of social class does not become clearly evident until well along in the elementary school years,[3] self-awareness in its simplest form probably occurs during the first year of life. During the preschool years, a child receives condemnation or support from other children. A child may receive approval, constant praise, and acceptance from his playmates, or he may be reminded of the disapproval of others by being "told that he is 'messy,' 'dumb,' a 'cry-baby,' or, a 'brat.'"[4] Often such designations are a reflection of the visible physical characteristics possessed by particular children. They may also be a reflection of how children appear to behave as seen by their peers or by adults.

Taunts of "fatty," "shorty," "clumsy Ox," "dumbbell," "smarty," and the like are often heard as one listens to a group of children at play or work. Such designations may be fitting descriptions of particular children in particular situations, but at the same time may cause emotional concern resulting in permanent psychological scars. Regardless of the beliefs one holds, it is almost impossible not to form impressions of others based on the image of their phys-

[2] Interested readers see Kaoru Yamamoto (ed), *The Child and His Image* (Boston: Houghton Mifflin, 1972).

[3] Celia B. Stendler, *Children of Brasstown* (Urbana, Ill.: University of Illinois Press, 1949).

[4] A. T. Jersild, *Child Psychology*, 5th ed. (Englewood Cliffs, N.J.: Prentice-Hall, 1960), p. 174.

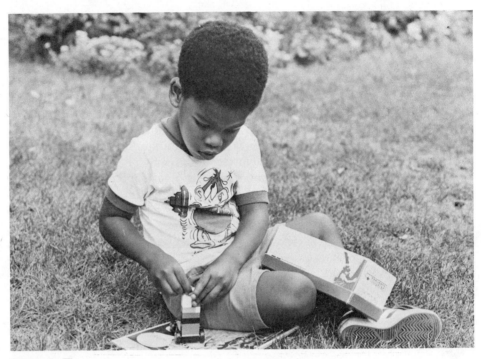

Figure 7
The importance of a healthy self-concept cannot be overemphasized. Children need to develop self-identity and view themselves as having competence and worth.

ical selves. As a result, a great deal of psychological suffering occurs even though no harm is intended or even perceived.

In recent years studies of body image, identification, motivation, self-control, self-actualization, selfhood, and similar concepts have occupied the attention of many researchers and theorists. For example, Jahoda categorizes the self-concept as (1) *accessibility to consciousness,* or the ability to achieve self-awareness; (2) *correctness,* or objectivity in being able to assess one's true characteristics; (3) *feeling about the self,* or acceptance including imperfections and faults; and (4) *sense of identity,* or clarity of the self image.[5] There is little research in this area covering the early years because of the difficulty of objective control and measurement. It seems clear, however, that the self emerges only in the presence of other human beings for the comparison with others serves as a guide to behavior. We fashion our self-identification early in terms of cues from others, such as the reflected appraisals of parents, siblings, playmates, and other persons present in our environment.

[5] M. Jahoda, *Current Concepts of Positive Mental Health* (New York: Basic Books, 1958), pp. 13–15.

Recognition of the importance of a healthy self-concept during the early years was recognized by the planners of Head Start programs for disadvantaged children. Included in the goals was: "To help children develop self-identity and a view of themselves as having competence and worth."[6]

The processes involved in the emergence of the self are varied and complex. In the early years, social and emotional factors are likely most important, although cognitive and intellectual development play an important role in both these areas. Demands of parents and of society in general include early learning. Young children must be provided rich and varied environments in order to develop feelings of competence in the world in which they find themselves. Fortunately, young children are curious and eager to learn and the rapidity with which they learn amazes adults. The important question for parents and teachers is, "What should be taught to children at each age level and why?" Choosing between required learning activities and the other essential activities of childhood can be a perplexing problem. Reported research has not been very helpful, for although complex and abstract concepts can be learned early, long-range effects have not been determined. It is doubtful that the time and effort expended on early reading or other academic pursuits make it a wise and efficient educational procedure.

EARLY DOCTRINES OF CHILD DEVELOPMENT

Although individual differences are the rule in growth and development, the teacher must have a thorough knowledge of normal development in order to know when growth or behavior deviates to the extent that special consideration and handling of a child or event is called for. It is commonly proclaimed by present-day educators that a knowledge of the characteristics of children at any age or developmental level will enable the teacher to select and pace activities suitable for any given child at any age. This is the central concept in the value of the child study movement and in child development research. That this concept is not without precedent may be found in the more philosophical doctrines of earlier great educators. A few examples might be enlightening before presenting a brief summary of the physical, mental, and personal-social characteristics of young children as found by researchers in the field.

Hinting at the concept of natural changes, Plato in the "Laws" states, "Up to the age of three years, whether of boy or girl, if a person strictly carries out our previous regulations and makes them a principal aim, he will do much for the advantages of the young creatures. But at three, four, five, or even six years the

---

[6] Office of Economic Opportunity, *Project Head Start—Daily Program I* (Washington, D..C.: U.S. Government Printing Office, 1965), p. 11.

childish nature will require sports. . . . Children of that age have certain natural modes of amusement which they find out for themselves when they meet. . . . The age of thirteen is the proper time for him to handle the lyre."[7]

Representative of sixteenth-century English thinking, Elyot would exercise extreme care in the selection of the child's nurse.[8] Since knowledge of value was written in Greek and Latin at the time Elyot lived, he would begin instruction in these languages before the "age of seven." However, pupils were not to be forced to learn but rather were to be "sweetly allured thereto with praises and such pretty gifts as children delight in."[9] Recognizing the need for education in keeping with the child's maturation and regardless of his or her economic status, Comenius wrote "when boys are only six years old, it is too early to determine their vocation in life, or whether they are more suited for learning or for manual labor. At this age neither the mind nor the inclinations are sufficiently developed, while, later on, it will be easy to form a sound opinion of both. Nor should admission to the Latin School be reserved for the sons of rich men, nobles and magistrates, as if these were the only boys who would ever be able to fill similar positions. The wind blows where it will, and does not always begin to blow at a fixed time."[10]

An early proponent of child study, Locke, characteristic of modern thinking, stated in 1689, "Follow a child from its birth, and observe the alterations that time makes, and you shall find, as the mind by the senses comes more and more to be furnished with ideas, it comes to be more and more awake; thinks more, the more it has matter to think on. After some time, it begins to know the objects which, being most familiar with, have made lasting impressions."[11]

More explicitly, in regard to instruction, Pestalozzi states, "The elementary method limits itself to employ the impressions which nature puts at random before the child's senses, but extends the natural process along definite lines adapted to his capacities and requirements."[12] Foreshadowing modern readiness concepts, he wrote, "This principle [adapting the instruction to intellectual capacity and mental development] necessitated the subject matter being presented at the psychological moment in order, on the one hand, not to hold him back if ready, and on the other, not to load him and confuse him with anything for which he is not ready."[13]

Froebel, also, was aware of developmental processes, for he affirmed, "It is

[7] B. Jowett (trans.), *The Dialogues of Plato*, vol. 2 (New York: Random House, 1937), p. 549.

[8] Sir Thomas Elyot, *The Boke Named the Governour*, 1531 (London: J. M. Dent, 1907), p. 19.

[9] Ibid. Cited by R. R. Rusk, *The Doctrines of Great Educators* (London: Macmillan Publishing Co., 1926), p. 55.

[10] A. Comenius (Komensky), *The Great Didactic*, 1657, Ch. 29; quoted in Rusk, op. cit., p. 101.

[11] John Locke, *An Essay Concerning Human Understanding*, Book 4.

[12] J. A. Green (ed.), *Life and Work of Pestalozzi* (London: W. B. Clive, 1913); quoted in Rusk, op. cit., p. 179.

[13] J. H. Pestalozzi, *How Gertrude Teaches Her Children* (Syracuse, N.Y.: C. W. Bardeen, 1898), p. 26.

highly important that man's development should proceed continuously from one point, and that this continuous progress be seen and even guarded."[14] He further adds, "Human education needs a guide which I think I have found in a general law of development that rules both in nature and in the intellectual world. Without law-abiding guidance, there is no free development."[15]

In a more modern vein, Montessori asserted, "By education, must be understood the active help given to the normal expansion of the life of the child."[16] She goes on to state, "It is necessary then to offer those exercises which correspond to the need of development felt by an organism, and if the child's age has carried him past a certain need it is never possible to obtain, in its fullness, a development which missed its proper moment."[17] Although today considerable opposition can be found to the latter statement, Montessori implied the importance of pacing activities to psychological and developmental needs.

Montessori predated the modern critical or sensitive periods concept, which hypothesizes that there is a time when certain developmental events take place. Furthermore, the environmental impact or nurturance at that time is the most effective, for better or for worse. This concept is basic to today's views of Early Childhood Education and is precisely why we have programs for young children. Such concepts as "readiness" and "teachable moment" are educational applications of this biological concept of critical periods in maturation. Kennedy[18] emphasizes the need for consideration of the "critical period" hypothesis in relation to the early development of children.

Early attempts at describing the characteristics of childhood, mostly biographical in nature, were made by Galton,[19] Preyer,[20] Taine,[21] Tiedemann,[22] and Darwin.[23]

This type of observation led to later adaptations, such as the questionnaires of G. Stanley Hall[24] and the more recent extensive longitudinal observations as represented by the "ages and stages" development by Gesell and Ilg,[25] and by many others.

---

[14] Froebel, *Education of Man;* quoted in Rusk, op. cit., pp. 236–237.
[15] Baroness B. von Marenholz-Bülow, *Reminiscences of Frederick Froebel,* 1877; quoted in Rusk, op. cit., p. 238.
[16] Maria Montessori, *The Montessori Method* (New York: Frederick A. Stokes, 1912), p. 104.
[17] Ibid., p. 358.
[18] W. A. Kennedy, *Child Psychology* (Englewood Cliffs, N.J.: Prentice-Hall, 1971), p. 102.
[19] F. Galton, *Hereditary Genius,* 1869.
[20] W. Preyer, *Die Seele des Kindes,* 2 vols., 1888.
[21] H. Taine, "On the Acquisition of Language by Children," *Mind,* 2 (1877), pp. 252–259.
[22] C. Murchison and S. Langer, "Tiedemann's Observations on the Development of the Mental Faculties of Children," *J. Genet. Psychol.,* 34:2, 1921), pp. 205–230.
[23] C. Darwin, "Biographical Sketch of an Infant," *Mind,* 2 (1877), pp. 285–294.
[24] G. S. Hall, "The Contents of Children's Minds," *Pedag. Sem., 1*:2 (1891), pp. 139–173.
[25] A. Gesell and Frances Ilg, *Child Development* (New York: Harper & Row, 1949).

Although many of the early writers projected their views from the stand-point of philosophy, they provided an excellent basis for extensive present-day research. The following statement by Olson is representative of present-day growth philosophy for education.[26]

> The general philosophy as applied to the growing child is a simple one. . . . Each child is to be assisted in growing according to his natural design, without deprivation or forcing, in an environment and by a process which also supply a social direction to his achievement. For the student of child development, education is a process by which children are assisted in growing; and the adequacy of administration, of the physical environment, of curriculum experiences, and of methods of teaching should be appraised in terms of the extent to which this function is realized.

There are infinite possibilities and challenges afforded adults who, as they work with young children, attempt to see each child for what he or she is, to see the influences of natural endowments and natural growth processes at work, and to discover and put into practice methods and use of materials which provide the best possible educational environment for the growing child.

GROWTH, LEARNING, MATURATION, AND DEVELOPMENT

It is all too easy to speak of growth, learning, maturation, and development as a single concept, although in reality each has a separate meaning that should be understood. Concepts of growth, borrowed from biology, deal basically with an increase of some dimension such as height, circumference of the head, and similar physical characteristics. Present-day educational literature sometimes uses the term to express change in function and includes such expressions as growth in vocabulary, growth in reading, or growth in social understanding. Often these and similar expressions are used in such a way as to imply development, a concept which will be dealt with presently.

It is helpful to think of maturation as a process, its characteristics and temporal patterns peculiar to the organism involved, that represents the innate forces producing growth and change in a fixed direction. When environmental forces such as the effects of food or exercise interact with the innate force responsible for maturation, development takes place. Development may then be thought of as the changing end product that results from the interaction of maturation and the environmental factors or nurture. Thus, there is the implication that development represents a "stage" that has been achieved at any particular point of time in the maturation process.

[26] W. C. Olson, *Child Development*, 2nd ed. (Boston: D. C. Heath, 1959), p. 449.

Figure 8

In no other area of growth and development are differences so obvious as in that of physical growth. These children all attend the same kindergarten. Their unique features and differences in height and body build illustrate the folly of the often-used description of "fiveness." Although a general description of a five-year-old may be helpful as a reference point, it is generally agreed that individual differences due to innate and experiential variations make the concept of "five" or "fiveness" misleading, and often suggest practices that do not enhance the opportunity for optimum development of each child.

A great deal has been written about learning. Psychologists devote much of their efforts to research on the process. In this frame of reference, learning is usually thought of as any observable or inferred change in response behavior caused wholly or in part by experience. As a result, several theories of learning have been developed; much is known about the conditions of learning, but the process itself still remains a mystery. In the context of education, learning is assumed to have occurred when a person has acquired relatively permanent knowledges and skills. It is generally assumed that such knowledges and skills happen as a result of practice, although learning certainly takes place as a result of single experiences. Because there is so much to learn, young children, unhampered by a large number of previous experiences, find the world a very fascinating place. As a result they learn easily and acquire knowledges and skills at a very rapid rate when their environment provides an opportunity for them to do so. While learning theory is outside the scope of this text, the student of Early Childhood Education should become familiar with the various theories of learning and their implications for education. (See Chapter 8.)

Early compensatory education for children from culturally different and low-income families is an attempt through direct intervention to enable such children to "catch up" in school learning. Previous experience and child-development research and theory would indicate a pessimistic outlook for much success. The availability of funds for such programs in the early 1960s spurred a vast amount of controlled research in this field. Notable is the work of Bereiter and Engelmann,[27] Bloom,[28] Deutsch,[29] and Hunt.[30] While early reports indicate a high level of achievement success by using direct methods and by eliminating other developmental areas common in most preschool programs, follow-up studies will be necessary to determine the effectiveness of such programs. A review of many studies done two to five years following intensive educational efforts would seem to cast doubt on the effectiveness of compensatory programs. However, some report sustained gains.[31] It is highly possible that gains may not be manifest until later childhood or adolescence.

It must be kept in mind that most children involved in these efforts continue to live in the same environments that brought about the deprivation in the first place. It seems highly unrealistic to expect a child to maintain gains resulting from short intensive learning programs without rather drastically restructuring the home and community living conditions and bringing about greatly improved family life. Many emerging programs are attempting to do just that. (See Chapter 8.) It must also be kept in mind that these programs are designed for children with severe learning deprivation and not for the majority of American children.

The expression "normal development," when applied to an individual child, means that the nurture has been such that the child concerned has achieved whatever stage of development is under consideration at about the

---

[27] C. Bereiter and S. Engelmann, *Teaching Disadvantaged Children in the Preschool* (Englewood Cliffs, N.J.: Prentice-Hall, 1966).

[28] B. S. Bloom, A. Davis, and R. Hess, *Compensatory Education for Cultural Deprivation* (New York: Holt, Rinehart and Winston, 1965).

[29] M. Deutsch, "Facilitating Development in the Preschool Child: Social and Psychological Perspectives," *Merrill-Palmer Quart.*, 10:3 (1964), pp. 249–263.

[30] J. McV. Hunt, "The Psychological Basis for Using Pre-School Enrichment as an Antidote for Cultural Deprivation," *Merrill-Palmer Quart.*, 10:3 (1964), pp. 209–248.

[31] *Educational Programs That Work*, 3rd ed. (San Francisco: Far West Laboratory for Educational Research and Development, 1976).

same time and with similar characteristics as has been achieved by most children his or her age. Developmental changes may be thought of as occurring because of the complex interaction of the forces of nature and nurture. The teacher and school have as a major purpose to provide many types of experiences which the child might not otherwise encounter, but which are designed to assist nature in the child's developmental process.

As adults work with preschool-age children and observe the numerous and varied movements, expressions, behavioral attitudes, and seemingly endless and often meaningless activities, they will have a better understanding of the needs of children if they are familiar with characteristics of growth, development, and maturation common to all children. For example, because movement and activity are essential to normal physical growth at this time, the prudent teacher avoids experiences that require long periods of quiet attention to the tasks at hand.

Likewise, all young children possess varying degrees of curiosity. Yet, not all children confront new and novel situations with bubbling enthusiasm and excitement. Standing quietly and closely observing details by intently gazing at a new object or event may be one child's way of expressing curiosity, while another child in the same situation may jump up and down screaming joyously.

Most preschool children are functioning either in what Piaget[32] describes as the sensorimotor stage or the intuitive phase of the preoperational stage of cognitive development. The sensorimotor stage (about the first eleven months) takes place prior to speech and thus lacks representation, a process characteristic of the preoperational stage, which usually lasts from seven to eight years.

The use of any one, or of several sensory modalities simultaneously, may be appropriate as children explore new experiences in ways that are unique to each. An observing adult soon learns and respects the mode of sensorimotor expression peculiar to each child in the group while at the same time encouraging new and different ways of discovering meaningful concepts. In each case, the child grows in confidence as he learns more about the world by experiencing it through his available sensory-motor repertoire at any given point in time.

The following observations depict activities and behavior common to children of normal development for the ages described. A range of individual differences is included, but these discussions are not intended to portray the characteristics of those who deviate widely from the expectancies of the respective age groups.

---

[32] Jean Piaget, *The Child and Reality: Problems of Genetic Psychology,* translated by Arnold Rosin (New York: Viking Press, 1974).

OBSERVATIONS IN A CHILD DEVELOPMENT CENTER

Early one morning, Dorothy, Robert, Mary, and Billy—all three years old—were happily playing in a large outdoor sand enclosure. To the casual observer, nothing of importance was going on. Mary and Dorothy seemed to be piling and shaping the moist sand into separate, rather large, indescribable objects, while Robert and Billy were scooping up the sand with their hands, tossing it in the air, and letting it fall wherever it happened to go. All were talking constantly but not to each other. Billy's "ridem-em cowboy" and Mary's "mother says, 'No! No!'" seemed to have no relationship to what they were doing. After a few minutes Robert, without warning, climbed out of the enclosure, falling on his hands as his feet did not quite clear the low wall which kept the sand inside. Without concern, he got up and ran to stand and watch another boy and girl simultaneously trying to claim a tricycle. Dorothy, Billy, and Mary appeared to be unaware that Robert had left their company. Suddenly, Billy's "whoopee" accompanied by a shower of sand from his rapidly rising arms attracted the attention of the teacher as Mary began to cry loudly, and Dorothy quietly rubbed the sand from her moist eyes with the convenient skirt of her dress. The teacher reassuringly put her arm about Mary's shoulders as Mary clung tightly to one of the teacher's legs, and then proceeded to remedy the situation by quietly asking Dorothy whether the sand got in her eyes and suggesting to Billy that he had not said "good morning" to the rabbit in the nearby hutch. Soon, with the teacher's guiding suggestions, all four children were engaged in new activities. Apparently, the unfortunate end of the sand play was over with and forgotten by all concerned.

What can be learned about the maturation, growth, learning, and development of normal three-year-olds from the above incident? Do these observations agree with summary findings of research intended to discover the characteristics of normal three-year-olds? Did the teacher act wisely in terms of the implications of established research findings?

Professional personnel working with the young child have long been concerned with the problem of physical growth and development for they have observed that behavior of the moment is often related to the physical makeup of the child. The observer of the sand incident noted the use of large, somewhat uncontrolled muscle movements, such as the seemingly purposeless piling of sand and the upward swinging of the arms with an aimless release of sand from the hands. Large-muscle activity is the rule during the early years. Out of these large-muscle, aimless, and seemingly endless activities there gradually emerge patterns of coordination and control.

Physical growth has been so well charted that most events, like the eruption of a particular tooth, the start of walking, or a later growth spurt can be predicted with considerable accuracy. In fact, the helpless, uncoordinated, and

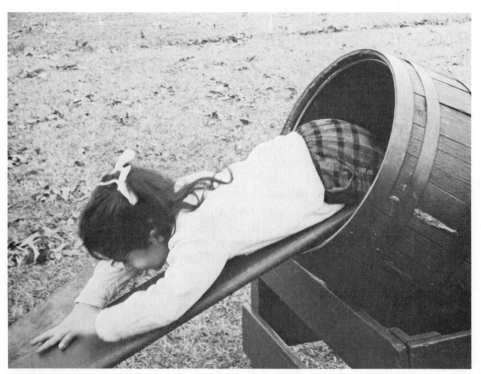

Figure 9

Physical activity and physical growth are major concerns in children's centers. Play may be just fun to the little girl coming down the slide from the barrel. Climbing up through the barrel and holding back as she comes down the incline head first provides unlimited opportunity for tensing and flexing numerous muscles and provides the much-needed movements for normal growth of the young child.

unskilled infant is able to progress through a succession of predictable and orderly developmental tasks with advancing age. Of course, this progress assumes the prerequisite nurture supplied by the parent and the home.

Stages of development, as previously indicated, always follow in a particular sequence. Children do not stand before they sit, not do they draw a square before they draw a circle. This orderly progression of events moves forward at different rates of speed, with some children growing and developing at a faster rate than others. In general, girls pass through these periods of maturity more rapidly than boys. It was noted that Dorothy and Mary seemed to be making "something" from the moist sand, while Billy and Robert were just actively, and more or less purposelessly, playing with the sand. Robert's fall wasn't merely an accident, rather it was a consequence of body proportions in which the legs and lower body parts are not developed proportionately to the upper body region—this produces a high center of gravity and falls occur at the slightest excuse. For the same reason, three-year-olds tend to run rather than walk in order to get where they want to go. Longer legs would mean longer steps!

The plan of physical growth is so well coordinated that the emergence of each stage seems to depend on the mastery of the previous one through activity and exercise. The result is a continuous orderly process. The motivation for this process is one of the marvels of life itself. There is a certain urgency about growth inherent in the child. The growing, developing child is the end product of meeting this urgency through interaction with the environment.

Physical disproportions at ages three and four, as compared to later years, dictate many of the expectancies adults should have for the three-year-old child. Eyes, for example, are a part of the body proportions that are "oversize." It is just so much easier for objects, such as sand, to get into them! Because of their peculiar shape and developmental status, farsightedness is the expectation. Large objects, long play runways, big sheets of paper, and lots of room for active play are essential partly because the eyes play an important role in eye-muscle coordination. Growth inconsistencies, improperly proportioned body parts, lack of fine control and of personal learning experiences add to the picture and account for many of the characteristics of the motor activities of the young child. The encouragement of formal reading instruction, work requiring fine muscle skills, or extended periods of concentration is wisely postponed until development catches up with the demands of these activities. However, children will seek to use these skills on their own as maturation occurs.

The teacher of young children should become familiar with what research has found to be true of the age group of children she or he is working with. Such books as those by Breckenridge and Vincent,[33] Landreth,[34] Stone and Church,[35] Cantor,[36] Merry and Merry,[37] Smart and Smart,[38] and Garrison and Jones[39] will enable the teacher to acquire an excellent grasp of research important to an understanding of the growth and development of the young child, as well as what to expect later. (See also Chapter 4.)

[33] Marian E. Breckenridge and E. Lee Vincent, *Child Development*, 4th ed. (Philadelphia: W. B. Saunders, 1960).

[34] Catherine Landreth, *The Psychology of Early Childhood* (New York: Alfred A. Knopf, 1958).

[35] L. Joseph Stone and Joseph Church, *Childhood and Adolescence,* 2nd ed. (New York: Random House, 1968).

[36] Pamela Cantor, *Understanding a Child's World* (New York: McGraw-Hill Book Company, 1977).

[37] Frieda K. Merry and R. V. Merry, *The First Two Decades of Life,* 2nd ed. (New York: Harper & Row, 1958).

[38] Mollie S. Smart and Russell C. Smart, *Children: Development and Relationships,* 2nd ed. (New York: Macmillan, Publishing Co., 1972).

[39] Karl C. Garrison and Franklin R. Jones, *The Psychology of Human Development* (Scranton, Pa.: International Textbook Co., 1969).

But the child as a person is not just a physical being. While developing physically, their personal-social and mental development is moving forward at a pace that challenges the abilities of adults working with them. Through language, children express their very being as well as the outside world as perceived. Mary's "Mother says 'No! No!'" is a sure sign that socialization is taking place. Already she is learning that doing or saying what adults closest to her think is wrong will bring disapproval. The importance of language to the child's early development cannot be overemphasized. Language development is treated in detail elsewhere in this text.

Unfortunately, science has not been able to determine such orderly laws for the personal-social and mental areas of development as it has for physical development. It is likely that the unique personality characteristics so treasured by all account for the fact that personality descriptions tend to defy lawful prediction. However, great strides are being made in personality research. Such publications as *Child Development, Childhood Education, Your Today's Child,* and *Young Children* enable teachers to keep abreast of new research findings as they apply to young children.

The fact that the other children did not notice Robert's leaving is characteristic of three-year-old children. It is true that they are happier in the presence of a few other children their own age, yet seldom do they play together. This type of play in the presence of, but not with, others their own age is known as parallel play. While three-year-olds are less demanding than they will become later, they usually stay with others only a few minutes and then leave for a new group or to explore new worlds.[40]

Murphy found that the ability to perceive the need to sympathize with another when in distress does not occur until four years of age. This could explain why no one except the teacher came to Dorothy's aid when sand got in her eyes.[41] At no time was there evidence of cooperative endeavor on the part of the children in the observation report. Again, this type of effort is seldom observed in children under four years of age.[42]

Even as early as three, sex roles are being learned, as evidenced by Billy's cowboy-type expressions and actions. However, sex-role identification is at a minimum. Little boys and girls can play together, fight with each other, share the same toilet facilities, and are seemingly unaware of sex differences. Modesty played no part whatever when Dorothy used the skirt of her dress to wipe the sand from her eyes. However, using a picture-interview technique, Fauls and Smith found that five-year-olds had well-established sex-role per-

[40] Gesell and Ilg, op. cit., pp. 209–210.
[41] Lois Barclay Murphy, *Social Behavior and Child Personality: An Exploratory Study of Some Roots of Sympathy* (New York: Columbia University Press, 1937).
[42] M. B. Parten, "Social Participation Among Pre-school Children," *J. Abnorm. Soc. Psychol.* 27:2 (1932), pp. 243–269.

ceptions in keeping with the expectations of the social group of which their parents were a part.[43] Obviously, much social learning occurs very rapidly during the preschool years. It is felt by many that the attitudes toward others and toward right and wrong developed during these years strongly persist throughout childhood and adolescence and even during the entire life span. The implications for the need of well-qualified teachers and caregivers of irreproachable character for preschool children are clear.

The question might be raised as to whether the teacher handled the sand-throwing incident correctly. What were the characteristics of three-year-olds that the teacher took into account? It should be pointed out that although the children were playing alone, the teacher must have been supervising carefully, for we was present when needed. She knew that in times of distress, three-year-olds need the reassurance of adults. She knew that crying and running to cling to the nearest adult are ways in which children of limited language facility bring their immediate needs to the attention of those they have learned to trust. The teacher knew that Billy wasn't being naughty and intentionally throwing sand at the girls in order to be mean. She was aware of the fact that three-year-olds do not carry grudges, that they forget their hurts quickly, and that most hurts are more surprise than real injury. One of the surest ways to aid developmental processes is to quietly and immediately re-direct children's activities in positive directions. The professionally informed will recognize the teacher's handling of the situation as a case of positive child discipline despite the complete absence of physical punishment, threats, or depriving of privileges. Each child was reassured by word or act and enabled to quickly return to normal and satisfying activities. It should be recognized that what was right to do for the discipline and guidance of three-year-olds might not necessarily be the proper management of children of other ages and in other situations.

In discussing the reported observation of three-year-olds, little has been said about two very important facets of development: language and learning other than social. Although accounts vary, three-year-olds are reported to have a vocabulary of approximately 1,000 words.[44] They chatter incessantly, as was observed by the recorder of the typical observation reported earlier. It is theorized that this continuous use of words is the young child's way of testing his or her new-found power—the ability to communicate. The rapid learning of language and its ability to make possible the control of environment, is one of the most challenging and important aspects of development during the preschool years. At this stage, language is, at least partly, an imitative process.

---

[43] Lydia B. Fauls and W. D. Smith, "Sex-Role Learning of Five-Year-Olds," *J. Genet. Psychol.*, 89:2 (1956), pp. 105–107.

[44] Mary K. Smith, "Measurement of the Size of General English Vocabulary Through the Elementary Grades and High School," *Genet. Psychol. Monogr.*, 24:2 (1941), pp. 311–345.

The adults present must avoid baby talk and be conscious of the fact that their enunciation and pronunciation is always the model that the child is following.

Although there is no lack of communication among children and adults in low-income families, it is more often nonverbal in nature, making more use of gestures, stares, foot stomping, or physical handling. When communication is verbal, the adult model uses fewer words and often the enunciation and grammatical structure are limited.

The mere repetition of sounds or words on the part of younger children represents the beginnings of verbal communication. The child soon learns that speech is useful in bringing approval or disapproval. In this way language is a strong force in the socialization process. At the same time it is directly functional, for through it the child is learning to communicate first with and about himself or herself, and then with and to others. Many studies refer to these patterns of speech as the egocentric and socialized functions of language. There seems to be a gradual replacement of the egocentric expressions so prevalent in the early stages of language development by those of a socialized nature so that egocentric speech practically disappears by the time the child is seven or eight years of age.[45]

It is probably more realistic to point out that language and other forms of learning develop together than it is to argue whether language is a product of learning or that learning results from language development. Whatever the genesis, it is generally agreed that language plays an essential role in the rapid acquisition of knowledge, attitudes, and other ways of responding during the early preschool years.

It is not within the scope of this book to present a detailed review of the voluminous research in child development on the characteristics of preschool-age children. The preceding observational report and discussion concerned itself with some of the major findings of importance to the teacher or caregiver of young children. A similar report of the findings of major importance to the kindergarten teacher follows.

OBSERVATIONS IN A KINDERGARTEN

A student observer arrived at the kindergarten shortly after the opening of school one morning late in the school year. The day before she had observed a group of 14 three-year-olds. She had noticed that at no time were the three-year-olds all together as a group, and she was rather surprised to find 25 five-year-olds grouped comfortably and quietly in a semicircle around the teacher intently making plans for the day. During the discussion the teacher wrote in large letters on newsprint on the easel "quiet corner," "wheel toys," "pic-

[45] R. I. Watson, *Psychology of the Child* (New York: John Wiley and Sons, 1959).

Figure 10

Individual or group play takes many forms, and objects of every description take on new meaning as they are given fascinating roles by the unlimited imagination possessed by children between the ages of three and six. Such explorations and experiences provide the basic new materials upon which later school learning is built.

ture making," "clay," "science," "story time," "juice," "outdoors," "rest," and "lunch." Three girls chose an activity by pointing to the words, "quiet corner," and went to a special corner set aside for this purpose. Three boys and one girl chose "wheel toys" and immediately proceeded to walk leisurely to the large covered porch where the tricycles, wagons, and similar toys were kept. Soon all the others were actively taking part, knowing that the teacher would warn them in plenty of time when it was story time, outdoor play time, time to rest, and time for lunch.

Obviously, great developmental strides had been made since these children were three years old. They could now plan as a group; they could be given more responsibility; they were learning that words had meaning and that choices meant certain responsibilities.

During the course of the morning, the observer made certain notes that agreed with what she had learned in her child development courses. The following discussion includes the major characteristics of five-year-olds most of which were recorded as a result of one morning's observation in a typical kindergarten setting. The observer was struck by the fact that kindergarten children appeared more grown-up and had lost their "baby" looks. There seemed to be little difference in the size of boys and girls; some of each were larger than others, "perhaps the boys are slightly taller and heavier."

During outdoor play, both boys and girls exhibited good large-muscle control. They could run easily without tripping, they seemed especially good at climbing, swinging, and performing acts of daring on parallel bars, jungle gyms, suspended planks, and rope ladders. Those who climbed the sturdy branches of the several large oak trees near the building exhibited great assurance. "At one time, they looked and sounded like a flock of birds in the trees, as they went through their well-practiced 'acts,' singing merrily as they did so," recorded the student. Another significant comment was "At no time during the morning did any of the children appear to miss mother or home. Once, a little girl picked herself up after getting in the way of two boys playing horse, looking shyly as if deciding whether to cry, ran to the teacher and held her hand momentarily, then hurried back to join her group at the outdoor easel."

The morning's observation produced some additional statistics. Two boys

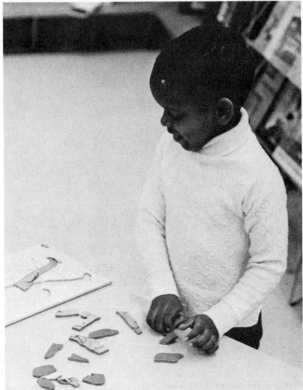

Figure 11
Interesting puzzles provide opportunities to recognize contrast, shape, form, and generalizations so important in the early phases of mental development. This boy studies intently the remaining pieces of the puzzle as he tries to decide where they will go to complete the picture.

and one girl were left-handed; all the rest were obviously right-handed. No one seemed concerned about the fact that three of the children used their left hands predominantly. All the children participated in preparing, and serving, and drinking juice and eating crackers just before going out to play. All seemed to be ready for, and to enjoy, the "nap" just before lunch. The morning produced surprisingly few conflicts and squabbles, which were usually resolved quickly, often without the teacher's help.

In comparison to three-year-olds, most five-year-olds handle language well, using it to question, to answer, to suggest, and to get permission to do things. Both vocabulary and sentence structure have greatly improved. The five-year-old has become quite independent and responsible, able to run errands, follow directions, and carry out rather complicated tasks. The five-year-old's conscience seems to be developing rapidly, for the child quickly judges and reports the small deeds of others as right or wrong.[46] Gesell and Ilg have provided a detailed account of the typical five-year-old.[47]

EMOTIONAL DEVELOPMENT

Various studies of certain aspects of the emotional development of young children show that emotional control and generally more mature behavior gradually develop during the preschool years. For example, Goodenough's classic study of expressions of anger in young children showed a gradual decline with age of undirected general outbursts of anger and a corresponding increase in anger resulting from conflicts or situations which might be described as a reasonable excuse for anger. Of interest to teachers was the finding that there were more anger expressions just before mealtime, when the children were tired, were coming down with an illness, or when some atypical home condition, such as the presence of visitors, existed.[48]

Likewise, Jersild and Holmes found that most of the specific situations which evoked fear responses in two- and three-year-old children did not produce like responses from five-year-olds.[49] These developmental differences, like so many others, apparently are due to a combination of the effects of maturation and learning. At any rate, the five-year-old represents a rather well-organized, somewhat calm and delightful period of life, as if in preparation for the demanding expectations of the more academic school years ahead.

[46] Gladys G. Jenkins, Helen Schacter, and W. W. Bauer, *These Are Your Children*, 3rd ed. (Chicago: Scott, Foresman, 1966).

[47] Gesell and Ilg., op. cit., Ch. 20.

[48] Florence L. Goodenough, "Anger in Young Children," *Univ. Minn. Inst. Child Welf. Monogr. Ser.*, 9 (1931).

[49] A. T. Jersild and Frances B. Holmes, "Children's Fears," *Child Develop. Monogr.*, 20 (1935).

DEVELOPMENT OF MOTOR SKILLS

Hicks studied the learning skills of young children involved in ball throwing at a moving target over a period of eight weeks. One group practiced 10 throws each week while another group, which was matched with the experimental group on initial ball-throwing ability, was not given the practice. When tested at the end of the experiment, both groups had made gains, but the experimental (practice) group did not make significantly better gains than the second (control) group. Apparently, children not in the control group were practicing the same skills in the course of daily living. Of course, it could be questioned whether the practice periods were often enough or intensive enough over a period as short as eight weeks to produce measurable differences in learning a complex skill.[50] Psychologists speak of learning that goes on without specific intent to learn in keeping with the maturation process as autogenous learning. Much of the learning of preschool children falls within this category.

SUMMARY

Rather than list a set of characteristics of the young child at various age levels, it should prove more meaningful to illustrate some of the principles this chapter has developed. Young children are not alike; each has unique qualities and features that become evident early in life. Beginning with innate differences, variations in growth and maturation processes interacting with the multiplicity of possible environmental differences, both physical and human, result in development that further differentiates, and thus accounts for the individuality of personality. An excellent example of this differentiation is found in the usually retarded language and achievement levels of children from culturally different homes. These basic components of individuality are well established during the preschool years. Because these processes take place very rapidly during the early years of life, major developmental differences occur during this period at shorter intervals than at any later period of life, which accounts for the dramatic and challenging changes observed in young children.

Today much emphasis is placed on the importance of how children view themselves, that is, on the development of the concept of self. There are those who would build a young child's learning experiences entirely around this concept. However, it is becoming increasingly clear that a healthy self-concept

[50] A. Hicks, "The Acquisition of Motor Skill in Young Children: A Study of the Effects of Practice in Throwing at a Moving Target," *Child Develop.*, 1:2 (1930), pp. 90–105.

is dependent on how well a child's behavior fits social and environmental expectancies, for only such behavior receives the reinforcement provided by approval, praise, and acceptance. For example, "Sesame Street" has become a symbol of good child-rearing practice by middle-class families in America, even though the program was not designed with this audience in mind. A young middle-class child who is not exposed to "Sesame Street" would be likely to feel somewhat inferior among peers and parents who are familiar with the program. It would seem realistic, therefore, to view each child's self concept in relation to all aspects of development, including cognitive development, rather than as an isolated concept.

Students of child growth and development have found that development corresponds rather closely with maturational change and growth patterns. To the person who understands the processes of growth, maturation, and development, there are always small signs as to what will occur later. For example, not long ago a mother called who was very concerned because the child was not walking when other children of the same age were. The child was observed during the interview. Certain signs were noticed, such as creeping and moving in a circular direction, attempting to pull himself up on every occasion, and a general effort to arrive in an upright position. These signs indicated that within a few weeks the child would be walking and that development was occurring as a result of maturation and growth. The mother was reassured, and she reported several weeks later that her child was walking. The important point here is that when one understands the developmental process and watches for the little signs that precede an actual act, anxieties can easily be relieved. It is also important to know that readiness is often primarily a biological function that cannot be hurried. Nevertheless, it is necessary to keep in mind that biological development does not proceed on its own without suitable environmental nurture. Unfortunately, lack of readiness has often been mistaken, in the past, for an inherent biological lack, rather than a lack of adequate environmental stimulation to enable maturation to occur on schedule. However, when the stage or maturation point is arrived at and the act can be completed, the child will complete the act and do it with enthusiasm and with a high degree of motivation. Psychologists call this indigenous motivation, which means that when one is able to do something at the proper stage of maturation, one will do it, and with zest and vigor. Everyone has observed young children arriving at this stage.

Another important factor is that growth, although it occurs rather uniformly for an individual, make take place in one child at a speed or rate different from that of other children. So far as is known, this is an inherited characteristic. Each growing child possesses an individual pattern and rate of growth. When arriving at a certain place in this pattern the child can "tune in" and achieve the goal just the same as a radio can be tuned in to get a program that was present all the time but was not coming in until it was tuned in to the proper wavelength. Similarly, certain activities and certain behavioral acts cannot be achieved until the proper "wavelength" represented by development can be tuned in to the circumstances provided in the environment. The teacher, caregiver, or parent can no more change this process than the color of one's hair can be changed. True, hair can be dyed and temporarily it will appear different, but it will grow out to be the color it should be at a particular time; the change is only temporary. The same kind of thing often happens when youngsters are pushed and undue pressures put upon them, or when remedial work is carried on for long periods of time. Always, the individual functions in keeping with his or her stage of development.

While a "stage" represents a point in development at a particular time, growth and maturation proceed as a somewhat erratic continuum. The concept of threes, fours, fives, and so forth, merely represents specific points on the continuum from birth to maturity. This ongoingness of development is hard to describe primarily because developmental research on which such descriptions are based is developmental in name only, as it represents a succession of points rather than a true continuum.[51]

Perhaps the best way to summarize is to indicate that there is likely to be no "static," or discipline problems, when the wavelength is right and the activities are tuned in to the child's stage of development. It is important to realize further that all behavior is caused and that undesirable behavior results when the individual is not properly "tuned in" to activities which are consistent with his or her stage of development and thus, the ability "to do."

Some three-year-olds may be able to do the tasks normally expected of five-year-olds, and some five-year-olds can perform only the tasks usually expected of three-year-olds. But in general, the expectancies adults have for each child should be in keeping with those suitable to his or her age group and particular stage of development. The concept of "threeness," "fiveness," and so on, so common in the literature, has served a useful purpose by pointing out the direction we can reasonably expect a child's development to take. However, educational programs for groups based on such concepts without provision for a wide range of individual differences in development, would most surely fail to provide for the optimal development of each child as a person.

Suggested Activities

1. Prepare a detailed class report on the development of children on such topics as "readiness to learn," "a typical four-year-old," "learning sex roles," "early speech

---

[51] R. B. McCall, "Challenge to a Science of Developmental Psychology," *Child Develop.*, 48:2 (1977), pp. 333–344.

development," "motor development of five-year-olds." Use the references given in the text and any other that you can find on the topic.

2. Discuss and decide on a specific topic, such as some of those in 1 above, "readiness for the first day of school," "teeth and the preschooler," "children's diseases," "socialization," "motor development and materials and equipment," "sibling relationships," "development of creativity," "crying," and so on. Prepare and report on one research study from the current periodicals related to the above topics. Discuss each report and use the study as a basis for continuing discussion.

3. Arrange with a nursery school or kindergarten teacher to observe for 15 minutes a planned activity with a group of young children. Immediately afterward, write down what you learned about children and about yourself from the experience. If several members of the group do the same thing, such observations can provide the information for a lively class discussion.

4. Select a child to observe over a period of time. Evaluate his or her concept of self. Document with descriptive observations how you arrived at the conclusions of your evaluation.

5. If the birthrate increases and children become more "valuable" again as predicted, what changes in child-rearing practices and types of preschool programs would you anticipate finding in the late 1980s?

6. Have a class committee plan and lead a discussion on the topic, "The later results of preschool educational experiences that can be expected to be evident in the third grade." Be sure to be specific regarding expectations.

Related Readings

America's Children, 1976. Washington, D.C.: NCOCY, 1976.

Bloom, B. S., et al. *Compensatory Education for Cultural Deprivation.* New York: Holt, Rinehart, and Winston, 1965.

Brockman, Lois M., and H. N. Riceluti. "Severe Protein-Calorie Malnutrition and Cognitive Development in Infancy and Early Childhood," *Develop. Psychol.,* 4:3 (1971), pp. 312–319.

Bromwich, Rose M. "Stimulation in the First Year of Life: A Perspective on Infant Development," *Young Children,* 32:2 (January 1977), pp. 71–82.

Corcoran, Gertrude B. *Language Experiences for Nursery and Kindergarten Years.* Itasca, Ill.: F. E. Peacock Publishers, 1976.

Elkind, D. *Child Development and Education: A Piagetian Perspective.* New York: Oxford University Press, 1976.

Erikson, Erik H. *Toys and Reasons.* New York: Library of Human Behavior, 1977.

Flavell, J. H. *Cognitive Development.* Englewood Cliffs, N.J.: Prentice-Hall, 1977.

―――. *The Developmental Psychology of Jean Piaget.* Princeton, N.J.: Van Nostrand–Reinhold, 1962.

Hunt, J. McV. "The Psychological Basis for Using Pre-School Enrichment as an Antidote for Cultural Deprivation," *Merrill-Palmer Quart.,* 10:3 (1964), pp. 209–248.

Hurlock, Elizabeth B. *Child Development,* 5th ed. New York: McGraw-Hill Book Co., 1972.

Kallstrom, Christine. *Yellow Brick Road (Ages 5–6)*. Austin, Texas: Learning Concepts, 1977.

Kaplan, A., and Joan Bean (eds.). *Beyond Sex-Role Stereotypes: Readings Toward a Psychology of Androgyny*. Boston: Little, Brown, 1976.

Mussen, P. H., et al. *Child Development and Personality*, 5th ed. New York: Harper & Row, 1974.

The Nature and Nurture of Behavior: Readings from Scientific American. San Francisco, Calif.: W. H. Freeman and Co., 1973.

Oleron, P. (translated by R. P. Lorion). *Language and Mental Development*. Hillsdale, N.J.: Lawrence Erlbaum Assoc., 1977.

———. "The General Problems of the Psychobiological Development of the Child," in *Discussions on Child Development*, edited by J. M. Tanner, and B. Inhelder. New York: International Universities Press, 1960.

Raman, Pattabi (ed.). *Nutrition in Human Development*. Stamford, Conn.: Greylock Publishers, 1977.

Roedell, W. C. *Social Development in Young Children*. Washington, D.C.: DHEW, NIE, 1976.

Samuels, Shirley C. *Enhancing Self Concept in Early Childhood*. New York: Human Sciences Press, 1977.

Todd, Vivian E., and Helen Heffernan. *The Years Before School*, 3rd ed. New York: Macmillan Publishing Co., 1977.

Travers, J. F. *The Growing Child: An Introduction to Child Development*. New York: John Wiley and Sons, 1977.

———. *The New Children: The First Six Years*. Stamford, Conn.: Greylock Publishers, 1976.

chapter 4

The young child and research

This chapter highlights the importance of research using children as subjects as a vehicle for determining public policy in relation to programs for young children and their families. These programs include health and other social services, as well as the implementation of educational programs for infants and young children. This chapter is not intended to be a review of research using children as subjects nor is it intended to be a critique of research methodology. Relevant research is documented in every chapter throughout this book in the form of discussion, rather than in-depth analysis or critique.

RESEARCH AND PUBLIC POLICY

Perhaps the most significant development with respect to children and research during the 1970s was the consensus among members of the research community of the indispensability of the adequate and proper use of research findings in determining public policy for services and programs for children. Researchers were showing increasing concern for the individual obligation of each to see that their own research findings were properly interpreted and disseminated to the appropriate policymaking groups or individuals. Significant deliberations of the prestigious Society for Research in Child Development meeting held at the 1977 biennial meeting in New Orleans centered on the role of the Society and its individual members in policy formation in relation to children.

PUBLIC INTERVENTION

The changed child's world (see Chapter 2) clearly pointed to the need for public intervention in family life and child-rearing if the best interests of a large number of American children were to be served. Policy decisions, for political reasons, though a reality in American life, are not always in the best interests of children and their families. These developments as would be expected, had a profound effect on both the nature and purposes of the research being carried out. The then current need for early education and alternate parenting as more and more mothers of young children reentered the work force or continued pursuing their career objectives was reflected in the program of the Society for Research in Child Development meeting referred to earlier. Of the 376 papers accepted for presentation, 91 were on infancy, 71 on socialization, 67 on cognition and memory, 55 on language and speech, 25 on perception, 16 on adolescence, 16 on biologic and genetic factors, 16 on socioeconomic and ethnic factors, 14 on clinical and intervention problems, and only 6 on intellectual development.[1] At that time, researchers using children as subjects were assigning high priority to the social and developmental needs of infants and young children in order to assure more successful care and educational programs for three-, four-, and five-year-olds.

PROTECTION OF HUMAN RIGHTS

In recent years, there has been increasing concern for the protection of human rights. The right-to-privacy laws (Privacy Act of 1974) have been felt in educa-

[1] *Report of the Program Committee*, SRCD Biennial meeting, New Orleans, March 17–20, 1977 (Topeka, Kansas: Menninger Foundation, *SRCD Newsletter*, Summer, 1977), p. 12.

tional circles as confidentiality of records, except under certain conditions, has been abolished by law. Concern for the protection of children participating in research projects has received much attention. At the January 1977 meeting of the National Commission for the Protection of Human Subjects of Biomedical and Behavioral Research held in Bethesda, Maryland it was decided that research including children is "important for the health and well being of children and can be conducted in an ethical manner."[2] The Commission was established under the National Research Act of 1974 to identify ethical principles underlying research involving human subjects. Although many attempts have been made to provide adequate guidelines for research using children as subjects, at the time of this writing the National Commission had not finalized such a statement.

The panel of the Commission did, however, recommend that the Secretary of Health, Education and Welfare support and conduct research with children within a broad framework, including approval of minimum-risk projects by institutional review boards, and that those posing greater than minimal risk be approved by a national ethical advisory board. It was suggested that appropriate consent from children and parents be secured and that participation be severely limited for children who had no parents.

It is interesting to note that at the time of the above deliberations, HEW was currently supporting 3500 research projects involving children at a cost of $391 million, more than half of which were supported by the Education division. Researchers agree that most research involving children does not present a serious risk to them, and that it is extremely valuable for the social good of society as a whole.[3]

It is generally thought that research with children should protect the integrity of the family and the importance of parenting, as well as facilitate efforts that will involve both children and parents in decision making that affects their own lives. Since current emphasis in human research is on its usefulness to social policymaking, such involvement and restraints as discussed here are essential, for the lives of all Americans are affected by these decisions.

Behavioral scientists often use animals as subjects because custom and human values tend to discourage the use of human subjects in controlled experimentation. In many cases, the information obtained from such experimentation is likely to be as valid when interpreted in terms of human behavior; still, the question remains: Would humans react in the same way? College students provide a readily accessible source of subjects for research and have been used extensively as such. Preschool-age children as research subjects (except for hospital and institutional populations, such as orphans, seriously

---

[2] Susan Lawrence, "Panel Takes up Children as Subjects," *APA Monitor* (February 1977).
[3] Ibid.

ill, and physically disabled children) have traditionally been much more difficult to secure.

Today, with thousands of young children in Child Development Centers, which usually require some participation on the part of parents, opportunities for research with children and their families are almost unlimited. It has been the experience of researchers in centers where parents participate that it is easier to secure their consent to have their children take part in research efforts. Such has not been the case where parents were only responsible for seeing that the children were delivered to the custody of the school or center. It enhances the self-concept of parents when they feel that they are actively participating in an effort that may produce new and better ways of providing a chance for their own children to have a richer, more rewarding life than they themselves have been able to enjoy.

CHILD RESEARCH IN PERSPECTIVE

Beginning in the 1920s, several universities established nursery schools and kindergartens to provide preschool-age children for research. This practice has continued, and many universities now have such laboratory groups of children. However, it was not until the advent of Head Start in 1965 that a large number of groups of preschool-age children became readily available for research purposes. Research sponsored by the Office of Economic Opportunity included provision for follow-up studies of Head Start children in the first three grades of the public schools in a program called Follow Through. This program provided funds for continuous evaluation and research, the results of which are continually being updated.

Research and evaluation of programs conducted by other government agencies, and foundations during the present decade are providing a wealth of information about how young children, particularly culturally different children, learn and give clues to the improvement of educational practices for all youngsters. As would be expected, an all-out search for quick panaceas for the faults of the entire educational program took place at once, and often extravagant claims were made on the basis of short-term, sometimes poorly designed, and small-sample research.

There is no question that innovation and experimentation are to be encouraged, but the Early Childhood Education teacher should carefully weigh the evidence presented before making radical departures from accepted procedures that have in the past enabled most preschool children to make a successful transition to the more formal public school program.

Most such programs are conducted at a much greater cost than are regular programs. Consequently, more and better equipment and materials and usually more faculty and helpers are called into play. Often the teacher or experimenter is imbued with confidence and a missionary zeal. Without comparable conditions and support of existing programs, it is unfair to make comparisons and claim superior achievements. Many such research programs have deliberately excluded the stimulation of areas of development other than the one being studied, usually the cognitive or intellectual area. It is not surprising that children learn specific facts or skills more rapidly when they are formally taught, rather than when expected to learn them incidentally. The important question is whether these specific facts and skills are the "right" ones and whether they will truly be effective in the later school and personal life of the child involved. When areas of development, earlier shown to be necessary correlates to learning and personality development, have been purposefully omitted or relegated to roles of secondary importance, will the end product be in keeping with the goals of American education? Observations of the preschool programs in the early 1960s have indicated that the cognitive and intellectual development of young children, in some instances at least, have received less attention than have such areas as social, physical, and emo-

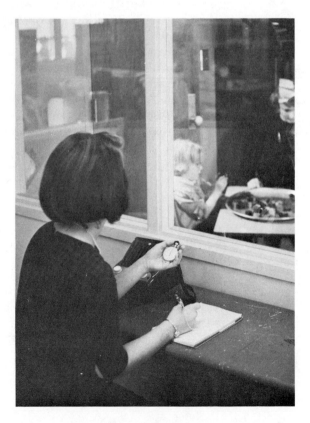

Figure 12

An observation booth with a one-way vision mirror lends itself to conducting research about children.

tional development.[4] Calling attention to this lack can well serve a useful purpose in helping bring about a better balanced program of education for young children, provided that other areas of development are not neglected. It is well known that the medical profession soon discovered that the quick acceptance and widespread use of antibiotics and other miracle drugs had made it harder to cure the very diseases the drugs were developed to cure, because through overuse of these medications the organism tends to develop an immunity. Child development specialists caution that too intensive emphasis on academic learning, too early, might likewise make later learning more difficult to achieve.

Although it has been claimed that early research in child development neglected the cognitive areas, it can also be said with equal vindictiveness that much of the research in the second half of the 1960s tended to ignore areas of development other than the cognitive area. The futility of an either-or approach was becoming evident as research merged into the 1970s. It was becoming accepted that whatever the research orientation or focus, the ultimate goal was the extension of knowledge that would enable children to have an opportunity for optimum personal development, assuring a "good" life for all.

Research, of necessity, cannot be global in nature. Rather, research must focus on specifics that can be defined and controlled but, at the same time, can be fitted into the larger stream of theory and ongoing practice.

RESEARCH REVIEWS

To expect the busy teacher or center worker to select helpful guidelines from thousands of research reports is asking the impossible. It is the responsibility of scholars and professional organizations to digest and integrate research findings into useful terms for research to serve its function and to justify its cost. One such effort worthy of note is a volume edited by Hartup.[5] For an encyclopedic, up-to-date review of research in child psychology, see Mussen.[6]

Although large sample research using young children was not extensive prior to the 1950s, important reviews have been made. Excellent analyses of research in all areas of development in young children can be found in *The Manual of Child Psychology*.[7] Descriptions and evaluations of the most com-

[4] F. M. Hechinger (ed.), *Pre-School Education Today* (Garden City, N.Y.: Doubleday & Co., 1966). Also, C. Bereiter and S. Englemann, *Teaching Disadvantaged Children in the Preschool* (Englewood Cliffs, N.J.: Prentice-Hall, 1966).
[5] Willard W. Hartup (ed.), *The Young Child, Reviews of Research*, Vol. 2 (Washington D.C.,: National Association for the Education of Young Children, 1972).
[6] Paul H. Mussen (ed.), *Carmichael's Manual of Child Psychology*, 3rd ed., Vols. 1 and 2. (New York: John Wiley and Sons, 1970).
[7] Ibid.

mon techniques and methods used in studying many aspects of child growth and behavior, as well as other valuable content, are included in the *Handbook of Research Methods in Child Development.*[8]

Prepared under the auspices of the Society for Research in Child Development, the *Review of Child Development Research* series provides the student with a reference to important research studies in child development as well as excellent source of additional readings.[9]

Sears and Dowley have traced the effect of research on teaching and procedures used in the nursery school.[10] They draw attention to the fact that nursery education in the United States has had as its primary objective the welfare of persons other than the children, with a resulting lack of emphasis on the child as an individual. Use should also be made of such standard library resources as the *Annual Review of Psychology,* the *Encyclopedia of Educational Research, The Handbook of Research on Teaching, The Review of Educational Research, Child Development Abstracts and Bibliography,* and *Psychological Abstracts.* It is always wise to consult the current issues or volumes of these sources for the latest information available. Another valuable source is *Resources in Education,* the official journal of the *Educational Resources Information Centers (ERIC).* Publications of the *1980 White House Conference* on Children and Youth will be an invaluable interpretation of the most pertinent research with children.

EFFECT OF RESEARCH ON PROGRAMS

Dissemination and application of research findings have always been difficult. Five Regional Information Exchanges have been created by the National Institute of Education. One such effort is the cooperative venture of CEMREL, Inc., St. Louis, Missouri, with the Mid-Continent Regional Educational Laboratory, Kansas City, Missouri. CEMREL, now operating as a private, nonprofit corporation, serves as an educational laboratory partially sup-

[8] P. H. Mussen (ed.), (New York: John Wiley and Sons, 1960).

[9] Editors of the respective volumes are:

Vols. 1 and 2, M. L. Hoffman and Lois Wladis Hoffman (New York: Russell Sage Foundation, 1964 and 1967).

Vol. 3, Bettye M. Caldwell and H. Riccuiti (Chicago: University of Chicago Press, 1973).

Vol. 4, Frances Degan Horowitz, E. M. Hetherington, Sandra Scarr-Salapetek, and G. M. Siegal (Chicago: University of Chicago Press, 1974).

Vol. 5, E. M. Hetherington, J. W. Hagan, R. Kron, and Aletha Hustin Stein (Chicago: University of Chicago Press, 1975).

Vol. 6, Willard Hartup (Chicago: University of Chicago Press, 1977).

[10] Pauline S. Sears and Edith M. Dowley, "Research on Teaching in the Nursery School," in *Handbook of Research on Teaching,* edited by N. L. Gage (Chicago: Rand McNally, 1963), Ch. 15.

ported by National Institute of Education funds. Of interest to Early Childhood Education are the following products: "Darcee Curriculum Guides," "How Does a Rainbow Feel?" and "The Arts in Early Education" by Nancy Richard and Stanley S. Madeja. The latter describes an extension of the earlier Early Education Arts Curriculum into kindergarten. "How Does a Rainbow Feel?" is a film produced by CEMREL's Aesthetic Education Program.[11]

The results of the several longitudinal studies of the 1920s and 1930s forced teachers to change their emphasis to concern for the growth and development of children. Following World War II, more concern for parent involvement developed, and the permissive, protective programs of small groups of children gave way to more structured programs of larger groups of children.

It was not until the late 1950s and 1960s that a genuine need for, and interest in, research on the early learning and development of cognitive skills took place. Landmarks in this area were the publication of Piaget's *The Origins of Intelligence in Children*,[12] Hunt's *Intelligence and Experience*,[13] Bruner's *The Process of Education*,[14] and Bloom's *Stability and Change in Human Characteristics*.[15] As a result of these and similar publications, researchers and programmers turned their attention to the early years of development. There were numerous experimental programs concerned almost wholly with the concept of learning as being the acquisition of specific material. Such acquisition was, and still is, widely lauded as superior to the kind of learning that grows out of meaningful experience and results from the interests and needs of children. Proponents of the acquisition concept point out that such early acquisition is necessary because the materials taught are the basic elements of what the child is expected to learn on entering a regular elementary school program.

Students of the history of education are not surprised by these developments, for history shows that educational programs have always been sensitive to contemporary social and cultural conditions. In a like manner, the accompanying research always has as its objective finding more efficient means of achieving the desired outcomes. The Space Age has brought about a need for highly structured areas of knowledge and public concern for the quality of education in the schools. The best development of each child as an individual thus became secondary to the aim of having children acquire as much specific knowledge as could be learned in the shortest possible time. Because research has

---

[11] *CEMREL Newsletter*, 2:1 (Winter 1976), pp. 1–8.

[12] J. Piaget, *The Origins of Intelligence in Children* (New York: International Universities Press, 1952).

[13] J. McV. Hunt, *Intelligence and Experience* (New York: Ronald Press, 1960).

[14] J. S. Bruner, *The Process of Education* (Cambridge, Mass.: Harvard University Press, 1961).

[15] B. Bloom, *Stability and Change in Human Characteristics* (New York: John Wiley and Sons, 1964).

Figure 13
Research may also be carried on in a naturalistic setting.

discovered that young children learn rapidly and acquire vast amounts of specific knowledge quickly, much attention was directed to the education of preschool children in the mid-1960s.

Concurrent with the increased Space Age needs, poverty and its attendant educational problems increased at an alarming rate. Children of poverty-stricken families have always suffered an acute educational disadvantage. However, it was not until the affluent 1960s that the disparities between the poor and the rest of society became critical enough to cause national concern. Educators applauded when the federal government took measures to attack poverty with educational programs, especially programs for very young children. This mammoth effort required not only educational programs, but large-scale research to ensure the effectiveness and improvement of these programs.

Research on language acquisition and communication skills

Crucial to all education is the acquisition of language and communication skills. Typical of the all-out attack on language acquisition is the work of Bereiter and Engelmann. They conclude:[16]

> Evidence was cited which suggests that lack of concrete learning has relatively little to do with the intellectual and academic deficiences of disadvantaged children and that is the lack of verbal learning, in particular the lack of those kinds of learning that can only be transmitted from adults to children through language, that is mainly responsible for these deficiencies. Thus there is justification for treating cultural deprivation as synonymous with language deprivation.

Bereiter and Engelmann presented evidence that the exclusion of every possible opportunity to experience other than the specifics being taught results in a much greater rate of learning than is normally experienced by children. It is their thesis that by teaching the essential and fundamental content for school achievement the culturally different children will quickly catch up with their more privileged peers and, thus, be able to compete favorably with them in regular school. The experienced educator, while impressed with the valuable contributions of this work, will view with caution the authoritarian evangelism with which the authors present their program.

Because highly developed speech and language distinguish humans from all other living organisms, the importance of these faculties has long held the attention of scholars and research workers. As both faculties are highly developed before American children are required to enter school, a knowledge of research findings in these areas can be of great value to the preschool teacher.

Language is not only a symbolic representation of objectives and ideas, it is also a means of expressing feelings and thoughts, including facial expression and gestures. Piaget early believed that thought precedes language but that as language competency develops language directs thinking.[17] The earliest and most frequent use of language by very young children is essentially emotional in nature and is used to express desires and feelings.[18] The use of words and symbols for objects or events comes later. Thus, it would appear that teaching letters of the alphabet, parts of words representing sounds and sound combinations, and written symbols before meaningful experiences that result in

---

[16] C. Bereiter and S. Engelmann, *Teaching Disadvantaged Children in the Preschool* (Englewood Cliffs, N.J.: Prentice-Hall, 1966), p. 42.

[17] J. Piaget, *Language and Thought of the Child* (New York: Humanities Press, 1951).

[18] Dorothea McCarthy, "Language Development in Children," in *Manual of Child Psychology*, 2nd ed., edited by L. Carmichael (New York: John Wiley and Sons, 1954).

feelings and thoughts on the part of the child would not be the most efficient means of promoting language success.

Language development is indeed an exceedingly complex problem, and much research attention is being given to it by psychologists, linguists, learning theorists, and grammarians. Reacting to papers presented at a conference on the acquisition of language, Deese comments:[19]

> The human being is able to transcend the effects of a reinforcement schedule through his ability to store and internalize environment behavior and intrabehavioral relations through the mediation of language; therefore, it is that aspect of language which makes it different from elements of behavior simply and entirely under the control of reinforcement contingencies, which makes language unique and worth studying in its own right.

Interesting theories regarding the origin, structure, and modification of language have been provided by linguists in recent years and have generated testable hypotheses for research. Notable in this respect has been the work of Brown.[20]

Bernstein[21] believes that language shapes both thought and social class initiating and reinforcing behavior appropriate to each specific class. Lower-class children use what he calls restricted codes, while middle-class children use elaborated codes that correspond roughly to the English expected by the schools. Thus children outside the mainstream group experience difficulty with the language used in the classroom. Recent efforts to treat standard English as a second language for language-different groups is an example of the application of these findings.

Brown found that children begin using two-word sentences at 18 to 24 months of age. Most significant is the fact that almost universally from the very start, the child expresses the basic grammatical relationships among subject, predicate, and object of the verb, even though words have been left out. Programs that stress language development accept simple, incomplete, but grammatically accurate, expressions on the part of the children. Thus, the young child may say "Where book?" for "Where is my book?" or "Leo run?" for "Will Leo run?" or perhaps meaning "Can Leo run?" No one knows for sure why language usage develops in this way, but research does show that early language development is an orderly process governed by rules present in the language modeled by the adults in the child's immediate environment. These rules vary from class to class and from culture to culture. Current theory has it

[19] James Deese, "Comments and Conclusions," in *The Acquisition of Language,* edited by U. Bellugi and R. Brown, *Mongr. Soc. Res. Child Develop.,* 29:1 (1964), p. 180.
[20] R. Brown, *A First Language* (Cambridge, Mass.: Harvard University Press, 1973).
[21] B. A. Bernstein, "A Sociolinguistic Approach to Socialization: With Some Reference to Educability," in *Language and Poverty: Perspectives on a Theme,* edited by F. Williams (Chicago: Markham, 1970, pp. 25–61).

that no one set of standards is superior to another, as long as the language used serves its purpose of meaningful communication.

Because language development is so crucial during the formative years, most students reading this book will have had a specialized course in preschool language development. For those who wish to investigate the applications of theory and research presented here, help will be found in the work of N. Chomsky,[22] Oleron,[23] Tough[24] and the general references at the end of this chapter.

OTHER APPLICATIONS OF RESEARCH

The coming of Head Start in the mid-1960s had a strong impact on educational research. The favorite effort was to "raise the IQ," often losing sight of the important gains made by Head Start children in areas other than cognitive development. For example, the "Kirschner Report"[25] on the impact of Head Start was optimistic that fundamental changes in educational and health institutions had taken place in the short period of less than five years. In both instances the traditional "middle-class" orientation had become more responsive to "the needs and desires of the poor."[26]

Cognition, or the process of knowing, has long been a subject for theory and research, especially by European scientists. Because cognition embraces thought and concept formation or meaningful understanding, an increasing number of American researchers and theorists have turned to studies of cognition in young children in an effort to determine more effective educational procedures. While the age-old battle concerning the effects of heredity and environment on intelligence and learning ability is far from resolved, much emphasis today is placed on environmental effects. The Russian scientist, Zaporozhets, summarizes thus:[27]

> At the beginning, a new way of becoming acquainted with an object is usually carried into practice by organs that are capable of performing both practical and cognitive functions, such as the hands' touching and manipulating an object or by

---

[22] Noam Chomsky, *The Logical Structure of Linguistic Theory* (New York: Plenum Publishing Corp., 1975).

[23] Pierre Oleron (translated by Raymond P. Lorion), *Language and Mental Development* (Hillsdale, N.J.: Lawrence Erlbaum Assoc., 1977).

[24] Joan Tough, *Listening to Children Talking: A Guide to the Appraisal of Children's Use of Language* (London: Ward Lock, 1976).

[25] *A National Survey of the Impact of Head Start Centers on Community Institutions* (Washington, D.C.: prepared for the Office of Child Development, HEW, by Kirschner Associates, 1970).

[26] Ibid., p. 19.

[27] A. V. Zaporozhets, "The Development of Perception in the Preschool Child," in *European Research in Cognitive Development, Monogr. Soc. Res. Child Develop.*, 30:2 (1965), pp. 98, 100.

the muscle apparatus of the larynx. . . . In reality, as we have tried to show in our paper, a given form of perception is the product of a continuous development that goes on in the child under the influences of practical experiences and learning.

Flavell[28] an American exponent of Piaget, Ojemann and Pritchett,[29] and Deutsch,[30] among others, have presented evidence to show that cognitive development can be modified and/or accelerated by manipulating the child's environment in specific ways. As a result, many preschool programs are becoming more structured than in the past. Considered modifications of the more permissive, relatively unstructured programs of the past, placing more emphasis on learning and intellectual development, do result in better educational experiences for young children. It is only when undue stress is placed on learning, or on a single component of development, that the quality of a good school program is endangered. The early childhood teacher must have preparation to enable her to understand and interpret research if she is to provide the best possible educational experiences for young children.

To say that interest in the importance of early education to the child's later development had waned since the first edition of this text would be a gross misstatement. The National Society for the Study of Education devoted its 400-page Seventy-first Yearbook to Early Childhood Education.[31] While reading the Yearbook, one cannot help but be impressed by the documented dependence on research for the viewpoints expressed by the various contributors. It would be highly premature to say that a theory of Early Childhood Education had emerged at the time of the publication of this text. Indeed, it would be more accurate to say that the research of the 1960s and 1970s, while clearly building on and adding to earlier findings, was only a beginning, albeit a fruitful and encouraging one. The Yearbook's chapter on research and evaluation[32] points the way toward more fruitful research strategies and methodology to provide information enabling the development of innovative and functional education programs for young children.

By the late 1970s, Early Childhood Education had become firmly entrenched. A new dimension had been added as well: the handicapped. Titles like *Instructional Materials for the Handicapped: Birth Through Early*

---

[28] J. H. Flavell, *The Developmental Psychology of Jean Piaget* (New York: Van Nostrand-Reinhold, 1964).

[29] R. Ojemann and K. Pritchett, "Piaget and the Role of Guided Experience in Human Development," *Perceptual and Motor Skills, 17* (1963).

[30] M. Deutsch, "Facilitating Development in the Pre-School Child: Social and Psychological Perspectives," *Merrill-Palmer Quart., 10*:3 (1964), pp. 249–263.

[31] Ira J. Gordon (ed.), *Early Childhood Education*, The Seventy-first Yearbook of the National Society for the Study of Education, Part II (Chicago: University of Chicago Press, 1972).

[32] Ibid., pp. 261–290.

Childhood[33] appeared. In addition, research was providing more reports of successful programs.[34]

Some federally funded programs have won the HEW Seal of Approval. However, not all evaluations of the research effort are so optimistic.

Project Longstep[35] deals with the effect of educational innovation over a five-year period on children in grades 1, 4, and 6. These studies mirror much of the earlier research on innovation in educational programs. The findings might well have some impact for such programs geared toward younger children. In essence, the primary hypothesis that substantial gain in achievement performance would be positively associated with innovative emphasis was not supported by the research data.[36]

EDUCATIONAL ASSESSMENT

Perhaps the concept *educational assessment* is more fitting than research per se in determining the effectiveness of specific educational and teaching strategies when dealing with programs for young children. This should in no way detract from the value of basic research as a means of providing assumptions and hypotheses for making decisions for change. However, assessment rather than research may well provide the most valuable data on which to make decisions to continue, discontinue, or modify existing procedures and programs. For an elaboration of educational assessment see the ASCD publication edited by Beatty.[37] (See also Chapter 21.)

SUMMARY

The technological, economic, and social developments of recent decades have brought about a re-evaluation of the effectiveness of the American educational program. This has led to general acceptance of the importance of education during the early childhood years. However, there is little accord as to the best methods and curriculum to be used.

[33] A. R. Thorum, et al., *Instructional Materials for the Handicapped: Birth Through Early Childhood* (Salt Lake City: Olympus Publishing Co., 1976).
[34] *Educational Programs That Work*, 3rd ed. (San Francisco: Far West Laboratory for Educational Research and Development, 1977).
[35] A. B. Chalupsky and G. J. Coles, *Exploring the Impact of Educational Innovation: Overview of Project Longstep* (Palo Alto, Calif.: American Institutes for Research, 1976).
[36] Ibid., p. 7.
[37] Walcott H. Beatty (ed.), *Improving Educational Assessment and an Inventory of Measures of Affective Behavior* (Washington D.C.: Association for Supervision and Curriculum Development, 1969).

Influenced by an abundance of sponsored research, many innovative and experimental schools for young children have come into being. Recent research has pointed particularly to the importance of language and cognitive development during the early years. Much of this effort has been aimed at enabling children who have been deprived of normal early experiences to catch up with, or compensate for, the lack of learning competencies thus brought about.

Research on the early years of life is long overdue and should be welcomed and encouraged. However, as is true of all research, findings should be implemented only as they apply to conditions under which the research was conducted; they should not be generalized. Educators should not view all research efforts with alarm. Rather, with the present improved research technology and support, early childhood educators should view these developments as the frontier movement in education today and point the way to innovation and improvement in the entire educational system.

We are long past the point of abandoning research efforts solely to raise the IQ in favor of recording sophisticated observable change resulting from the implementation of clearly stated objectives, whether they be in the physical, affective, or cognitive domain. We believe that any program that ignores major areas of the growth and developmental needs of the child will not succeed in producing individuals who can function intelligently in a democratic society.

How are research findings used to (1) determine public policy in regard to the rights of children, and (2) to implement and design programs for specific purposes? These concerns have had an impact on the type of research that is being conducted. For an excellent resource of research in progress refer to current issues of *Research Relating to Children*.[38]

Suggested Activities

1. Invite child psychologists and research personnel to discuss with the class the latest research findings in relation to Early Childhood Education.
2. Have various members of the class report on research findings published in current journals.
3. Organize a discussion or debate on the pros and cons of the more structured programs for young children. Use research findings to support each view.
4. Select one instrument for assessing a teaching strategy. Use it with children and evaluate its effectiveness.
5. Why have researchers become concerned about "public policy" and their part in its formulation? Invite a member of the state legislature and/or a member of Congress and/or a member of the local school board to meet with your class. Ask them to dis-

---

[38] *Research Relating to Children.* ERIC Clearing House on Early Childhood (for sale by the Superintendent of Documents, U.S. Government Printing Office, Washington, D.C. 20402).

cuss the basis on which they make their decisions on public policy matters when the education of preschool children is concerned.

Related Readings

Chomsky, N. *The Logical Structure of Linguistic Theory*. New York: Plenum Publishing Corp., 1975.

Dare, P. *A Four-Year Longitudinal Study of Follow Through Children*. San Francisco: Far West Laboratory for Educational Research and Development, 1973.

Educational Programs That Work, 3rd ed. San Francisco: Far West Laboratory for Educational Research and Development, 1977.

Educational Research: Limits and Opportunities. Washington, D.C.: U.S. DHEW, NIE, 1977.

Gage, N. L. (ed.). *Handbook of Research on Teaching*. Chicago: Rand McNally, 1963, Ch. 15.

Harris, C. W. (ed.) *Encyclopedia of Educational Research*, 3rd ed. New York: Macmillan Publishing Co., 1960.

Hoffman, M. L., and Lois W. Hoffman (eds.). *Review of Child Development Research*, 2 vols. New York: Russell Sage Foundation, 1964, 1967.

Jencks, C., et al. *Inequality: A Measurement of the Effect of Family and Schooling in America*. New York: Basic Books, 1972.

Karnes, Merle B. "Evaluation and Implications of Research with Young Handicapped Children," *Compensatory Education for Children, Ages 2–8, Recent Studies of Educational Intervention: Proceedings*, edited by J. C. Stanley. Baltimore: Johns Hopkins Press, 1973b.

Mussen, P. H. (ed.). *Handbook of Research Methods in Child Development*. New York: John Wiley and Sons, 1960.

Renner, J. W., et al. *Research, Teaching, and Learning with the Piaget Model*. Norman,: University of Oklahoma Press, 1976.

Resources in Education. Listed in ERIC/ECE *Newsletter*, 9:3 (1975), p. 7. (See current issue for ERIC/ECE listing.)

Review of Child Development Research, Vols. 1–6. Chicago: The University of Chicago Press (Society for Research in Child Development Series).

Ryan, Sally (ed.). *A Report on Longitudinal Evaluations of Preschool Programs*, Vol. 1. Washington, D.C.: U.S. DHEW, OCD, 1975.

Stein, A. H., and Friedrich, L. K. "Impact of Television on Children and Youth," in *Review of Child Development Research*, Vol. 5, edited by E. M. Hetherington. Chicago: University of Chicago Press, 1975.

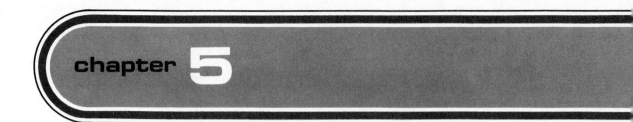

chapter 5

The behavior of young children: guidance and discipline

"You know . . . that the beginning is the most important part of any work, especially in the case of a young and tender thing; for that is the time at which the character is being formed." These words, as expressed by the philosopher Plato, have been emphasized by the findings of research in the areas of child growth and development. The early years are particularly important because habits and attitudes formed at this time may affect many aspects of a child's later life. The guidance given the child at the time that he or she has an experience may determine whether the resulting habits and attitudes are good or bad, even in adult life. Children learn, with or without instruction, and persons working closely with young children often are not aware that they offer guidance almost continuously. The effectiveness of this guidance depends on an understanding of the young child, the environment, and the goals and aspirations of the adults with whom the child comes in contact.

Problems related to the guidance of behavior and to discipline do not solve themselves. In order to enhance wholesome behavioral development the teacher must have clearly in mind the behavior it is hoped that the child will acquire. It is important, then, to consider such related factors as objectives and values, the environment, and the behavior that is considered normal and healthy for the age of the child.

OBJECTIVES AND VALUES

Attitudes and habits are developed as children work and play together in an environment that provides opportunities for physical, mental, and social growth. "Understanding," "getting along," and "cooperating" are not taught during designated periods of the day but are experienced as the child participates in such activities as science experiments or getting ready for lunch. The concern is not only for the experiences that a child may have, but also for what happens to the child while participating in these experiences. For example, as the child plays with other children, certain questions arise. Is the youngster developing the ability to "trust others," "get along," "take turns," or "have fun" and, as a result, learning to like people and to feel adequate as a person? Or, are the other children too much for the child? Are they a threat? Is the child becoming bossy, aggressive, or withdrawn? What is happening to the child's self-concept? Is the child coming to think of himself or herself as a person who can tackle hard jobs or one who says "I can't"? As one who tries new activities, or one who hangs back? As one who has friends, or one whom nobody likes?

If objectives and values are to be realized, there is need for consistency between purposes and actions, both verbal and nonverbal. Adults who guide the behavior of children need to examine their values and goals in relation to practice. A thoughtful consideration of the following questions is helpful: What are the values it is hoped the child will come to accept? Are they, for example, honesty, cooperation, and respect for the worth and dignity of the individual? What type of person will the child become? Will he or she be understanding, adequate, cooperative, enthusiastic, aggressive, submissive, self-directing, or inquiring? Answers to questions such as these can serve as guidelines for examining practices. It is important that every teacher answer them. Teachers of young children will find a basis for answering such questions on pp. 90–93. As teachers answer the questions for themselves, they may find that procedures are inconsistent with the desired ends or values. It is easy to say one thing and do something else. The following example illustrates how conflicts between purposes and practices may result in undesirable outcomes in the behavior of children.

In a meeting of kindergarten teachers, one member asked, "How do you make children sit still during story time?" There were several questions in reply. "What types of stories do you read?" "How long are the stories?" "When do you have story time?" The first teacher, impatient with the questions, replied, "It doesn't matter when or what I read. I intend to see that the children sit still and listen when I read a story." If one were to ask this teacher her purposes in reading the story, the following would probably be included: (1) to develop an appreciation of good literature, (2) to stimulate interest in reading, and (3) to provide pleasure and information. Her actions, however, tended to defeat the objectives she was trying to accomplish. By giving little or no attention to the selection read, by insisting that children sit and listen to material that might have little meaning for them, story time was becoming not only an ordeal for the teacher, but a very uninteresting activity for the children. Such emphasis could easily cancel the values of appreciation and pleasure.

Values, however, can reinforce each other. A story, carefully chosen and well read, can provide pleasure and information, as well as develop interest,

A   B   (Courtesy of Head Start.)

Figure 14
An atmosphere in which the self-concept may be enhanced is one in which the child can make an error and not lose face, one in which each child can help to purpose and plan.

appreciation, and listening skills. In recognizing the importance of a consistent approach to goals, values, and practice in guiding behavior, it is necessary to examine the opportunities during the school day for learning values and the ways in which concepts are acquired.

At times children have not shown much ambition or enthusiasm for learning what has been expected of them. The "natural" learning capabilities and aspirations of each child must be considered.[1] The way in which children perceive a situation also affects their learning. As a child perceives, so a child behaves. A new baby in the home may be perceived as a threat by the child even though no threat is involved. The success of guiding young children in acquiring self-discipline is influenced by how the child feels toward or perceives the adult's actions—as those of a hostile, indifferent adult or as one who is warm, loving, and caring.[2]

It is important to consider how the teacher develops goals for and with children and their parents. Teaching objectives are related to broad educational goals and are planned for both the group and the individual. The teacher may be concerned with helping the group set standards for behavior as she/he and the children plan together for using the new tools. In helping an individual achieve the same goal, the teacher may plan to support attempts to make a particular decision, and to carry it out. For example, Emmie was having trouble in sawing the wood and started to leave. The teacher offered to hold the board and with this help Emmie was able to finish the job.

The teacher has the responsibility of helping the child become aware of the goal currently being developed. For example, the teacher may be trying to help the child gain confidence in his or her ability. When the child says, "I can't do this," the teacher may reply, "Do it your own way. What can you do first?"

In selecting a goal for emphasis, the teacher might choose a focus because of the interest and readiness of the children or because there has been little opportunity to work toward achieving this objective. Attainment of goals may often involve teacher support and clarification as well as participation in selected activities.

The behavior of the child may tend to obscure her goals. The wise teacher understands. Kim picked up Jane's mitten and ran to the jungle gym. Jane told the teacher. The teacher said, "She was trying to play with you. I think she wanted to be your friend." The role of the adult in working with children involves observing, supporting, clarifying, enhancing, and sharing.[3]

---

[1] D. Russell, "Goals for American Education: The Individual Focus," *Educ. Leadership,* 28:6 (1971), pp. 592–594.

[2] D. K. Osborn and Janie D. Osborn, *Discipline and Classroom Management* (Athens, Ga.: Education Associates, 1977), p. 34.

[3] Sandra B. Horowitz, *From Theory to Practice: A Personal Diary of a Teacher of Young Children* (College Park, Md.: University of Maryland, 1971), pp. 19–22.

Parents and teachers usually share the same goals for children though they may have different methods of attaining them. They are mutually dependent. Parents and teachers must work together in order to understand the role of each and to reinforce important learnings that come from the experiences that each provides.

The goal of good schools for young children is to provide a succession of situations, of activities, whereby children may have the opportunity to develop at their own rate and in their own way in personal affective skills and values, academic learnings and cognitive skills, group values, and parental relationships. The following examples will illustrate behavior that can be observed and that seems to indicate progress in the realization of particular goals.

PERSONAL VALUES, SKILLS, AND AFFECTIVE RELATIONSHIPS

Learning to like and trust others.
  For example:
    In the housekeeping center Lynn said, "I made a cake like yours. You make good things to eat."
Expanding the concept of what it means to be human.
Gaining a positive image of self.
Accepting children of differing ethnic and cultural traits.
Learning to manage feelings.
  For example:
    Ron was building an elaborate structure with blocks. Roy ran up and knocked down one of the walls. Ron turned as if to give chase. He seemed to be angry. Suddenly he stopped short, paused a moment and said, "And I was making it for you."
Developing the ability to organize, to plan, and to follow through on simple tasks.
Increasing in ability to make wise choices and decisions in a consistent manner.
Developing a sense of the importance of and relationship between independence and dependence.
Developing the ability to set standards for personal behavior and to live by them.
Establishing routines and patterns of living.
Developing spiritual values.
Developing physical adequacy and mental health.
Finding both satisfactions and limitations in the field of make-believe.
Expecting and accepting failures as well as successes.

GROUP VALUES AND RELATIONSHIPS

Feeling wanted, valued, and cared for by peers and the adults in one's life.
Making voluntary contacts with other children without regard to sex, race, or class.
Understanding that a cultural trait which is different is not inferior or nonhuman.
  For example:
    Harry took one of Gale's blocks. Gale asked, "Why doesn't he know how to play?"

The teacher replied, "He is learning to speak English. He comes from another country. He may not know how to ask for the block."

Developing a willingness to share privilege with groups differing from themselves.

For example:

Gloria said, "They *are* boys, but let's let them use the wagon."

Becoming a social person; developing ability to interact with age mates.

Developing the attitude toward and the ability for being a part of a social group.

Knowing what is acceptable socially and having the desire to apply this knowledge consistently in functional situations.

Learning to distinguish between private or personal property and that which belongs to the group.

Learning the necessity of sharing and cooperating with others.

For example:

Debbie, wanting to play with the bear which Lisa was using, said, "Lisa, will you let me have the bear when you're finished?" Lisa said, "I'm not ever going to finish today." Debbie said, "Lisa, you're supposed to say 'yes' when I ask you like that." Lisa smiled and said, "Let's build a house for this bear."

Participating in the group while preserving one's own distinct ethnic and cultural traits.

ACADEMIC LEARNINGS

Satisfying natural curiosity which results in creative learnings.

Pursuing an interest wholeheartedly to greater depth and breadth.

Developing new interests and building upon recent ones.

Bringing into consciousness those things in the child's environment that he or she does not perceive (physical and biological).

Developing the beginnings of good work-study habits; learning successes are earned through repeated effort.

Learning to think; learning how things are done.

Developing meaningful vocabularies basic to thinking; developing language as a satisfactory means of communication.

Applying mathematical and scientific information to the solution of a problem.

Expanding knowledge through exploration, investigation, assimilation, and reflection.

Building new or expanding concepts and correcting misconceptions.

For example:

Sally, while examining the seed experiments, remarked that the formica table top was soft. Hearing her comment, the teacher asked her to tap the table with her fist, and then to tap the cotton used in the experiments. Sally tapped both the table and the cotton. She replied, "Oh, the cotton is soft, the table is hard." The teacher asked her what word could be used to tell how the table felt when she slid her hand across it. Sally slid her hand over it, thought for a moment, and said, "Smooth. The table is hard and smooth." She then proceeded to touch and tap other materials and objects.

> She explained that the jar was hard and smooth, the wall was hard and rough. The egg carton was rough, but not as hard as the jar.

Having experiences with many types of media and using them wisely.

Becoming interested in and appreciating books.

PARTNERSHIP WITH PARENTS

Learning to relate self to family and close associates.

Selecting clothing, toys, and activities (books, television, and radio programs) appropriate to the child's developmental level.

Developing an understanding of changes in oneself while progressing through the normal developmental sequence.

Participating in educational experiences that cannot be offered through the home situation; extending these experiences through cooperative planning involving teacher, parent, and child.

Beginning to recognize one's sex role through identification with family members and other age mates.

For example:

> Mitchell rode up on his tricycle and said, "Well, goodbye. I have to go downtown to work. I'll see you tonight." Away he went on his tricycle. In a few minutes he was back. He got off his tricycle, dropped on a bench and said, "Boy, I'm tired. That garage work is mighty hard. Yeh, man, it sure is hard."

Although goals have been identified in the areas of personal and affective skills, cognitive and academic learnings, group values and parental relationships, this does not mean that each child must develop the same values, learnings, and skills in the same way or at the same time. One child may have feelings of fear, while another may have feelings of impatience and anger. For example, the teacher observed that both Louise and Lester need help in managing their feelings. Lester seems to feel afraid of making a mistake or doing anything wrong. Every day he sits quietly looking at a book or builds carefully with blocks, activities in which he feels safe and in which he can succeed. He is not yet able to try new activities. Louise wants her turn to ride the tricycle and pushes Laney off the saddle. Although the goal for both children is in the area of personal skills, the skill needed by each child is different.

The goals for each child are based on belief in (1) the worth, value, and dignity of each individual, and (2) the recognition that group interaction and understanding are fundamental needs basic to American society. Translated into practical application, this means that each child needs to develop in keeping with his or her potential so that each can, through critical and creative thinking (1) select and set worthwhile goals, (2) arrive at purposes that will give direction to behavior, and (3) plan and carry out the necessary actions to realize these goals in terms of his or her own purposes. Accepting these objectives for children, the goal of the teacher then becomes one of determining:

1. How does the child feel about himself/herself? What is happening to this child? What kind of picture of self is he or she building—self-confidence and respect or defeatism and failure?
2. How can opportunities for experience be provided so that the child will learn to set realistic goals and select appropriate means for arriving at them?
3. How can an atmosphere of mutual trust be developed so that each child retains the right to be different as he or she thinks, discusses, and plans for experiences at the level of his or her ability and within clearly established limits?
4. How can a climate of increasing freedom coupled with an acceptance of increasing responsibility be established?
5. How can a stable environment be built by means of consistent patterns of freedom to do and to explore the new? How does one avoid overstimulation? How does one adapt the program to the child's needs?
6. How can the habit of placing value on accomplishments be developed in each child? How can each child be helped to value personal achievement according to standards and criteria appropriate for the purpose at this time but which will eventually lead to broader purposes and higher standards and criteria for achievements?
7. How can the teacher find new and better ways to work with each child?
8. How can opportunities be provided and experiences interpreted so that the child achieves the desired goals of personal values and skills, academic learnings, group values and relationships, and partnership with parents?

The program developed in schools for young children provides for activities that will contribute to the physical, mental, and social development of children. The objectives both for the program and for the activities are the changes expected to take place within each child through new experiences. Provision is made for continuous growth in social and emotional development through a balanced program that will meet the developmental needs of the preschool-age child. But since all children do not develop at the same rate, do not come from the same backgrounds, do not have the same needs and aspirations, the program is flexible and varied. The learning environment is made up of many people and many factors. Every environment is a learning environment. As has been said, "No environment in itself is good or bad. It is good or bad, effective or ineffective, only in terms of response to it."[4] It is important, then, to examine the people, places, and things that surround the child in terms of his or her reactions to them.

---

[4] R. R. Leeper (ed.), *Creating a Good Environment for Learning* (1954 Yearbook, ASCD) (Washington, D.C.: ASCD, 1954), p. 5.

THE ENVIRONMENT

The school environment can help or hinder the realization of goals for young children. The environment may be loving or frightening, stimulating or boring, conducive or inhibiting to the development of purposes and goals. What makes the difference? No one single factor can be identified, for it is the interaction, the cause-and-effect relationship, of many elements that characterizes the total situation. One such element, group size, is considered here.

The effect of group size on the behavior of children is significant. McConkie and Hughes studied two groups, one with 37 and one with 26 children, each attending school for a half-day, occupying the same room space, and taught by the same teacher. It was found that the larger group had less opportunity to work at its own problems and received less individual guidance. More aggressive behavior was also observed in the larger group. Its tempo revealed greater excitement, more noise, and a less permissive atmosphere. Twenty percent of the children in the larger group initiated no personal contact with the teacher, while only 4 percent of the smaller group had no such contact. The smaller group utilized space and materials better and played more cooperatively.[5]

The size of the group, then, should be considered in relation to the realization of the goals desired. If children are to grow in self-direction, wise use of materials, and cooperative behavior, provision should be made for a group situation small enough in number to make such behavior possible.

Another factor concerns the availability of materials and equipment. If the child is to grow in decision making, opportunities for choice are important. Interest or learning centers can offer the child possibilities for working at the easel, with blocks, or even with puzzles. To encourage independence and responsibility in the use and care of materials, storage space must be accessible to the child.

The extent of aggressive behavior may be influenced by the play material and space available. Two earlier studies report findings that are applicable today. Johnson reported her observation of nursery school children on the playground under different conditions. When only the stationary equipment (slides, climbing apparatus) was available, the children seemed to engage in more quarrels and to require more teacher intervention and direction than when movable equipment and toys were also available.[6] Jersild and Markey found that where play space was most restricted, conflicts were greatest in number.[7]

[5] Gwen W. McConkie and Marie M. Hughes, "Quality of Classroom Living Related to Size of Kindergarten Group," *Child. Educ.*, 32:9 (1956), pp. 428–432.
[6] Marguerite W. Johnson, "The Effect on Behavior of Variation in the Amount of Play Equipment," *Child Develop.*, 6:1 (1935), pp. 56–68.
[7] A. T. Jersild and F. V. Markey, "Conflicts Between Preschool Children," *Child Develop. Monogr.*, 21 (1935).

The influence of the home

The home environment also has an influence on the child and the realization of goals. Before children enter nursery school or kindergarten, they have experienced various types of behavior in response to parental guidance and expectations. Some children have become independent, while others are unable to make decisions. Some have become submissive, while others are rebellious. Certain behaviors may be highly acceptable in one ethnic or social group yet be considered unacceptable in another. The teacher, then, should be alert to the fact that the children have experienced different types of parental guidance that may have been influenced by various factors and in several ways.

How an adult was reared as a child plays an important part in how one treats one's own child. The adult may have come from a home where a strict father insisted that the child obey instantly, or from a very lenient home where neither parent could agree as to what the child was permitted to do. Thus, adults may carry over certain feelings from their own childhood that give direction in dealing with their children. Parents may have resented how they were treated as children and may now attempt to direct their children differently. One may be an outgoing person who yells at a child but quickly gets over one's anger. Another parent may show no anger but demand that the child obey without question.

The parent may have read much of the literature written during the years when permissiveness without limits was in vogue and may have been influenced by ideas of permitting children to do exactly as they please. Feelings regarding the words *guidance* or *discipline* play an important part in dealing with children. The word *discipline* has different connotations. Some people feel that it means keeping order in a group, while others interpret it as a technique of maintaining order. To still others, discipline means punishment. The authors see discipline as a means of helping the child develop inner controls to do what is approved and act in approved ways. This goal may be shared by parents and teacher, but what is meant by the goal and how to achieve it may be completely different. Discipline should be discussed with parents. Children often find themselves in conflict when the guidance given at home and school is inconsistent. Both parents and teachers should realize that controls or limits are necessary for children to adjust to societal standards. Children feel more secure if they know what is expected of them and understand what conformity means.

The child may come from a home in which he or she has learned to expect physical punishment, threats, and abuse. This child may have difficulty in adjusting to a teacher who does not shout, threaten, or hit. This child may need help in learning to make decisions, having been told quite firmly how to behave at home. Since our society leans toward independent decision making and choice of behavior, such a child may have ambivalent feelings and difficulty in adjusting to the expected behavior for school and peers. Other children, having received much attention and constant direction, may have become overly dependent upon what the parents think is correct behavior. Still other children are insecure and appear shy and withdrawn. They need activities to help them develop a feeling of security and self-confidence.

There has been a tendency to equate certain modes of behavior with social classes. While the socioeconomic level of the family can either limit or extend the opportunities of the child, it is the emotional and intellectual climate that determines the child's outlook. Home environment may be so harmful with regard to physical punishment that a family welfare agency may have to intervene. Today, child abuse has been openly recognized by the courts and the medical profession. There still are parents who are unable to restrain themselves physically and as a result there are some unfortunate instances of bodily injury to children.[8] Bain points out that "Gross physical abuse is only one segment of a much wider problem of parental neglect. The unloved child, the emotionally deprived child, becomes part of our group of neurotic, disturbed, retarded, or delinquent adults."[9]

Parents are entrusted by nature and society to care for the child and provide appropriate limits for behavior. However, there are times when families cannot fulfill their responsibilities alone. When children's needs are unmet who takes responsibility?

Child advocacy is the term being used to describe the growing emphasis placed on identifying unmet needs of children, suggesting ways to meet these needs, and on stimulating public support for projects already in operation.[10] Child advocacy is a concept and a process designed to make the needs of children real to the public, to give us, at local and national levels, a structure with which to deal with these problems, and to insure needed services to children, youth, and their families.[11]

The ultimate goal for the child and all individuals is the acquiring of self-discipline. Gradually children learn how to make decisions and to know whether their behavior is acceptable to others. At first the teacher or parent may help the child to make wise choices by offering two definite alternatives where either one is acceptable. Gradually the child can move to more difficult decision making where the alternatives are less clear. For example, it is raining and yet, with proper clothing, Charles may play out in the rain. The adult

[8] M. G. Paulsen, "Legal Protections Against Child Abuse," *Children, 13*:2 (1966), pp. 43–48.
[9] Katherine Bain, "Commentary: The Physically Abused Child," *Pediatrics, 31*:6 (1963), p. 897.
[10] Shelia B. Kamerman, A. J. Kahn, and Brenda G. McGowan, "Research and Advocacy," *Children Today, 1*:2 (1972), pp. 35–36.
[11] S. A. Ward, "Components of a Child Advocacy Program," *Children Today, 1*:2, (1972), pp. 38–40.

might say, "It is raining, but if you wear your boots and raincoat, you can go out to play in the rain, or you can stay inside and play with your trucks. You decide which you'd rather do."

Young children need to move toward independent thinking, for as they mature, they move away from the parental home to the school, to peers, and to a larger society. They will no longer have an adult always beside them to make choices. It will be easier to know which path to take as they approach adolescence and adulthood if they have begun to make appropriate decisions in their early years.

LEVEL OF MATURITY

Time is an important dimension in a child's behavior, for a relationship exists between a child's behavior and level of maturity. If the adult recognizes that each child develops at a different rate, the same behavior will not be expected of each child in the group. Opportunities for experiences appropriate to the child's level of maturity will be planned. There will be differences in many abilities. Examples follow.

1. *The ability to share and wait for turns.* One child may be able to take turns with four other children in riding a tricycle, but be unable to wait for 20 children to ride before having another chance.
2. *The ability to listen attentively.* The length of time one can listen varies, as does the content one has the background to enjoy.
3. *The ability to participate in a group.* Some children are comfortable in small group activities, but are not yet ready to cope with the total group of 25 children. Refusal to come "to a group story" may not indicate lack of interest in stories on the part of a child, nor an inappropriate story, but could indicate fear of the large group.
4. *Muscular coordination.* Some children can skip, while others can only run; some can cut exactly on the line, while others can only tear paper.
5. *Reaction time.* Some children take longer to respond or react than others.

The good teacher provides opportunities for the child to engage in activities in terms of these differences. As certain behavior such as negativism or inattention appears, the teacher remembers that these are to be expected of children at certain stages of development.

The very young child of two or three may be extremely negative to any and all requests. This negative "No, I don't want to!" or, "No, I won't" is expected at this age. The child is beginning to be self-assertive and may express this self-awareness in a negative way. The power of "no" has been discovered. The child begins to realize that adults are disturbed by "no" and thus uses it constantly, even when he or she really would like to carry out the activity requested. The wise teacher either rephrases the request, ignores the negativism, or redirects the activity. The teacher makes no issue when announcing, "Time to each lunch," but simply takes the child by the hand and together they go to eat. The child is not indulged by being allowed not to eat; neither is he punished for saying "no" when in reality he may not mean "no" at all. The child is helped to do what needs to be done.

Knowing that manners cannot always be counted on with four-year-olds does not mean that manners are ignored. It simply means, for example, that on leaving a party, the parent does not ask the child, "What do you say?" and risk a scene and embarrassment. Rather, the adult may say, "Jerry and I enjoyed the party. Thank you for inviting us." The adult sets the example which later the child will make a part of his or her own behavior.

Knowing that most five-year-olds can listen in a group for only 10 to 15 minutes, the teacher should plan listening experiences involving stories, sharing, and music accordingly. To expect the child to sit attentively for a longer period is to expect more than he or she is capable of doing. One teacher kept five-year-olds in a circle for 45 minutes. After the first few minutes they were very restless, falling out of chairs, playing and wrestling with their neighbors. By insisting that they remain for that length of time, the teacher was not only causing difficulties in the form of discipline problems, but was teaching children to be rude, impolite listeners rather than to listen attentively while others were speaking.

Hymes, however, warns that the teacher must be careful not to become too easygoing and content with too little on the one hand, or become too demanding and maintain unrealistic expectations on the other. For example, if the children are wiggling, it may be because of their age or their maturity level. Yet the reason may be entirely different. The children may be bored. The teacher, then, must determine the cause of the behavior and take action that is consistent with the cause.[12]

The developmental point of view is based on knowledge and understanding of the growth and development of the child. According to Hymes, this approach does not mean that anything goes; nor does it call for lowering of standards. Teachers have the highest possible standards for the age group they teach. The child development approach means accepting the behavior that is normal and healthy for a specific age. The teacher recognizes the maturity level of each child and lives with it.[13]

[12] J. L. Hymes, Jr., *Behavior and Misbehavior* (Englewood Cliffs, N.J.: Prentice-Hall, 1955), p. 53.
[13] Ibid., p. 52.

GUIDANCE AND DISCIPLINE

Although each teacher may have special strategies and techniques, it is important that teachers understand something of the philosophy of the approach they choose as the basis for guidance and discipline.

Butler reports that techniques advocated during the past several years come from two quite divergent sources.[14] One point of view, expressed by Maslow, Rogers, Kelley, and Combs in *Perceiving, Behaving, Becoming,* holds that the way a person behaves at a given moment is a direct expression of the way things seem to that person at that particular moment. Thus, the child does not behave according to the facts as they seem to an outsider. The child behaves in terms of how things seem to be or how they are perceived at that moment.[15]

These authors believe that the attributes of dignity, integrity, and autonomy are concomitants of the environment which impinges positively on the individual. They hold that "situations where the conditions for social development are kept open and fluid are most favorable for the development of these characteristics."[16] An atmosphere in which the self-concept may be enhanced is one in which:

Human development in dignity and honesty is put first.
Each child's spiritual integrity—his right to be—is recognized.
Individuality is considered an asset rather than a liability.
Genetic growth patterns are respected and used as a basis for teaching.
Each child helps to purpose and plan.
Each can act freely, knowing those around him accept him as he is.
Each can make an error—or even do wrong, and not lose face thereby.
Each child can grow each day and know that he is growing.
Each can hold his head up high and meet the other's gaze.
Each can make friends, enjoy other people, learn how to extend a hand to help.
Each can learn the warm flood of gratitude that comes from being regarded with warmth.
Each can venture into unknown worlds and stretch his wings to find new truths.
Above all where each child can experience success in subject matter, human relationships and the discovery of self as a person of worth and dignity.[17]

"From a quite different point of view the theory of operant conditioning sees a preschool as essentially a behavior-modifying environment in which

[14] Annie L. Butler, *Current Research in Early Childhood Education: A Compilation and Analysis for Program Planners* (Washington, D.C.: American Association of Elementary-Kindergarten-Nursery Educators, 1970), p. 117.
[15] A. W. Combs, chm., *Perceiving, Behaving, Becoming* (1962 Yearbook) (Washington, D.C.: ASCD; 1962), pp. 67–68.
[16] Ibid., p. 221.
[17] Ibid., pp. 232–233.

the teacher plays an important role in choosing behavior that will be systematically reinforced," says Butler.[18] Operant conditioning is usually based on the use of consequences to strengthen or weaken behavior in such areas as decreasing aggressive responses and threatening or violent behavior, increasing social skills, and learning to take responsibility for simple tasks. The behavior that is compatible with desired ends is reinforced.[19]

Katz points out, however, that the application of these techniques must be thought through carefully. She says, "Stop, look, and listen before you condition."[20] Limitations of this approach are seen in the example described by Katz. Three children manifest disruptive behavior for which behavior modification is likely to work. When used without concern for the origins of the behavior, however, the positive results may be questioned.

> Child 1 learned to be disruptive because such behavior resulted in attention or some other reinforcement. For this child operant conditioning seems appropriate. The reinforcement which usually followed his disruptive behavior could be consciously withheld.
>
> Child 2's disruptive behavior may express some kind of emotional injury, some kind of internal stress. Although behavior modification may work and the undesirable behavior disappear, the injury could remain. A new manifestation of the stress may appear. A therapeutic response seems indicated in this case.
>
> Child 3 may lack the social skills or alternative ways of responding to the situation. This child can be helped by clarifying or explaining alternative solutions for solving the problem at hand. The teaching strategy appears to be appropriate.

Katz does not reject the principles of behavior modification but warns against the indiscriminate application of conditioning techniques. She emphasizes the fact that before applying the principles the teacher should know the child.[21]

For the teacher who decides to use reinforcement techniques Osborn and Osborn make suggestions:[22]

1. The child should be observed carefully.
2. The behavior to be changed should be identified and attainable goals set up.
3. The desired behavior should be rewarded.
4. The undesirable behavior should be ignored.
5. The reward (or reinforcement) should follow closely after the appropriate behavior.

[18] Butler, op. cit., p. 120.
[19] W. C. Becker, D. R. Thomas, and D. Carnine, *Reducing Behavior Problems: An Operant Conditioning Guide for Teachers* (Urbana: ERIC Clearinghouse University of Illinois, 1969), pp. 4–5.
[20] Lillian G. Katz, "Stop, Look, and Listen Before You Condition," *ERIC/ECE Newsletter*, 5:6 (1971), pp. 1–2.
[21] Ibid.
[22] Osborn and Osborn, op. cit., pp. 40–49.

6. Reinforcement, in the beginning, should be continuous.
7. Reinforcement should be consistent.
8. The child should be reobserved and goals evaluated.

Different approaches to guidance and discipline come from different philosophies and beliefs. Butler concludes, however, that

> The important question is how one goes about building satisfying interpersonal relationships: whether one chooses to develop the relationships that encourage the child to want to change his behavior and give the guidance and support necessary to do this, or whether steps must be taken to urge him forward in the desired direction; whether the child should be motivated by some real desire to change, or whether he responds to tangible rewards for desired behavior until the behavior becomes a habit.[23]

In guiding behavior, then, the teacher recognizes that options are available. One can choose to develop relationships within the classroom that encourage the child to want to change behavior. Likewise, the teacher may choose to encourage the formation of desirable habits of behavior by providing rewards or reinforcement.

Helping the child become a group member

The transition from home to school may bring many new or different activities for the child. Being a part of a group is definitely one of them. A child new to the group may withdraw and watch the others, or become aggressive and push and grab toys. Too often the teacher may not realize that children new to the group need more individual help as well as introduction to various group activities. Some children require a longer period of adjustment to become a part of the group, while others feel at home almost immediately.

Some of the difficulties that teachers encounter with young children are related to different behavior expectations of the home and the school. At home the child may have been encouraged or at least permitted to fight; use the language heard; take things without asking. The teacher, then, accepts the child and begins at the child's level in helping him or her learn to take turns, to share toys, and to become an active participant in a group. The child may use words for which he or she does not know the meaning:

> Tip, a four-year-old boy, called out happily to the teacher, "You look like a bastard!" The teacher, somewhat taken aback, responded by asking, "What do you mean when you say that I look like a bastard?" Tip replied, "You look funny." "Tip," said the teacher, "You need to explain what you mean when you say 'bastard.' People don't know that you mean *funny*." Tip said, "O.K. I'll just say, 'You have a funny face.'"

[23] Butler, op. cit., p. 121.

Other difficulties that teachers encounter with young children are related to assisting the child in learning to take turns, to share toys, to become an active participant in a group. Children need this kind of guidance, for most of them have been the center of attention at home. They have lived in a family setting where the other members were not of the same age as themselves. Thus, we find some three- and four-year-olds grabbing toys from others and hitting, pinching, biting, or using physical force to obtain what they want. Others stand back, watching, or withdrawing, or appealing to an adult for help. Comments frequently heard are "Tommy won't let me ride the tricycle," "Nancy doesn't want me to be the daddy." The teacher can help the children by suggesting, "Tommy, you've had the tricycle quite a while; two more trips around the circle, then it's Billy's turn." In other activities the teacher can often guide a child by merely saying, "You could do it this way." So often the manner in which the teacher suggests new ideas to children will encourage them to tackle a project or stick to one they are working on.

Establishing routines

When entering one of the many programs, children who are unaccustomed to group activities may find it hard to engage in the expected routines, such as washing, toileting, going out or coming indoors, resting, and eating at lunch time. Many of the children will imitate the others, yet usually there are a few who need help in adjusting to a daily schedule.

Furthermore, some children come from homes where there are few, if any, routines other than doing whatever they find to do at whatever time is convenient for the parents. They are not accustomed to washing their hands before eating. Meals have not been served according to a schedule. Resting is unimportant. These boys and girls must first have help in understanding the "why" of doing things. They need encouragement and support while they are in the process of acquiring the desired behavior. In helping the child, it is important for the teacher to consider the possible effect of guidance on the child's concept of self and his or her home.

Children often become confused when an activity is shifted because of weather conditions, a field trip, or special event. Explaining the necessity for a shift in plans or letting children know ahead that a routine will be shifted helps avoid confusion.

Younger children who have never had a chance to engage in water play may enjoy spending a longer time washing hands and face than the teacher has counted on. The teacher may need to give such a child a special "water play" time. Some children may be hesitant about going to the toilet when others are in the bathroom, or may refuse to go at all. A teacher may need to supervise such children carefully until they become accustomed to groups in a bath-

A

B

(Courtesy of Head Start)

C

D

Figure 15
Teachers of young children consider it a part of their function to help children establish routines and habits dealing with dressing, cleanliness, elimination, eating, and rest.

The rigid conformance once required in nursery school or kindergarten routines has given way to a more relaxed and informal pattern that permits children to establish these requirements at their own pace, consistent with the demands of maturation attained at the time. Like most learned activities, changes occur gradually in keeping with the stage of development. It is, therefore, undesirable to expect the same level of conformity and perfection from all children.

These pictures illustrate activities characteristic of those in centers with a well-planned program designed to help children establish basic routines.

room. Some schools are equipped with child-size lavatories that may be a novelty to a child, who thus spends a longer time in the bathroom. The teacher must be aware of the home training in regard to toileting, as some parents have probably stressed modesty and others may have been rather free. New children are likely to have more frequent need to use the toilet facilities, because of the newness of the situation, nervousness, or when the weather becomes colder. Therefore, in planning a daily schedule the teacher would need to include more frequent toileting with new or younger children.

The routine of the rest period can provide a relaxing time or it may produce only a group of squirming, restless children. The length and number of rest periods should be determined by the length of time children are in school, how much sleep they get at home, when they go to bed, and when they get up in the morning. For children who are in the center for only two or three hours, the 15–20-minute period may be considered a quiet time. Some children may need or want to lie down on mats while others may choose a quiet activity, such as listening to music or looking at a book.

It is important for the teacher to remember that such a period provides not only physical relaxation but also a time for the child to be by herself or himself: in the group, yes, but not an active part of it. Rhodes found that when children in a morning kindergarten were provided with a rest period, there were fewer signs of fatigue.[24]

For children who are in the center all day, nap time is usually arranged just after lunch. Children seem to rest and sleep better if the amount of activity is reduced prior to nap time. Some children may sleep for an hour, while others may not nap at all. They may spend the time relaxing on their cots and engaging in a quiet activity. The teacher's attitude about rest makes a difference as to whether the children are able to relax. Some teachers feel that soft music and darkened rooms are conducive to rest, whereas in other schools the quiet attitude of the teacher with an expectation of relaxation may provide a better atmosphere.

The routine of eating should be considered in relation to both the midmorning snack and the noon lunch. Some children have not been used to washing hands before eating, to sitting down with a group their own age to eat, nor to a variety of foods, nor to conversation with other children while eating, nor to behavior appropriate for mealtime. The lunch hour can be a pleasant experience instead of a nagging time. Small portions and the teacher's expectancy that the children will feed themselves and complete their meals without undue urging will be conducive in helping those children who are having difficulty at meal time.

Throughout the school day children become engrossed in their work and play and are not conscious of time. Many teachers encounter difficulty with children who are not ready to put blocks away, to stop their activity at the work bench, or to return indoors for a story. Some children have become accustomed to what comes next in the daily routine and yet rebel at moving on to the next activity. Teachers can help children by warning them a few minutes prior to change of activity by quietly commenting, "It is almost juice time; we will need to start putting the blocks away very soon now." Sometimes there are too many blocks and the job is too big for the child. The teacher can help by gaining the cooperation of other children as well as assisting in the putting away. Recognizing that each child may be accustomed at home to a variety of differences in routines is important in helping children know what is expected in a school group.

Teaching techniques

Diverting the child by redirecting unfavorable behavior into more constructive channels is a challenge to every adult, whether parent or teacher. It sometimes takes foresight or ingenuity for the adult to use favorable diversion in suggesting to the child other ways of handling situations. Sometimes a reminder may be used, such as "Remember we said the shovel is used to dig with. How about getting the wagon and filling it with dirt?"

Sometimes children who are overstimulated need quiet time to look at books or to play alone. The difficult child who disturbs the entire group may need to be removed from the group for a short period of time. This removal should not be in the form of a threat, such as "If you don't behave I'll have to put you in another room." Rather, the teacher should suggest, "You seem to be having trouble playing with Bob. Perhaps you should play by yourself for a while." If a child is extremely difficult or disturbing to a group, the teacher may need to isolate the youngster in another room in order to calm the entire situation. If the child is removed from the group, there are several factors to be considered:

1. *Length of time.* Briefness of isolation is extremely important, because of the child's short span of attention. Five minutes can be a long time for a child.
2. *The child's understanding of purpose.* It is important that the child knows why he was removed, because many times he does not understand. Learning reasons for removal from the group can be helpful in preventing further behavior difficulties.
3. *Safety.* The safety and supervision of the child while outside the group should be assured.
4. *The child's reaction.* If the child is alone in a room or hall, is his security threatened? Is he frightened? Does the child enjoy the experience?

5. *Provision for learning.* If frequently excluded, does the child ever learn that the activity from which he was excluded can be an interesting and happy one? Is he being helped to learn "what to do" and "how to behave" in order to remain in the group?

6. *Reinstatement in the group.* When does the child return to the group? Does the child or the teacher decide? Is the child told, "Come back when you can behave," or does the teacher reinstate the child within the group by saying, "Jim is ready to hear the story now"?

One of the most important traits in a teacher of young children is sensitivity to each child's needs and how these needs relate to the group as a whole. Knowing the developmental characteristics of children at each age level will assist the teacher in becoming aware of these needs. When guiding the behavior of children under six in group situations, the teacher needs to be aware that:[25]

1. The tone of voice used should be positive yet not demanding, pleasant yet firm, calm yet forceful and matter-of-fact.

2. The teacher should give a feeling of expectancy that the request needs to be carried to completion. If she has to leave the group because of an unexpected situation, the children will know that the teacher will return and follow through with the activity.

3. The nonverbal behavior of the teacher should be consistent with her verbal behavior. The effects of a positive comment may be minimized if the teacher does not look directly at the child, while the effects may be reinforced if she places a hand on the child's shoulder.

4. The teacher places herself so that she can see the entire group at all times to know where they are and what they are doing. In giving directions, she may find it helpful to stand near the child who has difficulty in listening.

5. Reasons, rules, and directions should be clearly stated.

6. The teacher should be consistent in relations with the children. They learn what to expect and are more likely to comply.

7. The teacher should offer the child alternative solutions. Suggest acceptable behavior rather than merely probiting actions.

8. The teacher gives suggestions rather than commands; for example, "How about trying to do it this way," or "You might ask Larry to help you."

9. The teacher avoids favoritism by not giving too much attention to an attractive, a talented, a handicapped, or a disturbing child because doing so may result in neglect of others in the group.

It is expected that in a school situation teachers will not use threats with young children, nor will they use physical punishment. Parents may feel that these are necessary forms of punishment; nevertheless, they should not be used by teachers. The teacher who understands children is aware of other

---

[25] Osborn and Osborn, op. cit., pp. 61–63.

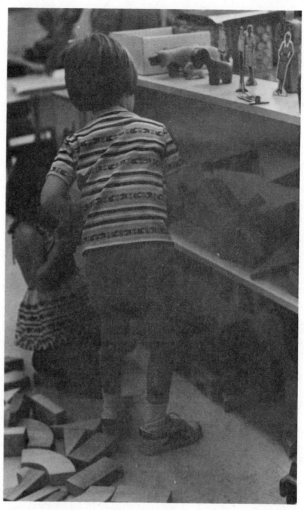

Figure 16
Children often become engrossed in their work and play and are not conscious of time. Teachers can help in the routines of putting materials away by quietly commenting, a few minutes prior to change of activity, "It is almost time for juice. We will need to start putting the blocks away very soon."

methods of guiding the child and does not have to resort to physical punishment.

Giving young children special privileges or attention may be legitimate if such practices do not become crutches on which teachers lean to gain cooperation from youngsters. Older children in elementary school are more likely to be helped in the area of discipline by the withdrawing of privileges than are preschool children. Praise, too, is an effective method of control. However, some teachers tend to use it too frequently, especially with the so-called "good children." Too often praise is withheld from those difficult children who really need more attention and would profit by having their efforts accepted.

For some children in the group, the activities may be too difficult, either because the child does not know what is expected or because he or she may be slower in some aspects of development. Insight may be gained through study of the home situation, or it may be necessary to secure outside assistance from a child guidance clinic in cooperation with the parents. Too often teachers are afraid to admit failure with a child; in reality, however, the admission of the need for help is an indication of a professional teacher. Recognition of serious behavior difficulties and prompt referral can ensure early treatment for the child.

Through careful analysis of the child's feelings, attitudes, and reactions, appropriate steps in guiding behavior can be evolved. In the following paragraphs, two different types of school situations involving the behavior of children are described as illustrations of the application of guidance principles. No attempt is made to answer all questions but rather to suggest a process which may be used by the teacher in answering questions.

Total Group Situation. The teacher determines the goals for behavior in a group situation such as music or story time. For example:

> Each child will be a good listener; participate in group activity; share turns; show consideration for others in group.

In working to achieve these goals, the teacher plans and provides for:

1. The activities to be within the attention span of the group, and individuals in the group.
2. A balance of types of activities within the period—active and quiet, listening with participating.
3. Physical arrangements that are comfortable; seating arrangements so that children can see the leader and are not directly facing the light; proper temperature.
4. Content of the group activity appropriate for maturity level of the children. Adaptations made for individuals.

Even with all the planning, there still may be need for guidance on the part of the teacher. For example:

> It is story time. Fred, a five-year-old, is wiggling and squirming. He annoys the children next to him by an occasional kick, a slap on the back, a whisper, or a pinch. Should the teacher reprimand, ignore, or send Fred from the group? To do any one of the three is to disrupt the listening climate for the group. Yet, something needs to be done for the sake of the group as well as for Fred.

Before making the decision, it will be well to remember that Fred's behavior may be due to any number of causes and that it is important to ask "why?" If he needs to be excused from the group, the way in which it is done and the follow-up will vary according to the cause of the behavior. The teacher considers, Is Fred tired? He was listening to a recording during the free activity period. This is much the same type of activity. Perhaps he has done enough listening for now. The teacher might say, "Fred, you have listened to the story on the record and you may find something else to do now. Remember, the rest of us are listening to the story. If you want to listen with us, you are welcome; but if not, choose something that will not disturb us."

Is Fred insecure in total group situations? Is such behavior evidence of his inadequacy to cope with the group? It is important that the treatment of this behavior not create more insecure feelings. Fred may be excused in much the same manner as described above. It is important, however, that Fred not be deprived of hearing stories and that he be helped to grow in his ability to participate within the group. The teacher may accomplish this by (1) finding time to read to Fred alone or with one or two other children, helping him to make "friends" with one of these children, (2) helping him to participate in an activity—in block building or in playing in the doll corner with a few other children, and (3) gradually increasing the size of the group in which Fred participates. The quality of the teacher's interaction with Fred is very important.

Is the content of the activity too difficult or perhaps boring for Fred? Does the vocabulary of the story relate to concepts and experiences which are not yet Fred's? If so, perhaps using pictures, a model, or giving an explanation might help.

The Activity or Work Period. The teacher determines goals for behavior during work time or the activity period. For example, each child will:

1. Find a job to do.
2. Gain satisfaction from the job or activities.
3. Take turns.
4. Put away materials.
5. Show consideration for others in the group.

There is much that the teacher can do in advance to set up an environment conducive to the desired behavior, such as the following:

1. Set up several centers of interest or activities in which the children can participate. For the youngest, these will be set up on arrival. The child simply goes to the activity of choice. The five-year-olds may participate in group planning and choose a job for which materials are available and accessible.
2. Balance activities to provide several that require a minimum of teacher supervision, thus enabling the teacher to give guidance in new activities or in those requiring more supervision.
3. Plan activities that are interesting and challenging but not too difficult or frustrating. Provide a variety of activities of varying difficulty so that each child can find something satisfying to do.
4. Provide materials in amounts that encourage sharing. For example, there need

not be a pair of scissors for every child, but neither will the child's capacity to wait and take turns be strained by insisting that the youngster wait while five other children cut. Perhaps the child begins sharing most easily by using the scissors with one or two others. To share, then, does not mean waiting indefinitely or losing one's turn completely.

Despite this planning, Paul, age four, knocks down the block structure which three other boys have built. The teacher questions, Was it an accident? If not, was it an attempt to play with the others? Is Paul's aggressiveness perhaps due to a change in routines at home? Is his place in the family threatened by the new baby? Did a visit from relatives keep him up late last night? Has Daddy or Mother lost a job? Was there food for breakfast? Is there money for the rent? To scold or exclude Paul may cause him to think, "Not even the teacher cares any more." Certainly, Paul cannot be permitted to annoy the other boys but the treatment should not make him more aggressive. A quiet comment, such as, "Paul, you were angry and knocked down the blocks. Pat and Hugh worked hard to build the house. They will build it again. You can work over here." Thus Paul is directed to an activity such as painting at the easel, pounding clay, or using hammer and nails. The teacher recognized that Paul felt aggressive but did not condone his behavior. She set the limits with positive guidance. "They will build it again. You can work over here."

Could Paul's aggressiveness be a way of saying, "I want to play with you"? If so, he needs help in learning acceptable ways of getting into a group. The teacher may say, "Boys, Paul wants to play with you. He will help you build the house again." In this instance, the teacher did not ask Paul, "What do you say when you want to play with the boys?" If he had been able to say it, he would not have resorted to the behavior he used. Rather, the teacher will supply the verbal request, "Boys, Paul really wants to play with you, but he had a strange way of showing it, didn't he?" Paul has experience, then, in another way of joining in play with the boys.

SUMMARY

Guiding the behavior of children, helping them develop a core of values, fostering good human relationships, and building healthy personalities are important yet exacting tasks for the teacher. Suggestions for this task, which have been presented, include the following:

1. Know the children. Review the general characteristics of children at this age level. Study each child's home environment, health status, goals, and interests.
2. Determine goals and values.
3. Plan a school environment and a program conducive to the understandings,

attitudes, and habits which it is hoped the children will develop. As Hymes has said, "A program in school that is dull and dreary, uninteresting and boring, makes it harder for children to be good."[26]

4. Establish positive, friendly relationships between the teacher and the children. Keep verbal and nonverbal behavior consistent.
5. When an incident does arise, remember the following steps in guiding the child:
   a. Realistically accept the child's feelings through the use of verbalizations.
   b. Set up the necessary limits for the child, so he or she does not and cannot continue to build up unacceptable behavior patterns.
   c. Provide the necessary release for unacceptable feelings at the moment they occur through the use of materials appropriate for release of tense and difficult feelings.
   d. Encourage and support the child while he or she is in the process of getting release.[27]
6. Try to find the cause of the child's behavior difficulty.
7. Plan a course of action which is appropriate for the cause of the behavior and consistent with the goals sought for the child.

Today, the child development point of view emphasizes the importance of helping the child become a self-directing individual. Both inner urges and outer pressures need to be considered.

Suggested Activities

1. Observe teacher–child contacts in a center for young children. Note the number of ways the teacher insists the child carry through on requests, when the teacher gives choices, when the child refuses, and the outcome of such.
2. Observe teacher–child contacts. Note the tone of voice used by the teacher when speaking to a child, the wording of requests, the teacher's poise, the children's behavior in terms of requests completed, requests refused. Analyze why the children behaved as they did during such contacts.
3. Select one child to observe, either in a home or at a center. Note the number of "don'ts" used, the number of "would you like to's" or direct commands given the child by an adult. Analyze how this child behaved as a result of the way the teacher or parent communicated with the child.
4. Observe children who are having difficulty belonging to or getting into groups. Note leadership qualities of certain children, shyness of others, aggressiveness, and the general outcome of "groupness" among the children. Did adults interfere or assist children or did the children handle the situations without adult help?
5. Observe a child who manifests aggressive behavior. Seek to determine the cause.

---

[26] J. Hymes, "They Act Their Age," *Discipline* (Washington, D.C.: ACEI, 1957), p. 22.
[27] Eleanor Evans, "Vents for Children's Feelings," *Discipline* (Washington, D.C.: ACEI, 1957), p. 26.

Does the application of behavior modification techniques seem appropriate? Why? Discuss your reasons with the class.

6. Observe one child in a center for young children. Identify ways in which his or her self-concept was enhanced. Share your observations with the class.

7. Visit a center for young children. Note ways in which the teacher guides the interactions among children. How are children guided in the use of materials? Note instances in which children were involved in making decisions. How were children helped to enhance their self-concepts?

8. The way in which a skilled teacher talks to children can help in teaching them how to discipline themselves. Formulate statements that could be used by a teacher when a child is angry, hits another child, grabs a toy, or kicks the teacher.

9. Take pictures of young children in a center. Mount them on paper. Write each child's name under the picture. Read stories and sing songs using children's names. How can this teaching enhance a child's self-concept and identity with the group? In how many other places in the room do you see children's names?

10. There are routine jobs in the classroom in which children participate. Observe in a center and note examples of children participating in routines. How did the teacher handle routines?

11. View film, *Discipline and Self Control.* Modern Talking Pictures, 2323 New Hyde Park Rd. New Hyde Park, N.Y. 11040.

Related Readings

Axline, Virginia. *Dibs in Search of Self.* Boston: Houghton Mifflin Co., 1964.

Baker, Katherine Read, and Xenia F. Fane. *Understanding and Guiding Young Children.* Englewood Cliffs, N.J.: Prentice-Hall, Inc., 1970.

Caldwell, Bettye M. "Aggression and Hostility in Young Children," *Young Children,* 32:2 (1977), pp. 4–13.

Cohen, M. D. (ed). *When Children Move from School to School.* Washington, D.C.: ACEI, 1972.

Evans, E. D. *Contemporary Influences in Early Childhood Education,* 2nd ed. New York: Holt Rinehart and Winston, 1976, pp. 87–137.

Galambos, Jeannette W. *A Guide to Discipline.* Washington, D.C.: NAEYC, 1969.

Hartup, W. W. "Peer Relations: Developmental Implications and Interaction in Same- and Mixed-Age Situations," *Young Children,* 32:3 (1977), pp. 4–13.

Hildebrand, Verna. *Guiding Young Children.* New York: Macmillan Publishing Co., 1975, pp. 57–88; 273–296.

Hughes, Marie M. "Teacher Behavior and Concept of Self," *Child. Educ.,* 41:1 (1964), pp. 29–33.

Hyman, I. A., et al. "Paddling, Punishing, and Force," *Children Today,* 6:5 (1977), pp. 17–25.

Katz, Lillian G. "Condition with Caution," *Young Children,* 27:5 (1972), pp. 277–280.

Krumboltz, J., and Helen Krumboltz. *Changing Children's Behavior.* Englewood Cliffs, N.J.: Prentice-Hall, Inc., 1972.

Leiserson, Marion Laurence. *Creating a "Loving" Environment for Young Children.* College Park, Md.: University of Maryland, 1971.

Lipton, A. "Classroom Behavior: Messages from Children," *Elem. Sch. J.*, 71:5 (1971), pp. 254–261.

MacMillan, D. L. *Behavior Modification in Education.* New York: Macmillan Publishing Co., 1973.

Mead, Margaret. "Rearing Children to Live in a Changing World," *Parents Magazine*, 41:1 (1966), pp. 33–35.

Miel, Alice. "Relating Freedom and Responsibility," *Child. Educ.*, 52:5 (1976), pp. 234–237.

Moore, Shirley. "Research in Review—Considerateness and Helpfulness in Children," *Young Children*, 32:4 (1977), pp. 73–76.

Mowbray, Jean K., and Helen H. Salisbury. *Diagnosing Individual Needs for Early Childhood Education.* Columbus, Ohio: Charles E. Merrill Publishing Co., 1975, pp. 109–120, 145–160.

Osborn, D. K., and Janie D. Osborn. *Discipline and Classroom Management.* Athens, Ga.: Education Associates, 1977.

Romatowski, Jane A. "What Is the Humane Response?" *Child. Educ.*, 53:1 (1976), pp. 21–26.

Schaar, Karen. "Corporal Punishment Foes Strike Out," *Children Today*, 6:5 (1977), p. 16.

Suchara, Helen T. "The Child's Right to Humane Treatment," *Child. Educ.*, 53:6 (1977), pp. 290–296.

Todd, Virginia E., and Helen Heffernan. *The Years Before School—Guiding Preschool Children*, 3rd ed. New York: Macmillan Publishing Co., 1977, pp. 561–563; 687–698.

Veach, Davia M. "Choice with Responsibility," *Young Children*, 32:4 (1977), pp. 22–25.

Zigler, E., and Susan Hunsigner. "Supreme Court on Spanking: Upholding Discipline or Abuse?" *Young Children*, 32:6 (1977), pp. 16–24.

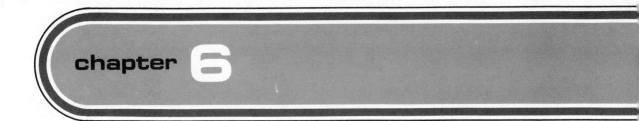

chapter 6

Educational programs for young children

The importance of early education to later development and the changing conditions that have brought the need for Early Childhood Education have been explored in Chapter 1. However, awareness of the importance of educational programs for young children as an integral part of the educational system has developed slowly and over a long period of time. Today, parents and educators know the significance of the child's early experiences, and recent research has confirmed what many people have long believed regarding the value of a good program in Early Childhood Education for all children. Recognition of the growing needs of culturally different children has brought a tremendous increase in federally sponsored programs and research as to their effectiveness. It is believed and partially supported by research that sound education during the early years will enable such children to function more effectively when entering elementary school.

DEVELOPMENT OF PROGRAMS FOR PRESCHOOL-AGE CHILDREN

Kindergartens have been a part of the public school system in the United States for more than a century. However, while housed in public school buildings, kindergartens have generally been thought of as something different from "real school." This is evidenced by the fact that attendance at kindergarten is usually voluntary rather than compulsory as it is in elementary school beginning with the first grade. Likewise, the curriculum followed often is not coordinated with that of the grades to follow. The kindergarten experience often is thought of as both an orientation to school and as a period of nurturing readiness for more formal learning activities.

The first kindergarten in the United States was established in 1855 at Watertown, Wisconsin. The first public kindergarten was established in 1873 in St. Louis. Prior to this date, kindergartens were established and maintained largely from private funds. Since 1950, as the percentage of children enrolled in all schools has been greater than ever before, there has been a proportionate increase in the number of children attending public kindergartens as well as an increase in the number of children attending private or church-related kindergartens. As reported in Chapter 1, there were 1.6 million children enrolled in private and public kindergartens in the United States in 1974.[1]

As a backdrop for exploring existing schools and centers for young children it might be beneficial to quickly review the development of prekindergarten programs in the United States.

Nursery schools were first introduced into the United States at Teachers College, Columbia University, and at the Merrill Palmer School of Motherhood and Home Training in Detroit, as experimental centers where children could be thoughtfully cared for and observed.[2] These schools emphasized educational guidance of parents and children, in contrast to programs of custodial care hitherto considered adequate for children of working mothers. The Iowa Child Welfare Research Station was established under a state legislative grant in 1917. Through a trust fund left by Lizzie Pitts Merrill Palmer of Detroit, the Merrill Palmer School was established in 1920. In 1922 a nursery school demonstration center for student study and practice was opened at the

[1] 1976 Databook: *The Status of Education Research and Development in the United States.* (Washington, D.C.: U.S. DHEW, The National Institute of Education, 1976, p. 6).
[2] Mary Dabney Davis, *Nursery Schools, Their Development and Current Practices in the United States,* Bull. 9 (Washington, D.C.: U.S. Office of Education, 1932).

Merrill Palmer School. Through the Laura Spelman Rockefeller Memorial, grants were made available in 1923 whereby child study centers were developed or expanded at various universities. These, and many other centers established soon after, have given stimulus to the growing interest in child development research, and education has assumed much larger significance in the programs for young children.

During the period from 1920 to 1932 the number of nursery schools reported to the United States Office of Education increased from three to 203. There were many more nursery schools that did not report. During this same decade the evidence supporting the need for schools for young children centered around the needs of the only child, limited play space for children at home, women seeking employment outside the home and needing care for their children, and parents seeking the best environment for the development of their children.

Since the heavy emphasis beginning in the 1960s on compensatory and intervention programs for children from low-income and culturally different families has continued, the traditional nursery school has become much less prominent on the Early Childhood Education scene. For example, the September 1977 issue of *Young Children* does not mention the nursery school in any substantive way. The words nursery school appear only in older references, titles, and in one case in an anecdotal account referring to a nursery school "about five years ago." In contrast, *Young Children's* predecessor, *The Journal of Nursery Education* for September 1964 (its last issue), includes the terms nursery school, nursery education, and nursery school education on virtually every page. Today, nursery schools as such may have a more limited clientele, often made up of children from upper-class and middle-class families who feel that nursery school attendance is essential for adequate social development and for admission to coveted private schools, or that it lays the groundwork for later development.

Today, as was often true in the past, the largest number of publicly supported programs for children is predicated on the principle that child care must be worked out satisfactorily if the family is to maintain itself in society. Since 1930, two national emergencies—the Great Depression of 1929 and World War II—greatly increased the demand for care services for young children. The provision in 1933 for children's centers as a part of the Federal Emergency Relief Administration was the first time that center programs for young children had become a part of a federally supported program. Although designed to help relieve unemployment and to supplement existing educational programs, the increasing concern for the welfare of the young child gave direction to the development of children's centers. Since then, many varied laws and guidelines have resulted from what was learned in the implementation of these programs. As women were mobilized for war emergency work and to replace men in service, attention was focused on the need for legislation to ensure that schools for young children provided an educational experience in a satisfactory environment. This was made possible through funds made available by the Lanham Act.[3] To put this act into operation,

> the War Manpower Commission issued a directive in August, 1942, instructing the Office of Defense Health and Welfare Services to present plans for the development and coordination of federal programs for the care of children of working mothers. Very soon thereafter the President made $400,000 of emergency funds available for transmittal to the U.S. Office of Education and the U.S. Children's Bureau to assist the states in establishing needed services. By June, 1943, 39 states had developed plans for extended school services to be developed under state and local educational agencies, and thirty states had similar plans for child-welfare programs to be administered by welfare agencies.

These war-created emergency programs were developed through the cooperative endeavor of the Federal Emergency Relief Administration and the U.S. Office of Education, assisted by the three professional organizations concerned with the education of young children—the National Association for Nursery Education, the Association for Childhood Education, and the National Council of Parent Education—to provide adequate care for children of working mothers. This program was later administered by the Work Projects Administration and the Federal Works Agency.[4]

In a democracy, the right of every child to have an equal opportunity is recognized. Therefore, it is essential to provide a good environment for each child; this means that an inadequate home environment must be compensated for by a rich and varied preschool curriculum.[5]

The 1960s have become known as the decade of the disadvantaged. A brief but inclusive definition of the culturally disadvantaged (the low-income deprived) is that these are individuals or a group of people who lack social amenities and cultural graces associated with the majority middle-class society. This goes back to the overwhelming numbers of the culturally deprived, who began to appear around 1860, when the population changed largely to rural-urban with the rural living in urbanized communities for which they were not vocationally equipped. Large groups of culturally deprived children were found in the slums of large cities, certain rural areas, Indian reservations, and migrant workers camps.

Today we do not think of these groups as culturally deprived or disadvantaged, for it has been shown that each has an exceedingly rich heritage that is different from, but not inferior to, that of the majority group. When compared

[3]Bess Goodykoontz, Mary Dabney Davis, and Hazel F. Gabbard, "Recent History and Present Status of Education for Young Children," *Early Childhood Education* (46th Yearbook), Part II, NSSE (Chicago: University of Chicago Press, 1947), p. 61.
[4]Ibid., p. 60.
[5]M. L. Goldschmidt. "Early Cognitive Development and Preschool Education." *Internatl. J. Early Child. Educ.*, 3:1 (1971), pp. 5–6.

to commonly accepted norms, many groups deviate because of their own backgrounds and values. Therefore, it is more appropriate to speak of culturally different, than of culturally disadvantaged people, even though these differences may put some at a disadvantage competitively in the everyday requirements of work and conduct. Different does not carry the negative and inferior connotations that disadvantaged does.

Great progress has been made in recent years in legislation for the assistance of the economically deprived child. It is now recognized that deprived children and their parents have a positive attitude toward education but are sometimes alienated from the regular public school situation because of frustrations and failure.

There is a coming together of forces in a concerted effort to develop programs to help such children. Many aspects of the social environment contribute to a child's behavior, but the most crucial is interaction with parents. The focal point is moving steadily downward and is now pointed to early childhood. Programs are being developed for the child of the low-income group in city slums, the child from a minority group, the child who is physically remote from more modal society, the child of migrant workers, and the child whose deviation is such that he or she qualifies as a handicapped child. Because these groups experience economic dependency in many cases, it is anticipated that special programs will not only assist in giving them a knowledge and appreciation of their culture and its values but will also encourage and motivate them to develop skills that will make them vocationally and socially independent.

COMPENSATORY AND INTERVENTION EDUCATION PROGRAMS

The Economic Opportunity Act of 1964 provided for varied ways through which children may derive the best possible benefits from child development, social welfare, teaching methods, and motivational techniques.[6] It authorized the establishment of programs for economically deprived children of preschool age designed to prepare them to enter public school. These programs are called Head Start Child Development Programs.

Head Start is a program designed to reach children of low-income families between the ages of three and five through a comprehensive preschool program. It provides language opportunities (speaking and listening), a wide variety of experiences, and adequate behavior models for the children. It is an attempt to break the poverty cycle in early ages since evidence indicates that the early years of childhood are the most crucial in educational development.

[6]D. Brieland, "Cultural and Social Change," *Young Children*, 20:4 (1965), pp. 223–229.

Bloom has pointed out that environment can mean as much as 20 IQ points in the developing child and is most critical in preschool years because children go 50 percent of the way in organizing their thinking patterns by the time they are four years of age and the next 30 percent by the time they are eight.[7]

Head Start is a total program to meet children's mental and emotional needs in preparing them to find success in their first school experience. It has many component parts—medical and dental examinations and corrections, immunizations, social services, nutritional care, and psychological services. The parents are involved in all aspects of the program, including decision making and often filling many nonprofessional positions. Other people interested in the community are encouraged to work as volunteers. Activities are planned by the center to help parents deal with general and specific problems of making a home and bringing up a family.

The planning for Head Start programs was based on first looking at the needs of children and then setting up appropriate goals. It was found that many children were lacking in language development and often had difficulty in expressing themselves because of limited vocabulary and inability to speak so as to be heard. Because of limited experiences they did not fit into social groups and were often unable to use simple toys or scissors, crayons, paper, pencils, and such, which are readily accessible to privileged children. The program that emerged placed emphasis on improving language, healthful living, developing curiosity, building self-image, and respecting authority as a means to self-discipline.

The 1965 summer program of Head Start began at 13,344 centers in 2,000 communities with an attendance of approximately 500,000 children.[8] One of every two economically deprived children eligible to enter public school in the fall of 1965 was helped. Forty thousand teachers and 500,000 volunteers were involved in the eight-week program. Local communities paid 10 percent (either cash or in kind). The federal government paid up to 90 percent of the cost.

This 1965 summer program was so successful that in August of that year it was announced that Project Head Start would become a year-round program. There were the following three types of programs:[9]

1. Programs, including health, education, social service, and parent activities, during the school year for the children who participated in summer Head Start.
2. Full-year programs for preschool children who would enter school in the fall of the year.

[7]B. S. Bloom, *Stability and Change in Human Characteristics* (New York: John Wiley and Sons, 1964), p. 88.
[8]Irwin Ross, "Head Start Is a Banner Project." *The PTA Magazine*, 60:7 (1966), p. 3.
[9]Keith Osborn, "Project Head Start—An Assessment," *Educ. Leadership*, 23:98 (1965), pp. 18–103.

3. Short-term summer programs for children who would enter school in the fall of the year.

The local programs were conducted by a Community Action Agency or were delegated to a group that had the capacity to organize and operate the program, such as the public schools, other public agencies, private nonprofit organizations, or institutions of higher education. In communities without a Community Action Agency other provisions were made for sponsorship of a Head Start program. Children were selected on the basis of an index of whether a family was earning a minimum-standard income, where the family lived (farm or nonfarm family), and number of children in the family. At least 90 percent of the children came from families that fell below the poverty line. The other 10 percent could come from the community at large but could not share in the medical benefits.

Groups were limited to 15–20 children per teacher. The Office of Economic Opportunity financed an eight-week teacher training course for a limited number of local people who were to teach in the program. Short-term courses were planned for other teachers.

Such programs as Institutional Development Studies,[10] the program in New Rochelle, New York,[11] the Early School Admission Project in Baltimore,[12] Early Training Project at Murfreesboro, Tennessee,[13] and the New York Housing Authority Project,[14] had given direction to the development of preschool programs before the need for compensatory education had attained such national scope.

Some educators questioned whether an eight-week program or even a year-round program could make up for four years of deprivation. Some leaders in the field suggested that emphasis in these programs be placed only upon academic learning. Others believed that the broader program would ensure greater achievement in academic learning and contribute more to the cultural development of the child.[15] Spodek raised the questions of the value of "massive intervention" and quality control of programs for such large groups of disadvantaged children.[16]

[10]M. Deutsch, "Early Social Environment: Its Influence on School Adaptation," *Pre-School Education Today* (Garden City, N.Y.: Doubleday & Co., 1966).
[11]Thelma G. Wolman, "A Preschool Program for Disadvantaged Children—The New Rochelle Story," *Young Children*, 21:2 (1965), pp. 98–111.
[12]Catherine Brunner, "Deprivation—Its Effects, Its Remedies," *Educ. Leadership*, 23:2 (1965), pp. 103–107.
[13]R. A. Klaus and Susan W. Gray, "Murfreesboro Preschool Program for Culturally Deprived Children," *Child. Educ.*, 42:2 (1965), p. 92.
[14]Alice M. Brophy, "Children's Centers—Three Decades of Progress," *J. of Nursery Educ.*, 13:3 (1964), pp. 173–177.
[15]Project Head Start," *NEA J.*, 54:7 (1965), p. 58.
[16]B. Spodek, "Is Massive Intervention the Answer?" *Educ. Leadership*, 23:2 (1965), p. 109.

Jenny W. Klein states that it took almost one hundred years before a comprehensive, federally sponsored intervention program emerged for preschoolers. Experimental and pilot programs, planned variations of Head Start, and other models provide information to show that early intervention may raise the quality of children's lives before the effects of poverty are established into a self-perpetuating cycle.[17]

The evaluative studies of Project Head Start are divided into census surveys, research, educational testing service, longitudinal studies, and national evaluation studies. The studies showed a need for more careful instrumentation particularly in research designs, the need to study long-term interventions, and the need to avoid quick judgments on the basis of data or the art of Early Childhood Education.[18]

In a recent review of the effect of Head Start programs, Moore[19] summarizes the following earlier findings:

1. Gains are short-lived, whatever the model, once the program is over.
2. Head Start children are less likely to be placed in special rooms or to be retained in the same grade than are similar non-Head Start children.
3. Early intervention is a complex process. It must involve the home and family and requires unusual resources.
4. Variation of results using the same model suggests that forces other than the model used are influential.
5. The more structured academically oriented models seem to produce the best results, at least temporarily.
6. The answer as to long-term effects of early programs is not in, and awaits much clarification from, long-term efforts now under way.

Since Head Start began, the effectiveness of compensatory and early intervention programs in producing lasting gains has been debated. New evidence based on longitudinal studies begun in the sixties, suggests that advantages of early childhood compensatory and intervention programs have been retained by most children over a period of years.[20] The "sleeper effects" were not evident in the scores of children participating in the original preschool program the first few years following the program. However, there is now evidence of gains that seem somewhat permanent.[21]

---

[17]Jenny W. Klein, "Head Start: Intervention for What?" *Educ. Leadership*, 39:1 (1971), pp. 16–19.
[18]Lois-Ellen Datta, "A Report on Evaluation Studies of Project Head Start." *International Journal of Early Childhood Education*, 3:2 (1971), pp. 58–68.
[19]Shirley M. Moore, "The Effects of Head Start Programs with Different Curricular and Teaching Strategies," *Young Children*, 32:6 (1977), pp. 54–60.
[20]*Education Daily*, February 25, 1977, p. 6.
[21]B. Brown, *Long-Term Gains from Early Intervention: An Overview of Current Research* (mimeogr.). Presented at the 1977 Annual Meeting of the American Association for the Advancement of Science, Denver, Colorado, February 23, 1977.

Seitz et al.[22] followed the academic progress of children from economically disadvantaged families living in the inner city. One group of children participated in Head Start and Follow Through programs while the control group received no special attention. For those children who responded positively there was no fade-out of gains. The gains evident when the program ended were still found four to five years later—these children were still performing at a higher level than were those in the control group in mathematics, general information, vocabulary, and IQ scores.

Several studies have reported that early compensatory and intervention programs produced marked reductions in the number of children placed in special education classes or retained in the grade. For example, Guinagh and Gordon found that 10 percent of the children in the treatment group were placed in special education classes, as compared with 30 percent of the control group.[23]

While the early Head Start evaluations were disappointing, in many ways they provided valuable cues for the development of programs with specific characteristics and goals. Furthermore, teachers generally report Head Start children as being better prepared for school than like children who had not attended Head Start. Head Start children also repeat fewer grades than children not in the program and, of course, the value of better health and personality adjustment resulting from the health and social services program to later learning is hard to estimate.

By the fall of 1977, more than 5.5 million children had participated in Head Start programs. Despite the fact that 37 percent of preschoolers' mothers work outside the home, 10,000 Head Start parents have become certified teachers.[24] In addition to its standard program, Head Start has consistently allocated a portion of its funds to research and development. Three significant programs emerged as a result, namely, Follow Through, Parent-Child Centers, and Home Start.

The objectives of the Follow Through program were twofold: comparing short-term and long-term effects of well-defined approaches to Early Childhood Education and assessing the cumulative impact of a continuous, systematically different program from preschool to primary grades.[25] The operation

[22]Victoria Seitz, Nancy Apfel, and Carol Efron, *Long-Term Effects of Early Intervention: A Longitudinal Investigation.* (mimeogr.). Presented at the 1977 Annual Meeting of the American Association for the Advancement of Science, Denver, Colorado, February 23, 1977.

[23]B. J. Guinagh and I. J. Gordon, *School Performance as a Function of Early Stimulation* (Final Report, Grant No. NIH-HEW-OCD-90-C-638), Institute for Development of Human Resources, University of Florida, 1976.

[24]Dorothy Levenson, "Whatever Happened to Early Childhood Education?" *Instructor* (October 1977), p. 71.

[25]*Implementation of Planned Variations in Head Start, 1969–70* (Washington, D.C.: Institute of Child Study, University of Maryland, and Office of Child Development, DHEW).

of the Follow Through program was delegated to the U.S. Office of Education. Selected school districts were asked to choose a model that had been shown promising as a vehicle for meeting the objectives of Head Start and for continuing that model program for former Head Start children into the early elementary grades. This study was done in order to determine the effectiveness of the program through time.

A recent study involving 352,000 Follow Through and comparison group children over a nine-year period conducted originally by Stanford Research Institute and continued by Abt Associates[26] found Follow Through ineffective in increasing test scores in the basics. Sixty-seven percent of Follow Through programs failed to produce gains in the program children over those not in the program. However, the basic skills models were superior as far as test results were concerned over the cognitive/conceptual skills and affective/cognitive models. The study also showed great variations within the use of the same models from site to site with the best results in middle-sized communities rather than in large cities or small communities. This is an important finding, as it points to significant influences on learning other than the model program used.[27]

A critique of the Abt Report made by House et al. reached different conclusions.[28] These workers found that models that emphasize basic skills are not necessarily better than other models or methods. However, one approach was not demonstrated to be better than another and participation in the Follow Through classes was neither superior nor inferior to regular schooling. Many of the goals of the Follow Through models were not measured, even though the development of effective evaluative instruments had been promised. House and his team agree with the Abt Report that the effectiveness of a teaching model varies from one community to the next. Individual teachers, schools, neighborhoods, and homes seem to influence children's achievement far more than the method used.

Additional evaluation conducted and/or sponsored by the U.S. Office of Education, but not completed at the time of this writing, may well shed additional light on the effectiveness of this program. By the time you read this, such results will likely be available to you and should be used in any evaluation of the Follow Through program.

Parent Child Centers were established in 1967 as an early intervention demonstration project involving 36 communities. Thirty-three of these were managed by the Office of Child Development, DHEW, while three were retained by the Office of Economic Opportunity as research demonstration pro-

---

[26]"Value of Federally Funded Programs in Basics Disputed," *ASCD News Exchange 19*:4 (1977), pp. 1–13.
[27]Ibid., p. 12.
[28]E. R. House, G. V. Glass, L. D. McClean, and D. F. Walker, "No Simple Answer: Critique of the "Follow Through" Evaluation," *Educ. Leadership, 35*:6 (1978).

grams. Head Start for children from three to five years of age had clearly shown that environmentally caused developmental deficits present by age three were difficult to overcome. In an effort to alleviate this problem, Parent-Child Centers (PCC) only enrolled children below the age of three and "graduated" them when they reached their third birthday. In reality, the family of the target child in each case was an active part of the program. In many cases, in order to assure the most profitable impact of the program, target children were accepted before birth.

PCC is a Head Start program with all components receiving maximum attention. It operates on the concept that normal learning and development must have a normal environment in which to function if critical early developmental processes are to proceed on schedule and without causing later retardation. Consequently, heavy emphasis is placed on working with the entire family, encouraging home improvement, and an all-out effort to bring target families into the mainstream of American life while still retaining their unique cultural and ethnic characteristics. Every effort is made in the interest of the target child in order that he or she be provided optimum opportunities for all aspects of growth and development. It will be interesting to see how these children fare later in middle and high school, as they were originally, almost without exception, at high educational risk.

Home Start, a three-year demonstration Head Start project involving 16 programs, was conducted from 1972 to 1975, buttressed by certain continuing efforts thereafter. Basically, Home Start, like PCC, provided all the services of Head Start, except that the programs focused on home rather than on a center operation, thus enabling parents to become "child development specialists" providing for the maximum education, growth, and development of their own children. A major goal was to demonstrate the effectiveness of providing support for parents in their major child-rearing efforts through home-based programs as well as to assess the financial feasibility of such efforts.[29]

RESPONSIBILITY FOR PREPRIMARY EDUCATION AND SERVICES

The American public has generally accepted responsibility for the education of all children age six and above and has been willing to support such efforts with tax dollars. When it comes to like responsibilities for the education of children below that age, the story is somewhat different. There are two significant beliefs rather firmly ingrained in the minds of most people that account for this situation. First, educational psychology has led us to believe that it

---

[29]*The Home Start Demonstration Program: an Overview*, (Washington, D.C.: U.S. Department of HEW, Office of Child Development, 1973).

takes a certain amount of maturity to be able to achieve the tasks (such as reading) expected of the school. While there is some validity to this belief, there is considerable evidence, as pointed out elsewhere in this text, that perhaps the child's most significant learning occurs prior to that time. Second, the American cultural and religious heritage suggests that the responsibility for the care and education of infants and preschool-age children belongs to, and is the responsibility of, the child's family. Yet families continue to have difficulty in fulfilling this role.

Beginning in 1909 and every 10 years thereafter the President of the United States has called a national conference on the needs of children and youth attended by citizens and professionals from all walks of life. It is of value to look at the recommendations made over the last three decades by these White House Conferences on Children and Youth.

At the 1950 White House Conference, the citizens attending expressed their approval of education for young children by this recommendation: "As a desirable supplement to home life, nursery schools and kindergartens, provided they meet high professional standards, should be included as a part of public opportunities for all children."[30]

At the 1960 Conference, three forums recommended that free public education be extended downward to include kindergartens as a part of the school system. It was further recommended that every organized group of young children away from home be under the supervision of at least one person qualified in the field of Early Childhood Education.[31]

The 1970 Conference had certain unique features, namely (1) the division into two groups, one conferring on children and another on youth so that the problems of children not become secondary to the problems of youth; and (2) the multidisclipinary approach, by bringing together groups from both inside and outside educational circles.[32] The conference participants recommended that each state set up community-coordinated child-care committees. These committees were to be composed of parents and professionals (both public and private) who serve in the field of child development. Ten such committees (4C) were already in existence when the White House Conference met in 1970.[33]

The Economic Opportunity Act of 1964 and the Elementary and Secondary Education Act (ESEA) of 1965 brought the federal government increasingly

[30]*Conference Proceedings* (Washington, D.C.: Midcentury White House Conference on Children and Youth, 1950).

[31]*Conference Proceedings* (Washington, D.C.: The Golden Anniversary White House Conference on Children and Youth, 1960).

[32]*Report to the President, White House Conference on Children* (Washington, D.C.: U.S. Government Printing Office, 1970), pp. 5–15.

[33]*Interim Policy Guide for the 4C Program, Pilot Phase* (Washington, D.C.: U.S. Department of HEW, OCD, 1969).

into the educational scene. For the first time, funds in unprecedented amounts were made available to every community in the nation. Both of these Acts and their subsequent implementation placed major emphasis on early education, particularly for children of disadvantaged families. The tremendous and immediate public response to Head Start pointed up the urgent need for such a program.

The influence of this federal legislation during the mid-1960s has given impetus to the changing trends in Early Childhood Education and should prove beneficial to children of all socioeconomic levels. The prospects for kindergartens in all public school systems are brightened. In addition, the child-care centers are rapidly changing to carefully planned educational programs under the direction of trained teachers.

In crowded situations, however, there has been a tendency for the teacher to teach two groups, one in the morning and one in the afternoon, and to increase the size of the group to as high as 45 to 50 pupils. Inability to meet the cost involved may prevent many children from attending a private school, thereby depriving them of the opportunity to attend preschool or kindergarten unless schools are made available through public funds.

Title XX

The Social Security Act, as amended in 1975 as Public Law 93-047 opened up new possibilities for children's service programs managed at the state and local levels. This new program, usually referred to as Title XX,[34] replaced among other titles, Title IV, which was of greatest concern to Early Childhood Education. The Act provides for local and state planning and accountability. Funding requires the prior approval of a state plan with the state and local community providing $1 for every $3 of federal funds. This program is widely used to provide direct or purchased care for children of welfare parents. Since approval of state plans is prerequisite to funding, as would be expected, care programs vary in number and quality from state to state and from program to program.

State responsibility

By 1974 only two states, Mississippi and Idaho, had no legislation permitting or mandating kindergartens. In 46 states, some form of state aid was provided to kindergartens. However, kindergarten attendance is far from universal,

[34]*Using Title XX to Serve Children and Youth* (New York: Child Welfare League of America, 1975).

since the legislation in 34 of the states is permissive and mandatory in only 14 states. Eleven states provided some form of funding for prekindergarten programs.[35] However, ECS also publishes a monthly newsletter keeping interested persons up to date on developments in Early Childhood Education in the various states. For example, a recent issue[36] includes proposed legislation to expand the Minnesota Early Childhood and Family Education Programs, which begin with prenatal education for the parents and continue until the child is through kindergarten; a new law establishing kindergartens in Georgia as "soon as possible"; plans for 10 pilot kindergartens in Arizona; an interagency agreement in Michigan providing a parent support system and a child health fund available to "all" preschool children; and a legislative review of legislation in Missouri to provide school-based parent/child Early Childhood Education for three- to five-year-olds. Missouri has been providing funds for preschool handicapped children. With monthly developments such as these, it is impossible to attempt to detail each state's efforts in Early Childhood Education or care-service programs for young children. It is best to consult the State Department of Education or the State Department of Social Services of a particular state for the latest information desired.

Private efforts

The inadequate provision on the part of public schools to meet the growing need for extensive care and early educational experiences for preschool-age children has meant heavy reliance on private care centers and schools. The rapid progress these have made raises questions as to what types of schools, program quality, and adult personnel qualifications, including teachers, are needed. Although many provide excellent facilities, have a good adult–child ratio, and employ properly trained personnel, there are a number that do not maintain standards necessary for the well-being of the children involved. In fact, some programs are detrimental to children, even if they fill an immediate need in the care of children.

Summary

In an attempt to summarize information on funding, certification of personnel, licensing, and agency responsibility for Early Childhood Education, a survey

---

[35]*Early Childhood Programs: A State Survey 1974–75*, Report No. 65 (Denver, Colo.: The Education Commission of the States, 1975).
[36]*Early Childhood Project Newsletter* (Denver, Colo.: The Education Commission of the States, April 1977).

conducted by the Education Commission of the States[37] was carefully studied along with other current reports. Since there is no uniform definition of types of programs, rationale for funding, or responsibility for maintaining quality standards of personnel and programs, no attempt will be made here to designate what each state does. In general, it can be said that most states require certification for "teachers" in early childhood programs for five- and six-year-olds and, of course, in grades 1 and above. In addition, most states have some minimum requirements for children's programs other than those in the public schools and show an effort to provide general funding for public school kindergartens, pilot programs, and other types of programs for children below kindergarten age. However, funds for the latter programs are provided chiefly by grants from the federal government, usually for children from low-income families. It would be impossible to generalize about requirements for day-care licensing, as each state is struggling with this concern. Where licensing exists, it is generally, concerned only with physical care and safety. For the latest information available at this time see the 1975 survey of the Education Commission of the states.[38]

TYPES OF PROGRAMS FOR YOUNG CHILDREN

Many types of children's programs are in operation today, and they vary as to purpose and program. Yet each type of program has a place in our society and has a contribution to make to the development of young children. Parents need help in selecting the best program for the child concerned (see Chapter 20).

Although the name of a center may not appear important, it should provide some guidance for selecting a school or center program. But the name is often misleading. This is because it is common practice to select challenging and interesting names for programs, even if the name selected is inconsistent with the purpose of a given program. In fact, the name may even convey the opposite impression of what the program really is. If you examine any local or state directory such names will turn up as "Finishing School for Tots," "Kountry Klub for Kiddies," or "Little Rascal's Heaven." Names such as "Community Child Development Center," or "School for Young Children" present a clearer indication of what one might expect to find.

While most of today's programs for young children are not schools in the usual sense, still many parents and their children talk about "going to school," regardless of the type of program involved. As indicated, there is a vast array

[37]*Early Childhood Programs: A State Survey, 1974–75,* op. cit.
[38]*Day Care Licensing: Policies and Practices—A State Survey, July 1975.* Report No. 72 (Denver, Colo.: The Education Commission of the States, 1975).

A

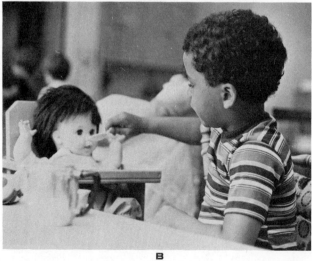

B

Figure 17
Today parents and educators have become more aware of the significance of the child's early experiences.

of services offered in the "world" of today's child. In any situation organized for children, learning takes place, whether desirable or undesirable. It is often difficult to distinguish a program designed primarily for the physical care of children from one that accepts the responsibility for a sound educational effort toward furthering the total development of each child involved.

It is little wonder that parents are confused and that Early Childhood Education specialists themselves often find themselves in disagreement about programs. In nearly every community we find "kindergartens" for three-, four-, and five-year-olds, Child Development Centers, nursery schools, comprehensive Family Day Care, Head Start centers, child-care centers, day care for exceptional children, schools for exceptional and handicapped preschool children, day-care centers, cooperative child care, cooperative nursery schools, play schools, day and "drop-in" nurseries, child-care programs for employees, babysitting services, and many more. For example, the Yellow Pages of the telephone directory of a city of 500,000 population lists 75 offerings under the heading Day Nurseries, 2 under Baby Sitters—Home Service, 91 under Schools—Nursery & Kindergarten (Academic), 6 Schools—Private, and 3 Child Development Centers. Of course, there are many duplications, which further adds to the confusion, and a large number are not even listed in the Yellow Pages. A brief definition of the most common types of preschool programs would appear useful to all concerned. The following descriptions are generally agreed upon by national organizations and authorities in the field of Early Childhood Education.

Nursery school

Nursery schools are often confused with day care centers, day nurseries, and nurseries. The nursery school is the first of a series of units making up an educational program. In public schools it usually is planned for four-year-olds; when operated under non-public school auspices it generally includes children of three and four years of age. Since the emphasis is on an educational experience that includes socialization education, children under three years of age are seldom accepted, except for children with special developmental deviations. The sessions are usually $2\frac{1}{2}$ hours in length and may or may not take place five days a week, especially for the younger children.

In addition to the public and nonpublic nursery schools, there are many that may be classified according to the purposes they serve. These include cooperatives, those that serve as laboratories for research for an agency or institution, nursery schools sponsored by and for children of special groups, and nursery schools for children with special needs that cannot be provided for in the typical classroom. A large number of nursery schools serve as laboratories for observation of normal growth and development either by high school or college students.

Kindergarten

The school unit that enrolls five-year-olds, in some cases six-year-olds, on a regular basis for a year prior to first grade is designated as a kindergarten. This experience has usually been thought of as a transition from home to formal education or school. Today, however, most children have had a group experience away from home by the time they enter kindergarten. Consequently, much effort is being put forth to develop kindergarten curricula as a regular initial phase of the school's instructional program. In a few cases this was true in years past. Thus, kindergartens provide for a continuous educational experience under the guidance of a qualified teacher and in close cooperation with the parents. Many are a part of public school; others operate as church related, privately owned, or sponsored special-purpose programs. Some, whether private or public, are full-day sessions, but many run half-day sessions. While not recommended, it is common for one teacher to have two groups of children, one in the morning and one in the afternoon.

Child development center

The designation of a comprehensive early childhood development program in the form of a Child Development Center was made popular by the Head Start program. The center is usually organized around activity rooms for various ages, from a few weeks after birth to age five or six, depending on the availability of kindergartens in the community. In addition, various amounts of space are available for play areas inside and out; facilities for food preparation and for conducting a health program; and provisions for parents to meet and to take part in instructional programs often of a home- and personal-improvement nature. Since total development of the child in the context of the home and family is usually the major emphasis, and while a key thrust is always a carefully planned educational experience, provision is made for a program for early diagnosis of problems not always recognized by parents, including dental, medical, and emotional. This type of program is both a concept and a community facility. It is a drawing together of all the resources in a community—both family and professional—which can contribute to the child's total development. The skills of professional workers in the fields of education, health, welfare, and related areas are utilized in building a program for each child. In planning, it is recognized that both professionals and nonprofessionals can make a meaningful contribution; therefore, it emphasizes the family as fundamental to the child's total development. The parents have an important role in developing policies and participating in the program. The concept of the child development center was used as a model for Head Start centers.

Unfortunately, there is a tendency on the part of many parents and paraprofessionals to feel that, when physical and safety needs have been met, all the child's needs have been met. As a result, some Child Development Centers, often underfunded, are nothing more than depots for children of welfare parents. This of course, need not be the case, for the Child Development Center concept is a sound one when adequately funded and operated by adequately qualifed professional and paraprofessional personnel.

Such a center's educational program should provide many opportunities to widen the child's horizons, to assist the child to express himself or herself orally, to succeed in a climate of confidence, and to develop within the child and the family a responsible attitude toward society and a feeling of belonging to a community. The teacher ratio, which needs to be lower, since these children require additional attention, is usually one teacher for 15 to 20 children with additional aides or teachers, or both. Time schedules are adapted to needs of individual children and their parents. A well-planned follow-through program with parents and children is a functional part of the activities. Special training for teachers and courses and clinics for parents are included. The parents are actively involved in planning and following through the activities.

School for exceptional children

The school for exceptional children is developed to meet the needs of an atypical child. Frequently, the entrance age is younger than three years, and special provisions are made for early diagnosis, treatment, and guidance of the atypical child. Teachers in these specialized schools require additional training, and clinical services are provided for teacher and parents as they work closely together in meeting specific mental, physical, or social needs of the child. (See other provisions in Chapter 23.)

Cooperative nursery school and / or kindergarten

Cooperative nursery schools and kindergartens serve a real purpose in our present-day life. Through this program many children have opportunities to participate in an educational program within the limits of the family's income. Often they serve a twofold purpose, providing an intensive program of parent education as well as worthwhile educational experiences for the children. Some cooperatives are operated by parents under church sponsorship; others are neighborhood or community ventures sponsored by parents only. Most of these schools provide for a director qualified in Early Childhood Education who is assisted by the parents. As they work with the children, parents receive guidance and close supervision from the director. The term "cooperative" itself implies that each parent contributes services or time to the ongoing program.

Child day care center and day nursery

Many of the child day care centers and day nurseries have the qualities desired for a good nursery school or kindergarten; many others place greater emphasis on custodial care and offer a very limited educational program. A number of these centers provide for care of children whose mothers work. Some are organized specifically to provide for children from less privileged homes. At times the necessity to be self-sustaining and/or to provide an income, especially in the private sector, makes it difficult to provide a satisfactory arrangement that will benefit the child. However, since the mid-1960s the infusion of federal and, to a lesser extent, state funds into programs for children of the poor, which enables mothers of young children to engage in gainful employment, has brought attention to the problems of children in care services (see Chapter 8).

Family Day Care still provides care for more children in the United States than does any other type. Families provide care for a few children, often along with their own children, for remuneration. This service may be either purchased with public funds or paid for by the parents of the children served. Recognizing public responsibility for child care, Congress has passed legislation allowing sizable tax breaks when care is paid for by working parents. These provisions are constantly being studied and revised to help parents out as increasing numbers of women have become gainfully employed over the past several years.

Because of the large number of homes involved, Family Day-Care programs range from inadequate babysitting services to those which provide the security and experiences very young children were usually provided in their own homes before so many mothers were not home during the day. In many ways, family day care has the potential of being better than that provided by often large and impersonal, but highly organized, publicly supported centers. This is especially true for infants and very young children when the continuity and security of the same caregiver or caregivers is so important to the forming of attachment bonds, self-identification, and later personality development.[38]

[38]J. Bowlby, *Attachment and Loss*, Vol. I (New York: Basic Books, 1969).

Play school

Play school programs are usually operated under the sponsorship of a church, an organized group of parents, a civic club, as part of a recreation program, or by a service set up for the care of underprivileged children. In many cases, play schools have expanded their facilities in order to incorporate activities formerly considered as those provided in a nursery school and/or kindergarten.[39] Closely related is a play program called a Drop-in Nursery, usually sponsored by a church, civic group, or shopping center. Children do not attend regularly but attend at the convenience of the parents, thus enabling the mother or father to have "some time off" or to do the shopping. Fees are usually on an hourly basis.

LEGISLATIVE TRENDS

The trend toward provision of educational opportunities for greater numbers of children under the age of six has focused attention on the need to ensure that schools and centers for young children meet acceptable standards. Parents have faith in the term *school;* therefore, they frequently place their child in a center called a school without further investigation.

As early as 1879 state legislators began to enact laws permitting local school authorities to establish kindergartens. In a 1928 survey, Davis found that children's centers were expanding in number and enrollment at a rapid rate. This survey indicated that parents were seeking the best possible environment for their children; in addition, it indicated that parents desired guidance and cooperation in the supervision of the child's development.[40]

However, the strongest demand for provision and protection of schools for young children has come since 1940. Many states have taken legislative action regarding standards for schools for young children.

Legislative and federal action that pertains only to schools supported through public funds is not adequate. Many of the leaders of nonpublicly financed programs are giving aggressive leadership toward securing legislative action related to supervision and control of all schools for young children. Practically all states now provide for some authority vested either in the state or local officials to exercise some leadership function and to provide, in some instances, more or less limited supervision over nonpublic schools, either through directly expressed or implied legislative action.

Administering the programs for Early Childhood Education is either per-

[39]Hazel F. Gabbard, "Status and Trends in Early Childhood Education," *Those First School Years,* Vol. 40 (Washington, D.C.: NEA, 1960) pp. 219–21.
[40]Davis, op. cit., pp. 1–15.

missive or mandatory, depending on the type of legislative enactment. Legal authorization usually provides for some or all of the following: (1) registration and approval of schools; (2) authorization to develop rules and regulations for approval of nonpublic schools; (3) establishment of standards for schools; and (4) regulatory, administrative, supervisory, and leadership powers for the State Department of Health, Education and Welfare.

Since the 1960s, as federal legislation relating to education of young children has been enacted, state legislation has followed in many areas. In addition, nonpublic funds have been made available for experimental and special programs.

IMPORTANCE OF COOPERATIVE EFFORT

Many organizations are interested in the educational welfare of children at the local, state, regional, and national levels. Representatives from these organizations are working together closely to provide educational opportunities that allow children to reach their highest potential as they enter the continuous program of education from childhood through adulthood. Their cooperative efforts have greatly aided in securing better legislation, improved facilities and staff, and additional funds for programs for young children.

Through the years, this willingness of leaders to work together for the development of the programs of good schools for young children has been evident. This cooperative effort in searching for better ways to provide educational opportunities for the young child has resulted in the present-day recognition of the implications of these experiences for the continued education of the child. Through analyzing the strengths and weaknesses of the present programs, a basis for improved educational opportunities can be established. America has faith in education and holds to the belief that all children should have access to the best possible educational opportunities according to each child's potential. This faith and belief should continue to give direction to the expansion of the present-day schools and to the development of new programs for young children in the world of today and tomorrow.

SUMMARY

The trends and issues in preschool programs which have been discussed include the following:

1. Extending public schools downward to include kindergarten, nursery school, child development centers, and programs for infants.
2. Changing patterns of school organization and adapting programs for specific

purposes, such as those for the culturally different or for exceptional children.
3. Changing emphasis in day care programs to educational programs as well as day care.
4. Changing curriculum for preschool children by differentiating goals, activities, and materials to provide for individual differences within the group.
5. Changing role of the teacher to that of a guide of child development as opposed to a director of activities.
6. Continuing need for church-related schools for preschool children.
7. Expanding cooperative programs for preschool children.
8. Changing parent participation to parent involvement and replacing formal parent education with a cooperative teacher-parent team approach, which utilies parents in the instructional programs of their children in both home and center.
9. Replacing nursery schools and kindergartens with child development centers that provide the comprehensive programs made possible by available funds from the Federal government and various foundations.
10. Defining types of programs.
11. Assessing the impact of Head Start.

In analyzing these trends, it will be noted that some are positive and good for children; others indicate situations which contradict all that is known about how children grow and learn. Shortened sessions and large groups of children are being accepted as emergency measures. Too frequently there has been a tendency to rationalize and accept these makeshift arrangements, rather than to evaluate the services in terms of the effect on children. The present confusion regarding what is good for children must be cleared up and, in order to do this, there must be some guidelines by which to evaluate trends, a cooperative effort on the part of all those who are concerned with educational programs for young children.

Suggested Activities

1. Make a survey of nursery schools and kindergartens in your community. Trace the historical development of a selected number according to types. List requirements for admission, length of day, and types of services offered.
2. Compile a directory of these schools with an annotation showing services offered and so forth.
3. Compile a report of laws pertaining to schools for young children in your state and in your community. Discuss the historical development of these laws and what provisions are made for enforcing them in your local community.
4. Have a panel discussion on present strengths and improvements needed in schools for young children in your area. Present statistical data to support this discussion.
5. Investigate the Head Start program, defining provisions made by the federal government and the relationship to state and local community. Describe programs in oper-

ation in your community, listing strengths and weaknesses. Describe follow-through activities.

6. Discuss pending legislation relative to schools for young children (at the national level, the state level, and the local level).

7. Perhaps the most significant development in Early Childhood Education at the time this book was last revised was the growing demand for full-day programs for children from infancy on. Visit three such programs and describe the educational component of each. Find out what their objectives are, the methods used to attain them, and the evaluative procedures used. If possible, one of the programs visited should be a "model" funded in one of the federal or state pilot programs. Make comparisons.

Related Readings

ASCD. "Federal Funds to Assist or to Control?" *Educ. Leadership, 24*:1 (1966).

Bissell, Joan S. *Implementation of Planned Variation in Head Start,* First Year Report, I, Review and Summary. Washington, D.C.: U.S. DHEW, OCD, 1971.

Concept of A Child Development Center, Relationship to Preschool and Day Care. Washington, D.C.: OEO, 1965.

Day, Carol M., and R. K. Parker. *The Preschool in Action: Exploring Early Childhood Programs,* 2nd ed. Boston: Allyn and Bacon, 1977.

Honig, A. S. "The Family Development Research Program with Emphasis on the Children's Center Curriculum," in *Compendium of Curricula for Toddlers and Infants,* edited by A. S. Bardwell. Columbus, Ohio: Ohio State University Press, 1973.

Light, N. S., chm. *Early Childhood Education, Part II,* 46th Yearbook (NSSE) Bloomington, Ill.: Public School Publishing Co., 1929.

Meek, Lois M., chm. *Pre-school and Parental Education, Part I, Organization and Development, and Part II, Research and Method,* 28th Yearbook (NSSE). Bloomington, Ill.: Public School Publishing Co., 1929.

Snyder, Agnes, et al. *Dauntless Women in Childhood Education 1856–1931.* Washington, D.C. ACEI, 1972.

Taylor, Katherine Whiteside. *History of Parent Cooperative Movement, 1916–1966.* Indianapolis: Parent Cooperative Preschools International, 1966.

Weber, Evelyn. *The Kindergarten: Its Encounter with Educational Thought in America.* New York: Teachers College, 1969.

chapter 7

Providing qualified personnel and maintaining standards in preschool programs

Assuring qualified teachers, caregivers, and other involved adults in programs for young children is one of today's greatest challenges, for the need still far exceeds the availability of good personnel. Laymen and educators regard teachers and all adults involved as the most significant factor in determining the quality of experience that a child will have in any program. Yet, throughout the nation it is still possible for persons without even minimal educational and personal qualifications to establish and operate programs for infants and young children. Certification of educational personnel and licensing of centers are the usual means of attempting to ensure safety for the children and some degree of competence in teachers, administrators, and other educational personnel. Regardless of the licensing and certification standards, professionals and especially parents must always be on the alert that these standards are being met, reporting any concern to the appropriate licensing or certification authority.

Perhaps the most effective means of assuring quality is the continuous functioning of a duly appointed or elected advisory committee. Experience has shown that unless one half of the membership of such a committee are parents of the children actually enrolled, the chances of it being effective in matters that really count, such as policymaking and the establishment of goals and objectives, is minimal. In some programs, the advisory committee is charged with the responsibility of seeking and recommending the hiring of specific personnel and, in some cases, firing as well. Involvement of parents in these vital roles is, to say the least, a break with tradition, but it is an effective means of assuring good programs for their children.

CHARACTERISTICS OF GOOD ADULT PERSONNEL

Throughout the years, love of children has been recognized as basic to successful work with them. However, love is not enough. The adults must also enjoy working with children, and the love of such adults should be different from that of the mother. Patience and understanding not only for what is happening, but why it is happening, are essential to guiding the development of the young child. Only an adult who is secure can build security within children. A warm, outgoing, but not dominating, person can work well with children and parents. However, a teacher may have all the desirable personal qualities yet not be a good teacher. Basic information, understanding, knowledge, skill, competencies, and appreciations can only be secured through training and experience. The teacher must apply this knowledge in daily work with children. Many programs that prepare one for teaching in the field of Early Childhood Education provide counseling and guidance in the development of these essential qualities while the training and experience are secured.

In the selection of teachers for preschool children, special attention is given to personal qualities, such as warmth, openness, humor, efficiency, confidence, appearance, creativity, speech, voice, and the ability to communicate well by speaking clearly and choosing words carefully.

In recent years, preparation for all fields of endeavor, including Early Childhood Education, has been influenced by the concept of accountability and its corollary, Competency Based Education. Notable examples are the Management-by-Objectives Head Start programs and the Child Development Associate program. The latter will be discussed later in this chapter.

Credentialing teachers today, however, places emphasis on the demonstra-

Figure 18
Patience and understanding not only of what is happening but why it is happening are essential to guiding the development of the young child.

tion of professional competencies as well as personal qualities.[1,2] The competencies may be acquired in a variety of settings including teacher education institutions, on the job training, and in the community through the utilization of human resources. The new direction is away from inflexible adherence to regulatory functions and toward constructive dynamic leadership at the local level. Widespread exploration and change is indicated. Among the changes are earlier exposure to teaching situations and a shifting in preparation from the campus to the school systems,[3] and other programs for young children.

Although characteristic of personal qualifications for many other careers and employment opportunities, Lay and Dopyers[4] stress as the major categories of qualifications for early childhood teachers Commitment, Sensitivity, Resourcefulness, and Organizational Ability.

Licensing standards for directors of child-care center staff vary from state to state. The director or head teacher is usually a college graduate with professional study in Early Childhood Education. Staff training is one of her or his

[1] W. C. Allen, et al., "Performance Criteria for Education Personnel Development: A State Approach to Standards," *J. Teacher Educ., 20*:2 (1969), pp. 133–135.
[2] D. W. Allen and P. Wagschal, "New Look in Credentialing," *Clearing House, 44*:3 (1969), pp. 137–140.
[3] *A Manual on Certification Requirements for School Personnel in the United States,* 1970 edition (Washington, D.C.: National Commission on Teacher Education and Professional Standards, NEA, 1970).
[4] Margaret V. Lay and J. C. Dopyers, *Becoming A Teacher of Young Children* (Lexington, Mass: D. C. Heath, 1977).

Figure 19
Only an adult who is secure can build
security within children. A warm, outgoing, but not dominating, individual
can work well with children and parents.

responsibilities. The age for the director varies from sixteen years in four
states to twenty-one years in the other states. The requirements also vary from
high school graduation or its equivalent to four years of college. However, all
states do require experience and also that the individual be equipped to do
the work required. The qualifications of the other staff members also vary
from state to state. The staff-in-training must be capable of doing work required and must have a sensitivity to children and their needs.[5]

NEW DIRECTIONS IN THE PREPARATION OF EARLY CHILDHOOD EDUCATION PERSONNEL

As the need for full-day services for young children from low-income families,
from families whose mother and father both work, from one-parent families,

[5] *Child Care Data and Materials*, Committee on Finance, U.S. Senate, June 16, 1971.

and from families of varied ethnic and cultural backgrounds increases, colleges and universities charged with the responsibility of providing for the preparation of teachers have responded by drastically changing the traditional "lab school" program and function. One example of such a change is the College of Education's Early Childhood Education Children's Center at the University of South Carolina in Columbia. This Center enrolls 40 four- and five-year-olds and operates in cooperation with the College of General Studies' Center for infants and children through age three, which is housed in the same building. Of the many changes, perhaps most dramatic is the provision of a full-day program in which one half of the children enrolled are selected from families who qualify for Title XX benefits, and one half from families on a fee-paying basis. In addition, in keeping with mainstreaming efforts for exceptional children, one of ten children is "referred" with special needs to be met, that is, with sight, hearing, speech, and/or other unique problems that must be dealt with or worked around.

Because of the availability of university and state agency personnel and services, an effort is being made to make the program truly interdisciplinary in scope and multidisciplinary in practice, with services being provided by many departments of the university and by various local and state agencies. This well-equipped laboratory facility includes a modern-approach playground and excellent observation and recording facilities, including videotaping. The program is adequately staffed by well-qualified personnel and provides unique opportunities for research in cooperation with faculty and students from other departments of the university. Excellent observation and participation opportunities are provided for parents, for students pursuing degrees in Early Childhood Education, for public and private school personnel, and for other professional and nonprofessional persons interested in observing an exemplary preschool program in action. Staffing is differentiated, and the adult–child ratio exceeds the much-debated federal interagency standards.[6]

The program at the Center is child-centered with teachers, parents, and ancillary adult staff members serving as facilitators of learning. It is experience-based, developmental in philosophy, and personalized for each child and his or her family. Obviously, a major goal is the provision of a high quality of experience in the development and refinement of instructional behaviors for Early Childhood Education students and professionals in training.

The Anna Boyd Child Development and Teaching Center is an example of the trend toward field-based teacher education. Proponents of excellence in teacher education have always sought opportunities to place students in actual, on-going children's programs. The familiar Student Teaching placement,

[6] The Federal Interagency Day Care Requirements (FIDCR) Appropriateness Study," *Young Children*, 31:5 (1976), pp. 385–392.

with major emphasis on experience in a public school or agency, has resulted from this need. Beginning in 1973, a unique opportunity to go beyond the traditional student teaching experience was provided when the College of Education's Early Childhood Education program at the University of South Carolina in Columbia, Richland County School District Two, and the South Carolina State Departments of Education and Social Services entered into a cooperative agreement to develop, fund, and operate a full-day Child Development Center and program designed to serve as a Teaching Center for the preparation of Early Childhood Education teachers. An elementary school building that was available and no longer needed, was renovated for this purpose.

The Anna Boyd Child Development Center is rather unique in that the university, in addition to providing funds for program development and supplies, furnishes a full-time resident instructor who co-directs the program and supervises 10 to 12 full-time Early Childhood Education seniors and several part-time practicum students in their "becoming teachers" activities. This is a key provision of the program as the university's Early Childhood Education degree requirements provide for the integration of all methods, materials, and curriculum courses except in Reading and Language Arts into the full-time student teaching experience. In addition, majors are required to participate in a practicum experience each semester of their four-year program. The resident university instructor and the district's co-director can thus provide flexibility and relevance in the continuous ongoing planning process, and in the execution and the evaluation activities of the program. This process involves the classroom teachers, the university students, resource persons, parents, ancillary personnel, and, at times, the children themselves.

Enrolled on a multi-age and family grouping basis, the 60 children who attend the Anna Boyd Center are from varying ethnic, racial, and socioeconomic backgrounds with varying degrees of experiential deviations, thus providing a multicultural context. The Center is community-based, involving parents and citizens at all levels of operation, including service on advisory committees. It is staffed by teaching teams. Each team consists of a certified teacher, a teacher's aide, two to four student teachers, and several practicum students. The teams have the benefit of guidance at all times provided by the resident co-directors both of whom are experienced specialists in Early Childhood Education.

CHILD DEVELOPMENT ASSOCIATE

A pilot program for training Child Development Associates (CDA's) was initiated in the fall of 1972, and the first CDA was credentialed on July 24, 1976. By April, 1977, 1,000 CDAs had been approved and, at press time in May

1977, another 1,000 were being processed. The CDA training is not based on courses taken or degrees earned. Rather, the credential is awarded by the Child Development Associate Consortium (CDAC) after the individual has been assessed by examining teams employed and selected by the Consortium. The CDAC is a nonprofit organization funded by the Office of Child Development, DHEW, for the purpose of providing competent personnel to work in preschool programs including Head Start. Of course, this program does not have the authority of law that certification of teachers does. Nevertheless, the promoters of the program envision wide national acceptance in programs other than Head Start. Indeed, several states have included the CDA credential as appropriate preparation for personnel in meeting state standards. As pointed out earlier, the training consists of acquiring competencies that have been prescribed and can be assessed. Fifty percent of the training must be field-based and the program is not time circumscribed.[7]

It is too early to predict the effectiveness of preschool personnel who have achieved the CDA credential. One can surmise, however, that there will be great variation among the credentialed, just as there is among teachers who are certified. Those who propose the CDA training as more innovative, put other preparation models on the level of mere course-taking and ignore the vast amount of research and innovation engaged in by the "traditional" teacher-preparation institutions.

PARAPROFESSIONALS AND VOLUNTEERS

A pilot study reported by Prescott[8] gives a factual description of day care facilities and the requirements for day care leaders and volunteers. It has long been recognized that one teacher cannot do all that is needed for each child. Paraprofessionals render many services under the supervision and direction of the head teacher.[9,10] *Aides* can assist with clerical services, housekeeping activities, group supervision, technical assistance, and some instructional activities as assigned by the teacher.[11]

Volunteers may or may not be trained personnel. They assist the trained

[7] "CDAC Reaches New Milestone: Thousandth Credential," *Dateline CDAC*, 3:2 (May 1977), p. 1.
[8] Elizabeth Prescott, *A Pilot Study of Day Care Centers and Their Clientele* (Washington, D.C.: Children's Bureau, Welfare Division, U.S. Department of Health Education and Welfare, 1965).
[9] D. Findley and K. T. Henson, "Teacher Aides: Should They Be Certified?" *Contemporary Education*, 42:4 (1971, pp. 177–180.
[10] A. J. Mauser, "The Paraprofessional: Panacea or Frankenstein?" *Contemporary Education*, 41:3 (1970), pp. 139–141.
[11] Sylvia Sunderlin and B. Willis, *Aides to Teachers and Children* (Washington, D.C.: ACEI, 1968).

teacher and also help with community service. They share what they can do best. The trend is to involve *parents* and *community groups* in the instruction and care of children.

All personnel must have an understanding of the objectives and concepts of Early Childhood Education, a personality that children and adults respond to readily, and an intense interest in the development of the children.

The number of persons working in a center depends on the number of children and the maturity of the children. The type of head teacher also affects the enrollment. However, all centers should have at least one qualified person.

Other personnel may include a career assistant, a career community assistant, career health specialist as well as trainees or aides, the volunteer worker, and paraprofessional personnel. Trainees or aides may assume office or administrative responsibilities as a part of their duties or they may have this type of work exclusively.[12] As the personnel give evidence of continued interest in children every opportunity should be given them to have additional responsibilities and additional work in courses and experience, as well as opportunities for developing career ladders for paraprofessionals.[13]

OTHER APPROACHES

As the need and demand for the education of prekindergarten-age children continues to grow, concern for properly prepared teachers, caregivers, and other adult personnel increases. The extensive use of untrained paraprofessionals, parents, volunteers, and elementary teachers without specialized preparation in Early Childhood Education is likely to result in inadequate programs for young children. This is not to say that this approach is necessarily unsatisfactory. What is needed in such cases is a carefully planned system of undifferentiated staffing, extensive preservice and in-service training, and retraining. Because of the nature of the needs of very young children, the contributions of professionals from varied disciplines, including psychology, sociology, health education, nutrition, anthropology, pediatrics, nursing, and possibly others, are needed. The most successful programs have this interdisciplinary instruction built into the program content, instead of having to depend on the "volunteer" efforts of professionals in these fields on a one-shot class-lecture basis.

Because the CDA program permits persons with less than a high school education as well as persons with advanced degrees to prepare for credential-

---

[12] Project Head Start, *Career Planning and Progression for a Child Development Center* (Washington, D.C.: U.S. Department of Health, Education and Welfare, 1970).

[13] Margaret Malone, *Summary of Selected Proposals Related to Child Care* (Washington, D.C.: Library of Congress, Congressional Research Service, Education and Welfare, June 1971).

ing, Berson and Sherman[14] report on the effectiveness of an alternate competency-based model for the preparation of teachers. Involved were paraprofessionals, undergraduates, and certified teachers. The model employed used an
adaptation of the following approaches: team teaching, involvement of paraprofessionals, competency or performance-based instruction, and preser-
vice/in-service teacher education.

After taking part in the program, the participants' performance was evaluated using scores on self-evaluation, on the Barth Assumptions About Learning and Knowledge Scale, and on scores on the CDA Competencies instrument. Berson and Sherman found statistically significant differences on the
self-evaluations of all groups. The Barth Scale showed that classroom teachers
and undergraduates gained during the program at a statistically significant
level, but that the paraprofessionals did not. These results indicated that approaches to teacher education other than the CDA competency-based model
can be effective in producing competencies among teacher trainees, and those
who are already classroom teachers.

STANDARDS, CERTIFICATION, AND LICENSING

The Economic Opportunity Act of 1964 required that a set of standards be established by the Secretary of DHEW and the Director of OEO. The result was
the publication in 1968 of a set of standards for Day Care (FIDCR).[15] Since its
inception there have been many attempts at revision of the requirements.
Title XX of the Social Security Act was passed in 1975, making the educational requirements of FIDCR optional but the staffing of adult–child ratios
mandatory as follows: under six weeks of age, 1:1; six weeks to three years of
age, 1:4; three years to four years of age, 1:5; and four years to six years, 1:7. In
April 1976 President Ford vetoed legislation providing funds to assist states in
meeting these requirements. At the time of this writing, this issue has not
been settled. Readers are urged to contact local social service and education
agencies and institutions for the current status of federal day care standards.

CERTIFICATION REQUIREMENTS

A number of reports concerning the preparation of teachers have been
made.[16-18] In 1967 the Association for Childhood Education International

---

[14] Minnie P. Berson and C. E. Sherman, "Divergent Views on Prekindergarten Teacher Education," *Educational Leadership,* 34:2 (November 1976), pp. 143–149.

[15] FIDCR, op. cit., 1968.

[16] C. L. Rampton (ed.), *Early Childhood Development, Alternatives for the Program Implementation in the States* (Denver, CO: Education Commission of States, 1971), pp. 4, 6, 13.

identified the areas to be included in the preparation of teachers for children three to eight years of age. The areas included (1) liberal education, (2) foundations of Early Childhood Education, (3) child growth and development, (4) nature of the learning process, (5) small group dynamics, (6) curriculum and method, and (7) professional laboratory experiences.[19]

The Ad Hoc Joint Committee on the Preparation of Nursery and Kindergarten Teachers of the National Commission on Teacher Education included desirable goals in its report for both preservice and in-service education.[20] These included independence, positive self-image, intellectual stimulation, creativity, socialization, physical development, emotional development, and staff collaboration and cooperation. The committee also sets forth proposals on personnel selection and programs for personnel at different levels.

By 1975, 48 states and territories had mandated certification for kindergarten teachers and administrators in the public schools. Mississippi and American Samoa had no certification, and Texas did not require certification for administrators. However, only eight states did not accept elementary certification for kindergarten teachers, seven required elementary plus minimal early childhood preparation, and 29 required only an elementary certificate. Most states had no form of certification for paraprofessionals.[21]

STANDARDS AND LICENSING

Because of the importance of preschool experience to the child's development, standards and licensing for these schools and centers are vital. Furthermore, facts uncovered by Forbes on how and why parents select schools reveal the need for standards. She found that (1) most parents selected centers because of friends' recommendations; (2) some parents selected centers because of enrichment activities; others, however, considered the convenience of the location; (3) although most parents talked by telephone or personally with the director of the center before enrolling their child, 19 percent did not

---

[17] U.S. Office of Education, *Compilation on Legislation on Title I—Financial Assistance to Local Agencies for the Education of Children of Low-Income Families* (Washington, D.C.: Department of Health, Education and Welfare, July, 1971).

[18] *State Agencies Administering Services Under Title V, Parts 1 and 2, and Title IV, Part B, of the Social Security Act.* (Washington, D.C.: U.S. Department of Health, Education and Welfare, Social and Rehabilitative Services, Children's Bureau, 1969).

[19] *Preparation Standards for Teachers in Early Childhood Education* (Washington, D.C.: ACEI, 1967).

[20] *Preliminary Report of Ad Hoc Joint Committee on the Preparation of Nursery and Kindergarten Teachers* (Washington, D.C.: National Commission on Teacher Education and Professional Standards, NEA, 1969).

[21] *Early Childhood Programs: A State Survey 1974-5,* Report No. 65 (Denver, CO: The Education Commission of the States, 1975).

visit the center or meet the director before enrolling their child; and (4) most of the children were attending the center because parents were not home during the day.[22]

The procedure for ensuring improved standards for schools for young children varies from state to state and within cities. Through programs of cooperative action, plans suitable for a given locality are developed and put into effect. Participants often include leaders from public, private, and church-related schools, and federal programs, as well as social workers, doctors, psychologists, directors of educational programs for teachers, and other community leaders. Through educational and interpretive programs on television and radio, and through newspapers and magazine articles, the general public is being informed as to values and problems of good schools for young children. As a result, parents are becoming more and more discriminating toward the schools their young children attend. They are cooperating with leaders in the movement to ensure that all schools for young children meet minimum standards.

Licensing is one form of ensuring standards in preschool centers. It does not guarantee optimum conditions, but indicates a level at which a center can operate safely and efficiently. Many persons consider the licensing of child care facilities as the responsibility of departments of welfare. In some situations, however, other agencies cooperate or assume the responsibility.[23]

No attempt will be made here to summarize the status of day-care licensing in the United States, for at the time of this writing the latest available information was that licensing was in ferment, as almost every state was in the process of reviewing or updating previous legislative status. The requirements varied greatly from state to state and for different kinds of facilities within each state.[24] Readers are urged to contact local or state agencies and area colleges or universities for current information regarding licensing legislation.

ORGANIZATIONS CONCERNED WITH YOUNG CHILDREN

Participation in the programs of professional organizations can be very rewarding to teachers, caregivers, and other personnel working with young children. One of the greatest benefits is getting to know others in the same type of

---

[22] Marcia Boyer Forbes, *Parental Selection of Schools for Pre-School Children.* Unpublished Master's Thesis, Florida State University, 1960.

[23] E. Class, *Licensing of Child Care Facilities by State Welfare Departments.* Washington, D.C.: U.S. Department of Health, Education and Welfare, Social and Rehabilitation Service, Children's Bureau, 1968.

[24] *Day Care Licensing: A State Survey 1975* Report No. 72 (Denver, Colo.: The Education commission of the States, 1975).

responsibility and sharing ideas with them. Most organizations help people keep up to date through conferences and publications. A brief history of the development of some of those organizations which have prospered and been influential in influencing the quality and type of services and educational programs available to young children today follows.

Growth of kindergarten associations

The organization of a Primary department in the National Education Association in 1870 stimulated interest in kindergartens. Prior to this, kindergartens were mainly under private auspices. During the period of 1880 to 1889, the kindergarten movement was expanded through private and church kindergartens and centers for young children in social settlements. During this same period, as the number of these groups became larger, kindergarten associations were formed to provide leadership and guidance for all programs for young children. This concept of cooperative action stimulated the development of many organizations at local and state levels among groups interested in young children.

Among the first of such organizations were the Golden Gate Kindergarten Association in San Francisco, the Sub-Primary Society of Philadelphia, the Des Moines Kindergarten Association, the Los Angeles Association, and the Louisville Kindergarten Association. Immediately following the development of these organizations, kindergarten associations were rapidly formed in Albany, New Orleans, Detroit, Denver, Asheville, Grand Rapids, Chattanooga, Buffalo, Minneapolis, and elsewhere.

From 1890 to 1899, the public kindergarten movement spread rapidly and training departments for teachers of young children were established. Kindergarten associations were developed in many areas as the movement expanded. The International Kindergarten Union was formed at the National Education Association Conference in 1892 to unify and give direction to the many local associations. The influence of the expanding number of associations resulted in a Kindergarten Exhibit at the Columbia Exposition in Chicago in 1893.

By 1895 it had become evident that the crowded conditions of programs of the National Education Association made it necessary to appoint a separate time and place for meetings of the International Kindergarten Union. Therefore, this group had its first independent meeting at Columbia University's Teachers College, New York. Interest in the child-study movement stimulated by the International Kindergarten Union was a significant factor in the development of the National Congress of Mothers in 1897.

By 1910 three large groups—The National Kindergarten Association, The International Kindergarten Union, and The National Congress of Mothers—

were working closely together for kindergartens for all children. At this time, teachers of the primary groups and the kindergarten worked cooperatively in planning programs for children that would supplement and not overlap the work of each group. At a meeting of the Superintendents and the National Education Association in Cincinnati in 1915, 30 primary teachers formed a National Council of Primary Education. One of the stated purposes of this council was to unify the work of the kindergarten and the primary school.

Nursery Schools. In 1920 the nursery school at Teachers College, Columbia University, was introduced to America through a course taught by a specialist from Miss McMillan's School in London. At this time, there were only three nursery schools in America: one in a college, one private, and one philanthropic. The Merrill-Palmer School in Detroit and several Child Development Research Centers were established in 1920 and 1924. During the next decade, nursery schools expanded until, in 1931, the National Association for Nursery Education was established. This same year the International Kindergarten Union appointed a committee to project plans for reorganization to include both nursery schools and primary schools; this resulted in the Association for Childhood Education, which included all three groups. This association has a predominant influence on the development of programs for all children under 12 years of age. Following is a description of the major organizations currently concerned with young children:

Association for Childhood Education International (ACEI)
3615 Wisconsin Avenue, NW, Washington, D.C. 20016

The purposes of the ACEI are as follows: to work for the education and well-being of children ages 2 to 12; to promote desirable conditions, programs, and practices in the schools (nursery through elementary); to raise the standard of preparation and to encourage continued professional growth of teachers and leaders in this field; to bring into active cooperation all groups concerned with children in the school, the home, and the community; and to inform the public of the needs of children and how the school program must be adjusted to fit those needs.

Individuals, local branches, state and province associations work together to support a unified movement for children through:

A plan of action developed at two-year intervals by analyzing existing conditions which affect children and suggesting appropriate action.

The annual study conference planned for members and others to discuss current developments, exchange ideas and experiences relating to children.

An information service to which anyone may write for help on a subject related to education and well-being of children.

Publications which include *Childhood Education*, the official journal, and bulletins on current problems in education.

Cooperation with other organizations.

The Childhood Education Center which is maintained at Headquarters in Washington, D.C.

Members include nursery, kindergarten, elementary teachers, parents, all community workers, and others concerned with the education and well-being of children.

National Association for the Education of Young Children (NAEYC)
1834 Connecticut Avenue, NW, Washington, D.C. 20009

The National Association for Nursery Education (NANE) established in 1931, in keeping with the trends in Early Childhood Education, became the National Association for the Education of Young Children (NAEYC) in October 1964. It is interesting to compare the stated purpose of the new organization in its first issue of the new journal *Young Children,* October 1964 with the statement of purpose appearing in the September 1977 issue. In October 1964, we find:

> The purpose of the National Association for the Education of Young Children is to provide a medium for the study, interpretation, and improvement of the education and development of young children.

In September 1977 the statement of purpose had been revised to read,

> The expressed purpose of NAEYC is to serve and to act on behalf of the needs and rights of young children (birth to eight years), with primary focus on the provision of educational services and resources.

Services and resources for members include:

Young Children—NAEYC's bimonthly journal.

Publications—Books and pamphlets on a wide range of topics concerned with young children.

Affiliate Groups—More than 210 groups affiliated with NAEYC offer a variety of services on behalf of children.

Conferences—NAEYC's annual conference attracts participants from every aspect of children's services. It has been observed that the annual national conference is the largest multicultural group to assemble in the field of education.

Day Care and Child Development Council of America, Inc.
1401 K Street, NW, Washington, D.C. 20005

The goal of the Day Care and Child Development Council of America is to promote the development of a universally available child-care system. This is done through public education, social action, and its publication and conference programs. The Council publishes *Voice for Children* and *Action for Children.*

Child Study Association of America
9 East 89th Street, New York, N.Y. 10010

Founded in 1888 as the Society for the Study of Child Nature, the Child Study Association of America is the oldest organization having a continuous parent education program. In 1912 it published the first selected list of books for children and in 1921 began publishing *Outlines of Child Study.* The *Child Study Quarterly* was published until 1960. The Association serves to strengthen the family through its training, research, and publications programs.

World Organization for Early Childhood Education

The World Organization for Early Childhood Education, known as OMEP after the initials of the French translation, Organisation Mondiale pour l'Education Prescolaire, was founded in 1948. OMEP is an educational organization that promotes the study and education of young children, fosters happy childhood and home life, and thus contributes to world peace. It strives to help all those who work with children to think clearly and wisely about the needs of young children and to provide opportunities for all professions and organizations to cooperate in serving those needs.

OMEP was initiated in 1946 by Mrs. Alva Myrdel (Sweden) and Lady Allen of Hurtwood (Great Britain), who met in Sweden to discuss how to create a greater understanding throughout the world of the educational needs of young children and how to unite all those working in this field. In July 1946, a group of interested people from different countries gathered together in London to prepare plans for an international organization in the field of Early Childhood Education. National committees, the units of this international organization, were then set up in a number of countries to work for a wider understanding of Early Childhood Education.

These national committees bring together for discussion and action as many disciplines as possible that have a concern for the education and well-being of young children and their parents. Of importance in this respect are educators and teachers; medical doctors and others concerned with mental health; representatives from training colleges, universities, and parent–teacher organizations; architects; recreation directors; administrators at both national and local levels; religious bodies; and others. These committees also promote research on Early Childhood Education; conduct surveys of nursery schools; encourage parent education; prepare and publish pamphlets for parents and the public on nursery schools and kindergartens; supply toys and books for children; foster the training of teachers for young children; hold national conferences; and publish a newsletter.

OMEP holds an international assembly biennially on aspects of preschool education. This is open to all members and to other interested persons. It has cooperated with UNESCO on projects of mutual concern, such as a seminar on the training of teachers, a world survey of nursery schools, a study of children's drawings, a seminar on parent education, and a bibliography on status and trends in preschool education. OMEP has consultative status with both UNICEF and UNESCO and sends a representative to the meetings of each. Cooperation is sought with other international organizations having similar aims. The *International Journal of Early Childhood* is published by OMEP.

OTHER NATIONAL ORGANIZATIONS

While the above professional groups may be thought of as the "old stand-bys," many other groups afford valuable assistance to programs for young children and to the personnel involved. Programs for young children have broadened in purpose and scope in recent years to include services to exceptional children, among which the following serve as significant examples.

Alexander Graham Bell Association for the Deaf, Inc.
1537 35th Street, NW, Washington, D.C. 20007

The Alexander Graham Bell Association for the Deaf acts as an information center for parents. This association has as its purpose the promotion of speech and lipreading with the use of residual hearing. Publishes the *Volta Review* as well as many educational materials.

The United States Children's Bureau, Administration for Children, Youth, and Families, Office of Human Development Services
P.O. Box 1182, Washington, D.C. 20013

The United States Children's Bureau publishes the magazine, *Children Today,* six times per year.

Bureau of Education for the Handicapped
U.S. Office of Education, Dept. HEW
7th and D Streets, SW, Washington, D.C. 20036

The Bureau of Education for the Handicapped is the official arm of the federal government dealing with the education of children with handicaps of all kinds.

Black Child Development Institute
1028 Connecticut Avenue, NW, Suite 514, Washington, D.C. 20036

The Black Child Development Institute focuses on black child development through technical assistance to predominately black day-care centers.

Child Welfare League of America
44 East 23rd Street, New York, N.Y. 10010

The Child Welfare League involves itself in all phases of child welfare, including adoption, day care, and foster family care. The league publishes *Child Welfare* and many educational materials.

Council for Exceptional Children
1920 Association Drive, Reston, Virginia 22091

The Council for Exceptional Children is a major professional association for those involved with exceptional children, especially in the education of children with special and deviate needs. The Council publishes *Exceptional Children.*

Education Commission of the States, Early Childhood Project
300 Lincoln Tower, 1860 Lincoln Street, Denver, Colo. 80295

The Early Childhood Project gathers, interprets, and disseminates findings concerning all phases of Early Childhood Education throughout the nation, serving as a valuable resource to persons in the field. The Commission's Early Childhood Project publishes *Early Childhood Project Newsletter* and numerous study reports.

National Association for Retarded Children
2709 Avenue E East, Arlington, Tex. 76011

The National Association for Retarded Children is primarily an organization for parents of mentally retarded children and for other persons interested in the concerns of the mentally retarded.

National Congress of Parents and Teachers
700 North Rush Street, Chicago, Ill. 60511

The National Congress of Parents and Teachers publishes *The National Parent–Teacher* and study guides for parent meetings and study groups.

Office of Child Development, Department of HEW, ACYF,
P.O. Box 1182, Washington, D.C. 20013

The Office of Child Development is the federal agency most involved with programs for children below school age, especially those dealing with children of low-income families. Consequently, this Office is of utmost importance to publicly funded programs for young children and infants. It is a source of many valuable educational materials and consultant services. Head Start and the Children's Bureau are the major divisions of the agency.

The above list of services, while carefully selected for their importance to readers of this text, represents only a sample of the organizations and agencies at the national level concerned with programs for young children. It does not mean that those omitted are not important, especially if they emphasize a particular area of concern.

Sources for Films on Early Childhood

Contacts should be made with media centers at the various state universities, state departments of education, and the National Audio-Visual Center, National Archives and Records Service, General Services Administration, Washington, D.C. 20409. Information regarding films may be secured from these sources. For example, films suitable for Head Start and other Child Development Programs may be obtained from this source.

Suggested Activities

1. Discuss requirements for teacher certification and plans for school accreditation in your area.
2. Have a panel discussion on relative merits of different organizations and contributions of each to teacher certification and standards for preschool children.
3. List and discuss local organizations interested in schools for young children in your area. Invite members of these organizations and groups to share their plan of action, problems encountered, and progress being made in their efforts to provide good preschools for all young children in your area.
4. Discuss how these preschools in your area are financed. List financial plans for full-time and part-time attendance in the preschools in the area.

5. List requirements for joining and participating in professional and community organizations in your area.
6. Select an instrument for the evaluation of teacher interaction with children. Analyze your interaction with a group of children using the instrument.
7. Examine a career ladder. Discuss the steps with your class or group.
8. With the burgeoning need for teachers and caregivers, or combinations of the two, find out all you can about the Child Development Associate Program that meets this need. If possible, find an employed CDA in the community, visit that program, and invite her or him to participate in a class discussion on the pros and cons of the effectiveness of the credentialed CDA with children.

Related Readings

Devries, E. D. "Theory in Educational Practice," in *Preschool Education: A Handbook for the Training of Early Childhood Educators,* edited by R. W. Colvin and E. M. Zaffire. New York: Springer, 1974.

Fleming, Bonnie Mack. *Resources for Creative Teaching in Early Childhood Education.* New York: Harcourt, Brace, Jovanovich, 1977.

Fuller, F. F., and O. H. Brown. "Becoming A Teacher," in *Teacher Education, The Seventy-fourth Yearbook of NSSE, Part II,* edited by K. Ryan. Chicago: The University of Chicago Press, 1975.

Hartman, Karen. "How Do I Teach Children in a Future-Shocked World?" *Young Children,* 32:3 (March 1977), pp. 32–36.

Schickedans, Judith A., et al. *Strategies for Teaching Young Children.* New York: Prentice-Hall, Inc., 1976.

Spodek, B., and H. J. Walberg (eds.). *Early Childhood Education.* Chicago: NSSE, 1977. (Published by McCutchan Publishing Co., Berkeley, Calif., 1977.)

Stallings, J. "Implementation and Child Effects of Teaching Practices in Follow Through Classrooms," *Monogr. Soc. Res. Child Develop.,* 40:163 (1975).

Welty, D. A., and Dorothy R. Welty. *The Teacher Aide in the Instructional Team.* New York: McGraw-Hill Book Co., 1976.

Wilson, LaVisa Cam. *Caregiver Training for Child Care.* Columbus, Ohio: Charles E. Merrill Publishing Co., 1977.

chapter 8

Emerging programs for young children

An assessment of developments in Early Childhood Education during the 1970s revealed clearly emerging trends. As a natural consequence of a decrease in birthrate in the United States, elementary school enrollments were generally lower than formerly, making once-scarce space available for kindergartens, federally sponsored Early Childhood Education programs, or Child Development Centers. This fact, coupled with a broader acceptance of the value of early educational experiences for later success in school, encouraged the establishment of more opportunities for kindergarten experiences in the public schools. Even more dramatic was the development of comprehensive child development programs for three- and four-year-old children. Pilot programs for even younger children, including infants, were cropping up. Although most of the programs for prekindergarten children sponsored by various federal agencies were not administered by the public schools, many were found in public school facilities, often in close cooperation with school programs. At the same time, more and more schools were developing programs for children below the kindergarten level. The designation Child Development Center rather than "school" has gained popular acceptance for such programs.

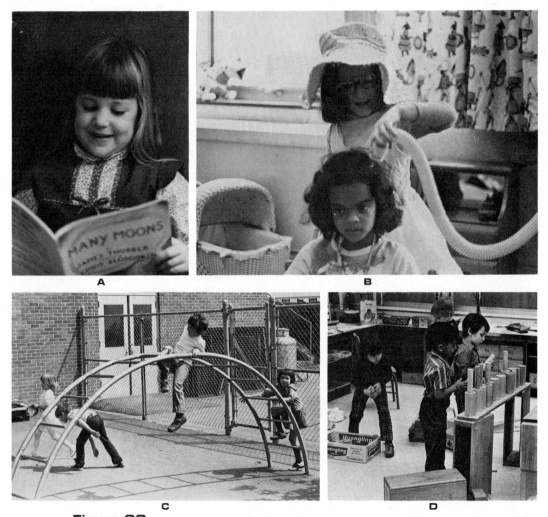

Figure 20
Learning environments are provided to enable the child to imitate and create, rather than merely to respond.

Most Child Development Center personnel, especially for the educational component, were not trained or "certified" in Early Childhood Education. However, many centers were adding qualified teachers, especially in supervisory roles, because earlier experience had shown a particular need for those in leadership positions. Clearly, at the time of the publication of this text, educational qualifications and standards had not been established except for kindergarten teachers employed in public schools.

Although most federally funded programs for young children were basically limited to children of low-income families, there was a growing demand for early education for all children. States and local governments were responding by making provision for such programs, especially public school kindergartens. The education of young children was fast becoming the responsibility of the public and private sectors of society, including business and industry. The importance of health and nutrition, family and personal development, and agency cooperation in providing services for young children and their families had been established. Program staffing patterns included parents, aides, and volunteers from the community and were truly interdisciplinary in nature. A coordinated educational effort never before known in American education, making effective use of various levels and types of competencies was emerging. Most significant to teachers and educators was the development of pilot and model programs with built-in research components to determine the effect of various curriculum approaches, teaching strategies and newly developed materials of instruction on the immediate and long-range cognitive and learning abilities of young children.

Psychologists had long observed the value of continuous, consistent procedures for learning and therapy, regardless of the theoretical orientation employed. Continuous learning programs, best exemplified by the federally sponsored Follow Through programs, were developed to determine long range values of common strategies and approaches on the learning and achievement of children aged four or five through nine. The Parent and Child Center programs were designed for the same purpose, extending the program downward to birth or during pregnancy. (See Chapter 6.)

THEORIES OF LEARNING

Education in America has been heavily influenced by stimulus–response (S–R) psychology. This behaviorist approach holds that the child is a purely reactive organism and reacts or responds rather than initiates; thus his or her behavior can be predicted from past experiences. Behaviorism as a psychological theory is represented by the well-known work of Ivan Pavlov, Edward Lee Thorndike, John B. Watson, Kenneth Spence, and Edwin Guthrie, among many others, and culminating in the work of B. F. Skinner.

In its simplest form, behaviorism teaches that all behavior is learned. The neurons automatically respond to incoming stimuli, and when such responses are strengthened by reward (reinforcement), learning takes place. However, without further reward or later reinforcement at certain intervals such responses are extinguished. In this manner, all responses (learning) can be shaped or modified by rewarding only predetermined desired responses. One of the strengths claimed by proponents of this approach is that "it works." The system is mechanistic and precise and resulting behavior is highly predictable. Accordingly, in this view, one's behavior is molded by outside forces and measurable only by observable overt responses. Current behavioristic terminology places stress on "operant" conditioning and "behavior modification." For a description of a utopian society based on behavioristic principles, see the novel *Walden Two*.[1] Hence the need in programs for carefully planned structure and drill, and for programmed materials of instruction reduced to small bits of information, to assure success each step of the way. However, there have always been those who believe that children are capable of actively participating in and influencing their own behavior as they interact with the environment.

Most markedly opposed to behaviorism is a group of philosophies and theories which together are known as the humanistic approach to psychology. Proponents of humanism insist that the uniqueness of each individual is because of the fact that each human being has the inherent potential to actively and creatively become what he or she is, by behaving in ways that are consistent with his or her view of self. One behaves as a total, dynamic unity, accepting, rejecting, or acting upon external stimuli in keeping with one's own internalization of present and past events in terms of one's developed goals for self-realization. Thus the child has inner motivations (as compared to outer stimuli) that trigger response patterns. Under this view, learning environments are provided to enable the child to initiate and create rather than merely to respond to a fixed set of conditions.

A few of the many well-known leaders in the humanistic psychology movement are Gordon Allport, Arthur Combs, Abraham Maslow, Gardner Murphy, and Carl Rogers. The emerging school programs are largely based on one or the other or some variation of these opposing psychological viewpoints. When planning and executing, programs, it is tempting to pick "the best" from each of the major theories—behaviorism and humanism. Educational research over a long period of time has indicated that most clearly defined learning theories produce good results when applied consistently by a teacher who believes strongly in the theory and applies it uniformly to provide continuity.

The early work in child development as exemplified by the work of Gesell[2]

---

[1] B. F. Skinner, *Walden Two* (New York: Macmillan, Publishing Co., 1948).
[2] A. Gesell and Catherine S. Amatruda, *Developmental Diagnosis*, 2nd ed. (New York: Harper & Row, 1952).

would lead to the conclusion that behavior emerges in a fixed order or sequence according to a genetically determined timetable. Therefore, a child's development can be described in stages in relation to chronological time. The literature of the 1940s and 1950s described "typical two-year-olds," "typical five-year-olds," and so on. This approach led to the belief that innate forces peculiar to each child determined his or her "ability" to respond at any given time and that environmental experiences, though necessary, played a minor role in the child's behavior and learning. Instructional activities were designed to fit the stage of development for each child or for groups of "normal" children at each particular stage of development. Little attention was given to the possibility that response patterns could be changed or speeded up by intervention at some earlier point in time. Traditionally, schools have waited until the child displayed "readiness" for certain learnings, or waited until a child fell behind the expected level of performance and then applied so-called remedial techniques in an effort to help the child "catch up." This is basically the approach of present-day "compensatory" programs.

It was not until the 1960s that the concept of intervention was used extensively to forestall expected deficiencies in learning. Placing major emphasis on intervention and compensatory techniques was the appropriately named Head Start program. It had been found that most children who didn't fit the expectations of the public school program were from lower-income families. Therefore, Head Start and similar programs were designed for children whose learning, physical, and social deficits were associated with problems faced by families with inadequate income. A new emphasis was also given to compensatory or remedial programs for children who were already behind in learning abilities when entering school. Both intervention and compensatory programs place more emphasis on environmental than on maturational influences than was previously true.

In recent years, the concept of critical periods in development has received much attention and has had a strong influence on programming experiences for young children. Biologists, who generally believe that the capacity to respond at any given time to specific aspects of the environment is genetically determined, were making breakthroughs of their own. Study of the genes, segments of the deoxyribonucleic acid (DNA) that fills the chromosomes in cell nuclei, suggested a master genetic code that provides a blueprint for life itself. Ribonucleic acid (RNA) is made in the nucleus of the cell by DNA and serves as the messenger to amino acids in the cell's cytoplasm, carrying out the genetic master plan. All the elements needed for any response an individual is capable of making are present in the DNA code at conception but do not go into operation until an appropriate environmental stimulus triggers the response. While all the possibilities of growth, development, and learning are inherent, environment at all times plays an important role.

It is environment that must always fit the unfolding of the code. Consequently, throughout life there are critical periods during which the presence or absence of appropriate environmental stimuli results in following or altering DNA's master plan. A dramatic example of critical periods in development was the sharply increased incidence about a decade ago of babies being born with deformed or no arms and legs. The cause was traced to the fact that the mothers of these children had taken the tranquilizing drug thalidomide during the first seven weeks of gestation. The effects of maternal rubella (German measles) on the offspring during the prenatal period are well known. For a more detailed account of the biological bases of behavior and the importance of critical periods see Beadle's lucid analysis.[3] There are also indications that chromosome aberrations may be directly responsible for certain behavioral characteristics. For example, in the case of Down's Syndrome (mongolism) the child inherits three chromosomes of a given kind instead of the usual two.[4]

New discoveries of this type as well as findings in the fields of biochemistry and nutrition offer strong evidence that behavior described as "good" or "bad" by parents and teachers may well bear no relationship to the connotations thus implied and is not subject to change by known instructional strategies. Emerging schools are now often staffed with professionals from many disciplines who can detect and advise on procedures for those children who show early developmental or learning deviations. It would be all too easy to make the same error made by researchers and practitioners of the 1920s to the 1950s and assume that growth, development, and learning, while sequential through time, are fixed at conception and "unfold" according to each individual's timetable. Rather, what the newer evidence indicates is that, though growth, development, and learning are indeed sequential through time, the expression of the genetic potentialities is determined by environmental influences at any given time during the life of the individual. Although behaviors in the learning sphere are much more difficult to pinpoint than in the area of physical development, it can reasonably be said that a child who doesn't progress from random vocalizing of vowels to consonants, to words within the first 24 months of life is likely to be severely handicapped in the the use of language later.[5]

During the mid-1960s American education was badly in need of a panacea to remedy everything from poverty and unemployment to reaching the greatest potential of the gifted. There was an almost universal acceptance that early education could serve this purpose. Unanswerable questions arose immediately: How early should early education begin? Age five? Age four? Three or earlier? Who should receive early education? All children—or just

[3] Muriel Beadle, *A Child's Mind* (Garden City, N.Y.: Doubleday and Co., 1970), pp. 11–24; 61–71.
[4] Ibid., p. 19.
[5] Ibid., p. 61.

those whose parents are poor and those who are "exceptional" in some way? What should be taught to young children? How should young children be taught and by whom? Which learning theory applies best to young children? Who should control schools for young children? The parents? The existing educational system? Or some other form of government or community organization? Because of these and similar questions, a wide variety of approaches and forms of control quickly emerged. They ranged from public or private Montessori schools to open classroom approaches and versions of the British Infant School.

As the nation approached the late 1970s, the envangelistic fervor of proponents of many varied schools of thought had somewhat abated. Fortunately, foundations and the federal and state governments insisted on research to validate or invalidate the effectiveness of sponsored innovations. At this writing the evidence is not all in, but certain trends are emerging. Among them:

1. Because of the uniqueness of each individual child, both genetically and experientially, no one approach is acceptable for all children.
2. Parents are important to the education of their young children and parent involvement in the program can be an essential ingredient for success.
3. Specific content itself is not as important as the use that is made of the content to establish positive attitudes toward learning and toward self.
4. Young children, including very young infants, can and do learn. Because many authorities now feel that the first five years of life, including infancy, represent a critical period with regard to basic attitudes and values about self and others, the development of language, and the establishment of basic interpersonal relationships, programs for young children should not be entered into lightly and without careful planning and judicious use of qualified personnel.
5. Although aides, volunteers, and other paraprofessionals are now accepted as necessary and valuable personnel, adequately trained teachers and supervisory leaders are the most promising avenue to successful programs.
6. Traditional teacher education programs have not adequately prepared teachers for the emerging new schools for young children. New and innovative practices in the preparation of teachers at both the preservice and in-service levels are being developed to fill this need.
7. As the age for starting education has moved downward from the traditional first-grade entrance at age six, there has been in each case mounting evidence that an earlier start was needed. Most prominent examples of programs designed to implement these findings are kindergartens for five-year-olds, Head Start, Home Start, a program to demonstrate alternate ways of providing Head Start type services, for three-, four-, and five-year-old children where kindergartens were not available, and Parent Child Centers for children from birth to three years of age. All represent efforts to enable large numbers of children to make use of learning opportunities provided by the nation's schools.
8. All recent programs place a new emphasis on the importance of early cogni-

tive development, at the same time giving recognition to the profound influence of good health and nutrition, healthy psychological and social development, and stable and accepting family relationships on successful learning.

9. Teachers and other staff personnel in these programs must be aware of the total needs of each child and be able to work with professionals in other fields to see that these needs are met. In fact, most programs now provide fully staffed components and consultative services in these areas to complement the educational process. Staffing of programs for young children is truly becoming interdisciplinary with differentiated but cooperative responsibilities.

10. The need for day care as mothers sought employment outside the home has brought about a re-evaluation of many former programs for young and school age children. Without sacrificing quality care, innovative educational experiences are becoming an accepted component of full-day and year-round programs for infants and young children.

TECHNOLOGY AND THE PRESCHOOL CHILD

It is commonly held that television, computers, teaching machines, tape recorders, and a host of other electronic devices, games, and kits of programmed materials offer hope of breaking the age-old boring procedures used in many of the public schools. In effect, it is claimed that modern technology has the potential of bringing about a "revolution" in education. Almost all these devices offer the self-evaluation and immediate feedback features much sought by educators, parents, and taxpayers. Seizing an opportunity beginning in the early 1960s and late 1950s, huge commercial firms, often conglomerates, sought to provide the necessary hardware and often the "software" or programs for the emerging revolution in education. As preschool programs gained priority, mainly because of federal and foundation funding, the availability of "complete" educational programs for young children greatly increased. Today, preschool teachers and administrators can choose from an almost endless variety of kits, programmed and talking books, packaged learning materials, computer-assisted or computer-managed instructional materials, prepared television tapes, and the usual array of what were formerly known as audiovisual instructional materials. The list is almost endless. Yet after twenty years the impact has been visible only where programs have been heavily funded and researched; these programs often stopped when outside funds were no longer available. The most common research finding is that children in these programs achieve as well as they would under less costly conventional methods.

There are two commonly recognized problems with the use of educational technology—excessive cost and the fact that technology lends itself best to instructional programming based on behavioristic theory. Many educators, however—especially classroom teachers—accept more readily procedures and materials based on humanistic approaches. This is especially true in relation to programs for young children. For a thought-provoking analysis of educational technology see *The Myth of Educational Technology*.[6]

Sesame Street

Although there are many programs for young children on commercial and educational television, none has captured the imagination of audiences (of all ages) to the extent that *Sesame Street* has. The multimillion-dollar program, funded by grants from the Carnegie Foundation, the Ford Foundation, the U.S. Office of Education, the Office of Economic Opportunity, and other federal agencies, went on the air on 163 public television stations on November 10, 1969. Its purpose was to determine whether television could teach preschool children via popular approaches used by commercial television. It is too early to assess long-term effectiveness of *Sesame Street* as a feasible means of teaching young children, especially children from low-income and slum homes. Berkman[7] suggests that "something just drastic" could happen to the generation of children, regardless of race or family income, who have watched *Sesame Street* regularly. He feels that schools, as they now exist, could "turn off" large numbers of children who are accustomed to *Sesame Street* exposure, necessitating a profound effect on early grade education. Edward L. Palmer,[8] vice-president and director of research at The Children's Television Workshop, which created and produced *Sesame Street*, has described the careful planning and research involved in this best-known effort to teach young children by television.

To the authors of this text, *Sesame Street* represents a pioneer experiment in Early Childhood Education—an attempt to bring about social change as well as early cognitive learning. It is a well-known fact that children have different learning styles in keeping with their early family and cultural influences. There is evidence that certain children, especially children denied early exposure to cognitive experiences that best fit them for the demands made upon them when entering school, learn best when exposed to more structured, repetitive bits of information. *Sesame Street*, with its deep roots in behaviorism, fits this requirement well. However, the authors feel that for most children real life experiences strongly buttressed in early sensory-motor

[6] D. Berkman, "The Myth of Educational Technology," *The Educational Forum*, 36:14 (1972), pp. 451–460.
[7] Ibid., p. 460.
[8] E. L. Palmer, "Television Instruction and the Preschool Child," *International Journal of Early Education*, 4:1 (OMEP, Dublin, Ireland: Irish University Press, 1972), pp. 11–17.

experiences, as indicated in Piaget's theory,[9] are essential for later, more complex forms of *learning*.

Although television and other forms of technology are of immense importance in assisting learning, they should never be expected to replace the human element in the instructional process. Nor should behaviorally oriented programs exclude the values and creative initiative inherent in teaching strategies based on humanistic theory.

In a recent review of the effects of television viewing on preschool behavior, Moore[10] summarizes the effect from a review of the research. Children, at least over the short term, do learn prosocial behavior from such programs as *Mr. Roger's Neighborhood,* changes in attitudes and behaviors from those like *Sesame Street,* and behave in less prosocial behaviors after viewing programs like *Batman* and *Superman.* The long-term effects have not yet been determined by research.

NATIONAL PROGRAMS

The U.S. Office of Education (OE) did not come into the "big time" in education until the early 1960s with the passage of federal legislation involving substantial appropriations. The major purpose of most education legislation at that time was to enable the public schools to provide quality education for children of low-income families and to find and research innovative and alternative ways of improving the instructional process. One such effort was the establishment of the National Laboratory on Early Childhood Education, which became The National Program on Early Childhood Education (NPECE) under the administration of CEMREL (Central Midwestern Regional Laboratory, Inc.) on June 1, 1970. Although the National Laboratory program is now defunct, CEMREL continues to operate as a private organization producing and testing innovative materials and programs in Early Childhood Education. The *CEMREL Newsletter,* a semiannual publication, is designed to disseminate news of the activities of CEMREL and to aid readers in keeping abreast of new developments in education.

Another important source of information is the Educational Resources Information Center, commonly known as ERIC. Although originally sponsored by the U.S. Office of Education, ERIC is now a function of the National Institute of Education, and has several clearinghouses, one of which is the ERIC

[9] B. J. Wadsworth, *Piaget's Theory of Cognitive Development* (New York: David McKay Co., 1971), p. 33.

[10] Shirley G. Moore, "The Effect of Television Viewing on the Prosocial Behavior of Young Children," *Young Children,* 32:5 (July, 1977), pp. 60–65.

Clearinghouse on Early Childhood Education located at the University of Illinois. The current address of the ERIC/ECE Clearinghouse and *Newsletter* is University of Illinois, Urbana-Champaign, 805 West Pennsylvania Avenue, Urbana, Illinois 61801.

ERIC should be thought of as the first place to look for information on any topic in Early Childhood Education. Ask your college or university librarian for help, as these valuable materials and services are available at most such libraries. Materials are available in either hardback copies of originals or in microfiche, a transparent film card that contains up to 98 pages. ERIC will also conduct a manual or computer search on almost any topic in Early Childhood Education upon request. Your librarian can also supply current addresses of Clearinghouses and Reproduction Services which may change from time to time.

INNOVATIVE PRACTICES

Changes are taking place in the areas of curriculum, organization, and instruction, and experimentation is under way in the content areas as well as in reading and language development. Children in some situations have been encouraged to inquire on their own and to learn through discovery. Team teaching and multiage and multicultural groupings have become rather commonplace in programs for young children.

Many of the programs have been motivated and influenced by the special problems and needs of children who come from environmental conditions thought to handicap them severely in their present development and later success in school. Goodlad and Klein point out, however, that the early education of all children, whether environmentally disadvantaged or not, should be guided by sound principles of learning and development.[11]

Some of the innovative practices based on particular points of view are briefly described here. Since no one innovation is the answer for all learners and all situations, each must be carefully evaluated before being adopted.

Open space centers

Open space centers provide the setting for a new kind of learning experience planned in terms of the potentialities of children and the environment. The open space concept in teaching is, as much as anything, a state of mind.[12] It is

---

[11] J. I. Goodlad, M. Frances Klein, and associates, *Behind the Classroom Door* (Worthington, Ohio: Charles A. Jones Publishing Co., 1970), p. 7.
[12] AASA, *Open Space Schools* (Washington, D.C.: American Association of School Administrators, 1971), p. 20.

the structuring of a living situation with a wide range of educational alternatives.[13] Facilities for such a center include large open spaces that can be used flexibly and in a number of ways. There are no separate, individual classrooms. The teacher does not work alone; but with an available team of adults, made up of teachers, aides, and volunteers.

Open education is considered by some as the legacy of the Progressive Education movement. Reminiscent of the critics of progressive education, it should be pointed out that open education is a carefully planned learning experience based on the observed needs of the children enrolled and is not a free-for-all, do-as-you-please smorgasbord, as critics would have one believe.

British infant school

The British Infant School, although English in origin, is thought by some to reflect many of the characteristics of Progressive Education in America.[14] The infant stage of British education includes children from four to seven years of age and utilizes vertical or family grouping. Children of varying ages are placed together in the same class as a deliberate educational policy.[15] Lavatelli points out that play is more explicitly used for cognitive growth than in the American child-centered schools.[16]

Rogers[17] lists the salient features of the British philosophy as follows:

> Children should live fully and richly now. Education is life, not preparation for life.
> The curriculum is a series of jumping off places and emerges through the mutual interests and explorations of children and teachers working together.
> Studies are interrelated and cut across subject matter lines.
> The teacher is "largely a stage setter," a stimulator who encourages and guides but who does not appear to direct.
> Teachers are concerned with how the child learns, the significance of the process; the development of independence and responsibility in children. Teachers care deeply about children and respect children's ideas.

[13] J. Macdonald, "The Open School: Curriculum Concepts," *Open Education* (Washington, D.C.: NAEYC), p. 26.

[14] B. Spodek, "Introduction," *Open Education* (Washington, D.C.: NAEYC, 1970), p. 7.

[15] Mary A. Mycock, "Vertical Grouping" in *Teaching in the British Primary School*, edited by V. R. Rogers (New York: Macmillan Publishing Co., 1970), pp. 34–35.

[16] Celia S. Lavatelli, *Piaget's Theory Applied to an Early Childhood Curriculum* (Boston: American Science and Engineering, Inc., 1970), p. 23.

[17] V. R. Rogers, *Teaching in the British Primary School* (New York, Macmillan Publishing Co., 1970), p. 7.

Piaget's theories

Lavatelli describes Piaget's theory as a developmental one, pointing out that, according to this theory, the thinking of all children tends to go through the same stages and usually when they are about the same age.[18] Using what Piaget identified as the important cognitive developments for children, Lavatelli has planned a curriculum centered on Classification, Space and Number, and Seriation, based on step-by-step development in these areas. Short structured periods are utilized along with self-directed periods of play. Directed learning activities are conducted by a teacher with a small group of children. The concepts acquired are reinforced during play. The children's observations are directed to phenomena they might otherwise miss.[19]

A developmental—interaction point of view

The Bank Street Program is based on a theory developed by Biber et al.[20] to promote cognitive growth. It emphasizes the identifiable patterns of growth, the child's interaction with the environment (people as well as material objects), and the interaction between the cognitive and affective spheres of development. It is based on "a consistent philosophy of education comprising values, goals, and strategies congruent with a humanistic approach. Central to this philosophy are concepts of competence, interpersonal relatedness, individuality, and creativity."[21] Cognitive categories for use in analyzing teaching techniques have been developed and illustrated.

Cognitively oriented curriculum

The academically oriented centers are primarily interested in the cognitive development of children and in speeding up the acquisition of academic skills. Most controversial is the Bereiter and Engelmann program for disadvantaged children with the emphasis on preacademic skills in reading, language, and arithmetic, discussed in Chapter 4. Weikart et al. have developed a cognitively oriented program in which attention is not explicitly paid to the affective development of the child. Proponents feel that these needs are met through the style of classroom operation that the curriculum creates.[22]

[18] Lavatelli, op. cit., p. 27.
[19] Ibid., p. 24.
[20] Barbara Biber, et al., *Promoting Cognitive Growth: A Developmental Interaction Point of View* (Washington, D.C.: NAEYC, 1971).
[21] Ibid., p. 7.
[22] D. P. Weikart, *The Cognitively Oriented Curriculum* (Washington, D.C.: NAEYC, 1971).

Process approach

Berman[23] holds that any carefully designed conception of curriculum must be based on some fundamental assumptions about human beings, whom she considers to be "process-oriented beings." Curriculum is therefore concerned with process and process skills that include Perceiving, Communication, Loving, Decision Making, Knowing, Organizing, Creating, and Valuing. Teachers at the University of Maryland Center for Young Children, using the process approach in developing a curriculum for young children, have focused on the process of "decision making." They developed suggestions for teacher statements, designed to focus the children's thinking on possibilities, outcomes, and awareness that choices have been made. Examples of the suggested statements follow:[24]

> Thinking of possibilities: "Where do you think you could work?" "What other way could you have . . . ?"
> Thinking of outcomes: "What else could you do to . . . avoid . . . ?" " . . . stop . . . ?" " . . . help . . . ?"

An interdisciplinary integrated approach

Project CARE—Correlating Art and Reading Essentials—developed by Evans et al.[25] is an excellent example of an interdisciplinary approach to instruction with built-in formative evaluation on the part of public school personnel. The aim of the project, currently in its second year, "is to develop and deploy by September 1979, a program for kindergarten and grade one children which employs a unified approach to teaching skills and competencies common to art and reading. . . . The Project will also develop materials and planned activities to train teachers and supervisors of curriculum in the skills necessary to fully utilize the program. The Project's final goal is to pilot–revise–field test–validate–package and disseminate the correlated art and reading program."[26]

Reading and art are viewed as natural partners, as both are a means of communication. It is expected that careful attention to mastery of skill develop-

[23] Louise M. Berman, *New Priorities in the Curriculum* (Columbus, Ohio: Charles E. Merrill Publishing Co., 1968).
[24] Louise M. Berman (ed.), *Decision Making in Young Children: Part I, Monograph II* (College Park: University of Maryland, 1971), p. 48.
[25] Elizabeth A. Evans, Project director, *Project CARE* (Tallahassee, Fl.: Leon County Schools–Kate Sullivan School, 1977), Unpublished Project Abstract.
[26] Ibid., p. 1-B.

ment in the beginning stages of both will help prevent later learning difficulties.

Project CARE is a planned comprehensive art program for kindergarten with its scope and sequence designed to correlate with concept formation and prereading needs. Expected learning outcomes deal with Concept Formation, Oral Language, Visual Discrimination, Eye–Hand Coordination, Comprehension, and Vocabulary.

The core art program consists of 10 units of instruction: Introduction, Shape, Color, Line, Texture, Color Mixing, Facial Expressions, Form, Action, and Resources. This Program is a three-year, carefully developed, interdisciplinary, integrated model with a clinically field-tested and validated, packaged, exportable product as an end goal. It is an example of the trend toward more teacher participation in the planning, execution, and evaluation of instructional programs.

The emergence of care programs

As documented throughout this text, the need for care services for large numbers of young children is clearly a part of the American scene as the 1970s come to a close. It is likely that this need is here to stay and will require long-range instructional and financial planning as well as long-range longitudinal research in order to discover the best means of programming to protect the optimal normal growth and development of the children involved.

Beginning in 1970, the U.S. Office of Child Development embarked on a program of involving nongovernment child development experts, day-care and Early Childhood Education practitioners, and parents in a series of workshops, task forces, and related assignments culminating in a series of bulletins on Day Care. Because this series probably represent the best source of information available at the time of this writing, each is documented here as a major resource rather than being relegated to the usual placement in footnotes or reference lists:

1. *Day Care: A Statement of Principles,* 1973: Contains 12 pages, covering Aims, The Basic Needs for Programming, Economic and Social Change, and Administration.
2. *Day Care Serving Infants,* 1971: Contains 87 pages including chapters on Guiding Principles, Organizing a Day Care Center, Daily Planning for Infants, and Appendices on Information Services, Equipment and Supplies, and Available Toys and Books.
3. *Day Care Serving Preschool Children,* 1975: Contains 164 pages of authorative information on all aspects of care for preschool children. This bulletin is a must for all who are interested in care programs for preschool children.

4. *Day Care Serving School Age Children,* 1972: Contains 69 pages of helpful information on this all too often neglected need. This source details the unique and special care needs of school-age children and provides examples of how they are being met.

5. *Day Care Staff Training,* 1971: Handbook contains 38 pages of guidance based on the premise that continuously trained personnel are vital to ensure good programs for infants and very young children. It is not necessarily true that an individual well qualified as an elementary teacher, social worker, or child development specialist will be properly qualified as a teacher or caregiver of young children. Hence, the need for a continuous in-service training program. Those prepared in Early Childhood Education have the same concern due to the rapidly changing needs and changing social conditions.

6. *Day Care Health Services,* 1972: Contains 80 pages of suggestions as a guide for program personnel including directors and participating physicians. This bulletin describes in detail Administrative Considerations, Professional Considerations—Medical, and the Dental Program including helpful ideas on record-keeping and reporting.

7. *Day Care Administration,* 1972: An invaluable resource, containing 167 pages of essential information for all who are interested in organizing, managing, owning, or directing day-care services for young children. Included are specifics of developing an operations manual.

8. *Day Care Serving Children with Special Needs,* 1972: Report includes 72 pages of helpful ways to serve children with special needs, including appendices on Community Resources, Funding Resources, and an extensive Bibliography arranged in 11 categories of need.

9. *Day Care Family Day Care,* 1975: Contains 118 pages detailing information essential to the operation of Family Day Care Homes. It is estimated that Family Day Care provides more than 91 percent of all day-care needs in the United States.

Obviously, it is beyond the scope of this text to present materials covered in the 807-page library on day care described above. Since these bulletins are published by an agency of the federal government they may be obtained from the Superintendent of Documents, U.S. Government Printing Office, Washington, D.C. 20402. While the cost is always very modest, it is wise to write for current prices as they may change from time to time.

INNOVATION AND CHANGE IN PERSPECTIVE

As mentioned previously, the emerging programs placed more emphasis on cognitive development than was formerly thought necessary in preschool education. When this need for effective curriculum development and programming in Early Childhood Education arose, there was a paucity of thoroughly researched programs to provide guidance for the rapidly developing programs. As a result, large-scale federal and foundation funds, usually in the form of research and development grants, were made available to universities, schools, individuals, and consulting and technical assistance firms (often hastily organized). Those conducting the programs were often without previous training or experience in Early Childhood Education. The newly developing multimedia industry also quickly rose to the challenge. As a result, packaged programs complete with sponsors and consultative services soon dominated the Early Childhood Education scene and continue to do so. Their goal was the development of exportable models and corresponding materials for sale or adoption by those conducting programs for young children.

An indication of the stress placed on certain areas is reported in the Spring 1972 *CEMREL Newsletter*. All forty-four children in CEMREL's experimental kindergartens received reading certificates at their graduation exercises as a result of participation in their Instructional Systems Program. Thirty of the children were awarded "special recognition" for having completed the entire series of 52 SWRL reading books. Some of the children read books considered "fourth grade level."[27]

It was the original intention of the writers to include descriptions of the models existing during the 1970s. However, because of the unusually large number of models, packages, and systems increasingly available, it was decided not to carry out the original intent. Instead, a selected few models whose names and brief descriptive statements indicate the variety that exists on the continuum from behavioristic to humanistic are listed. This list although, far from complete, will show the variation that exists among emerging programs. The examples listed fall roughly into four categories: (1) those stressing basic learning skills through the use of behavioristic techniques, (2) those stressing the importance of parents on the instructional team, (3) those employing individualized instruction, and (4) those based on humanistic approaches. Some, of course, do not fall clearly into any one of the above categories and are more eclectic in nature. The list follows.

> Systematic Use of Behavioral Principles Program (Focuses strongly on objectives, presenting tasks in a rapid-fire order)
> Behavioral Analysis Program (Uses the techniques of reinforcement to accelerate social and learning development during the early years)
> Behavior-oriented Prescriptive Teaching Approach (Employs intensive individualized instruction for the attainment of specific behavior objectives)
> Florida Parent Education Model (Emphasizes the use of "trained" mothers on the instructional team with the major thrust being in the home)

[27] "Kindergarten Children Demonstrate Reading Ability for Parents," *CEMREL Newsletter*, 6:2 (Spring 1972), p. 8.

Home-School Partnership—A Motivational Approach (Enlists parents as partners in the education of their children)

Parent Implementation Approach (Strives to make use of parents and other community residents as significant people in the learning process)

Responsive Environment Approach (Makes individual problem solving the essence of learning by providing an environment responsive to each child's needs)

Hampton Institute Nongraded Model (Individualizes instruction in the classroom on a nongraded basis)

Learning Research and Development Center Model (Uses individually prescribed instruction, IPI)

Bank Street College of Education Approach (Designed to enable each child to build a positive self-image of himself as a learner)

Education Development Center Approach (Rooted in the philosophy of the British Primary Schools to provide a broad humanistic education)

New Nursery School Approach (Stresses self-directed learning through the use of learning centers in the classroom)

Mathemagenic Activities Program (Provides sequentially structured materials to stimulate learning as a coherent interpretation of reality)

Cognitively Oriented Curriculum Model (Provides home and school experiences with learning materials derived from the theories of Piaget)

Cultural Linguistic Approach (An oral language program building on the strengths of another language or nonstandard English)

In actual practice there are only a few programs using exported models such as the above. Most programs for young children continue to stress the importance of children's needs. An effort is usually made to stress the importance of learning environment based on an understanding of child development. These programs usually have less structure than the models listed above and permit children more freedom to explore their feelings and environment in imaginative and play-type activities. The teacher or caregiver serves as an observing guide, encouraging the children to participate in activities allowed by a prearranged environment. Such programs emphasize personal and social development with less emphasis on skills believed to be needed "later." Although difficult to evaluate because of the lack of specifics, to some extent all show more concern for preplanned activities to reach more specific objectives than was generally true of programs a decade ago.

SUMMARY

One of the encouraging signs of the early 1970s was the emergence of a large number and variety of innovative and experimental programs in Early Childhood Education. The designation *Child Development Center* had become established for programs for children below the kindergarten level and pilot programs for infants and their families have flourished. Longitudinal programs, such as Follow Through, for children aged three to nine have offered an opportunity to study the effects of several well-defined and planned innovative approaches to the education of young children.

Philosophical and theoretical differences prevailed. Programs based on behavioristic and humanistic approaches, with many variations and combinations, have provided an opportunity to discover the most effective educational strategies for children with different learning styles from various socioeconomic backgrounds.

A significant characteristic of the emerging programs has been the greater involvement of parents in the education of their children. Equally important is the interdisciplinary nature of the training and experience of staff members and the extensive use of volunteers and paraprofessionals with differentiated responsibilities.

Because of the high cost of Early Childhood Education, exportable models, programs using educational technology, and packaged instructional materials have been developed in an effort to make early learning experiences available to a greater number of young children. Changing social values and the rising numbers of mothers of young children in the labor market have created a need for more day care facilities. Public and professional demands have mandated an educational component in all such programs.

It can truthfully be said that although Early Childhood Education was rediscovered in the 1960s, it came of age during the 1970s. These developments have placed unprecedented demands on training programs, stressing the need for consultative services, in-service training, and on-the-job training. Most colleges and universities have responded with greatly expanded, innovative approaches of staff members, both professional and paraprofessional, including parents and volunteers.

Suggested Activities

1. Visit a child development center, a nursery school, and a kindergarten in your community. Determine the philosophy or theory on which each program is based. Write a comparison of the three programs giving examples of activities that are clearly a result of the theory or philosophy followed.
2. Watch Sesame Street and at least two other television programs for young children. Evaluate what you saw in terms of interest level, theory on which the program is based, and the goals of each, in terms of meeting the needs of young children.
3. Ask your librarian how to use the services of ERIC as a resource for your studies in Early Childhood Education.
4. Talk with several first-grade teachers and ask them what they would like children to be able to do when they enter first grade.
5. Consult the Yellow Pages of your local telephone directory to determine the types

of schools for young children in your community. Visit at least three that appear to be different from the others, such as Montessori, academically oriented, or cooperative nursery schools. Evaluate each.

6. Find out from your state department of education and state OEO offices how many children below kindergarten age are participating in programs. Determine the goals of these programs and the kinds of activities used to meet these goals.

7. Ask your instructor to help you locate a research project (preschool) that you can correspond with by telephone and/or by letter, or perhaps that you can visit "on your own." Determine the "problem" being researched, the methods employed to find answers, and how the researchers view the project in relation to public policy.

Related Readings

An Administrator's Handbook on Educational Accountability. Arlington, Va.: AASA, 1973.

Biber, Barbara. "A Developmental Interaction Approach," in *The Preschool in Action,* edited by Mary Carol Day and R. K. Parker. Boston: Allyn and Bacon, 1977.

Cass, Joan E. *Helping Children Grow Through Play.* New York: Schocken Books, 1973.

Dennis, Wayne. *Children of The Creche.* New York: Appleton-Century-Crofts, 1976.

"The Federal Interagency Day Care Requirements Appropriateness Study." *Young Children,* 31:5 (1976), pp. 385–392.

Federal Interagency Day Care Requirements as Approved by U.S. DHEW, OCD, and the U.S. Dept of Labor. Washington, D.C.: Children's Bureau, OCD, DHEW, 1968.

Milhollan, F. *From Skinner to Rogers—Contrasting Approaches to Education.* Lincoln, Neb.: Professional Educator's Publications, 1972.

Palmer, W. C. "Observations on Education in the USSR," *Innovator* (University of Michigan School of Education), 8:7 (April 15, 1977).

Stevens, J. N., and Edith W. King. *Administering Early Childhood Education Programs.* Boston: Little, Brown, and Co., 1976.

Sulby, A. B., and A. Diodati. "Family Day Care No Longer Day Care's Neglected Child," *Young Children,* 30:4 (May 1975), pp. 239–247.

PART two

The curriculum: planning and teaching

Who Am I?

I am a child.
I live in suburbia, the ghetto, Appalachia, on the Reservation—
   I live anywhere.
I go to nursery school, Head Start, day care center, kindergarten—
   This is my first day. I am new.
I don't know what my teacher says.
I don't understand her so I don't listen.
   I don't know what to do.
I do nothing.

I don't listen.
   I don't sit still. I bother children.
I am naughty. I am unhappy. . . .

Today the teacher smiled at me!
   "Hello—I'm glad to see you this morning!"
I see some trucks—I roll them and roll them—
I take blocks and make a garage for my trucks.
   I lie on the rug and look at it.
My teacher says, "You made a big garage.
   You used some red blocks.
Let's count together and see how many red blocks you used.
Let's see how many wheels are on that truck 1-2-3-4.
   You can count!"
I feel very, very good!

That child next to me—
She wanted to make a garage too—I helped her.
   We made a garage. We put a big truck in it.
We had two garages and two trucks.
We counted eight green blocks.
   I feel good. I am happy.
My teacher likes me.

That girl and I play together. She likes me.
   I feel good!
I'm glad I'm me!

Adapted from "Who Am I?" by Theron Jacobson. *Educ. Leadership,* **23**:2 (1965), pp. 121–123.

Photo: Part two
These children helped to reseed their playground in the
spring. When they came back to the Center in the fall
they looked at the seeds on the grass.

chapter **9**

Curriculum and young children

"Curriculum Is What Happens—Planning Is the Key!"[1] Curriculum is what happens to young children in school. The word *curriculum* has not always had this meaning. At one time the term referred to a course of academic study, a set of activities prescribed for a certain purpose. Currently the word *program* is used interchangeably with, or in place of, curriculum. Programs include planned opportunities for experiences that may take place in the school but may often extend beyond the classroom into the home and the commu-

[1] NAEYC, *Curriculum Is What Happens* (Washington, D.C.: NAEYC, 1970).

nity. Planning for the curriculum or the program involves both the school and the parents.[2]

After the ferment, experimentation, and innovations that took place in Early Childhood Education during the 1960s a reordering of priorities appears to be under way. Attention in curriculum planning is beginning to focus on the child and the totality of his or her experience.[3]

Frazier says:

> The whole child seems to be newly before us today. Over the past 15 or 20 years, we may be thought to have let our historic commitment to rounded development go by the board. Immersed as we were in trying to understand and do better by cognitive functioning, we may have forgotten the rest of the child. What we found, of course, is that when it comes to behavior, the child insists on putting himself back together again. Detached from the hand or the heart, mind does not function very well.
>
> . . . Competence is based on control of mind, body, and feeling. And when we neglect any of these, or overlook their interrelationships, we find ourselves in trouble.[4]

The new challenge in curriculum planning, according to Frazier, is the recognition that all children have a right to learn what is taught; to learn whatever is necessary to keep options open to further learning; to learn that which will enlarge or enrich human experience. He speaks of an "equal rights curriculum" for all children—all children have an equal right to profit fully from a broadly based program. By "all children" Frazier includes minority children and children from the majority, those who live in the city and those in the suburbs, poor and affluent children, children from working-class and professional families, less able learners and the eager, able learners—all children.[5]

Some children have a richer, more relevant experience than others. Some are not taught things they need to be taught. All children have a right to learn about the environment, the full range of the arts, love and friendship, media and the marketplace, play and playfulness, political action, self-understanding, value clarification, the world of work, and a world view.[6]

Berman holds that any carefully designed conception of curriculum must be based on some basic assumptions about humankind, whom she considers to be "a process-oriented being." Curriculum, therefore, is concerned with proc-

---

[2] Millie Almy, *The Early Childhood Educator at Work* (New York: McGraw-Hill Book Co., 1975), pp. 55–56.

[3] Ibid.

[4] A. Frazier, *Adventuring, Mastering, Associating: New Strategies for Teaching Children* (Washington, D.C.: ASCD, 1976), p. 127.

[5] Frazier, op. cit., pp. 3–12.

[6] Frazier, op. cit., pp. 12–13.

ess and process skills that include Perceiving, Communicating, Loving, Decision Making, Knowing, Organizing, Creating, and Valuing.[7]

CURRICULUM PLANNING

Through the years, Early Childhood Education has responded to prevailing assumptions about the nature of human development, the ways in which learning takes place, and sociological concerns.[8] Today there are many concerns, among them being the totality of the child's development, humane education, the processes and skills involved in living, multicultural education, and mainstreaming of the handicapped. Incorporating such concerns into curriculum planning is indeed a complex operation. The possible interrelationships are many. Experiencing the curriculum should help all children to feel worthy, respected, capable, and competent as well as giving them the opportunity to gain desirable skills.

There are no required subjects in the traditional sense in programs for young children. Within the stream of each curriculum area there are skills whose mastery is related to the developmental levels of the child. For example, when the child has developed enough control of his muscles to make more precise movements, as he becomes more interested in what he is making than in the manipulation of materials, he is indicating that he is moving out of the "scribbling" stage of art development into the presymbolic. For some children this occurs at age four, but for others it may not take place until kindergarten or even first grade. Whether the child is three, four, five, or six, whatever the program, when the child is ready for the next step the alert teacher is ready to help the youngster take it.

A good program is not totally organized into a rigid schedule with separate periods for language arts, number activities, and science. Neither are certain activities labeled as appropriate for four-year-olds and some for five-year-olds. For example, while playing in the housekeeping center the child may use a variety of skills, such as language arts—conversation, asking questions, talking on the telephone, and listening; or mathematics—cooking, measuring a cup, quart, teaspoon, and reading numerals on radio or TV dials.

Table 9-1, based on a study of birds, emphasizes some of the conceptual learnings a child might acquire in a given subject area while participating in a variety of activities. Opportunities for the practice of some of the process skills

[7] Louise M. Berman, *New Priorities in the Curriculum* (Columbus, Ohio: Charles E. Merrill Publishing Co., 1968).

[8] Evelyn Weber, *Early Childhood Education: Perspectives on Change* (Worthington, Ohio: Charles A. Jones Publishing Co., 1970), p. 4.

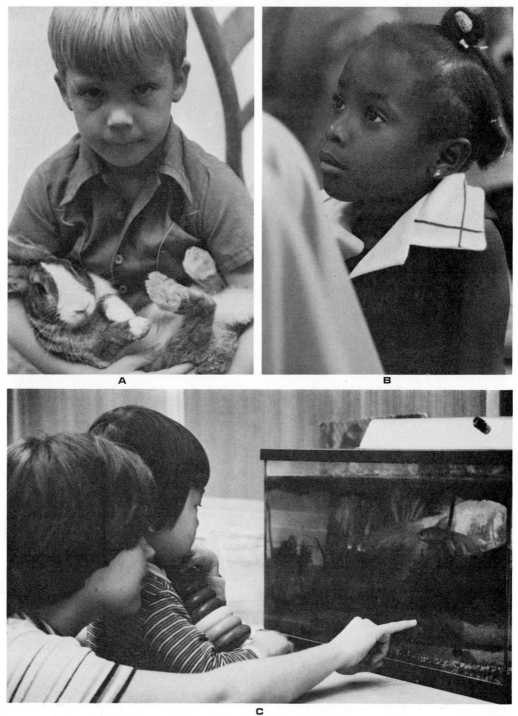

Figure 21
Children are an important consideration in planning the curriculum. Each group is different just as the child differs from other members of the group.

Table 9-1
Conceptual Learnings–The Birds*

Conceptual Understandings	Experience, Activity, and Play Possibilities
1. There are many kinds, colors, and sizes of birds. 1,2,3,5.	1. Identifying and classifying local birds. 2,5 and A,B,C.
2. All birds have feathers for protection. 3, 4,5.	2. Collecting feathers on a nature walk for use in making collages and in other activities. 1,5, and A,B.
3. Birds live in many different kinds of localities and homes as families. 4,5.	3. Making a bird house. 1,2,3,5. and A,B,C,D.
4. Birds depend on nature for their variety of food needs. 3,5.	4. Making a feeding station and observing birds at the station. 1,2,3,4,5, and A,B,D
5. Travel, communication, and self-preservation vary with the species of the bird. 1,3, 4,5.	5. Imitating the movement, habits, and sounds of a variety of birds. 1,2, and A,D.

Key: Subject Areas		Process Skills	
Music and the Arts	1	Communicating	A
Mathematics	2	Decision Making	B
Science	3	Patterning	C
Social Studies	4	Creating	D
Language	5		

* Adapted from *A Guide: Early Childhood Education in Florida Schools*, Bull. 76 (Tallahassee: Florida State Department of Education, 1969), pp. 46–49.

are also indicated. However, not all of the subject areas or the process skills have been included.

However, certain curriculum principles are important in planning the program. These principles apply to programs for all children. For example, although the immediate environment of the children is different, a good program develops from the environment, whether it is slum or suburb. The following are a few of the most important of these principles:[9]

1. A good program provides many opportunities for social adjustment and developing affective and cognitive skills. Most young children are individualists, and one of their most important developmental tasks is to learn to play and work with other boys and girls. They must learn through experience to share toys and equipment, to take turns, and to plan and act with individuals and groups. These experiences must be such that children build a positive self-image and gain confidence in themselves.

2. A good program grows out of the immediate environment of the children. They are interested in all that goes on about them. Their immediate environment points up and emphasizes such interest.

3. A good program allows plenty of time and adequate opportunities for children

[9] Adapted from *A Guide for Organizing and Developing a Kindergarten Program in Florida*, Bull. 53A (rev.) (Tallahassee: Florida State Department of Education, 1955), pp. 31–33.

to express themselves freely through many media. Young children like to work with things, to get their hands into water, to paint with their fingers or with brushes, to pound nails into wood, to "dress up" in the clothes of adults, to work with clay, and to build with blocks. Opportunities for talking are provided as children engage in these activities.

4. A good program allows children to use their whole body and to develop wholesome attitudes toward it. The program center is a place for children to use their voices in talking and singing. It is a place for laughter and dramatizing. It is a good place to dance, to engage in rhythms and movement, and to sing. The day should also be arranged to help establish the rhythm of bodily functions in the taking of food, resting, sleeping, eliminating, and in the establishing of acceptable health habits.

5. A good program utilizes the experiences of children and attempts to meet their needs as three-, four-, and five-year-olds, and at the same time builds a firm foundation for later experiences. The good program does not ignore so-called formal subject matter. On the contrary, it provides opportunities for experiences which build foundations for these fields. Cognitive development is a vital element.

6. A good program involves parents as well as children. When the program is planned, the teacher should take into account the fact that different families have special needs. Moreover, since young children are so closely identified with their parents, the teacher should make every effort to determine policies and plans with the parents. Provision should be made in the teachers' professional load for parents' meetings, conferences with parents, and for frequent home visits. Both the program and the school day should provide time for the work of teachers with parents. Parent involvement is an essential part of Head Start activities.

There is no one formula or method that can be used by the teacher to plan an effective program. This task calls for intelligence and understanding, imagination, and flexibility, rather than formulas. There is need for knowledge of research and the factors that influence the learning of children. These include (1) what the culture expects, (2) what the children are like and how they learn, and (3) academic content and skills. The first two factors are discussed in this chapter. The third factor is treated in subsequent chapters.

CULTURAL EXPECTATIONS

A child growing up in American society is confronted with certain "tasks" to be mastered if he or she is to make normal progress. These "developmental tasks are those major common tasks that face all individuals within a given society."[10,11] Within the society there is a variety of groups that differ from the

[10] Caroline Tryon and J. W. Lilienthal, "Developmental Tasks: The Concept and Its Importance," *Fostering Mental Health in Our Schools*, 1950 Yearbook (Washington, D.C.: ASCD), p. 77.

majority of the population. Children from these groups face the same developmental tasks as do other children. In helping these children achieve these tasks, the teacher must show respect for the children and their backgrounds.

Each task has certain stages of development appropriate to different age groups—infancy, early childhood, adolescence, adulthood, and old age. If one is successful in achieving the earlier tasks one is likely to be happy and successful in achieving later tasks. Failure in achieving these earlier tasks usually leads to unhappiness and difficulty with later ones.

These developmental tasks are set by both inner and outer forces, namely, the expectancies and pressures of society, the changes which take place in the physical organism through the process of maturation, and the individual's values and aspirations.[12] An active learner who is interacting with the social environment is meeting an individual need as well as a demand of society.[13] Havighurst includes such developmental tasks as learning to walk, to take solid foods, to talk, to control the elimination of body wastes; forming concepts and learning language to describe social and physical reality; getting ready to read; learning to distinguish right from wrong; and beginning to develop a conscience as characteristic of infancy and early childhood.[14]

Among the developmental tasks noted by Tryon and Lilienthal the following have been selected. The stages of development appropriate to early childhood are summarized and suggestions are made for helping the child achieve them.[15]

1. The task—achieving an appropriate dependence-independence pattern. The child needs to adjust to less private attention and to become more independent. This means that physically while learning to be independent in dressing, eating, and toileting, the child is also learning to share the teacher's attention with others in the group. In order to help the child in this respect, the school needs to:
   a. Maintain a warm, accepting atmosphere in the group. The child cannot adjust to less personal attention unless he is secure and receives much private attention. The group must be small enough for the teacher to give this attention to each child.
   b. Provide facilities that enable the child to become independent. For example, child-size bathroom fixtures, accessible lockers for hanging clothing, table and eating implements of appropriate size.
   c. Provide time in the program and facilities suitable for the child to put away materials or to hang up clothing. Explain to parents how important it is for the clothing to be such that the child can manage it independently.

---

[11] R. J. Havighurst, *Developmental Tasks and Education,* 3rd ed. (New York: David McKay Co., 1972), pp. 1–18.
[12] Ibid., p. 5.
[13] Ibid., p. vi.
[14] Ibid., pp. 8–17.
[15] Tryon and Lilienthal, op. cit., pp. 77–128.

2. The task—achieving an appropriate giving-receiving pattern of affection. The child needs to achieve an appropriate pattern of giving and receiving affection. At this stage, children learn to give as much love as they receive and to form friendships with other children of their own age. In order to help the child in this respect, the school program should:
   a. Provide opportunities for children to show affection for others in desirable ways—greetings, sharing toys, playing together.
   b. Avoid unfavorable comparison of one child with another. It is difficult for a child to share affection or love unless the child feels secure and loved.

3. The task—relating to changing social groups. It is important that the child develop the ability to relate to changing social groups. At this stage of development he is learning to feel a part of the school group, beginning to interact with age-mates, and to adjust to the expectations of the group. In order to help with this task, the school program should:
   a. Provide opportunities for the child to be a part of the group in planning and sharing, such as news and possessions.
   b. Stress cooperative and voluntary effort rather than domination and force.
   c. Provide opportunities for learning to give and to receive helpful suggestions and criticisms.

4. The task—developing a conscience. In early childhood this task involves developing the ability to take directions, to be obedient in the presence of authority, and gradually becoming able to be obedient in the absence of parents or teachers when conscience substitutes for authority. This is usually the period in which, as the child identifies with adults, he or she identifies with their values and standards of behavior. In order to help with this task, the school should:
   a. Offer explanations of or reasons for actions in simple, direct terms which can be understood by the child.
   b. Avoid moralizing.
   c. Provide opportunities for choices within limits.
   d. Provide opportunities to respond to signals and directions, and to learn respect for authority.

5. The task—learning one's psycho-socio-biological sex role. In early childhood the child is learning to identify with adult male and female roles. As children enter this stage, at the age of two, three, or four years, boys and girls exchange roles freely. During this stage, however, a change usually commences. The boys usually begin to identify with their fathers, then with men in general, while the girls begin to identify with their mothers and then with other women in general. In order to help with the task, the school program should:
   a. Provide opportunities for dramatic play.
   b. Provide opportunities for the child to find out about the work that mothers and fathers do. Visit some parents at work, or invite them to visit the school.
   c. Avoid use of sex stereotypes.

6. The task—accepting and adjusting to a changing body. Still another task includes managing a growing body and learning new motor patterns. The child needs to develop muscular control and skill in coordinating movements. At school, space, equipment and opportunities are needed for climbing, running,

sawing, painting, cutting, as well as opportunities for dressing, using buttons, and tying shoelaces.

7. The task—developing an appropriate symbol system and conceptual abilities. At this stage of development, children are increasing their vocabulary and improving sentence structure and pronunciation, so basic to the ability to communicate and to read. They are gaining concepts, not only of values but of ideas and things. At school, help in achieving these specific tasks can be provided by experiences gained through trips, stories, books, and opportunities for conversation and speaking in the group.

These tasks, expected of the young child in present-day culture, have implications for the teacher in planning the program.

WHAT THE CHILDREN ARE LIKE

The children, too, are an important consideration in planning. Each group is different, just as the child differs from the other members of the group. The teacher will do well to review the developmental characteristics of children in the age range to be taught (see Chapter 3, The Young Child as a Person). The child's social and physical development are important as are theories of intellectual growth. The teacher uses this information as an aid in looking at the children in the group to be taught. For example: the teacher opens the top file drawer in which the records of a group are kept: (see Chapter 21, Recording the Development of Children). She examines the first folder—a boy, age: four years, six months; height: 42 inches; weight: 38 pounds. The next folder is also a boy's—age: four years, five months; height: 41 inches; weight: $39\frac{3}{4}$ pounds. Now for a girl's record—age: four years, six months; height: 43 inches; weight: 44 pounds. The folders reveal that among 16 children there is variation in height, weight, and age. In Table 9-2 the range in heights, weights, and ages of four groups of children is given. These groups include children in a nursery school, a child development center, and a kindergarten.

Table 9-2
Variations in Four Groups

Group	Age Range	Height Variation	Weight Variation
Threes	2 years, 9 months	$36\frac{3}{4}$ inches	33 pounds
	3 years, 8 months	$39\frac{1}{2}$ inches	$45\frac{1}{2}$ pounds
Fours	3 years, 9 months	$36\frac{3}{4}$ inches	32 pounds
	4 years, 7 months	45 inches	48 pounds
Fours	4 years, 1 month	39 inches	35 pounds
	5 years, 1 month	47 inches	60 pounds
Fives	4 years, 11 months	$37\frac{1}{2}$ inches	35 pounds
	6 years, 1 month	48 inches	55 pounds

Note the overlap in height and weight among the groups and the variation within each group.

What do these heights, weights, and chronological ages mean for equipment, activities, and materials? Important as these factors are, there are still others to be considered. A closer examination of several folders reveals more details:

Karen and Kirsten are twins, five years old. They live in a six-room house with their parents and a sister who is three years older. The father attended college for two years, has no church affiliation, and is engaged in a business of his own—upholstering. The mother was born in Denmark and lived there until she married. She has no church affiliation and feels that for her civic and social activities can wait until the children are older. She speaks both English and Danish to the children.

In the testing situation both girls showed good discrimination in objects and forms and performed best on items requiring nonverbal responses. Test results, probably influenced by language, indicate that the girls are of low average intelligence. They are among the oldest children in the group, and above average in height and weight. Karen enjoys mealtime, while Kirsten often refuses food. The girls have had few trips in the community but spent last summer in Denmark with their grandparents.

The teacher notes: twins, mother of foreign background, limited language development, good muscular control, limited experiences in community.

Lisa, now four, is the older of two children. The walk to and from school each day with her mother serves as exercise for her mother who is expecting another baby soon. Once home, Lisa must remain in the apartment because her mother is not able to take her to a playground. Her father, a day laborer, is proud of Lisa, but has little time to spend with the children except during inclement weather when he can't work. Lisa is a bit larger than the other children in her group. She often takes leadership roles in small group activities and participates eagerly in school activities.

The teacher notes: mother pregnant, father can't work in bad weather, limited outdoor activity, assumes leadership roles, few experiences in the community.

Shaw knows that he is an adopted child. He lives with his foster parents and an older brother (also adopted) in a comfortable seven-room house. His father is a very successful businessman. Both father and mother are active in civic and church activities. Shaw accompanies his parents on trips to the beach and mountains. He is his father's hunting companion. He expresses himself well, enjoys books, likes school. Results of an individual intelligence test indicate that he is a gifted child. His height and weight are average but he is one of the youngest in the group. In situations which seem difficult, Shaw continues to try. His mother says, "He does not get hot and bothered. He has the patience of Job."

The teacher notes: adopted, gifted child, meets difficult situations confidently, good language facility, rich experience in immediate environment.

Gloria's oldest sister, a first grader, is responsible for bringing her and another sister, who is in kindergarten, to the center each day. Before the parents leave for work at 7:30 A.M. the mother gets the children up, dresses and feeds them. The girls stay in the apartment alone until a neighbor tells them that it is time to go to school. In the afternoon they are alone until the parents come in from work. The mother gives them money for candy and gum because they are left alone so much of the time. Gloria is a superior child and learns easily. She has difficulty in joining a group activity. At story time she sits on the lap of the adult assistant.

The teacher notes: both parents work, often left alone without an adult, given money as compensation, seeks adult attention, superior child, difficulty in group situations.

Jennie's father and mother are both students. The mother arranges her classes around the father's schedule so that one parent is free to care for the children, Jennie and a younger sister. The family lives in a small, dirty, cluttered apartment. The mother worked until the week before Jennie was born. Jennie is not permitted to cry at home. The father says, "Carsons do not cry." At school Jennie cries often and is afraid of children. An offer of friendship is greeted by, "He's bothering me." When she first entered the group, she became so excited by the children that she had a fever for several days. Her muscular coordination appears jerky. She tires easily. Mental test results indicate that she is a child of high average ability.

The teacher notes: preoccupation of both parents in their work—little time for children, cramped living space, normal emotional outlets denied, ill at ease with children, poor muscular coordination.

And there are others: Bob, whose father deserted the family; June, whose father is unemployed—only the "welfare" money is available to feed and clothe six children; Roger, whose father makes a great deal of money—there is plenty of money to buy things but little time for shared family experiences; Jan, who seldom stops talking and is at home in any group; and Pete, who seldom utters a word—occasionally, there is a faint smile of communication.

These children face common developmental tasks, yet because of various factors in their own lives, they will achieve them in different ways. Wise is the teacher who understands this and is able to plan a program to provide for experiences that meet common needs of the group as well as individual needs. In planning such a program, the teacher, then, becomes familiar with various factors involved in the lives of the children in the group and the expectations of the culture in which they live. The teacher reviews the research pertinent to these factors and determines the implications of these findings for the children he or she teaches. Within this framework of the child, the culture, and research findings, the teacher selects, plans, and organizes activities for the children in her particular group.

"At the very heart of curriculum planning," says Weber, "stands the problem designated by Hunt as the 'problem of the match.'"[16] The perfect match may mean boredom and little development. Differences that are too great may mean distress or negative motivation. Teachers must seek the match that will challenge the child to learn without undue stress.

> Young children have to have a balance between vigorous motor activities and quieter moments. They require individual and small-group situations. They depend upon significant adults working together—parents, teachers, aides, pediatricians. They need an expanse of space indoors and outdoors with adequate equipment and materials to challenge them and keep curiosity alive. They must have spontaneous and planned experiences which utilize their deep motivation to understand their world. They require a program that fosters intellectual growth. The need for integrating intellectual and affective growth is readily apparent.[17]

The authors of this text maintain their belief in the theories of child growth and development. The need for cognitive or intellectual development is recognized but emphasis is also placed on socialization, physical development, creativity, and the processes of learning. The task of translating these beliefs into daily activities and programs is not an easy one.

MULTICULTURAL EDUCATION AND THE CURRICULUM

For many American children the school culture is highly consistent with their own culture. This is not true, however, for many children of distinct ethnic groups who often find the school culture alien, hostile, and self-defeating.[18] Earlier, these children were considered culturally disadvantaged. This concept implied deficits in their cultural background. More recently these children are recognized as culturally different. The culturally different approach recognizes the dignity of the child's culture and seems to be a positive response to the needs of children of distinct ethnic groups.[19]

The school in our society has a difficult task—the task of helping all children develop "cultural literacy," to learn of and respect the many cultures in the United States, and in so doing to help them recognize and value the pluralistic nature of our country. Children must be helped to gain skills needed to function effectively within their ethnic culture as well as in the dominant culture.[20] While the school values and reflects cultural diversity there is also the "responsibility to teach a commitment to and a respect for the core values" of

[16] Weber, op. cit., p. 179.
[17] Ibid.
[18] J. A. Banks, "Cultural Pluralism and the Schools," *Educ. Leadership*, 32:3 (1974), p. 164.
[19] D. J. Puglisi, "Two Approaches to Minority Education," *Educ. Leadership*, 32:3 (1974), pp. 173–175.
[20] Banks, op. cit., p. 165.

our democracy, which include justice, equality, and human dignity.[21] The school should foster cultural differences that maximize opportunities for democratic living but oppose those that run counter to it.

In response to this need, culturally pluralistic education, or multicultural education has developed. This type of education encourages people to accept and respect their own cultural heritage as well as that of people of different backgrounds.[22] For such education, a curriculum that responds to the diverse needs of a pluralistic society is essential. The curriculum plays an important role in influencing children's attitudes and must therefore respect the dignity of all children.[23]

The basic principles for curriculum development apply to the development of a multicultural or culturally pluralistic curriculum. There are, however, suggestions that can be helpful in developing a curriculum or in modifying an existing one. One important way to begin is to emphasize similarities, rather than differences in young children. For example, children can be helped to understand such concepts as:

> *Children everywhere play games.* Begin with learning about games played by children in the group and then learning about games played by other children. Rather than emphasizing the different games the fact that all children play games is stressed.
>
> The same procedure may be used with other concepts: *Children everywhere celebrate holidays, All children eat food, Most children live in some type of family.*[24]

Be sure that the books, pictures, and other instructional materials are accurate and free of stereotypes.

Another way to begin is to evaluate the current curriculum. Grant has developed criteria for such an evaluation. She says that a culturally pluralistic curriculum should:[25]

1. Reflect the pluralistic nature of our society, both past and present.
2. Present diversity of culture, ethnicity, and custom as a strong positive feature of our nation's heritage.
3. Present the cultural, sexual, and racial groups in our society in a manner that will build mutual respect and understanding.
4. Portray people—boys and girls, men and women—whatever their culture, as

---

[21] Ibid., p. 166.

[22] Donna Gollnick, F. H. Klassen, and J. Yff, *Multicultural Education and Ethnic Studies in the United States: An Analysis and Annotated Bibliography of Selected ERIC Documents* (Washington, D.C.: American Association of Colleges of Teacher Education and ERIC, 1976), p. 10.

[23] Gloria W. Grant, "Criteria for Cultural Pluralism in the Classroom," *Educ. Leadership*, 32:3 (1974), p. 190.

[24] Joan E. Moyer and Guillermina Engelbrecht, "Multicultural Education: Where Do We Begin?" *Child Educ.*, 53:5 (1977), pp. 241–244.

[25] Gloria Grant, op. cit., p. 192.

displaying various human emotions, both negative and positive. Individuals of different cultural groups should be described working and playing together.

5. Provide a balanced representation of cultural groups.
6. Present members of various cultural groups in positions of authority.

⋮

9. Show that every cultural group has many individuals, such as educators, scientists, artists, writers, architects, and others, who have made important contributions to society.
10. Portray cultures other than from a "special occasion" point-of-view. For example: Is there usually a "piñata" when studying Mexico? Are native Americans presented mostly around Thanksgiving? Is the study of Blacks confined to Black History Week? Are Asian Americans usually studied around the Chinese New Year?

⋮

14. Provide experiences that will help build positive attitudes of a student's own cultural group and acceptance of other cultural groups.
15. Use words and phrases that are complimentary and honest for the culture.
16. Make certain that cultures are not presented separate or in isolation from each other. A pluralistic curriculum should provide experiences that show how people of one culture have adopted food, clothing, language, etc. from other cultures.

Suggested Activities

1. Visit a center for young children and evaluate the program in terms of the criteria presented on pp. 185–186. Discuss observations with the class. Note similarities and differences among programs observed by class members. Discuss possible reasons for these.
2. Visit a center in which culturally different children are enrolled. Compare the principles of learning and development and teaching strategies used in working with these children. How are individual needs met? How are children helped to participate in group activities?
3. Select one developmental task characteristic of early childhood. Observe a group of children and note evidences in their behavior which indicate attempts to meet the task selected. Share observations in class discussion.
4. Visit a center that has developed an innovative program. Note the curriculum, organization, and teaching strategies used. Discuss observations with the class.
5. View a film depicting one of the innovative programs. Compare the program you observed with the one presented in the film. Suggested films include *Children Are People,* Agathon Press, New York, N.Y., 1972; and *They All Learn,* Promethean Films South, Birmingham, Ala., 1974; *The British Infant School—Southern Style,* Promethean Films South, Birmingham, Ala.; *Early Childhood Programs* (filmstrips and tapes). Educational Products Information Exchange, 463 West Street, New York, N.Y. 10014. *Open for Children.* Odeon Films, Inc., 51 West 86th St. New York, N.Y. 10024.

Related Readings

Carini, Patricia. "Building a Curriculum for Young Children from an Experiential Base," *Young Children, 32*:3 (1977), pp. 14–18.

Combs, A. W. *Educational Accountability: Beyond Behavioral Objectives.* Washington, D.C.: ASCD, 1972.

Corwin, Rebecca, G. E. Hein, and Diane Levin. "Weaving Curriculum Webs: The Structure of Nonlinear Curriculum," *Child. Educ., 52*:5 (1976), pp. 248–251.

Crandall, J. *Early to Learn.* New York: Dodd, Mead, 1975.

Dittmann, Laura L. "Migrant Children in an Early Learning Program," *Young Children, 31*:3 (1976), pp. 218–228.

Elkind, D. "Humanizing the Curriculum," *Child. Educ., 53*:4 (1977), pp. 179–182.

Evans, E. D. *Contemporary Influences in Early Childhood Education,* 2nd ed. New York: Holt, Rinehart & Winston, 1975.

Frost, J. L., coordinator. *Developing Programs for Infants and Toddlers.* Washington, D.C.: ACEI, 1977.

Galin, D. "Educating Both Halves of the Brain," *Child. Educ., 53*:1 (1976), pp. 17–20.

Gross, Dorothy W. "Encouraging the Curious Mind: Through the Curriculum," *Child. Educ., 51*:1 (1974), pp. 5–7.

Harms, Thelma. "Change-Agents in Curriculum—An Overview of Innovative Programs in American Schools for Young Children," *Young Children, 29*:5 (1974), pp. 280–288.

Harvey, J. "Special Program Needs of the Culturally Diverse Child," *Early Childhood Education for Exceptional Children.* Reston, Va.: The Council for Exceptional Children, 1977, pp. 158–181.

Hawkins D. "Balancing Basics: The Three Rs Revisited," *Child. Educ., 50*:4 (1974), pp. 187–191.

Inhelder, B., and J. Piaget. *The Early Growth of Logic in the Child.* New York: Harper & Row, 1969.

Lagenbach, M., and Teanna West. *Day Care Curriculum Considerations.* Columbus, Ohio: Charles E. Merrill Publishing Co., 1977.

Leeper, Sarah H. "Reflections—Directions," *Child. Educ., 53*:1 (1976), pp. 5–8.

Moore, Shirley G. "The Effects of Head Start Programs with Different Curricula and Teaching Strategies," *Young Children, 32*:6 (1977), pp. 54–61.

Seefeldt, Carol (ed.). *Curriculum for the Preschool–Primary Child—A Review of the Research.* Columbus, Ohio: Charles E. Merrill Publishing Co., 1976.

———. *A Curriculum for Child Care Centers.* Columbus, Ohio: Charles E. Merrill Publishing Co., 1974.

Wassermann, Selma. "Teachers as Curriculum-Makers or Curriculum-Making in 9 Easy (?!!) Steps," *Child. Educ., 52*:5 (1976), pp. 242–247.

White, S. H., and A. W. Siegel. "Cognitive Development: The New Inquiry," *Young Children, 31*:6 (1976), pp. 425–436.

Wood, Mary M., and O. L. Hurley. "Curriculum and Instruction," *Early Childhood Education for Exceptional Children.* Reston, Va.: The Council for Exceptional Children, 1977, pp. 132–157.

chapter 10

Planning for learning

A center for young children, whether it is a nursery school, a kindergarten, Head Start, or a Day Care Program, is a place where children are engaged in interesting, stimulating activities, relevant to their lifestyles, not a place where children just do "busy work."

Each center for young children is unique. The type of program and the schedule planned for various activities depend on such factors as the educational philosophy of the staff, the amount of time the children spend in school, the special needs of the children enrolled, the physical facilities available, and the location in terms of climate. However, all centers aim to provide a happy place with opportunities for worthwhile play and work experiences so that children will grow and learn under the guidance of well-qualified teachers.

Each day is important and the child can live the day only once; therefore, the teacher is acutely conscious of the fact that how *this day* is lived helps determine how capable the child will be to direct his or her energies as one day slips into the next and on and on into adulthood. The teacher asks such questions as how to plan so that this child can acquire skills and work habits, yet be flexible enough to live in a rapidly changing society with ever-changing occupations. How to plan for a child who will live in this world with the expanded community concept? How to plan so that a pattern of work and play will be developed that will guide the child in knowing how to work, how to use leisure time, and how to relax and rest?

In order for children to have such opportunities, the teacher utilizes knowledge about each child, the level of the developmental tasks the child faces, and the sequence of skills within the various subject areas in selecting learning activities and materials to be used. It is in the selection and guidance of activities for young children that the teacher's education and skill are evident.

As planning begins, a teacher of a group of five-year-olds looks at the notes on each child. These notes are a part of the information that has been assembled from parent conferences, observation of the child, and anecdotal records. (See Chapter 9.)

Examples of what might be read are: Gloria needs help in group situations; Karen and Kirsten, the twins, have limited language development; Jennie needs to develop muscular control; and so on until the needs of each child in the group have been considered (see p. 190). The teacher studies these notes and ponders: What is the role of the teacher in working with these children? What shall be the teaching tasks, the children's activities? What materials will be needed? Which materials should be prepared or assembled in advance of the arrival of the group and which materials should be selected and collected by the children under teacher guidance? How can the teacher tell if the children are developing according to their potential as they participate in the planned and the incidental activities?

Using the long-range goals already developed (see Chapter 5), the teacher must analyze each child's achievement and discover his or her needs, plan a daily schedule, and select learning opportunities and activities. Suggestions for the teacher in each of these areas follow.

ANALYZING PUPIL ACHIEVEMENT

The teacher's concern in analyzing the child's present level of development or achievement is in securing information to be used as the basis for curricular planning for each child. Observation of children in a variety of situations can yield valuable information. The following questions may be helpful:

> What is the relation of the child to others in the situation? Does the child engage in solitary play, parallel play, cooperative play, share toys, take turns?
> How does the child use materials? Does the child show evidence of good coordination, a willingness to experiment with new media? Does he or she organize well?
> What is indicated about the experiential background of the child? Are there limited experiences, good vocabulary, secure home relationships?
> What concepts need to be clarified?

If the opportunities for learning are paced for each child, enthusiasm for learning can be developed through participation in many, yet diverse, activities. Within each curricular field and in the areas of physical, mental, and social growth there is a developmental sequence that can serve as a guide for the teacher. (See Chapters 11–19.) The teacher can identify the child's present level and when the child is ready for the next step the adult is ready to help. There is a need for instruments to help the teacher in analyzing the child's achievement. An analysis of each child can help the teacher in utilizing experiences and activities to facilitate learning. For example, if the teacher finds that Melissa does not recognize a dime or a quarter, she can be included when planning for a committee to buy bird food at the pet store so that she will have opportunities to become acquainted with and use money. This information—that Melissa does not recognize certain coins—can be shared at a parent conference and parents can be encouraged to provide similar meaningful opportunities.

An analysis of the entire class may reveal that only 10 percent recognize a dime and a quarter. Is this to be expected? In answering this question, the teacher can consult research and authorities in this area and then set goals. If such competency is to be expected for children at this age, the teacher will need to consider appropriate learning opportunities for the group as well as for individuals within the group. Thus, plans can be made for each child in terms of achievement. Results of periodic evaluation may be also used by the teacher to determine a child's achievement over a given period of time.

The following Achievement Checklist is planned to help in making an analysis of each child. It is not a test. No attempt was made to establish norms for different age groups. It consists of a list of items for assessing achievement that were selected from the literature and have been reviewed by specialists as being appropriate for the early childhood years. The checklist is intended to help the teacher gain a picture of the child's status that will serve as a basis for planning and guidance and as a means of assessing a child's progress. Other items relating to the curriculum can be added to the checklist.

Achievement Checklist for Young Children

Directions for Using: Below is a list of items which may be achieved by some three-, four-, and five-year-old children. Put a check (✔) in the appropriate column to indicate how frequently, in your experience with this child, he or she has achieved in each item.

Section I	Always	Sometimes	Never	Does Not Apply
Eats with spoon				
Eats with fork				
Holds silver correctly				
Holds cup with one hand				
Spills food or drink only once during meal				
Spills food or drink more than once during meal				
Goes to toilet without help with clothing				
Flushes toilet				
Hangs clothing in locker				
Puts on sweater that opens down front alone				
Puts on coat alone				
Buttons sweater				
Buttons coat				
Puts on slip-on sweater alone				
Manages zipper				
Ties shoe laces				
Climbs jungle gym				
Jumps from 12-inch height				
Skips				
Catches ball				
Pedals tricycle				
Climbs steps with alternate feet				
Puts three-piece puzzle together				

Achievement Checklist for Young Children (*Cont.*)

Section I	Always	Sometimes	Never	Does Not Apply
Puts puzzle of five or more pieces together				
Holds scissors correctly				
Cuts on a line				
Knows full name				
Writes given name				
Section II				
Follows simple directions				
Sits and listens to story for at least 5 minutes				
Sits and listens to story for at least 10 minutes				
Puts away blocks or toys when finished				
Responds to own name				
Recognizes locker				
Leaves mother after one "good-bye"				
Rides to school in car with someone other than parent				
Chooses to look at picture books				
Looks at books from front to back				
Looks at page from top to bottom				
Recognizes name				
Recognizes name of at least one other child				
Contributes to experience story				
Reads experience story with group				
Identifies words in experience story				
Can identify rhyming words				

Achievement Checklist for Young Children (*Cont.*)

Section II	Always	Sometimes	Never	Does Not Apply
Can match beginning consonant sounds				
Counts by rote 1–5				
Counts by rote 1–10				
Counts rationally 1–5				
Counts rationally 1–10				
Uses ordinal numbers first through third				
Recognizes money—penny, nickel, dime				
Recognizes geometric shapes—circle, square, triangle, rectangle				
Solves problem without number				
Uses number in problem solving				
Writes numerals 1–5				
Speaks without baby talk				
Uses personal pronouns				
Speaks in sentences (uses sentences of at least five words)				
Tells events or story in sequence				
Engages in conversation with other children				
Engages in conversation with adults				
Speaks in group situation				
Section III				
Sings alone				
Sings songs of at least two phrases				
Recognizes songs sung or played by others				
Manipulates and experiments with instruments				

Achievement Checklist for Young Children (*Cont.*)

Section III	Always	Sometimes	Never	Does Not Apply
Uses instrument as accompaniment to movements (beats drums as marches, but not necessarily in time with the steps)				
Knows names of at least two better-known musical instruments				
Listens and identifies sounds of different instruments				
Matches tones				
Draws or paints lines and circles				
Draws or paints squares				
Shows ground line in painting or drawing				
Names paintings or drawings				
Names (or recognizes) primary colors				
Names at least five colors				
Adjusts bodily movements to accompaniment of regular beat (can keep time to music)				
Adjusts bodily movements to accompaniment which involves contrasts (slow–fast, light–heavy)				

Directions for Scoring: Note items in which the pupil has achieved, the items that need continued practice, and those that need to be introduced. Plan learning opportunities in terms of analysis of achievement items. Ignore those items which do not apply.

The teacher studies carefully the data secured through the use of the checklist. Activities that will provide continued practice as well as introduce opportunities for new learnings are planned. The progress of the children is assessed periodically to assist in further planning. However, the teacher is constantly aware that, in order to achieve, all children need to feel secure and loved, to be free from fear, and to have some recognition and success as they participate in a variety of learning opportunities.

PLANNING LEARNING OPPORTUNITIES

As the teacher plans opportunities for experiences and activities for and with the children, the teacher takes into consideration their individual and group likes, needs, and abilities, as well as the child's home life and experiential background. With these factors in mind, the teacher will plan so that the children may:

1. Plan together—for the day, for the period, and for special events.
2. Make decisions—as to work, play, rest, and behavior.
3. Learn new skills—as an individual child and as a group.
4. Expand interests—in special areas or in new areas.
5. Have balance—between active and quiet activities and between indoor and outdoor play.
6. Have opportunities—to laugh together, to console one another, to help one another.
7. Have opportunities to work alone—to browse among materials or to think and muse quietly.
8. Visit places—within the school, at home, an interesting place in the community, or have a person from outside the school visit them.
9. Establish routines—of physical habits, work habits, discipline, or self-direction and self-control.
10. Develop social values—following through activity and receiving group acceptance, developing a balance between independence or initiation and consideration or aggression, developing pride in ownership yet willingness to share, acquiring a feeling of security for self but also a sense of responsibility to the group.
11. Develop readiness—in reading, speech, mathematics, writing, according to child's maturity.
12. Grow—through creative self-expression in music, rhythm, dramatic play, art activities, games.
13. Explore natural environment—through observing, investigating, experimenting, experiencing.

As the teacher considers these points, she or he knows that emphasis will not be placed on all of them each day, yet all are so interrelated that many of them will appear daily in some form. Certainly a group would not take a trip each day nor would someone from outside the school visit the group very often.

TEACHING STRATEGIES

How, then, does the teacher plan and teach in order to achieve the desired results? What are some of the strategies that may be used? Descriptions of a few teaching strategies follow. These are applicable to any subject area. Examples of use in various subject fields, such as social studies and science are included in chapters dealing with the subjects (see Chapters 14 and 16).

Reinforcing, Clarifying, Explaining, and Discussing Incidents That Affect Children During the School Day. Often opportunities for reinforcing, clarifying, explaining, and discussing incidents that affect children during the school day are lost. However, a comment by the teacher at the right moment can be most effective in utilizing both in- and out-of-school experiences that children mention in their conversation. In the following example, two four-year-olds complain to Miss D., "We don't like Steve. He knocks our blocks down."

> Miss D.: Why do you think he knocks them down?
> Hal: He's just mean.
> Joe (thoughtfully): He doesn't know how to play with other children.
> Miss D.: Why do you think he doesn't know how?
> Joe: He just came to nursery school.
> Miss D.: How could we help him?

In response to the question, two suggestions were made.

1. "We could say 'Please don't knock down the blocks. We don't do that at nursery school.'"
2. "We could ask him to play with us."

These four-year-olds were being taught to understand that rules can help us live happily together.

Cooperative Planning. Cooperative planning means that the teacher and children plan together, examine alternatives, and make decisions appropriate for consideration by the child. They can participate in planning for many different activities such as field trips, cooking, a visit by a resource person or what to do in the classroom. For example, the teacher says, "This is a rainy day. We can't go out on the playground. What could we do inside?" The teacher and children discuss the possibilities available, make choices, and plan for their use.

Cooperative planning does not mean that the teacher already has the plan in mind and is trying to have the children guess what it is or to manipulate them into making correct choices. As one example of such manipulation, conscious or unconscious, one teacher said, "I let the children plan the lunch menu every day." When asked how it was possible to do this, the reply was, "Oh, I have the meal already planned and partially prepared. But I ask the children what they want for lunch. If they don't name what I have planned, I say, let's not have that today. What about fish? Tuna fish? You know how good that is.' And they agree."

Figure 22
Cooking activities provide opportunities for exploring the physical world, discussing and planning, taking turns, following directions, learning quantitative measurement, using desirable health habits, developing scientific concepts, and beginning reading experiences.

Cooking. Activities related to cooking are of interest to young children. Not only are these experiences enjoyable but they also provide opportunities for discussing and planning, taking turns, following directions, learning quantitative measurement, using desirable health habits, developing scientific concepts, and beginning reading experiences.

Gelatin desserts can be made by children. Water is heated by the teacher, but the measuring and stirring are done by the children. Cake mixes can be used for making cupcakes for a birthday party. A simple butter icing may be used to decorate the cake. Ice cream can be mixed and frozen in the classroom.

If a stove is not available in the classroom, an electric hotplate may be used or the food may be cooked in the school cafeteria. The refrigerator in the cafeteria may also be used if one is not available in the classroom. In guiding cooking activities, the teacher should keep in mind the following suggestions:

Use "no-fail recipes."
Maintain constant, alert, adult supervision.

Exercise care in the use of the stove and hot liquids.

Discuss the safety rules.

Practice desirable health habits. Be sure that hands are washed and utensils are clean.

Relate cooking to various phases of the school program, such as health, science, social studies, and holiday celebrations.

Picture the ingredients to be used on a chart as a reference for the children.

Experiment with using various measures, such as one tablespoon or one-half cup, before the cooking activity.

Keep the project simple enough so that the children will have a successful and happy experience.

Allow time for children to do the work.

The entire group need not "cook" at the same time.

A cooking activity can contribute to learning in the various areas of the curriculum.[1] For example:

1. Language Arts
    a. Discussing plans.
    b. Listening to and following directions.
    c. Learning new words.
    d. Reading plans and recipes.
2. Social Studies
    a. Learning about home activities.
    b. Working as a member of a group.
    c. Learning where foods come from and how they are transported.
    d. Understanding about division of labor.
3. Science
    a. Learning how foods grow.
    b. Understanding how matter changes form.
4. Mathematics
    a. Measuring ingredients.
    b. Understanding quantities.
    c. Learning how foods are sold; measuring; weighing.
5. Health and Safety
    a. Developing the concept that many foods help us grow strong.
    b. Practicing reasonable cautions—"cooking can be done safely."
    c. Practicing desirable health habits, such as handwashing.
    d. Helping improve self-image, because child is really doing something worthwhile.

Field Trips.   Visits may be made to spots within walking distance of the school, or sites farther away which necessitate transportation. In either case, one should use the following checklist in preparing for the trip:

[1]Tricia Godshall, "Discover Cooking With Preschoolers" (mimeogr.), Project Florida Head Start, University of Miami, Coral Gables, n.d.

1. Formulate purpose of trip. Too many trips are taken merely because they are novel or unusual and provide an activity for the group. Trips should be made only after the teacher has clearly in mind reasons for taking the trip, and feels that the trip offers the most effective method of helping the children to develop certain understandings and appreciations and to acquire certain knowledge and facts. In deciding whether the trip is the most effective method to use, it is important that the teacher consider such factors as the following:

   a. Length of time required for transportation and the visit. Considering the age of the children, is it too long? Will they become too tired? Will it interfere with the routines for eating and resting?

   b. Complexity of the concepts and difficulty of the facts to be gained. Are they appropriate for the maurity of the children? Could they be acquired more effectively when the child is older?

   c. Experience background of the children. Have the children had, or are they likely to have, this experience with their parents?

Figure 23

(Courtesy of Head Start.)

These children have had a trip to the fire station. They met firefighters and saw the fire engine. Now they are engaged in dramatic play. The hats add interest.

d. Security of the child. Is the security of the child threatened by leaving school with "a stranger," an adult who is helping with the trip?

2. Obtain administrative permission. Investigate school policies covering field trips and observe these in planning for the trip.

3. Obtain written permission of the parents. The following is a sample form that may be used and covers trips for the entire school year:

....has my permission to go on
                    (Child's Name)
excursions away from Nursery School. I understand that these excursions will be planned and adequately supervised.

                                      ....
                                      (Parent's Signature)

It is important, however, to notify parents of each trip away from school. Such notice helps parents to understand the value of the trip and to know the details involved that may influence the clothing the child wears that day, and the schedule for bringing and picking up the child.

4. Visit site before taking children. This is essential in order to determine whether or not the site is appropriate and can fulfill the purposes of the trip. Safety hazards should be noted. Talk with adults who will serve as guides and talk with the children.

5. Arrange transportation. When private cars are used, be sure that the parent has adequate liability insurance. Two adults should be in the car, one in the back seat. The number of children per car should be limited so that there is room for each child to sit down. If the group is walking, the number of adults will vary with the age of the children. With three-year-olds there should be at least one adult for every two children. For four- or five-year-olds, there should be at least two adults for every five or six children.

6. Invite parents to assist. Select parents whose presence in the school situation does not overstimulate their own child. In order to help the adult "keep up" with the children assigned to her, each child might have a name tag, the color of the children's tags matching the color of the tag worn by the adult. Discuss with the parents the purposes of the trip. To provide consistent guidance, talk with them regarding the standards of behavior that have been developed for the trip.

7. Plan with the children. Talk about what we hope to see, to observe, to learn. Be sure that they know why they are taking the trip. Discuss reasons for standards of behavior, such as listen to the adult who is with you; sit down in the car; and when you get out of the car, wait for the group and the adult. Count the children before leaving school and frequently during the trip.

8. Evaluate the experience. Variety is needed here. Too often the group only discusses the trip or paints pictures about it. On one field trip a child was overheard to say, "Don't look 'cause when we get back we'll have to read and write." Although preschool children do not read or write about the trip, the comment reflects the child's reaction to the exclusive use of one type of evaluation. Children's comments, conversation, and dramatic play all can be used to determine whether or not the purposes of the trip have been fulfilled.

Organization and Use of Centers of Interest and Learning Centers. The terms *learning center* or *station* are often used and the question arises as to the difference between them and the term *centers of interest* as used in programs for young children. A center of interest is just what the name implies—a place in the nursery, kindergarten, or Child Development Center in which the child can engage in activities related to one of many interests. These centers provide interrelated experiences that may be adapted to the child's interests, maturity, and experiential background. Through such experiences the child can grow in appreciation of his or her world, relationships, and roles. In such a center the children can manipulate objects, build, and engage in conversation and role-playing, and can learn at their own level. The use of blocks may range from manipulation by some children to the building of a structure related to a topic of interest. One child may rock the doll as she or he plays alone, while three others may engage in cooperative play and role-playing. Opportunities for practicing physical and social skills as well as cognitive development are available. Some children, however, do not utilize them.

The learning center has evolved as an attempt to individualize instruction for more effective education of children. Perhaps the main distinction between the learning center and centers of interest lies in the fact that the learning center emphasizes cognitive growth and provides for self-evaluation. In a learning center the cognitive aspects are pinpointed. Exploring behavior by itself is not considered to be learning, and provision must be made for opportunities by which the child's mind can be stretched.[2] There are certain tasks to be performed, such as: "Find four blocks that are just alike." Self-evaluation can take place as the child puts the blocks in a frame or storage shelf to test for size.

In using centers with young children, whether called *interest* or *learning*, it is important that the intellectual growth of the child not be affected adversely —activities should not be boring and dull on the one hand, or too structured and demanding on the other.[3]

The role of the teacher in planning for and supervising the centers is an important one. Suggestions for the teacher in planning and organizing centers follow:

1. Select centers that are appropriate to the child's level of development and interests and vary these from time to time. Be sure that the centers are attractive, inviting, uncluttered, and safe. Enough equipment should be available so that the child does not have to wait too long for a turn. Some centers, such as block building and the doll corner are available each day. Variety may be provided by the addition of different materials on certain days. For example, toys related to transportation—trucks, trains, and airplanes—may be placed in the

[2]D. E. Day and D. W. Allen, "Organization for Individual Work," *Learning Centers: Children on Their Own* (Washington, D.C. ACEI, 1970), p. 31.
[3]Ibid., p. 32.

Figure 24
The learning center has evolved as an attempt to individualize instruction. The learning center emphasizes cognitive growth and provides for self-evaluation. This girl is listening and responding as she places shapes on the board.

block-building area. Conversation may be encouraged by including toy telephones in the doll corner. Specific learning tasks may be added. The materials and/or tasks selected will vary with the emphasis that the teacher considers to be important at the time.

Other centers of interest may be set up for a few days only. Such centers may relate to a holiday or to the unit of study (see pp. 326–333, 369–373) that is in progress at the time.

2. Arrange for several learning centers to be available and to be set up before the child arrives at school. The child's attention span is short and he may participate in several centers of interest during the morning. A wide variety of activities should be available. The following list of centers suggests the types that the teacher might make available:

Housekeeping Center or Doll House. (This center is available every day.) Activities related to the home, kinds of homes, members of the family. A learning task may be planned to involve classification. For example, "Hang the clothing here. Put the cooking utensils on the table." Vary the tasks from time to time.

Block Building. Construction of houses, trains, identification of community helpers who work on the train. Provide caps for conductor and engineer.

Puzzle Table. (See p. 412 for suggestions as to use of puzzles.)

Library Table. (See pp. 275–278 for suggestions as to use of books.) Books displayed for the day may relate to the unit which is under way.

Sound Center. During a unit on *Sounds*, the center might include musical instruments, rubber bands, sandpaper, and blocks with which the child could experiment in making sounds.

Art Center. The easel, the clay or dough table, scraps of paper for tearing and pasting may be available also.

Mathematics Center. Scales for balancing, containers for measurement, and felt figures for comparing can be utilitized. A suggested task might be, "How many nuts balance one apple?"

3. Set up centers around the room in order to utilize space and minimize conflicts. For example, use blocks in an area which is not in the direct line of traffic.

   Related centers should be near each other. Maintain a balance between quiet and noisy centers and between those that accommodate a group or an individual.

4. Maintain a classroom atmosphere that is conducive to effective use of the centers and one in which the child is free to move from one activity to another. Suficient time is needed for the child to engage in the activity and to move around without being hurried or pushed. In supervising the centers of interest, the teacher observes the responses of children in the situation. This information can be of great help in analyzing pupil achievement (see pp. 197–202).

5. Guide the children's activities so that the experience may be satisfying and valuable. For example, the teacher may help each child find some activity, help a child get into a group, help in quarrel situations, raise questions which may clarify the situation, assist in problem-solving situations, and clarify use of materials.

6. Watch for indications of leads into future activities.

PLANNING FOR TEACHING

Very few teachers can plan and teach exactly as they might wish. In most situations, planning and teaching are influenced to some degree by regulations of the state, the county, Head Start, the parent cooperative, or the private school. There is usually a "handbook" and a curriculum guide. The teacher should become familiar with these, not to be followed slavishly, but as a framework of learnings to be taught.[4]

Neither is the choice of a topic for teaching based exclusively on the interests of the child, nor is it entirely dependent upon the occurrence of some incident. The teacher utilizes both the child's interest and incidents within the framework of learnings to be taught.

[4]J. Jarolimek, *Social Studies in Elementary Education*, 5th ed. (New York: Macmillan Publishing Co., 1977), pp. 25–27.

Often the question is asked, "What can the children do tomorrow?" and the reply is in terms of activities in which the children may participate. The most important question for the teacher to ask, however, is, "What am I trying to help the children learn, to understand, to experience?" When this has been answered, activities can be planned and incidents utilized.

The teacher should be more concerned about justifying some of the topics routinely used. He or she should ask frequently: What contribution will the study of this topic make toward helping this child become more competent for living in this modern world? Is this worthwhile? Why? What difference will this make in the life of the child? Honest answers to such questions can help make the content and learnings more meaningful.

Once the learnings and the topic have been selected, the teacher will do further planning. The educational long-range goals have already been developed. These are reviewed frequently to see how each lesson fits into and furthers the achievement of the goals.

Good planning is based on goals the teacher hopes to achieve (see pp. 90–92). Plans may take a variety of forms. Some teachers make lesson plans from day to day with little thought for continuity or reinforcement of learning. Others choose a more integrated approach, which helps avoid a fragmented program. The latter approach includes long-range planning as well as daily lesson or teaching plans. A description of this type of planning follows.

A Plan for Developing Key Concepts. A plan for developing key concepts is a means of organizing materials for instructional purposes.[5] Such a plan, traditionally thought of as a *unit*, is usually a collection of teaching materials and suggested activities organized around a topic such as "Our Homes," "Money Is Used for Many Things," or "Many People Help Us." These plans (or units) may be developed well in advance by the teacher or committee of teachers as is done in some school systems. Such plans or units do not necessarily limit the teacher, because from these resources the teacher is free to select and work out a lesson or teaching plan with a specific group of children.

The Lesson or Teaching Plan. The lesson or teaching plan may be developed from the materials related to the Key Concept (or unit plan). The teacher selects certain phases to emphasize for a period of time and provides opportunities through which learning can take place.

A plan of work may be for a part of a day, one day, or for several days, depending on the maturity and interest of the group. Whatever the length of time involved, whether it be a unit or a teaching or lesson plan, good planning includes (1) objectives or purposes, (2) activities or opportunities for learning

---

[5]Ibid.

experiences through which these objectives may be realized, (3) materials needed, and (4) plans for evaluating to determine whether or not the purposes have been achieved. Examples of units are included on pp. 326–333, 369–373.

INSTRUCTIONAL RESOURCES

The use of instructional technology in children's centers has greatly increased in recent years. Educational media may be used to help children visualize and understand ideas more clearly.

Models, Collections, and Museums. The resources of models, collections, and museums may be used for instructional purposes. Models and collections may belong to one of the parents, one of the children, or someone in the community. A file of such resources, identifying possible uses and values, can be most helpful. Expensive and rare collections which may be easily broken or damaged should not be brought to the nursery school or kindergarten. Museums, especially those for children, will often plan a special exhibit. Others have collections which may be borrowed by the teacher for use at school. For example, one Junior Museum has "Treasure Chests" for loan to schools and some are appropriate for the young child. The chests include pictures, books, filmstrips, and objects related to a specific topic.

Films, Slides, Filmstrips, and Television Programs. Films, slides, filmstrips, and television programs can contribute to children's understandings when used for specific purposes. In using them, the teacher will find the following suggestions helpful: Always preview films, slides, and filmstrips and listen to recordings before using them with children. Judge their value and appropriateness in terms of length, difficulty, and number of concepts presented, vocabulary used, voice of the narrator, and relation to the teacher's purpose. Slides and filmstrips make questions and comments possible at the time each picture is shown. To use a film which shows only one scene directly related to the purpose and which contains many other concepts may be confusing to the child. One slide or a flat picture might be a better choice for effective teaching.

Clarify with the children the purpose or the reason for viewing the film, slide, or filmstrip. Relate the visual material to the problem or question with which children are concerned. Use the visual materials more than once if possible. The second viewing often answers questions and clears up misunderstandings. Observe the behavior of the children, their attention, questions, and comments as indications of the value of the experience to them.

It is important that the teacher go with the child to books to "find out." The teacher may say, "I think I know where to find this." The teacher and child look at pictures together.

Bulletin Boards. "Typically used for display purposes," says Jefferson, "the bulletin board's seasonal pictures and flat objects 'cutely' arranged prove meaningless to young children."[6] The most effective use occurs when the bulletin board reflects current interests of the group and when children are engaged in the activity. Such boards are called *involvement bulletin boards.*[7] Jefferson suggests the following as appropriate uses for the bulletin board with young children.[8]

1. Preparation for and summary of field trips.
2. Learning about current events and happenings.
3. Helping children learn colors and distinguish shapes.
4. Special projects.

Resource Persons. Resource persons may be invited to talk with the children, to show pictures, materials or other items, or to share a skill, such as singing, playing a musical instrument, or cooking. Such persons may be the parents or family members of a child in the group, some person in the community, or another teacher. If the person is to talk with the children, the teacher needs to be sure that he or she can talk with them in a manner they can understand. Don't ask someone to come and talk about a general topic, such as "rocks." Before the visit, be sure your guest speaker understands the questions raised by the children and the length of time in which to talk.

Packaged Materials. Commercially prepared materials are now available in many areas, such as concept development, auditory and visual perception, and language. The *package,* however, is different from such materials. The package is a full program and the primary purpose is to create a curriculum along with the necessary accessories,[9] a system of instructional media and materials along with a plan for their use. Some plans are very flexible while others are quite restrictive.

The packages have usually been field tested before general distribution. If a teacher is considering the use of packaged materials, it may be well to examine the objectives and how these are to be accomplished; the background research; opportunities for active participation by the children, and creative use by the children and teacher; initial cost and cost of replacement of parts; nec-

[6]Ruth Jefferson, "Bulletin Boards for Young Children," *Involvement Bulletin Boards* (Washington, D.C.: ACEI, 1970), p. 60
[7]Ibid.
[8]Ibid., pp. 60–62.
[9]Carolyn Wakefield, *Evaluation of Packaged Materials for Young Children,* Unpublished Graduate Paper, University of Maryland, College Park, 1971.

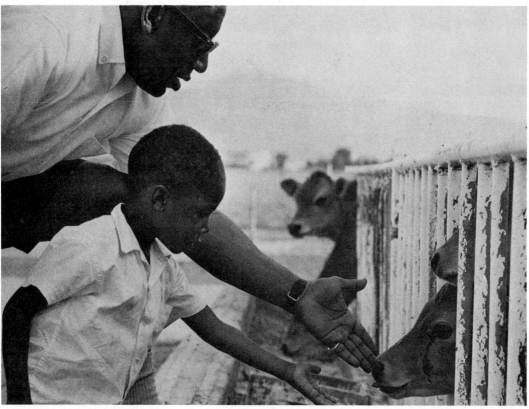

Figure 25   *(Courtesy of Head Start.)*

At the dairy the child sees the cows and watches as they are milked. A friendly adult encourages him to reach out and to talk about what he sees. Field trips have been effective in encouraging language development.

essity for teacher training; and the relationship to other courses and activities in the school or center.[10,11]

In summary the words of Murphy are appropriate.[12]

> Gimmicks for learning are a dime a dozen and there is a new bandwagon every year! . . . Not that all old methods are bad or that all new methods are good.

[10]Ibid., pp. 6–7.
[11]Detailed criteria for the selection of packaged instructional materials may be found in the following publication: *Selecting Educational Equipment and Materials for Home and School* (Washington, D.C.: ACEI, 1976), p. 29.
[12]Lois B. Murphy, "Multiple Factors in Learning in the Day Care Center," *Child. Educ.*, 45:6 (1969), p. 311.

Rather, we need to choose carefully and combine wisely the methods that will help children to become intelligent members of a democracy. To do this, we need to learn what each approach can offer and what are its hazards.

PLANNING THE DAY

Planning the day's schedule is important as it assists the teacher in developing an effective educational program. The day's schedule, while it may vary in length, is much the same in a school or a day-care center because each is based on what is good for children. There are conditions, however, which affect the teacher's plans. These include:[13]

The chronological age, developmental level, and experiential backgrounds of the children.
The length of the allotted school day.
Weather conditions
Bus schedules, car pools, transportation variations.
Space and physical facilities, location of bathroom and playground.
Class enrollment
The ratio of adult leadership to the number of children.

A good day begins with a friendly informal exchange of greetings followed by some activity that has concern for the health of the child. Some schools require that the parent wait until this has been given the necessary attention before leaving the child at school. The daily school period varies according to the situation and purpose. The length of the day is not significant, provided there is proper balance between rest and play, with attention to indoor–outdoor play, and active and quiet activities. The general plan may vary from day to day; however, some orderly planning is important to the security of the child and the teacher. The schedule should not be so inflexible that special events and unexpected happenings cannot be a part of the program.

An example of a plan that includes blocks of time follows:

1. Arrival. (Approximately 15 minutes.)
2. A period in which the children decide what they want to do and move freely from one activity to another. (For many children, toileting should be the first activity; this is especially true for the very young child. Others may need food.) The teacher plans and prepares for this period in advance. Many and varied activities and materials are used. Block building, painting at the easel, dramatic play, drawing with large crayons and chalk, looking at books on library table, working with clay, and many other indoor or outdoor activities are planned for each day and varied from day to day. (Approximately 60 minutes.)

[13]*A Guide: Early Childhood Education in Florida Schools*, Bull. 76 (Tallahassee: Florida State Department of Education, 1969), p. 41.

3. A period for routines of toileting, eating, and resting or relaxing. The rest period may be a story hour or there may be quiet music. Some children may go to sleep during this period. Freedom from glare and bright lights is important. The teacher is alert to notice that the lights appear different at her eye level and she checks light in terms of the child's eye level. The teacher should remain quiet and as a rule seated during this period. After relaxing, the child may get up quietly and prepare for the next activity. Rest should be pleasant and happy and not regarded as punishment. (Approximately 20 minutes.)

4. A period of total group activity that may involve singing, experimenting with rhythm instruments, listening to records or a story (if not used in 2), or dramatization of a story read. (Approximately 15 minutes.)

5. Outdoor play (if not in first period and weather permits). Activities with large-muscle equipment, wheel toys, construction, balls, and ropes. All of the work-play periods are closely supervised and the activities are guided by the teacher. (Approximately 60 minutes.)

6. Evaluating and planning for the next day. Through these activities the teacher receives suggestions for the next steps, and the children leave with a feeling of accomplishment and anticipation for returning the next day, which holds new challenges for them. They get ready to go home. (Approximately 20 minutes.)

7. Dismissal.

Some teachers find it desirable to develop a form to be used in planning and recording the activities for the day and for the week. Whatever the form used,

PLANNING FORM

When? Date and Time	What? Activity-Purpose	Where? Location(s)	How? Methods- Techniques	What? Materials Equipment	Who? Is Responsible	For Future Use*
Monday-9-6-79 9:00-9:15	Arrival of children — Each child: (1) is greeted in a pleasant manner and helped to feel "wanted".	Gate	Greets child and parent (or adult). Makes informal health check Comments on something child is wearing. Asks Sue about new baby brother		Teacher	Call Mrs. Narvo. Tell her Paul used tools today. Get caps for conductors on block train. Puzzles 1 and 5 have pieces missing.
	(2) puts away wrap. (3) finds and begins an activity.	Inside – near classroom door	Greets each child. Remind child to remove and hang up wrap. Talks with child about possible activity.	Blocks Puzzles Clay Easel Paint	Aide	Cheryl painted today-first time. *Be sure to include these notes in planning for tomorrow.

Adapted from ACTIVITY PLANNING FORM distributed by Head Start Regional Training Officer, Nancy Goldsmith, University of Maryland, College Park, Md. (Mimeographed).

it should allow space for specific notes to serve as reminders as the day develops and to record points to remember in future planning. The example on page 217 was developed for use in planning, with all persons involved in the daily activities, including the teacher, parents, and aides. Plans for *arrival* are given here. Plans may be developed for each activity or for part of the day.

Teachers in centers that operate either a morning session or an afternoon session, or both, find that they can adapt this schedule to suit the local situation. In schools that, operate on a full day, the schedule will need to be adapted to include a 30- to 45-minute lunch period at school. This period will be followed by an afternoon session that includes a nap period of approximately 1½ hours and a period of outdoor play of approximately the same length.

Two examples of a suggested daily schedule and plan follow. One schedule, for a center that operates all day, can be adjusted for sessions of varying lengths (note suggested dismissal times) and may be adapted and used in daycare centers, Head Start programs, kindergarten, or nursery groups. The second schedule is for a group of three-year-old children in a half-day program.

Table 10-1

Daily Schedule

8:30–9:00	Children enter center. Informal health check. Free play with materials such as puzzles, table toys, crayons, blocks. Outdoor play if weather permits. This is a good time to give special attention to individual children.
9:00–9:15	Clean up. Put materials in order for later morning work time. (Some materials might be left so that play can resume after breakfast or juice time.) Each day a few children with one adult help set up for breakfast or juice.
9:15–9:30	Breakfast or juice and crackers. Clean up.
9:30–9:45	Short discussion of day's plans, what was done the previous day, or other topics of interest to children. Include some music and physical activities.
9:45–10:30 indoors and/or outdoors	Work time. Housekeeping and dramatic play, carpentry and woodworking, water play, table games and toys, sharing and caring for pets, blocks, art activities, such as finger painting, easel painting, wood, collage, crayons, clay, play dough.
10:30–10:50	Clean up. Adults work with children.
10:50–11:00	Bathroom. If center set-up permits, children go to bathroom on their own as the need arises. If children must go at a specific time with adult supervision, it is possible to go in small groups.
11:00–11:30	Outdoor activities. If adults are available, stagger coming inside so that not all children arrive indoors at one time.
11:30–12:00	Clean up and getting ready for lunch. Quiet activity—story or rest. Getting ready for dismissal for those leaving before lunch.

Table 10-1 (Continued)

12:00–12:45	Lunch. If possible, children should be able to leave table when they are finished. They may participate in a quiet activity until the bus or car arrives or begin rest time if the program continues into the afternoon.
12:45–1:00	Getting ready for dismissal for those leaving at this point. Getting hats, coats, and art work. Listening to story or records.
12:45–2:00	Rest time. Children should *not have* to go to sleep. They should rest on mats or cots quietly. If possible, they should rest in small groups or the room should be divided so that there are just a few children in each area. Provision should be made both for those children who wake up early and for those who sleep longer. An adult can take those waking early outside or to another area for quiet activities. Another adult should stay with the sleepers.
2:00–2:15	Afternoon snack.
2:15–2:45	This time can be used in a very flexible way. Be sure to provide for individual needs. Some children need physical activity, others need quiet kinds of involvement. Outdoor time if weather permits: Activities such as water play, hiking, digging, science activities.
For indoors:	Table activities, manipulative materials, science activities, music, rhythms, stories, filmstrips, movies.
2:45–3:00	Dismissal for those leaving at this point. Some changes will be necessary if there is more than one class per center. Plans need to be made for the staggered use of the bathroom and playground so that facilities are used by only one class at a time.

Adapted from Sample Schedule distributed by the Head Start Regional Training Officer, Nancy Goldsmith, University of Maryland, College Park, 1970 (mimeogr.).

Alternate Afternoon Plan For Children Remaining at the Center Until 5:30 or 6:00 P.M.

2:00–2:30	Toileting, dressing, looking at books, playing with puzzles until all resters are awake.
2:30–2:50	Afternoon snack, table conversation, clean up.
2:50–3:20	Music, rhythms, singing, playing instruments, dancing, listening to records.
3:20	Outdoor play or special activity such as cooking, digging, and planting gardens, experimentation with science aspects of the environment.
4:20	Story, filmstrips, movies, slides. Quiet games, review of the day, plans for next day.
5:00	Dismissal for some.
5:15	Light evening snack. Quiet games, songs, individual time with the teacher until picked up to go home.

Half-Day (Three-year-old children)	
9:00–9:45	Dramatic play, blockbuilding, easel painting, science (feeding fish, turtle, etc.), puppets, stories, singing.
9:45–10:00	Clean up, handwashing, toileting.
10:00–10:15	Snack or juice.
10:15–10:40	Rest on mats.
10:40–11:00	Put away mats, story, singing, rhythms.
11:00–12:00	Outside play, short trips.

From *A Guide: Early Childhood Education in Florida Schools*, Bull. 76 (Tallahassee: Florida State Department of Education, 1969), pp. 45 and 44, respectively.

EVALUATING DAILY PLANNING

The teacher uses the following questions to check activities and to determine how effective the plans were as developed and used with the children:

	Yes	No	Comments
1. Was there a balance of activities as to type and place? Were these activities planned in terms of weather, space, length of session, and maturity of each member in the group?	—	—	
2. Was provision made for each child to have time of his own to do as he chose? Were the periods kept short where the child was expected to sit in one place?	—	—	
3. Was there a balance between large group, small group, and individual work-play?	—	—	
4. Were there new materials, new activities, and new situations for learning provided for each child according to his interest and growth pattern? Were these paced to his need?	—	—	
5. Was enough of the familiar included in the day in terms of routine, activity, and learnings to give the child security?	—	—	
6. Did the children have freedom to create, to explore, to experiment? If so, what happened—how did each child use this time?	—	—	

	Yes	No	Comments
7. Were the activities and experiences goal-centered and so planned that the attitudes and feelings, the skills and information were satisfactorily developed? Were the desired results obtained or were the activities a form of busy work?	—	—	_____
8. Was time provided for necessary routines so that no child became tense or frustrated?	—	—	_____
9. Was special consideration given to planning for certain children with special needs?	—	—	_____

A plan for the next day should include an evaluation of the day's work in terms of the activities of each child. The teacher may list needs which have been observed in the space for "comments" (see above chart).

PLANNING FOR THE CHILD'S FIRST DAY

As a child leaves home and enters an organized group for the first time, whether it be a first experience of this nature or entry into a new school group, the teacher is concerned as to what will be expected of the child in the daily program. He or she considers what can be done to assist the child in making the transition with security, yet with anticipation, curiosity, and challenge from the unknown, the untried, the inexperienced.

Most schools find it better to induct the children on a staggered basis; that is, some on Monday and Wednesday, others on Tuesday and Thursday, and all on Friday. Other schools take two weeks to induct all the children. In one kindergarten the following schedule was used:

Monday	—Group 1 (12 children)	9:00–11:00 A.M.
Tuesday	—Group 2 (13 children)	9:00–11:00 A.M.
Wednesday	—Group 1	8:30–12:00 noon
Thursday	—Group 2	8:30–12:00 noon
Friday	—Total Group	8:30–12:30 P.M.

Children need to be a part of a group, but what happens to them as they enter the group for the first time has significance for their sense of belongingness. It is the responsibility of the teacher to plan for this induction into the group so that the child comes to feel a part of a happy working situation. Children can learn this only if they experience it to be true.

Even though the daily planning is flexible throughout the year, the first day of the school (and also the first day for the child who enters later) demands even greater flexibility in planning. It is important that this day be a happy one for the child, the parent, and the teacher so that they may continue to "live and learn together" happily. On the first day, the regular routine can be observed, but much more time and individualized attention will need to be given in greeting the children and parents, for helping children to place their wraps and possessions in lockers, and for gaining security in the setting. Even though each child and parent have visited the school previously, this time and attention are important on the first day. Name tags for children, parents, and teacher help to give security and assist the teacher in getting acquainted. An inspection tour of the room will orient and interest the child. Outdoor orientation will include instruction and guidance for the children in use of equipment.

After routines of toileting and handwashing, the children have a brief period of outdoor play. The bathroom routines will need guidance as to place and procedure. However, no child should be coerced to use the bathroom. Children will develop proper habits as they gain security in the new environment. The same is true of outdoor play. It may be that the children will feel more secure in the room. If so, all should remain uless there are two people to supervise, one indoors and the other outside.

Following the getting-acquainted period for each child, the children will need time to look, to handle, and to explore interesting materials and equipment. Provision should be made for centers of interest that will encourage manipulating, creating, building, exploring, and experimenting. Some will begin free play, others will move from activity to activity. This freedom of movement is important for release of tension and gaining security. After most of the children are actively interested in some center, the teacher will call them together by striking a gong, triangle, or a note on a piano, or singing a quiet call to come and sit down together. This then becomes a period for talking, sharing, listening, finger plays, singing, or storytelling. As a rule, midmorning lunch and rest are omitted the first day as the children are too excited to make these events practical. Therefore, the quiet period needs to be a time for relaxation.

The dismissal should be a happy time with discussion of plans for tomorrow, such as feeding the fish, building a train, or riding a tricycle. Care should be taken that each child leaves with a parent or with the person designated in writing by the parent. Kindergarten children who live in the immediate vicinity can go home on their own, provided the school is in an uncongested traffic area and parents have given their permission.

By allowing the child's day to gradually be increased in length, time is granted for the young boy or girl to become adjusted to the new environment and to the change in the pattern of living which results from attending school.

WORKING POLICIES AND PLANS

Much of the planning for the year takes place before the school opens. While the teacher may not have been involved in some of the planning, it is important to become familiar with the policies and plans of the center. Current practice usually provides time for continuous planning throughout the year. Plans for the physical facilities, the necessary equipment, and basic supplies are related to the broader plans involving policies related to the number and type of children to be accepted. Policies will need to be developed and plans made regarding the following:

1. Registration—procedures, amount, and plan for payment of fees, scholarships, insurance and medical costs, and refund, if necessary, of fees paid.
2. Composition of Group—balance between boys and girls, limiting size of group to facilities and personnel, age range of group as related to staff and space.
3. Operation—the school day (hours and days), vacations, holidays, opening and closing dates, induction of children, provision for children who arrive early and for those who leave later, getting acquainted with children before entering school, lunch (if provided), and midmorning snack. The staggered entrance schedule can be a factor in helping the child make a satisfactory adjustment to school; this plan provides for the teacher to have a smaller number of children to orient to the new situation and, more important, the child has a smaller group to which he or she must adjust. Parent contacts and visits help the child and the teacher as well as the parents to plan for the child's adjustment in the school situation.
4. Health and Safety—health examination and inoculations before entering school, securing child's health history, daily health inspection and teacher observation of health, provision for isolation or transportation home if needed, and information relative to contacting parents and preferred physician if needed (see pp. 324–325).
5. Transportation of Pupils—how provided, cost, regulations, provision for safe drivers, insurance coverage, and plans for emergencies. (See p. 325.)
6. Working with Parents—initial interview, parents' stay at school during orientation and induction, mutual agreements and acceptance of responsibility between parents and teachers, reports to be made to and from school, scheduled parent conferences and informal contacts, parent observation and participaton, follow-up at home of school activities, contact and work with parents who cannot or do not visit school, and provision for parent meetings and study groups.
7. Cooperation—with other schools in community, with community agencies, and institutions; coordination of school calendar and records with community calendar; provision for satisfactory transfer or transition to another school.
8. Interpreting the School Program—to parents, to general public, to other school groups.

9. Staff Responsibilities—working hours, provision for health examination and insurance, sick leave, substitutes.
10. Consultant Service—for child problems, for staff problems, for professional growth of staff.

SUMMARY

Good planning provides opportunities for desirable learning experiences that are educationally significant. It provides for continuity and balance day by day, but it also provides for relating the experiences so that the teaching objectives, the ideas, the teaching procedures or activities, the materials and resources are so organized that the insight and understanding of the child is continually deepened and broadened. For some children, the depth and breadth may be less deep and narrow, for others it will be deep and broad, and for others, deeper and broader. To plan and to guide the learning opportunities so that this will occur is the challenge of teaching.

Suggested Activities

1. Observe groups of three-, four-, and five-year-olds. How do their interests and maturity levels differ? What are the implications of these differences for planning for different age groups?
2. Observe the same groups and identify differing interests and maturity levels among the children of the same age groups. What does this imply to the teacher in terms of planning?
3. Plan a day's tentative activities for three-, four-, and five-year-olds. Include goals. List materials needed, and teacher preparation required.
4. Indicate how the plan might be modified for a full day program.
5. Assess achievement of at least two children using Achievement Checklist on pp. 199–202. Make plans for each child in terms of the data secured.
6. Select one teaching strategy. Plan for and use it with a group of three-, four-, or five-year-olds. Evaluate the effectiveness of your teaching. Make follow-up plans.
7. Examine a daily schedule in a center for young children. Evaluate the schedule in terms of the criteria listed on pp. 218–221. Are there differences? What might be possible reasons for the differences?
8. View the films *Organizing Free Play* and *Organizing the School Day.* Modern Talking Picture, 2323 New Hyde Park Rd., New Hyde Park, N.Y. 11040. (Available in Spanish.)
9. View the film *Setting the Stage for Learning.* Churchill Films, 622 North Robertson Blvd., Los Angeles, Calif. 90069. Discuss.

Related Readings

Almy, Millie. *The Early Childhood Educator at Work.* New York: McGraw-Hill Book Co., 1975, pp. 55–77; 109–142.

Association for Childhood Education International. *Migrant Children: Their Education.* Washington, D.C.: ACEI, 1971.

Berk, Laura E. "How Well Do Classroom Practices Reflect Teacher's Goals?" *Young Children, 32*:1 (1976), pp. 64–81.

Cannon, Gwendolyn M. "Kindergarten Class Size—A Study," *Child. Educ., 42*:1 (1966), pp. 9–13.

Elliott, B., and Mary Jo Woodfin. "Evaluating and Recording Children's Activities: Diagnosing Educational Need," *Learning Centers—Children on Their Own.* Washington, D.C.: ACEI, 1970.

Fennel, Margaret, and Elizabeth Kelly. "Children on Their Own—Centers and Stations for Learning," *Learning Centers—Children on Their Own.* Washington, D. C.: ACEI, 1970.

Frazier, A. *Adventuring, Mastering, Associating: New Strategies for Teaching Children.* Washington, D.C.: ASCD, 1976.

Galen, Harlene. "Cooking in the Curricula," *Young Children, 32*:2 (1977), pp. 59–69.

Gambrell, Linda B., and R. M. Wilson. *Focusing on the Strengths of Children.* Belmont, Calif.: Fearon Publishers, 1973.

Goff, Regina. "Mind-Content and School Readiness with Special Reference to Low-Income Children," *Child. Educ., 51*:5 (1975), pp. 290–294.

Katz, Lillian G. "Children and Teachers in Two Types of Head Start Classes," *Young Children, 24*:6 (1969), pp. 342–349.

———. "What Is Basic for Young Children?" *Child. Educ. 54*:1 (1977), pp. 16–19.

Keliher, Alice V. "Effective Learning and Teacher-Pupil Ratio," *Child. Educ., 43*:1 (1966), pp. 3–6.

Lewis, Anne. *Conference Time.* Arlington, Va.: National School Public Relations Association, 1970.

Lindberg, Lucile, and Rita Swedlow. *Early Childhood Education: A Guide for Observation and Participation.* Boston: Allyn and Bacon, 1976, pp. 243–249.

Linder, R. "Learning to Identify Children's Interests," *Child. Educ., 52*:6 (1976), pp. 296–299.

Madden, P. "Experiencing Joy in Teaching," *Child. Educ., 54*:1 (1977), pp. 12–15.

Mcaffee, Oralie, Evelyn W. Haines, and Barbara B. Young. *Cooking and Eating with Children—A Way to Learn.* Washington, D.C.: ACEI, 1974.

Mendelson, Anna. "Picture That," *Early Years, 2*:5 (1972), pp. 20–23.

Moore, Shirley. "Research in Review: The Effects of Head Start Programs with Different Curricula and Teaching Strategies," *Young Children, 32*:6 (1977), pp. 54–61.

Mugge, Dorothy J. "Taking the Routine Out of Routines," *Young Children, 31*:3 (1976), pp. 209–217.

Raskin, L. M., W. J. Taylor, and Florence G. Kerckhoff. "The Teacher as Observer for Assessment: A Guideline," *Young Children, 30*:5 (1975), pp. 339–344.

Strattner, Mary, J. "Deaf and Hearing Children Learn Together—an Australian Model," *Young Children, 29*:4 (1974), pp. 231–234.

Zeitlin, Shirley. *Kindergarten Screening—Early Identification of Potential High-Risk Learners.* Springfield, Ill.: Charles C Thomas, 1976.

chapter 11

The language arts

The language arts are a part of daily living and are functional in every activity and experience. Speaking, listening, reading, and writing are interrelated and the skills are developed as the child participates in many varied activities throughout the day—at home as well as at school. Crosby says,

> Research in human growth and development and in learning reveals that for most physically and emotionally normal human beings, learning to communicate beyond the stage of crying or random babbling involves learning to listen, to speak, and to write, in the order listed. Listening and speaking serve as a base for reading and writing and, if rooted in experience, furnish a rich background of meaning for written and printed symbols.[1]

[1] Muriel Crosby, "Identifying Oral Language Relationships," *Children and Oral Language* (Washington, D.C.: ASCD, 1964), p. 9.

Each aspect of the language arts, however, is discussed separately in this chapter in order to identify the trends, research, and development of skills in each area. The activities involving children are included to illustrate the contribution of the activity to the development of the skills. Questions that may arise as the teacher analyzes the value of the activity are identified and discussed.

SPEAKING · LANGUAGE DEVELOPMENT

A great deal of money has been spent to support research and federal programs for children from low-income families. The language used by these children has received much attention, since language skills are considered a prerequisite for school success. Today this focus on language has been broadened to include children of minorities and culturally different groups. From infancy the child hears language almost continuously, but the language that is learned and applied is that used in the speech of persons who are significant in the child's world.[2]

Before they go to school, children have much practice with spoken language. Estimates of the number of words spoken per day by the child range from 7,500 at three years to 10,500 at five.[3] The child has thus developed much of the skill in speaking before he or she receives any formal instruction. Noel states that by the time the child arrives at school age, he or she has already learned to speak with whatever sound system, grammar, and vocabulary heard most often at home or in the neighborhood.[4] Other studies by Strickland[5] confirm the fact that the language patterns of children are largely set by the time they enter school.

Young children bring their language to school from a variety of backgrounds. How the teacher or caregiver accepts and treats the child's initial language influences the child's concept of self and family, and the child's progress in school.

The pace at which children acquire language varies greatly, but considerable evidence indicates that the pattern of development is similar for all.[6]

[2] Courtney B. Cazden, *Child Language and Education* (New York: Holt, Rinehart, and Winston, 1972), pp. 2–3.

[3] Dora V. Smith, "Growth in Language Power as Related to Child Development," *Teaching Language in the Elementary School* (Chicago: NSSE, 1944), 43rd Yearbook, Part II, pp. 52–97.

[4] Doris I. Noel, "A Comparative Study of the Relationship Between the Quality of a Child's Language Usage and the Quality and Types of Language Used in the Home," *J. Educ. Res., 47*:3 (1953), pp. 161–167.

[5] Ruth G. Strickland, *The Language of Elementary School Children: Its Relationship to the Language of Reading Textbooks and the Quality of Reading of Selected Children* (Bloomington: School of Education, Indiana University, 1962).

[6] L. G. Butler, "Language Acquisition of Young Children: Major Theories and Sequence," *Elementary English, 51*:8 (1974), pp. 1120–1123.

From the birth cry to mature language, verbal development follows a definite pattern. According to Lenneberg, "it is only under conditions of intellectual or environmental deprivation that this pattern varies."[7]

Children discover rules and how the language works and learn grammar gradually on their own. They use content words such as nouns, verbs, and adjectives before they use function words such as prepositions and conjunctions. While learning to form noun and verb endings at a certain period of their development children may say "foots" instead of feet and "goed" instead of went. These apparent errors should be seen as evidence that the child is beginning to understand the form of language. Correct usage of the exceptions to the rules will come later.[8] Nursery school children often substitute "-ed" for irregular forms of the past tense, for example, "growed" or "throwed."[9]

During the early years, children's language development reflects their mental processes, interests and relationships with the world. The use of the pronoun "I," which begins at about two years of age, reflects interest in one's self. As the child advances in age, there is an increase in the number of other pronouns used such as *he, we, you,* and *they,* and a trend toward more socialized speech in which children speak and respond to one another.

At about age five or six the language abilities have developed so that children can usually handle language situations in an almost adult manner.[10] However, as the five-year-old encounters new experiences in kindergarten and makes the necessary adjustments, pressures may be reflected in his or her speech. The child may temporarily revert to patterns of speech practiced at an earlier age.

By the age of three a child's articulation improves and becomes fairly clear. There is a sequence in the child's ability to pronounce the consonant sounds, and an understanding of this may be of help to parents and teachers. Ages at which 75 percent of the subjects correctly produced specific consonant sounds in the Templin study are listed.[11]

3 years: m, n, ng, p, f, h, w
3.5 years: y
4 years: k, b, d, g, r
4.5 years: s, sh, ch
6 years: t, th, v, l
7 years: z, zh, j

[7] E. L. Robbins, "Language Development Research," *Interpreting Language Arts Research for the Teacher* (Washington, D.C.: ASCD, 1970), p. 5.
[8] Courtney B. Cazden (ed.), *Language in Early Childhood Education* (Washington, D.C.: NAEYC, 1972), p. 4.
[9] Dora V. Smith, "Developmental Language Patterns of Children," in *Effective Language Arts Practices in the Elementary School: Selected Readings,* edited by H. Newman (New York: John Wiley and Sons, 1972), p. 9.
[10] A. T. Jersild, *Child Psychology,* 6th ed. (Englewood Cliffs. N.J.: Prentice-Hall, 1968), pp. 424–425.

Figure 26
The telephone conversation involves
communication with language—listening to others and expressing one's own
ideas.

Growth in vocabulary

Growth in the vocabulary of the young child has been studied by a number of
investigators. The reports are of interest in noting the changes that have occurred.

One of the early vocabulary studies was done by Madorah Smith in 1926.
Her estimates of the size of the vocabulary of young children have been
widely used. She found the vocabulary to consist of 896 words at three years,
1,540 at four, 2,072 at five, and 2,562 at six.[12] In the 1950s Loban found that at

---

[11] Mildred C. Templin, *Certain Language Skills in Children*, Institute Child Welf. Monogr. Series XXVI (Minneapolis: University of Minnesota Press, 1957), p. 53.
[12] Madorah E. Smith, "An Investigation of the Development of the Sentence and the Extent of
Vocabulary in Young Children," *University Iowa Studies Child Welf.*, 3:5 (1926), p. 54.

kindergarten level, subjects varied in vocabulary from 180 to about 5,000 words with 3,000 words as the average.[13] Since Smith's study, changes may have occurred in the speech of young children as a result of increased TV viewing, number of experiences, and changes in child-rearing practices.

An extensive study of language skills in children was completed by Mildred Templin in 1957. In comparing her work with earlier studies, she reports, "In the areas of articulation and vocabulary, one is impressed with the stability of results over a period of time among studies using comparable methods, but carried on with different samples and by different investigators. . . . Differences occur, however, in the increased loquacity of children in child–adult situations and in a tendency for children of the same age to use more mature language than they did twenty-five years ago."[14] More mature speech is interpreted as the use of fewer one-word remarks and simple and incomplete sentences and the use of more complex sentences and adverbial clauses.

More recently, however, concern for the size of the child's vocabulary has not been important. Studies seem to focus on how the child acquires and uses language, and on the language of minority and culturally different children.

Factors that influence language development

Robbins reports many studies supporting the notion that there are influences in the child's environment that interfere with language development. Research done by Hess and Shipman, Jensen, May, Olem, and Reissman indicates "a direct relationship between the quality of the child's environmental circumstances and his language facility."[15]

It has been found that the speech patterns of the child from the less-favored economic or culturally different environment are different from and often conflict with the language used in the school. Crosby says, "the child's natural language, often dynamic, descriptive and forceful is frequently not the language of acceptability in the school. Aware of the rejection of his natural language, the child is nevertheless unskilled and inexperienced in using the standard, informal English of the school."[16]

Recent studies have compared the language abilities of children from upper and lower socioeconomic levels on elements other than those found in standard English. Robbins says, "Their findings support the view that there are no significant differences between the language abilities of low and high socioeconomic children when nonstandard language criteria are used."[17] The prob-

---

[13] W. Loban, *The Language of Elementary School Children* (Champaign, Ill.: NCTE, 1963), p. 37.
[14] Templin, op. cit., p. 150.
[15] Robbins, op. cit., p. 11.
[16] Crosby, op. cit., p. 5.
[17] Robbins, op. cit., p. 11.

lem, then, becomes one of *different* language usage, and is treated in much the same manner as teaching another language to a young child.

Intervention programs have been developed to counteract the influence of the environment on the child's language development. Butler reports that these programs range from those in which children are encouraged to express themselves to those in which they are "bombarded with language."[18] The program for Mexican-American children at the University of Arizona is one in which opportunities for wide experiences, language lessons, and teacher models are all included. Children engage in activities—field trips, cooking, art, construction—which stimulate conversation. Modeling of language is considered important and teachers use complex sentences when appropriate to lift the child's language. Lessons help the children understand the position of words in language learning.[19]

The quality and type of the teacher's interaction with the child are very important. Katz, after studying children and teachers in two types of Head Start classes, concluded that perhaps teacher style was a more important factor than the method. She observed that the teachers in this study did not follow through on the specified teacher behavior. They tended to neglect the praise and supportive aspects of their role and the behaviors that seemed to interfere with the learning of children were increased.[20]

The skill with which children use oral language will vary from child to child. Certain environmental factors as well as the child's mental and physical abilities have an influence on language development. Some of these factors are discussed here.

Family. The child's family is an important consideration. An only child or a singleton seems to have the advantage, probably because of the greater opportunity for association with adults. The number of children in the family affects the growth of vocabulary. At five and one-half years of age, the singleton uses 94 words, the twin 89 words, and the only child 104 words in 50 remarks.[21]

Considerable evidence in the literature cited earlier tends to indicate that there exists a marked relationship between socioeconomic status of family and the child's linguistic development. Children from more favored environments use more words meaningfully at earlier ages. In a more recent study, Templin found consistent differences in the language performance of chil-

[18] Annie L. Butler, *Current Research in Early Childhood Education: A Compilation and Analysis for Program Planners* (Washington, D.C.: EKNE, 1970), p. 135.
[19] Ibid., pp. 133–134.
[20] Ibid., p. 39.
[21] Edith A. Davis, *The Development of Linguistic Skill in Twins, Singletons with Siblings, and Only Children from Age Five to Ten Years,* Institute Child Welf. Monogr. Series 14 (Minneapolis: University of Minnesota Press, 1937), p. 114.

Figure 27

Parental attitudes toward children and habits of family
life are significant factors for language development.
This family enjoys a snack together. Jonathan and
Mother share some time together.

dren from upper and lower socioeconomic levels. Differences in the linguistic
environment provided by homes of the two levels were recognized.[22]

If children hear very little speech or if the speech of the significant persons
in their lives is limited and restricted, they are likely to have a language deficit when compared with others from a more favorable environment. A language deficit does not necessarily mean that the child is limited in the ability
to learn language. The deficit may indicate the inadequacy of the environment in which the learning took place.[23]

Shaw, one of the children described earlier, has these benefits; Roger,
while coming from a wealthy home, lacks family contacts and experience, as
do Jennie and Jan. The research of Milner regarding patterns of parent–child
interaction seems important here.[24] Striking differences were found in the patterns of family life between first-grade children scoring high and low on language tests. Families of "high scorers" usually had breakfast together, en-

[22] Templin, op. cit., p. 147.

[23] R. D. Hess and Doreen J. Croft, *Teachers of Young Children* (Boston: Houghton Mifflin, 1972),
p. 178.

[24] Esther Milner, "A Study of the Relationships Between Reading Readiness in Grade One
School Children and Patterns of Parent–Child Interaction," *Child Develop.*, 22:2 (1951), pp. 95–
112.

gaged in conversation with the children at mealtime and before school. These children also received more overt affection from significant adults in the home. Milner's study points up the fact that parental attitudes toward children and habits of family life are the really significant factors for language development and they may vary with socioeconomic status.

In an effort to describe how mothers influence language development, Hess and Shipman studied parent teaching styles and found social class differences.[25] Lower-class mothers who had the lowest IQ's and who were poorly educated were the least effective in teaching their children.

What can the school do for Gloria, Roger, and Jennie, who lack the intimate parent–child interaction growing out of shared experiences? Certainly the school cannot and should not replace the home. The teacher can, however, provide opportunities for these children to talk with her, and for her to show an interest in their conversation. The teacher must help each child feel important as an individual and that he or she can make a contribution to the group. The task includes helping children to appreciate the speech of others, and providing opportunities to handle materials, to talk about them, to listen to the comments of other children, to ask questions, and to express feelings—all a part of learning.

Another Language—Bilingualism.   Americans are becoming increasingly aware of the importance of languages in communication and understanding between nations in the world today. Recognition of these facts has resulted in a heightened interest in teaching foreign languages to young children. To achieve this end an English-speaking child is given instruction in a foreign language for short periods of time spaced throughout the school week.

As concern for multicultural education has increased, new appreciation has been given to the language of minority groups in the United States. Recent concern has been focused on the child who comes to school from a home in which the language spoken is one other than English. Often these children are Mexican Americans, Puerto Ricans, or American Indians.[26] More recently many of them are Vietnamese. Children from homes in which nonstandard English is spoken may face problems similar to the non-English-speaking child. A number of language-related factors have been identified as reasons for the school difficulties experienced by these children. The young child who does not speak English is unable to understand the language of the teacher or to express his or her feelings in a strange language. The child's reaction may be one of frustration, fear, aggression, or a feeling of inferiority.

[25] R. Hess and Virginia Shipman, "Parents as Teachers," in *Piaget's Theory Applied to an Early Childhood Curriculum,* edited by Celia S. Lavatelli (Boston: American Science and Engineering, Inc., 1970), pp. 59–61.
[26] Judith Socolov, General Editor, *Early Childhood Education Project* (New York: The Modern Language Association of America, 1971), p. 1.

The child, eager to learn, may find it necessary to stop and learn English words for everything that has been taught in another language.[27]

The non-English-speaking child has often been forced to learn the second language immediately upon entering school before the first language is well established. When the second language is introduced before the child has developed adequate cognitive skills in the native language, both the native and second language usually develop in limited ways and may lead to intellectual and academic retardation.[28] The time, then, at which the second language is introduced is very important.

Other research suggests that the way in which the two languages have been learned helps determine whether bilingualism becomes a handicap and, if so, the extent of the handicap. The socioeconomic and cultural background of the non-English-speaking child is just as important as it is for the English-speaking child.[29]

In summary, when the second language is introduced, how it is introduced and to whom it is introduced are factors that affect the speech of the non-English-speaking child.

Suggestions for teaching an English-speaking child a second language are also applicable to teaching the non-English-speaking child English, just as they are to teaching the child who needs help in learning standard English.

There are those who recommend patterned drill as the most effective procedure for helping bilingual children. Others favor the "natural" method and hold that young children can acquire the structure of the language with sufficient exposure to a rich vocabulary and interactions with adults that include a complex syntactical model. Lavatelli recommends that a model for language training should incorporate the following features.[30]

1. Provision should be made for some language training in small group sessions in order to facilitate two-way communication between teacher and child.
2. The speech of the teacher should serve as a model in the sessions. Children should be encouraged to use the sentence structures which she is modeling.
3. The process of modeling should be carried on in a "natural conversational manner" during free play activities as well as in small group sessions.
4. The teacher should keep in mind the child's level of linguistic development as well as "the possible contribution of the structure to logical thinking."
5. The environment should be warm, friendly, and supportive.

Penfield recommends "the mother's method," the direct method of teaching language which is employed in the home. There, language for the child is

---

[27] Ibid., pp. 164–165.
[28] Ibid., p. 171.
[29] Ibid., p. 173.
[30] Celia S. Lavatelli, *Piaget's Theory Applied to an Early Childhood Curriculum* (Boston: American Science and Engineering, Inc., 1970), pp. 77–78.

only a means to an end, not an end in itself. "When he learns about words he is learning about life, learning to get what he wants, learning to share his own exciting ideas with others, learning to understand wonderful fairy tales and exciting facts about trains and trucks and animals and dolls."[31]

According to this point of view, then, there should be no question of teaching the child of this age to read or write in the foreign language. The oral–aural method of instruction is encouraged. Children first learn a foreign language orally as they do their own language.[32]

Some suggestions for teaching a foreign language to young children include the following:

1. The language experiences should be those which can be used in daily living. Translate as much as possible of the new language into action. Greetings, dramatizations, songs, nursery rhymes, role playing, and games may all be used effectively. The use of familiar experiences and everyday activities for games and dramatizations help to make them more meaningful. Avoid having children answer questions or recite in chorus since it is difficult to hear whether or not individual children are pronouncing words correctly.
2. Keep vocabulary of second language in relation to the spoken English of the child. A word should not be introduced in the second language until it is first a part of the child's vocabulary.
3. Create visual impressions of how the person who speaks another language acts or behaves. Suggestions include the following:
   a. Invite a native speaker to visit class.
   b. Visit a home or center where the language is spoken natively.
   c. Use films.
4. Create a "climate of sound" in which the child hears words of the second language spoken correctly. It is important that children use their learnings throughout the day.

Travel Experiences. The development of concepts to which symbols of communication can be attached is important in the language development of young children. For them, this development of concepts is largely one of direct, personal experience. Bean reported that travel and events which broaden the child's experiences are accompanied or followed by increases in vocabulary.[33] While the kindergarten teacher cannot force the growth of language, he or she can provide experiences and events through which the children can increase their vocabularies. The trips around the neighborhood, to the train, to the fire station, and to the farm; picture books for the child and

---

[31] W. Penfield and L. Roberts, *Speech and Brain-Mechanisms* (Princeton, N.J.: Princeton University Press, 1959), p. 254.

[32] O. E. Perez, *Spanish in Florida Elementary Schools* (Tallahassee: Florida State Department of Education, 1960), pp. i–iii.

[33] C. H. Bean, "An Unusual Opportunity to Investigate the Psychology of Language," *J. Genet. Psychol.*, 40:2 (1932), pp. 181–202.

story books to be read to him; films, filmstrips, and recordings can be provided. For example, referring to the children in Chapter 9, Shaw has frequent trips to the beach and mountains and hunts and fishes with his father. The twins, Karen and Kirsten, as well as Lisa and Gloria, have few trips in the community.

Olson and Larson report field trips as the most frequently used activity in an experimental curriculum for culturally different kindergarten children. "Trips were assumed to be valuable in eliciting linguistic responses from children; language output could not be expected without provision for input. The planning and evaluation experiences relating to field trips provided opportunities for the growth of language facility."[34]

Personal Factors. In addition to the environmental factors, there are personal factors which have an influence on the child's language development.

INTELLIGENCE. Differences in language development are closely related to the differences that exist in intellectual development. In the groups described on p. 190, there is the possibility of a wide variation in speech development. Shaw has been identified as a gifted child and Gloria as a superior one. These two seem to have the ability to learn from their environment and to communicate to others what they have learned.

It is important to remember the limitations regarding intellectual measurement. Growth in language depends upon other factors in addition to those discussed in this chapter. Children from different backgrounds may not have had the opportunities for developing their intellectual potential. According to Almy, these children may have had perceptual experiences but lacked verbal labels to apply to them.[35]

Studies have shown that intelligence tests may not accurately reveal the potential of the highly creative individual. Getzels and Jackson suggest that the term *giftedness* should be used to include other potentially creative groups besides the children of high IQ.[36]

SEX. In nearly all aspects of language development that have been studied, there seems to be a slight difference in favor of girls. Olson, in comparing the growth curves in language for boys and girls from the same family, found that, age for age, the girls regularly exceeded the boys. He further states that many

[34] J. L. Olson and R. G. Larson, "An Experimental Curriculum for Culturally Deprived Kindergarten Children," *Educ. Leadership*, 22:7 (1965), pp. 557.

[35] Millie Almy, "New Views on Intellectual Development in Early Childhood Education," *Intellectual Development: Another Look* (Washington, D.C.: ASCD, 1964), p. 21.

[36] J. W. Getzels and P. W. Jackson, "Giftedness and Creativity," *Newsletter* (Chicago: University of Chicago, November 1960), pp. 5–6.

of the differences may be due to maturity rather than sex.[37] Boys at a given age attain achievements and behavior at about the same rate as somewhat younger girls. Young found sex differences in language development more marked among children of lower socioeconomic levels than among those from superior homes.[38] Templin found differences between the sexes less pronounced.[39] Many believe today that the differences are not due to sex or maturity but to environmental influences.

HEALTH. Loban found a low but positive correlation between health and language proficiency. He pointed out that the health measures which he used were crude and that the correlation might well be higher.[40]

Educational Factors. If educational influences can help make the child's association with language pleasant he or she will be more likely to have a positive attitude toward language.

EFFECTS OF SITUATION. It was found by Van Alstyne that over half the time preschool children tended not to talk to other children while using certain play materials.[41] Some materials seemed to be more conducive to conversation than others. Play with dolls, blocks, crayons, and clay was accompanied by conversation for a high percentage of the time; painting, using scissors, and looking at books were low in conversation value. McCarthy in reporting this study comments:[42]

> It is interesting, in view of the sex differences previously shown, that the doll-corner activities and dishes, which are typical girl activities, were among the highest in conversation value. It might be concluded that certain differences in language are due to the situation, but it must also be remembered that certain situations may attract children of different levels of language development.

More recently, Crowe recorded the conversation of kindergarten children in nine activities.[43] She found that housekeeping play and group discussion

---

[37] W. C. Olson, *Child Development,* 2nd ed. (Boston: D.C. Heath, 1959), p. 155.

[38] F. M. Young, "An Analysis of Certain Variables in a Developmental Study of Language," *Genet. Physchol. Monogr.,* 23:1 (1941), pp. 3–141.

[39] Templin, op. cit., p. 147.

[40] Loban, op. cit., p. 87.

[41] Dorothy Van Alstyne, *Play Behavior and Choice of Play Materials of Preschool Children* (Chicago: University of Chicago Press, 1932).

[42] Dorothea McCarthy, "Language Development in Children," *Manual of Child Psychology,* 2nd ed. (New York: John Wiley and Sons, 1954), p. 595.

[43] E. G. Crowe, "A Study of Kindergarten Activities for Language Development," C. B. Cazden, "The Neglected Situation in Child Language Research and Education," in *Language and Poverty,* edited by F. Williams (Chicago: Markham Publishing Co., 1970).

held the greatest potential for language use, in both the amount and maturity of speech. Block play, dancing, and woodworking held least. Crowe suggests that adult participation, a concrete topic of conversation, physical arrangements, and noise seem to influence speech.

The Language Program. Some of the characteristics of the spoken language of young children and the factors which influence it have been identified. With an awareness of these, the program can be planned to facilitate the language growth of children. Important elements include the teacher, the climate, and the goals.

Hess and Croft report that children seem to acquire vocabulary and pronunciation of words by imitation and repetition while the grammar seems to be

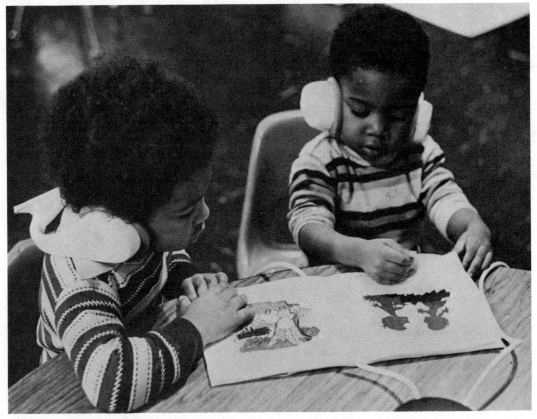

Figure 28
Using the earphones these children listen to the story while looking at the illustrations in the book.

acquired on their own as they learn to speak.[44] It is important, then, to provide opportunities for children to have much verbal interaction with one another and with adults on a one-to-one basis. Teachers can provide such opportunities as they elaborate and qualify their answers to children's questions, read aloud from a variety of materials, and make tapes, records, books, and pictures available. It is important, however, that the teacher provide time for the children to talk about what they hear and see.

THE TEACHER. It is important that the teacher take time to listen to the child. If preparations for the day have been made in advance, the teacher can be free to greet each child as he or she arrives. Here is an opportunity to practice the social courtesies of greeting, such as, "Good morning" or "Hello." The child, fresh from home, often has news to share. It can be fun for the child to talk to the teacher. It can be frustrating, too, trying to tell the teacher something very important while she is stirring paint, or cutting paper without even a glance in the child's direction, and making only a noncommittal, uninterested reply, such as "Yes" or "Oh." Perhaps the teacher is busy and doesn't have time at that moment to listen. If so, then she may say to the child, "I am busy, but I will talk with you as soon as I have finished." And she or he must be very sure to remember the promise and not keep the child waiting too long.

Speech instruction, according to Anderson, begins with the teacher's voice. The tone of voice, the manner of speaking, and the vocabulary she or he uses all have an influence on the quality of instruction.[45] A voice can invite conversation, or discourage it. A harsh, loud voice can irritate and embarrass while a soft, well-modulated voice can help one to be relaxed and comfortable.

The teacher's speech should set a good example in enunciation and pronunciation. It is easy to fall into habits of slovenly speech. Teachers should use the tape recorder and listen to their own speech.

THE CLIMATE. The atmosphere of the kindergarten, nursery school, or child development center reflects the attitude of the teacher. The atmosphere should be supportive, one in which a child is free to converse, to enjoy experiences, to use language, to make mistakes, and to correct them.

Lavatelli says that "the child should hear directed at him a wide variety of well formed utterances to which he must make a response."[46] She also suggests that for children from different backgrounds there should be some time during the day when a child can be part of a small group, under the guidance

[44] Hess and Croft, op. cit., pp. 182–184.
[45] P. S. Anderson, *Language Skills in Elementary Education*, 2nd ed. (New York: Macmillan Publishing Co., 1972), p. 83.
[46] Butler, op. cit., p. 133.

of the teacher, and have an opportunity to listen, to respond and be responded to.[47]

As the teacher works in a relaxed, happy school atmosphere, she or he keeps in mind certain objectives of the language program for children.

THE GOALS.   As the teacher works with children she or he will help each child to accomplish the following:[48]

1. Develop fluency and naturalness in expression. Opportunities for many experiences will introduce new words and provide the child with something to talk about. These, together with the stimulation of an understanding teacher, can help the child gain desired fluency and spontaneity and build a functional vocabulary.

2. Develop the ability to speak distinctly in a pleasant voice with good control both as to volume and tone—a voice free of baby talk and incomplete enunciation, not too high, too loud, or too soft. The teacher may give guidance by such comments as, "I'm sorry, I didn't hear what you said. Tell me again and speak just a little louder, please." Such guidance helps the child realize that "too soft" voices can't be understood, and the child is helped to feel adequate and secure enough to speak louder.

3. Form habits of correct usage. Constant criticism can interfere with the fluency and spontaneity of expression. Constructive helpfulness, gauged to the needs of the individual child, is essential. For example, a child may say, "Jim comed to my house." The teacher may smile and repeat, "Jim came to my house."

   Children learn grammar gradually. They usually learn irregular verb forms first, since words like "went" and "came" are among the most common verbs in the English language. As children reach the stage of discovering the rule for the past tense, they may overgeneralize and say "goed" and "comed." Finally the mature pattern is achieved. Identification with particular models of speech is very important. The child uses the language that is heard as examples from which to learn, not as examples to learn in themselves.[49]

4. Use language as a social tool. The teacher needs to help each child learn to talk freely and easily, to listen courteously, and to use socially accepted phrases such as "thank you" and "excuse me."[50] The school in which children are helped to develop an awareness of and concern for others offers opportunities for practice. If the teacher sincerely uses the accepted terms in her speech and actions, the children in this environment will use them also. Use of such words without an appreciation of their meaning is futile. The teacher may also use comments such as, "Voices that are too loud bother others. There are voices for the playground and voices for the kindergarten room. We are inside now."

[47] Ibid.

[48] H. A. Greene and W. T. Petty, *Developing Language Skills in the Elementary School,* 5th ed. (Boston: Allyn and Bacon, 1975), pp. 90–94.

[49] Cazden, op. cit., pp. 5–6.

[50] Greene and Petty, op. cit., p. 92.

5. Develop the ability to name, describe, and classify objects common in the environment. The teacher may talk with one child alone and give an opportunity to name what he or she sees, feels, hears, or smells. Different children may be asked to categorize objects on one, two, or three dimensions: for example, find two green objects, two green circles, two large green circles.[51]

6. Develop the ability to communicate with others. This skill involves not only expressing one's ideas, but understanding what has been said; being able to repeat in one's own words what another has said and being able to respond appropriately to the meaning of another person's statement. The teacher may give directions such as "Lucy, please put the cups on the table."[52] Children may also be helped in this regard by having the opportunity for retelling a story in their own words after they have heard it read.

7. Organize ideas in expression. Often, the child's mind races ahead while speaking, and the result is a disorganized comment or story. For example, listen as Joe was telling about a hunting trip: "We got up early. We ate breakfast—and, oh! We got dressed in our hunting clothes—and, oh! My mother bought me a new rain coat and boots." At this point the teacher may say, "You were telling us about your hunting trip," helping him get back on the track, to organize his ideas, and to relate his experiences in proper sequence.

8. Learn about the language. Strickland has identified elements in the field of linguistics which appear highly valuable for younger children. She proposes that development of concepts about language begin in kindergarten. While the concepts may seem formal and meaningless for the kindergarten child, the examples indicate many opportunities for learning in relation to daily activities. Some of the concepts and examples, as adapted, follow:[53]

Language is a system of sounds.

The patterns of sound convey meaning to those who know the language.
(Learn familiar words in another language—e.g., "Thank you.")

Pitch, stress, and juncture are a part of the sound system of the language and help to convey meaning.
(Use same words to convey different messages—e.g., *When* do you expect him? When do you expect *him?*)

The sounds convey meaning only when put together in patterns of words and sentences.
(Help child speak in sentences. Note how meaning and emphasis are influenced by position of words in sentence—e.g., The boy in the yard ate his lunch. The boy ate his lunch in the yard.)

A language changes; old words may be given new meanings and new uses. Likewise, old words are dropped and new words are coined of old parts to represent new meanings or modifications of old ones.

---

[51] Louise M. Berman (ed.), *Toward New Programs for Young Children* (College Park.: University of Maryland, 1970), pp. 16–17.

[52] Ibid., pp. 17–20.

[53] Ruth G. Strickland, *The Contribution of Structural Linguistics to the Teaching of Reading, Writing, and Grammar in the Elementary School* (Bloomington: School of Education, Indiana University, 1963), pp. 7–9.

(Note old words in Mother Goose Rhymes—*"fetch* a pail of water."
What does it mean today?
Note new words; "telstar," "supersonic."
Note new meanings for old words; "capsule.")

READING AND THE YOUNG CHILD

As the importance of early learning opportunities to a child's development has been recognized, interest in early reading has become apparent. There are those who believe that teaching reading to young children will give them academic advantage in later grades. In 1964 the U.S. Office of Education held a Conference on Teaching Young Children to Read. While reports indicated that approximately one fourth of the school systems maintaining kindergartens offered reading instruction, there was a lively controversy regarding the practice.[54] Despite the controversy there has been an increasing number of programs that are attempting to teach reading to pre-first-grade children. A discussion of some of the important points of view regarding early reading follows.

Doman describes a plan for parents to use in teaching their babies to read, a plan which grew out of his work with brain-injured children. In recommending that the age of two years is the best time to begin and that any parent willing to go to a "little trouble" can achieve results, Doman overlooks individual differences in both babies and parents.[55] Moore recommended the use of specially designed typewriters in teaching two- to five-year-olds to read.[56]

Nila B. Smith expresses the point of view of those who do not advocate early formal reading instruction:[57]

Many studies have been directed toward the proper age for beginning instruction. Whether or not to teach reading to the preschool child is the question in the minds of many people at present. Can preschool children learn to read? Is it desirable for them to do so?

Of course they can learn to read. Both Dr. Durkin and Dr. Almy found that many children read before they come to school. Back in 1926 Terman in his study of gifted children found that over 1 percent of his subjects learned to read before they were 3 years old, and that $2\frac{1}{2}$ percent read before they were 5.

We have plenty of evidence that young children can learn to read. All of us know preschool children who are reading. There is no question in regard to

---

[54] Mary C. Austin, "Current Reading Practices," *Teaching Young Children to Read* (U.S. Office of Education, Washington, D.C.: U.S. Government Printing Office, 1964), pp. 16–20.

[55] G. Doman, *How to Teach Your Baby to Read* (New York: Random House, 1964).

[56] Maya Pines, "How Three-Year-Olds Teach Themselves to Read and Love It," *Harper's Magazine*, 226:1356 (1963), pp. 58–64.

[57] Nila B. Smith, "Trends in Beginning Reading Since 1900," *Teaching Young Children to Read* (U.S. Office of Education) (Washington, D.C.: U.S. Government Printing Office, 1964), pp. 14–15.

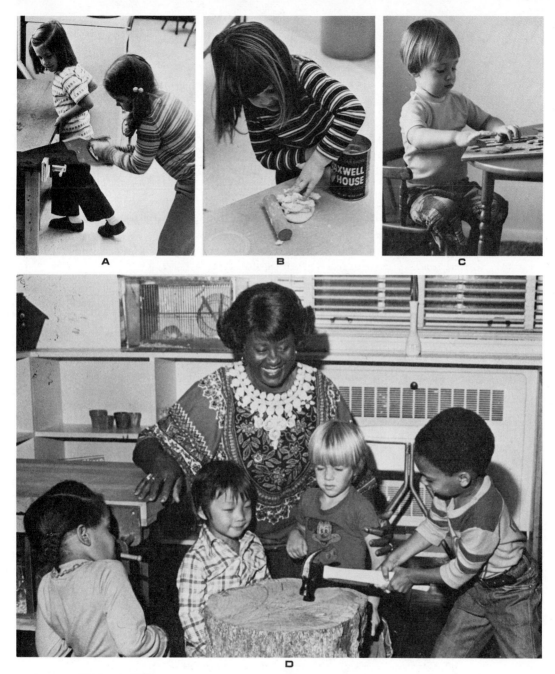

Figure 29

Working with puzzles, manipulating clay, painting, and hammering nails into wood offer opportunities for visual discrimination, training in visual perception, and the development of eye–hand coordination—all important skills in learning to read.

whether or not they *can* read; the main consideration is whether they should be *taught* to read at an early age.

Smith affirms that young children in kindergarten who want to read and are ready to read should be given the help they request. This procedure is quite different from introducing formal reading instruction to all kindergarten children. Smith reports that between 1915 and 1935, investigators found that from 20 to 24 percent of first-grade children were failing because of inability to read. If such large numbers of children failed when taught reading at the age of six years, Smith questions what would happen if formal reading were taught to all kindergarten pupils today. Smith has identified certain misconceptions, adapted below, which she maintains are held by those who advocate formal reading instruction for young children:[58]

1. They seem to consider reading as a growth separate and apart from all other growth, a phase of learning that can be worked on whenever the adult is ready. They overlook the fact that reading is an integral part of the total growth and development of the child.
2. They seem to hold an oversimplified concept of the reading process, thinking that when a child can pronounce a printed word he is reading. They forget that pronouncing words is not reading. There are important meanings to be gained from the words.
3. They seem to believe that all children are alike, disregarding individual differences. Some threes, some fours, and some fives can learn to read, but not all of them can. There are differences in ability as well as home environment and experiences—all of which influence a child's readiness for reading.

One of the areas of the controversy relates to the permanence of early reading gains and the results of the effect of early instruction on later school achievement.

Keister reported in 1941 that, while five-year-olds could acquire reading skills at a normal rate and maintain them through the first grade, the skills seemed to lack permanence, tended to disappear between first and second grades, and the loss was not made up in the following years.[59]

After reviewing research in early reading, Mason and Prater made preliminary conclusions that include the following.[60]

1. When exposed to the same program, younger children make less progress than older ones with similar levels of intelligence.
2. The control of attention is likely to be difficult for young children, and attempts to force learning may lead to emotional reaction.

[58] Nila B. Smith, "Early Reading: Viewpoints," *Child. Educ.*, 42:4 (1965), pp. 230–231.
[59] B. U. Keister, "Reading Skills Acquired by Five-Year-Old Children," *Elem. Sch. J.*, 41:8 (1941), pp. 587–596.
[60] G. Mason and Norma Jean Prater, "Early Reading and Reading Instruction," *Elem. English*, 43:5 (1966), pp. 483–488.

The Denver Study, a five-year research project, compared the effectiveness of beginning reading instruction in kindergarten with beginning reading instruction in the first grade. Some conclusions of the researchers follow.[61]

> Beginning reading skills can be taught quite effectively to large numbers of typical kindergarten pupils. . . . The permanence of gains made as a result of being taught beginning reading in the kindergarten depended upon subsequent instruction; . . . and that the early reading program presented no blocks, physical or emotional, to later reading.

As the result of a six-year study of children who had an opportunity to learn to read in a language arts program at the age of four, Durkin reports no negative effects on later achievement in reading. She believes that future achievement depends on the type of instruction offered in the later grades.[62] Research findings relating to early reading gains are conflicting, and, according to Durkin, the studies have been criticized for flaws in methods and statistical treatment.[63] When reading was introduced in the kindergarten there were usually no changes made in materials or methodology. Reading was taught much as it was in the first grade.

Any analysis of the controversy regarding early reading should distinguish between prereading activities and formal reading instruction. It is also important to note whether formal reading instruction is intended for all children or whether it is recommended for those children who are ready for or are already reading. Instruction for all five-year-olds on a wholesale basis is questionable and may well be harmful for some children.

Other issues involved in the controversy relate to the nature of reading readiness, the question of when to begin the teaching of reading, the meaning of the term *formal reading instruction,* and how reading is taught.

Prereading and readiness experiences

Perhaps no one educational term is more discussed and less understood than *reading readiness.* Some kindergarten teachers, even today, say they offer a reading readiness program, as if a child could be readied for the process of reading. There are others who believe that reading readiness cannot be developed by means of a program but depends entirely upon maturity. A hands-off policy is advocated, and they believe that, aside from attempting to maintain

---

[61] P. McKee and J. E. Brzeinski, *The Effectiveness of Teaching Reading in Kindergarten,* Cooperative Research Project No. 5-0371 (Denver: Denver Public Schools and the Colorado State Department of Education, 1966), pp. 80–86.

[62] Delores Durkin, "A Six-Year Study of Children Who Learned to Read at the Age of Four," *Reading Research Quarterly,* X:1 (1974–1975), pp. 9–61.

[63] Dolores Durkin, *Teaching Young Children to Read,* 2nd ed. (Boston: Allyn and Bacon, 1976), p. 19.

sound healthy bodies, there is little that the teacher or parents can do for the child. These two extremes point up the argument of nature versus nurture, or maturity versus training.

An examination of what is meant by the term *reading readiness* may help the reader understand the distinctions made in this text. A child is ready for reading when his or her capacities are mature or adequate in relation to the requirements of a specific learning situation, in this instance, learning to read.

"Readiness," as Krogman explains, "implies a best-time for initiating a specific task situation."[64] Readiness for reading, then, has to do with the "best-time" for beginning reading instruction. Reading instruction, however, involves many tasks or learning situations of varying difficulty. The focus, then, is upon the relationship between the child's particular abilities and the learning opportunities available. The child, having reached a certain stage in development now has the opportunity to acquire certain visual skills, such as looking at the page from left to right, top to bottom, and to see likenesses and differences in letters. As children use books, listen to stories, and help to dictate stories to the teacher, they are processing information, learning that printed words have meaning, that words say something. They are attaching the label of reading to the experiences. The child matches these experiences to those of having mother read aloud. A concept of reading is being formed.

Beginning reading involves a sequence of learning situations. For example, in relation to visual discrimination a child may be able to match colors, without concern for shape or size, and is ready to engage in activities involving this ability. This does not necessarily mean, however, that the child is ready for the more difficult discrimination required in seeing likenesses and differences in words.

This explanation implies that readiness for reading depends on nature and nurture, maturity and training. Olson uses the equation, "Maturation × Nurture = Development," which may well be applied to readiness for reading.

There are some factors involved in readiness which are wholly dependent on maturation. The teacher cannot say to a child, "focus your eyes" or "coordinate your muscles" and expect such a response. That is impossible. Such development depends on maturity. When this has been achieved, appropriate experiences may be supplied and the child learns happily and successfully. Olson states, "Synchronization between maturity and opportunity seems to be the safest guide to educational practice."[65]

Durkin reports that "a child's readiness to learn to read . . . is the product of maturation (nature) and of environmental factors (nurture).[66]

The environmental factors in a child's life have become especially signifi-

---

[64] W. M. Krogman, "Physical Growth as a Factor in the Behavioral Development of the Child," *New Dimensions in Learning* (Washington, D.C.: ASCD, 1963), pp. 15, 21.
[65] W. C. Olson, op. cit., pp. 14, 17.
[66] Dolores Durkin, *Teaching Them to Read* (Boston: Allyn and Bacon, 1970), p. 38.

cant as the importance of early learning opportunities been recognized. The "War on Poverty" and the Head Start programs are evidences of society's concern.

It is difficult, if not impossible, to isolate single factors involved in readiness, because of their interrelationship. A child with superior mental ability, rich experiential background, and good language development may not learn to read because of visual difficulties. On the other hand, adequate vision alone cannot insure success in reading. Such physical factors as age, vision, hearing, eye-hand coordination, and general health are considered important. Likewise, a child's concept of his or her ability to learn to read and his or her interest in reading affect the progress that will be made. The quality of instruction that the child receives is also very important. Durkin emphasizes the importance of a child's capacity in relation to the instruction that will be available.[67] A look at these factors seems important here even though the combination of factors and their interrelationship will vary with each child.

Age.   Chronological age has not been found to be a realistic index to readiness. Some children will begin reading at about six years of age. Some children, however, will be ready earlier; some not until later. Durkin reminds us that beginning reading in the first grade, at the age of six, is a product of convention, not of evidence that six years of age is an especially good time to begin reading.

Vision.   The young child is usually farsighted and only gradually will the eyes mature sufficiently for him or her to maintain them in focus at the distance required for reading. The child may be able to see distant objects clearly, but the same object becomes blurred when examined closely at near vision. A child may look at a picture in a book on the table, seeing it clearly, and still have difficulty in looking at the small letters involved in a word.

According to Gesell, a child of five may have trouble in adapting to the blackboard and in making adjustments from far to near and near to far.[68]

Park and Burri found that the percentage of children with vision below 20-20 declined from approximately 50 percent in the prereading stages to 20–35 percent in the early elementary and junior high school period.[69] Good fusion, stereopsis, and the power to maintain binocular single vision also improve during this period.

One concern in relation to preschool reading has been the harmful effect upon a child's vision. Durkin points out, however, that these early concerns

[67] Durkin, *Teaching Young Children to Read*, op. cit., p. 76.
[68] A. Gesell, Frances Ilg, and G. E. Bullis, *Vision: Its Development in Infant and Child* (New York: Paul B. Hoeber, 1948), p. 289.
[69] G. E. Park and Clara Burri, "Eye Maturation and Reading Difficulties," *J. Educ. Psychol.*, 34:9 (1943), pp. 535–546.

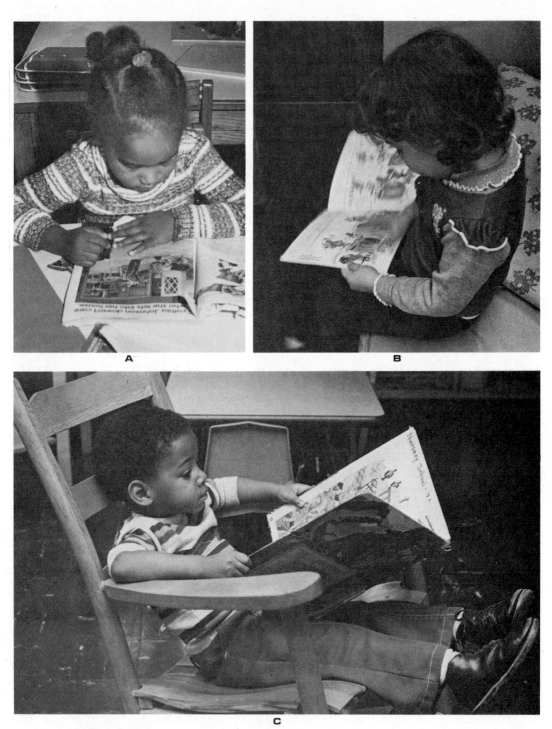

Figure 30
Handling, using, and loving books can help the child become interested in learning to
read and to know that reading can be fun.

were not supported by research data and were not stated by medical personnel. And the lack of adequate research is still evident. Durkin recommends that until research on this question is available, caution should be exercised. She says that young children who show an interest in reading are probably visually ready for reading. When young children are not interested in reading, one "ought to keep in mind the dearth of facts about the effect of early reading on vision and be cautious."[70]

Early childhood programs offer many opportunities for experiences that provide visual discrimination and training. Many such activities are used daily, but the teacher is often unaware of their value in readiness for reading. The children's responses to these activities suggest their readiness for more complex situations or their need for some less difficult. A few activities are identified here to illustrate the opportunities available as the child plays, uses tools, paints, or looks at books. Note the progression from the simple to the more complex. From such a sequence, the teacher who is alert to the child's needs can select appropriate materials for learning encounters appropriate for each child.

VISUAL PERCEPTION. Choosing colors for painting; choosing colored paper for mounting or cutting; and commenting on clothes children are wearing are activities usually included in schools and centers for young children. These offer opportunities for making gross discriminations.

The teacher may say, "Jane has a new *blue* sweater. It is just like Helen's. I have a blue bracelet. Everybody who is wearing something blue, stand up."

Games may be used in which matching involves only one color. Each child may be given a scrap of red paper (block, ball) and asked to find one other thing that is the same color as his or her paper and bring it to the teacher.

Objects may be matched according to two or three attributes. The teacher may say, "Find a red ball." "Find a little red ball."

Pictures, flannel figures, or shapes may be used. Place a triangle on the flannel board. From several shapes given to the child, ask him or her to find the shape just like the one on the board. Other attributes such as size and color may be introduced with comments such as, "Find the largest red circle."

Activities involving letters and words may begin with showing the child his or her name on a locker or painting and later matching it with his or her name on an experience chart; or noting words that begin alike in the recipe for making apple sauce.

VISUAL RECALL. Looking at pictures accompanying a story, remembering what was seen, and talking about the picture often occur in situations with children. The teacher may use a question such as: "Look and see what else we

---

[70] Durkin, *Teaching Them to Read*, op. cit., pp. 50–51.

need to make the cookies." The teacher may use the simple game of "hide and seek" in the circle. The children close their eyes while the teacher indicates the child who is to leave the circle and hide. Children open their eyes and the teacher says, "Who is missing?"

The same game may be used with cards on which the children's names have been written.

EYE–HAND COORDINATION. Working with puzzles; rolling, throwing, catching balls; manipulating clay; painting; and hammering nails into wood offer opportunities in developing eye–hand coordination. The child can be helped to acquire other visual skills, such as looking at the picture book from front to back and top to bottom and the pictures from left to right across the page. Such skills can be acquired most effectively as the child examines picture books and observes the book as stories are read. Experience charts, records of trips, lists of committee responsibilities all may be used in developing the left to right eye-movement.

One child in first grade had developed the habit of looking at words from right to left. This was observed in the following situation: The sentence— "Here is the dog"—was on the board. The teacher gave the pointer to Herb and asked him to read it. He moved the pointer from *dog* to *Here* as he read the sentence. When asked to find the word *dog*, he pointed to *Here;* and to *dog* when asked to find *Here.* Visual examinations by competent specialists failed to reveal any difficulty. The doctors reported that the child had learned to look from right to left. A parent conference revealed that in kindergarten Herb had done many exercises for visual discrimination. Evidently these had not been closely supervised, and he had found the picture that was different by beginning at the right side of the page. Well-meaning teachers who use formal readiness material without proper supervision may be encouraging the development of harmful habits.

In addition to the incidental situations in the kindergarten, which may be utilized by the teacher, various training programs have been designed to develop perceptual abilities.[71,72]

Hearing. As children live the first five years of their lives, they hear many sounds about them, but by the time they enter nursery school or kindergarten there are wide differences in their experiences with sounds and their awareness of sounds. Some children have listened to frogs croak, cows moo, sheep bleat, and dogs bark; others recognize the sounds of planes, trains, and trucks.

[71] Marianne Frostig, *Frostig Program for the Development of Vision Perception* (Chicago: Follett Publishing Co., 1964).
[72] *Fostering Growth in Perceptual Skills* (Darien, Conn.: CCM Threshold Learning, Inc., 1970).

For some there have been poetry, stories, and music. Others have had no one to share with them the fun of hearing different sounds or noises.

Some children are handicapped by faulty hearing, while others have normal hearing acuity but have not learned to discriminate differences in sounds. In either case, this deficiency in auditory acuity can be responsible for continued baby talk or faulty pronunciation. If a child does not hear the difference between two words, it will be difficult for him or her to distinguish between their printed symbols. The teacher should be alert to detect hearing difficulties, make adjustments for the child, and recommend correction to the parents.

Before learning to read, the majority of children will profit from learning about sounds with special reference to language. This should not be interpreted to mean formal phonetic drill but rather opportunities for experiences by which children become aware of sounds, and the ways in which sounds differ and are alike, and become able to discriminate, identify, and match sounds. Such experiences can offer beginning instruction in phonics. For example:

Sounds can be loud or soft—"Turn up the record player so that the record will be a little louder. I can't hear it." Or, "How do you feel when you hear this music?" "It is very soft and slow. I feel sleepy." Or, "Talk softly. The baby [doll] is asleep."

Sounds can be high or low. Match tones in music. The teacher strikes a note on the piano. She says to the child, "Find a sound that is low," or vice versa. In singing, call attention to the way in which the song goes up and down.

Sounds can be made by people, animals, and things. Ask the children to close their eyes, listen, and name the sounds they hear. Make a recording of the children's voices. Ask them to listen and identify the voices. Make a recording of sounds heard on the playground. Ask children to identify a sound and decide if it was made by a person, animal, or thing. Show pictures of animals and ask children to make a sound appropriate for each. Ask children to find a person, animal, or thing in the classroom that can make a sound. Listen to the sounds of each.

Sounds can be the same. Use poetry containing words that rhyme; stories with initial consonant sounds, such as choo choo, chug chug. The teacher may say, "milk," and ask the child, "Can you think of a word that begins with the same sound as milk?" Play a musical pattern on the piano or bells, such as *do do sol*. This may be done by child or teacher and the child repeats it.

Other Physical Factors. The general health and nutritional status influence the child's energy level. A child who has frequent colds and is absent often must continually make adjustments to school. He or she may get settled and begin to feel comfortable with the group, then be ill and out of school for four days. Upon returning the child finds that the group is not as familiar as it was last week. Two days after the return, he or she feels secure again. This happy state lasts only a few days and the child is out again and the process must be repeated.

Muscular control and development affects what the child can do. Jennie, you recall, has "jerky" muscular movements and is afraid to climb the jungle gym. This inability to climb successfully further limits her social contacts with other children.

Emotional-Social Factors. It is easier for a child who is emotionally secure in the school situation to learn to read. He or she is free to devote attention to the job at hand. Jean, a six-year-old, returning home from her first day in first grade expressed this truth. Bounding through the front door, she called, "Mommie, a little girl cried at school today." For Jean, who had been so eager to go to school, the little girl's tears had evidently been quite a surprise. Her mother asked, "Why did the little girl cry?" Jean thought for a moment, then replied, "I guess she hadn't been to kindergarten. She didn't know her mother would come at 12 o'clock and everything would be all right."

Programs for young children can make a great contribution to the social and emotional adjustment of children. They can learn to feel secure in a situation away from home with adults other than their parents. Children can learn that the teacher is friendly, that everything is all right. The child can learn that groups can be friendly too—they can be a member and speak, sing, listen, or sit in the group! Children can begin to direct their own behavior, to follow directions, to select and use materials, to assume responsibility for jobs in the room. A child lacking in this confidence and security is seldom ready for reading. It is difficult, if not impossible, to teach a crying child, or a child on the verge of tears, to learn to read.

Of the children described in the kindergarten, remember Jennie, who is not permitted to cry at home but cries often at kindergarten; Gloria who needs adult attention; the twins, who have each other; and Shaw, who continues to try, even in difficult situations. Who can doubt that emotional-social factors are involved here, as in every group of young children.

No book can tell you specifically what to do for these children. Perhaps for a time Jennie needs the opportunity to cry, to experience this natural outlet for her feelings. But since crying is not accepted at home, she needs to learn other outlets. Because she has good ability she may be helped to use words: "Please don't do that"; "I don't like it." When she can't have her way, she can be helped to find a substitute. The teacher can, while providing individual activities, also arrange for her to play and become friendly with one child, and gradually increase the size of the group to help her overcome her fear of children. This last suggestion may also prove one way of helping Gloria and the twins to include other children in their lives—not forcing them immediately into the total group but gradually building readiness for group activities, increasing slowly the number of children with whom they become involved.

Mental and Intellectual Factors.   Learning to read involves the ability to see and hear and other factors which have been identified, but it is more than these. It involves learning to associate meaning with symbols and to interpret what is read. Such skill requires the intellectual capacity and the mental maturity necessary to reason, to form meaningful associations, and to remember word forms. In one of the earlier studies, Morphett and Washburne found that among the first-grade children studied, those with mental ages between 6.5 and 7.0 years profited most from the initial reading instruction.[73]

There were, however, objections to this concept. The degree of mental maturity required for success in beginning reading depends to some extent on the way in which beginning reading is taught, the materials used and the child's interest in learning to read. Gates and Bond report a low correlation of mental age with reading achievement. They conclude that the optimum time for beginning reading depends not entirely on the child, but also on the reading instruction he or she receives. They indicate that the general and social returns to the child from learning to read are important also.[74]

Durkin points out that different types of instruction in reading make different demands of the child.[75] The teacher then, chooses the type of reading instruction appropriate to the child's abilities and needs.

There appears to be a positive relationship between mental development and language development. Factors involved in the development of speech were discussed earlier in this chapter. Language is mentioned here to indicate the relationship to reading. It is oral language that relates the child's experience to the abstract word symbols. Language development is also related to home and experiential background. Children who have trips and visits in the community, associations with people, and knowledge of things around them will probably have more words in their vocabulary and more things to talk about. Almy found a significant, positive relationship between success in beginning reading and the child's experiences in kindergarten, in play, and with adults, which involved being read to and looking at books, papers, and magazines.[76]

McCormick reviewed research and concluded that reading aloud to chil-

[73] Mabel V. Morphett and C. Washburne, "When Should Children Begin to Read?" *Elem. Sch. J.*, *31*:7 (1931), pp. 496–503.
[74] A. I. Gates and G. L. Bond, "Reading Readiness: A Study of Factors Determining Success and Failure in Beginning Reading," *Teach. Coll. Rec.*, 37:8 (1936), pp. 679–685.
[75] Durkin, *Teaching Young Children to Read*, op. cit., pp. 76–77.
[76] Millie C. Almy, *Children's Experiences Prior to First Grade and Success in Beginning Reading* (New York: Teachers College, 1949).

dren significantly improved their vocabulary, knowledge, and reading comprehension.[77]

Children's capacity for learning to read is also influenced by their own concept of their ability, which is influenced by previous experiences. Some present views of intellectual development assume that the position a child has reached indicates the intellectual progress already made, but the prediction of future development depends on knowledge of the experiences in store for the child.[78]

Attention Span. In learning to read the child needs to be able to focus attention on the specific instructional task. For example, in recording an anecdotal record, one student wrote, "tension span" instead of "attention span." Perhaps in reality this was not an error. Tensions do build up and the span indicates the length of time before they interfere with the child's ability to attend. The attention span indicates the length of time for which a child can focus thoughts on, listen to, or concentrate on a given topic. Olson states that it has been difficult to determine the attention span of children at different ages, but there is rather general agreement that the attention span of children for toys and play materials increases with age. A range of 7 to 20 minutes has been identified for the preschool period. Individual differences are great and the time seems to vary with the appropriateness of the material for the age.[79] Durkin says that the attention span of the same child varies according to the activity in which the child is engaged.[80]

Again there is the relationship between maturity and experience. The program can provide opportunities for the child to focus attention on a topic. It is important, however, that the content and length of time expected be appropriate for the maturity and the interests of the child.

Summary. The following statements regarding readiness are important to its understanding.

1. Readiness refers to a combination of abilities and understandings. It is not a single package consisting of specific abilities in specified quantities.
2. Readiness is the product of nature and maturation as well as nurture and the environmental factors in the child's life.
3. Readiness is concerned with the relationship between the child's capacity and the type of reading instruction available.[81]

---

[77] Sandra McCormick, "Should You Read Aloud to Your Children?" *Language Arts*, 54:2 (1977), pp. 130–143.
[78] Almy, *Intellectual Development: Another Look*, op. cit., p. 13.
[79] W. C. Olson, op. cit., p. 95.
[80] Durkin, *Teaching Young Children to Read*, op. cit., p. 29.
[81] Ibid., p. 76.

A   B

Figure 31
Reading aloud to children can help to develop their interest in reading, improve their vocabulary, and increase their general knowledge. Young children never tire of having stories read to them once they discover the magic contained between the covers of a book.

Teaching reading

One of the questions often raised in regard to teaching reading is *when* to begin the instruction. Durkin points out that there is no single, unequivocal answer.[82] The time for beginning reading depends on both the child's capacities and interest and the type of reading instruction available. Rather than concern for the time to begin reading, the problem becomes one of assessing readiness and providing instructional opportunities that "provide the best match for the capacities and interests of the children to be taught."[83] More time needs to be spent considering *"how* to begin" rather than arguing about when the instruction should begin.

The term *reading instruction* does not necessarily mean formal instruction —a situation in which all the children are taught the same prescribed material at the same time and at the same rate. Such procedure is not appropriate for the kindergarten or any grade level. Durkin reminds us that reading instruc-

[82] Durkin, *Teaching Them to Read,* op. cit., p. 58.
[83] Ibid., p. 43.

tion may take a variety of forms.[84] Reading instruction can include anything that a teacher does to help a child:

1. Use and understand oral language through activities such as trips, conversation, reading stories.
2. Use materials that display written language and help the child begin to understand the meaning of the reading process through activities such as experience stories, signs, labels, recipes.
3. Develop an understanding of the purposes of writing and spelling in dictating letters, charts, and develop the ability to write.

How does one teach young children to read? Hymes suggests that reading be taught to fit the child. There are many differences among children of the same chronological age and these must be considered in planning for reading instruction. Children can't be lumped together. Each child remains an individual. The teacher teaches as much as each child can comfortably, naturally, and easily learn.[85]

When reading instruction was begun first with the fives and later with the fours little attention had been given to adapting the reading process to the very young—to fitting it to the child. First-grade procedures were usually used. The books, methods, and materials formerly used for the six- and seven-year-old children were moved down to the kindergarten. Today, however, there is a growing awareness that reading for the pre-first-grade child is different. The program can be one of trips, jobs and activities, pets, visitors, creative experiences, and play. The program needn't be one in which children are sitting quietly rather than being active. It can grow out of the children's activities and experiences relevant to them.[86]

The language-experience approach to reading instruction seems very appropriate for the young child. Such an approach integrates listening, speaking, writing, and reading. The children's oral language and experiences are used as the basis for developing reading materials. Children learn to read in conjunction with talking, listening, and writing. One of the important types of reading material used in the language-experience approach is the experience story.

The experience story (plans, news, stories) may be developed individually or in a group situation, with the children's ideas being recorded by the teacher. The content of the stories should be familiar, growing out of the experiences of the children.[87]

---

[84] Ibid., p. 74.

[85] J. L. Hymes, Jr., "Teaching Reading to the Under-Six Age: A Child Development Point of View," in *Claremont Reading Conference 34th Yearbook* (Claremont, Calif. 91771: Claremont Graduate School, 1970), pp. 79–83.

[86] Ibid., p. 83.

[87] Mary Anne Hall, *Teaching Reading as a Language Experience* (Columbus, Ohio: Charles E. Merrill Publishing Co., 1970).

Nihar's Birthday Plans
Chocolate cupcakes
Chocolate frosting
Tropical Punch
Play tic-tac-toe
Bean Bag throw
Read Lentil
Sing "Ten Little Indians"

Figure 32
Children learn to read in conjunction with talking, reading, and writing. The experience story is one of the important types of reading materials used. The experience story often includes plans, recipes, and news. The teacher recorded the birthday plans for Nihar.

The experience story may be used in a variety of ways, depending on the maturity and interests of the children. For one child, participation in expressing ideas for the teacher to record is enough. Others may be learning that written words have meaning, that words express ideas which have been recorded; beginning the development of the skills of reading, such as focusing on print, reading from top to bottom and left to right, and making the return sweep across the page; and having practice in matching and letter recognition. Still others are developing a sight vocabulary and learning to identify words. In writing an experience story the teacher may find the following suggestions helpful.[88]

1. Use manuscript writing.
2. Leave a margin of at least three inches between the title of the story and top of page and between the title and the first line of the story.
3. If a sentence is too long for one line divide the sentence between phrases.
4. Place large pictures near the top center of the chart.
5. Leave a margin of one and one half or two inches on the left side of the story.
6. Place smaller pictures along right margin or at bottom of the chart.
7. Children may become restless while waiting for the teacher to write the story carefully on the chart. If so, record the comments quickly and transfer them to the chart later.

Suggestions for language arts activities that can contribute to reading are included on pp. 269–288. Art and music activities can make a contribution as

[88] V. E. Herrick and Marcella Nerbovig, *Using Experience Charts With Children* (Columbus, Ohio: Charles E. Merrill Publishing Co., 1964).

well as activities in social studies, science, mathematics, health and safety, and play.

Learning centers may be utilized. Suggestions for developing comprehension by using tapes or recordings in a center follow:[89]

> Children listen to riddles and identify the appropriate pictures.
> Children listen to a story and arrange pictures of the story in proper sequence.
> Children listen to a story and respond to questions that may be answered by the selection of an appropriate picture.

Summary. A pre-first-grade reading program which provides instruction appropriate to the abilities and interests of children may be described as follows.

> Abundant exposure to language would be a central goal of such a program. Situations in which children will talk spontaneously are planned. The teacher reads to the children as well as writes down what they say. As children gain in language competence, they approach the time when they are able to learn to read words and comprehend what they have read. Children reach this point at different times. Some are even ready when they first come to school. For this reason a school program offers a spectrum of activities ranging from concrete experiences to adventures in reading to accommodate the different levels of development of its children.[90]

LISTENING

Listening, as one of the language arts, is an important facet of communication. Children hear many sounds. Just hearing, however, does not guarantee listening. Listening involves recognizing sounds, giving them meaning from one's experience, reacting to or interpreting them, and integrating them with one's knowledge and experiences. It is a major means of learning. Dawson says, "It is through listening, then, that the young child gains much of his vocabulary, most of his sentence patterns, and nearly all of his imitatively acquired ways of enunciating and inflecting. Listening, of course, also contributes to his constantly growing stock of ideas."[91]

Types of listening include the following:

1. Passive or marginal listening is prevalent as children are engrossed in one activity but listen just enough to be aware of what is being said. Listening is not the focus, it is marginal.

---

[89] *Some Suggestions for the Development of Sensory and Language Skills at the Kindergarten and Primary Level* (Rockville, Md.: Montgomery County Public Schools, 1970), p. 71 (mimeogr.).
[90] *Prereading, Bulletin 246* (Rockville, Md.: Montgomery County Public Schools, 1974), p. 101.
[91] Mildred Dawson, *Learning to Listen*, Language Arts Notes, No. 3 (Yonkers, N.Y.: World Book, n.d.), p. 1.

    2. Appreciative listening is involved when the child enjoys a story, a poem, or a recording.
    3. Attentive listening is involved in situations when the child listens to directions or announcements.
    4. Analytical listening occurs when the child analyzes what he hears in terms of his own experience. One may hear the child pondering, "I wonder why."[92]

Each child comes with some ability to listen but the range in ability varies greatly. Jennie, described in Chapter 9, is inclined to "tune out" sounds and ignore them because much of the talk at home has been impatient and nagging, such as "Be quiet, I must study." Many children who live in the inner city have also learned to "tune out" sounds, because their environment may be noisy. There are many street sounds as well as those from neighboring apartments. When a large family lives in cramped space there is likely to be much talking and voices are raised in order to be heard above the confusion. A child from such an atmosphere may have had little opportunity for "peace and quiet" and listening.

To grow as an accurate and critical listener, children must be taught how to listen and how to use the results of listening. Some suggestions for teaching this type of listening are

    1. Remember that young children are easily distracted. Because they have a short attention span, the teacher tries to adjust to this and at the same time to help the child grow in ability to attend, without undue pressure.
      a. Plan brief periods of any one activity. The length of stories, recordings, music periods should be within the child's attention span.
      b. Vary methods of presentation with attractive materials. Pictures, bright colors, interesting objects, help to gain attention.
      c. Permit wiggling and twisting. Monroe suggests that trying to hold his body still takes conscious effort on the part of a little child and may therefore be distracting.[93] Rather than insisting that "we sit up straight, feet on the floor, hands in our laps," the teacher may suggest that each child sit comfortably. The teacher may use a finger play, such as:

> Open, shut them, open, shut them
> Give a little clap
> Open, shut them, open, shut them
> Fold them in your lap[94]

    and immediately begin the story or activity.
      d. Arrange the physical environment so that children are comfortable and that outside noises and interferences are at a minimum.

[92] *Language Arts for Today's Children,* National Council of Teachers of English (New York: Appleton-Century-Crofts, 1954), pp. 80–81.
[93] Marion Monroe, *Growing into Reading* (Chicago: Scott, Foresman, 1951), p. 177.
[94] For other finger plays see Margaret A. Stant, *The Young Child: His Activities and Materials* (Englewood Cliffs, N.J.: Prentice-Hall, 1972), pp. 125–129.

2. Help the children understand that listening is important. For example, don't repeat explanations, directions, or announcements over and over.
   a. If children know that the teacher will repeat for them whenever they are ready, why should they stop to listen with the group?
   b. Make activities so interesting that children will want to listen and will miss something if they don't.
3. Teach the children to listen.
   a. Speak in a voice that is adequate, but low enough to require listening if the child is to hear what is being said. Don't try to talk above the noise of the children nor speak so softly that you cannot be heard.
   b. Don't talk too much. The voice that goes on and on becomes monotonous and the children tend to "tune it out."
   c. Allow time for the child to get ready to listen. After saying "Children," or "Boys and girls," allow a moment or two for the child to put down the block or crayon. Often the announcement is made while the child's effort is expended in balancing the block rather than listening.
   d. Give explanations simply and in well-organized sequence.
4. Set a good example of attention. A teacher who is preoccupied with personal problems, such as writing a note or getting a drink of water while a recording is being played, does not emphasize the importance of listening. "A teacher who looks attentively into the face of the child who is talking, listens closely to what he is saying, tries to understand his exact meaning, however poorly phrased, and gives him the most thoughtful reply she is capable of, will hold that child's attention better than any device that can be suggested."[95]
5. Create a relaxed, happy atmosphere and relationship among the children and between them and yourself (see pp. 86–111). A child who is relaxed and free from emotional strain can listen more easily than the child who is uneasy, hostile, or afraid.
6. Help the children develop an awareness of sounds, the sounds they hear every day. The teacher may begin by calling attention to types of sounds, such as those of nature, or the traffic, or human sounds. One approach is to say to the children, "Close your eyes. Listen carefully and tell me what you hear." They may identify the sounds and describe them as loud, soft, close, far away, sharp, and so on.
7. Provide many opportunities for a wide variety of meaningful listening experiences. There should be listening for pleasure, appreciation, and information. The teacher may use stories, poetry, records, directions, tapes, musical instruments, television, radio, and conversation with adults and other children.
8. Arrange opportunities for children to listen for certain purposes, such as answering questions, solving riddles, completing rhymes, putting ideas in sequence, identifying words which do not rhyme, and detecting irrelevant sentences.[96]

[95] Monroe, op. cit., p. 178.
[96] P. C. Burns, Betty L. Broman, and Alberta L. Lowe, *The Language Arts in Childhood Education*, 2nd ed. (Chicago: Rand McNally and Co., 1971), pp. 71–73.

WRITING

A nursery school teacher exclaimed in shocked tones, "Writing! Why the nursery school has nothing to do with writing!" Perhaps she was thinking in terms of formal instruction in writing, or perhaps she did not recognize the opportunities available for developing an awareness of writing and its values.

Before discussing when writing begins and the opportunities for beginning, it is important to emphasize the why of writing. The purpose of writing is to communicate or to express an idea. This purpose is so often lost in the beginning stages of practice. Handwriting is a tool, a means to an end. With this purpose in mind, one may examine the beginnings of writing, which occur long before the child takes pencil in hand to write.

The child scribbles and draws pictures. The child can deliver or receive simple notes, invitations, or letters; dictate individually or participate as the group dictates and the teacher writes captions for pictures, experience charts, plans, invitations, thank-you notes, charts about pets, experiments, or some other phase of group interest.

At home the child has had the fun of receiving a letter. In reply he or she has scribbled a note to Grandmother, often talking as he or she writes. The teacher offered to write the name for four-year-old Mary on her letter. The child replied, "You don't need to write it. I can do it. Here it is." (She pointed to a penciled scribble.) That signature sufficed for a while, but there came a time in nursery school when the scribble wasn't sufficient—another child claimed Mary's picture, the one she had painted at the easel. The teacher said, "Next time, I'll write your name on the picture. Then we will know it is yours." Writing was important now—to communicate her name to others.

For a time Mary made no attempt to write her own name, but each time she asked the teacher to do it for her. She became aware that her name was written in other places too—her locker, her books, her sweater, and that there were other names that belonged to other children. *Such awareness also contributed to readiness for reading.* She learned that when the teacher wanted to tell Mother about a trip or something else at nursery school, sometimes she used the telephone, but sometimes she wrote her a note, either by hand or on the typewriter. The teacher said, "This is a message I have written to your mother."

Along with the experiences that helped establish a need for writing, the child used clay, finger paint, easel paints and brushes, blocks, crayons, hammers and nails, puzzles, paste, and many other media. Through these experiences she was doing exercises that involved arm and finger movement, eye–hand coordination, and muscular control, all of which are essential to learning to write. Mary had these experiences in nursery school. For some children,

Figure 33
Manuscript writing is recommended for use with young children. Individual guidance in writing is given the child at the time he or she asks and is ready for it. The amount of actual writing will depend upon the child's experiences and interest, his or her intellectual, physical, and emotional maturity.

these experiences with writing do not come in the nursery school or Head Start program, but are delayed until kindergarten or even first grade.

Anderson has identified three kinds of experiences that contribute to writting readiness.[97]

1. Manipulative experiences are planned to strengthen the muscles used in writing and to gain control over the writing tools.
2. Many activities are planned to increase the child's vocabulary.
3. Practice activities are related to the basic movements of writing, usually beginning at the chalkboard.

The amount of actual writing will depend on the child's experiences and interest, as well as intellectual, physical, and emotional maturity. Actual writing begins with attempts at writing letters, usually the letters in the child's name. The letters written with pencil, crayon, chalk, or paint will probably be of varying size, scattered over the page with little evidence of fine motor control. As this control develops, the child can use smaller spaces and letters. Young children should not be expected to copy letters or words from a large chart or the chalkboard. Eye–hand coordination usually is not fully developed, and it is difficult for the child to look up at the copy and down again at

[97] Anderson, op. cit., pp. 178–179.

the paper. A copy of the child's name or the needed word should be available at the table.

Formal writing instruction is not included in nursery school and is not usually undertaken in kindergarten. Individual guidance is given the children at the time they ask and are ready for it. Their purposes will suggest the content. Following are some suggestions for guiding children who indicate readiness.

Materials

Provide large sheets (preferably 18 × 24) of unlined paper, such as newsprint, for the children to use. They may write with crayons, chalk, or pencil. If pencils are used it is easier for most children to use pencils with large, soft leads. As a child shows evidence of maturity and increased muscular control, fold the paper once in the middle for a crease, then smooth it out. Children may write their name in the top and the bottom. Later, they may use the crease as the line on which to write the letters. After a child manages this easily, the paper may be folded into quarters.

Type of writing

Manuscript writing (sometimes called print-script[98]) is recommended for use with young children because:

1. Letter forms are based largely on circles and straight lines, which require only simple strokes. This makes writing easier for the child who is just gaining skill in the use of the small finger muscles and is soon able to use writing for communicative purposes.
2. Letter forms more closely resemble printed forms than do the cursive script letters. The writing helps encourage and reinforce beginning reading, and the child is not confused by two types of writing.

Manuscript writing should be distinguished from the other types of writing in use. It is often referred to as printing. While some of the letter forms are the same as printing, others are different. Below are listed samples of writing. Note differences in a, g, t, y.

Manuscript	and get yes
Print	and get yes
All capitals	AND GET YES
Cursive script	and get yes

[98] Ibid., p. 176.

In writing children's names, capital letters are used by many kindergarten teachers because they are all one size, as **TOM** . The child does not have to make the adjustment in writing between upper- and lower-case letters. First-grade teachers sometimes complain because children coming from kindergarten use the capital letters only, and it is necessary for them to change to the manuscript forms. One teacher tried using the manuscript forms with kindergarten children. Lockers and other labels were done in manuscript. When a child asked for help with his name or a word, it was written in manuscript. The teacher used upper- and lower-case letters, but no attempt was made to have the child use them. Some children were able to use "tall and small letters," such as the name **Jack** . On the other hand, a child might write **JaCK** making no difference in the height of the letters, but using the manuscript forms. As the child gained in muscular control, he began to use both sizes of letters and gradually reduced their sizes.

Sometimes there was the comment, "That's not the way my mother writes my name." The teacher replied, "There are different ways to write. This is the writing we use in kindergarten." Some children, however, had not been taught to write with only capital letters, and for them to begin with the manuscript forms eliminated one type of writing.

Explain to parents the writing forms being used. It may be a good idea to provide a manuscript alphabet for them. If letter samples are displayed for reference by the children, they should be placed conveniently in the room at the child's eye level.

Reversals

As the young child writes, one often notices that letters or numbers are reversed, as **Ƨ** or **S** . The letters in a word may be written correctly, but in reverse sequence, such as **nhoJ** for **John**. Such errors are common and are often indicative of inexperience in writing from left to right, limited visual memory as to how the number, letter, or word should look, and lack of mature eye-hand coordination. Watch the child as he or she writes. The right-handed child who has not yet learned to begin at the left side of the paper may put his pencil down at the extreme right side of the paper. There is no room to go to the right, so he writes to the left and as a result, **nhoJ** . This is not strange, nor necessarily indicative of visual difficulty. It does indicate, however, that this child needs guidance in establishing the left-to-right sequence.

As children practice and use writing, with proper guidance, such reversals usually disappear. If they persist, it may be advisable for the child to be referred for a visual examination.

Handedness

Theories regarding handedness appear to be conflicting. This confusion is reflected in practice. One theory holds that handedness is determined by cerebral dominance inherent in the child, while another takes the position that the child is born with no preference but learns to favor one hand over the other. If one accepts the first theory, then the teacher would not interfere with the child's hand preference. According to the second theory, the child can be taught to use his right hand without strain but this should be done before habits are formed that must be broken at a later time.

Olson states that "Perhaps the teaching profession has been oversold through an earlier literature which often painted the dire effects of handedness on speech and emotion."[99] Consequently, the child has been allowed to select the hand of preference. According to present thinking, this is probably wise.

The teacher, however, may sometimes permit the child to become left-handed accidentally. Some children, upon entering nursery school or kindergarten have not yet developed a hand preference, and as they begin to work with materials, may inadvertently use the left hand. The teacher can suggest, "Try using the scissors in your right hand." If the child makes the transfer easily, well and good. If the child persists in using the left hand, it is probably wise not to insist on changing.

By writing the child's name in the left-hand corner of the paper instead of the right the teacher can give the child a clue as to where to begin to write. Such procedure can also help the child in developing the "left to right" skill needed in reading.

If the child shows a decided preference for his left hand, the teacher needs to help him make necessary adjustments in the position of the paper and pencil or crayon. It is not necessary for the left-handed child to write in a cramped position. The paper should be in front of the child, parallel to the edge of the table but slightly to the left of the center of his body. The pencil, crayon, or chalk should point in the direction opposite that of the right-handed child.

Most children, by the end of kindergarten, will regard writing as a means of communication and will be able to write their names.[100] There will be wide variations, however, as with all skills, because of the quality of the program and the teacher, as well as the child and his background.

[99] W. C. Olson, op. cit., p. 88.
[100] Anderson, op. cit., pp. 173–174.

TEACHER INVENTORY

The confident teacher of young children possesses certain information important to the child's development in the language arts. Anderson has developed a self-evaluation form for language teachers, a partial inventory that may be used in directing efforts toward improving one's understanding, knowledge, and skills. An adaptation of the form follows.[101]

> Do I know
>> how children master language before coming to school?
>> how language instruction fits into the school day?
>> books that should be read to children?
>> how to share a picture book with little children?
>> how to direct children in a simple verse choir?
>> how to help a left-handed child learn to write well?
>> why I teach handwriting as I do?
>> why it is important to listen to children?
>
> Can I
>> select and purchase books intelligently for a center for young children?
>> hold children's attention as I read or tell a story?
>> involve children in dramatic play and creative dramatics?
>> teach a finger play to a child and explain its importance to the parents?
>> read poetry well?
>> use manuscript (print-script) writing?
>> write legibly so as not to be embarrassed when writing a note to a parent?

If some of your answers are "no," you should devote special attention to the discussion and practice the suggestions found in Chapters 11 and 12.

Suggested Activities

1. Listen to and record the speech of three four-year-old children for a period of fifteen minutes each. Compare as to the total number of words spoken, the number of different words spoken, the length of the sentences used, the interests revealed, and consonant sounds which were mispronounced. Identify possible reasons for similarities or differences.
2. On the basis of your observation of the children's speech, plan a language learning activity for one of the children. Use the activity with the child. Evaluate.
3. Observe in a center. Record incidents in which the teacher elaborated on a child's comment in order to increase the child's vocabulary.
4. Observe in a kindergarten. Note activities and experiences used to help the child understand that "writing is communicating."
5. Observe a kindergarten teacher and note the ways by which he or she gained the attention of the group of children.

[101] Ibid., pp. 8–9.

6. Observe a total group situation in the kindergarten. Identify children who had difficulty in listening. Discuss possible causes of the difficulty.
7. Practice manuscript writing. Write a note to a friend using this type of writing.
8. Record an experience story dictated by a child. Transfer the story to chart paper.
9. View the film, *Foundations of Reading and Writing.* Campus Films, 20 East 46th Street, New York, N.Y. 10017. Compare with your observations.

Related Readings

Anderson, P. S. "Speech and Listening," *Language Skills in Elementary Education,* 2nd ed. New York: Macmillan Publishing Co., 1972, pp. 57–118.

Barbe, W. B., and Virginia H. Lucas. "Instruction in Handwriting: A New Look," *Child. Educ.,* 50:4 (1974), pp. 207–209.

Becenti, Mabeth. "Children Who Speak Navajo," *Young Children,* 25:3 (1970), pp. 141–142.

Broman, Betty L. "The Spanish-Speaking Five-Year-Old," *Child. Educ.,* 48:7 (1972), pp. 362–364.

Brzeinski, J. E., and Howard, W. "Early Reading—How, Not When!" *Reading Teacher,* 25:3 (1972), pp. 239–242.

Cazden, Courtney B. (ed.). *Language in Early Childhood Education.* Washington, D.C.: NAEYC, 1972.

———. "Studies of Early Language Acquisition," *Child. Educ.,* 46:3 (1969), pp. 127–131.

Childhood Education. "Valuing Diversity in Language," *Child. Educ.,* 46:3 (1969), entire issue.

Ching, Doris C. *Reading and the Bilingual Child.* Newark, Del.: International Reading Association, 1976.

Chomsky, Carol. "Write Now, Read Later," in *Language in Early Childhood Education,* edited by Courtney B. Cazden. Washington, D.C.: NAEYC, 1972, pp. 1–2.

Day, Barbara, et al. "Reading and Pre-First Grade—A Joint Statement of Concerns About Present Practices," *Educ. Leadership,* 34:5 (1977), p. 325.

Eisenson, Jon, and Mardel Ogilvie. *Speech Correction in the Schools,* 4th ed. New York: Macmillan Publishing Co., 1977.

Ekwall, E. E. *Psychological Factors in the Teaching of Reading.* Columbus, Ohio: Charles E. Merrill Publishing Co., 1973.

Enstrom, E. A. "Paper Placement for Manuscript Writing," *Elementary English,* 40:May (1963), pp. 518–522.

Freshour, F. "Parent Education & Reading Readiness & Reading Achievement," *Reading Teacher,* 24:8 (1971), pp. 763–769.

Gillham, Isabel. "Self Concept and Reading," *Reading Teacher,* 21:3 (1967), pp. 270–273. Also included in *Psychological Factors in the Teaching of Reading,* edited by E. E. Ekwall. Columbus, Ohio: Charles E. Merrill Publishing Co., 1973, pp. 80–84.

Gonzalez-Mena, Janet. "English as a Second Language for Preschool Children," *Young Children,* 32:1 (1976), pp. 14–19.

Granger, R. C. "The Nonstandard Speaking Child: Myths Past and Present," *Young Children, 31*:6 (1976), pp. 478–485.

Jersild, A. T. "Handedness," *Child Psychology*, 6th ed. Englewood Cliffs, N.J.: Prentice-Hall, 1968, pp. 156–160.

————. "Language Development, Perceptual Development," *Child Psychology*, 6th ed. Englewood Cliffs, N.J.: Prentice-Hall, 1968, pp. 414–442.

Lavatelli, Celia S. (ed.). *Language Training in Early Childhood*. Urbana: University of Illinois Press, 1971.

Lowes, Ruth. "Do We Teach Reading in the Kindergarten?" *Young Children, 30*:5 (1975), pp. 328–331.

Mayne, Lucille. "An Individual Study of the Reading Acceleration of Two Kindergarten Children," *Elementary English, 40*:4 (1963), pp. 406–408; 442.

Mendelson, Anna. "The Listener," *Young Children, 31*:3 (1976), pp. 184–186.

Ollila, L. O. (ed.). *The Kindergarten Child and Reading*. Newark, Del.: International Reading Association, 1977.

Paul, Rhea. "Invented Spelling in Kindergarten," *Young Children, 31*:3 (1976), pp. 195–200.

Pialorsi, F. P. (ed.). *Teaching the Bilingual: New Methods and Old Traditions*. Tucson: University of Arizona Press, 1974.

Rakes, T. A., and Emily Canter. "Children's Language: Theirs to Use!" *Elementary English, 51*:8 (1974), pp. 1087–1090.

Salzar, R. "Piaget and Reading Instruction," *The Reading Teacher 24*:7 1971), pp. 630–640.

Sandberg, J. H., and Joanne D. Pohlman. "Reading on the Child's Terms," *Young Children, 31*:2 (1976) pp. 106–112.

Scherwitzky, Marjorie. "Reading in the Kindergarten: A Survey in Virginia," *Young Children, 29*:3 (1974), pp. 161–169.

Smith, J. A., and Dorothy M. Park. *Word Music and Word Magic: Children's Literature Methods*. Boston: Allyn and Bacon, 1977.

Stauffer, R. G., and J. J. Pikulski. "A Comparison and Measure of Oral Language Growth," *Elementary English, 51*:8 (1974), pp. 1151–1155.

Sullivan, D., and J. H. Humphrey. *Teaching Reading Through Motor Learning*. Springfield, Ill.: Charles C Thomas, 1973.

Weaver, Susan W., and W. L. Rutherford. "A Hierarchy of Listening Skills," *Elementary English, 51*:8 (1974), pp. 1146–1150.

Weiser, Margaret. "Parental Responsibility in the Teaching of Reading," *Young Children, 29*:4 (1974), pp. 225–230.

————. "Awareness—One Key to Reading Readiness," *Young Children, 25*:6 (1970), pp. 340–344.

Williams, Jean. "The Relationship of Self Concept and Reading Achievement in First Grade Children," *Journal of Educ. Research, 66*:8 (1973), pp. 378–381.

Winn, Marie. *The Plug-in Drug*. New York: Viking Press, 1977.

chapter 12

Growth through language activities

The child develops skill in the language arts by participating in various experiences and activities. One activity can contribute to growth in several of the arts and, for that reason, activities have not been labeled as appropriate for reading, speaking, listening, or writing. Rather, the activities of storytelling, using poetry, sharing, and dramatizing are discussed, and the ways in which each contributes to growth in the language arts are noted. Certain activities have not been labeled for child development center, nursery school, or kindergarten because of the wide range of individual differences from group to group. Using information pertaining to development and experience of the children in the class, the teacher can select and adapt the activity most appropriate for them.

In working with children from culturally different backgrounds, the teacher will find the language arts activities essential. It is especially important, however, that the teacher utilize the information pertaining to the maturity and experiential background of the children in the selection of the story, poem, book, or materials for dramatic play.

Although activities discussed in this chapter are labeled language arts activities, it is emphasized that these activities are applicable and usable in many different learning situations. Poetry may be read and stories told which relate to social studies, mathematics, and other subject areas. Books with science content may be read to the children. Role-playing and dramatization are techniques useful in a variety of learning situations.

STORYTELLING

Young children today enjoy a good story just as children always have. Although the content of the story may vary from generation to generation, the use of storytelling to entertain, to teach, and to develop appreciation of literature continues to be an important art.

While many other values are recognized, the discussion in this chapter will relate primarily to storytelling as an activity that offers opportunities for developing skills in the language arts. Specifically, the child may learn to listen and have experience in speaking while talking about the story or telling original stories. The child may learn to keep in mind a sequence of ideas, increase vocabulary, and enlarge the background of experiences. These points are emphasized, not to limit the creative possibilities of storytelling nor to formalize the art, but rather to indicate ways in which this creative activity can make a contribution—a fact often overlooked.

Teachers without training in speech or dramatics may hesitate to undertake telling stories to children. Others have questions regarding the selection and use of stories. Rather than use a general discussion for guidance, questions that are often asked in regard to storytelling have been identified and suggested procedures have been discussed.

Selecting an appropriate story for young children

A checklist that may be used by the teacher in the selection of stories includes the following criteria:

1. A simple, well-developed plot, centered in one main sequence of events, structured so that a child can anticipate to some degree the outcome of events, with action predominant. A slight surprise element which makes the children wonder what will happen next can add much to the story.

Figure 34
These children have listened to a story and are responding to questions by placing the appropriate pictures on the board.

2. A large amount of direct conversation.
3. Use of repetition, rhyme, and catch phrases that the child memorizes quickly and easily.
4. Use of carefully chosen, colorful language.
5. Situations involving familiar happenings. The new, unusual, and different may be included, but there must be enough of the familiar with which the child can identify. The "familiar happenings" will not be the same for all children. Children from culturally different homes have often had different experiences. In selecting stories for them, their experiential background should be considered.
6. Simple and satisfying climax.
7. One main character with whom the child can easily identify. Too many characters can be confusing.
8. A variety of ethnic, cultural, and racial backgrounds. Such stories should present realistic pictures, not ridiculous stereotypes of racial or ethnic groups.

Children's books are often a source of stories to be told. Criteria listed for selecting a story are also applicable to the contents of a book. In addition, the following questions may be helpful.[1]

1. Does the book help the child gain some insight into his or her own personal life or the lives of other people?
2. Does the plot or action of the story hold the child's interest?
3. Does the content add to the child's joy in living and a feeling that life is good?
4. Are the characters honest, well described, unforgettable?

[1] Mary Hill Arbuthnot, *Children and Books*, 3rd ed. (Glenview, Ill.: Scott, Foresman, 1964), p. 19.

5. Does the story include humor, dramatic elements, and beauty of language appropriate for the child and the story?
6. Is the information accurate? Will the information help expand the child's experiential background?

These questions should be considered as generalizations and not applied too rigidly. There may be books or stories which do not measure up in every detail, yet may be good for a special child or occasion.

Deciding whether to tell or to read a story

The question is often asked as to whether a story should be read or told to the child. Examining the values involved, there appears to be a place for both telling and reading. Telling the story enables the teacher to establish and maintain eye contact with the children and thus encourage listening. Since no script is involved, the teacher can easily make explanations or adaptations in length or vocabulary for the children. The story that is told seems more direct, informal, and intimate than one that is read. Reading the story, however, has the advantage of the example of the teacher reading from the book, helping the child to recognize that reading can be fun and to associate pleasure with reading. It is important that the teacher set a good example in holding the book and turning the pages, seated so that the book is at the eye level of the children. The teacher should be familiar enough with the story to be able to read it well. The book should not be a crutch to avoid the effort of learning the story.

Preparing and telling a story

Some teachers say that it is hard for them to learn to tell a story. Often a person thinks that it is necessary to memorize a story, word for word. There is no one way to tell a story, but the following suggestions for preparing and telling the story may be helpful:

1. Picture the story to yourself, since the story should be learned as a series of pictures. Read the story slowly, forming a picture in your mind of each character and event. Close the book and think through the story in terms of the pictures you have made. Read the story again for language. The words fit themselves to the pictures and the story takes form.[2]
2. Use direct quotations when a character speaks.
3. Plan a good beginning to gain the attention of the audience. Avoid unnecessary descriptions and explanations.

[2] Ruth Sawyer, *The Way of the Story Teller* (New York: Viking Press, 1962), pp. 131–148.

4. Use a conversational tone of voice, speaking slowly and distinctly. Avoid excessive use of "and," "er." Avoid a sing-song uneven tone and a voice pitch which is too high. Too many gestures tend to detract from the story. Avoid exaggerated facial expressions.
5. Look directly at the children. Include all members of the group, not just those directly in front of you.
6. Sit on a low chair.
7. Use timing effectively, vary the tempo. As action increases and things begin to happen, hurry the tempo. Before a moment of question, surprise, or awe, a pause can be most effective.
8. Keep the story, or the listening period, within the limits of the child's attention span. A range of 7 to 20 minutes has been identified for the preschool period (see page 254).
9. Following the story the children may have a few questions or comments. Take time for these, but do not force discussion by use of questions. This procedure often detracts from the child's enjoyment of the story. If, during the story, a child interrupts to relate an incident, one should encourage him or her to keep it until the story is finished. Occasionally such a contribution is valuable and should be allowed, but many such interruptions can spoil the story.

Helping children listen to the story

Often children want to crowd around the teacher to see the pictures as the story is read or told. The teacher is concerned with getting them to sit down and listen. Before beginning the story, arrange for the children to sit in comfortable positions, in a group or in a semicircle, in front of the storyteller. Be sure they can hear and see easily. They may be seated either on the floor, on a rug, or in chairs.

Give the children an opportunity to see and enjoy the illustrations as the story is being told. This may be done in several ways. In telling a story, the teacher can hold the book in front and slighty to the side, always at the eye-level of the children. Using the book in this way enables the child to see the pictures while the story is being told and helps to hold attention.

The teacher may not find it necessary to show the pictures throughout the story. She can show the picture and say, "See the picture. Now I will tell you the story," or, "Just as soon as I tell you a part of the story I will show you the picture." The teacher then pauses briefly at the appropriate time to share the picture. The teacher who forgets to show the picture invites trouble. The child who crowds up may be reminded quietly to sit down so that everyone can see.

When reading the story the teacher may also hold the book to the side to show the pictures to the children. If this practice is followed, the teacher will need to group the children so that all may see and so that it will not be necessary to turn the face and voice away from them. As the children become able to listen to the longer story with more plot, the teacher may not find it necessary to show the pictures while reading.

Using aids in storytelling

Aids can be used to make the story more effective and to offer variety. Figures or dolls representing the characters may be used by the teacher during the story or placed on the library table along with the book. The latter enables the child to handle the figures as he or she looks at the book. If dolls representing the characters are not available, pictures of the characters can be cut, mounted, and placed in small stands or racks. A flannel board is effective also, since figures cut from felt or flannel can be used on the board. Pictures made by the teacher or children can be prepared by gluing strips of sandpaper to the back of the picture. The story "The Peddler and His Caps" is appropriate for such use. It is important, however, that the aids be manipulated in such a way as not to distract the child's attention from the story. After a flannel board story has been told, the figures and board can be left out for the children to use in retelling the story or in creating one of their own.

Using fairy stories or tales

The fairy tale, according to Bettelheim, is a unique form of art. Children can be entertained by the fairy tale, helped to understand themselves and develop their personalities, and encouraged to learn the advantages of moral behavior.[3]

Bettelheim says that we cannot know the age at which one child may be interested in a particular fairy tale. Usually the parents, teacher, or other adults begin by reading or telling to children a tale that was their favorite. This tale, however, may not be appropriate for a particular child or group of children. The reactions of the children should be noted, especially those of younger children.[4]

As a rule, the traditional fairy tales with cruel witches and stepmothers, kings, and queens are not used with young children. The child at this age usually is not yet able to distinguish easily between fact and fancy, and the

[3] Bruno Bettelheim, *The Uses of Enchantment—The Meaning and Importance of Fairy Tales* (New York: Alfred A. Knopf, 1976), pp. 12–13.

[4] Ibid., pp. 17–18.

Figure 35
An interesting story and a good storyteller encourage children to listen.

gruesome details, easily accepted later as "make-believe," often trouble the young child. This does not mean, however, that fanciful tales are to be omitted. Some stories relate imaginative experiences of children. In other stories that are children's favorites, one will find animals speaking. Children often talk with animals or toys, and conversation of this type is within their range of experiences. Most fables are not suitable to use with young children. However, in some instances, if the moralizing is omitted, the storytelling value is high.

USE OF BOOKS

Not by accident does a child develop a love for books, a feeling that books can be friends and companions, an awareness of the fun and enjoyment that can come from books, an appreciation of good literature, the knowledge that books can be sources of information, and an interest in caring for books. All these attitudes, which it is hoped the young child will develop, evolve as the child has many pleasurable experiences with books both at home and at school.

Opportunities for the children to listen to and enjoy stories, read and told, to handle, use, and love books can help them to learn that reading can be fun and to become interested in learning to read. In selecting a book, the contents, illustrations, and physical makeup are important items to be considered.

Types and content of books

Young children should be introduced to a variety of types of literature recommended for young children. Picture books and Mother Goose Rhymes, books of poetry, information, counting, concepts, the alphabet, animal stories, humor, everyday experiences, and inspiration, and other books that stimulate creative expression, are essential.

Illustrations

Attention should be given to the illustrations, remembering that young children usually read their books via pictures. The artist is really the co-storyteller and his or her work complements rather than supplements that of the author.[5] The content, mood, and feeling of the illustrations should be relevant and match the plot and tone of the story. Just as the story's text includes things familiar to the young child with few details yet plenty of action, so should the illustrations. This is especially true of books for young children, since they are largely picture books without text or with a very simple story. Children like brightly colored illustrations but these need not be used to the exclusion of well done black-and-white or muted ones.

Format

Book bindings should be sturdy and firmly stitched. The covers should be attractive in order to encourage the child to care for them. A binding that comes off the book at the first careless handling can be most discouraging for the child. It is well to talk with children about how books should be cared for and where they are kept.

Among the collection of books are those for holidays and special occasions that will not be used as often as some of the others. These books may be purchased in the less expensive editions, but the same criteria for content and illustrations apply. For the favorites that are used day in and day out, a good binding is an economy. The pages should be of strong, heavy paper to prevent

---

[5] V. E. Herrick and L. B. Jacobs, *Children and the Language Arts* (Englewood Cliffs, N.J.: Prentice-Hall, 1955), p. 199.

their tearing easily as the child turns them. The size of type and spacing of words are important.

Most of the books should be light enough and of a size that is easy for the child to handle. Some large books may be included for occasional use and enjoyment on the rug or the table.

Using book collections

The well-selected collection of books is not enough. To be effective in the lives of children, it must be well used. All of the books need not be displayed all the time. Change the books on the library table and in the library corner often. Unless this is done, the child may become so accustomed to seeing the book that it becomes a fixture rather than an exciting adventure. Display books attractively on a table or on a low shelf. Flowers, a plant, or cut-outs of characters in the story may be used to advantage.

Plan ahead so that the time spent in looking at or using books becomes important. Avoid using books when there is nothing else to do or just to "fill in." For example, the child may say to the teacher, "I've finished. I don't know what to do." Too often, an indifferent reply is made, "Go and get a book," and the child responds in the same indifferent manner.

Arrange for children to borrow a favorite book to take home and share with their families. In one kindergarten, choosing a book is a part of getting ready to go home. If the child wants a book, she or he brings it to the teacher and together they write the name on the book list. The list is posted, and when the book is returned the child checks his or her name off the list. Such a procedure helps children to develop responsibility in using and caring for books. Children may be encouraged to bring books from home to share with the group. A visit to the library can help to develop an interest in books and an understanding of how books are cared for. The teacher can provide suggested book lists for parents. The books may be purchased or secured from the local or school library.

Bulletin boards may be used to display children's paintings, drawings, or other art products of their favorite book. Jackets of favorite books may be used in the display.

The teacher, then, must not only select a good collection of books but must use them effectively with children. Personal interest in and knowledge of the classics as well as current books, skill in using books with and reading them to children, and a true appreciation and enjoyment of books determine in large measure the extent to which children gain the values which may be derived from books. In selecting books for the collection, there are several sources which the teacher may consult:

1. Published book lists and catalogues. One that is inexpensive and revised frequently is *A Bibliography of Books for Children.*[6] The American Association of School Librarians and the Association for Childhood Education International have published *Excellent Paperbacks for Children.* The list is revised frequently.[7]
2. Reviews of books for children published in professional periodicals. The teacher may supplement the nursery school or kindergarten collection by borrowing books reviewed from a library. In some cities a teacher may borrow as many as twenty books for a two-week period. When these are returned, others can be selected.

Movement and children's literature

Huck suggests that basic rhythmic movements may be introduced through Mother Goose rhymes. "Jack and Jill" may be used for children to walk to, "Ride a Cock Horse" for galloping, "Jack Be Nimble" for jumping, and "Wee Willie Winkie" for running.[8]

POETRY

Experiences with poetry can be happy and spontaneous ones for children. They enjoy the sounds around them, create sounds, laugh at unusual combinations of words, sense the rhythm of running, skipping, and speaking. The spontaneous language of children is often poetic in nature. Dorothy, telling about the little bird that had fallen out of the nest, said, "The little bird was shivering with scaredness." Poetry, if well selected and correctly used, can help the child to listen carefully; to learn new words and ways of expressing one's feelings; to develop increased auditory awareness or acuity; to improve the quality of one's own voice; and to feel secure in the group as one participates in saying poetry with the group. Poetry can bring laughter and happiness to the child.

The success of the teacher in presenting poetry to children depends on several factors: (1) the selection of verses which are appropriate for the age of the child and for use in a wide variety of situations; (2) the teacher's own appreciation of poetry and the manner in which she shares poetry with the children; and (3) the extent to which poetry is used.

[6] *A Bibliography of Books for Children* (Washington, D.C.: Association for Childhood Education International, 3615 Wisconsin Ave., NW, 20016, 1977).

[7] *Excellent Paperbacks for Children* (Washington, D.C.: Association for Childhood Education International, 3615 Wisconsin, Ave., NW, 20016, 1978).

[8] Charlotte S. Huck, *Children's Literature in the Elementary School,* 3rd ed. (New York: Holt, Rinehart and Winston, 1976), p. 664.

Selecting poetry for use with children

Children enjoy a wide variety of poems including those about the here and now; situations familiar to the children—playmates, clothing, and pets; poems about nature—the seasons, the wind, the falling leaves or signs of spring; poems that are fanciful and imaginative; holiday poems; humorous verses, and those filled with the repetition of unusual sounds with a singing quality. One should use poems related to the experience at hand, but it is undesirable to force correlations which do not fit.

The content of the poem should be sufficiently related to the child's experiences that he can understand something of the meaning expressed by the words.[9] How many children today are likely to understand Stevenson's likening the sound of the wind to the passing of "ladies skirts across the grass"?

Jacobs says:

> Children enjoy good poetry that:
> Gives them an exhilarating sense of melodious movement.
> Makes the everyday experiences of life vibrant.
> Tells wonderful stories.
> Releases health-giving laughter.
> Carries them into extravagant or fanciful situations.
> Extends their appreciation of their natural world.
> Creates memorable personages or characters.
> Sings its way into their minds and memories.[10]

Sharing poetry with children

First of all, if children are to appreciate and enjoy poetry, it is imperative that the teacher appreciate poetry and share his or her enjoyment in presenting the poems to them. Arbuthnot suggests that in exploring a new poem, the teacher read it aloud first in order to become familiar with the words, mood, and tempo.[11] Unless this is done, the teacher may not find the sound pattern or rhythm of the poem and as a result the reading will be dull and meaningless.

The poem may either be read or shared from memory. The teacher who knows a number of poems can share them informally with a small group or even with one child on the playground, while taking a walk, observing a pet, or whenever there is an opportunity. But no one teacher can memorize all the poems that will be needed. Familiarity with children's poetry and knowing where to find it, will mean being able to share the poem at a later time, merely

[9] Arbuthnot, op. cit., p. 195.
[10] L. B. Jacobs, "Enjoying Poetry with Children," in *Literature with Children* (Washington, D.C.: ACEI, 1972), pp. 33–34.
[11] Arbuthnot, op. cit., p. 205.

recalling the incident or mood to which it refers. However, not all poetry should be related to some thing or incident. Sometimes it is shared just for fun or pleasure

Memorizing poetry

Forced memorization of poems has turned many children away from poetry.[12] A teacher who often reads well-selected poetry to children in a simple, natural, and an appreciative manner will soon find that the children will "say" the poem while it is being read. Many children will learn poems in this manner without the pressure to memorize.

Choral speaking (or a verse choir) for young children is largely speaking poetry in unison. Children may experiment with different ways of saying a verse, once it has been learned in the manner suggested above. For instance, the boys may say the verse, then the girls. Use questions such as, "How does it sound?" If questions or conversation are used, as in the verse "Sing-Song" by Christina Rossetti, try having one child speak those lines and the entire group the remaining lines. Some poems may be broken up and each child say a line or two. Mother Goose rhymes such as "Pease Porridge Hot" or "This Little Pig" are examples.

SHARING TIME AND GROUP DISCUSSION

The word *sharing* is often used in nursery school and kindergarten with reference to the use of toys and materials. It implies the willingness to "take turns" or to "let Jane have some clay." Sharing may also refer to communicating— between children or between teacher and child. For the child who is beginning nursery school, this communication may involve only a few words accompanied by a facial expression that emphasizes the thought. On the first cool morning, Mary arrived dressed in a new blue sweater. "Look," she said as she displayed the sweater, her eyes sparkling and her face alight with an expression of joy and well-being. As this informal communicating and sharing continues, the child uses more words to express her thoughts. As children become more secure in a group situation, they want and need to talk together, and a time in the school day for planning and sharing may be designated. This activity is usually considered appropriate for kindergarten groups, although some more mature nursery classes may begin such a period. The time for beginning such a group activity, however, will depend on the children involved —their interests, attention span, and readiness to participate in a group situation.

[12] Herrick and Jacobs, op. cit., pp. 211–217.

This period for sharing often goes by the name "Show and Tell," which has been somewhat discredited. Such a name implies an activity in which the child shows some object and tells about it. There are those who claim that it is an artificial situation and becomes a monotonous routine, thus losing its language value. Sharing time implies communication. Objects may be shown and talked about, but plans, incidents, and news may be discussed too by the teacher as well as by the children.

Discussion time, however, with teacher and children, is usually problem-centered. Plans may be made for a trip or a special project for the morning. The choice of activities may be discussed. This type of sharing time and discussion can be rich in opportunities for developing skills in the language arts. The child can learn to:

1. Speak distinctly and clearly.
2. Speak in front of a group.
3. Tell an incident in sequence.
4. Listen politely.
5. Take turns in speaking.
6. Speak in complete sentences.

Encouraging children to participate

Some children never speak in the group, and the question is often asked, "How may they be encouraged to participate?"

First, it is important to determine why the child does not participate. Is he or she afraid of a group situation? Could it be that the child has nothing to share? Is the child bored, uninterested? Not knowing the other children well, might she or he feel no need to communicate with them? The answers will depend on the reason.

Only gradually does a child come to feel secure in a group situation. Both Jennie and Gloria seemed to remain on the fringes. Fear of the group will not be overcome by forcing participation. Rather, the teacher may encourage sharing with them at times other than the organized period. Gradually, one or two children may be included by comments such as, "That is a beautiful book. Let's show it to Joe," or "Such good news! Tell Bob." The number of individuals may be expanded to form small groups, gradually increasing the size. One must remember that sharing does not always mean speaking. First attempts may involve showing a book or toy without a comment. With maturity and security, speaking will come later.

For a child who has nothing to share, the teacher may be alert during the day to help the child identify something worthy of sharing with the group. For example, as the child arrives in the morning, he or she tells the teacher that on the way to school there was a squirrel scampering up a tree. A few questions, such as "What was it carrying in its mouth?" may help the child clarify and identify the details of the incident. The teacher may say, "That is a very interesting story. Please tell the other children at sharing time."

A child may become bored or lose interest because he or she does not have an opportunity to speak. This can happen when a few children are permitted to dominate the situation, speaking loudly and often. The teacher can help these children learn to take turns. A reminder, "You had a turn, Joe," may help. Consistently, the teacher must remind the children of those who have shared and those who still need a turn. A child with several items to share may need to be reminded, "You have told us about one thing. The other children need a turn before you tell us more."

Encouraging good habits of listening

The teacher may refer to the suggestions on pp. 258–260 regarding listening. In addition, it is important to help children learn what is involved in good listening. The teacher may say to the child who is ready to share, "Look around the circle. See if everyone is ready to listen before you begin to speak."

DRAMATIZATION

The word *creativity* is often used only in connection with the arts. The discussions on using books, poetry, storytelling (pp. 270–280), and the creative arts, (pp. 419–461), present creativity as related to these areas. Many activities considered simple and unimaginative may offer opportunities for creative expression. If language expression is to be creative, it must be based on thoughts and ideas that are the child's own. The child should therefore be given opportunities for experiences to develop many ideas and thoughts. In the language arts, the creative expression of the child may take many forms. Some children may express their feelings in pantomime, while others may use puppets. Dramatization can offer many activities through which creativity in oral language may be encouraged.[13]

Dramatization may include dramatic play, creative dramatics, and using puppets. While there is no clear-cut distinction, each does have a unique characteristic. The relationships and differences are discussed in the following sections.

[13] H. A. Greene and W. T. Petty, *Developing Language Skills in the Elementary Schools*, 5th ed. (Boston: Allyn and Bacon, 1975), pp. 179–183.

Dramatic play

Dramatic play is spontaneous and free of teacher direction. This type of play is one in which the child may try living life as an adult; find out how it feels to have certain responsibilities, such as feeding the baby or cooking dinner; clarify concepts regarding the role of mother, the firefighter, or the doctor; and practice certain basic language skills, such as speaking, using conversation, listening, learning new words, clarifying the meaning of words, and social amenities. Dramatic play offers opportunities for children to come to understand their world and the people in it. In this section, the focus is on the aspects of dramatic play as they relate to the language arts.

The teacher's responsibility includes providing many interesting opportunities for the children, since the child's creative efforts are limited to experience—trips, contacts with various people, recordings, books, pictures, and films; and providing space, materials, and time for the activity. Once this has been done, usually nothing more is required. If a child does not participate readily, the teacher may help the child enter the group by suggesting some role the child can assume. Conversation between the teacher and child can yield leads to dramatic play and to more talking among the children.

The teacher does not direct the activity. The children do this. The teacher

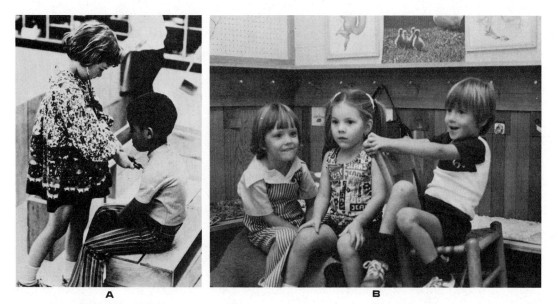

A   B

Figure 36

In dramatic play children may try living as adults and find out how it feels to have certain responsibilities. In this instance, Cynthia is the doctor. Who knows where these three are traveling in their dramatic play?

seeks to guide the dramatic play so that the experience is satisfying to the children. This means that the teacher may need to help in the settlement of a dispute and solving problems that arise. Timing of teacher help is very important, lest the play become disrupted and the children discouraged. The teacher also observes possible leads for further study and notes concepts which may need to be clarified.

John, Lisa, and Myron, who were building a train of large blocks, were engaged in a heated argument as to the location of the engine. John, the engineer, insisted that it was first, but Myron and Lisa were certain that it should be after the coaches. In talking with the children, it became evident that they did not know the purpose or the names of the various cars on the train or the people who work on the train. Here was a lead. A trip, a film, pictures, stories, models were all used to clarify the concept.

Puppets

Puppets are often used by children in dramatic play or dramatizations. The child who hesitates to speak with others or before the group may speak freely through a puppet. With young children the puppets are generally used informally without screens or stories. Usually the conversation is supplied by the individual child or perhaps two children. Puppets are made available and the child chooses to use them as he or she wishes or needs to do so.

Puppets for the young are kept simple. Pictures of people or animals glued on sticks, sacks filled with air and with ends twisted to make a handle, or commercial hand puppets are all useful.

Creative dramatics

In this group activity, an experience is acted out by the children as they are guided in thinking, feeling, and creating their own dialogue and action. There are no lines to be memorized, no formal audience, no costumes, or technical aids. The dramatization may be original as to the idea or it may be based on a poem or story written by someone else.

Creative dramatics contributes to language arts skills as children speak, communicate, and listen. Auditory discrimination may also be built. According to Siks, "A child's ability to discriminate grows through such satisfying experiences as becoming a train engine that moves fast or slow; a train with a light load or a heavy load . . . a train that is near or far away."[14] As children

---

[14] Geraldine B. Siks, *Creative Dramatics, An Art for Children* (New York: Harper & Row, 1958), p. 280.

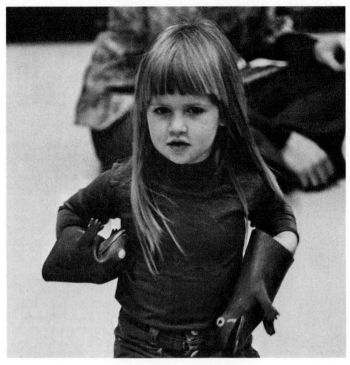

Figure 37
Puppets are generally used informally by young children without screen or stories. Conversation may be supplied by the individual child or perhaps by two children.

play out appropriate stories and verses, they enjoy and learn to appreciate good literature. Lease and Siks offer suggestions for introducing creative dramatics to young children.[15] They suggest that the teacher begin with:

1. Rhythmic movement. Create the mood by several statements before asking the question. "Let's pretend that we are going outside to pick up nuts. Let's see how many nuts we can find. What is one way you can look for the nuts?" Some may crawl on hands and knees, others walk slowly looking down on the ground, some skip, others run.

   The children may also do characterizations in rhythmic movements. For instance, they may characterize animals by the way they walk and sound, the weather, the wind blowing, rain falling.

2. Songs. Many children's songs suggest action, pantomime, or characterizations. The teacher may sing while the children do the actions. The teacher may use a recording to which the children respond or let one group of children sing while the remainder pantomime. Singing games offer opportunities for beginning experiences in this area also.

3. Finger plays. As children participate in finger plays, vivid pictures may be

---

[15] Ruth G. Lease and Geraldine B. Siks, *Creative Dramatics in Home, School, and Community* (New York: Harper & Row, 1952), p. 37.

formed in their minds and they may be guided to feel and act as characters felt in the finger play.

4. Dramatic play as discussed on pp. 283–284.
5. Pantomime poetry or verse. Nursery rhymes, Mother Goose, and other poems that are short, the characterizations limited, and the action direct, are appropriate.

After children have had considerable experience in the activities already described, they are ready to play the role of an individual character. The teacher selects a verse already familiar to the group, for instance, "The Caterpillar," and says it to the children.

Fuzzy wuzzy, creepy crawly
    Caterpillar funny,
You will be a butterfly
    When the days are sunny

Winging, flinging, dancing, springing
    Butterfly so yellow,
You were once a caterpillar,
    Wiggly, wiggly fellow.[16]

Then the teacher may say something like this: "Here is some nice green grass. Let's all be caterpillars crawling on the grass." After the children have enjoyed being caterpillars, the teacher may say, "What creepy, crawly caterpillars. Now you have become a butterfly. How do you think the butterfly feels? Let's all be butterflies here on the grass." The questions will lead to lively discussion and creative thinking. It is important, however, that the teacher not spend too long in talking and planning with very young children. They are eager to *do*, to play the role. The teacher, in talking about the characters, will do well to discuss how the butterfly feels, rather than what is says or does. As Lease and Siks say, "When children are thinking and feeling in character, the action will be spontaneous."[17]

Following group participation in the roles of the different characters, one child will be chosen to be the butterfly and one to be the caterpillar. This may be repeated several times with different children playing the different characters. Some children may pantomime a Mother Goose rhyme, for example, "Little Miss Muffett," while others try to guess what it is.

6. Dramatize or play a story. Folk tales provide stories which are short and in which the actions and feelings of the characters are easily identified. Suggestions pertaining to pantomime are relevant here. Once the children are familiar with the story, the teacher may plan briefly with the children for one scene of the story. Do not try to plan for the entire story at one time. Characters are identified and children asked to play the different roles. They may be helped

---

[16] Lillian Schulz, "The Caterpillar," in ACEI, *Sung Under the Silver Umbrella* (New York: Macmillan Publishing Co., 1962), p. 77.

[17] Lease and Siks, op. cit., p. 39.

Figure 38
Using the typewriter, Chris can write her name.

to assume roles of the different characters by questions directed to the entire group. For instance, if the story were *Three Billy Goats Gruff,* comments such as the following might be used. "What kind of goat was the first billy goat? How did he feel when he heard the Old Troll? Tell us about the Old Troll. What kind of creature was he?"

Emphasis is not placed on remembering what the character says. Once the child has a feeling for the character and senses how the character feels, then the child's speech as well as actions will be spontaneous. The child may easily forget *what* to say if taught only the words. If one is playing the *role,* then there are several different ways, however to express the character's feelings. The child is seldom at a loss for words.

SUMMARY

Teachers who have used activities such as stories, poetry, and dramatic play without analyzing, understanding, and noting ways in which they contribute to growth in the language arts may not be articulate in resisting questionable practices. Table 12-1 summarizes the contributions of each activity included in the chapter, not to prove the academic value of the activities described, but to emphasize the fact that creative, spontaneous language experiences can also contribute to foundation learnings.

Table 12-1

Contributions of Language Arts Activities

	Reading Readiness	Listening	Speaking	Writing
1. Dramatization	Visual and auditory discrimination, enriched vocabulary; clarification of concepts; interest in books and reading.	Appreciation and enjoyment of good literature; listening while others speak.	Discussion and planning, speaking in front of group, taking turns in speaking; feeling secure and a member of the group.	Recognition of value of writing; list of characters on chart.
2. Poetry	Auditory acuity; hear likenesses and differences in sounds.	Appreciation and enjoyment of poetry.	Encourages distinct speech; encourages speaking before the group; choral reading may help the child feel a part of the group.	Use of writing to record one's ideas.
3. Storytelling	Experience in listening; enriched vocabulary; clarification of concepts; interest in books and reading.	Appreciation and enjoyment of good literature.	Conversation about the story.	Recognizing that a story is recorded for others to share at a later date.
4. Sharing	Enriches vocabulary; clarifies concepts; listens; keeps in mind a sequence of ideas.	Experience in listening to other children.	Takes turns in speaking; speaks distinctly and clearly; tells an incident in sequence; speaks in front of group; speaks in complete sentences; develops a sentence sense; takes part in group planning; asks questions.	Awareness of importance of writing through dictating plans or invitations.

Suggested Activities

1. Select, prepare, and tell a story appropriate for a four- or five-year-old group of children. Evaluate your performance in terms of the criteria on pp. 272–273. Select another story and prepare figures for use on a flannel board to accompany it.
2. Begin to keep a poetry file. Choose three topics appropriate for the young child, such as Play, Bed-Time, Holidays, Minorities. For each topic, select and record several poems.
3. Examine a collection of books for young children. Select and evaluate three each of picture books, and books that deal with concept development, holidays, and minority groups, in terms of criteria presented on pp. 271–272.
4. Visit a center for young children and become acquainted with several of the children. For the group, select a story and read it to them. On another occasion, select a poem and say or share it with the group. Evaluate.
5. Observe young children engaged in dramatic play. Note the roles that the children seem to be assuming and the topics for play. Compare your observations with those of others in your class. Discuss differences observed. Note the teacher's role. Note materials provided for dramatic play.
6. Visit a materials center or a distributor's display. Examine current kits and packaged materials for young children in reading, writing, speaking, and language development. Evaluate in terms of the goals of your center.
7. View the film, *Dramatic Play, An Integrative Process*. Campus Films, 20 East 46th Street, New York, N.Y. 10017, 1972. Compare with own observations.

Related Readings

Anderson, P. S. "Rediscovering Children's Literature," *Language Skills in Elementary Education*, 2nd ed. New York: Macmillan Publishing Co., 1972, pp. 121–168.

Batinich, Mary. "Language Experience Activities," *Reading Teacher*, 23:6 (1970), pp. 539–546.

Beyer, Evelyn. "Language Learning—Fresh, Vivid and Their Own," *Child. Educ.*, 48:1 (1971), pp. 21–24.

Cazden, Courtney (ed.). *Functions of Language in the Classroom*. New York: Teachers College, 1972.

Cohen, M. D. (ed.). *Literature with Children*. Washington, D.C.: ACEI, 1972.

Coody, Betty. *Using Literature with Young Children*. Dubuque, Iowa: Wm. C. Brown Co. Publishers, 1973.

Cullinan, Bernice E., and Carolyn W. Carmichael (eds.). *Literature and Young Children*. Urbana, Ill.: National Council of Teachers of English, 1977.

Fassler, Joan. "Children's Literature and Early Childhood Separation Experiences," *Young Children*, 29:5 (1974), pp. 311–323.

Fisher, Carol J., and C. Ann Terry. *Children's Language and the Language Arts*. New York: McGraw-Hill Book Co., 1977, pp. 283–289.

Fitzgerald, Alice Irene. "Literature Approved by Today's Kindergarten Children," *Elem. English*, 48:8 (1971), pp. 953–959.

Gilpatric, Naomi. "Power of Picture Books to Change Child's Self-Image," *Elem. English, 46*:5 (1969), pp. 570–574.

Hall, Mary Anne. *Teaching Reading as a Language Experience.* Columbus, Ohio: Charles E. Merrill Publishing Co., 1970.

Hawkins, Roberta. "Nursery Rhymes: Mirrors of a Culture," *Elem. English, 48*:6 (1971), pp. 617–621.

Hayes Eloise. "Expanding the Child's World Through Drama and Movement,"*Child. Educ. 47*:7 (1971), pp. 360–367.

Herrick, V. E., and Marcella Nervobig. *Using Experience Charts with Children.* Columbus Ohio: Charles E. Merrill Publishing Co., 1964.

Hildebrand, Verna. *Guiding Young Children.* New York: Macmillan Publishing Co., 1975, pp. 260–272.

Hollingsworth, P. M. "Let's Improve Listening Skills," *Elementary English, 51*:8 (1974), pp. 1156–1157, 1161.

Huck, Charlotte S. *Children's Literature in the Elementary School,* 3rd ed. New York: Holt, Rinehart, and Winston, 1976.

Monson, Dianne L., and Bette J. Peltola (compilers). *Research in Children's Literature.* Newark, Del.: International Reading Association, 1976.

Ostler, Renee, and P. L. Kranz. "More Effective Communication Through Understanding Young Children's Nonverbal Behavior," *Young Children, 31*:2 (1976), pp. 113–120.

Sadker, Myra D., and D. M. Sadker. *Now Upon A Time: A Contemporary View of Children's Literature.* New York: Harper & Row, 1977.

Siks, Geraldine B. *Drama with Children.* New York: Harper & Row, 1977.

Swift, M. S., Mary Uelli, Tracey Warner, and D. Klein. "Preschool Books and Mother–Child Communication," *Reading Teacher, 25*:3 (1971), pp. 236–238.

Tanyzer, H., and Jean Karl (eds.). *Reading, Children's Books, and Our Pluralistic Society.* Newark, Del.: International Reading Association, 1972.

Todd, Virginia E., and Helen Heffernan. *The Years Before School—Guiding Preschool Children,* 3rd ed. New York: Macmillan Publishing Co., 1977, pp. 409–480.

Toothaker, R. E. "Curiosities of Children That Literature Can Satisfy," *Child. Educ., 52*:5 (1976), pp. 262–267.

White, Doris (compiler). *Multi-ethnic Books for Head Start Children, Part I: Black and Integrated Literature.* Urbana, Ill.: ERIC Clearinghouse on Early Childhood Education and National Laboratory on Early Childhood Education, 1969.

chapter 13

Mathematics

Mathematics programs for young children vary greatly. In some programs proficiency in counting, writing numerals, and other mathematical skills is the primary objective. Another focus, however, is the almost exclusive use of the incidental activities in which the child participates each day as the basis for whatever mathematical skills may be developed.

THE MATHEMATICS CURRICULUM

A mathematics curriculum organized primarily around one of these positions tends to ignore the possible interrelationships of various phases of development and the questions relating to content, teaching, and learning. A balanced program can be planned in such a way as to provide for an intellectual orientation as well as a recognition of the broader aspects of the child's development. The balanced program should:[1]

> Emphasize the thinking processes and concept development.
> Emphasize language acquisition and use of oral language in relation to the child's real-life activities—not as rote verbalizations.
> Introduce new language and written symbols slowly.
> Build a child's self-confidence in perception and the ability to find information and to draw conclusions from it.
> Encourage the child to perceive, describe, and extend patterns.
> Provide for balanced emphasis on concepts, skills, and abilities.
> Provide opportunities for the child to explore, manipulate, make decisions, and experiment.

In order to provide for a balanced program the teacher needs a knowledge of what to teach and an understanding of the children to be taught. First let us look at the children to be taught. There are many theories concerning children's development and many implications of such theories for math education. Piaget's work has helped produce programs that emphasize the development of broad intellectual powers, rather than the mastery of narrow academic skills. He has identified certain stages of development and has established approximate chronological age boundaries for each stage. Only the preoperational stage which includes the ages covered in this text will be discussed here.

The preoperational stage begins at about age one or two and lasts until approximately age seven. Because of individual differences, some children will enter the stage earlier while others may not leave the stage until later. This is the stage of representation and symbolism. Children begin to manipulate symbols or representations of the world in which they live. Playing house, store, garage, doctor, all *let's pretend* activities, involve imagining and represent the real thing. Words are being used to represent things also.

This is the stage of intuitive thinking. The child at about the age of five thinks that things are what they seem, not what they are. If an object seems bigger, then it is bigger, and the child has difficulty with conservation. Gradually the child establishes the "invariance of number." Regardless of how the five acorns may be arranged there are still five acorns. The amount of liquid poured into containers of different shapes remains the same. The child acts on objects to discover their properties. In order to reach a coherent generalization, the child needs to apply reasoning to manipulative materials, to test and find out. Many opportunities, then, are needed for the child to act on objects, to manipulate, explore, make choices and decisions. The child is developing

---

[1] Glenadine Gibb and Alberta M. Castaneda, "Experiences for Young Children," in J. N. Payne, ed. *Mathematics Learning in Early Childhood* (Reston, Va.: National Council of Teachers of Mathematics, 1975), p. 124.

thinking processes, not just correct answers. Gradually, and over a period of time, the child moves into the next stage.[2]

Such information about the child can be of value to the teacher in serving as a guide for expectations, for diagnosing a child's situation, and in individualizing instruction. Too often there is concern for moving the child faster and faster through the stages of development and accelerating learning. Parents and teachers often brag about how advanced their children are. Piaget, however, reports that most of the efforts to accelerate the development of logical thinking have not been successful.[3]

Now for a look at the content of the math program. In centers for young children, teachers recognize that the child may encounter numbers in many ways: selecting nails and hammering wood, setting the table for lunch, and counting cookies and apples. The activity in and of itself can contribute little to the child's mathematical understandings. The interaction of the child and the activity is significant. As the child passes out apples for lunch, does the teacher say that one apple is given to each child? Is there an opportunity to give one to Mary, one to Tony, and so on, thus working out a one-to-one correspondence? Or is the child merely told to count five apples and give them to the children without having the opportunity to think through the process and gain knowledge of the one-to-one correspondence? As the child's thinking is challenged, the teacher will at the same time be helping in the development of intellectual capacity and mathematical understandings. The teacher works not only to provide a rich environment, but one in which the child has many opportunities to interact with objects and people, to have many experiences, and to develop ideas and concepts.

Emphasis on the child's learning through his or her own activities, instead of scheduling a special period for math, does not mean that the teacher has not planned for mathematics. The teacher plans and organizes so that the learning is developed through incidental and not accidental activities which provide opportunities for learning. A child may manipulate and observe materials without understanding their mathematical significance. Interaction between teacher and child is essential. The child may play with a rectangular block and not know the word "rectangle," unless this word is used in context.

To avoid gaps in certain areas of number experiences, it is essential that the teacher give attention to the conditions of learning as related to mathematics, developmental sequence of mathematical concepts and skills, and to questions related to planning for and organizing activities.

Many preschools do not have a special period for mathematics. This does not mean that the teacher has not planned for each child. The teacher may give help individually, in small groups, or by working with a large group in

---

[2] Richard W. Copeland. *How Children Learn Mathematics: Teaching Implications of Piaget's Research* (New York: Macmillan Publishing Co., 1974), p. 26.
[3] Ibid., p. 41.

which each child contributes according to maturity. Accurate records are important. The teacher keeps records of skill and concept development and of how each child uses what is taught in the course of participating in other activities and in free play.

Analyzing mathematical learnings

The teacher recognizes that the children are ready for experiences that build on and extend previous experiences; these experiences are limited but bear repetition in different settings. The child counts spoons, children, and napkins. This change in the setting is important so that the concept, and not the setting, can be learned. Therefore, the skillful teacher utilizes all the natural settings that occur in the daily life of the school and uses the quantitative words correctly in situations. For example, she says: "It is 10 o'clock—time for our lunch," or "It is 12 o'clock—the time your mother will meet you," or "In 10 minutes your father will come."

When going on excursions, the teacher may use a compass with the children to guide their directions or to determine the direction an airplane is flying. The teacher is careful to use such words as *high, low, higher than, lower than, slow, fast, faster, far away, near.* On a trip children observe street signs pointing directions and listing distances. As the children play they estimate, then measure, and compare distances that they jump or run.

Often the large thermometer in the room is read and records made on a calendar as the changes in weather are noted or the date is discussed. Countdown for games and division of materials for work and play become opportunities for developing number learnings if the teacher is alert and plans the activities in terms of the readiness of the children. Selected songs, games, and finger plays develop interest in, and provide for, motivated repetition of concepts presented.

Concepts of quantity and of contrasting sizes and shapes are introduced and used informally; however, provisions for these activities are consciously planned by the teacher. Guided observations and discussions assist the children to know many quantitative words and to apply them in meaningful situations.

Planning and organizing for experiences

Only through listing the attitudes, skills, and understandings desired can a teacher select and plan wisely for the continuous development of number concepts. He or she must plan in terms of the development of individuals and small groups of children as well as for the larger group.

As activities are planned, the teacher records and analyzes the types of home and school experiences that have contributed to the child's number readiness. The teacher builds on and supplements these experiences and plans with the parents so that additional opportunities may be provided in the home for the child to apply and to reuse what has been learned at school.

In one kindergarten, a list of five names written under the word "thermometer" was observed on the teacher's desk. Upon inquiry, the teacher explained that as the result of a recent activity, she had found that these five children did not know how to measure the temperature in the classroom. She had listed these children as those who would need special activities and guidance in the use of the thermometer.

In the same room was another list of children's names written under the figure "25¢." Explanation of this list indicated that these children should be included in activities related to the trip to the store, and that guided experiences should be provided for them to use 25¢ in *real* money (as a quarter, five nickels, or two dimes and a nickel) in functional situations.

All planning for experiences should be flexible yet should make provision for situations that will require use of mathematics and quantitative thinking in a broad program. This program must be comprehensive yet balanced.

MATHEMATICAL PROCESSES, UNDERSTANDINGS, AND SKILLS

The teacher is so familiar with the curriculum and the developmental skills that each experience is taken advantage of as it occurs. In addition, the teacher projects and develops many creative situations through which the desired mathematical learnings are functionally introduced, used, reused, and evaluated. These meaningful experiences offer opportunities to develop simple understandings that later unfold as the child meets more and more difficult situations. Therefore, the teacher needs to make a careful listing of abilities, the skills, possible teaching opportunities and procedures, plans for parent cooperation at school and at home, and ways of evaluating the progress for each child and for groups of children.

Three processes that underlie the concept of number are classifying, comparing, and ordering. Experiences in these processes provide necessary background for the higher degree of abstraction required later.[4] These processes are related to and involve measurement, vocabulary, counting, fractions, shape and space, and organizing and presenting data and patterns.

A discussion of the concepts, abilities, and understandings to be used as a frame of reference or as a basis for planning, and for analyzing the present

[4] Gibb and Castaneda, op. cit., p. 98.

development and the progress of young children in arithmetic skills and understandings may be found on the following pages. Emphasis should be placed upon simple beginnings and expansion of these skills and understandings according to the developmental pace of each child. The child should not be forced to acquire skills; these are acquired as the child understands and finds use for them in daily living. Hence, no designation is made as to specific experiences for nursery school, Head Start, Day Care Center, or kindergarten for three-, four-, or five-year-old children.

Classifying

Young children participate in classifying as they name objects, such as a shoe or a box, put together things that are alike, and engage in a variety of sorting activities. But in order to be able to classify, the child must understand the meaning of the words used by the adult in giving instructions, such as "alike," "put together," "go together." Concepts and words for attributes, purposes, positions, locations are necessary. The development of concepts and vocabulary is an essential part of early mathematics learning.

Copeland reports that children usually sort first by shape, then by color, and last of all by size.[5] Language related to sets is seldom a part of the child's everyday conversation. Classifying, however, can be used to help the child develop concepts and language related to sets. Blocks, a tea set, a pair of shoes may not be thought of as sets, but are considered as single entities. Gibb and Castaneda say that when children are able to classify objects and see the col-

[5] Copeland, op. cit., p. 54.

Figure 39

The first activities with shapes should be planned to help the child develop a general concept of shape, later to describe likenesses and differences in shapes, and finally learn the names for the most common shapes.

lections thus formed as entities, they can then classify sets of objects as equivalent or nonequivalent.[6]

1. Talk about how objects such as toys, fruit, and clothes are alike and how they are different. Include not only words of size, shape, and color, but also words that relate to use, location, and position.
2. Use activities to develop meaning for words and phrases used in the classifying process, such as alike, put together, belong together, combine. (See pp. 230–240 for suggestions for developing language skills.)
3. Develop meaningful vocabulary relevant to the activities of the young child. (See pp. 203–216 for suggestions for developing vocabulary.)
4. Have collected objects, such as buttons, seeds, nails, blocks, felt shapes, and checkers available in boxes. Do not use all the objects each time you take the boxes out. Make a selection each time. Ask child to find two objects that are the same. Talk about how objects are the same. Pick out one object. Ask child to find an object that is the same. Discuss.
5. Make a collection of felt cut-outs using a variety of shapes and colors. Ask children to put together the felt cut-outs that are alike in some way or are the same. Discuss. Repeat, using other objects that can be sorted such as buttons, washers, cups, nails, various toys, cups, spoons.
6. Ask child to select two toys that are in some way the same. Ask other children to guess how the two toys are "the same." Repeat, using dolls, children, books.
7. Show several crayons, telling the children "This is a set of crayons." Repeat with other objects.
8. Using the collection suggested above, selected one object, such as a doll. Ask a child to start a set with it. Name the set and select other members of the set.

Comparing

In the process of comparing, the child establishes a relationship between two objects, using a specific attribute as a basis. For example, when a child says that one crayon is longer than another, the relation, "is longer than" is established. Just as in classifying, it is essential in comparing that the child have an understanding of the attributes used such as longer, shorter, or taller than. The comparing process serves as foundation or base for ordering and measuring.

1. Select two objects, such as dolls or blocks, that differ only in height. Ask the children which doll is taller or shorter. Talk about what they had to do to be sure.

[6] Gibb and Castaneda, op. cit., p. 98.

Figure 40

(Courtesy of Head Start.)

In dramatic play Wanda and Billy use the vocabulary related to money. They have opportunities to recognize and understand the relative value of coins and bills.

2. Put three jars of paint on the easel. Give a child three brushes. Ask if there is a brush for each jar. Talk about how one can find out.
3. Cut out and mount on pieces of cardboard in three distinct sizes three beds and three dolls. Be sure that each item is the same in every way except size. Ask a child to put dolls to bed in one that is the correct size for each doll. Use other cut-outs, such as clothes, cars, people, and houses. Use real objects if available.

Ordering

Ordering by the young child means arranging objects or sets of objects so as to have an origin, a direction, and to reflect some rule. A child may be asked to order five pencils of different lengths from the longest to the shortest. The rule would be that each pencil after the first must be shorter than the pencil it follows.

Children should be asked to order objects only on the basis of attributes they understand and can compare. The child can order the pencils from the longest to the shortest only if the meanings of shortest and longest are understood. It is suggested that in beginning activities no more than five objects should be used.

TEACHING SUGGESTIONS

1. Show a child a set of objects arranged in some order. Give a duplicate set and ask that it be arranged in the same order as the one you showed first.
2. Select three spools. Paint each a different color. Thread the spools on string, tying a knot between each to prevent slipping. Put the spools inside an empty cardboard tube and pull the spools through the tube. Ask children to watch and tell which spool comes first, and so on. Repeat with spools in different order.
3. Ask a child to order a set of objects according to a specified relation, for example," longest to shortest."
4. Show five straws that have been ordered according to height. Show five more objects. Arrange first, third, and fifth object according to height. Ask children to put in the two remaining objects so that the set is ordered like the first set. Repeat, using children.
5. Show three objects of differing height. Indicate the object of medium height. Ask a child to choose one of the two remaining objects, compare it to medium one, describe the comparison, and place the object to one side of the medium object. Ask another child to repeat this activity for the remaining object.

Measurement

Young children differ greatly in their experiences with and ideas of time, money, and linear and liquid measure with little mastery evident. As age, socioeconomic level, or mental ability increased, so did the child's familiarity with measurement.[7] The teacher, therefore, needs to study the composition of the group in relation to the factors mentioned when planning activities involving measurement.

In early measuring activities the child makes a visual estimate. Joe was sawing legs for a table. When offered the yardstick to help him get the legs the same length he replied, "I can just look and tell they are the same." Not until after the legs were attached to the table and the table wobbled did he ask for "that stick." The child at this stage uses measuring instruments but may not use them correctly. Later, after experimentation the child can begin to use measuring instruments more effectively. Joe reached the stage at which he carefully measured the table legs.

[7] G. Mascho, "Familiarity with Measurement," in *Mathematics Learning in Early Childhood,* edited by J. N. Payne, op. cit., p. 61.

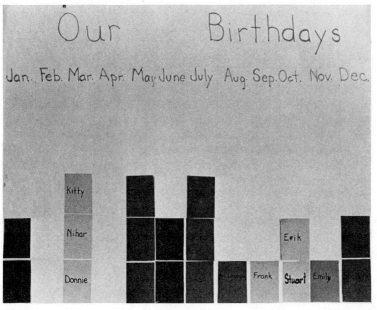

Figure 41
A graph of birthdays offers opportunities for counting, comparing, discussing, and reading.

After the jello didn't jell, the fives were very careful to measure exactly one cup of water. The teacher should not hurry the children. Rather, time and opportunities are provided for children to build concepts related to measurement.

TEACHING SUGGESTIONS

1. Develop and use vocabulary related to weight, temperature, time, money, size, capacity, and distance, such as measure, big, fat, wee, tiny, short, wide, deep, low, high, hole, pound, ruler, teaspoon, tablespoon, cup, quart, pint, speedometer, round, circle, square, cube, cone, triangle, thermometer, clock, hour, minute, buy, sell, penny, nickel, dollar, scales. (*Note:* Do not confuse the group by introducing both standard weights and measures and their metric equivalent at the same time, even though the latter will be the rule by the time they grow up. Choose and stick to one system. See pp. 308–309.)
2. Ask questions about size.
3. Discuss paper, pencils, rulers, yardsticks, and so one, in terms of shape, size, and purpose.
4. Use ruler and yardstick in woodworking activities.
5. Estimate how many small glasses in a quart, cookies in a box.
6. Emphasize vocabulary as trips and excursions are planned and taken, or in giving directions or playing games.
7. Experiment with filling different types of containers.
8. Use much water play and sand activities involving weighing and measuring capacity.

9. Measure the distance a child runs, jumps, or throws a ball.
10. Post a large thermometer and call the children's attention to it.
11. Check temperature and record on calendar periodically, but not necessarily daily. Summarize findings.
12. Discuss various ways of telling temperature. Observe and discuss habits of people, animals, trees, and so on, according to changes in temperature. Feel two objects. Note differences in temperatures. Observe school nurse taking temperature. Post pictures of cool things and warm things, and discuss.
13. Respond to different rhythmic time patterns.
14. Call attention to the clock in relation to jobs as discussed. Ask questions requiring clock—use words hour, minute, and so on. Raise questions such as "What time for lunch, to go swimming, how long until lunch?"
15. Read and discuss books such as *All Kinds of Time* by Harry Behn or *Mike Mulligan and His Steam Shovel* by Virginia Lee Burton. However, this discussion should not destroy the child's enjoyment of the story by overemphasizing the number words and concepts.
16. Post an attractive calendar. Fill in days and dates on calendar on bulletin board. Discuss days, dates, and special events. Note special days for celebrations.
17. Lift different objects. Discuss why some are heavier than others although smaller. Weigh on scales, balancing scales.
18. Use wheel or slanted board to raise objects. Weigh and record each child's weight. Weigh other objects. Read labels giving weight.

Counting

Counting is one of the first number ideas taught to children but, according to Copeland,[8] the numbers that children recite may have little meaning for them. The first counting is often a rote activity. When the child understands and uses number ideas, such as one-to-one correspondence or matching, he or she is counting rationally. The child should be asked to count only with number names that are meaningful, and the process should follow the establishment of meaning for one, two, three, four, and five. Usually cardinal number is what is meant. Children at this (preoperational) level usually have difficulty in grasping the relationship between cardinal and ordinal number.[9]

Gibb and Castaneda say that a premature effort to teach counting may result in the undesired effect of teaching the child to associate number names with single objects rather than sets of a certain number. The child may count, "one, two blocks." Later, when asked to bring two books to the table, the child may count, "one, two" and bring only the second book.[10] Activities involving

[8] Copeland, op. cit., p. 82.
[9] Copeland, op. cit., p. 100.
[10] Gibb and Castaneda, op. cit., p. 113.

matching or one-to-one correspondence first utilize people and/or concrete objects, such as napkins to spoons, children to chairs. After children can match objects to objects in pictures, they can begin learning to match number names or numerals to objects.[11]

TEACHING SUGGESTIONS

1. Count by rote which may or may not have meaning for the child.
2. Do not mistake counting by rote as evidence of readiness to work with numerals.
3. Use rhyming words, finger plays, singing games such as, "one two, buckle my shoe," "This Little Piggie."
4. Identify pairs, two's as in shoes, mittens, bicycles. Extend to three's as in tricycle or in games.
5. Begin with having the child touch each object. Count only with number names meaningful to child. Repeat this in various settings until this need to touch or to point to objects is no longer necessary.
6. Provide for many manipulative counting situations with beads, buttons, cookies, napkins, children, chairs. Match beads to boxes, children to chairs.
7. Determine the number of places, quantity of milk, silverware, napkins, and so on, needed at the table. Match milk to napkins, and so on.
8. Read and use numbers. Identify numbers on the television. Observe figures on a page. Dial telephone numbers. Play with number cut-outs. Write home address. Provide for play with figure cut-outs.
9. Play games involving "more" or "less."
10. Make certain no pressure is exerted on the child to attempt to write figures before his or her small muscles are coordinated and he or she can perceive relationships. Call figures by name; do not refer to them as numbers.

Fractions

The idea that a fraction is a bit, a piece, or a part of something is essential. This concept can be acquired by children at an early age—a part of an apple, a part of a banana. In order to develop the correct concept of a fraction, the teacher helps the child with the following questions:

What is the unit or the whole?
How many pieces are in the unit or the whole?
Are all the pieces the same?[12]

The number of pieces in the whole can give the child the name for a part of the fraction. For example, an apple divided into four pieces leads to the name

---

[11] Copeland, op. cit., pp. 93–94.
[12] Arthur Coxford and Lawrence Ellerbuch, "Fractional Numbers," in *Mathematics Learning in Early Childhood*, edited by J. N. Payne. op. cit., pp. 192–193.

Gingerbread Boys
1 Stick margarine
1 cup brown sugar
1 egg
Mix
Add 2 boxes Gingerbread Mix
1 cup flour
Mix
Bake 350°
12-15 minutes

Figure 42
The recipe for "Gingerbread Boys" is available for reference as the children work. This activity can involve use of measurement, simple fractions, counting, and reading.

"fourths." Ordinal names help in learning the names of fractions. Pieces of the whole should be equal. Children need help in recognizing equal size parts and in dividing the whole into equal parts.

TEACHING SUGGESTIONS

1. Use vocabulary to express parts of a whole, such as: 1/2, 1/2 cup, cup; both, divide, piece, middle, double, alike.
2. Provide for sharing in terms of "half an apple," "a whole cookie," "half a sandwich."
3. Plan situations requiring use of half a sheet of paper.
4. Use vocabulary in comparing blocks and other objects as to size as "half as big," and so on.
5. Prepare cocoa, jello, or cookies, using measuring spoons and cups.
6. Weigh objects with balancing scales. Measure height and weight using scale and discussing fractional parts.

Shape

Children begin to explore space and shape very early in life. They crawl around and through objects, and up and down stairs; roll balls; finger the edge of a low table while walking around it; they play with blocks, dishes, and wheel toys. Gibb and Castenada say that these early experiences help the child develop an awareness of the likenesses and differences in the shape of many objects.[13] With adult guidance, children learn to describe what they see and feel. The description may be put across in a variety of ways—pictorially and through movement, as well as verbally. Words are not always necessary.

The first activities should be planned to help the child develop a general concept of shape, later to describe likenesses and differences in shapes, and finally to learn the names for the most common shapes. Too often the naming of shapes is one of the first activities.

TEACHING SUGGESTIONS

1. Show the children a shape, such as a circle mounted on cardboard. Ask them to form the shape. Give them a piece of elastic, tied together to put around the outside of them to indicate size of circle or shape.
2. Show the child a shape. Ask the child to use rubber bands or pegs to form a shape on the pegboard.
3. Take the class for a walk. Show a shape (cut from paper) to children. Ask them to find this shape on the walk. Observe and discuss objects and places in the environment.
4. Discuss shape and size of small musical instruments. Discuss the shape and size of containers, wheels, balls, and so on, for different purposes in terms of use.
5. Build with blocks, put away blocks, and so on, and discuss shape and size in terms of use.

Patterns

If the child is to gain mathematical insight the ability to recognize a pattern is essential.[14] This recognition and awareness of patterns may be developed through the use of real objects, pictures, designs in weaving, symbols, and drawings. Give the child practice in seeing, describing, completing, and repeating patterns.

TEACHING SUGGESTIONS

1. Show different arrangements of objects. Talk about how the arrangements are alike and how they are different.

[13] Gibb and Castaneda, op. cit., pp. 107–108.
[14] Gibb and Castaneda, op. cit., p. 111.

2. Make a pattern of objects, such as one red, one white, one blue plastic spoon. Ask a child to make a pattern just like the one shown directly below it. Use blocks, beads, pipe cleaners, anything of distinctive shape, color, or some other attribute.
3. Provide objects. Ask one child to make a pattern. Ask another to make one just like it and directly below it.
4. Ask children to look at a picture and identify the pattern.

Vocabulary

A beginner's math program emphasizes the development of concepts and the acquisition of oral language. Appropriate words are needed for expressing number ideas.[15] It is important, then, for the teacher to remember that the young children he or she teaches are still in the process of learning language and may not be able to verbalize how a problem was solved. Many opportunities are needed for the child to acquire a mathematical vocabulary. (Suggestions for vocabulary development are found on pp. 203–216.)

TEACHING MATERIALS AND RESOURCES

Teaching materials can be used by children in exploratory activities and in developing and using a mathematical idea and concept. Activities that involve

[15] Gibb and Castaneda, op. cit., p. 97.

Figure 43
In the Mathematics Center Marsha places the correct card on the horses. "Yes, there are seven horses."

the use of materials can contribute to mathematics learnings, but an intelligent and balanced use is necessary. Trafton says, however, that they are not "cure-alls." The real experiences of the children as well as manipulative and audiovisual materials may be effectively used.[16]

Manipulative materials

Manipulative materials used within the home can be collected and used in the classroom—egg cartons, empty berry containers, bottle tops, small and large boxes, buttons, and empty spools. Children's socks, shoes, gloves also provide valuable resources. Here is a list of other manipulative materials that should be readily available in the classroom:

Empty spools, enameled in red, blue, or green.
Straws and tooth picks of various colors.
Balls of several sizes.
Large wooden beads of many colors.
Blocks of varied size and shape.
Empty milk or fruit cartons in quarts, pints, half pints.
Measuring cups marked into thirds, fourths, and halves.
Separate measuring cups holding $\frac{1}{3}$, $\frac{1}{2}$, and $\frac{1}{4}$ cups.
Measuring spoons.
Bottle caps, aluminum washers, colored plastic clothespins.
Play money in coins and paper dollars.
Scraps of cloth of varied sizes, colors, shapes, and materials.
Simple tools as hammer, saws.
Scraps of lumber.
Nails of several sizes.
Paper bags of many sizes.
Cardboard clock.
Stop watch.
Clock with alarm.
Clock with second-hand.
Timers for stove and for egg.
Sundial.
Scales of several types—balance, kitchen, bathroom, postal.
Cubes of soap.
Cake pans of various sizes and shapes, and muffin tins.
Peg boards, flannel boards with toys and figures.
Magnetic board.
Toy telephones, cash registers, adding machines.
Various types of dials—TV, washing machine, and radio.

[16] P. Trafton, "The Curriculum" in J. N. Payne, ed. *Mathemathetics Learning in Early Childhood,* op. cit., p. 39.

Puzzles with geometric designs.
Calendar.
Thermometer.

The mathematical materials provided and distributed by publishers of professional materials may be added if funds are available.[17]

Pictorial materials have a place, and a carefully selected picture file is of great value in illustrating the use of arithmetic in daily life. A collection of books, stories, finger plays, and poems that expand arithmetical concepts is a valuable resource for the teacher to read and for the children to look at or to take home to be shared. Such materials need to be selected carefully as to relationship with and treatment of the concepts to be developed as well as to the maturity of the child. This material should be artistic both in content and in the method of presentation. The mathematical problem should be involved in the story, and the content and use should be essential to the solution of the problem in the story. Through use of these materials the child acquires facility in use of vocabulary and builds understanding for use in more complex situations.

Books

Teachers have found children's books to be of value in developing mathematical concepts. Here are a few good examples:

Cole, William. *What's Good for a Three Year Old?* Holt, Rinehart and Winston, 1974.
Hoban, Tana. *Count and See.* Macmillan Publishing Co., 1972.
Kohn, Bernice. *Everything Has a Shape.* Englewood Cliffs, N.J.: Prentice-Hall, 1964.
————. *Everything Has a Size.* Englewood Cliffs, N.J.: Prentice-Hall, 1964.
Lathan, Jean L., and Bee Lewi. *The Cuckoo That Couldn't Count.* New York: Macmillan Publishing Co., 1961.

For additional suggestions as to appropriate titles consult your librarian or *A Bibliography of Books for Children.* Washington, D.C.: ACEI, 1977.

EVALUATING MATHEMATICAL LEARNINGS

Evaluation is an essential part of any school program, but it becomes increasingly important in a program based largely on incidental teaching. Since the experiences are a part of the child's life, it is necessary to check to see whether

[17] For additional suggestions, see *Selecting Educational Equipment and Materials For School and Home* (Washington, D.C.: ACEI, 1976), pp. 64–65.

he or she is making progress in all the areas of the number program. The teacher will do a better job of guiding mathematical learnings if he or she makes the following evaluations:

THE PROGRAM

1. Has provision been made for activities involving all abilities listed on page 295 counting, measurement, vocabulary, and so on? It is easy to have had many experiences in one area and comparatively few or even none in another area.
2. Is teaching in terms of the readiness of the children? No two children will be at the same level of readiness; even if two appear to give the same response, one may have a more complete understanding.
3. Has there been practice in the repetition of a skill in a functional setting? If so, the teacher checks to see if this repetition is found throughout the day as the children work and play together.
4. Is there a variety of materials and methods designed to develop the desired number concepts? Consider, for example, the use of rhymes or finger plays in counting.

PROGRESS OF THE INDIVIDUAL CHILD

The teacher observes the child in various activities in order to determine the degree to which mathematical skill and understanding in the areas described on pp. 296–305 have been acquired. Progress is noted for each child in ability (1) to match objects, (2) to determine if there is enough, too many, or too few, (3) to count without skipping but using number names in correct order, (4) to match number names with objects or to give a correct number of objects for a number name, and (5) as he or she strings beads, to count them by one's or in groups of two's or three's.

As the teacher evaluates, findings are summarized and recorded in order to aid

CHECKLIST FOR COUNTING

Date_____

	counts 1–5 by rote	counts 1–10 rationally	childs touches each object as counting	child matches objects using one-to-one correspondence
Julie	X	X	X	X
Jan	X	—	—	—
Marcus	X	X	—	X
Marguerita	X	X	—	X

X = accomplished
— = needs continued experience

in planning for and working with the child. The record may be in the form of a checklist, which can make individualization of instruction more effective. A checklist may be developed for each area of the math program. See example of checklist at bottom of page 308.

METRIC SYSTEM

As the metric system becomes more widely used in our country, eventually children will need to learn to use metric units of measure. The basic units of the system include the meter (length), the liter (capacity), the gram (weight), and the degree Celsius (temperature).

The concepts, abilities, and understandings presented in this chapter are basic to mathematics whether the present (formerly English) system or the metric system is used. One word of caution is needed, however. The two systems should not be introduced simultaneously. If, for example, the teacher begins with the English system, this system should be used until the child has achieved beginning understandings. Concepts related to the metric system may then be introduced but without reference to, or comparison with, the English system. As the child works with the two separately, through the process of discovery he or she will come to see that 1 meter is a little longer than 1 yard. Young children should not be taught to convert from one system to another. Children may hear the weather report refer to the temperature at 23° Celsius. Such an incident may be used as the basis for discussing the two systems of measuring temperature. This discussion is not intended to suggest that young children be taught to convert from one system to another.[18]

Suggested Activities

1. Contact a group of children in the neighborhood, in the home, and/or in an organized group. Talk with them informally, and jot down examples of number vocabulary used. Note their ability to count, to recognize common coins, and to select coins in terms of relative values. Note differences among three-, four-, five-, and six-year-olds and differences among children of the same age group.
2. Observe a group of three-, four-, and five-year-olds. List the vocabulary used by the group in terms of size and weight, distance, time, temperature, and shape.
3. List some suggested activities suitable for two- or three-year-old children at varying stages in the development of mathematical concepts.
4. Discuss the differences among the relative value of the incidental, the social, the drill, and the meaningful approach in the development of mathematical concepts

---

[18] Edith Robinson, M. Mahaffey, and D. Nelson. "Measurement" in *Mathematics Learning in Early Childhood,* edited by J. N. Payne, op. cit., pp. 249–259.

and abilities and understandings. Justify your statements as to relative values of these approaches.

5. Observe in a center for three-, four-, and/or five-year-olds. List materials available for the children and how these materials were utilized in the development of mathematical abilities and understandings, such as classifying, patterning, ordering, comparing, measurement, and problem solving. Describe the method and organization used by the teacher to guide the children in their selection and use of these materials. What did the teacher do to enhance the children's learnings?

6. Observe children engaged in activities such as block building, dramatic play, and painting. Discuss the opportunities available in these activities for classifying, counting, ordering, patterning, using fractions, comparing, building vocabulary, and using shapes.

7. View the film, *Foundations of Mathematics*. Campus Films, 20 East 46th Street, New York, N.Y. 10017. Compare your observations with the film.

Related Readings

Callahan, L. G., and V. J. Glennon. *Elementary School Mathematics: A Guide to Current Research*, 4th ed. Washington, D.C.: ASCD, 1975.

Cockscroft, W. H. *Your Child and Mathematics*. New York: John Wiley and Sons, 1971.

Copeland, R. W. *How Children Learn Mathematics: Teaching Implications of Piaget's Research*, 2nd ed. New York: Macmillan Publishing Co., 1974.

———. *Diagnostic and Learning Activities in Mathematics for Children*. New York: Macmillan Publishing Co., 1974.

Davis, R. B. "The Strange Case of the New Mathematics," *Child. Educ., 50*:4 (1974), pp. 210–213.

———. *The Changing Curriculum: Mathematics*. Washington, D.C.: ASCD, 1967.

Heard, I. M. "Mathematical Concepts and Abilities Possessed by Kindergarten Entrants," *Arithmetic Teacher, 17*:4 (1970), pp. 340–341.

Inhelder, B., and J. Piaget. *The Early Growth of Logic in the Child*. New York: Harper & Row, 1969.

Kamii, Constance, and Rheta De Vries. *Piaget, Children, and Numbers*. Washington, D.C.: NAEYC, 1976.

Leeb-Lundberg, Kristina. "The Block Builder Mathematician," in *The Block Book* Elisabeth Hirsch, ed. Washington, D.C.: NAEYC, 1974, pp. 33–58.

Lindberg, Lucile, and Rita Swedlow. "Mathematics," in *Early Childhood Education: A Guide for Observation and Participation*. Boston: Allyn and Bacon, 1976, pp. 242–262.

Nuffield Mathematics Project. *I Do and I Understand*. New York: John Wiley and Sons, 1967.

O'Brien, T. C. "New Goals for Mathematics Education," *Child. Educ., 50*:4 (1974), pp. 214–216.

Payne, J. N. (ed.). *Mathematics Learning in Early Childhood*. Reston, Va.: The National Council of Mathematics, 1975.

Rea, R. E., and R. E. Reys. "Mathematics Competence of Entering Kindergartners," *Arithmetic Teacher, 17*:1 (1970), pp. 63–74.

Swenson, Esther S. *Teaching Mathematics to Children*, 2nd ed. New York: Macmillan Publishing Co., 1973.

Walton, Jeanne. *Logical-Mathematical Thinking and the Preschool Classroom.* College Park, Md.: Head Start Regional Resource and Training Center, 1974.

Wilderman, Ann M., and J. A. Rudnick. "Measure Up . . . The Metrics Are Coming!" *Child. Educ.*, 52:6 (1976), pp. 312–315.

chapter 14

The social studies

Pollution, rapid change, energy shortages, unemployment, space stations, housing problems, and violence—these are all realities of the present-day world that intrude even into centers for young children.

Education for facing such social problems cannot be delayed until the children are older. The early years are very important and instruction must begin during these years. Hess and Easton attempted to discover the concepts, attitudes, and values held by children about the political world. Data collected seem to indicate that the child's political world begins to take shape before he enters elementary school and is subject to rapid change. Many basic political attitudes and values are firmly established by the end of elementary school.[1]

[1] R. Hess and D. Easton, "The Role of the Elementary School in Political Socialization," *The School Review*, 70:3 (1962), pp. 257–265.

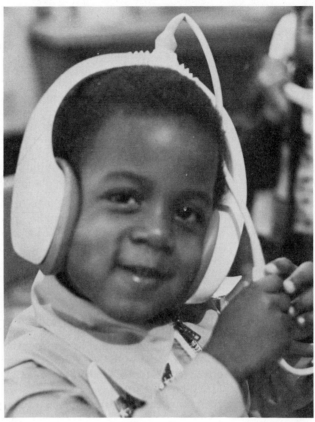

Figure 44
Realities of the present day are evident
in children's centers. Joseph is ready
for a trip on the space shuttle.

Lambert and Klineberg reported views which children hold of their own
and foreign peoples. Such findings seem to imply the necessity of early concern for the development of international views and attitudes essential to intercultural and international understanding. For example, by age six children
stressed differences rather than similarities of people from other countries.[2]
Goodman reported that the onset of bigotry and racially related value systems
is to be found in children as young as four years.[3] Findings such as these
should influence both the content and the techniques of social studies for
young children and emphasize the importance of social studies in the child
development center, the nursery school, and the kindergarten.

Social studies education, says Jarolimek, has the task of helping the young
to grow in their understanding of and sensitivity to the physical and social

[2] W. E. Lambert and O. Klineberg, *Children's Views of Foreign Peoples.* (New York: Appleton-
Century-Crofts, 1967).
[3] Mary Ellen Goodman, *Race Awareness in Young Children,* rev. ed. (New York: Macmillan Publishing Co., 1964).

forces at work around them so that they may develop the ability to cope with and to some extent manage their futures. Social education is concerned with human beings. Such education must help children generate hope in the future and confidence in their ability to solve social problems:[4]

> Learning about people, how and where they live, how they form and structure societies, how they govern themselves and provide for their material and psychological needs, how and why they hate each other, how they use and misuse the resources of the planet that is their home—all this is what social studies education is really about.

In order to accomplish the goals of the social studies, teachers of young children need answers to the following types of questions.

1. Why are social studies included in the program for young children?
2. What is taught in social studies in the nursery school and kindergarten?
3. What are some common fallacies about social learnings for young children?
4. How does the teacher plan and organize her work for teaching in this area?
5. What learning situations—teaching strategies, activities, and experiences—are best for children of these age groups?

WHY TEACH SOCIAL STUDIES?

Through content and experiences, the social studies are designed to develop intelligent, responsible, self-directing people who can function as members of groups—family, community, world—with which they become identified. The aims and objectives of the social studies program can be stated as follows:[5]

1. Develop understandings of cooperative group living with an awareness of and appreciation for the rights of others, personal property, honesty, courtesy, responsibility.
2. Broaden the child's social environment through guided opportunities to live, play, work, and meet with other children and adults of various backgrounds, religions, and races.
3. Explore the child's here-and-now interests in the environment, focusing on home, school, and neighborhood; stress the interdependence of man in neighborhood and community.
4. Aid the child's understanding of his or her dependence on parents, older siblings, teachers, school personnel, neighborhood and community helpers, and how he or she can help others.
5. Expand the child's horizon to include new understandings relating to children in other countries of the world and their ways of living.

---

[4] J. Jarolimek, *Social Studies in Elementary Education*, 5th ed. (New York: Macmillan Publishing Co., 1977), p. 4.

[5] *A Guide: Early Childhood Education in Florida Schools*, Bull. 76 (Tallahassee: Florida State Department of Education, 1969), p. 23.

Social studies are concerned, then, with behavior, goals, values, skills, and knowledge. The objectives may be classified in three categories: understandings, which deal with knowledge and knowing; attitudes, which deal with values, appreciations, ideals, and feelings; and skills that must be related to the social skills of living and working together, skills that make for civic competence.[6] Concepts, skills, and behavior are all interrelated. In guiding behavior, it is necessary to consider the feelings and needs as well as the ideas, attitudes, and skills of the child. As Ojemann pointed out, if a child is in a position where his security, self-respect, or activity is seriously threatened, it will be difficult for the child to cooperate with others.[7]

In setting up learning situations and planning teaching strategies, the teacher must make sure that each child has opportunities to gain some measure of self-respect, satisfaction, assurance, and emotional security through the desired behavior. This is easier said than done. To indicate something of the difficulty involved, it is important to examine some of the fallacies to which teachers are prone.

The first fallacy is *to view beliefs and social action as separate*. The tendency has been to act and teach as if children will behave as they are told, not as they observe others behaving. The admonition, "Do as I say, not as I do," is perhaps a futile one. It is from the environment that the child learns of people and things.

What a child comes to recognize as important usually depends on what values are set on the event by parents, teachers, and other adults. Rasey and Menge state, "Children see their world as through a glass, darkly or brightly, as their adults reflect or transmit it to them." Speaking of the teacher, they point out:[8]

> Whether he wants the responsibility or not, the fact remains that our own choices and preferences are themselves contagious, and ways of life of young humans always have a considerable admixture of the choices and preferences of those in their human environment.

Research in this area supports the belief that the values and attitudes of children reflect those of parents, teachers, and other adults in the community.

According to Trager, the Philadelphia studies have shown that if the culture practices and condones rejection, children tend to behave and think in terms of rejection.[9] Even in kindergarten, children accepted adult concepts and attitudes toward racial and religious groups. "One of the most socially wasteful

[6] Jarolimek, op. cit., pp. 7–8.
[7] R. Ojemann, "Social Studies in Light of Knowledge about Children," *Social Studies in the Elementary School* (56th Yearbook NSSE), (Chicago: University of Chicago Press, 1957), p. 78.
[8] Marie Rasey and J. W. Menge, *What We Learn from Children* (New York: Harper & Row, 1956), p. 39.
[9] Helen G. Trager and Marian R. Yarrow, *They Learn What They Live: Prejudice in Young Children* (New York: Harper & Row, 1952), p. 392.

learnings children get from their schooling is the habit of viewing beliefs and social action as separated one from the other."[10]

There appears to be a direct relationship between the attitudes of parents and children. Parents who are accepting of themselves, their children, and other people have a positive influence on their children while those with negative attitudes have a negative influence.[11]

One who teaches young children needs to be reminded of the implications of the old saying, "What you are speaks so loud I can't hear what you say." The school situation must be planned so as to help children to observe and practice behavior consistent with the beliefs and values which it is hoped they will choose.

Another common fallacy is *to assume that all children are at the same stage of maturity and have had the same experiences.* In planning teaching strategies in the social studies, the question is frequently asked as to when the child should begin the study of history or geography. The reply is often made in terms of age or grade levels. The answer, however, should be when concepts of time, geographical location, and distance are sufficiently developed so that the child can profit from such studies. Since the development of such concepts depends on both the nature of the child and the experiences had, the time will not be the same for all children of a given age. However, the experi-

---

[10] Alice Miel and Peggy Brogan, *More Than Social Studies* (Englewood Cliffs, N.J.: Prentice-Hall, 1957), p. 133.
[11] Reported in Celia Stendler and W. Martin, *Intergroup Education in Kindergarten-Primary Grades* (New York: Macmillan Publishing Co., 1953), p. 11.

A   B   C

Figure 45
Early contact with children from different cultures and other countries can contribute to the development of multicultural and international understandings.

ences provided in early childhood contribute to the development of the concepts essential to the study of history, geography, and other social studies.

Life experiences which have an influence on achievement include[12] patterns of physical growth, development of interests, child's emotional organization, quality of child's relations with others, social class, ethnic background, family, and family values.

Backgrounds of children vary widely. Lacey found that the differences in concept development within a grade group seemed to be of more importance than the differences between grades.[13] Harrison used fifty common terms relating to time and found that children of high intelligence in the kindergarten scored almost as many correct responses as children of lower intelligence in the third grade.[14]

The third fallacy is *to assume that when a child uses labels or words he understands the meaning of the word or concept.* Since there is no inevitable connection between the meaning of a concept and the word that stands for it, it is quite possible for a child to use the word with little understanding of the meaning or even the wrong meaning. For example, a "train-bearer" to a four-year-old meant a little boy carrying a "choo-choo" train. One group of five-year-olds talked about being kind to one another. That they did not understand the meaning of kindness was evidenced by the fact that immediately following the discussion, these same children forced another child out of the playhouse.

Another fallacy is *to assume that the values that adults hold for the child are the same as the child's values.* The question, then, becomes one of asking how the child learns what he ought to do. Just because the child knows the desired response does not mean that he will behave in that way. The child may answer as he thinks adults want him to answer. Fite and Jersild found that during an interview a three- or four-year-old may say that fighting is bad, yet actually engage in fighting.[15] Combs says that "Our greatest failures are those connected with the problem of helping people to behave differently as a result of the information we have provided them."[16]

Children need opportunities to discover the personal value and usefulness of the concept. Until children find that they can solve problems satisfactorily, get a turn at the slide, or use the blocks without fighting, they will probably

[12] Sybil K. Richardson and Faith W. Smitter, "The Learner," *Learning and the Teacher,* 1959 Yearbook (Washington, D.C.: ASCD, 1959), pp. 29–34.
[13] Joy M. Lacey, *Social Studies Concepts of Children in the First Three Grades* (New York: Teachers College, 1932).
[14] M. Lucile Harrison, "The Nature and Development of Concepts of Time Among Young Children," *Elem. Sch. J.,* 34:7 (1934), pp. 507–514.
[15] M. D. Fite and A. T. Jersild, "Aggressive Behavior in Young Children and Children's Attitudes Toward Agression," *Genet. Psychol. Monogr.,* 22:2 (1940), pp. 151–319.
[16] A. W. Combs, "Personality Theory and Its Implications for Curriculum Development," *Learning More About Learning* (Washington, D.C.: ASCD, 1959), p. 9.

continue to hit, grab, and push. The child needs help in finding different ways of solving a problem and of evaluating the various methods. To correct these fallacies and to plan effectively for learning situations through which the objectives of the social studies may be realized, it is essential to observe the following basic principles:

1. Children must have an opportunity to clarify what they say and to relate this to what they do; to live what they learn; to experience and to practice kindness, courtesy, sharing; and to make choices. Verbalization alone is not adequate.
2. Meaningful experiences closely related to the activities of the child and behavioral goals are essential. The child must find in the desired behavior some satisfaction, some enhancement of self-respect, security, and personal worth.
3. Standards, teaching strategies, and learning activities must be adapted to the differences prevalent in the group. Each child needs the opportunity to participate in challenging activities, to make choices, and assume responsibilities suited to his or her background.

WHAT TO TEACH: CONTENT

Social studies for young children focus on the immediate environment and experiences of the child. The use of themes to indicate areas of study for different age levels has been widely practiced. Themes for young children have been related to the child's experiences in the here and now. "Living Together in Home and School" is typical of the themes selected for kindergarten and first grade. "Community Helpers" is often the topic for the second grade. At successive grade levels the child studies about the state, the nation, and the world, both historically and geographically.

Such an organization has value as revealed by the research related to the development of time and space concepts in children. Ames found that while four-year-olds can indicate that an event took place before or after a meal, they cannot tell the time of day or the day of the week.[17] Oakden and Sturt found that not until age eleven are concepts of historical time sufficiently developed to place historical characters in chronological order.[18] Dunfee, however, reports that

> A review of the studies of time concepts seems to indicate that children may be able to understand time and chronology concepts at an earlier age than previously predicted and that many children are receptive to planned instruction in these relationships.[19]

[17] Louise B. Ames, "The Development of the Sense of Time in the Young Child," *J. Genet. Psychol.*, 68:1 (1946), pp. 97–125.

[18] E. C. Oakden and M. Sturt, "Development of Knowledge of Time in Children," *Brit. J. Psychol.*, 12:4 (1922), pp. 309–336.

[19] Maxine Dunfee, *Elementary Social Studies: A Guide to Current Research* (Washington, D.C.: ASCD, 1970), p. 29.

The authors recognize the limitations of the child's concept of time and experiential background. They are aware, however, of the impossibility of limiting the child's learnings to those of the home and school. Many children, by the age of five, have lived in other countries or have some member of their family living abroad. By means of television the child becomes aware of holidays and hears something of their historical significance. Few, if any, children move sequentially from home to school, to community, state, nation, and the world in their experiences. Fraser states:[20]

> The principle of selecting and arranging learning experiences in terms of children's experiential backgrounds remains valid. Implementation of the principle requires a realistic appraisal of the experiences and needs of today's children.

An appraisal was made by Wann who, with a group of teachers, studied three-, four-, and five-year-old children in their own classrooms over a period of five years. He reported[21]:

> The readiness of young children for challenging intellectual experiences was evident throughout the study. The young children were eager to gather information to apply to their conversations and their play situations. They were attempting to see relationships, to make generalizations, to discriminate, to classify. They were curious and concerned about the daily occurrences of group living, about friendship and family, neighbor and neighborhood. They were interested in the faraway in time and space. . . . They were trying to interpret and have interpreted for them the many facets of the world around them. Not all children were at the same point of intellectual development. Some had more information on a greater variety of topics, others had less.

The store of information young children have today, their continual quest for knowledge, and their struggle to organize information into a meaningful conceptual framework have significant implications for school programs. It is apparent that teachers of young children must support their efforts to acquire information and to organize it.

In view of the changing experiences and concepts of children, it appears wise to enlarge the scope of the social studies for young children to include understandings from all the major areas of social studies and provide for the growth of children through constantly enlarging experiences. Simple ideas introduced in the early years will lay a foundation for understanding more complex ones in later grades. Such a "spiral approach" introduces concepts to the young child and provides for reteaching these concepts in a more complex sit-

[20] Dorothy M. Fraser, "The Organization of the Elementary School Social Studies Curriculum," *Social Studies in the Elementary School*, Part II (NSSE) (Chicago: University of Chicago Press, 1957), p. 141.
[21] K. D. Wann, Miriam S. Dorn, and Elizabeth A. Liddle, *Fostering Intellectual Development in Young Children* (New York: Teachers College, Columbia University, 1962), p. 98.

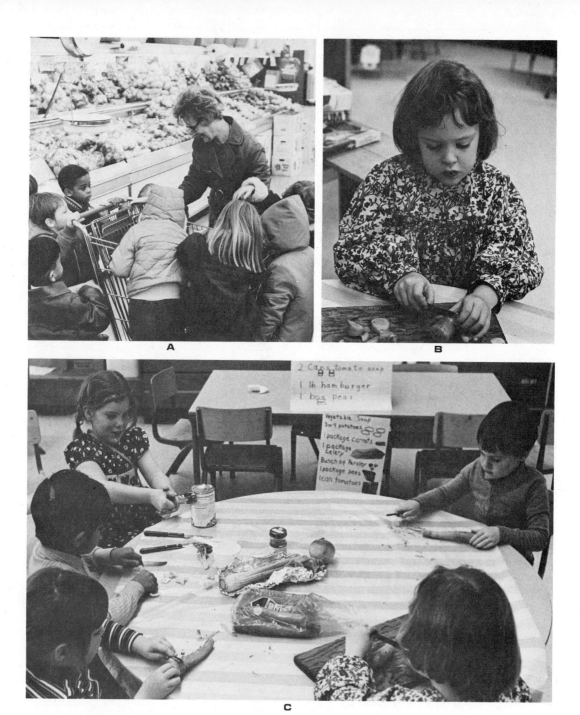

Figure 46

Concepts in the areas of economics, conservation, geography, and civics can be developed as children engage in this learning episode. Cooperative planning, a trip to the grocery store, preparing vegetables and cooking soup, are among the teaching strategies used.

uation at a later date. According to Bruner, in the spiral curriculum "ideas are first presented in a form and language, honest though imprecise, which can be grasped by the child, ideas which can be revisited later with greater precision and power until finally, the student has received the reward of mastery." [22]

As an example of this approach, certain areas of the social studies are listed. The name associated with the area (for example, history or anthropology) is used in order to indicate that the concepts or beginnings, may be developed with young children. The study of history or anthropology is appropriate for young children, but the concepts selected for study and the procedures used are not the same as those used for older children. For each area some of the appropriate concepts are listed, along with suggested opportunities for experiences that can contribute to the development of concepts, understandings, values, and skills.

The possible interrelationships among the areas should be noted. While developing the concept that each person has worth and dignity, there are also possible learnings in anthropology and sociology as well.

[22] J. S. Bruner, *On Knowing* (Cambridge, Mass.: Harvard University Press, 1962), p. 62.

Table 14-1
Learnings in Social Studies

Area	Examples of Concepts To Be Learned	Some Learning Activities That Can Contribute to Concept Development
1. Moral education.	Each person has worth and dignity. We are not all alike.	Introduce each child in class. Talk about how children are alike and yet different. Use books, songs, pictures, discussion, snapshots.
2. Civics.	Rules can help us live happily together (respect for rules and regulations).	Participate in discussion of "limits" or "rules" for the slide. Make plans for taking a walk. Note "how we cross the street," "why we walk on the sidewalk." Accept "limits" set by group.
3. Conservation.	Money is used to buy food, clothing, and school supplies. They can be used freely but without waste (respect for personal and public property). Water has many uses. Water can be conserved.	Take care of one's own possessions. Hang coat in locker, wear apron while painting. Use paper towels as needed. Help clean up after work period. Turn off water faucets.

(Continued)

Table 14-1 (continued)

Area	Examples of Concepts To Be Learned	Some Learning Activities That Can Contribute to Concept Development
4. Economics.	People do different types of work (appreciation of contribution of others). People live in different types of homes (understanding of how others live). Money is used to buy what we need.	Learn about the work that parents do, use stories, pictures, trips, visitors, and discussion. Learn about homes in which the children live; trailer, apartment, one-story houses. Make use of pictures, art products, trips, stories, discussion.
5. History— American heritage.	Understanding that great men had great ideas. They were honest, brave, kind (historical understanding). An event is a part of a chronological series. Simple time relationships exist. Our society changes.	Celebrate holidays. Emphasize historic significance. Use stories, films, trips, role-playing, music, bulletin-board displays. Discuss and clarify meaning of honest, brave, kind. Learn how time is measured. Use clock and calendar. Discuss important events in lives of the children. Observe changes in neighborhood or town. Discuss reasons for change.
6. Geography— where we live. Relationship of scientific and social change.	People travel in different ways. Messages are sent in different ways. Weather affects the way we dress and where we play (readiness for geography).	Learn about the ways people travel. Take a bus or train ride. Visit the airport. Send messages—use telephone, mail a letter. Observe evidence of seasonal changes.
7. International understandings.	People live in other countries. Children live and play in other countries. (Recognition that people are different—not necessarily that one is better than another.)	Learn games and songs of children in other lands. Compare them with games and songs of the kindergarten children. Invite persons from other lands to talk with children.
8. Anthropology.	People live according to certain values, skills, and traditions.	Talk about how each family celebrates birthdays. Role play social skills. Make choices and examine alternatives. Consider what each child values most. Examine behavior of group.

Table 14-1 (continued)

Area	Examples of Concepts To Be Learned	Some Learning Activities That Can Contribute to Concept Development
9. Sociology.	The family is the basic social unit in our society. All families are not alike.	Learn about members of the family. Play roles of family members. Use pictures, books, and songs.
10. Environmental education— ecology.	Water and air can be polluted. Many familiar sounds cause noise pollution. Waste disposal is a severe problem.	Observe effects of air pollution on one's eyes and breathing. Note effects of water pollution on where children can swim. Identify sounds which contribute to noise pollution. Plan to reduce noise at school and home. Plan for cleaning room. Observe disposal of school waste.

PLANNING AND TEACHING

A teacher will find many opportunities for helping the child develop desirable habits, attitudes, and skills and to gain useful information. Suggested strategies for planning and teaching are discussed on pp. 203–216, and the reader is urged to refer to this section for a more detailed treatment. Certain strategies are illustrated here with examples from the social studies.

Reinforcing, Clarifying, Explaining, and Discussing Incidents that Affect Children During the School Day. For example, one Monday morning the kindergarten children were telling about what they had done over the weekend.

> Jack: "I went to Sunday School. I go to the Presbyterian Sunday School."
> Joseph: "I don't. We go to the Episcopal Church."
> Several children joined in, identifying the church that they attended. Then Edith spoke. "I don't go to Sunday School. My mother doesn't take me." The teacher replied, "On Sunday, Jack and Joseph went to church with their parents. Edith stayed at home. We can do that because we live in our country, the United States. In our country, mothers and fathers can choose whether or not they want to go to church. They can choose the church, too."

While children at this age do not understand the term "religious freedom," a discussion such as this can provide the experience on which generalizations can be developed later. This opportunity for children to talk about different religions can contribute to fulfilling the second objective on p. 90.

Cooperative Planning. An example of cooperative planning follows: The kindergarten children had been given a collie puppy. It was their very own puppy, and it must have a name. The teacher and children sat down together.

> Teacher: "Several of you have already suggested names for the puppy. Hugh wants 'Candy.' Glenn wants 'Collie'; Joan wants 'Spot.' How shall we decide?"
> Glenn: "We could vote."
> Teacher: "Yes, we can vote. That means I will write down each name: Candy, Collie, and Spot. Then I will ask each of you to tell me the name you like best. We will count to see how many children like each name. The name that most of you like will be the name of our puppy. Do you want to do it that way?"
> Children: "Yes."
> Teacher: "Think for a moment about the names: Candy, Collie, and Spot. Decide on the one you want."
> Each name was written on a piece of newsprint. As each child's name was called, the teacher made a mark by the choice. Together they counted the marks:

> Candy—20.
> Spot—3.
> Collie—2.

> Teacher: "Candy has 20 votes. That is more votes than for the other two. So Candy will be our puppy's name."
> Glenn, who wanted "Collie," angrily stamped his foot and said, "Why vote, if you can't get what you want?"
> Teacher: "Glenn, we vote to give everyone a chance to say what one wants. You didn't get your choice this time. We will vote again some other time on another idea. Maybe you will win then."

This learning activity can help the children develop understandings of cooperative group living and an appreciation for the rights of others, the first objective on page 90.

Field Trips. The use of field trips is discussed on pages 206–208. The suggestions for planning and evaluating are also applicable to the social studies.

Trips may be made in connection with the study of a variety of topics in the community. Trips may be made to centers such as the library, the fire station, or the post office; sources of food supply, such as the farm, the orchard or grove, the dairy, the supermarket; transportation to locations such as the airport, the railroad terminal, bus station, a street or highway; the home, which could include a look at the various types of homes and the actual construction of a building.

Instructional Resources. See pages 213–216 for detailed discussion relating to the use of instructional technology.

Resource Persons. In the following examples, parents and members of the family served as resource persons. The teacher said, "Stephen's grandfather is visiting us today. He doesn't speak English but he will play his violin for us."

At another time she said, "Mrs. Olson is Swedish and in her family they make a gingerbread house every year at Christmas time. She is here today to help us make one."

Centers of Interest and Learning Centers. See pages 209–211. As children participate in the centers, there is opportunity for them to gain the following values related to social studies:

> Sharing materials, toys, and turns.
> Using materials freely but without waste.
> Respecting the rights and feelings of others.
> Understanding their own rights and how to stand up for them.
> Respecting limits or rules which have been made for the good of the group.
> Learning and following everyday routines.
> Learning about the physical and social environment.
> Communicating with others.
> Making choices and decisions.
> Cooperating with others.
> Formulating and clarifying ideas.

Units. Currently units may be referred to as plans for developing key concepts. Unit, and teaching or lesson plans are discussed on pages 326–334. In selecting the topic for study, a balance among various areas of the social studies is desirable. It is possible for an undue proportion of time to be spent in activities that contribute most directly to one area. For example, geographic understandings may be emphasized to the extent that the child may have few learning opportunities in other areas of social studies. Children need contact with history and anthropology too.

Examining the background of the children can give leads to topics. McAulay found in interviewing 70 second-graders that 63 of the children could name at least two duties of the policeofficer and 65 at least one duty of the firefighter. Units had been planned on both topics.[23] The same situation exists in many children's programs today.

The teacher should not be upset by the fact that children already have some information about a topic selected for study. The teacher needs to find out what the children already know and to make plans for the educational needs of each. There is so much to learn and know that children should not be bored with the repetition of information already familiar to them. This type of orga-

---

[23] J. D. McAulay, "Social Studies in the Primary Grades," *Social Educ., 18*:8 (1954), pp. 357–358.

nization offers flexibility and makes possible a variety of learning opportunities that can be adapted to individual needs and interests

A plan for organizing a unit of work, and a unit developed according to the plan, are described. The unit selected relates to "Feelings." At the beginning of the school year there is the opportunity to utilize the interests of children in getting acquainted with one another. The teacher can help them develop beginning learnings in the area of citizenship education, to learn that each person has feelings, and that feelings affect behavior.

A PLAN FOR DEVELOPING KEY CONCEPTS (UNIT)

Outline for Planning	*Topic—Feelings: How Do I Feel?* *How Do Others Feel?* *For Four- or Five-Year-Olds—* *Early in the Year*
1. *Purposes:* These give direction to planning. Here the expected outcomes are stated. Simply state the purpose or task "What am I trying to do? What do I hope to accomplish?	a. *Purposes:* To help the child achieve beginnings of self-understanding; to develop the ability to identify and express one's feelings or emotions; to become aware of the feelings of others; and to begin to understand how feelings influence behavior.
	b. *Concepts To Be Developed.* I have feelings. I can be happy, thankful, angry, afraid. Other children have feelings too. They can be happy, etc. The way we feel affects how we act. If I am happy I may be kind. If I am angry I may cry, hit, snatch. The way I treat other children affects how they feel.
2. *Initiating the Plan:* Plan to initiate the study in such a way as to arouse the curiosity and interest of the children. Regardless of the plan for beginning, children should be involved in the planning. Several means of initiating a plan are listed:	
a. Teacher Suggestion. The teacher may propose certain questions about the topic, leave questions unanswered, provoke some discussion, and then say that the answers to the questions will be found during the study of the topic.	When the children come together for a group session, the teacher can introduce each child individually. She might ask, "What were you like when you were a baby?" "How much have you grown since you were born?" "What does it mean to grow?" "How do you feel now that you are five years old?" "How did you feel when you came to school?"

Outline for Planning	*Topic—Feelings: How Do I Feel?* *How Do Others Feel?* *For Four- or Five-Year-Olds—* *Early in the Year*
	The teacher may use a story, such as *The Growing Story,* following it with questions such as those above.
	Questions such as "How do you feel?" may need to be followed by words such as *afraid? happy? lonely?* Thus the teacher can help the child find the meaning for these terms and also for his or her feelings.
b. Incidents. Some incident or happening in the life of a child or in the local community, state, nation, or world might be the means of creating interest in a particular topic. For example, a good time to have a unit on the circus is when the circus comes to town. Holidays, festivals, and seasons of the year also offer leads.	The incident—It is the first day the children are together. As the teacher greets each child, she pins on a name tag and says, "This is your name." She may ask, "What do you like about your name?"
c. Audiovisual Materials. Use of any of the following: motion pictures, filmstrips, slides, flat pictures, recordings, radio, field trips, TV, or resource persons.	
d. Ongoing Experience. A preceding topic may lead directly into a second one. If interest in the preceding topic was high, it should be sufficient to carry over.	
e. Arranged Environment. Arrange a display of some type in which books, objects, pictures draw attention to a particular topic. For example, if the topic to be studied is on "Our Homes," the teacher would arrange books, pictures, and models of different types of homes on a table or bulletin board. The arrangement should be set up the day before and children should be permitted some time to view the display, to talk freely about the things they see. They may identify the specific questions and topics to be considered.	Polaroid pictures could be taken of each child and mounted on the bulletin board. Actions in pictures could be labeled in connection with teacher questions such as "What were you doing there?" "How did you feel doing that?"

(Continued)

Topic—Feelings: How Do I Feel?
How Do Others Feel?
For Four- or Five-Year-Olds—
Early in the Year

Outline for Planning

3. *Learning Opportunities:* There must be a relationship between the learning opportunities and the purposes. It is through the activities that the purposes are attained. Learning activities should be numerous and varied so that individual differences can be met. The following is a list of possible activities. They are not listed in order of importance. One plan may not include all of them. Activities are classified according to subject areas to illustrate how a topic such as *Feelings* can offer opportunities for academic learnings in the various subject areas. It is important to remember that one activity can contribute to learnings in several areas.

a. Language Activities. Discussion, dramatization, conversation, telling stories, listening to stories and poems, and writing letters and stories (dictated to the teacher), looking at books.

Make a tape recording of children's voices. Ask children to listen and to identify their own voice. The teacher may ask, "How did you feel when you heard your voice? How did your voice sound?"

Listen to stories, poems, recordings about a child or children.

Look at books about a child or children. Books such as *What Mary Jo Wanted* and *Will I Have a Friend?* could provide identity figures for the children and encourage them to express their feelings about characters in the stories and their own personal wants and attitudes. Possible teacher questions might include "Why do you think Mary Jo wanted a puppy?" "What does it mean to share?" "What is a friend?" "How do we make friends?" "How do friends feel about each other?"

Role playing could emphasize the feelings of children and how these feelings influence their behavior. Pictures can provide a good beginning. Possible questions include "What do you think is happening here?" "How do you think the children feel?" "Why?" "What do you think the children might do next?" "Show us." The *Let's Start Collection* can be helpful.

	Topic—*Feelings: How Do I Feel?*
	How Do Others Feel?
	For Four- or Five-Year-Olds—
Outline for Planning	*Early in the Year*

Feelie Boxes can be fun. Objects of different shapes are included. The child is asked to reach into the box and respond to the questions "How does it feel?" "What shape do you think it is?" "Is it a happy shape?" "How do you know?"

Make picture books using titles such as "How I Feel Today," or "My Friends." Pictures may come from magazines or they may be drawn or painted.

Create poems or stories (dictated to teacher).

Note children's names under photographs.

Play games: Identify child by his voice. "Who am I?"

Practice use of courteous terms such as "thank you" and "excuse me." Discuss meanings of terms and relate them to how one feels.

Develop meanings for vocabulary words such as happy, thankful, angry, lonely, friend, enemy, afraid, hope.

Dramatize while others identify the feeling.

b. Community Resources. Field trips to places of interest such as city hall, library, post office, airport, bakery, grocery, and farm. The immediate school environment is a laboratory in itself. Many individuals in the community can be brought into the classroom as resource persons. Don't overlook parents as resource people; they have much to offer.

Take field trips around the school and in the community.

Take pictures on trip. Dictate stories to go with pictures.

Make picture books using titles such as "People at the airport."

c. Audiovisual Experiences. Films, filmstrips, slides, radio, recordings, television, models, charts, graphs, flat pictures, dioramas, wall murals.

View films and filmstrips. *The Joy of Being You* and *All Kinds of Feelings* are filmstrips that can be used to introduce children to their own feelings, how they may be expressed, and the meaning of feelings such as joy or loneliness.

Listen to and respond to recordings. The song *Growing* (album by Hap Palmer) encourages children to feel what it is like to grow.

(Continued)

Outline for Planning	*Topic—Feelings: How Do I Feel?* *How Do Others Feel?* *For Four- or Five-Year-Olds—* *Early in the Year*
d. Handicrafts and Arts. Painting, clay modeling, paper mache modeling, and construction out of paper or wood.	Paint and draw pictures of self and others. Children can trace around each other on large sheets of paper placed on the floor. Details may be filled in later. Teacher questions might include "Is your face happy?" "How do you think your friend feels in his picture?" Use finger paint. Questions that may be asked include "How does the paint feel on your hands?" View reproductions of famous paintings. Ask questions that relate to how the painter might have felt when painting the picture and how the people in the picture feel. Make paper bag puppets. Faces could be happy, sad, or lonely. Make a picture time line of growth from babyhood to the age of five years. Make a silhouette of each child and label with child's name.
e. Music and Physical Activities. Songs, rhythms, games, listening to records, playing instruments.	Play musical selections on piano or record player. Ask children to listen to and respond to questions such as "How does the music make you feel?" "Sleepy?" "Lazy?" "Happy?" "If you feel like that music how would you act? Show us." Sing songs about self and other children. Songs such as "If You're Happy and You Know It" can be used for encouraging responses. Feelings such as *sleepy* or *hungry* can also be used. Use an adaptation of the game "Simon Says." Ask a small group of children to face a mirror and to make facial expressions to match certain feelings. For example, "Simon says to make a happy face (or to make a frown or to be afraid)."
f. Number Activities. Opportunities for counting, measuring, weighing, development of concepts and vocabulary.	Weigh and measure children. Chart differences over time period. Involve children. Make a time line, using pictures of the children from birth to time of school entrance.

Outline for Planning	Topic—Feelings: How Do I Feel? How Do Others Feel? For Four- or Five-Year-Olds— Early in the Year
	Make cookies for someone to make him or her happy.
g. Growth in Social Skills and Attitudes. Opportunities for leadership, cooperation, a dramatization, a film, or a discussion period may be used.	Make choices.
	Share materials and equipment.
	Take turns. Discuss how one feels when one shares or takes turns, and how the other child feels. Avoid moralizing.
	Cooperate in clean-up.
	Learn other children's names.
	Practice courtesy in asking for and receiving materials, turns, etc. Relate to feelings.
4. *Evaluation:* Ask the question "How can I know whether or not the purposes stated in the beginning have been realized?"	See evidences of desired behavior on p. 326.
	Observe dramatic play. Note conversations and comments of children for indications of self and others that have developed.
	Observe children's behavior for evidences of planning, sharing, assuming responsibility, using courteous forms of speech.
	Observe children's art products. See pp. 436–440.
5. *List of Materials:* List the materials needed to teach the unit. The materials should be accessible and ready to use when needed.	Use anecdotal records. See pp. 492–493.

BOOKS

Anglund, Joan W. *A Friend Is Someone Who Likes You.* New York: Harcourt, Brace, Jovanovich, 1958.

Balian, Lorna. *I Love You, Mary Jane.* Nashville, Tenn.: Abingdon Press, 1967.

Beim, Jerrold and Lorraine Beim. *Two Is a Team.* New York: Harcourt, Brace, Jovanovich, 1945.

Bromhall, Winifred. *Peter's Three Friends.* New York: Alfred A. Knopf, 1964.

Bryant, Bernice. *Let's Be Friends.* Chicago; Children's Press, 1954.

Cohen, Miriam. *Will I Have a Friend?* New York: Macmillan, Publishing Co., 1967.

Cole, William. *Frances Face-Maker.* New York: World, 1963.

Ets, Marie H. *Just Me.* New York: Viking Press, 1965.

Evans, Eva K. *People Are Important.* New York: Capitol, 1957.

Green, Mary M. *Is It Hard? Is It Easy?* Reading, Mass.: Addison-Wesley, 1960.

Guilfoile, Elizabeth. *Nobody Listens to Andrew.* Chicago: Follett, 1957.

Iwasaki, Chihiro. *Will You Be My Friend?* New York: McGraw-Hill Book Co., 1974.

Keats, E. J. *The Snowy Day.* New York: Viking Press, 1962.

——. *Whistle for Willie.* New York: Viking Press, 1964.

Keesler, L., and Ethel Keesler. *Kim and Me.* New York: Doubleday & Co., 1960.

Krauss, Ruth. *The Growing Story.* New York: Harper & Row, 1947.

Kushin, Karla. *Just Like Everybody Else.* New York: Harper & Row, 1959.

Ness, Evaline. *Exactly Alike.* New York: Charles Scribner's Sons, 1964.

Orbach, Ruth. *I'm Dan.* New York: Charles Scribner's Sons, 1970.

Udry, Janice May. *Let's Be Enemies.* New York: Harper & Row, 1961.

——. *What Mary Jo Shared.* Chicago: Whitman, 1966.

——. *What Mary Jo Wanted.* Chicago: Whitman, 1968.

Vreeken, Elizabeth. *The Little Boy Who Would Not Say His Name.* Chicago: Follett, 1959.

Yashima, Taro. *Youngest One.* New York: Viking Press, 1959.

FILMSTRIPS

The Joy of Being You. (6970), Scholastic Kindle Filmstrips, 902 Sylvan Avenue, Englewood Cliffs, N.J. 07632.

All Kinds of Feelings. (6968), Scholastic Kindle Filmstrips, 902 Sylvan Avenue, Englewood Cliffs. N.J. 07632.

RECORDS

Learning Basic Skills Through Music. Vol. I, Educational Activities, Inc., Box 392, Freeport, N.Y. 11520.

POETRY

Aldis, Dorothy. *All Together.* New York: Putnam, 1952.

Frank, Josetts (ed.), *Poems to Read to the Very Young.* New York: Random House, 1961.

Hopkins, Lee Bennett (ed.). *Me: A Book of Poems.* New York: Seabury Press, 1970.

Jacobs, Leland B., *Alphabet for Girls.* New York: Holt, Rinehart, and Winston, 1969.

Livingston, Myra C. *Whispers and Other Poems.* New York: Harcourt, Brace, Jovanovich, 1957.

Untermeyer, Louis (ed.). *The Golden Treasury of Poetry.* New York: Holden, 1959.

PICTURE SETS

Let's Start Picture Collection: School Experiences. Scholastic Magazine, 902 Sylvan Avenue, Englewood Cliffs, N.J. 07632, 1968.

Let's Start Picture Collection: Urban Environment. Scholastic Magazine, 902 Sylvan Avenue, Englewood Cliffs, N.J. 07632, 1969.

Role Playing Photo-Problems for Young Children. Holt, Rinehart, and Winston, New York.

SONGS

McCall, Adeline. *This Is Music.* Boston: Allyn and Bacon, 1966.

Nelson, Mary J., and Gladys Tipton. *Music for Early Childhood.* New York: Silver Burdett Co., 1952.

Pitts, Lilla Belle, et al. *The Kindergarten Book.* Boston: Ginn Co., 1949.

Seeger, Ruth Crawford. *American Folk Songs for Children.* New York: Doubleday & Co., 1948.

Winn, Marie (ed.). *Children's Songs.* New York: Simon & Schuster, 1966.

Zetlin, Patty. *Castle in My City—Songs for Young Children.* San Carlos, Calif.: Golden Gate Junior Books, 1966.

Suggestions for parts of the unit adapted from C. K. Ducolon, Loving: A Process Approach, unpublished graduate paper, University of Maryland, College Park, May 1971.

The *teaching plan* may be developed after the teacher becomes acquainted with the children. Looking at the plan, "Feelings" the teacher may decide to use the concepts, "I have feelings," "Other children have feelings." Selections which are appropriate may be selected from the unit. The *teaching plan* is developed from the overall plan and includes detailed plans for the day. For example, Albert enters kindergarten a few days after the other children. The teacher decides to use this incident in developing beginning understandings of the concept, "I have feelings. Other children have feelings too." The plan for this part of the day might include the following:

1. Purposes: To help each child achieve beginning understandings of his or her feelings and feelings of the other children, as evidenced by such statements as "I didn't know anybody when I came to kindergarten. I was lonesome. Now I am glad."
   "Albert has some friends now. He likes to play with me."
2. Initiating the plan: When Albert came to kindergarten he was introduced individually to the children. Later in the morning as the children come together for a group session the teacher might say.
   "Albert came to kindergarten today for the first time. How did you feel when you came to school? Happy? Afraid? Lonely? How do you think Albert felt? Why?"
3. Learning Opportunities: Discuss questions. Discuss ways to help children feel happy at kindergarten. Jot down children's comments. Make into experience charts later. Summarize suggestions. Read story, *Will I Have A Friend?*

4. Materials:
   Book: Cohen, Miriam. *Will I Have a Friend?* New York: Macmillan Publishing Co., 1967. Paper and marker for experience chart.
5. Evaluation: Observe children's behavior for evidences of concern for the feelings of others. Note conversations and comments of children.

At other times, on other days, the teacher may continue to provide opportunities for experiences through which the children may learn about feelings. The teacher may select other concepts and provide appropriate learning opportunities. Little by little, experience by experience, the understandings, attitudes, and skills are learned. As one teacher was told, "just keep on keeping on."

Suggested Activities

1. Select one concept to be developed with young children from the areas listed on pages 321–323. Make a plan (or unit) for teaching the key concepts using the suggested outline found on pages 326–331. Indicate the age level for which the plan or unit is intended. Select another concept. Plan a series of learning encounters for developing this concept.
2. Observe in a children's center. Describe ways in which the teacher is helping the children or a child develop an understanding and acceptance of others, how they live and feel.
3. Note the ways in which the backgrounds of children in a group that you visited differ. Describe ways in which the teacher is making provision for and utilizing these multicultural backgrounds.
4. Discuss in class the time concepts of young children. Observe a group of young children and note the words used in relation to time. Were the words used accurately? Note instances of how the teacher helped develop an awareness of time with the children.
5. Select a site that you consider to be appropriate for a field trip for young children. Visit the site and evaluate it in terms of the checklist on pp. 206–208. What learnings might the children gain from the trip?
6. View the film, *Sugar and Spice.* Odeon Films, Inc., 51 West 86th St., New York, N.Y. 10024. Discuss how you feel about this film in helping children understand and assume sex roles.
7. Invite someone from another country to come and teach a group of young children a game from that country.
8. Invite the mother of a child from a different ethnic background to come to the center. Perhaps she could cook some food or serve some food appropriate to her background.
9. Read stories to children about children in other countries, the games they play, their homes, their food.
10. View the film, *Head Start to Confidence.* Modern Talking Pictures, 2323 New Hyde Park Rd., New Hyde Park, N.Y. 11040.

Related Readings

Abrahams, R. "Cultural Differences and the Melting Pot Ideology," *Educ. Leadership,* 29:2 (1971), pp. 118–121.

Brody, Charlotte. "Social Studies and Self Awareness," in *The Block Book.* Washington, D.C.: NAEYC, 1974, pp. 59–68.

Clark, Kenneth B. *Prejudice and Your Child.* Boston: Beacon Press, 1963.

Cohen, M. D. (ed.). *Learning to Live as Neighbors.* Washington, D.C.: ACEI, 1972.

Danilov, V. J. "Museums as Educational Partners," *Child. Educ.,* 52:6 (1976), pp. 306–311.

Endsley, R. C., and K. Osborn, "Children's Reactions to TV Violence: A Review of Research," *Young Children, 26*:1 (1970), pp. 4–11.

Goodman, Mary Ellen. *The Culture of Childhood.* New York: Teachers College, 1970.

Kranz, P. L., and R. Ostler "Adult Expectations of Children—Do As I Say, Not As I Do," *Young Children 29*:5 (1974), pp. 277–279.

Jantz, R. K. "Social Studies," in *Curriculum for the Preschool-Primary Child, A Review of Research,* edited by Carol Seefeldt. Columbus, Ohio: Charles E. Merrill Publishing Co., 1976, pp. 83–123.

Lane, Mary B., F. F. Elzey, and Mary Leivos. *Nurseries in Cross-Cultural Education.* San Francisco: San Francisco State College, 1971.

Lindberg, Lucile, and Rita Swedlow. *Early Childhood Education: A Guide for Observation and Participation.* Boston: Allyn and Bacon, 1976, pp. 166–186.

Mitchell, L. S. *Young Geographers.* New York: Bank Street College of Education, 1971.

Morris, D. N. "Rallying Around the Children of the World," *Child. Educ.,* 53:5 (1977), pp. 235–240.

Moyer, Joan E. *Bases for World Understanding and Cooperation—Suggestions for Teaching the Young Child.* Washington, D.C.: ASCD, 1970.

Moyer, Joan E., and Guillermina Engelbrecht. "Multicultural Education: Where Do We Begin?" *Child. Educ.,* 53:5 (1977), pp. 241–244.

Mukerji, Rose. "TV's Impact on Children: A Checkerboard Scene," *Phi Delta Kappan,* January 1976.

National Institute of Education. *The Development of Career Awareness in Young Children:* NIE Papers in Education and Work, No. 1. Washington, D.C.: U.S. Department of Health, Education and Welfare, 1976.

Nilsen, Alleen P. "Alternatives to Sexist Practices in the Classroom," *Young Children, 32*:5 (1977), pp. 53–58.

Redl, Fritz. "The Nature and Nurture of Prejudice," *Child. Educ.,* 45:5 (1969), pp. 254–257.

Richards, Betty. "Mapping: An Introduction to Symbols," *Young Children, 31*:2 (1976), pp. 145–156.

Rohrer, Georgia K. "Racial and Ethnic Identification and Preference in Young Children," *Young Children, 32*:4 (1977), pp. 24–33.

Seefeldt, Carol. *Social Studies for the Preschool—Primary Child.* Columbus, Ohio: Charles E. Merrill Publishing Co., 1977.

———. "Is Today Tomorrow? History for Young Children," *Young Children, 30*:2 (1975), pp. 99–106.

Simmons, B. "Teacher Beware of Sex-Stereotyping," *Child. Educ., 52*:4 (1976), pp. 192–195.

Spodek, B. "Social Studies for Young Children: Identifying Intellectual Goals," *Social Education 33*:1 (1974), pp. 40–45.

chapter 15

Children and values: moral education

Educating for values is no simple task. The responsibility for value development is shared by the school, the home, organized religion, and various agencies of the community. This does not, however, lessen the task of the school, for value development is an integral part of the learning process.[1] Values and the valuing process are related to the moral development of children. Berman writes,

> Most persons responsible for inducting the young into the culture are concerned that they learn what the culture prizes. Through exhortation, but more frequently

[1] ASCD, *Toward Better Teaching*, 1949 Yearbook (Washington, D.C.: ASCD, 1949), pp. 154–155.

through example, the young become dimly aware of the most pervasive values peculiar to a given group of people.[2]

Such learning, however, is complicated by the very nature of American society. There are groups differing as to race, national origin, religious beliefs, and social and economic levels.

Many persons believe that the family plays a crucial role for children in the development of values and awareness. Raths points out, however, that the changes in the family are dramatic, if not frightening. The consequence, he says, has been a growing confusion and conflict in relation to values.[3]

There are both general and personal values. General values reflect the basic orientation of our society which is democratic. Personal values are those that have to do with making choices and decisions in our personal lives. Children can be helped to think about their choices in terms of a "values framework."[4]

WHAT ARE VALUES?

Values form the basis for inner direction by the individual. They have been defined by many authorities in many ways. Several definitions follow.

> A value is the comparative weight, esteem, or price attached by the individual to a given idea, person, or object.[5]
> Values are standards applied to thought or action, principles, preferences on a scale of priorities, or commitments to what one feels is desirable.[6]
> Our values show what we tend to do with our limited time and energy.[7]

Values, says Raths, are based on the three processes of choosing, prizing, and acting. He has identified criteria, all of which must be met if something is to be called a value. One must choose freely from alternatives, after considering the consequences of each alternative. One cherishes values and is willing to affirm them publicly. One acts upon values, and repeats them. They are incorporated into one's behavior and tend to persist.[8] The following guidelines can be helpful to the teacher in understanding how children develop values.

[2] Louise M. Berman, *New Priorities in the Curriculum* (Columbus, Ohio: Charles E. Merrill Publishers, 1968), p. 155.
[3] L. E. Raths, M. Harmin, and S. B. Simon, *Values and Teaching: Working with Values in the Classroom* (Columbus, Ohio: Charles E. Merrill Publishers, 1966), pp. 15–20.
[4] J. Jarolimek, *Social Studies in Elementary Education*, 5th ed. (New York: Macmillan Publishing Co., 1977), pp. 67–69.
[5] ASCD, op. cit., p. 154.
[6] *Report to the President*, (Washington, D.C.: The White House Conference on Children, 1970), p. 63.
[7] Raths, op. cit., p. 27.
[8] Ibid., pp. 28–30.

Values Grow Out of and Change with Experience. For children, values build up as the result of their many experiences both in and out of school. For example:

> It was May. Jane was sharing with the teacher some feelings about nursery school. She said, "You know, when I first came to nursery school I didn't hang up my sweater. I didn't play with the other children. I hit them. Now I put things in my locker and I like to play with Mary and Brenda." The teacher replied, "You have learned many things in nursery school. You have learned to care for your belongings. You have learned to play with Mary, Brenda, and the others."

The Importance of an Experience in Relation to Value Building Varies According to the Individual Child, His or Her Maturity, Family, Friends, and Background of Experiences. A situation may be helpful to one child in formulating values, but it may not have the same results for another child. For example:

> One morning the five-year-olds were moving with music. Maria skipped gracefully and Rose said, "Maria can skip. She's good. Look at Albert. He's so funny." This situation, including Rose's remark, offered Maria an opportunity for building a positive self-concept while for Albert the effect was probably negative.

Some of the Values an Individual Holds and Exhibits May Conflict with One Another. The child may value friendship and want very much to play with other children. The child, however, may not recognize that aggressive behavior patterns stand in the way. For example:

> Ted wanted to play with Robert and Juan, two five-year-old boys who were using the blocks. Ted picked up a ball and threw it at the block structure. When talking with the teacher he asked, "What else could I do? I wanted to play with them."

In considering values it is important to remember that, "the formative school years present a challenge to the educator to contribute to the development of values desirable in a democracy. This whole area of appreciations, interests and goals, character and morality, social and spiritual values is basic to the entire educational process."[9]

WHICH VALUES TO TEACH?

"In a pluralistic society, diversity is an important value that our educational institutions should express."[10] But Fantini's statement describes the dilemma

---

[9] ASCD, op. cit., p. 9.
[10] M. D. Fantini, "Public Schools of Choice and the Plurality of Publics," *Educ. Leadership,* 28:6 (1971), p. 585.

faced by the teachers of young children. When values are divergent and in conflict, what can the teacher do? The following quotations offer criteria for the selection of values to be taught.

> For a pluralistic society to survive, certain common values must be accepted, such as mutual respect and concern for the welfare of others. These common values take precedence over the freedom to be different. Pluralism is not a justification for polarization and estrangement.[11]

> In this society with its many values, some confused and conflicting, two values are basic: a belief in the potential worth of each individual, and reliance upon the method of individual and group intelligence in the solution of problems. When either of these basic values is challenged, democracy is threatened. The teacher, as the agent of a democratic state, has a responsibility to help students develop attitudes and beliefs that are consistent with these fundamentals of democracy.[12]

Pressure to have the teacher of young children work for acceptance of values held by the majority violates one of the democratic values—reliance on intelligence, which involves examining different points of view and evolving one's own values.

Recent efforts on the part of some persons interested in respecting a diversity of values have apparently gone to the extreme of accepting any behavior that is different by reason of racial, class, or ethnic origin as "good." Prejudice or violence or aggressive behavior, for example, may be strong in certain situations. In relation to this, Forum 3 of the White House Conference on Children reported:[13]

> Any manifestation of pluralism, cultural identity, or individuality becomes invalid when it contradicts or conflicts with the "inalienable rights" and "privileges of others." This basic American understanding is crucial to any consideration of values and must be a fundamental lesson in value learning for every American child.

There has been a tendency to consider middle-class values as those of children in suburbia and lower-class values as belonging to children of the inner city. Such a tendency not only overlooks migrant and rural children but those of differing social, ethnic, and minority groups as well. The tendency implies a stereotype, assuming that all persons of the same class have the same values. To the contrary, values that are held by the family and that affect the child may differ greatly from the stereotype. Families in the inner city as well as those in suburbia and rural areas may value cleanliness and good health for their children. Families in the inner city may not have the resources necessary to maintain cleanliness and good health but that does not mean that these qualities are not valued.

[11] *Report to the President*, White House Conference, op. cit., p. 64.
[12] ASCD, op. cit., p. 155.
[13] *Report to the President*, White House Conference, op. cit., p. 64.

However, beliefs and feelings about what children should be and do differ widely. The teacher needs to know the behavior patterns expected of each child and the cultural beliefs about what the child should do and be. Such knowledge can help the teacher in dealing with value conflicts between the home and the school.

As the teacher placed a hand on Jimmy's shoulder, he yelled, "Take your hand off my shoulder." The teacher's gesture of affection was interpreted by the child as an aggressive act.

Aggressive behavior may be valued in each of two homes, yet the value may be expressed in different behavior patterns. In one home the child shows aggression verbally, talks loudly, and perhaps ignores others who want a chance to speak. In another home the child may be encouraged to hit and fight in order to "get along." The difference may be in the behavior manifestations rather than in the value itself.

The teacher must begin with the children where they are and must use the resources of each child and his or her cultural background in order to help identify and clarify values.

The values common in our democracy need to be considered, because these are the values that the schools hope to develop. "These values are a part of our political and religious heritages."[14] One list of these values has been used in developing a statement appropriate for young children.[15] The terms such as *Moral Responsibility* and *Devotion to Truth* are adult terms, expressed in adult language. However, these have been used to suggest that the foundations of such concepts have their beginnings in the very early years. The adult terms for the values and teacher goals are used, but the behaviors, attitudes, and comments are those of children.

It is important not only that the values be known, but that the teacher recognize behavior, comments, and attitudes of children that are conducive to the realization of the values. A statement of values, including teacher goals expressed in terms of children's behavior, attitudes, and comments, follows.

HUMAN PERSONALITY

Teacher's goal: Help each child—
1. To have a sense of personal worth and to know that:
   "My Daddy and Mother love me.
   My teacher loves me too.
   I can climb high on the jungle gym.
   I am Ann's friend."
2. To feel secure in the nursery or kindergarten and to feel that:
   "I belong to this group.

[14] Jarolimek, op. cit., p. 67.
[15] National Education Association and American Association of School Administrators, Educational Policies Commission, *Moral and Spiritual Values in Public Schools* (Washington, D.C., 1951).

The children like to play with me.
The children miss me when I am not here.
The teacher misses me when I am absent.
The children are glad to see me when I come in the morning.
Ann is my friend."

3. To develop self-understanding as expressed through:
"I like to play with Sue.
Sometimes, when children won't let me play with their toys, I get mad and hit them.
I can talk with Jim, instead of hitting him.
Children don't like for me to hit them."

4. To gain insight into the behavior of others and to understand that:
"Jim can't fix the block house. It is going to fall. I will help him.
Tom is crying. He fell and cut his foot.
Joe hasn't been to school before. He doesn't know how we play."

MORAL RESPONSIBILITY

Teacher's goal: Help each child—

1. To develop a willingness to try new activities and experiences as evidenced by such statements as:
"I don't know how to paint on the easel, but I can try.
I haven't been to the airport. I might be afraid. But Miss Jones will go with us—mother, too. I can have fun."

2. To recognize ownership and understand that:
"Some things belong to me. Some things belong to others. Some things are for all of us to use.
I will share only the things that belong to me or that are for all of us to use.
I will ask if I may use something that belongs to somebody else.
I will use materials carefully."

3. To develop consideration for the welfare and convenience of others. For example:
"Miss Jones is reading a story. The children want to hear. I will not play the record player now.
It is lunch time. I will come to the table. I will not keep the other children waiting."

4. To develop a willingness to let others have turns and practice such behavior as evidenced in:
"Here is a ball. You can play with it.
Jim, you can ride the tractor now."

5. To gain an understanding of what it means to do a job. For example:
"I will get the things I need to work with. I'm going to paint. I need an apron.
I will finish my job.
I will put materials away."

INSTITUTIONS AS THE SERVANTS OF PEOPLE

Teacher's goal: Help each child—

1. To develop an understanding that each person has a job to do. For example:

Figure 47

(Courtesy of Head Start.)

Frances is gaining some insight into the behavior of others. She understands that Tracey is crying because he fell and hurt his hand.

"There are many jobs to be done at school.
   The teachers teach children. They read stories to us. They watch us when we play.
   The custodian cleans our room. The custodian sweeps the floor. The custodian washes the windows."
2. To understand that some jobs help all of us. For example:
   "The police officer helps us cross the street. He or she reminds the cars to drive slowly in front of our school.
   Mrs. Brown cooks the food for our lunch at school."

COMMON CONSENT

Teacher's goal: Help each child—
1. To develop the willingness to talk things over. For example:
   "If I talk to somebody, I don't have to hit, or to snatch the toy."
2. To gain an appreciation of the value of planning together. For example:
   "We all have good ideas.
   Now we all know what we are going to do."
3. To develop an understanding of how we plan together. For example:
   "We can talk about what we want to do. We can ask questions.
   We talk about what we can do.

We decide what we will do.
There are different ways to do things."
4. To gain an understanding of the individual's responsibility for following a plan. For example:
"We made a plan. I helped.
I will do what we decided.
Jim forgot. He came down the slide 'head first.' What did we decide to do?"

DEVOTION TO TRUTH

Teacher's goal: Help each child—
1. To learn that some things are true and some things are not true, and to understand that:
"Some children tease just for fun.
Some stories are make-believe and I enjoy them.
Sometimes I can pretend or make-believe.
Sometimes children do not understand what their mother said and tell something that is not true.
Sometimes children 'make up' a story just to get others to listen.
Sometimes children are afraid to tell what really happened."
2. To learn how we can find out the truth. For example:
"We can go and see for ourselves.
We can look at pictures.
We can look at movies.
We can ask grown-ups.
We can listen while grown-ups read to us."
3. To develop understanding of what it means to be honest. For example:
"I will try to remember what happened.
I won't blame Jim when he hit me. I will remember that I was angry and I pushed Jim.
Jane didn't make me fall and skin my knee. I wasn't looking where I was going.
I tripped and fell.
I will try to find right answers.
When I am asked a question, I will tell the truth.
I can ask myself if this is the best I can do."

RESPECT FOR EXCELLENCE

Teacher's goal: Help each child—
1. To learn to do one thing well, such as walk straight, rest comfortably, drive a nail all the way into the board.
2. To come to recognize his or her best effort, as evidenced by such statements as:
"I can do it better now. Watch me.
I will try.
I don't like this picture. I tore it.
I'm tired now. I'll make another boat tomorrow."

3. To appreciate the achievements of others, as evidenced by the following statements:
   "Jan built a big block house.
   Look, Joe can skip.
   I like your picture. That's good."
4. To set standards for himself or herself. For example:
   "I want to tie my shoe. Please help me."
5. To enjoy learning, as evidenced by such statements as:
   "It is fun to say new words.
   I have learned a poem. I can say it."

BROTHERHOOD

Teacher's goal: Help each child—
1. To develop an understanding that children are different, yet alike. For example:
   "We are different in the way we talk, look, dress, worship, the food we eat, the games we play, and the homes we live in.
   But we do talk, eat, wear clothing, worship, play, and live in homes.
   I live in a brick house. Joe lives in an apartment. I am happy in my home. He is happy in his.
   Jane's hair is curly and blond. Tina's hair is straight and black."
2. To develop a willingness to treat other children as one wants to be treated. For example:
   "I will take turns.
   I will share my toys."

SPIRITUAL ENRICHMENT

Teacher's goal: Help each child—
1. To develop sensitivity to and appreciation for beauty. For example:
   "The bird is hopping on the grass.
   The sun is so gold and shiny.
   Oh, look. See the little new leaf."
2. To engage in creative activities, with resulting comments such as:
   "I know what we can do. I thought about it. [creative thinking]
   The little bird was shivering with scaredness. [creative language]
   The music makes me want to dance and dance." [creative movement]
3. To experience successful achievement. For example:
   "You were a good helper, Joe. You put the blocks away.
   I did it! I did it! I did it! I painted a house."
4. To develop an understanding that there is law and order in our natural world which we can regard with reverence and wonder. For example:
   "There are seasons. It is spring. The flowers are blooming.
   The sun sets in the evening. The sun rises in the morning."
5. To develop an appreciation of kindness, friendliness, cooperation, and loyalty in others. For example:
   "When I was lonesome, Pam played with me.

Miss Helms helped me fix my truck.

Sam let me look at his book. He was kind to me."

6. To learn that God is very great. He created beauty for us to enjoy. One child said:

"See the little new moon. God made it. I wish the sky was full of little new moons."

Many early childhood experiences can build spiritual values if the teacher is consciously working toward that end. The teacher's role is an important one.

DEVELOPING VALUES

According to Havighurst, "Moral character is learned and therefore is a proper object of education. It is learned, however, in various ways and at various levels of complexity."[16] This concern for the development of moral values, beliefs, and character among the young is not new. Through the years various methods have been used in teaching morals. "In colonial times great reliance was placed upon reading, memorizing, and repeating religious material such as the Lord's Prayer, the Creed, the Ten Commandments, and a catechism."[17] The earliest textbooks were filled with selections which presented moral precepts designed to be memorized.

Later, plans for systematic instruction in such areas as morals, manners, patriotism, and citizenship were developed and used. Grades were given in desirable character traits—reliability, judgment, and industry. Organizations sponsored contests to prepare the best theme or to deliver the best address on a patriotic topic.

The Character Education Inquiry, begun in 1924, raised questions regarding the methods of character education which were then in use. Hartshorne and May reported that "the main attention of educators should be placed not so much on devices for teaching honesty or any other 'trait' as on the reconstruction of school practices in such a way as to provide not occasional but consistent and regular opportunities for the successful use by both teachers and pupils of such forms of conduct as make for the common good." Kohlberg says that the findings of recent research support these conclusions.[18,19]

---

[16] R. J. Havighurst, "Moral Character and Religious Education," *Relig. Educ.*, 51:3 (1956), pp. 165–167.

[17] Alice Miel and Peggy Brogan, *More Than Social Studies* (Englewood Cliffs, N.J.: Prentice-Hall, 1957), p. 122.

[18] H. Hartshorne and M. A. May, *Studies in Deceit* (New York: Macmillan Publishing Co., 1928), p. 414.

[19] L. Kohlberg, "Development of Moral Character and Ideology," in *Review of Child Development Research*, Vol. 1, edited by M. L. Hoffman and Lois W. Hoffman (New York: Russell Sage Foundation, 1964), p. 426.

According to Miel and Brogan, in the early 'thirties, as schools participated in the "activity movement," attempts were made to plan enterprises that would build character. During the 'forties, educators concerned themselves with ways of helping children develop moral and spiritual values. "More attention was given to children's ability to identify with storybook characters, and there was keen interest in promoting good human relations through intercultural or intergroup education."[20]

One of the forums of the 1960 White House Conference on Children and Youth considered the topic, Beliefs—Religions, spiritual and secular beliefs and personal codes of conduct which affect the development of the young. "The Forum affirmed 'the importance of personal faith in God, the strengthening of moral and religious values, and the necessity for a continuing re-examination of personal conduct in order that the Nation's children may realize their full potential for a creative life in freedom and dignity.' The ethical principles to be set before our young people 'have as their ultimate source the belief that man is created by God and is therefore possessed of dignity as an individual.' Churches, synagogues, character-building agencies, and all citizens were called upon to cooperate in encouraging moral and religious training, values, and beliefs among our children and youth."[21] Throughout the years along with the concern for the development of moral and spiritual values, there has been the concern for the role of the public school in this area of instruction.

Schools for young children are operated under various auspices. Some are public schools while others are private or church-related. Still others are sponsored by an organization or community agency. Centers supported by public funds, in keeping with the ideas that have been expressed, avoid sectarian emphasis. The church-related and private centers, however, may present spiritual and moral values from their denominational point of view. Regardless, however, of the sponsorship of the school, certain principles are basic to the development of these values in young children.

Jones points out that the capacity to grow spiritually must be nourished just as the capacity to grow physically. The nourishment, however, must be provided in terms of the needs and capacities of a child of a given age. "Overstimulation may be as detrimental to the child's development as is malnutrition."[22] It is important then to provide the needed spiritual nourishment to each child at each stage in his or her growth.

By the age of four the child is becoming assertive. The child has a lively mind and asks many questions, some of which relate to God, the universe, and

[20] Miel and Brogan, op. cit., p. 126.
[21] *Conference Proceedings* (Washington, D.C.: The Golden Anniversary White House Conference on Children and Youth, Inc., 1960), p. 192.
[22] Mary Alice Jones, *Guiding Children in Christian Growth* (Nashville, Tenn.: Abingdon Press, 1949), p. 11.

who made it. Gesell says that, "the vast intangible creative force called God is often grasped rather well by the mind of the four-year-old."[23] The child is beginning to understand relationships, and needs help in comprehending the difference between the activity of God and the work of man. Children, for example, are told that "God gives us food." They should, however, be helped to see that man, using the sun, rain, and soil provided by God, can grow plants or fruit which can be used as food. Man may work with God.

At this age the child often shows a marked interest in death but has little understanding of its meaning. Comments, however, may sound plausible because the child's vocabulary exceeds his experiences. The finality of death is not yet understood. By five years of age, the child has the tendency to bring God within the scope of the everyday world. The age of six is described as the peak period of the child's interest in a creative power to which he or she can relate. The child thinks of God in terms of creation. Prayers are becoming important.[24]

Some children think of God as kind and loving, while others think of Him as stern, terrifying, and awe-inspiring. Jersild points out that a child's concept of God as father will be influenced by experience with one's own father or others in a paternal role. Concepts of sin and forgiveness will be influenced by the ways the child has been treated after misbehaving.[25]

Harms reported that, regardless of different backgrounds and experiences, children show a similar pattern of development in their religious concepts.[26] "The growth in understanding right and wrong is a slow process, dependent upon a growing ability to think, to reason, to make comparisons, to foresee consequences."[27] By the age of three, the child usually knows that some behavior is considered good and some bad by adults he or she knows. At five years the child is able to make some generalizations when the situations are similar. The child up to seven or eight years of age usually accepts, almost entirely, the values of his or her parents and family. Young children coming from different homes bring with them the values of their parents.

There are several approaches to the moral development of children. A discussion of each follows.

Cognitive-Developmental Approach. Both Piaget and Kohlberg are exponents of the cognitive-developmental approach to moral development. This approach involves analysis of the thought structures which underlie the moral concepts of persons at different age levels. Such analysis is used to de-

---

[23] A. Gesell and Frances Ilg, *Child Development, II* (New York: Harper & Row, 1949), p. 86.

[24] Ibid., I, p. 128.

[25] A. T. Jersild, *Child Psychology*, 6th ed. (Englewood Cliffs, N.J.: Prentice-Hall, 1968), p. 520.

[26] E. Harms, "The Development of Religious Experience in Children," *Am. J. Sociol., 50*:2 (1944), pp. 112–122.

[27] Jones, op. cit., p. 29.

fine a general development.[28] Piaget has evolved two broad stages of moral development which include the following:[29]

1. "Moral realism, morality of constraint or heteronomous morality." In this stage the child feels that he must comply with rules because they are "sacred and unalterable." Behaviors are viewed by the child as totally right or wrong and he thinks that others view them the same way. The rightness or wrongness of an act is judged on the basis of the consequence or punishment. For example, severe punishment may be interpreted to mean that the deed was very wrong. Violations of rules are followed by accidents or misfortunes.
2. "Autonomous morality, morality of cooperation or reciprocity." In this stage rules are not viewed as unchangeable but as established and maintained through mutual agreement and thus subject to modification in response to the situation. In determining right or wrong, one considers the role of "intention." "Did he mean to do it? or was it an accident?" Now the child is more likely to consider the welfare of others and considers punishment as related to a consequence of an act. For example, an act that causes much damage may deserve more punishment. In making the transition from one stage to the next, Piaget holds that both maturation and experience are involved.[30]

Kohlberg has developed levels of moral orientation and stages within each level.[31] The *Preconventional level* has two stages. People in the first stage are concerned with avoiding punishment or gaining rewards. They defer to authority figures. In the second stage there is concern for one's own needs and sometimes the needs of others.[32] The two other levels are The *Conventional level* and the *Principled level* (principled moral thought).

Generalizations that have grown out of Kohlberg's research include the following.[33]

1. People think about moral issues in six qualitatively different stages arranged in three levels of two stages each. . . .
2. A stage is an organized system of thought. . . .
3. These stages are natural steps in ethical development, not something artificial or invented. . . .
4. All people move through these stages in invariant sequence, although any individual may stop at a particular stage. . . .
5. Higher moral stages are better than lower ones.

There are those, however, who believe that Kohlberg's approach, that of moral reasoning, is not sufficient. The child's emotional development is also

[28] M. L. Hoffman, "Moral Development," in *Carmichael's Manual of Child Psychology*, 3rd ed., edited by P. H. Mussen (New York: John Wiley and Sons, 1970), p. 264.
[29] Ibid., pp. 256–266.
[30] Ibid., p. 266.
[31] Ibid., pp. 276–277.
[32] E. Fenton, "Moral Education: The Research Findings," *Social Education*, 40:4 (1976), p. 189.
[33] Ibid., pp. 189–193.

important. The cognitive and emotional development are interdependent. Beck suggests that an interactive approach that involves both intellectual and emotional development is needed.[34]

Clarifying Strategies. Raths identifies four basic approaches to the development of values current in schools today: the lecture method, use of peer group pressure, finding or setting examples for children to respect and emulate, and a reward and punishment rationale.[35] Raths contends that these methods are rather ineffective, "partially because they are based on the assumption that the knowledge of moral and ethical choices necessarily leads to ethical conduct."[36] Such an assumption, he holds, seems to have little basis in fact. Raths recommends the use of clarification procedures by which the teacher strives to (a) establish a climate of psychological safety, and (b) apply clarifying strategies.[37] In establishing a climate of psychological safety, the following procedures are suggested:

1. Express nonjudgmental attitudes. In order to provide an atmosphere in which children are free to express themselves without threat of disapproval or ridicule, teachers should refrain from using expressions such as "That's poor." "Can't you do better than that?" "That's good." Rather use comments such as "You've finished the picture." "You climbed on the jungle gym."
2. Manifest concerns. The teacher should be concerned with the ideas the child expresses. This may be done by listening to the child and remembering what was said. If the teacher shows no interest in listening, the child is not likely to be interested in sharing thoughts.
3. Provide opportunities for the sharing of ideas. Children need to be able to express their opinions, feelings, beliefs about moral issues significant to the young child. Such issues might include "taking care of our things" or "taking turns."

Two clarifying strategies, with examples pertinent to young children, follow:

1. Asking questions. The teacher may try to clarify the ideas or feelings expressed by the children by asking questions. For example: Leroy was feeding the rabbit. Douglas pushed him away and stuck the carrot into the hutch. Leroy yelled, "I hate you." "I hate the rabbit." "I hate nursery school." The teacher, using the clarifying strategy might say, "You don't like for Douglas to take the carrot away from you and feed the rabbit. Is that what you mean?" or "You don't like to come to nursery school. Is that what you mean?"

   The five-year-olds were planning a trip to the apple orchard. Sandra exclaims,

---

[34] J. R. Fraenkel, "The Kohlberg Bandwagon: Some Reservations," *Social Education, 40*:4 (1976), pp. 221–222.
[35] J. D. Raths, "A Strategy for Developing Values," *Educ. Leadership, 21*:8 (1964), pp. 509–514.
[36] Ibid., p. 511.
[37] Ibid., pp. 512–514.

"I have a good idea. We can get the school bus to take us." The teacher may say, "In what way is that a good idea?"

2. Acceptance without judgment. The purpose of an exchange of ideas between teacher and child is to clarify children's ideas. It is important that the teacher find a way to accept these ideas without communicating agreement or praise of them, except in cases where the health or safety of the group is involved. For example: Nancy, with her sandy hair cut very short, was gently stroking Mary's long dark hair. She said, "It's so soft. It's so long. I wish I had long hair like Mary's." The teacher might reply, "I can see how you would feel that way."

Instant changes and miracles are not likely, according to Raths. He says, "It may take a long sustained effort to help children develop serious purposes and aspirations through the clarifying process. For a free society, opportunities to clarify and to choose must be created again and again."[38]

Process Skills. Berman suggests that one way to develop values is to provide the time, setting, and encouragement for children to reflect upon life, its meaning and what the child can, wishes, or ought to do.[39] "Loving" has been identified as one of the process skills that should help the young child handle himself or herself and the world more effectively and to gain a better understanding of others.

If teachers want children to become loving individuals, opportunities must be provided for them to learn what it means to love and be loved. See p. 328 for suggested learning opportunities. Leiserson has developed suggestions for creating a loving environment for young children.[40] These suggestions may be familiar. They are used in this context, however, to indicate how the creating of a loving environment can be related to guiding the behavior of children, or teaching social studies, music, or any phase of the curriculum. Loving is a vital part of the curriculum. An adaptation of her suggestions follows:

In a loving environment the teacher:

1. Looks at each child as a unique person and gives the child opportunities to develop a positive self-concept. One may say, for example, "Erik's feeling very grown-up. His new shirt is size 5."[41]
2. Helps each child feel accepted and that he or she belongs to the group. One learns the children's names quickly, is courteous, and shows the children that she or he is happy to see them. For example, one may say, "I'm glad that you are feeling better. We missed you yesterday."[42]

---

[38] Raths, op. cit., p. 514.

[39] Berman, op. cit., p. 173.

[40] Marion L. Leiserson, *Creating a "Loving" Environment for Young Children* (College Park, Md.: University of Maryland, 1971), pp. 3–12.

[41] Ibid., p. 3.

[42] Ibid., p. 5.

3. Gives support and assurance to the child and lets him or her know the expectations in regard to the school environment. For example, one may say, "It isn't safe to climb on top of the brick wall. There's concrete below if you should fall."[43]

4. Lets children learn by experience, sometimes through mistakes and at other times through successes. The child may say, "My caterpillar crawled out because I did not have the top on the jar."[44]

5. Helps child understand that he or she creates his own emotional environment; helps him or her see the effect of actions on others. The teacher said, "She was knocked down when you bumped her. Is there something you could do to make her feel better?"[45]

6. Listens to children. What the child has to say is important and the comments indicate concepts that have been developed. After the child tore the paper cover of a book the teacher explained, "After the story you can help me mend the cover."

     Child: "What does *mend* mean?"

     Teacher: "It means to fix or repair it."

     Child: "Okay, but can I sit on your lap now and hear the story? Then I can be quiet."[46]

7. Helps the children to assume responsibilities. One may say, "Do you remember what our plants need to grow? Could you take care of them today?"[47]

8. Appears relaxed, pleasant, and in control of the classroom. Lets the children know that she is available if help is needed. The teacher might say, "Sometimes boots are tight. I'm here if you need help with them."[48]

SCHOOL PRACTICES

As one consciously works to build values, questions often arise regarding practices. Practices in public schools must be in accordance with the legal interpretation regarding religious instruction. If certain practices are contrary, they should be omitted. Some of these questions are identified and discussed here:

1. Shall we say "Grace" at mealtime if there are children of different faiths in the group?

     Grace at mealtime is one way of helping children develop a spirit of appreciation and thankfulness. If Grace is used, however, it is important that the teacher keep in mind the following:

     a. Grace, if it is to develop the value of appreciation, should be said happily

---

[43] Ibid.
[44] Ibid.
[45] Ibid., p. 8.
[46] Ibid., p. 9.
[47] Ibid., p. 10.
[48] Ibid., p. 11.

Figure 48
The teacher works to develop a willingness on the part of the boys to let others have a turn. She may need to give assurance when a child wants to ask for a turn.

and reverently. Take time for the children to be seated, relaxed, and ready. Avoid statements such as "Hurry and be quiet so we can say Grace and you can have your juice." Such comments emphasize not the purpose of the Grace, but characterize it as something "to get through with" in order to be able to eat.

b. If the Grace is to be said by all the children, select a form which is acceptable to all faiths. To thank God is usually acceptable to both Christian and Jewish parents. If there are children in the group who come from homes without affiliation, it may be well to use a statement such as, "We are thankful for our food," or "We are glad that we have food to eat."

c. Grace is only one way of expressing appreciation. There are many other opportunities throughout the day.

The children may learn a poem to use as a prayer, or sing a song that expresses thanks. On other days, each child may say "thank you," whispered quietly, or a child may volunteer to say Grace for the group, expressing thanks in one's own words.

2. Should a special time each day be set aside for a "devotional" or "worship" period?

Heinz has said that "Worship has a very special place in the kindergarten. . . . Worship can come from a fleeting moment of wonder, as when it was discovered that a moth had emerged from the cocoon."[49]

There are times, however, when a teacher makes definite plans for guiding children into worship. In making such plans, it is well to remember that worship cannot be forced. Music, pictures, stories, poetry, and Bible selections can be used as aids in creating an atmosphere and helping children worship. The suggestions made in regard to planning other group situations, and the selection of materials are appropriate here.

3. How may selections from the Bible be used with young children?

Much of the language in the Bible is difficult for the children to understand. In choosing selections from the Bible to be used with young children, Heinz formulated questions which may be of help to the teacher. Does the selection—

a. Help the child to grow in appreciation and understanding of God?
b. Add to a feeling of security and love, or does it promote fear?
c. Create a feeling of wonder and beauty for the child?[50]

Jones suggests the following verses from the Bible as appropriate for the young child:[51]

He has made everything beautiful in its time.
A child is known by his doings.
God is Love.
Love one another.

The way in which these verses are used is very important. They may be used many times, not for memorization, but as they relate to the experience which the children are having. A verse thus used can help a child express thoughts of God.

4. How can differences in the religious backgrounds of children be respected in celebrating religious holidays such as Christmas?

Celebration of religious holidays should be planned in such a way as to respect the worth and dignity of each child and not to threaten one's security or place in the group. If children have been helped to become aware of the differences among the children in the group and to know that they are all accepted, this awareness can be used as an approach to understanding different religious beliefs and the way in which people in other lands celebrate Christmas. If children from Christian and Jewish homes are in the group, both

---

[49] Mamie W. Heinz, *Growing and Learning in the Kindergarten* (Richmond, Va.: John Knox Press, 1959), p. 122.
[50] Ibid., p. 128.
[51] Jones, op. cit., p. 100.

may have an opprotunity to share their beliefs. A Jewish child and mother can tell the others about Hanukkah, while another child and mother may share a crêche and tell of the birth of Jesus. In both celebrations, gifts are given even though the origin of the gift giving is different. It is suggested that the interpretation of a religious belief be given by a person of that faith in order that the interpretation be accurate. In this way each child can accept his or her own religious beliefs and yet understand those of others, thus furthering intercultural understanding among young children.

Mary, relating her Christian activities, said, "I mailed Christmas cards to everybody in my kindergarten but three." The adult to whom she was talking asked, "Why didn't you mail cards to the three children?" Mary replied, "They are Jewish. They don't believe in Christmas as we do. They have Hanukkah. I didn't want to hurt their feelings."

A   B

Figure 49
Young children are able to set standards for themselves and work to achieve them. Jody has learned to tie his shoes. Mary has learned to wait for her turn.

If society is to survive, there must be values in which the majority of citizens believe. Kagan states "That too many Americans have lost the feeling that what they do has lasting importance at all has become the focus of attention of the honest critics of our day. . . . These critics plead for more "inner directed persons interested in the independent thinking a democracy requires."[52]

Values form the basis for this inner-direction by the individual. It is in the early years that the foundation for moral and spiritual values is laid. "So far as we can tell," say Sears, Maccoby, and Levin, "there is a learning of internal control that goes on mainly in the years before puberty, perhaps chiefly in the first six to ten years, determining the extent to which conscience will operate throughout the rest of life."[53]

According to Dewey: "A child's moral upbringing has an affect upon him which will remain largely untouched by anything that happens to him thereafter. If he has had a stable upbringing, whether on good principles or on bad ones, it will be extremely difficult for him to abandon those principles in later life—difficult but not impossible."[54]

Suggested Activities

1. Reread the description of the broad stages of moral development evolved by Piaget and Kohlberg pages 348–349. Visit a center for young children and describe situations in which a child's or children's behavior illustrate the first stage.
2. Arrange for a panel to discuss in class the role of the public school in developing values and moral conduct.
3. Visit a center for young children. Look for situations in which the teacher uses a clarifying strategy, as described by Raths, pp. 350–351, in developing values. Share your observations with the class.
4. Reread the section, "What Are Values?," pp. 338–339. Visit a children's center and describe situations which illustrate the characteristics of operational values with children. Share your observations with the class.
5. Conduct a class discussion on the topic, "Which Values to Teach Young Children."
6. Visit a kindergarten and note the ways in which the teacher seeks to develop "a climate of psychological safety."
7. Identify values that you have chosen, cherish, and affirm. What do you believe to be the source of these values?

[52] H. E. Kagan, "Teaching Values to Our Children," *Children and Youth in the 1960's* (Washington, D.C.: White House Conference on Children and Youth, Inc., 1960), p. 57.
[53] R. R. Sears, E. E. Maccoby, and H. Levin, *Patterns of Child Rearing* (Evanston, Ill.: Row Peterson, 1957), pp. 367–368.
[54] R. E. Dewey, F. W. Gramlich, and D. Loftsgordon, *Problems of Ethics* (New York: Macmillan Publishing Co., 1961), p. 480.

8. Visit a center for young children. Observe how the teacher tries to create a "loving" environment. How do her techniques compare with those on pp. 351–352?
9. Discussions about decisions to be made offer opportunities for children to talk about what they think is important. Observe such a situation. What did the children identify as being important?
10. Reread the statement of values common in our democracy, pp. 341–346. Select one of the values, such as, *Moral Responsibility*. Plan opportunities to help children grow in accepting moral responsibility.

Related Readings

Barcus, F. E., and Rachel Wolkin. *Children's Television: An Analysis of Programming and Advertising.* New York: Praeger Publishers, 1977.

Berkowitz, L. *The Development of Motives and Values in the Child.* New York: Basic Books, 1964.

Combs, A. W. (Chm.). "Convictions, Beliefs and Values," *Perceiving, Behaving, Becoming.* Washington, D.C.: ASCD, 1962, pp. 198–212.

Fenton, E., (Guest Ed.). "Cognitive-Developmental Approach to Moral Education," *Social Education 40*:4 (1976), entire issue.

Jacobs, L. B., Barbara Biber, and L. E. Raths. "Value-Outcomes of the Curious Mind: A Symposium," *Child. Educ., 51*:5 (1975), pp. 245–248.

Jarolimek, J. *Social Studies in Elementary Education,* 5th ed. New York: Macmillan Publishing Co., 1977, pp. 66–71.

Jersild, A. T. "Moral Development and Religion." in *Child Psychology,* 6th ed. Englewood Cliffs, N.J.: Prentice-Hall, 1968, pp. 506–524.

Jones, Jessie Orton. *Small Rain.* New York: Viking Press, 1943.

———. *This Is the Way.* New York: Viking Press, 1951.

Joyce, W. W. (ed.). "Moral Education in the Elementary School: A Neglected Responsibility?" *Social Education,* 39:1 (1975), pp. 23–39.

La Veck, G. D. *The Acquisition and Development of Values.* Bethesda, Md.: National Institute of Child Health and Child Development, 1968.

Leeper, R. R. (ed.). "Values: The Challenge, The Dilemma," *Curricular Concerns in a Revolutionary Era.* Washington, D.C.: ASCD, 1971, pp. 2–26.

Lerner, M. *Values in Education.* Bloomington, Ind.: Phi Delta Kappa Foundation, 1976.

Meyer, J. *Reflections on Values Education.* Waterloo, Ontario, Canada: Wilfrid Laurier University Press, 1976.

Metcalf, L. E. (ed.). *Values Education* (1971 Yearbook, NCSS) Washington, D.C.: NCSS, 1971.

"Moral Development," *Theory Into Practice XVI*:2 (1977), entire issue.

Osborn, D. K., and Janie D. Osborn. "Television Violence Revisited," *Child. Educ.,* 53:6 (1977), pp. 309–311.

Piaget, J. *The Moral Judgment of the Child.* New York: Free Press, 1965.

Religion and the Schools: From Prayer to Public Aid. Washington, D.C.: National School Public Relations, NEA, 1970.

Redbird-Selam, Helen Marie, and L. B. Selam. "Cultural Conflict in the Classroom," *Social Educ.*, 36:5 (1972), pp. 513–519.

Sayre, S. A., and P. Ankney. "Piaget, Justice and Behavior in the Classroom," *Child. Educ.*, 52:5 (1976), pp. 238–241.

Tanyzer, H., and Jean Karl (eds.). *Reading, Children's Books and Our Pluralistic Society*. Newark, Del.: International Reading Association, 1972.

chapter 16

Science

The young child and science seem to go together. The child is active, curious, and likes to manipulate and experiment with objects. Children ask many questions about how, why, where, and when. Children possess those characteristics that are important to the study of science.

Have you observed a young child watching intently as the squirrel nibbles the acorn held tightly in its paws, or as the jet streaks across the sky? Have you heard a young child ask, "Why does it rain? How does it work?" Have you listened as one mused, "Don't be afraid. I love you. Pretty little white chicken!" or perhaps chanted, "The sun is shining! The sun is shining! It is hot, hot, hot!" As young children watch, wonder, study, and question, they are

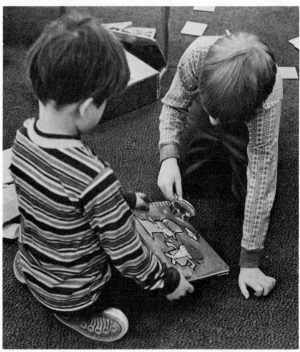

Figure 50
These boys participate in the processes of science. They are also developing skills of observation and description.

experiencing science as a part of everyday living. Such experiences can help children to gain an appreciation of the world around them; to keep alive the sense of wonder; to understand the orderliness of the universe; to develop a method of thinking and finding answers to questions.

In science education today the processes of learning are emphasized. The "process approach" offers opportunities for the child to participate in the processes of science as inquiry, as exploration, and as discovery, and to begin development of skills in observation, description, problem solving, classification, comparison, verifying, creating, hypothesizing, seeing relationships, logical reasoning, and inferring. Each child should progress, at his or her own rate, from concrete learnings (facts) through conceptual images (concepts) to more abstract generalizations. For example, a child experiences daily changes in the weather, in night and day, in plants and animals, and from such concrete facts develops a concept of change. This concept can serve as a basis for future understanding of the generalization that living things and the environment change all the time.[1,2]

[1] *A Guide: Early Childhood Education in Florida Schools*, Bull. 76 (Tallahassee: Florida State Department of Education, 1969), p. 24.
[2] Ruth L. Roche, *The Child and Science—Wondering, Exploring, Growing* (Washington, D.C.: ACEI, 1977), p. 2.

In teaching children who live in the inner city it is especially important that the science program be based on the child's environment. Skeel reminds the teacher that the environment of the inner city is not one of "butterflies and fishes." These may become a part of it but are not the most effective topics for beginning. Begin with questions important to the child, such as, "What happens to the garbage?" or "Why does it rain?" From these topics the child's environment may be extended in many of the ways discussed in this chapter.[3]

SOME GOALS IN TEACHING SCIENCE

Blough holds that the major objectives for teaching science are essentially the same at every level of learning. "They vary only to the degree that they are attainable at a given level."[4] The teacher needs to be aware of them even though she may make only a small step toward achieving them. She must understand the ultimate purpose if she is to make an effective beginning.

Four generally recognized goals are presented in the following outline, with suggestions for realizing them:[5]

1. To develop in children the ability to solve problems through the use of methods of science. To help children begin to become problem solvers and achieve these skills the teacher may do the following:
    a. Make as much use as possible of the natural curiosity of children and of their many questions.
    b. Help children say exactly what they want to find out. The statement of the questions or problems is important.
    c. Help children grow in suggesting ways to find out. Call these ways by names: looking, experimenting (or trying out), and listening.
    d. Keep trying things together. For example: "Remember what we did the other day to find out? Could we try it again?"
    e. Label these experiences *science*.
    f. Remember that the process of discovery is as important as what is discovered.
    g. Guide discovery by suggesting processes without telling the answer.
2. To develop in children an attitude—commonly called a scientific attitude. Elements of such an attitude are: Don't jump to conclusions, look at a matter from all sides, evaluate sources of information, be open-minded, don't be superstitious. To help the very young to take the beginning step in the direction of developing this attitude the teacher may use comments and questions such as the following:

[3] Dorothy J. Skeel, *Children of the Street, Teaching in the Inner-City* (Pacific Palisades, Calif.: Goodyear Publishing Co., 1971), pp. 71–72.
[4] G. O. Blough, "Content and Process in the Kindergarten," address to New England Kindergarten Conference, November 1966 (mimeogr.).
[5] Ibid.

    a. "Do you think that was a true story?"
    b. "Let's measure and find out."
    c. "Shall we try it *again* and see what happens?"
    d. "Let's *look at more* pictures and books."
    e. "Let's each take a turn at looking and see if we all see the same thing." (Observe carefully and often.)
    f. "How much does it weigh?"
    g. "What can we find out by looking?"
    h. "What can we do to be sure?"
    i. "Wonder who said that."
    j. "Let's see who wrote the book?"

3. To help children gain scientific knowledge and information. Subject matter can be overemphasized, but it can also be neglected. It should be selected from the environment of the children. Since process and content are so closely related, the following suggestions are similar to those for problem solving.
    a. Keep the learning of information at the children's level but *don't underestimate* children's abilities and interests.
    b. *Intend* to have children begin to learn some science ideas.
    c. Help children put ideas together. Recall related information and help children go as far as they can in seeing relationships.
    d. Keep a record of some of the things children have learned. They can't read it. They don't need to, but they can listen to it.

4. To develop in children an interest and appreciation in the science around them. To help in developing this interest and appreciation, suggestions for the teacher follow:
    a. Keep the interest children have, add to it, and broaden it.
    b. Try for satisfying experiences so that interest will grow.
    c. Urge children to show and discuss, to listen and to think, to manipulate, and to wonder.
    d. Present materials and problems that will open new interests children have not thought about.
    e. Remember you cannot help another person get interested in or have an appreciation for science unless you yourself are interested.

CHARACTERISTICS OF AN ADEQUATE SCIENCE PROGRAM

Evidences of science can be found in almost every center for young children. This does not mean, however, that one can find a well-balanced science program in all schools for young children. Science to many teachers has sometimes meant only a haphazard approach to nature study. This approach has been based on the incidental method and has utilized the casual consideration of some object: a leaf, a pet, or a rock brought into school by one of the children. This procedure is often justified because the child brings to school that which is of interest to him and the child's interests form a reliable basis for the science curriculum. The incidental interests of children can provide excellent teaching and learning opportunities. They should not be ignored.

Interests are important in program planning, but dependence on them for the total program often results in gaps in content. Some areas receive overemphasis while others are untouched. Furthermore, children's interests are limited by experience. Children may not bring a certain object to kindergarten or discuss a specific topic when they know nothing about it. They might, however, become very interested if they had the opportunity to become acquainted with the topic. A good science program includes incidental teaching and a flexible, general framework as well.[6]

How, then, can teachers utilize the incidents and yet provide a well-balanced science program that is flexible and adaptable to the needs and interests of children? It is important first to consider the requirements for an adequate science program for young children. These include:

1. *Planning which is both definite and flexible.* It is important that planning be both definite and flexible. This does not mean a detailed outline of specific learnings to be followed rigidly. Rather, there is a framework which is flexible enough for children and teachers to plan cooperatively for experiences that meet their particular needs. Such a framework often helps the teacher to utilize incidents more effectively because he or she sees in the situation possibilities for developing certain concepts. Without such planning many incidents may not be utilized or too many incidents of a similar nature may be emphasized; thereby the science program may tend to be limited in scope.

2. *Understandings from all major areas of science.* These understandings include all major areas of science, the earth and universe, living things and their activities, man and his environment, and matter and energy. Children are interested in all of these areas. Simple ideas which are introduced in a children's center lay a foundation for understanding more complex ones later as children grow through constantly enlarging experiences. At one time the belief that science for children should deal primarily with biological concepts was prevalent. Investigators have found that children are also interested in the physical sciences.[7] They have found, too, that young children are able to generalize to some extent. This skill does not appear suddenly but is one that develops steadily with maturation and experience.[8]

[6] G. O. Blough and J. Schwartz, *Elementary School Science and How to Teach It*, 5th ed. (New York: Holt, Rinehart and Winston, 1974, pp. 71–72.

[7] H. Mutsfeld, "Science Experiences Afford Opportunity for Experimentation," *Child. Educ.*, 29:2 (1952), p. 81.

[8] J. G. Navarra, *The Development of Scientific Concepts in a Young Child* (New York: Teachers College, 1955).

Some of the areas and some generalizations appropriate for young children are listed. Some suggested activities, through which the learnings may be achieved are also included. For each activity the teacher will develop goals, concepts, and vocabulary to be utilized for the children with whom she is working.

Area	Examples of Facts and Concepts To Be Learned	Some Activities and Learning Encounters That Can Contribute to Concept Development
Matter and Energy (Physics)	Air is around us. Air fills space. Wind moves many things. Heat changes some things. We breathe air. Fire needs air to burn. Air has water in it. Substances can change form (water is found in more than one form). Electricity makes light. A magnet will pull some things but will not pull other things. Sounds travel a long distance. Many things make sound. Machines do work for us. Some machines burn fuel; some use electricity; some are run by the wind. Water evaporates. Some objects float in water.	Blow up toy balloons. Observe things that are being moved by the wind. Visit Windmill. Churn milk. Make butter. Cook different foods and observe changes. Make ice cream. Observe ice or snow melt. Experiment with magnets. Visit a building under construction. Collect pictures of machines used to help man. Find simple machines at school. Use a pulley to lift a heavy object, such as a chair. Compare to lifting by hand. Make an inclined plane using a walking board. Experiment with musical instruments. Note differences in sounds. Listen and identify sounds. Do water painting. Observe what happens to picture. Collect pictures of how electricity is used at home. Discuss ways to conserve electricity.
Living Things and Their Activities (Biology)	Living things need air, water, warmth, and food. Animals eat different foods. Animals move about in different ways. Some plants grow on land; some plants grow in water. Some plants grow from seeds; some plants grow from bulbs. Some trees lose their leaves in winter; some do not.	Hatch chicken eggs. Visit a zoo and observe different animals. Plant a garden. Care for plants. Construct a bird feeder. Observe birds. Collect different seeds. Dramatize and compare ways in which various animals move.

Area	Examples of Fats and Concepts To Be Learned	Some Activities and Learning Encounters That Can Contribute to Concept Development
	Animals and plants make adaptations to changes in seasons. All animals have young animals. Some young animals need care; some do not. Some animals migrate in winter.	Collect examples of homes of various animals. Visit farm or zoo and see young animals. Care for pet at school. Keep aquarium in classroom.
Our Earth and the Universe (Astronomy)	The moon, sun, and other stars are in the sky. Man has put satellites in orbit around the earth. Man has traveled in rockets into outer space. Stars move in the sky. The sun gives light and heat. The earth is composed of water and soil. Air is around the earth. There are different kinds of soils.	Observe and measure shadows at different times of the day. Engage in shadow plays. Compare objects in sun and shade. Talk about how they feel.
Humans and Our Environment (Ecology)	Humans use plants and animals for food, clothing, and shelter. Animals help us work. We use animals for pleasure. We can travel in many ways. We use and control light. We use and control heat. Living things are dependent on one another. We can help keep the earth clean. Litter pollutes the environment.	Collect samples of different soils. Make a trip to the store. Note vegetables (plants) used for food. Note meats (animals) used for food. Pick up and put away toys on the playground. Clean up the classroom. Visit a farm. Observe and note foods grown. Talk about how to save energy. Collect pictures of where heat comes from. Place trash cans on the playground. Wage an anti-litter campaign. Collect pictures of ways water is used in the home; how homes are lighted and heated.

3. *Integration of science learnings with other experiences of the young child.* In studying "living things and their activities," the science learnings may be closely related to health and social studies. With the change in weather, living things make adaptations to the cold or heat. Children may discuss the relation of proper clothing to health status. The ways in which clothing

is secured relate to social learnings. Experiences are needed that help the child see how science is related to his own life; for example, electricity for light, cooking, cooling, and heating. The social implications of science in relation to community activities help children to understand why transportation is important and why the city provides water.

4. *Variety and balance in the activities in which children participate.* Field trips, experiments, instructional media, observations, learning centers, and resource people afford opportunities for a wide variety of science experiences. This does not mean that every science experience will include a field trip or an experiment. The teacher will choose carefully the activities most appropriate for developing the basic generalization under study.

HOW TO TEACH SCIENCE TO YOUNG CHILDREN

A variety of teaching strategies are described on pages 203–216. Refer to these in planning learning strategies for science. Examples of some of these strategies as applied to science follow.

1. Clarifying, explaining, reinforcing, and discussing comments made by children and sharing ideas and things brought to school by them are valuable techniques. Jane entered the kindergarten wearing a new red jacket. She greeted the teacher and said, "I wore my coat because it is cold. It is very cold—almost to freezing." The teacher said, "Yes, it is cold. How do you know it is freezing?"

   Jane: "The weatherman said so on TV."
   Teacher: "How does the weatherman know it is freezing?"
   Jane: "Because he is a weatherman."
   Teacher: "He reads the thermometer and finds out how cold it is. There is a thermometer in our room. Let's put it outside and see what happens." The teacher and Jane cross the room together.

2. The science center is a part of the room that reflects what children are doing in science. The pets or animals may be kept here. There may be an aquarium or a terrarium. Books with pictures that answer children's questions can be displayed. Materials for manipulation and experimentation are placed there. These may include magnets, dry cells, a magnifying glass, and a tuning fork.

3. The Learning Center. See pp. 209–211. Activities for a science learning center may include matching seeds, types of food, animals and their homes, mother animals and their babies.[9]

4. Caring for living things affords opportunities for children to broaden the

---

[9] Barbara Day, *Open Learning in Early Childhood* (New York: Macmillan Publishing Co., 1975), pp. 106–108.

experiential learnings they have developed regarding both plants and animals. Animals and plants can be compared, differences and likenesses noted. An awareness of the many kinds of plants and animals and an understanding of what is involved in the care of living things can be fostered through observing, using books, looking at pictures and discussing.

Caterpillars, guinea pigs, hamsters, birds, dogs, chickens, mice, fish, tadpoles, cats, and even goats have been cared for at school, either in the classroom or outside near the building. It is important that cages be kept clean and proper food and water be provided. Arrangements for care over the weekend should be made. Often arrangements can be made with parents for a child to take one of the pets home.

When using animals with young children the teacher may need to be responsible for their handling, encouraging but not forcing the children to observe and to "pet" them. A child, not knowing how to handle the pet, usually squeezes it, causing the animal to react by biting or scratching. Then the child may become frightened or hurt and as a result the desired learnings are not accomplished. Also, the animal may be injured.

5. Observations may be closely related to any of the activities for science experiences that have been described. Observations, however, may be planned as an activity for the nursery school or kindergarten room. Children will watch birds, fish, bees, ants, rabbits, turtles, or rats intently, sometimes talking to one another, but often looking and musing alone.

A   B

Figure 51
Caring for pets affords opportunities to broaden the experiential learnings. Questions may be used to sharpen or focus observation. How does the animal eat its food? Where does it sleep in the cage?

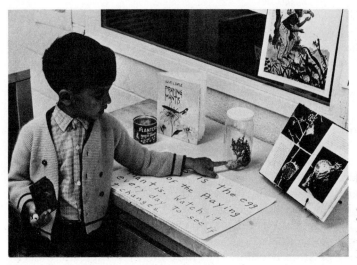

Figure 52
Science affords meaningful encounters with the environment. The praying mantis eats a grasshopper. "What did the grasshopper eat? How can you find out?"

Listen to three-year-old Ann as she watches the white rats:
"Long tails, long tails, long tails!"
Questions may be used to sharpen or focus the observation. For example: "How does the animal eat its food? How does it move? What does it eat? Where does it sleep in the cage?"

6. Resource persons who are invited to talk with the children about some aspect of science may be parents of a child in the group, another teacher, or some other person in the community. Before the visit be sure that the guest understands the questions raised by the children and the length of time to talk.

7. Experiments are planned to test, to try out ideas, and to help the child to come to accurate conclusions. They are not arranged to provide a display of magic and arouse fears and doubts in the child's mind. If there is a problem to be solved, children may be helped to use an experiment in finding the solution. The following steps may be used:

   a. State the problem of the experiment in order that children know what they are trying to find out.
   b. Decide on what is to be done to solve the problem or answer the question.
   c. Get the materials needed.
   d. Do the activities agreed upon.
   e. Observe carefully what happens.
   f. Answer the question.

   The following example is used to illustrate these steps. With young children, the problem of the experiment often grows out of their questions. Instead of answering the question with a pat "yes" or "no," the teacher sees in the question an opportunity for experimentation and problem solving. For example:

> Jim is showing Sam how his magnet will attract and pull nails to it. He comments, "My magnet will pull anything."
> Sam replies, "Oh no, it won't. I know."
> "Miss W., will this magnet pull anything?"
> Miss W. answers, "Let's see. Will a magnet pull iron nails?"
> "Yes," the boys reply.
> "Iron tacks?" "Yes."
> "A pencil?" Sam is not sure, though Jim is confident.
> Miss W. asks, "How can we find out if a magnet will pull a pencil?"
> "We can try it and see," said Sam.
> "Yes," said Miss W. "Are there other things you would like to try?"
> "Oh yes." Looking around the room the boys name blocks, iron screws, chalk, crayons, and scissors. "Let's see if the magnet pulls them."
> The boys take the magnet from one object to another and test the pull. Miss W. asked, "Did the magnet pull the blocks?" "No."
> "The iron screws?" "Yes." "Chalk?" "No." "Crayons?" "No." "Scissors?" "Yes."
> "Your magnet won't pull everything. It won't pull chalk, crayons, or blocks," concluded Sam.
> Jim looked down at the floor, crestfallen that his magnet had let him down. Miss W. said, "That's right, the magnet won't pull everything. But, Jim, your magnet will pull some things. What kind of things will it pull?"
> Jim's face brightened as he said, "My magnet won't pull everything, but it will pull some things. It will pull iron and steel things."

The teacher should encourage the child to tell what he finds out. She encourages him to speak in sentences and explain his findings clearly. For example, "Can you explain it better?" "Begin, 'I found out. . . .'"

8. The unit (A Plan for Developing Key Concepts), as a means of organizing materials, is discussed on pp. 325–333. The plan may also be used as a means of organizing science materials. As an example, a unit related to ecology is presented below. One value of the unit plan for organizing is that materials and activities are included to provide for a range in ability, maturity, and interests appropriate for a group of children, whether they be three, four, or five years of age, or whether they live in the city or the suburb.

A PLAN FOR DEVELOPING KEY CONCEPTS (UNIT)

Generalizations from the area, *Humans and Their Environment*, have been developed into the following plan (unit). One concept may be selected and developed in a learning activity or a series of encounters. Appropriate activities and materials may be selected and utilized.

ENCOUNTERS WITH THE ENVIRONMENT

1. *Purposes:* To help the children begin to:
   a. Develop an awareness of, and an appreciation for the environment as evidenced by statements such as:
      "See the tiny green leaves. Spring must be here."
      "This yard is a mess. There is paper all over it."
   b. Know that living things and the environment change all the time. Some changes are caused by nature, some by man. For example:
      "Look at the crack in the walk. It is getting bigger."
      "The rain washed the sand out of the box."
   c. Understand that living things depend upon one another and upon their environment. For example:
      "The plant grows toward the sun."
      "We picked oranges from the tree."
   d. Conserve resources in our environment. For example:
      "Turn off the faucet. The water is dripping."
      "You didn't eat all your apple. Don't throw it away."
2. *Initiating the plan:* Leads into *Encounters with the Environment* may come from:
   a. Incidents. For example, a child's comment. "There is so much junk here I can't work." The teacher may say, "you can't work at the table. Why?" During the conversation other children may be involved and questions raised. "Where do the books belong? Where are the puzzles kept? How can we have space to work and play?" Follow with discussion and planning. Another child may announce to the teacher, "My Daddy rides to work on the bus (car pool, train). Gas costs too much. Follow with discussion and planning.
   b. Teacher suggestion. Arrange for a walk. Questions may be raised: "What happened to the sand in the box? Why did the leaves fall from the tree? Why did the sidewalk crack? What changes have people made?" Follow with discussion and planning.
3. *Learning opportunities:* Take a walk or a field trip. On various trips ask children to observe: (1) evidences of change on the playground, (2) evidences of beauty in the environment, (3) things that make them feel happy, and (4) evidences that living things depend on one another and their environment.
   a. Develop meanings for such words as *environment, living things, waste, change, depend.*
   b. Rake leaves. Make a compost heap or observe what happens to leaves left in the gutter or a corner of the yard.
   c. Plant a garden. If possible, pick and cook vegetables.
   d. Visit an orchard. Pick apples. See how many ways the children can use the apples.
   e. Visit a farm. Pick vegetables. Gather eggs. Watch as cows are milked.
   f. Pull up a weed by the roots. Observe how it looks next day.

g. Ask children to identify natural things by touch: grass, water, leaf, peach, each other.
by smell: flower, grass, soil, leaf, apple.
by taste: apple, orange, banana.[10]

h. Record natural sounds such as a bird singing or fussing, wind blowing, cricket chirping, leaves rustling. Play recording. Listen carefully and identify sounds.[11]

i. Make gifts for parents using "recoverables from the recycling heap." Examples: Make paper weights. Children collect smooth, clean rocks and decorate with poster paint. Make wall plaques (piece of plywood and shellac) or a pencil holder (tin-can base). Children collect scraps of string, yarn, cord. Cover wood or can with glue. Pull, wind, twist pieces of string, and so forth into design.[12]

j. Make miniature trash receptacles. Decorate milk cartons, coffee cans, paper bags. Use at home, at school, or in the car. Involve parents.

k. Collect samples of soil from different places (around the building if possible). Compare as to color, moisture, temperature. "How do they feel? How are they different?" Spread out samples of soil on the paper. Pick out animals (earthworms, crickets) and put them in a jar. Ask questions such as, "How many different kinds of animals did you find? Were there the same number in each kind of soil?"[13]

l. Take a trip to the zoo. Focus on foods of animals. Find out the native foods of animals and the food given them in the zoo. Ask where the zoo foods come from. Ask children to name foods which they give their pets. Ask them to find out where the foods come from.[14]

m. If changes are taking place near the children's center (buildings being torn down, highways being built, construction) ask children to observe changes. Take photographs.[15] Ask questions such as, "Are there as many homes now?" Stores? Plants? Trees? Animals?" Observe how tools and power help men work.

n. Observe birds and try to find out what they are eating. "Are they eating seeds? Insects? Berries?"

o. Collect leaves that have been damaged by insects. "Why did the insect damage the leaf?"[16]

p. Dig up a plant from hard, dry soil. Plant it in loose, fertile soil and keep it watered. Observe what happens. Discuss reasons.[17]

q. Turn the hose on the playground on hard soil and again on soft, loose soil. Observe the running water and the materials it carries away. Discuss

---

[10] R. Caras, "Time to Join the World," *Early Years*, 2:9 (1972), p. 36.
[11] Ibid.
[12] Maija Kaljo, "Love, Nature and the Recycling Heap," *Early Years*, 2:9 (1972), pp. 38–39.
[13] Beth Schultz, "Your Town: A Biotic Community with People," *Environmental Education in the Elementary School* (Washington, D.C.: NSTA, 1972), p. 35.
[14] Ibid.
[15] Ibid., p. 34.
[16] Ibid., p. 35.
[17] Ibid., p. 36.

meaning of *erosion*. After a rain, collect muddy water from the street or yard. Observe sediment that settles to the bottom. "What is it? Where did it come from?"

r. Observe that the praying mantis eats a grasshopper. "What did the grasshopper eat? How can you find out?"[18]

s. Plant bean seeds. Expose some seedlings to more light than others. "What are the differences? Why?"

t. Discuss water conservation. Keep records of ways in which water was conserved.

4. *Evaluation:* Observe dramatic play. Note comments and conversations of children for awareness of interdependence, environment, change.

Observe children's behavior for evidences of assuming responsibility, caring for materials.

Observe children's art products.

5. *List of Materials:*

BOOKS

Alexander, Anne. *Noise in the Night.* Chicago: Rand McNally, 1966.

Atwood, Ann. *The Wild Young Desert.* New York: Scribners, 1970.

Borten, Helen. *Do You Hear What I Hear?* Eau Claire, Wisc.: E. M. Hale, 1966.

Busch, Phyllis S. *Puddles and Ponds: Living Things in Watery Places.* New York: World, 1969.

———. *At Home in Its Habitat: Animal Neighborhoods.* New York: World, 1970.

———. *Swamp Spring.* New York: Macmillan Publishing Co., 1969.

Darling, Lois, and Louis Darling. *Worms.* New York: William Morrow & Co., 1972.

Dayton, Mona. *Earth and Sky.* New York: Harper & Row, 1969.

Hawes, Judy. *What I Like About Toads.* New York: Thomas Y. Crowell Co., 1969.

Hazen, Barbara S. *Where Do Bears Sleep?* Reading, Mass.: Addison-Wesley, 1970.

Hurs, Edith Thacher. *Wilson's World.* New York: Harper & Row, 1971.

May, J. *Alligator Hole.* Chicago: Follett, 1969.

———. *Blue River.* New York: Holiday House, 1971.

Merz, R. *The Mockingbird Book.* New York: Harper & Row, 1962.

Miles, Miska. *Apricot ABC.* Boston: Little, Brown and Co., 1969.

Peet, B. *The Wump World.* Boston: Houghton Mifflin Co., 1970.

Pelgreen, J. *Backyard Safari.* New York: Doubleday & Co., 1971.

Podendorf, Illa. *Food Is for Eating.* Chicago: Children's Press, 1970.

———. *Every Day Is Earth Day.* Chicago: Children's Press, 1971.

Pringle, Laurence P. (ed.). *Discovering the Outdoors.* Garden City, N.Y.: The Natural History Press, 1969.

Pringle, Laurence P. *From Field to Forest: How Plants and Animals Change the Land.* New York: World, 1970.

Seuss, Dr. *The Lorax.* New York: Random House, 1971.

---

[18] Beth Schultz, "Ecology for the Child," *Environmental Education in the Elementary School* (Washington, D.C.: NSTA, 1972), p. 14.

Showers, Paul. *Listening Walk.* New York: Macmillan Publishing Co., 1961.

Shulevitz, Uri. *Rain Rain Rivers.* New York: Farrar, Straus & Giroux, 1969.

Simmons, Diane. *Gardening Is Easy When You Know How.* New York, Arco Publishing Co., 1974.

Tresslet, Alvin. *The Beaver Pond.* New York: Lothrop, 1970.

———. *It's Time Now!* New York: Lothrop, 1969.

Van Leeuwen, Jean. *One Day in Summer.* New York: Random House, 1969.

FILMSTRIPS

Plant and Animal Relationships: The Forest, The Pond, The Desert, The Swamp, The Seashore, The Grasslands. Encyclopedia Britannica Films, Inc., 1150 Wilmette Ave., Wilmette, Ill.

Discovering Life Around Us Series: A Visit to the: Seashore, Farm, Garden, Weeds, Pond. Encyclopedia Britannica Films, Inc. 1150 Wilmette Avenue, Wilmette, Ill.

POETRY

Association for Childhood Education International. *Sung Under the Silver Umbrella.* New York: Macmillan, Inc., 1952.

Arbuthnot, May Hill (ed.). *Time for Poetry.* Chicago: Scott, Foresman, 1961.

Behn, Harry, translated by. *Cricket Songs.* New York: Harcourt, Brace, Jovanovich, 1964.

Bramblett, Ella. *Sheets of Green.* New York: Thomas Y. Crowell, 1968.

Fischer, Aileen. *In the Middle of the Night.* New York: Thomas Y. Crowell, 1965.

———. *In the Woods, in the Meadow, in the Sky.* New York: Charles Scribners Sons, 1965.

Ferris, Helen (ed.). *Favorite Poems Old and New.* New York: Doubleday & Co., 1957.

Stevenson, R. L. *A Child's Garden of Verses.* New York: Watts, 1966.

SONGS

McCall, Adeline. *This Is Music.* Boston: Allyn and Bacon, 1966.

Nelson, Mary J., and Gladys Tipton. *Music for Early Childhood.* New York: Silver Burdett Co., 1952.

Pitts, Lilla Belle, et al. *The Kindergarten Book.* Boston; Ginn Co., 1949.

Winn, Marie (ed.). *Children's Songs.* New York: Simon & Schuster, 1966.

Zeitlin, Patty. *Castle in My City—Songs for Young Children.* San Carlos, Calif.: Golden Gate Junior Books, 1966.

Suggested Activities

1. Select one generalization to be developed with young children from the areas listed on pages 364–365. Develop a plan (unit) for teaching the key concepts related to this generalization, using the suggested outlines found on pp. 325–333 and 369–373.

2. Select a site which you think might possibly be appropriate for a field trip by a four-year-old group. Visit the site and evaluate it. Share your conclusions with the class. What possible learnings might children gain from this trip?
3. Visit a center. Observe and list evidences of science activities. Identify the areas, listed on pages 364–365, to which the activities contribute. Note the generalizations which are being developed. Share your findings with the class.
4. In your class conduct an experiment that you consider to be appropriate for young children, using the steps listed on p. 368.
5. Select an activity or learning encounter listed on pp. 364–365. Plan and develop it with young children. Evaluate.
6. Listen to and evaluate five recordings with science content for use with young children.
7. Visit a library or a center with a collection of children's books. Select and evaluate five books with science content for use with young children. Indicate the areas of science (pp. 364–365) in which the books may be used.
8. View and evaluate filmstrips for use with children. Describe how you might use the filmstrips.
9. Make a collection of flat pictures for use in science with the young child.
10. Visit a children's center and note ways in which a child or the group is encouraged to observe, classify, engage in problem solving, and to hypothesize.
11. View the film *Foundation of Sciences*. Campus Films, 20 East 46th St., New York, N.Y. 10017. Discuss.
12. View the film: *Water Play for Teaching Young Children*. Modern Talking Pictures, 2323 New Hyde Park Rd., New Hyde Part, N.Y. 11040.

Related Readings

ACEI. "The World's Bounty," *Child. Educ., 40*:8 (1964), entire issue.
———. "Outdoor Education," *Child. Educ., 44*:2 (1967), entire issue.
———. "The Living World," *Child. Educ., 47*:4 (1971), entire issue.
Althouse, Rosemary, and C. Main. "The Science Learning Center: Hub of Science Activities," *Child. Educ., 50*:4 (1974), pp. 222–226.
———. *Science Experiences for Young Children.* New York: Teachers College, 1975.
Bennett, L. M., and Gloria Bassett. "Games and Things for Preschool Science," *Science and Children,* 9:5 (1972), pp. 25–27.
Blough, Glenn, and Schwartz, Julius. *Elementary School Science and How to Teach It,* 5th ed. New York: Holt, Rinehart and Winston, 1974.
Day, Barbara. *Open Learning in Early Childhood.* New York: Macmillan Publishing Co., 1975, pp. 85–115.
Davis, A. R. "Science for Fives," *Child. Educ., 53*:4 (1977), pp. 206–207.
Durgin, H. J. "From Curiosity to Concepts: From Concepts to Curiosity-Science Experiences in the Preschool," *Young Children,* 30:4 (1975), pp. 249–256.
Gega, D. C. "Directions—Elementary School Science," *Teacher, 94*:3 (1976).
Good, R. G. *How Children Learn Science: Conceptual Development and Implications for Teaching.* New York: Macmillan Publishing Co., 1977.
Gratz, Pauline. "Maintaining a Supportive Physical Environment for Man," *Educ.*

Leadership, 27:2 (1969), pp. 173–175. Also in *Curricular Concerns in a Revolutionary Era.* Washington, D.C.: ASCD, 1971, pp. 261–263.

Harbech, Mary B. "Opinion: Is Science Basic? You Bet It Is," *Teacher,* 94:3 (1976), pp. 22–26; 30.

Holt, Bess-Gene. *Science With Young Children.* Washington, D.C.: NAEYC, 1977.

Keyes, Carol R. "A Science Open House Is Worth Copying," *Young Children, 31*:5 (1976), pp. 346–349.

Lindberg, Lucile, and Rita Swedlow. *Early Childhood Education.* Boston: Allyn and Bacon, 1976, pp. 218–239.

Moffitt, Mary W. "Children Learn About Science Through Block Building," in *The Block Book.* Washington, D.C.: NAEYC, 1974, pp. 25–32.

Riechard, D. E. "A Decade of Preschool Science: Promises, Problems, and Perspectives," *Science Education* 57:4 (1973), pp. 437–451.

Shephardson, R. D. "Simple Inquiry Games," *Science and Children, 15*:2 (1977), pp. 34–36.

Shymansky. "Mum's The Word—More About Science and Silence," *Science and Children, 14*:1 (1976), pp. 26–27.

Victor, Edward. *Science for the Elementary School,* 3rd ed. New York: Macmillan, Publishing Co., 1975.

Williams, D. L. "On Science for Young Children," *Science and Children, 13*:2 (1975), pp. 34–35.

chapter 17

Health and safety

Health is a state of physical, mental, and social well being and depends upon the interaction of these dimensions. Health is dynamic, in that it is ever changing.

Health is influenced by the interaction of many hereditary and environmental factors and conditions over which the individual may exercise varying amounts of control. Some aspects of everyone's health can be improved.[1]

The health of young children has been identified as an area of special concern in Project Head Start because, "a child who is in poor health will function at a

---

[1] Joint Committee on Health Problems in Education of the NEA and AMA, *Why Health Education* (Chicago: AMA, 1965), pp. 2–3.

level considerably lower than that of a well child."[2] The comprehensive goals of Project Head Start include finding and remedying any existing health defects; ensuring a child's future health by providing preventive services (such as immunization, health education); and improving the health of all members of the child's family and of the community.[3] Such goals, however, are appropriate not only for children in Head Start, but for all children. "Health" in any center for young children is most effective if it is incorporated into all the activities of the center. Health education cannot be limited to such activities as "daily inspections," "handwashing," "special demonstrations," and "play in the out-of-doors."

The definition includes these aspects, of course, but also emphasizes the importance of a healthful environment that offers opportunities to practice and acquire desirable information, habits, and attitudes and to participate in activities that contribute to healthful living. These are broad inclusive terms that must be analyzed and the implications for teachers of young children noted. Health and safety are considered together because of the interrelationships involved.

A HEALTHFUL ENVIRONMENT

The environment determines to a considerable extent the quality of healthful living possible in the situation. Too often emphasis has been placed upon the physical aspects of the environment, assuming that adequate space, toilet facilities, and appropriate equipment assured healthful living. There is increased recognition, however, that the best physical environment can be wasted unless the teacher is alert to its utilization and opportunities for learning. The sunshine may be glorious, but if the teacher plans no time in the out-of-doors the children cannot experience its values. Playground equipment that offers opportunities for exercise and muscular growth will be useless if the children are kept inside. Well-planned bathrooms with wash basins and toilets, exactly the right size, may not contribute to the development of desirable habits and attitudes if they are not kept clean and pleasant.

The recognition of each child and his or her parents as persons of worth, the provision for each child of an educational program appropriate to his or her developmental level, and the maintenance of a warm and accepting human environment all contribute to the positive mental health of each child. The total program of an adequate center for children can be considered as a mental health service and a significant part of a healthful environment.[4]

[2] Project Head Start, *Head Start, A Child Development Program* (Washington, D.C.: U.S. Government Printing Office, 1970), p. 2.
[3] Project Head Start, *Project Head Start, Health Services—A Guide for Project Directors and Health Personnel* (Washington, D.C.: U.S. Government Printing Office, 1969), p. 5.
[4] *Project Head Start, Health Services,* op. cit., p. 48.

(*Courtesy of Head Start.*)

Figure 53
The early school years are fraught with health and safety hazards. Thorough examinations are important in the early detection of illness and existing health defects.

Effective use of an adequate environment can benefit the young child greatly. It is essential that attention be given not alone to the adequacy of the environment but to the effective use of it in developing physical, mental, and social health. This concept of a healthful environment maintains that children will learn when they are involved in situations concerning health and safety and are then helped to practice consistently what they have learned. The effectiveness of this approach depends on such factors as the school personnel, the emotional tone of the situation, physical facilities, policies, and program.

PERSONNEL

According to Rasey, children learn from people and things and of the two, human beings appear to be more crucial. What a child considers important usually depends upon the values placed on the event by the people with whom one comes in contact. "Children see their world as through a glass, darkly or brightly, as their adults reflect or transmit it to them."[5]

All adults in the school situation are important to children. Personnel includes all persons who have any responsibility for any part of the program. Their responsibilities include maintaining and utilizing a healthful environment as well as good personal health.

The teacher or caregiver however, is the key person in the situation. It is

[5] Marie I. Rasey and J. W. Menge, *What We Learn from Children* (New York: Harper & Row, 1956), p. 39.

essential that he or she be in good physical health. Energy and vigor are pre-requisites for alert, active, yet intelligent, patient, and sympathetic guidance of children. Regular physical examinations, an adequate diet, sufficient rest, appropriate recreation, and comfortable clothing are as important for the adults as for the child. Yet these alone are not enough. Mental health is most important. Jersild points out that for a teacher to know those whom he teaches, he must know himself.[6]

Witherspoon has formulated the following questions that may be used by the teacher or other adults for self-examination:[7]

> Do I see children as they really are? Or, are my concepts clouded by my own experiences as a child?
> Can I show kindness and affection toward others? Or, do I feel that this is unnecessary?
> Do my actions and deeds reflect confidence and integrity? Or, are they merely an attempt to "save face" in order to protect me from myself?
> Recognizing that how I feel about my life and my environment is the only frame of reference that enables me to evaluate my actions, am I happy with my lot in life? Or, do I feel that this life has been unkind to me?
> Do I view myself as physically healthy, ambitious, and enthusiastic? Or, do I see myself as tired all the time even though I am healthy in the physical sense?
> Do I usually finish each day with a feeling of pride of accomplishment? Or, do I go home merely feeling that I have done my duty whether anything was accomplished or not?
> Is working with young children what I most like to do? Or, do I see teaching as a job?
> Am I sure that others think of me as their friend? Or, do I feel that I am not quite sure whether I have any friends at all?
> Do I face crises calmly and confidently so that I can face reality whatever it may be? Or, do serious "accidents" always happen to me?
> Do I recognize when I need help? Or, am I afraid of what others will think of me if I seek assistance?

If one can answer "yes" to the first part of these questions, children in the classroom have a person who can help them to become confident, alert, and imaginative. If one truthfully has to answer "yes" to some (or all) of the last parts of these questions, there is need for self evaluation and resolve to improve. The self-concept of the teacher or caregiver is as important as that of each child in the program.

The teacher's knowledge of the growth and development of children influences expectations of them. What the teacher expects has a great effect on the mental health of the child and the emotional tone of the classroom. Expressing undue concern when a three-year-old has an accident and wets his pants,

[6] A. T. Jersild, *When Teachers Face Themselves* (New York: Teachers College, 1955), p. 26.
[7] R. L. Witherspoon, "Teacher, Know Thyself," *Child. Educ.*, 35:2 (1958), p. 56.

insisting upon the use of "good adult manners" by the four-year-olds, or expecting each five-year-old to cut out an object evenly and smoothly along a line can result in anxieties and negative attitudes, neither of which are conducive to positive mental health. Adults who understand three's, four's and five's do not indulge them, but pace expectations and activities to their developmental level.

Alert supervision by the teacher is imperative in order to safeguard the health and safety of the children. This means careful observation of the child for signs of illness such as flushed face, paleness, listlessness, irritability, coughing, sneezing, running nose; adjusting wraps to changes of temperature or activity; closing or opening windows to prevent drafts or improve ventilation; raising or lowering shades for proper lighting; seeing that cups, spoons, and other eating utensils are not used in common; removing safety hazards; paying close attention to children who are climbing in high places or to children using such tools as hammers, saws, hoes, or shovels. As Read says, "the skillful teacher never relaxes her watchfulness."[8]

Attitudes can greatly facilitate or hinder the team approach to health. Such

[8] Katherine H. Read, *The Nursery School* (Philadelphia: W. B. Saunders, 1960), p. 88.

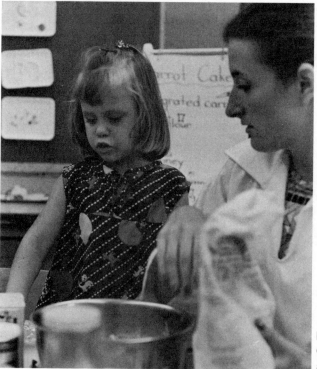

Figure 54
Children can be involved in planning and preparing foods.

an approach makes it possible to utilize the contributions of the parents, the physician, the nurse, and the psychologist, as well as the teacher and/or caregiver. No one person can do the job adequately alone. Persons working with young children need to know the resources available within the community and understand how they may be used for children. It is recognized that one cannot do everything alone and that it is a sign of strength, not weakness, to ask for help. Through this approach, common understandings regarding the goals of the health program and the role of each member of the team can be developed.

PHYSICAL FACILITIES

Physical facilities, equipment, and grounds are discussed on pp. 499–515. In this section the emphasis is placed on the the use of the facilities to promote health and safety.

Facilities for rest

All centers should make some provision for relaxation or rest periods. Facilities for resting in all-day schools include cots, sheets, blankets, and storage space. Spacing of the cots is important (approximately 3 ft apart) so that children will not lie with faces too close together. Shades should be drawn to facilitate rest. Quiet music is sometimes played during the rest period. The cots may range in size from 27 by 48 inches for four-year-olds, 27 by 52 inches for four- to five-year-olds, to 27 by 54 inches for children of five to seven years of age.

In schools not operating an all-day program, rugs and towels are often used for a midmorning rest. Such practice may be questioned on two important points:

1. If the floor is not warm and free from drafts, the rug or towel may not provide adequate protection for the child. Pads, from $\frac{1}{2}$ to 1 inch thick, are now being used in some schools. These are not as expensive as cots and yet provide more adequate protection from the cold floor. The pads may be made of foam rubber or cotton, with a washable cover. A plastic cover can be easily cleaned, whereas a cotton slip must be laundered frequently.

2. If rugs or towels are stacked together, the side of the rug next to the floor may be placed in contact with the "face" side of the next rug. This hazard can be minimized by having the floor side clearly marked, folded to the outside, and stored in each individual's locker. In order to prevent the "head part" from being folded to the "foot part," teach the child to first fold the rug lengthwise. If mats are used, the floor side should be marked also. Sheets can be used and

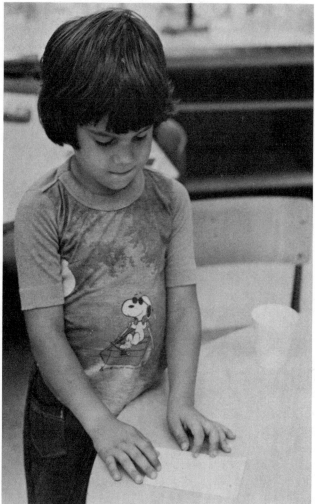

Figure 55
Theron is setting the table for snack time.

stored in each child's locker. Children should be involved in the process of getting out and storing cots or mats.

Drinking fountains

Drinking fountains, if used, should be low enough for the child to reach easily. It is important that the child be taught to drink so as not to put his or her mouth on the fountain. This is not easy for the child and supervision is necessary. For these reasons, individual paper cups are used in some schools.

Lockers

It is recommended that each child have a locker in which to keep clothing and supplies. Individual lockers are of value in helping the child establish proper habits of caring for clothing and supplies. Moreover, there is less danger of spreading contagious diseases when children's wraps are kept separate in individual lockers. It is often desirable to provide some lockers or storage cabinets on casters for use in partitioning off areas and for increased flexibility of activities in the room.

Furniture

Furniture should be of appropriate size for each child. This means that not all furniture within the classroom will be the same size. As children differ in height, so should the tables and chairs. It is important that tables and chairs be matched and that a high chair not be used at a low table. Help the child to decide whether or not he has the right chair by using such questions as:

1. Can your feet reach the floor?
2. Is there room for your knees under the table?
3. Are you comfortable?

Play equipment

Play equipment and toys that are sources of danger should be repaired or removed. Broken toys with sharp edges and protruding nails, unsteady ladders, splintery boards and blocks are examples. Loose gravel, sticks, or stones on the playground as well as roots, stumps, and holes can be safety hazards. Constant vigilance is essential.

Temperature, ventilation, and lighting

Temperature, ventilation, and lighting are important factors to consider in helping the child acquire desirable habits and attitudes. Although maintaining proper temperature, lighting, and ventilation is the responsibility of the teacher, it is important that opportunities for learning by the children be utilized. Comments and the activities which follow illustrate the teaching opportunities. For example, the comment, "John, I feel too warm—let's check the thermometer," helps John learn the following:

1. The thermometer is used to measure temperature.
2. The correct temperature for the room.

3. To become aware of feeling uncomfortable when one is too warm.
4. Some things to do when one is too warm.

In schools where the temperature is regulated by an engineer at a central control, the teacher assumes responsibility for reporting undesirable temperatures.

Another example involves Jane, who is looking at a book in the bright sunlight. The teacher may adjust the shade while the child is unaware of what she has done. Or the teacher may say, "Jane, your book is in the sunshine. The glare makes you squint your eyes. Let's fix the shade," or, "Move your chair over here, out of the sun." This situation can help Jane learn the following:

1. Looking at or reading books in direct sunlight is not a desirable health practice.
2. Why she squints and how the eyes feel in such a situation.
3. Some things to do to correct the situation.

POLICIES

Policies relating to health and safety should be formulated, made available to parents and all personnel involved, and consistently enforced. Policies are needed in the following areas:

Physical Examinations for Children, Teachers, Aides, and Other School Personnel. Such examinations should be made within one month prior to the date the child enters school or the adult begins work at the school. Forms for recording the results of the examination may be secured from the local health authority or developed by the school. Records should be filed so as to be easily accessible.

Immunizations. Those required should be specified by a health authority. Records of immunizations should be kept up to date.

Communicable Diseases. Policies should cover procedure when a child or adult has been exposed, the length of time a child should stay out of school when he has a communicable disease, and on what authority he is readmitted to school. Usually it is wise to follow the policies set by the local health authority.

Accidents and Sudden Illness at School. Such policies should include the procedure for contacting parents or a person designated by the parents (if they cannot be reached), and for contacting the child's physician, or providing the authority to use another physician if the child's cannot be reached. The extent of the school's liability and insurance coverage in such situations should be clearly defined and made known to the parents.

Health Information. Policies are needed regarding procedures for informing parents of defects observed by the teacher or the nurse, results of screening tests, information regarding height and weight, and of the incidence of a contagious disease in the group.

Morning Inspection. The routine for morning inspection needs to be understood by parents and children. Such a policy will probably state that the parent or adult bringing the child must wait until the child has been checked and admitted to the group. Inspection is usually done in such a way as not to embarrass the child. The adult may make a quick check while greeting the child.

Transportation. If transportation is provided, then a policy is needed as to the number of children transported in each car, the responsibility of the driver for the conduct of the children, the conduct expected of the children in the car, and the procedure for having a child delivered to someone or at someplace other than home. If parents and their cars are used for field trips, policies are needed to ascertain the amount of liability insurance the driver of the car should carry, number of children and adults per car, and the conduct expected of the children.

PLANNING FOR NUTRITION: LUNCHES AND SNACKS

Children's centers can offer many opportunities for developing habits of good nutrition. Some centers serve only a snack in the morning or afternoon. In addition to snacks, however, some all-day centers may serve breakfast as well as lunch, while others serve only lunch. Whatever food is served, whether a snack or a meal, the menus should be well planned and nutritionally balanced, the food tastefully and carefully prepared, and served attractively in comfortable, pleasant surroundings.

The schedule for snacks and meals depends on the child's home routine. The teacher or caregiver needs to talk with parents regarding such routines. Children who have had a good breakfast are usually ready for a light snack about ten o'clock in the morning. Children who have had no breakfast will need a heftier snack when they arrive at school.[9] A quiet activity before lunch helps the child get ready for the meal situations. (Suggestions for routines related to eating are included on pp. 104–105.) Suggestions for snack or mealtime include:

1. Adults should set good examples.
2. Maintain a relaxed, pleasant atmosphere.
3. Encourage child to try new foods—at least a bite.

[9] Margaret McWilliams, *Nutrition for the Growing Years,* 2nd ed. (New York: John Wiley and Sons, 1975), p. 236.

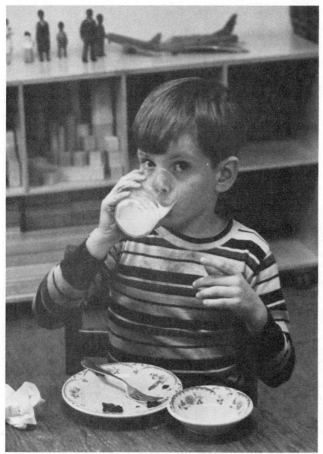

(Courtesy of Head Start.)

Figure 56
Encourage the child to try new foods.

4. Involve children in planning and preparing foods.
5. Encourage children, as they can, to assist in serving—for example, pouring milk or juice.
6. Use eating utensils appropriate to the size of children.

PRACTICES AND PROGRAM

Direct instruction in health is not usually undertaken with very young children. Rather, teaching is done in connection with the daily school activities and routines.

This does not mean that all teaching is incidental and that no planning is necessary. To illustrate how goals in health and safety can be identified and opportunities used to achieve these goals, instructional areas are suggested.[10]

For each of the areas there are listed concepts, beginning understandings, and learnings that it is hoped the child will achieve. Activities and learning encounters through which these may be realized are also listed. From these concepts and activities the teacher can select those that are appropriate for the group of children being taught. At regular intervals the teacher should review the activities in which the children have participated, note areas in which there has been little or no activity, evaluate progress toward goals, and plan for additional activities and learning encounters in needed areas.

Area	Examples of Concepts To Be Learned	Some Learning Activities That Can Contribute to Concept Development
The Body and Its Care	Children grow at different rates. The nose is an organ for breathing and smelling.	Weigh and measure children. Discuss sizes of children in group. Talk about different sizes in plants and animals. Identify some things by smell. Talk about keeping objects out of the nose.
Family Health and Living	Families are different in size, ages of the members, and in their customs. Families live in different kinds of homes. Growth and reproduction are common to all living things.	Talk about how birthdays and other holidays are celebrated in each child's family. Make family pictures. Invite family members to visit the school or center. Show pictures of mothers and babies. Show pictures of mother animals and their babies. Learn names for mother animals and their babies.
Food and Nutrition	Good foods help children grow. We eat food for growth, energy, and enjoyment. Foods come from plants and animals.	Plant a vegetable garden. Prepare, serve, and eat a variety of foods and beverages, such as fruit, fruit juices, and raw vegetables. Visit a farm, a dairy, a grocery store, or supermarket.

[10] *A Guide: Early Childhood Education in Florida Schools,* Bull. 76 (Tallahassee: Florida State Department of Education, 1969), pp. 37–38.

Area	Examples of Concepts To Be Learned	Some Learning Activities That Can Contribute to Concept Development
		Arrange snack trays according to colors. For "green" include green foods with a variety of flavors—green grapes, apples, peppers. For "yellow" include yellow apples, grapefruit, pineapple, and cheese.[11]
Environmental and Community Health	Children can help keep the community clean. There are doctors, nurses, and dentists who help us keep well. Hospitals are built to care for people who need special care.	Engage in cooperative planning by teacher and children for care of center, playground, and equipment. Engage in dramatic play. Arrange for a visit by a public health nurse. Visit the school clinic.
Safety	Getting in and out of a car safely helps to prevent accidents. One must not tease pets or play with strange animals.	Talk about safe ways to get in and out of cars. Dramatize getting in and out of cars safely. Demonstrate getting in and out of cars safely. Care for pets.
Mental Health and Human Relations	Each child is alike and different from all other children. Kindness, thoughtfulness, and courtesy help us live together happily. Young children, as well as adults, have responsibilities.	Talk about ways in which children are alike and different. Share toys and materials. Talk about treatment of classmates. Send letters, dictated to the teacher, of thanks and appreciation. List jobs to be done in relation to a certain activity. Choose jobs to do.

Areas of concern for the health and safety of young children in the various types of centers include the school environment, personnel, physical facilities, practices, and the program, all of which are interrelated. As children experience a healthful school environment, use desirable health and safety practices, and participate in a school program appropriate to their needs and maturity, they have opportunities to develop into individuals who experience physical, mental, and social well-being.

[11] McWilliams, op. cit., pp. 243–247.

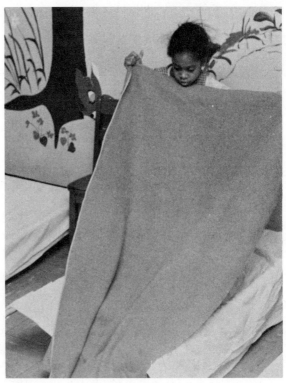

Figure 57

Shawne is spreading her blanket, getting ready for a nap. In this center there is a separate room for sleeping.

Suggested Activities

1. Visit the local health unit. Secure a copy of regulations and policies pertaining to communicable diseases. Discuss in class.
2. Identify agencies or organizations in the community that may serve as health resources; for example, the county or city health unit, the speech and hearing clinic, mental health clinic. For each one determine the services available, the cost, and referral procedures.
3. Visit a playground for young children. Identify any possible safety hazards. Note provisions made for children's safety.
4. Select one concept to be developed from the areas listed on pages 387–388. Plan a learning encounter appropriate for developing this concept and utilize your plan with a group of young children. Evaluate the activity.
5. Reread the material relating to policies. Visit a center for children and talk with the teacher regarding the center's policies on the topics listed on pp. 384–385.
6. Observe in a center for young children. Note provisions made for handwashing, toileting, developing a positive attitude toward health practices, snacks or lunch. What was the role of the teacher?
7. Observe the role of the teacher or aide in providing for the safety of the children.

8. View the following films:

Jenny Is A Good Thing. Modern Talking Pictures, 2323 New Hyde Park Rd., New Hyde Park, N.Y. 11040. Available in Spanish also.

Play in the Hospital. Campus Films, 20 East 46th St., New York, N.Y. 10017.

To Prepare a Child and *A Hospital Visit with Clipper.* Children's Hospital, Washington, D.C., National Medical Center.

Patterns for Health. Modern Talking Pictures, 1212 Avenue of the Americas, New York, N.Y. 10036.

Related Readings

Aaron, J. E., F. Bridges, and D. O. Ritzel. *First Aid and Emergency Care.* New York: Macmillan Publishing Co., 1972.

Althouse, Rosemary, and C. Main. "Foods," in *Science Experiences for Young Children.* New York: Teachers College Press, 1975.

Bell, J. E., and Elisabeth A. Bell, "Family Participation in Hospital Care for Children," *Children, 17*:4 (1970), pp. 154–157.

Bing, F. C. *Make Nutrition Fun* (k-3). Chicago: Nutrition Dynamics, Inc., 1974.

Brooks, Mary M. "Play for Hospitalized Children," *Young Children, 24*:4 (1969), pp. 219–224.

Calderone, M. S. "Sex Education and the Very Young Child," *PTA Magazine, 61*:2 (1966), pp. 16–18.

Chow, Marilyn. "Health Care: Its Symptoms," *Day Care and Early Education, 2*:5 (1975), pp. 3–7.

Cohen, M. D. (ed.). *Children and Drugs.* Washington, D.C.: ACEI, 1972.

Collins, Ruth H. "Planning for Fire Safety," *Young Children, 32*:5 (1977), pp. 28–32.

Dairy Council of California. *Little Ideas: An Early Childhood Nutrition Education Program.* Chicago: National Dairy Council, 1973.

Dayton, D. H. "Early Malnutrition and Human Development," *Children, 16*:6 (1969), pp. 210–217.

Foster, Florence P. "Nutrition and Educational Experience: Interrelated Variables in Children's Learning," *Young Children, 27*:5 (1972), pp. 284–287.

Highberger, Ruth, and Linda Carothers, "Modification of Eating Behavior in a Day Care Setting," *Home Economics Research Journal, 6*:1 (1977), pp. 48–52.

Hildebrand, Verna. *Guiding Young Children.* New York: Macmillan Publishing Co., 1975, pp. 149–167.

Johnson, Beverly H. "Before Hospitalization: A Preparation Program for the Child and His Family," *Children Today, 3*:6 (1974), pp. 18–21.

Larson, Lora Beth, and Donna M. Massoth. "A Nutrition Education Program for Texas Migrant Families," *Journal of Home Economics, 65*:8 (1973), pp. 36–40.

Lin-Fu, Jane S. "Childhood Lead Poisoning . . . An Eradicable Disease," *Children, 17*:1 (1970), pp. 3–9.

Lindberg, Lucile, and Rita Swedlow. *Early Childhood Education—A Guide for Observation and Participation.* Boston: Allyn and Bacon, pp. 111–119, 268–269.

Millar, T. P. "The Hospital and the Preschool Child," *Children, 17*:5 (1970), pp. 171–176.

Nutrition and Intellectual Growth in Children. Washington, D.C.: ACEI, 1968.

Schlick, Mary. "Kim, The Child Approved Nutrition Teacher," *Journal of Home Economics, 68*:3 (1976), pp. 21–23.

Scrimshaw, N. S., and J. E. Gordon (eds.). *Malnutrition, Learning, and Behavior.* Cambridge, Mass.: The MIT Press, 1968.

Todd, Virginia E., and Helen Heffernan. *The Years Before School: Guiding Preschool Children.* New York: Macmillan Publishing Co., 1977, pp. 203–247.

Waetjen, W. B., and R. R. Leeper (eds.). *Learning and Mental Health in the School.* Washington, D.C.: ASCD, 1966.

Wallace, Helen M. "Some Thoughts on Planning Health Care for Children and Youth," *Children, 18*:3 (1971), pp. 95–100.

West, Anne R. "Bringing the Hospital to Preschoolers: Teaching Young Children About Hospitals and Health Care," *Children Today,* 5:2 (1976), pp. 16–19.

chapter 18

Play activities

Play is the one activity that is included, almost without exception, in all early childhood programs. But, says Butler, "there are vast differences in what is meant by play and what is believed to be its relative value."[1]

There are teachers who feel that free play has little merit and should be replaced with educational play. In the direct-instruction type of program, play usually involves use of equipment to teach specific concepts and teacher-directed games to stimulate language and thought. Play is directed by the na-

[1] Annie L. Butler, *Current Research in Early Childhood Education: A Compilation and Analysis for Program Planners* (American Association of Elementary-Kindergarten-Nursery Educators, 1970), p. 13.

ture of the equipment. Spontaneous play is usually limited to short periods of outdoor activity, which are not considered to make any significant contribution to learning. In what are termed the *more open* centers, "self-initiated play is the major vehicle for learning."[2]

Almy says that psychoanalytic theory has long regarded spontaneous play as a reflection not only of the child's emotional needs but also of developing intellectual competence.[3] There are teachers, however, who are so preoccupied with the emotional aspects of play that they neglect its intellectual connotations. Utilizing the cognitive values of spontaneous play does not necessarily mean pushing or pressuring the child but rather nurturing basic abilities as they develop. The teacher needs to diagnose cognitive functioning as revealed in play. By observing and evaluating the child's curiosity and interest in investigation, problem solving, and mastery, the teacher can give guidance in play and in other curricular areas.

The several points of view regarding the value of play are related to differences in what is considered good education for the young—whether the emphasis should be on cognitive learning or on a more broadly based curriculum. Another cause of the confusion regarding the value of play, says Frank, "arises from the old distinction between work and play, with the feeling that, while work is good, play is somewhat questionable, if not bad or sinful."[4] Baker says that often play is considered as an alternative to work. But he reminds us that a four-year-old is working physically hard as he or she carries buckets of sand from one place to another in play. The leisure/labor, play/work dichotomy, according to Baker, must be prevented from rising too early in the child's life. This can be done, he suggests, by adults identifying with children in their play and treating them as adults and helpers and by avoiding giving the impression that play is "time out."[5]

PLAY OF THE YOUNG CHILD

Froebel, the father of the kindergarten, recognized the importance of play in learning. His ideas were of practical value. However, his conception of play did little to explain the nature of a child's play. In order to clarify the meaning of play, one should examine the research and theories regarding its nature and function. Some of the earlier theories may be helpful.

[2] Ibid., p. 14.
[3] Millie Almy, "Spontaneous Play: An Avenue for Intellectual Development," *Young Children*, 22:5 (1967), pp. 265–277.
[4] L. K. Frank, "Introduction," in Ruth E. Hartley and R. M. Goldenson, *The Complete Book of Children's Play* (New York: Thomas Y. Crowell, 1957), p. viii.
[5] D. Baker, "Worlds of Play," *Child. Educ.*, 53:5 (1977), pp. 247–248.

A   B   C

Figure 58

The outdoor environment offers many opportunities for physical activity. Outdoor play can help to lessen pressures on children. Physical activity and physical growth are major concerns in centers for children.

1. The *recapitulation* theory states that the individual in his or her play development passes through stages that are typical of those through which the race has passed. When applied on the playground, this theory resulted in somewhat arbitrary division of ages and the experiences appropriate for them. Investigations, however, have shown that children of a given age differ widely in the development of their play interests and that there is much overlapping between age groups. According to another theory, not all the energy produced by the child is needed for growth, and play is the result of an accumulation of *surplus energy.*
2. The *recreation* theory maintains that through play, tensions may be released and relaxed.
3. The *anticipatory* or *preparatory* theory "considers play as primarily a preparation for future life and work; in make-believe, children are practicing for future roles."[6]

---

[6] W. C. Olson, *Child Development*, 2nd ed. (Boston: D. C. Heath, 1959), p. 94. See also; Susanna Millar, *The Psychology of Play* (New York: Jason Aronson, 1974), pp. 13–22.

Each theory presents an aspect of the truth regarding play. Hurlock reported earlier experimental studies of children's play by Bott, Arlitt, Van Alstyne, Parten, and others.[7] A brief summary of the review follows.

> The child at three usually enjoys an activity as an end in itself, but by five shows interest in the end result. Imaginative play reaches its peak between five and eight years of age. The dramatic play of four-year-olds centers around living conditions, animals, and family relations.
>
> Play that involves skilled muscular movement is very popular during childhood. The young child likes to test the powers of muscular control by such activities as hopping on one foot or walking along the edge of a curb.
>
> An important element in children's play is construction and building. The young child begins to save and collect things.
>
> The average attention span for the eight most popular play materials was 7.0 minutes for two years, 8.9 for three, 12.3 for four, and 13.6 for five.
>
> No definite preference was shown for playmates of the same or the opposite sex. Apparent sex differences in play are due to training.
>
> Among three- and four-year-old children raw materials such as sand and blocks, were ranked as first choice. Dolls representing children were favored by the five-year-old children.

Frank expresses the point of view held today by many of those who work with young children: "Play is the way the child learns what none can teach him. It is the way he explores and orients himself to the actual world of space and time, of things, animals, structures and people. . . . Play is the child's work."[8] Play can be satisfying and pleasurable and these are good values for young children.

From his observation of children, Piaget states that games (synonymous with play) "reproduce what has struck the child or evoke what has pleased him or enabled him to be more fully part of his environment."[9] Piaget's theory of play is closely related to his theory of the growth of intelligence. Play begins in the sensorimotor period. Symbolic or make-believe play is characteristic of the age from two to seven years.[10]

Vygotsky points out that play is the leading source of development in the preschool years. At this age special needs and incentives arise, which are important to the child's whole development. Incentives and motives should not be disregarded. The child has a great number of tendencies and desires that cannot be realized immediately. When such tendencies appear in develop-

---

[7] Elizabeth B. Hurlock, "Experimental Investigations of Children's Play," in *Child's Play*, edited by R. E. Herron and B. Sutton-Smith (New York: John Wiley and Sons, 1971), pp. 51–70.

[8] Frank, op. cit., pp. vii, viii.

[9] J. Piaget, *Play, Dreams and Imitation in Childhood*, trans. Gattengo and Hodgson (New York: W. W. Norton, 1962), p. 155.

[10] Millar, op. cit., pp. 53–54.

ment, according to the viewpoint from the affective sphere, play is invented. If needs that cannot be realized immediately did not develop in the preschool years there would be no play.[11]

Play, says Vygotsky, is wish fulfillment—not as isolated wishes, but in terms of generalized effects. A child plays without realizing the motives of the play activity in which he or she is engaging. An imaginary situation is created by the child. Vygotsky holds that rules for play grow out of the imaginary situation. A child playing the role of Mother follows rules of maternal behavior.[12] Play, for the child, is purposeful activity.[13]

Jersild identifies characteristics and purposes of a child's play. Apart from being a self-chosen activity, any new play experience often involves an element of risk.[14] This is true when a child seeks to climb, build, ride a bicycle, use a hammer or saw, or even paint on an easel. One five-year-old expressed it this way: "I don't know how, but I guess I can try."

Repetition is also an important aspect of children's play. Through repetition the child can consolidate skills and, as he or she becomes more expert, can begin to experiment on his or her own. The child learns to ride a tricycle and is content to ride it up and down the sidewalk or porch, repeating the skill already learned. Soon, however, the child experiments as he or she backs up, turns around, rides fast and slow. In a short time the tricycle becomes a part of dramatic play. A traffic sign and a policeman are added.

Play may serve as a means of helping the child solve a problem. A child may select a toy that represents an object he or she fears or one toward which there is resentment. Play serves as a means of self-assertion through which a child can declare his or her needs. If the child wants affection he or she can be the "baby" in the dramatic play. In this role the child can receive attention and affection as he or she is fed, rocked, or put to bed.

Closely related to this is the role of play in self-revealment. Observing a child at play one may note the joys, fears, or hopes revealed. Although this is the basis for play therapy, even the teacher who is not a trained therapist can learn much from watching the child as she or he plays.

There appears to be a connection between play and creativity.[15] Others

---

[11] L. S. Vygotsky, "Play and Its Role in the Mental Development of the Child," in *Play—Its Role in Development and Evolution,* edited by J. S. Bruner, et al. (New York: Basic Books, 1976), pp. 537–538.

[12] Ibid., pp. 539–541.

[13] Ibid., p. 552.

[14] A. T. Jersild, *Child Psychology,* 5th ed. (Englewood Cliffs, N.J.: Prentice-Hall, 1960), pp. 424–425.

[15] J. L. Dansky and I. W. Silverman, "Effects of Play on Associative Fluency in Pre-School Children," in *Play—Its Role in Development and Evolution,* edited by J. S. Bruner, et al. (New York: Basic Books, Publishers, 1976), p. 650.

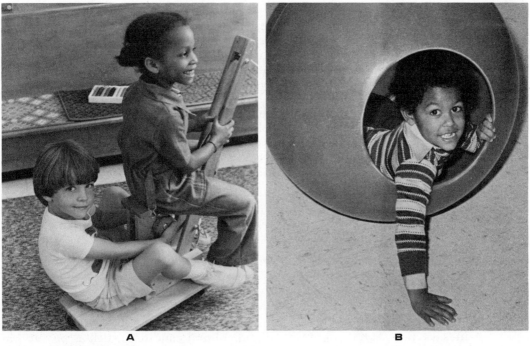

A   B

Figure 59

Adventure play involves overcoming obstacles, and gaining new skills through exercising and using the coordination that exists.

have found that creativity and inventiveness in the child's play are associated with later facility in divergent thinking.[16]

Through play children learn many things. They are helped to develop social relationships and skills. They learn to use play materials and equipment with others; to take turns; to lead and to follow; to ask for what they want or need; to understand the role of mother, baby, father, or the doctor. As children climb, walk, skip, and jump, they are exercising muscles and gaining in physical fitness. Contact with other children and the need to communicate with them help to stimulate language growth. The following incidents illustrate some of the values of play:

> Dan opened the door of the storage room and rolled the wagon in. Quickly he loaded it with blocks, just as many as he could pile on the wagon. As he pulled the wagon through the door, blocks fell in every direction. Without annoyance or concern he pushed the wagon in again and repeated the process. But this time,

[16] Corrine Hutt and Reena Bhavnani, "Predictions from Play," in *Play—Its Role in Development and Evolution*, edited by J. S. Bruner, et al. (New York: Basic Books, 1976), pp. 216–219.

with an empty wagon, he stopped and looked. He rolled the empty wagon in and out the door. No difficulty. Then he rolled the wagon back in again and loaded it carefully. Not one block extended beyond the edge of the wagon. He pulled the wagon safely out into the yard without losing a single block. Dan had encountered a problem and worked out a solution, all in play.

An elaborate train had been built from blocks and Jane, Pete, Joe, and Charles were ready to "play train." Roles were assigned and the conductor and passengers took their places. The engineer, however, went to the back of the train. As the teacher watched, the train was ready to pull out of the station. She said to Joe, "You are the engineer. What is your job?" Joe replied, "Oh, I'm just the engineer." Pete added, "He drives the train." Teacher, "If the engineer drives the train, where does he need to be?" The light dawned. Joe crawled onto the engine.

Observation of these children at play helped the teacher see that Joe and perhaps Jane and Charles did not know the role of the engineer. This evaluation of their knowledge of trains indicated to the teacher the need for pictures, stories, and perhaps a field trip in order to clarify their understanding. Interest and curiosity are aroused and questions raised which result in increased vocabulary and clarification of concepts. Play can serve as a means of helping the teacher to evaluate the learning, attitudes, and understandings of the child.

Bruner emphasizes the connection between play and human culture. Play, he says, reflects the culture or the subcultural condition, such as poverty, in which it takes place.[17]

Herron and Sutton-Smith report that children in Head Start Programs do not always evidence the same kind of capacity in make-believe as do some children in other middle class centers. Neither do they seem to show as much interest in make-believe stories or show the same capacity for thinking about things that are remote in time and place.[18] They raise the question as to whether the middle-class parent, by playing with the children, reading and talking to them, and providing play equipment, is actually encouraging the development of representative capacity and critical thinking.

Often inner city children have inadequate space or materials at home for physical movement and play activities. It is especially important that these children have opportunities for play.[19]

THE DEVELOPMENTAL SEQUENCES OF PLAY ACTIVITIES

Jersild says, "Generally speaking, the younger the child is, the more will the things he chooses to do give an indication of what he can do or can learn to

[17] J. S. Bruner, Alison Jolly, and Kathy Sylva, *Play—Its Role in Development and Evolution* (New York: Basic Books, 1976), p. 21.

like to do in the selection of equipment, materials, and supplies."[20] The teacher then needs to know the developmental sequences of play activities and how to use the information in the selection of activities and equipment. Strang says that "the play life of a child is an index of his social maturity and reveals his personality more clearly than any activity."[21] This is illustrated in the following incident:

> On a warm, sunny fall day, the four-year-olds were busy in the nursery school yard. Three had climbed up into the tree house. Others were at the jungle gym and the tire swing. Some were running around on the grass and some were building with blocks. A student observer remarked, "I'm going to teach four-year-olds." When asked the reason for her choice, she replied, "Oh, they are so easy to work with. Just look. Everybody is busy and happy." The instructor sitting beside her asked, "What do you think would happen if the teacher suddenly called the children together to play a game of baseball?" In amazement the student replied, "Why, she wouldn't do that!" "But if she did? Would they be playing as happily or contentedly?" For a moment she was puzzled, but then she smiled slowly as she asked the instructor, "Are you saying to me that the four-year-olds are playing this way because the teacher has structured the situation and planned it according to what the children can do?" The student answered her own question. "That's it," she said, "Fours aren't just naturally good. They are playing this way because of the way the teacher plans for and guides their play."

And so it is! The teacher needs to know the developmental sequence of play and to recognize the variations in maturity and interests that will be found among individual children.

Parten classified children's play behavior into six categories: unoccupied, solitary, onlooker, parallel, associative, and cooperative. The sequence includes ages three through five years.[22] Although ages are identified in relation to the developmental sequence of play, the teacher who understands children knows that each child progresses at his or her own rate. Some fives are not ready for cooperative play, while some fours cooperate easily and well.

More recently Millar has described a sequence in the development of social play. This classification begins with solitary activity and is followed in order by parallel, associative and finally by cooperative play.[23]

At first children usually play alone and engage in solitary play. As an "on-

[18] R. E. Herron and B. Sutton-Smith, *Child's Play* (New York: John Wiley and Sons, 1971), p. 2.
[19] Dorothy J. Skeel, *Children of the Street: Teaching in the Inner City* (Pacific Palisades, Calif.: Goodyear Publishing Co., 1971), pp. 80–81.
[20] Jersild, op. cit., p. 424.
[21] Ruth Strang, *An Introduction to Child Study* (New York: Macmillan Publishing Co., 1951), p. 495.
[22] Mildred Parten, "Social Participation Among Pre-School Children," *J. Abnorm. and Soc. Psychol.*, 27:3 (1932), pp. 243–269.
[23] Millar, op. cit., p. 178.

looker" the child watches as the others play. In parallel play the child plays alongside another child but is primarily interested in his or her own activity. Associative play is characterized by an increased interest in playing with other children. Two or three may play together in a group but both the group and activity change constantly. Dramatization and imagination are beginning to enter into play. The child is willing to wait a turn and, with supervision, will put toys away. The block play is concerned largely with manipulation, rather than building any one thing.

As children continue to grow and play they may choose a friend of the same sex for a specific play activity. A marked increase is noted in the constructive use of materials. The child uses blocks to build something. In the dramatization of play, one likes to dress up and finds props such as a cowboy hat, nurse's cap, or doctor's bag important. One may suggest turns but is often bossy in directing others. Such a child is not yet ready to make the social adjustment necessary for participation in group games.

The five-year-old usually can engage in cooperative play, the size of the group ranging from two to five children. Piaget believes that really cooperative play does not develop until after the age of seven or eight.[24] There is a definite interest in finishing an undertaking, even though it may need to be carried over from one day to the next. The request, "May I leave my block house and fort up? I haven't finished. Do I have to put the blocks away now?" is familiar to the kindergarten teacher. Dramatic play can be creative, both in actions and costumes which may be created from materials at hand. By this age there is usually fairly good control of body movement. The five-year-olds like climbing and other activities involving the large muscles. As a rule they are not ready for organized group games.

The first dramatic play of the young child usually centers around the situation most familiar and important to him or her, but the situation may vary according to the background of the child. For many children the situation will be the home. From this, the child branches out to individuals important to her or his immediate world—the doctor, the grocer, and the police officer. Other roles are added as experiences with books, stories, and television reveal cowboys, spaceships, boats, and airplanes. The characteristics of play that have been described can be used by the teacher as guides in the selection of equipment, materials, and activities. (See pp. 401–414.)

Hartley, Frank, and Goldenson report, from records of children three to five-and-a-half years old, eight functions that dramatic play serves in usual group situations of preschool centers. Through dramatic play the child has the opportunity[25]

---

[24] Ibid.

[25] Ruth Hartley, L. K. Frank, and R. M. Goldenson, *Understanding Children's Play,* (New York: Columbia University Press, 1952), pp. 27–28.

"(1) to imitate adults; (2) to play out real life roles in an intense way: (3) to reflect relationships and experiences; (4) to express passing needs; (5) to release unacceptable impulses; (6) to reverse roles usually taken; (7) to mirror growth; and (8) to work out problems and experiment with solutions."

Matterson describes three categories of children's play.[26] *Creative play* is encouraged by providing raw materials of all kinds such as sand, paint, and scraps. In *imaginative play* a child can create situations for himself or herself and work out reactions and solutions. Dress-up clothes encourage this type of play. *Adventure play* involves overcoming obstacles, gaining new skills through exercising and using the coordination that exists.

SELECTION OF PLAY EQUIPMENT AND MATERIALS

The goals of the program and the activities planned for the child indicate the basis for selecting equipment and materials for play. This selection should not be a haphazard process but one that is shared by all members of the staff and parents.

A variety of materials are provided. These are the media through which children develop physical strength and motor coordination, dramatic play, creative activities, and social skills. The variety is also necessary to meet the needs of children from different cultural and ethnic groups. Plans must be made for children with special needs, such as handicapping conditions.[27]

An ingenious teacher with imagination can improvise and collect materials that children greatly enjoy. Toys, especially wagons and tricycles in good repair and outgrown by older children, may be donated to the school. Parents handy with tools can contribute equipment. Before deciding to make, rather than buy equipment, the cost, durability, and safety should be considered. There are some intangible values, however, that may accrue from using homemade materials, and these should not be overlooked, for example, parent involvement and conservation.[28]

However, there are equipment and supplies that must be purchased. Other materials, such as art supplies, should be included in the yearly budget. Items to be bought as a part of a long-time purchasing plan include wheel toys, blocks, puzzles, equipment for dramatic play, musical instruments, and stationary outdoor equipment such as the jungle gym. The stationary equipment

---

[26] E. M. Matterson, *Play and Playthings for the Preschool Child* (Baltimore, Md.: Penguin Books, 1967), pp. 5–8.
[27] For help in this type of planning contact the Bureau of Education for Handicapped Children, Department of Health, Education and Welfare, Washington, D.C. 20202.
[28] Oralie McAfee, "To Make or Buy?" in *Selecting Educational Equipment and Materials for Home and School*, edited by M. Cohen (Washington, D.C.: ACEI, 1976), pp. 25–27.

is expensive and should be selected carefully in terms of the total amount of money available.

Criteria for selection and purchase are needed. Questions that may be asked in evaluating equipment and materials have been adapted from the ACEI criteria for selection.[29]

> For what age level is the item most suitable?
> Is the material of which it is made durable, resistant to effects of weather, easy to maintain, store?
> Is the size correct?
> Is the article strong enough?
> Are the edges rounded, not sharp? Are there protrudng parts? splinters? electrical and mechanical hazards?[30]
> Is the paint nonpoisonous?
> Is the article flame-resistant?
> Is it nonsexist?
> Is the item suitable to the child's culture and environment?
> Can the article be used for more than one purpose? By more than one child?
> Does the article stimulate in children curiosity, interest, manipulation, initiative, resourcefulness, problem-solving, imagination, creativity?
> Does it develop muscular coordination, freedom of movement, manual skills?
> Does it develop techniques in reading, writing, numbers?
> Does it promote growth toward independence, exploration, group activity, social relationships, international relationships?

OUTDOOR PLAY

Outdoor play can help lessen the pressures on children which often result from living under crowded conditions. "Healthy children," says Baker, "are likely to be those who spend a great deal of time outdoors where they can play actively and imaginatively.[31] "Baker continues,

> For a child, time spent watching clouds in the sky or the patterns of light and shadow through trees or discovering some of the many objects to be found outdoors are experiences of wonder. They feed the eager curiosity of childhood, which is the basis for learning.

Children need to play outdoors. The children who live in apartments or crowded housing units especially need to have opportunities for outdoor play;

---

[29] *Selecting Educational Equipment and Materials for Home and School* (Washington, D.C.: ACEI, 1976), p. 28.
[30] Contact the U.S. Consumer Product Safety Commission, Washington, D.C., for suggestions on safety in play and materials.
[31] Katherine Read Baker, "Extending the Indoors Outside," *Housing for Early Childhood Education* (Washington, D.C.: ACEI, 1968), p. 59.

they need to feel the wind on their faces or hair, to see blossoms floating by, to watch things grow, to feel the grass under their feet.

The outdoor environment offers many opportunities for physical activity, for exploring, discovering and learning. Outdoor play is not always vigorous. Provision should be made for outdoor play that involves musical instruments, easel painting, clay modeling, or even following a slow moving animal. Boxes and crates are simple outdoor equipment that provide a challenge and an opportunity for the young child to imagine, to recreate, and to enjoy the land of make believe.

Space

Outdoor space should be so arranged and equipped that it provides opportunities for enriching experiences rather than restricting activities. If the outdoor space is adjacent to indoor play space, much of the equipment can be used in either indoor or outdoor activities. A minimum of 75 to 100 square feet of play area per child should be provided for outdoor play. If several groups of children use the area and the space is limited, a schedule for using the yard should be provided so that all children are not outdoors at one time.[32] This space should be adjacent to the playroom and located on one side of the building so as to be easily supervised. The covering of outdoor space may vary and include both grass and paved surfaces. All play space should be durable and easily cleaned, be able to shed water and dry quickly, be free from safety or fire hazards, and be made of resilient surface so it will not injure a child if he or she falls on it. Shade is essential, and a balance between sun and shade should be established. Trees are valuable for shade, light, and sound control.

Bengtsson points out, however, the importance of the playground itself and suggests that consideration be given to the proportions of the area.[33] There may be need for some type of enclosing wall, screen, or shrubs to create some secluded areas and give a feeling of security and intimacy. A clear view for supervision is important, but at times children like to carry on play free from interruption. The smaller units within the area can provide shelter from the wind and the sun.

In hot, extremely cold, and rainy climates it is well to have a part of the space covered. Shelters from prevailing winds can be provided. A covered terrace or porch should be approached by a ramp (no steps) located near the playroom and entered through double doors off the playroom.

Landscaping is particularly important for the young child. Children need to

---

[32] *Plan of Action for Children 1953–55* (Washington, D.C.: ACEI, 1953).
[33] A. Bengtsson, *Environmental Planning for Children's Play* (New York: Praeger Publishers, 1970), 154.

have corners for play, secret places for being alone and for small group activities but not away from the watchful eyes of the teacher. Hardy plants that bloom at different seasons provide a pleasing effect but they should be placed so as not to interfere with the child's play. Adequate landscaping helps to provide for protection from the weather.

The surface of the outdoor play area is particularly important. Grass is the best possible surface and some grassy surface should be provided for all centers. A part of the area may be sloping, but all areas should be well drained. Surfaces for wheel toys, which are important to the child's development, need a hard base.

Outdoor space should be securely fenced with a nonsplintering material and kept in good repair. The construction should be such that it will have childproof exits. It needs to be sufficiently high and constructed so that it will not invite climbing. A gate that can be locked should be provided.

All play space should be free from rocks and glass. All sandboxes or places reserved for digging need to be protected from animals and covered when not in use. Concrete sandboxes which may be emptied and covered when not in use are cheaper if used over a long period of time. However, this type of sandbox should have adequate drainage before pouring. A digging area that is not part of the formal garden provides freedom for use and yet protects the child.

Features such as slopes and mounds or even an undulating asphalt surface provide variety and help make the area more interesting. For the safety of children a fence with adequate fastenings on the gate is essential.

Baker suggests that the area be located on the south side of the building where there will be sun and light throughout the day.[34] The play area should include:

1. a balance of space in the sun and shade.
2. a hard surface area where wheel toys can be used, balls bounced, and block structures built.
3. a balance of open and secluded areas.
4. a grassy plot for playing, running, and romping.
5. a spot for pets, gardens, and digging.
6. an area for sand play and manipulative activities.
7. a space for water play.

This outdoor space should be used as an integral part of the school.

Play equipment and materials

In selecting appropriate equipment and supplies the maturity level of the child furnishes one fundamental criterion. As children mature they may con-

[34] Baker, op. cit., p. 60.

tinue to use familiar materials, but in a different manner. In order, however, to challenge improved skills, new, fresh materials and more complex equipment are also needed. The many ways in which children actually use play equipment are sometimes quite different from what the designers had in mind.[35] The young child likes to work and rework materials. The observations seem to suggest that the provision of simple, manipulable, and imaginative materials is important.

Stationary equipment should be placed and installed around the outer edge of the yard so that supervision is easy and each separate piece is far enough apart to prevent accidents. The equipment must be carefully and safely installed and maintained in good repair. Sand, sawdust, or tanbark should be placed under all climbing and swinging apparatus in order to break falls.

Because of the expense and space involved, few play yards can include all items listed here or available on the market today. Those chosen should be carefully selected in terms of the criteria listed on page 402 and the total budget. Items that encourage large muscle development that are usually included on the play area are listed below:

1. The Jungle Gym. The jungle gym is an arrangement of strong metal pipes or wooden rungs. For outdoor use a metal gym is recommended; a wooden structure may be used indoors. The distance between rungs of the gym should be such that it can be managed by the children using the gym. Also useful are modifications of the gym—the climbing frame and a rope with knots tied about 18 in. apart suspended from a well-braced frame.
2. The Sand Area. The sandbox should be large enough for children to get into. A minimum of 50 to 60 square feet of space is desirable. A ledge or shelf around the edge helps to keep the sand contained and may be used as a seat or walking board. The sandbox must be covered when not in use in order to keep dirt, refuse, and animals out of the sand. In constructing a sandbox it is recommended that the floor be covered with brick or about 4 in. of gravel to facilitate drainage and then filled with from 18 to 24 in. of sand. The outdoor sandbox should be located so as to be in the sun for a part of the day. Utensils for sand play, such as shovels, pails, and small dishes are needed. Inspect these utensils frequently and discard broken or rusty toys.
3. Swings. Some teachers prefer not to include swings because of the safety hazards involved. As the younger child jumps from the swing, he or she may fall and be struck by the seat of the swing. Even a five-year-old is likely to forget and run in front of the swing. A safer type of swing for the younger child has a canvas strip for the seat. For the four- or five-year-old a swing may be made by attaching an old tire (with holes punched to prevent accumulation of water), to the end of a strong rope, suspended from well-braced frames. On the playground, swings should be placed so as not to be in line of traffic as the children run from one piece of equipment to another. It is important to arrange for a protective barrier to prevent a child from accidentally running in front of the

---

[35] Jeanette Galambos Stone, *Play and Playgrounds* (Washington, D.C.:NAEYC, 1970), pp. 15–63.

moving swings. A deep layer of soft sand under the swings is recommended.[36] The sand should extend well to the front and rear of the swings.

4. Slide. A standard slide that is metal and rust-proof with a safe climbing ladder is recommended. The height of the ladder and slide should be in relation to the age of the children. The slide should be placed so that it can be easily supervised, yet not in line of traffic to and from other equipment. A slide may be constructed as a part of a play platform.

   A slide of generous width does not require as much courage to climb and can be used in a variety of ways.[37] It is wise to arrange a slide so that a ladder is not needed, perhaps bedded in a natural slope of the ground.

5. Platforms. A play platform with a railing and fence around the top offers possibilities for dramatic play. Suggested measurements are: height, 5 to 7 ft.; platform, 4 by 6 ft. The steps may be from 20 to 36 in. wide, and the risers should be of appropriate height for the children using them—approximately 3 to 6 inches. Ladders are often used in place of steps.

6. Merry-Go-Round. Although this piece of equipment is popular with the children, it is one that requires very close and careful supervision to assure safety for those using it. The apparatus offers opportunity for pushing and running at the kindergarten level. Most younger children do not have the muscular control and coordination required.

7. Miscellaneous. For example, a large sewer pipe, set lengthwise and firmly in cement affords opportunities for climbing over and through it. A tree trunk can be used for the same purpose. Old tires may be used to make units to crawl and climb in, to roll, to lift, or to carry. Old equipment such as cars or boats, can stimulate eager minds and bodies.

Movable equipment for the playground includes the following:

1. Walking Boards. Cleats should be bolted to the bottom of the plank about 6 in. from the end to keep the plank from slipping when placed on boxes or sawhorses. It is suggested that planks be of varying lengths, ranging from 4 ft. to 6 ft. long, 1 in. thick, and from 8 in. to 10 in. wide. From 8 to 12 planks are needed for each group.

2. Sawhorses. A suggested size is from 1 ft. 6 in. to 3 ft. high and of varying widths, from 18 to 36 in. These may be used with ladders for climbing and with cleated boards for walking. From 4 to 6 sawhorses are recommended for each group.

3. Ladders. These may be metal, rope, or wood but should be light and sturdy enough to be moved or dragged around easily by children. Cleats or hooks should be attached to each end. Recommended sizes include 3-, 4-, or 5-ft. lengths by 14-in. width.

4. Balls. Lightweight balls in both medium and large sizes are recommended. Include rubber balls 8 to 24 in. in diameter. Beanbags may also be used for throwing and catching.

5. Jump Ropes. Include both long ones to be turned by an adult and short ones

[36] Bengtsson, op. cit., pp. 203–205.
[37] Ibid., p. 200.

for individual children. For younger children not able to jump the rope, lengths of rope of various sizes have many play uses.

6. Wheel Toys. The wagon and tricycle (12-in. and 16-in. ball-bearing wheels) and a wheel-barrow may be used both indoors and outdoors.

7. Tools for Gardening. Include items such as shovels, rakes, watering cans, trowels, and hoes. These items should be durable and child-size.

8. Miscellaneous. Such items include kegs, packing boxes, drag boxes, boats, car or jeep bodies, a large airplane or truck tire or tube. All such equipment should be safe for use—free of nails, splinters, glass, rough and broken edges, and rusted edges. Inspect often and discard equipment no longer safe for children to use. Adequate provision needs to be made for storage of out-door equipment when not in use. The storage area should be adjacent to the play area.

9. Building blocks and tools for woodworking may be used out-of-doors also. See pages 410 and 412 for recommendations.

10. A wading pool, hoses, a tube, and a table with metal or plastic pans provide opportunities for water play.

Games

Nursery school children are usually not ready for organized games and only very simple games are appropriate for the kindergarten. Games suggested for use in the kindergarten include those that require little group cooperation, have few rules or directions, and do not include the competitive element or refined coordinated movements not yet developed by the child. Choose games in which many children can participate at the same time rather than those in which most children are inactive while only a few are active. Tag, Loobey Loo, Here We Go Round the Mulberry Bush, and Musical Chairs are examples of games that involve all children and are loosely organized. Imitative games, such as Follow the Leader and Simon Says, are also appropriate.

As the teacher begins using games, the directions should be given one at a time, followed by the activity. For example, the first direction may be, "Take hands and make a circle." The teacher then moves among the group helping each child as needed. This is done before the next direction is given. In games which involve choices, some children may not be chosen. In order that all children may have a chance to play the game, ask those who have not had a turn to raise their hands. Ask the child who is making the choice to select a child whose hand is raised.

Activities

Water play is enjoyed by children in whatever form it may be available. Hartley, Frank, and Goldenson say that water play offers more varied experience and keener pleasure to the development of sensation and feeling than any other material except finger-paint.[38] Water play offers opportunities for flexibility, experimentation, and exploration. Materials such as a spray, small buckets and pans, a water hose, are inexpensive and contribute much to the activity.

Many indoor activities such as the following, can be moved outdoors or to an open porch or patio. Using books and telling stories are discussed on pages 270–280. A table with books may be set up in a quiet, shaded spot. Small rugs or mats may be used for the children to sit on during a group story period.

Imitative activities include the imitation of actions or movements of another child or person, an animal, or a machine. The child gives his or her interpretation of the way another person or thing moves or acts. The teacher may name the activity by saying, "Show me how you would fly if you were a bird," and the child creates his or her own response. The child, however, may imitate a person, animal, or thing and ask others to name or identify it.

Story plays usually involve a series of bodily movements based on a story or a plot[39] They are generally a sequence of events created by the teacher with the help of the children. All of the participants do all of the actions together as the story is told. Story plays are related to the experiences of the children, have a simple plot, and include activities that promote the use of large muscles. Story plays may be developed on topics such as playing on the beach or playing in the leaves.

Musical and rhythmical activities are presented on pages 448–459, art activities on pages 436–442, and dramatic play on pages 283–284. Suggestions made in those sections are applicable for the outdoor play area.

Picnics and snacks may be enjoyed on the playground also.

Supervision

Children should be supervised on the playground at all times. The teacher must be alert to the entire situation. Even when talking or occupied with one child the teacher does not turn her or his back on or forget the group. Remove objects that might cause a child to trip and fall. Definite limits relating to the use of apparatus must be set and consistently maintained. For example:

1. We run on the grass, not in front of the swings.
2. We need both our hands for climbing on the jungle gym. We leave blocks, boards, and dolls on the ground.
3. We slide down the slide. We climb up the ladder.

---

[38] Hartley, Frank, and Goldenson, op. cit., p. 185.
[39] Clarice D. Wills and Lucile Lindberg, *Kindergarten for Today's Children* (Chicago: Follett, 1967), pp. 243–245.

Evaluation

Questions that may be used in evaluating outdoor activities include the following:

1. Are the equipment and space adequate for the development of motor skills and muscular coordination?
2. Is the equipment placed so as to facilitate supervision and minimize the possibility of accidents?
3. Is there a variety of play equipment available—both stationary and movable? Is it varied in size and complexity to challenge children and lead to the development of new skills?
4. Does the teacher's supervision and guidance of the activities result in the continued physical, social, emotional, and intellectual growth of the child?

INDOOR PLAY

Adequate provision for indoor play requires consideration of such factors as the following:

Space

Indoor space required for good school living varies in each situation. For example, in warmer climates more time can be spent out-of-doors and it is possible to place all climbing apparatus outside and to use porches and patios. Less indoor space may be necessary. Arrangement of furniture and equipment also affects the space available. It is important, however, that the space be adequate to provide for a variety of equipment and activities and to enable children to move about freely without feeling cramped or crowded.

Acording to Jefferson, authorities differ as to recommendations for indoor floor space, "but the range from 35 to 60 square feet per child will provide a fair-sized room for a group of from 15 to 25 children."[40]

Equipment, supplies, and activities

Climbing Apparatus. In sections where weather conditions necessitate children remaining indoors for a considerable part of the time, indoor apparatus should be provided. Hardwood, movable apparatus, such as a jungle gym or slide, may be used. Walking boards can be used indoors as well.

[40] Ruth E. Jefferson, "Indoor Facilities," *Housing for Early Childhood Education* (Washington: ACEI, 1968), p. 41.

Blocks. Blocks are one of the basic play materials for young children. As children begin to use blocks, they are largely concerned with manipulating them —stacking, pushing, carrying, and lifting. After a time, this manipulation begins to be meaningful. A long row of blocks, carefully arranged on the floor, becomes a road; and a toy car, or even another block, is driven over the road. Gradually the child begins to plan structures and to test her or his own ideas. "Look, I'm going to build a tall bridge."

Play with blocks can provide opportunities for the following:

1. Physical release and the development of muscular coordination through lifting, carrying, and piling.
2. Emotional release through dramatic play. The child may express feelings of happiness, aggression, hostility, satisfaction of achievement, or fear.
3. Creative expression and the development of a sense of design and form.
4. Cognitive growth through the development of concepts and language opportunities.
5. Development of concepts of size, shape, and number values.
6. Development of readiness for reading through conversation, observation of size and shapes, and the need for additional information from books for his or her dramatic play.

In the guidance of block play, the teacher has an opportunity to observe what the child has absorbed of life going on around her or him as to ideas, information, relationships, and possible confusions. Rather than criticize or correct any errors, the teacher has the responsibility of creating a situation in which the child can learn and enrich his or her experiences. The child, however, does need to be held to the highest standards that he or she is able to attain. The teacher may use questions to help the child evaluate his or her structure. For example, "How do people get into your house?"

When clean-up time comes the presence and help of the teacher or another adult makes the task easier. For example, the adult may hand down the "high" blocks to the child and thus avoid a collapse of the block structure. Other children who have finished clean-up may help put the blocks away. Indoors, blocks should be stored on open shelves near the floor area where they are used. Provide ample floor space for block play. Traffic patterns need to be considered in selecting the space for block play, avoiding entrances to the classroom or the bath room.[41]

In selecting blocks, it is recommended that they be hollow and large enough to make structures that children can actually use. Suggested numbers and sizes recommended for a group of children, ages four to six years, include:

24 hollow blocks, $5\frac{1}{2}$ in. × 11 in. × 11 in., basic unit.
60 interlocking large floor blocks (to be added to original purchase).[42]

[41] Elisabeth S. Hirsch, "Block Building—Practical Considerations for the Classroom Teacher," in *The Block Book*, edited by Elisabeth S. Hirsch (Washington, D.C.: NAEYC, 1974), pp. 89–96.
[42] ACEI, *Selecting Educational Equipment and Materials*, op. cit., p. 62.

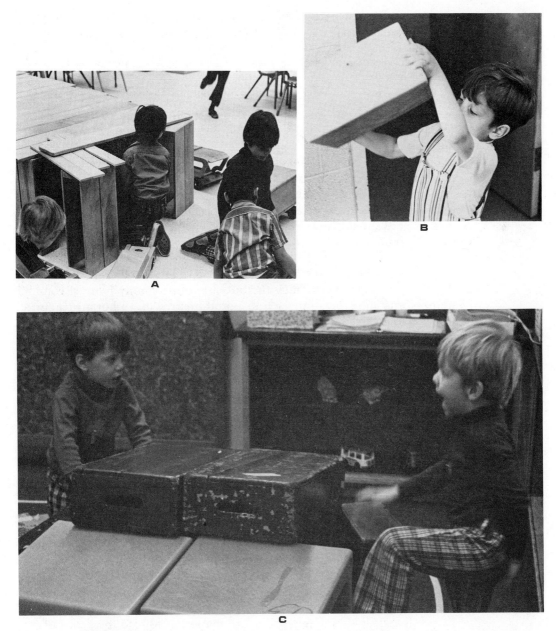

Figure 60
Blocks are one of the basic play materials for young children. A variety—hardwood, hollow, large interlocking, and unit floor blocks should be included in centers. In addition to providing for large muscle activity, blocks provide endless opportunities for the creation of shapes and forms.

350 unit floor blocks, assorted shapes and sizes.[43]
1 set building blocks, straight cuts, 500 or more, various sizes.
8 boards, 6 in. by 3 ft. long.
1 set of blocks which fasten together to make permanent structures large enough to accommodate children.
1 or 2 sets "stay-put" blocks fastening together with snaps, bolts, or pegs.

A waterproof finish will make the blocks suitable for outdoor use as well. Small trains, cars, farm animals, and people may be included in the block building area.

A good set of blocks represents a considerable financial investment but will last for many years. Cardboard blocks, which are much less expensive, are available and may be assembled for use. These are lighter in weight and do not provide the same experience in lifting as the heavier wooden blocks. There is one advantage, however; less noise is involved when they fall. A collection of wooden boxes can be assembled and used out-of-doors for building and construction.

Accessories for block building can contribute to the dramatic play in which the child may engage. These may include miniature family figures, community helpers, zoo and farm animals, transportation toys, and other unstructured materials such as spools, cans, baskets, boxes, or crates.[44]

Puzzles. The wooden jigsaw puzzle, framed or interlocked, is preferred. For the youngest nursery school child, the puzzle may consist of two or three pieces, such as of an animal, to be fitted into a frame. The number of pieces increases with age and the fours can handle from five to eight pieces in the frame. Framed puzzles are still preferred for the fives, but some children of this age can handle puzzles of the interlocking type.

A frame into which the puzzle can be slipped for storage is recommended. Put the same color on the backs of all pieces of one puzzle. This helps in identifying the parts of one puzzle and minimizes confusion when several children are using puzzles at the same table. Values of puzzles include opportunities for eye-hand coordination, use of small muscles, recognition of shape and color, and use of visual memory.

Equipment for Dramatic Play. The teacher's role in guiding dramatic play has been presented on pp. 283–284. At this point, the emphasis is placed on materials and equipment conducive to dramatic play. Among the most important materials are blocks, mentioned above. Equipment conducive to dramatic play is not listed. Rather, suggestions are made to indicate the types of materials that may be used creatively. Equipment related to family living and

[43] For suggestions regarding Unit Blocks, see. NAEYC, *The Block Book*, op. cit., pp. 105–108.
[44] *A Guide for Early Childhood Education in Florida Schools* (Bull. 76) (Tallahassee: Florida State Department of Education, 1969), pp. 61–62.

housekeeping usually includes dolls and accessories. The dolls should be unbreakable and washable, both boys and girls, and representative of different races and occupations.

Include authentic multicultural materials. Often these can be supplied by the child or parents. These materials can help the child from a different background.

Clothing for the dolls as well as a bed (large and sturdy), a bathinette, and a carriage are all appropriate. Clothes for dressing up (including hats, gloves, pocket books, ties, and gloves) help children to assume various roles.

Materials for housekeeping include a variety of furniture, the amount depending on the space available. Children often find uses for a table, chairs (including a rocker), dishes, a sink, a stove and cooking utensils, and a broom and other cleaning supplies. The toy telephone encourages conversation and language development.

Games and toys may be used separately or in relation to block play or other types of dramatic play. A cash register may be used at "the store." A set of family dolls and toy animals is frequently used. Accessories such as a firefighter's hat, a conductor's or a painter's cap, or an astronaut's helmet contribute to the play of children. Wooden animals, people, airplanes, trucks, trains, and boats can be stimulating too. Color cones, peg boards, dominoes (picture or large size with regular dots), pounding peg boards, picture lotto games, and wooden beads for stringing are only a few of the games and activities that can be provided.

The teacher's imagination and ingenuity offer many leads for creative materials. Although some equipment may be purchased, much can be improvised. Parent involvement can be especially helpful in this area.

Workbench and Tools. "Most children have a natural interest in working with wood and tools. It is one area of play content that most children do not have to be urged to try."[45] Early attempts at woodworking are largely manipulative. Have you observed a child drive one nail after another into a soft piece of wood or saw a board, just to be sawing? As in other activities, the manipulation begins to have meaning and the child realizes that the board she or he has sawed looks like a boat. Then the child usually begins to have ideas that she or he wants to test. The results may be crude and show little similarity to the finished product they represent, but the value of the activity does not lie in the finished product. Woodworking provides opportunities for eye-hand coordination; use of large muscles; emotional and physical release; social growth through sharing, taking turns, working together, caring for tools; and experimentation.

Suggestions for the use of tools include the following:

---

[45] Rowenna M. Shoemaker, *All in Play* (New York: Play Schools Association, 1958), p. 29.

1. Have an adult supervise the workbench at all times when it is in use by the children.
2. Arrange plenty of space for the child who is working.
3. Limit number of hammers and saws in use at one time.
4. Store tools in a safe place. A tool board (a peg board) may be mounted on the wall or on the inside of a door and serve as a convenient and safe way to care for tools. The shapes of tools may be outlined on the board in order to make storage easier. Hooks for tools should be strong.

In selecting tools for use by young children, it is important to remember that they should be of excellent quality. Questions that may be used as criteria for the selection of tools are listed below:[46]

1. Are the tools suitable for the age and interests of the child using them? Consider the child's stage of motor control and muscular strength. Do they serve the number of children involved?
2. Are the tools of good quality, adequate for long and hard use? Can they be resharpened, reconditioned, and broken parts replaced?
3. Will they build a child's respect for tools as a functional means to an end, stimulate interest, and encourage a wide variety of experiences?
4. Do they afford the means for developing in children appreciation for fine furniture and construction, in wood, in many forms?

Tools and supplies suggested for woodworking include the following:

Hammers (claw), 6 oz. to 10 oz. in weight for nursery school; 13 oz. to 16 oz. for kindergarten.
Saws (crosscut) 12 in. and 16 in.
Screwdrivers.
Clamps.
Workbench—the bench should be the correct height for the children. If a carpenter's workbench is not available, use sturdy wooden worktables or low broadtopped sawhorses with vises.
Pliers, screwdriver, ruler, yardstick.
Hand drill and bits.
Soft wood.
Dowel rods, different sizes.
Nails—large heads, assorted sizes.

Games. The comments and suggestions for outdoor games, p. 407, are also applicable for indoor use.

Cooking. See pp. 205–206.

---

[46] *Creating with Materials for Work and Play,* Leaflet 5 (Washington, D.C.: ACEI, 1957), p. 3.

Figure 61
Wheel toys afford children opportunities for the development of muscular coordination, manipulation, initiative, and even problem solving.

Evaluation

Questions that may be used in evaluating indoor play activities include the following:

1. Are materials and equipment conducive to dramatic play? Are they arranged in such a way as to be available to the children? Is there enough space for several groups or centers of interest to be active at the same time?

2. Is there time for individual and small group play, or is the time so tightly scheduled that there is little opportunity for participation in play activities?
3. Is there a variety of play equipment available—wheel toys, blocks, games, dolls, housekeeping equipment? Is it varied enough in complexity to challenge children and lead to new skills?
4. Does the teacher's guidance of the activities result in the continued physical, social, emotional, and intellectual growth of the child? For example, the children used blocks, barrels, and boxes in building a train. Are they encouraged to explore this interest in trains and gain more information? Are accessories added? Are pictures made available?
5. Are the experiences that children are having sufficiently rich and varied to provide a background for creative play? Are pictures and books available to help children recall and relive experiences?

The understanding of the importance of play in a child's life is closely related to the concern for the healthy development of all children. Play activities should be appropriate to the developmental level of the children in the group and a balanced program provided. Equipment should be carefully selected.

Although play is fun for the children, it is also work for them. They need resourceful, creative guidance, adequate space, materials, and equipment.

Suggested Activities

1. Discuss in class the values of play for young children. Observe young children at play and note the values that you think they may be gaining.
2. Visit a center for young children and observe the children at play. Note examples of basic intellectual skills being used, such as investigation, or classification. Share your findings with the class. Note factors in the situation that you think may influence the achievement of cognitive values of play. Describe the teacher's role.
3. Visit a program for young children. Observe and describe situations which are examples of parallel play and cooperative play.
4. Visit a local toy store. Select and evaluate five toys in terms of the criteria presented on pp. 401–402. Share your findings with the class.
5. Construct a game or piece of equipment that may be used in dramatic play of a young child.
6. Observe and describe examples of creative, imaginative, and adventure play as described by Matterson, p. 401.
7. Visit a playground for young children and do the following:
   a. Evaluate the play area in terms of comments on p. 404.
   b. Note any safety hazards.
   c. Describe any play materials or equipment that seems to be unusual or especially creative.
   d. Draw a diagram of the play area showing location of equipment. Comment.
8. Reread the opportunities for learning through block play, pp. 410–412. Observe

children involved in block play. Note shapes of blocks and accessories used. Note teacher's role. Describe and give examples of learning that the children seem to be achieving.
9. View the following films: *Blocks—A Medium for Perceptual Learnings.* Campus Films, 20 East 46th St., New York, N.Y. 10017. *Concept Development in Outdoor Play.* Campus Films, 2 Overhill Rd., Scarsdale, N.Y. 10583.

Related Readings

Almy, Millie. *Spontaneous Play—An Avenue of Intellectual Development.* New York: Bulletin of the Institute of Child Study, 28:2 (1966).

Andrews, Gladys (Fleming). "Movement—A Way of Learning," *Physical Education for Children's Healthful Living.* Washington, D.C.: ACEI, 1968, pp. 37–47.

Anker, Dorothy, Jackie Foster, Joan McLane, Joyce Sobel, and Bernice Weissbourd. "Teaching Children as They Play," *Young Children, 29*:4 (1974), pp. 203–213.

Baker, D. "Worlds of Play," *Child. Educ., 53*:5 (1977), pp. 245–249.

Caplan, F., and Theresa Caplan. *The Powers of Play.* Garden City, N.Y.: Anchor Press/Doubleday, 1973.

Cartwright, Sally. "Blocks and Learning," *Young Children, 29*:3 (1974), pp. 141–146.

Council for Exceptional Children. *Homemade Innovative Play Equipment* (Handicapped Children in Head Start Series). Reston, Va.: CEC, 1973.

Dennis, L. "Play in Dewey's Theory of Education," *Young Children, 25*:4 (1970), pp. 230–235.

Dimondstein, Geraldine. *Children Dance in the Classroom.* New York: Macmillan Publishing Co., 1972.

Ebbeck, F. N. "Learning from Play in Other Cultures," *Child. Educ., 48*:2 (1971), pp. 68–74.

Friedberg, M. P. *Playgrounds for City Children.* Washington, D.C.: ACEI, 1969.

Garvey, Catherine. *Play.* Cambridge, Mass.: Harvard University Press, 1977.

Hartley, Ruth E. "Play, The Essential Ingredient," *Child. Educ., 48*:2 (1971), pp. 80–84.

Hill, Dorothy M. *Mud, Sand, and Water.* Washington, D.C.: NAEYC, 1977.

Hirsch, Elisabeth S. (ed.). *The Block Book.* Washington, D.C.: NAEYC, 1974.

Hurlock, Elizabeth B. "Experimental Investigations of Childhood Play," *Mental Hygiene, 52*:3 (1968).

Jameson, K., and Pat Kidd. *Pre-School Play.* New York: Van Nostrand–Reinhold, 1974.

Kritchevsky, Sybil, Elizabeth Prescott, and Lee Walling. *Planning Environments for Young Children: Physical Space* 2nd ed. Washington, D.C.: NAEYC, 1977.

MacKinnon, D. W. "Parents and Teachers as Play Observers," *Child. Educ., 51*:3 (1975), pp. 139–141.

Markum, Patricia M. *Playscapes.* Washington, D.C.: ACEI, 1973.

Matterson, Elizabeth. *Games for the Very Young.* New York: Heritage Press, 1971.

"Research and Thought About Children's Play," in *Leisure Today,* a supplement of the *Journal of Health, Physical Education and Recreation, 43*:6 (1972), entire issue.

Rubin, K. H. "Play Behaviors of Young Children," *Young Children, 32*:6 (1977), pp. 16–24.

Stone, Jeannette G. *Play and Play Grounds*. Washington, D.C.: NAEYC, 1970.

Strom, R. D. "The Merits of Solitary Play," *Child. Educ.*, 52:3 (1976), pp. 149–152.

Sutton-Smith, B. "The Role of Play in Cognitive Development," in *The Young Child: Reviews of Research*, edited by W. W. Hartup and Nancy L. Smothergill. Washington, D.C.: NAEYC, 1967, pp. 96–108.

Tyler, Bonnie. "Play," in *Curriculum for the Preschool—Primary Child—A Review of the Research*, edited by Carol Seefeldt. Columbus, Ohio: Charles E. Merrill Publishing Co., 1976. pp. 225–246.

Winsor, Charlotte B. "Blocks as a Material for Learning Through Play," *The Block Book*. Washington, D.C.: NAEYC, 1974. pp. 1–8.

chapter 19

Creative expression: art, music, and movement

The young child, if encouraged to do so, approaches all experiences creatively. On a warm, spring day, brushes and pails of water were available in the yard for water painting. Sam painted the box industriously. Turning, he said, "I'm painting Mr. Nobody." As he moved his brush up and down in the air, he sang

```
          painting   ↓   no    ↓
    I'm         ↑       Mr.  ↑    body:
```

The teacher reinforced his rhythm by singing

```
          made   ↓   happy   ↓
    Sam      ↑      a    ↑    song.
```

Mike and Peter were talking about their birthdays coming up next week.

PETER: I'll be five years old.
MIKE: That's nothing. I'll be five years old too.
PETER: But I'm taller than you and I'm bigger too.
MIKE: I'm just as tall as you are. See.

The boys backed up against each other, each trying to prove his point. The teacher walked over and said, "Boys, if you want to know how tall you are, you can use the yardstick." She demonstrated its use and left Mike and Peter to figure out their problems—a creative experience in measurement.

Creativity is a complex process that usually involves a range of qualities including awareness, originality, fluency, flexibility, commitment, and complexity.[1] The creative product may be something tangible, such as a poem; or it may be intangible, such as a new way of attacking problems.[2]

Too often creativity is considered to be solely in the province of the fine arts. Recent findings in creativity, however, indicate that many aspects of the school program can be learned more effectively in creative ways.[3] Although creativity is discussed in connection with art and music, this is not intended to imply that the creative process is limited to these two areas of the curriculum. Creativity in the language arts are presented on pages 282–287. A look at creativity and the principles underlying its development indicates that whatever the curriculum area there is opportunity for creative teaching and learning.

FOSTERING CREATIVITY

According to Torrance:[4]

> From the best research evidence available and the observations of many investigators, creative imagination during early childhood seems to reach a peak between four- and four-and-a-half years, and is followed by a drop at about age five when the child enters school for the first time. This drop has generally been regarded as the inevitable phenomenon in nature. There are now indications, however, that this drop in five-year-olds is a man-made rather than a natural phenomenon.

It seems urgent, then, that school experiences and opportunities of young children be examined. What happens to discourage creativity?

[1] Louise M. Berman (ed.). *Toward New Programs for Young Children* (College Park: University of Maryland, 1970), pp. 45–52.
[2] Louis M. Berman, *New Priorities in the Curriculum* (Columbus, Ohio: Charles E. Merrill Publishing Co., 1968), pp. 139–140.
[3] E. P. Torrance, "Adventuring in Creativity," *Child. Educ.*, 40:2 (1963), p. 79.
[4] Ibid., p. 83.

A

B

Figure 62

In any group of children aged three to five years, all three stages of development in art are likely to be represented. One easel painting is largely the result of manipulating the brush and making strokes with little or no use of concepts or percepts. In the others, the child has painted forms with some relationship to reality and beginning concern for organization.

C

Obstacles to creative thinking

Hendrickson and Torrance have identified several cultural obstacles to creative thinking. These and some of the authors' examples follow:[5]

Peer Pressures for Conformity. Children exert a powerful influence on one another, even at an early age. This influence may affect choice of activity, clothing, or actions. One four-year-old wore cowboy boots to nursery school and soon "everybody" was wearing boots—even though they were hot and unsuitable for climbing and rhythmic activities. Parents reported pressure at home from their child to buy the boots and to wear them. Not until the teacher worked with the parents was it possible to relieve this pressure.

Pressures Against Questioning and Exploration. Even though the questioning stage is a phase of the young child's development, attempts are often made to squelch the asking of "What, why, and when." Rather, the emphasis is all too often on listening to and following directions. Have you heard an adult say, "Don't ask me why. Just do as I say"? Listening to and following directions are important skills but so is questioning. Instead of discouraging the child from asking questions, the teacher should help the child learn how to ask the right questions. Closely allied with this obstacle is the tendency to equate questioning with misbehavior. The child who asks the question is often considered impudent or impolite.

Emphasis on Sex-Role Differences. In our culture certain traits and activities have been associated with masculinity or femininity. Comments such as, "The girls may play in the doll house. The boys may use the blocks," or "Girls don't work with tools," tend to limit opportunities for exploration and discovery. Some children have sacrificed their creativity in order to maintain expected sex roles. While the situation is changing through the efforts of the women's liberation movement, teachers must be careful not to perpetuate the old stereotypes.

A Success-Oriented Culture That Makes Errors Fatal and Makes Children Afraid To Take a Chance on Trying a New Approach. One five-year-old had encountered this obstacle early. Each day he chose to play with blocks but consistently avoided the easel. After much encouragement to Joel to try the easel, the teacher said to him, "Today you are going to paint on the easel." In dismay Joel replied, "I can't. I don't know how. I might make a mistake." The teacher reassured him, "It's all right if you make a mistake. Go ahead and try."

[5] P. R. Hendrickson and E. P. Torrance, "Some Implications for Art Education from the Minnesota Studies of Creative Thinking," in *Creativity and Art Education* W. Lambert Brittain, ed. (Washington, D.C.: National Art Education Association, 1963), pp. 20–25.

With relief in his voice, Joel said, "Okay. I don't know how, but I guess I can learn." Joel had older brothers who adored him but who teased him when he made a mistake. Joel soon learned to avoid the teasing by doing the things he could do well and without a mistake. Pressures for conformity and adult standards may also cause children to be afraid to try.

Work-Play Dichotomy. In an austere, no-fun, all-business atmosphere, there is evidence that creative thinking abilities are usually least used. The philosophy of the old adage, "Work while you work and play while you play," seems to prevail still with many persons rather than a recognition that play can be the child's work.

How can the curriculum and methods be planned in order to overcome these obstacles?

Planning for creativity

The teacher is the first concern. To foster creativity in children, the teacher must be an adequate, fully functioning person. According to Combs, such persons have the following characteristics: "(a) a positive view of self, (b) identification with others, (c) openness to experience and acceptance, and (d) a rich and available perceptual field."[6] Acquiring these characteristics requires that "We all do more efficiently and effectively what some of us now do only sometimes and haphazardly."[7]

Carlson suggests that the teacher can develop inner resources through:[8]

1. Eliminating negative, hostile thoughts, fears, and feelings.
2. Building more positive satisfactions through undertaking new experiences.
3. Participating in original thinking processes.
4. Developing a more active *awareness* of environmental learning experiences.
5. Discovering new dimensions of learning.

Next, the methods of the teacher, the ways of working with children, and the program should be examined. Suggestions for change follow:[9]

1. Discard regimented routines, such as following directions for drawing, using patterns or models to be imitated, or ditto outlines.
2. Identify points in one's practice that are examples of stereotyped, habit-bound teaching performance. Project an alternative that is less rigid, more flexible.

[6] A. W. Combs, "A Perceptual View of the Adequate Personality," *Perceiving, Behaving, Becoming* (1962 Yearbook) (Washington, D.C.: ASCD, 1962), p. 51.
[7] Ibid., p. 62.
[8] Ruth K. Carlson, "Emergence of Creative Personality," *Child. Educ.*, 36:9 (1960), p. 404.
[9] E. P. Torrance, "Conditions for Creative Learning," *Child. Educ.*, 39:8 (1963), pp. 369–370; Laura Zirbes, "What Creative Teaching Means," *Child. Educ.*, 33:2 (1956), pp. 53–54; and Carlson, op. cit., p. 403.

3. Be attentive to the unusual questions children ask.
4. Respect the unusual ideas of children.
5. Show children that their ideas have value.
6. Give credit for self-initiated learning.
7. Provide chances for learning and discovery without threats of immediate evaluation.
8. Encourage aspects of behavior often attributed to the creative process. An adaptation from *Toward New Programs for Young Children* follows.[10]

   Awareness—of the five senses, detail, perceptions, alternatives. Suggestions follow.

   Provide a wide range of environmental stimuli such as trips, walks, and opportunities for touching, smelling, hearing, tasting, and seeing. Show a "surprise box" that contains an object. Ask questions such as "Can you tell what is in the box? How can you tell without looking?" Use questions about materials which children are using, such as, "How does it feel? How does it taste?" Sensitize child to feelings of others. Use comments such as "Mary fell down. How do you think she feels?"

   Originality—in manipulating constructive materials, in questioning and wondering, in using new and novel responses. Suggestions follow.

   Make a collage tray available. Include materials such as leather, styrofoam, feathers, fabrics, cotton, and wood scraps. The teacher may say, "The materials are for you to use. See what you can make."

   Fluency—in the production of ideas and possible solutions to a problem. Suggestions follow.

   Give the child a box of objects and say, "What can you do with these? Observe number of ideas and time required for expression. Encourage verbalization of problem for clarification. The teacher may say, "Tell me what the trouble is. Why do you think the bridge fell?"

   Flexibility—in using information in a variety of ways, developing and using a flexible schedule. Suggestions follow.

   Provide opportunities for the child to experiment with many types of materials to see how many ways he or she can use one material. Help the child expand verbally his or her experiences by comments such as "Why were you surprised?" "What else did it remind you of?"

   Involve child in planning a change of schedule.
9. Release the child's fears, hostilities, aggressions, and substitute a feeling of confidence, security, and satisfaction with his or her school activities.

The creative being does not emerge suddenly. The creative person develops gradually and grows by meeting problems and situations, recognizing them, and being able to solve or face them successfully. Experiences in art, music, movement, and other activities in children's centers can contribute to the development of a creative person.

---

[10] Berman, *Toward New Programs for Young Children*, op. cit., pp. 43–50.

ART ACTIVITIES

There are evidences of art activities, of clay, paints, and crayons in almost every child development center, nursery school, and kindergarten. In some situations one can see children working individually or in small groups, moving about freely, engaging in a variety of creative activities, such as painting, pasting and using scraps, cutting, tearing, or working with chalk. In other rooms, however, one can find all the children seated, quietly engaged in the same activity, coloring pictures, all very much alike. These two extremes indicate that even though there are art activities in almost every program, children are having quite different experiences and are acquiring quite different values and attitudes.

Art activities are considered an important part of any program for young children. Most children enjoy art activities, but there are also other reasons for including them.

Values of art activities

Art for young children is a means of self-expression. Art is used to express what they do, see, feel, think, and talk about. Art activities provide opportunities to explore and experiment, to express ideas and feelings about themselves and the world around them. They strengthen ability to imagine and to observe, and increase sensitiveness to self and to others. As the child works with materials he assumes responsibility for choosing and shaping them, uses judg-

A   B   C

Figure 63
Easel painting provides a means for the child to experiment, explore, develop eye–hand coordination, and to express feelings which the young may find difficult to put into words—each in a different way!

ment and control, and gains success experiences that aid in establishing a self-concept of worth as an individual.

Art experiences have therapeutic values. Through art materials the child can express feelings that are otherwise unacceptable and can learn to handle such feelings in an acceptable manner. Since the young child's speech is limited, strong feelings can often be expressed through art experiences which involve psychomotor activity. Materials such as clay for pounding, paper for tearing, and nails for hammering offer opportunities for handling negative feelings through positive action.

John, who pounds the clay with such vehemence, has learned that this is an acceptable way to work off the anger he feels toward the child who has the train he wanted to run. As he pounds and squeezes, he drains off his angry feelings to make them more manageable.

Helping a child to turn feelings into creative channels gives an outlet that can be used throughout life. To offer patterns or models could block this means of expression and prevent future growth; asking what has been drawn or telling how to do it might be just as detrimental. By leaving the child free to use materials in his own way, the teacher can sometimes gain insight into a child's private world by observing how such materials are used, the results obtained, and the feelings about the results.

Children grow socially through art experiences. As they participate in self-chosen activities, groups form easily from common interests. They learn to share materials, tools, and ideas, to make decisions, and to experience the give and take of group living. They learn to respect the rights, property, opinions, and feelings of others. As individuals interact with each other, group leadership qualities develop and children become aware of the importance of cooperation and self-control. These values are derived when children are free to choose materials and use them in their own way.

Intellectual growth takes place through art activities as the child invents new ways of using materials and refines methods previously used. As Jonathan, for example, becomes absorbed in work, he finds a need for more mature speech in order to talk about it, to explain, or to inquire. Concepts are developed as the child explores the properties of materials such as clay or paint, and learns such terms as *slick, pliable, soft,* and *hard.* The child can develop an art vocabulary, using words such as *artist, texture, color,* and *space.* The greater the variety of materials with which Daniel works, the greater his confidence in his ability to express himself. As he grows in ability to define problems and seek solutions, he grows in creative ability.

Opportunities for physical growth, exercise, eye–hand coordination, and motor coordination are also available. As children use fingers in painting or drawing with crayons and in manipulating clay, they are developing muscular control that will be used later in handwriting. Selecting shapes, choosing colors, and determining sizes offer opportunities for visual discrimination.

Environment for growth

The role of the teacher in art activities is to create an environment that fosters optimum growth, a setting that is challenging and stimulating, and that gives opportunities for the beginnings of aesthetic appreciation. Following are suggestions for the teacher in creating such an environment.

Individual Attention.   Children grow in depth and quality of ideas, in spontaneity and clarity of expression when they are accepted as individuals. The teacher helps each child to experience some success every day, to develop a healthy attitude toward mistakes, and gradually to assume responsibilities in the care of materials. The teacher guides, supports, and extends the child's thinking. The teacher must create a feeling of security that leaves the child free to think, imagine, select, and make decisions.

The teacher offers help when needed, raises questions to stimulate thought, and gives wholehearted approval of the child's honest attempts. Through wise guidance, the child is increasingly able to take part in planning activities and in assuming more and more responsibility for maintaining the orderliness and attractiveness of the room. This requires time and planning so that the child will know where materials are kept, can take these out as needed and can return them when finished. This also requires a teacher who is friendly, sincere, and understanding. Suggestions for becoming a more creative teacher are found on pp. 423–424.

Provision of Adequate Space, Time, and Materials.   Space is needed to enable children to move freely, to work alone or in small groups, at tables, easels, or on the floor, inside and out-of-doors; to permit children to obtain, arrange, and care for equipment and materials easily. The teacher must provide time for unhurried, satisfying explorations, time to make and carry out plans, time for each child to work at his or her own rate, and to clean up when he or she has finished. The teacher must also provide a variety of materials from which the child may choose. These materials are discussed on pp. 436–442.[11] The care and use of art supplies should be discussed with the children.

To meet the needs of all the children, the teacher makes allowance for their short attention span by offering them a choice of several activities. The teacher provides the class with large sheets of paper, large brushes (in a variety of sizes for five-year-olds),[12] chalk, and wax crayons, and generous amounts of clay and dough, scissors, and woodworking and scrap materials

---

[11] For a detailed list of suggested materials see *Selecting Educational Equipment and Materials for Home and School* (Washington, D.C.: ACEI, 1976), pp. 53, 62–64.

[12] Carol Seefeldt, *Curriculum for the Preschool-Primary Child: A Review of Research* (Columbus, Ohio: Charles E. Merrill Publishing Co. 1976), p. 190.

because of the limited eye–hand coordination and muscular development. Because taste and touch are so important to young children, the materials used are safe and washable. The teacher provides many opportunities for kinesthetic experiences with ample provision to indulge in tactile operations where the child uses hands for a tool. Because supervision is necessary the teacher offers one "messy" or new medium requiring close supervision along with several familiar media which the children can handle largely by themselves.

In making a selection of the types of materials for the day's use, the teacher may choose the scrap material and puzzles because they are familiar to the children and can be handled by them with few requests for help. The teacher can give time and attention to finger painting, which does require supervision. The introduction of a new material could have been handled in the same manner. The housekeeping center, blocks, and easel painting are available every day.

The children are permitted to move freely from one activity to the other, which encourages them to make choices and to assume the responsibility of finding something to do.

The art area should be accessible to water needed for mixing paint and cleaning up, should have adequate light, and should afford space away from the classroom traffic. Cleaning materials and space for drying paintings are also needed.[13]

Creative Expression. Children need rich experiences to stimulate creative expression. This should begin with their everyday living and their love of play. Through discussions of what they have seen or felt, or by talking with them about their play, the teacher can help them to vividly recall happenings they had only vaguely noticed before. (See pp. 423–424.) They should be encouraged to talk about themselves and their feelings toward others, and to dramatize these feelings. Through bodily action, children often are stimulated to express themselves in other media. By providing a variety of materials, the teacher enables them to select the media best suited to their individual need.

Planned trips are another means of stimulating creative expression. The teacher must not only plan these excursions, but later help the children to relive and recall them more fully through discussions and questions. The wise teacher does not necessarily expect to see these experiences depicted in the child's art. The child has been given ideas for creative thinking. Juliette must have freedom to choose what she wishes to express. As the children work following a trip, the teacher observes their behavior and seeks ways of helping them change habits and attitudes and to deepen their awareness of their en-

[13] *A Guide: Early Childhood Education in Florida Schools*, Bull. 76 (Tallahassee: Florida State Department of Education, 1969), p. 35.

vironment. The teacher can call attention to flowers, trees, birds, asking, "Are the two the same shape, color? Tell me how they are different." Children's creations indicate their frustrations and problems as well as their ideas of themselves and their surroundings.

Parental Attitudes Toward the Child's Creative Expression. The teacher must also act as interpreter of the child's work to parents. Often adults mistakenly stifle creative growth through imposing mature standards and ideas. The understanding teacher helps parents to appreciate the art qualities of children's drawings and to be familiar with the developmental stages the child goes through. In this way they may savor and enjoy each succeeding phase as well as provide a home atmosphere conducive to such wholesome growth.

The teacher can suggest suitable materials and ways of presenting them to the child at home. A suggestion that space be provided for the child to display artistic endeavors often opens new avenues of enjoyment for both parent and child. One parent of a nursery school child kept the paintings on the kitchen bulletin board where all might enjoy and discuss them.

Some inner city parents, as well as some in suburbia, show little, if any, appreciation of their children's art and often little, if any, space is made available for displaying what the child brings home. Consequently many children are not encouraged by the home and may become downhearted and disinterested. Display and appreciation of art products at school for such children become very important.

Parents should be encouraged to take children on trips around the neighborhood or community. These experiences will be reflected in the artwork.

As parents become involved in school activities, serving as aides or attending meetings at school, the teacher has the opportunity to show them their children's art. Appreciation of the child's work can be encouraged and an explanation given of how the child is expressing growth and ideas. In talking with parents, the teacher may suggest comments and questions that might be used with the child. The importance of conversation as a means of language development should be emphasized. A decorated folder may be given to the parent for keeping samples of the child's work.

The teacher should talk with parents about the use of coloring books. Parents sometimes need help in seeing the poor art qualities present in coloring books as well as the physical inability of the small child to stay within lines. They need to realize that patterns may rob the child of self-confidence and deaden imagination and spontaneity so important to all learning. Models made by teachers or other adults can sometimes rob the children of the opportunity for self-expression. Telling children how to paint can keep them from using their own ideas and initiative.

Comparing the artwork of one child with that of a sister or brother can make for negative feelings and attitudes.

Consideration of Developmental Level. The teacher should know the characteristic stages of growth in children's art and the developmental levels through which such growth evolves. (See pp. 431–432.) It is important that the teacher know and use the findings of research related to children and art. It has been found, for example, that middle-class children, when using finger paints, evidence more anxiety about getting dirty and staying dirty and show less interest in the products they produce while dirty than do lower-class children.[14] Such findings can give clues to the teacher for working more effectively and understandingly with children of differing home backgrounds.

There is a pattern of developmental levels through which a child's artistic expression evolves. These levels of maturation determine the selection of media, the size of paper and tools, and the kinds of experiences that will prove most effective for stimulating future growth.

[14] Thelma G. Alper, H. T. Blane, and Barbara K. Abrams, "Reaction of Middle and Lower Class Children to Fingerpaints as a Function of Class Differences in Child-Training Practices," *J. Abnorm. and Soc. Psychol.*, 51:3 (1955), pp. 439–448.

Figure 64
As Linda is manipulating the hammer and pounding nails she is gaining in eye–hand coordination, skill in using equipment and materials, and attaining feelings of success which contribute to a positive self-concept.

Lowenfeld identified these stages as scribbling, presymbolic, and symbolic. He emphasized that exceptions with regard to the period over which any stage is extended are quite frequent.[15]

The stages, as identified by Lowenfeld, are described here in order to picture the sequence of development. Although each child progresses through these stages, he or she does so at his or her own rate. In a group, ages three to five years, there are likely to be children in all three stages of development. Activities geared to only one of these would limit children who happen to be in other stages. The same child may not develop in all media at the same rate, owing to experience with and interest in the media. It is important for the teacher not only to understand the general stages of growth in art but also the development levels in each medium.

The scribbling stage begins when the child is first introduced to pencil, crayons, clay, or other media and usually extends to about the fourth year. The first efforts of the child are exploratory and largely muscular activity. Sarah is interested in the tool or material and what it can do. If using a crayon, she swings her arm and watches the resulting marks on the paper and soon becomes aware that she can control them by lifting the crayon up or repeatedly drawing lines consciously up and down and across the paper. Tasting is as important as feeling at this stage, so precautions must be taken to see that the materials are safe.

From uncontrolled muscular activity the child gradually develops the ability to make circular patterns. The development of motor control and muscular coordination is the major growth at this age level. To be able to hold a tool and make it go in the direction desired is a step in development. Until this level is reached, the child is not ready or able to perform other tasks requiring coordination such as eating and dressing. When the child begins to name scribbles or tell stories about them, he or she has taken still another step in development. The child is no longer thinking in terms of physical action but in terms of images and symbols. These symbols hold meaning for the child if not for the adult, so confidence and encouragement must be given. A simple "Tell me about your picture" gives the child a feeling of pride in the work and encourages him or her to imagine and to verbalize.

Between the ages of four and seven, a different mode of painting begins in which the child consciously creates forms. The child continuously tries out new concepts in an effort to establish his or her own individual pattern or symbol. This stage, known as the presymbolic, is characterized by his or her constantly changing symbols. This presymbolic stage begins as the child strives for a relationship with reality in drawings. A circle for a head with lines representing arms or legs gives a resemblance to a man. As Jerry becomes more aware of his relationship to the environment he feels a need to enrich

[15] V. Lowenfeld and W. L. Brittain, *Creative and Mental Growth*, 5th ed. (New York: Macmillan Publishing Co., 1970). pp. 64–97.

his new-found symbol and produces a large variety of symbols for the same object. This shows flexibility and ability to adjust. Because the child is most flexible at this time, it is important that the teacher stimulate and increase his or her awareness through individual experiences. When the child sees himself as part of the environment, he places everything on the base line.

McFee has identified three stages in the child's development in art. The first stage is largely manipulation with little or no use of concepts or percepts. McFee does not suggest ages for this stage because she holds that the time at which it begins or ends depends on the opportunities the children have. She quotes Dubin's study, which indicates that young children can change their level of graphic representation by being encouraged to conceptualize about what they are doing.[16]

McFee's second stage covers the time when the child symbolizes experiences. The third stage relates to realism, the time when the child is concerned with styles of design and organization.

McFee says that a teacher should consider the individual and environmental influences on the child, as well as physical and psychological growth.[17]

Providing opportunities in art

Authorities advocate the use of a creative approach as the most appropriate method for working with young children. The teacher who uses a creative approach encourages children to choose their art activity, the way in which they will express or do it, and the way in which they will organize ideas or materials. This does not mean that children proceed without guidance; it does mean that they will make decisions and choices.

There should be many art activity areas available to children each day. These should be changed frequently, taking into account the weather, season, curriculum, and the moods of the children and the teacher. Occasionally changing places where the child finds art activities may encourage new ideas and ways of doing things. However, some things remain in the same place— some things are left unchanged in order to help the child feel secure.[18]

There are times when it may seem wise for all the children to use the same topic, which may be selected by either the children or the teacher. This may sound rather formal; however, each child is free to choose how he or she will develop and organize the topic. As time for the Easter egg hunt approached, the children needed baskets for their eggs. They made their baskets, but what

[16] June King McFee, *Preparation for Art*, 2nd ed. (Belmont, Calif: Wadsworth, 1970), pp. 240–241.

[17] Ibid., p. 220.

[18] Clare Cherry, *Creative Art for the Developing Child* (Belmont, Calif.: Lear Siegler/Fearon, 1972), p. 3.

a variety of baskets! Some were very intricate, made by cutting and folding paper. Others were oatmeal boxes, gay with fingerpainting papers glued on. Other oatmeal boxes were painted with tempera paints. Berry baskets were painted and handles attached. Each child made a basket according to the level of his or her ability and perception. How did the teacher manage this with so many children and only one adult to help?

The teacher and the children talked about the many possibilities for making baskets. The materials were secured and arranged in areas around the room. One table had scissors, colored sheets of construction paper, rulers, and paste. On another table there were boxes, paint, heavy cord for handles, scissors, colored paper, finger paintings, magazine pictures, and paste. Berry baskets, paint, cord, and scissors were in another work area. The teacher also set up blocks, puzzles, and easels. These activities were familiar to the children and required a minimum amount of supervision.

Not every child could work on baskets at the same time, because space and teacher help were not sufficient for this. The teacher and children discussed the materials available and the children went to work in the area where the materials they needed were available. Some worked on baskets. As one child finished a basket another child took his or her place. A part of the group worked with blocks, puzzles, and at the easel. After experimenting, each child was free to move to another center if he or she wished. The teacher observed and was available as needed.

Contrast this situation with a directed lesson in which every child not only made a basket but made the same kind. The teacher gave directions, step by step. When each child finished the step, he or she had to wait until directions were given for the next step. Sue and Jim finished quickly and found it difficult to wait while the teacher helped Jerry. Jerry knew that "he was holding everybody up," and felt inept and embarrassed.

In both situations the children had experience in following directions and using art media. The creative situation, in addition, offered an opportunity for choices and decision-making, working at one's own pace, expressing one's own ideas, assuming responsibility, and building confidence in one's self.

There are those who reject the creative method for such reasons as these: "The child must learn to follow directions." "The child must learn to color within the lines." "With only one teacher it is impossible to let children do whatever they choose. One teacher can't supervise all of them." "Parents expect their child to make what the other children make." Such statements indicate a mistaken concept of the creative approach as being one of "confused pandemonium."

Two mothers were observing in a kindergarten as the children were preparing for the work period, or as some call it, "the art activity period." The teacher and children talked together about activities available for the day. The teacher turned to John and asked, "What do you plan to do?" To another child

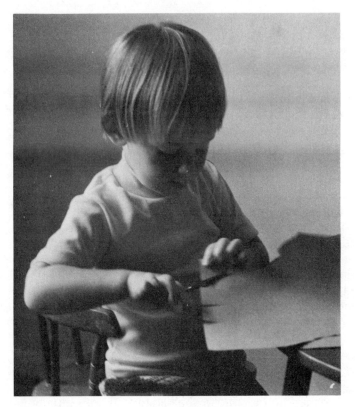

Figure 65
As Andrew uses scissors he is building muscle control and eye-hand coordination.

she said, "What do you want to do?" Then she said, "Those who have made a choice may go to work. If you have not decided, wait just a minute and I will help you."

The mothers were aghast. "Does she let them do whatever they want do do?" "No," was the reply. "The child chooses within the limits of the activities available. The teacher has selected those appropriate for the day. But the child does make a choice and the ability to make a decision is an important skill. Note that all children have not yet acquired this skill. The teacher must help them."

As the mothers watched, they saw children assume responsibility for getting the materials they needed, using them, and putting them away. As a child finished one job, he or she was free to move to another. Jim finished a picture at the easel and went to play with three other boys in the block corner. Children shared materials and took turns. Some had to wait for their turns at the fingerpainting table or wait to use the dry cell batteries in the electricity center. The teacher moved quietly among the children, reminding a child to put on an apron before painting and talking with another about some work.

Types of activities

Through a variety of well-planned activities in an environment where the child is free to explore and experiment, one progressively becomes aware of the environment and is better able to communicate this awareness to others. Moving at one's own pace, a child develops and refines the large muscles, strengthens the smaller ones, increases eye-hand coordination, and gains shape and color concepts which build toward reading readiness. The child develops socially through sharing materials, taking turns, assuming increasing responsibilities for using these materials and cleaning up afterward. Three-year-old Jane at the dough table showed this social growth when she said "I want to share with you." Tom, in the block corner also evidenced it when he told the teacher, "Look at my house. It has room for some more people." As a child works and plays with paints, clay, blocks, and tools, he or she is building perceptual and thinking abilities as a basis for further learning. As one gains skill in using materials, one grows in self-confidence.

Materials for art activities are unlimited. A creative teacher can provide for art activities even with a limited budget. There are possibilities in materials such as cloth, straw, boxes, gift wrappings, and feathers. It is important to help children see beauty and value in the world around them—in seedpods, leaves, grasses, and sand. Such materials may be called "junk" by some but to the creative teacher they offer opportunities for enriching experiences for boys and girls. The use of such materials is limited only by the vision of the teacher. The creative teacher experiments with new ways of presenting them and evaluates their true worth to the children using them.

There was no doubt in the teacher's mind about the feeling of achievement Jerry experienced when he confronted the powdered tempera in small dishes with a jar of water and brushes nearby. He wet his brush, dipped it into the dry paint and then applied it to the paper. With shining eyes he exclaimed, "I made paint." She also shared Judy's delight in the kinesthetic sensation of finger paint that equaled her enchantment with the color as she sang, "Purple hands, purple hands, look at my purple hands."

Art experiences for the young child are basic to developing a happy, wholesome, and creative personality. Through these early experiences in art children develop the ability to imagine, feel, explore, and express ideas. They learn to share materials, to cooperate, to assume responsibility, and to grow in awareness of themselves as individuals and of their relationship to those around them. They become involved in making choices, judging outcomes, and solving problems. Working with materials a child may become sensitive to one's own needs and the needs of others. Gaining skill in using materials, a child attains feelings of success that help establish a self-concept of worth as an individual and as a member of the group. Finished creations reflect one's unique personality and insights.

The following chart gives some of the basic materials for optimum creative growth. The chart also presents types of activities and attempts to suggest developmental levels in each type of media. It also lists the important values of each activity and suggests some of the responsibilities of the teacher in making the art experiences meaningful to the child. Following the chart are recipes for some of the materials that are suggested for use with the young child. It is hoped that these will encourage the teacher to experiment with ways of using these and other materials.

Modeling (Clay, Dough, Sawdust and Wheat Paste, Salt Ceramic)

Characteristics of Work	Values Derived	Teacher Techniques
The Child: Beats and pounds followed by breaking and rolling (consciously controlled). Names product. Begins to pull out or add on details such as nose, ears, arms, legs. Product has meaning for adult.	Develops large and small muscles and eye-hand coordination. Provides direct sensory experiences deeply satisfying to children. Stimulates different kind of thinking, builds concepts of form, allows changing of these concepts. Provides another outlet for emotional release and aggressive impulses.	Provide frequent opportunities to explore material. Encourage feeling, handling, and verbalizing. Do not model or show how to make something. Keep materials soft and pliable by storing properly.

Pasting, Using Scraps, and Styrofoam

Characteristics of Work	Values Derived	Teacher Techniques
The Child: Feels, manipulates, and explores. Uses paste lavishly showing little interest in its purpose. Uses with other materials such as scraps and sand.	Provides tactile experience and opportunities for manipulation and coordination. Offers emotional release and opportunity to acquire motor skill.	Furnish enough to allow child freedom to explore its uses and experiment. Help child find its use as a tool for creative expression. Use with scraps, sand, paper, crayons, cotton, cloth, styrofoam, and feathers.

Cutting and Tearing

Characteristics of Work	Values Derived	Teacher Techniques
The Child: Cuts and tears aimlessly exploring possibilities of material. Practices for skill trying to control scissors and direction of tearing. Names the forms. Forms have meaning for adults. Combines colors and textures.	Builds muscle control, eye-hand coordination. Provides another means of self-expression. Offers opportunities to grow creatively and in awareness of form concepts. Provides another means for release of tension.	Provide scissors when child can handle them; be sure they will cut. Teach the child proper safety rules. Help child to discover the possibilities of tearing. Provide variety of colors and textures of paper, fabrics, and materials.

Finger Painting

Characteristics of Work	Values Derived	Teacher Techniques
The Child: Feels and experiments with paints. Uses fingers, hands, and arms, overlays and mixes all colors. Exploration is long, accompanied by smearing and finally frenzied smearing. Experiments with patterns. Develops an appreciation for form and color.	Allows release from home pressures to keep clean by offering an acceptable means just to mess. Frees inhibited children for greater spontaneity. Provides social growth and openness to contact. It provides kinesthetic and tactual sensation and opportunity for large muscle activity. It encourages creative expression through its direct contact between child and product and a chance for self-discovery.	Provide free choice of paper, paint on formica-top table, or oilcloth. Allow child freedom to experiment. Encourage this freedom by painting to music, talking about swing of body. Allow time to continue as long as interest is sustained. Allow child to mix the paints. Provide several choices of colors. Encourage children to clean up themselves. Make hand or foot prints on paper. Vary paints.

Painting (Working with Paint, String, Soap, Sand, Chalk, Crayon)

Characteristics of Work	Values Derived	Teacher Techniques
The Child: Uses it to explore, to spread and overlay. Makes lines and circles, then form, using squares and blocks of color. Names the painting, the adult sees meaning. Shows evidence of relating objects.	Allows the child opportunity to work alone. Offers opportunity to experiment, explore, and express feelings which the young child finds difficult to put into words. Provides a means for motor expression. Helps the withdrawn child to give form to feelings and accept help. Permits messing in a controlled form and helps the too-neat child ease into finger paint and clay.	Furnish large sheets of paper, large brushes, and a choice of rich bright colors including red, yellow, and blue. Easel of suitable height, away from traffic, should be available at all times so that children can paint satisfying experiences or frustrations as they feel the need. Locate activity in area that cannot be harmed by paint. Use linoleum or plastic on floor. Provide opportunities for painting on tables, the floor, and outdoors. Include variations such as *spatter painting* (Hold wire screen over paper; dip toothbrush in paint and rub over screen); *straw painting* (Put blob of paint on paper; blow through straw on the paint to create design); *string painting* (Dip string into paint; drop string on paper; pull around to make design); *printing* (Use objects such as paper cups, pencil erasers, cut vegetables, ends of tubes or straws, cookie cutters; dip into paint and print on paper; add a few drops of glycerin or oil of wintergreen to paint mixture to keep it from becoming smelly).

Using Blocks

Characteristics of Work	Values Derived	Teacher Techniques
The Child: Plays with single blocks. Stacks them. Creates a building and then names it. States kind of building and then builds it. Uses knowledge gained in dramatic play.[19]	Their flexibility and ease of handling make an excellent first medium for the child. Their cleanness and sturdiness are nonthreatening to children from homes with parents' admonitions against dirt and breaking. They offer opportunities for playing alone, parallel to, or in cooperation with others. Offer sense of achievement and power to cope with physical world. Offer emotional release through tearing down or dramatic play. Offer physical release through lifting, carrying, and piling. Cultivate creative expression and a sense of design. Offer opportunities for problem solving, growth in number concepts, and language.	Provide ample space and materials. Allow opportunity to leave structure up when desired. Warn children ahead of time to clean up. Watch for ways of helping timid child to participate. Offer help when needed to prevent frustration. Avoid setting patterns. Listen to and observe child while building to gain insights into behavior and growth.

Using Tools (Hammers, Saws, Nails, Screwdrivers)

Characteristics of Work	Values Derived	Teacher Techniques
The Child: Handles and manipulates tools. Uses tools in hammering,	Offers opportunities to develop eye-hand coordination and muscle control.	Arrange for ample space. Provide for real tools, not toys.[20]

[19] Frances M. Guanella, "Block Building Activities of Young Children," *Arch. Psychol.* 26:174 (1934), p. 92, cited by D. H. Russell, *Children's Thinking* (Boston: Ginn Co., 1956).
[20] For a detailed list of tools for woodworking see: ACEI, op. cit., pp. 52, 64.

Using Tools (Hammers, Saws, Nails, Screwdrivers)

Characteristics of Work	Values Derived	Teacher Techniques
nailing, sawing. Concerned with activity—simply hammering nails in wood or sawing wood.	Provides another outlet for emotional release.	Provide scraps of soft wood—flat and in a variety of shapes.
Tries to make something. Object may not be recognizable.	Stimulates thinking and problem solving.	Help boys and girls enjoy working with tools.
Makes recognizable object.	Builds concepts of size and form.	Provide nails in a variety of sizes.
		Accept product that satisfies child. Don't strive for perfection in end product.
		Supervise activity at all times.
		Use tools only in woodworking area.

Recipes

Fixative

For chalk:
1. Glue thinned with water to the consistency of milk.
2. One part shellac. Two parts denatured alcohol.

For chalk, pastello, and charcoal:
1. Gum arabic, thin with water until consistency of thin mucilage. Spray—repeat twice.
2. Spray powdered milk mixed with water.

Colored Dough

3 cups flour
¾ cup salt
dry paint or 2 tsp. food coloring
½ cup water

Sift flour and salt together into a pan. Mix coloring with water and add gradually to flour and salt mixture. Knead as you would bread dough until the mixture is smooth and easy to handle. The more the mixture is kneaded, the smoother it becomes. If mixture becomes sticky add more flour. When not in use, place in plastic bag and keep in a cool place. (Should last at least two weeks.) Children can make this recipe.

Play Dough (Cooked)

2 cups flour
1 cup salt
4 teaspoons cream of tartar
2 tablespoons oil
2 cups water (substitute 2 teaspoons of water with 2 teaspoons of peppermint or wintergreen flavoring for scented dough)
food coloring

Heat all ingredients in a pan over moderate heat. Stir frequently until mixture pulls away from pan. The mixture looks very lumpy before it pulls away, but it smoothes out again. Knead until smooth. Will keep in airtight container and does not require refrigeration.

Sawdust	*Wheat-paste Mixture*
4 cups sawdust	2 cups wheat flour
2 cups wheat flour	3½ cups cold water
1 cup water	

Produces a very pliable media—used like dough but not as firm a consistency. (Liquid starch—mixed with sawdust and powdered paint or with tissue paper.)

Paste

1 tbsp. powdered alum
1 cup flour
1½ pts. boiling water
Few drops oil of cloves

Mix flour and alum in cold water. Add boiling water and cook for two minutes. Add a few drops of oil of cloves.

Finger Paint

½ cup dry starch
1⅓ cups boiling water
½ cup soap flakes
Vegetable coloring, show card or poster paint
1 tbsp. glycerin

Mix the starch with enough cold water to make a smooth paste. Add boiling water and cook the paste until glossy. Stir in the dry soap flakes while the mixture is still warm. Cool. Add glycerin and pour the mixture into jars. The mixture can be kept for a week if it is covered with a damp cloth or a tight lid. Add color later.

Two or three tablespoons of liquid starch may be poured on the wet paper, one-half teaspoon powdered paint added and mixed as the child paints with it. Color may also be added to wheat paste, paste, or liquid soap.

Sand Painting

Add ¼ part paint powder to 1 part sand and combine in large shakers. Use extra container to empty excess sand. Children shake on paper they have covered with paste. This is also excellent outside on the bare ground.

Soap Painting

Fill small dishes with soap powder. Add a little powdered paint and water. Mix thoroughly until it has a medium texture (not too stiff nor too soft). Children apply to various kinds of paper with fingers or brushes.

Figure 66
Lee experiences the kinesthetic and tactual sensations of finger painting.

Evaluation

To know if the children are achieving the values and skills it is hoped they will derive through art activities, the teacher has to collect evidence for the purpose of evaluation. Techniques which may be used follow:

Samples of Children's Work. Samples of work can be used to observe progress as the child moves through the developmental sequence from scribbling to forms which one consciously creates. A folder of the child's paintings and drawings and samples of other work, such as clay and wood, may be used for this purpose. It is important to date each product. Such samples may be helpful to the teacher in talking with parents.

Conversation. Informal conversation often takes place while the child works. This gives clues as to the child's ideas and feelings about one's self, one's work, and others. For example:

> One of the children stops painting long enough to ask for more red paint. The teacher puts a spoonful on the paper and the child moves the red paint into a yellow area. Martha looks up with a smile of wonder and pride and says, "Did you know I could make orange? I put red and yellow together and made orange."

There may be other conversation between the teacher and the child regarding the child's work. Questions such as, "What is it?" may be asking the child to identify an object when there was no object in mind. Perhaps the child was only manipulating and using materials. Comments such as, "I like your car," may indicate to the child that the teacher has not recognized the object just made. Use comments that do not put the child in an embarrassing position. "Tell me about your picture," or "You have used such pretty, bright colors—I like the red," are much more appropriate for the young child.

Jefferson points out that it is not necessary to discuss everything that children produce in art. Children may be apprehensive if they know everything they produce will be discussed.[21] Negative comments during a discussion may be embarrassing for a child. He or she may lose feelings of confidence as well as an enjoyment of art.

In considering a discussion of art products, it is well to remember that the young child may not appreciate pictures made by other children. According to Munro, research and experience indicate that while children make schematic pictures, they tend to prefer more realistic ones. This means that they do not prefer to look at the type of pictures they make themselves.[22]

Anecdotal Records. Children's reactions during art experiences constitute a significant part of the child's behavior at school and serve as a source for understanding the young child. Anecdotal records of this behavior can be helpful. Their uses are discussed in Chapter 21.

Records of Work Choices. A record of choices of activities which the children make from day to day can help identify the child who uses only one or a limited number of media; the child who skips from one material to another, not following through with the selected task; the child who uses a variety of ma-

---

[21] Blanche Jefferson, *Teaching Art to Children* (Boston: Allyn and Bacon, 1959), pp. 88–89.
[22] T. Munro, "Children's Art Abilities: Studies at the Cleveland Museum of Art," in *Readings in Art Education,* edited by E. W. Eisner and D. W. Ecker (Waltham, Mass.: Blaisdell Publishing Co., 1966), pp. 179–180.

terials freely and wisely. Such evidence can be used in helping the child. An example is shown in Table 19-1. List activities for the day across the top of the sheet. Write the child's name under one or more activities in which the child participates.

Table 19-1
Work Choices

Date	Blocks	Easel	Puzzles	Clay	Tools
5-9-78	Tom Ruth Bill	Ruth Jane Hal	Ruth Jane	Jane Hal	Tom Ruth Joe

Teacher's Evaluation. A weekly summary for each child can include the teacher's reactions to the child and his or her art activities, such as "Free in movement, Restricted in movement. Dependent. Experimental."

Interpretation of Children's Art Products. The psychological interpretation of children's paintings or drawings is wisely referred to the psychologist. There are, however, studies and scales which may be used to help the teacher gain greater insight into the children's products.[23]

MUSIC ACTIVITIES

The child's world is filled with music. On the TV children hear the musical accompaniment for the commercials. The country singer plays a guitar or picks a banjo and sings a plaintive folk song. On the radio one record after another is played. Some children have their own record players and a collection of recordings. Even with so much music of varying types in the lives of children, Smith says that their musical tastes are not fixed and definite when

[23] Florence L. Goodenough, *Children's Drawings: A Handbook of Child Psychology* (Worcester, Mass.: Clark University Press, 1931); D. B. Harris, *Children's Drawings as Measures of Intellectual Maturity (A Revision and Extension of Goodenough Draw-A-Man Test)* (New York: Harcourt Brace Jovanovich, 1963); Rhoda Kellog, *What Children Scribble and Why* (San Francisco: San Francisco Golden Gate Nursery, 1955); and Beatrice Lantz, *Easel Age Scale* (Los Angeles: California Test Bureau, 1955).

they come to school.[24] It becomes increasingly important to consider the role of music in all centers for young children.

Shelley says that "An imaginative and balanced music program in which a young child learns how to 'play with music' can contribute to the child becoming an active learner."[25] Musical activities, chanting, singing, playing instruments, moving, listening, creating and recreating music, and the materials available should be such that the child is actively involved in making music. As children have the opportunity to interact with an enriched musical environment, they can learn to listen, expand the power of concentration, improve speech, develop language, and acquire tonal and rhythmic repertoire —all prerequisites for developing a musical child.

Shelley suggests the following guidelines for creating an environment for musical growth.

1. Have a flexible schedule so that music may be enjoyed when the need or occasion arises. Begin the day by singing songs which create good feelings.
2. Let music be informal. Welcome the child's ideas.
3. Work at a comfortable pace allowing for repetition. Children enjoy repetition.
4. Work with individuals, small groups, large groups.
5. Show appreciation of every effort a child makes to participate and contribute to the group. Do not force a child to participate. Appreciate the child's point of view.
6. Accept the child at his/her level, but encourage and challenge.
7. Encourage creative response in all music activities. Use questions such as, "Is there another way you could do that?" "What would happen if . . . ?"
8. Provide for many and varied sensory experiences which will stimulate the child to use higher levels of thinking. Encourage the child to identify, discriminate, analyze, recall, synthesize, and make value judgments.
9. Help the child use nonverbal skills, such as movement. Help the child create simple orchestrations to reveal understanding of the mood, style, and structure of music.
10. Allow time for free exploration and manipulation of materials and equipment. Have instruments available so that children can touch, manipulate, play, and discover on their own.

Music helped Matt to grow socially. He was a very aggressive five-year-old, eager for attention regardless of how it was gained. He swaggered up to Miss S. who was standing near the piano. "I'll bet you don't know 'Ten Little Indians,'" he boasted. The teacher smiled, sat down, and played the song. "Is that the song you mean?" Matt nodded. She replied, "Sing it with me." Together they sang several songs. Matt not only enjoyed singing but found in singing an acceptable form of recognition.

---

[24] R. B. Smith, *Music in the Child's Education* (New York: The Ronald Press, 1970), p. 4.
[25] Shirley Shelley, *Music and the Whole Child-Implications for Curriculum Planning* (mimeogr.), EDEL 640, University of Maryland, November 17, 1977.

Figure 67
Donald uses the xylophone in the music center. Tuned bells and the autoharp are also effective instruments for exploring music.

Jim gained in physical development as he galloped across the playground, sometimes alone, sometimes with other "horses," and often with the teacher. Jane became aware of the quality of sounds and gained in auditory acuity as she experimented with instruments. The drum, the bells, and the sticks all sounded different, and she learned to distinguish among them. Lois remembered the words of the song she sang as she rocked the doll. Ann listened at nursery school and sang the songs at home. Sam created his own song.

Music can contribute in many ways by offering opportunities for listening, creating, singing, rhythmic responses, and playing instruments. Through these activities, the child experiences pleasure, joy, and creative expression; develops listening skills and auditory discrimination; gains in physical development and use of the body; and increases the range and flexibility of the voice. The child grows in appreciation of music and can learn to be discriminating in the choices made.

Shull states, "Many educators are apparently unaware of vocal music by many distinguished composers written especially for children to sing."[26] Shull found a considerable body of songs and music of distinguished composers appropriate for use with young children. Listening to classical music may also be enjoyed by young children.[27]

The first responses of young children to music may appear awkward and

---

[26] C. N. Shull, *A Study of Children's Vocal Literature Written by Selected Distinguished Composers,* Unpublished Dissertation, Florida State University, Tallahassee, June 1961.
[27] Eunice Bailey, *Discovering Music With Young Children* (New York: Philosophical Library, 1958), pp. 39–42.

uncertain, but as they grow physically and socially as well as in the enjoyment and understanding of music, their responses are gradually refined. A variety of free and pleasurable experiences in music invite participation by the child. To provide a balance, activities should include singing, creating, listening, and experiences with rhythms, movement, and instruments. For each activity there is a sequence of development from the first simple responses to those which are more complicated and refined. Knowledge and understanding of this sequence can enable the teacher to pace experiences to the level of the child's development.

For example, because the child in not ready to participate in one activity, the teacher may decide he or she should not be forced and leave him or her alone. True, one should not be forced, but activities can be paced to development, and and the child can be helped to take the next step. "Not forcing" does not necessarily mean leaving the child alone, unchallenged, and untouched for weeks or months. For example, a four-year-old, unable to skip, should not be subjected to drill in the practice of skipping each day. It does not mean, however, that nothing is done. Rather, the teacher who understands the growth and development of the child, as well as the stages of development of the skill of skipping, can arrange many worthwhile experiences. There will be opportunities to climb, run, and jump, all of which can help the child gain control of the large muscles. As children experiment with bodily movements, they will set their own tempo, which the teacher can emphasize. The child listens to music, responds, and the rhythmic response is accepted. Gradually, in keeping with the child's rate of maturity, he or she reaches the point where skipping is possible.

Nye and Nye make suggestions for helping children from a culturally different background musically.[28] In reality, the suggestions are applicable to all children.

1. Examine and analyze a child's background. Involve the child in planning and exploring songs he or she would like to sing or know; instruments and rhythmic movements the child might use with a song.
2. Provide opportunities for the child to use divergent and creative ways of interpretation.
3. Find out and understand conditions in which the child may live. There may be complete indifference to musical values and experiences.
4. Involve parents in music activities at school. Help them to find out about musical programs and experiences available to them in the community and of appropriate programs for viewing on TV.
5. Encourage the child in self-evaluation. Evaluate the child's progress in order to meet his or her needs.

[28] R. E. Nye and Vernice T. Nye, *Music in the Elementary School,* 3rd ed. (Englewood Cliffs, N.J.: Prentice-Hall, 1970), pp. 558–571.

Developmental sequence of music activities

The description of the developmental sequence presented here attempts to give a picture of the stages through which each child passes at one's own rate, and to help identify the next step that he or she is able to take. Such a sequence can prove helpful in making plans for a variety of individuals and situations. Wide differences among the group should not lead the teacher to the conclusion that some children can benefit from musical activities and others not. Smith says, "all young children have musical capacities, and all should have the opportunity to develop this potential."[29] Guidance and the introduction of new ideas at the appropriate time are necessary to help the child move to the next level.[30]

Singing

Developmental Sequence	*Suggestions to the Teacher*
The Child: 1. Plays with sound of own voice. Changes sound and pitch of voice. Repeats sounds.[31] 2. Sings egocentric phrases about self, parents, toys. 3. Enjoys listening to song sung by another; sings spontaneously as one plays. 4. Responds with actions to song sung by another. 5. Joins in with an occasional word or phrase as another sings. 6. Sings with an adult or group but not always in time with them (may be a measure behind and may not use the same words). 7. Sings along with adult or group, able to match tones. 8. Sings alone. 9. Selects and requests favorite songs. 10. Recognizes songs sung or played by others.	1. Children are at differing levels in the developmental sequence. Don't expect same response of all children. Give each child opportunity to participate at own level. a. Join in with a child who is singing. Add an idea to child's song. Don't make child feel his or her song is inferior. b. Sit with one or two children. Show picture. Sing, for example, "See the red _____". Encourage child to sing response, "apple."[32] c. Record some of child's chants or songs. Play for child to hear own voice. d. Some will listen as they are in block corner while others come to piano for a song. Accept child in doll corner at his level, but don't leave the child there all year. Work to help the child take the next step and the next. Perhaps sing a song (lullaby or one appropriate to the activity) for the child in the doll corner. He can rock the doll as you sing.

---

[29] Smith, op. cit., p. 9.
[30] Barbara L. Andress, et al., *Music in Early Childhood* (Reston, Va: Music Educators National Conference, 1973), p. 24.
[31] Ibid., p. 42.
[32] Ibid., p. 44.

Singing

Developmental Sequence	Suggestions to the Teacher
11. The child's voice range centers around G above middle C, but the voice he or she uses often varies with the activity and the purpose for singing.[33] Smith reports a range from middle C to G above.[34]	e. Some learn words easily and sing with teacher, accept this along with the response of an occasional word and a happy, eager expression. Avoid such statements as: "Now let's *all* sing." "Jane knows *all* the words. Jane, sing them for us. Now listen so you can learn the words too." Jane can sing alone for the group, yes—but not as a model which may discourage others.
12. Acquires a repertoire of songs.	2. Include songs of varying length, tonal range, and content.

13. Sings tunefully.	3. Provide many opportunities for singing throughout the day. Avoid "sing-song-ing" every comment to the child, but chanting some comments offers opportunities for individual and group responses.
	
	"Mary has a new doll.
	Who gave it to you?"
	
	Ma-ry
	    has a
	        new doll.
	Who
	   gave
	     it
	       to
	         you?

	4. Limit length of group musical experiences, taking into account the attention span of the group. A few songs, well selected, sung happily, and enjoyed can be of much more value than a longer period in which children may lose interest.

[33] A. T. Jersild and Sylvia F. Beinstock, "A Study of the Development of Children's Ability to Sing," *J. Educ. Physchol.*, 25:10 (1939), p. 491.

[34] Smith, op. cit., p. 17.

Singing

Developmental Sequence	Suggestions to the Teacher
	5. Select songs within the expected voice range of the young child. Many songs are written too high for the majority of children. The range within the song should not extend beyond three or four adjacent notes. A little more difficult songs vary in total range but a limited-range pattern should be repeated several times.[35]
	6. Include songs
	a. of a variety of types—patriotic songs, ethnic songs, religious songs and hymns, songs about holidays, the here and now, everyday experiences, counting, folk songs, familiar songs.
	b. of a pleasing melody and musical appeal.
	c. that are brief, simple, and repeat certain phrases.
	d. containing words that are easily sung.

[35] Ibid., p. 18.

Figure 68

Kim and Stanley choose a record for use in their dramatic and rhythmic activity. They have learned to use the record player and handle records carefully.

Listening

Developmental Sequence	*Suggestions to the Teacher*

The Child:
1. Is engrossed in one activity but listens just enough to be aware of what is being sung or played.
 	
2. Enjoys a short song, a recording, or an instrument, alone or with an adult (range of attention span varies from 2 to 20 minutes).
 	
3. Enjoys a short song, recording, or an instrument along with a few other children —gradually the size of the group expands to include the entire nursery or kindergarten group.
 	
4. Listens and analyzes what is heard. Can distinguish between loud and soft or happy and sad music. Can listen for details and for answers to questions. Can listen to his own singing and playing in order to correct or to match tones. Can listen to accompaniment for rhythmic responses.
	1. Include a variety of musical listening experiences.
	
	   a. Different purposes:
	     Mood—fast, slow, happy, sad, rhythmic response.
	     Stories in music.
	     Sounds of contrasting timbre, such as metal, wood, paper.
	
	   b. Different types:
	     Recordings—vocal and instrumental. Include a variety—chants, patriotic, ethnic, folk songs, and some examples of rock music.
	     Instruments—teacher plays piano, a father plays a horn, another child plays with a rhythm stick.
	     Singing—teacher sings, mother sings, another child sings.
	
	   c. Individual and in a group.
	
	   d. Resource people—sing or play an instrument.
	
	2. Provide record player and records that children can use.
	
	3. Watch child who spends too much time listening. The child may be using this as an escape from group adjustment—may need help getting into the group.
	
	The suggestions listed for language arts (pp. 258–260), are applicable in listening to music.

Rhythmic Experiences

Developmental Sequence	*Suggestions to the Teacher*
The child expresses rhythm through: 1. Making random movements, using large muscles. 2. Moving rhythmically in one's own way for short periods of time.	1. Provide space and opportunity for movement. 2. Observe child's movements and tempo. Accompany the child with piano, percus-

Rhythmic Experiences

Developmental Sequence	*Suggestions to the Teacher*
3. Moving rhythmically in own way, the child responds when teacher emphasizes his or her movement with an accompaniment.	sion instrument, or by clapping in his or her own tempo. The child sets the pace. Avoid accompaniments that include melodic and harmonic elements.[36]
4. Moving at fast tempo before conforming to slower tempos.	3. Help child with transition from moving rhythmically in his or her own tempo to moving to an accompaniment. For example, the teacher might say,
5. Adjusting bodily movements to accompaniment of regular beat. Can "keep time."	"Tim, I've been beating the drum as you walk. I will do it again and beat every time you take a step. Then I am going to beat differently—maybe faster or maybe slower. Listen and see if you can walk when I beat the drum."
6. Listening before participating.	
7. Adjusting bodily movements to accompaniment which involves contrasts (slow and fast, light and heavy).	4. Provide accompaniments in faster tempos, using those that invite the slower, more deliberate movements at a later time. Vary soft and loud tones.
8. Acquiring musical concepts of terms—high-low, short-long, fast-slow, and expressing them through movement.	5. Use even foot patterns such as walking, marching, running before the uneven patterns like galloping and skipping.[37]
	6. Play accompaniments to which child can respond. Be sure that rhythm is regular and easily detected. Ask child to listen first and then respond to the music. Avoid getting children on floor and saying, "Do what the music says" without first giving them an opportunity to listen. Avoid saying, "I am going to play some skipping music" (or galloping music). Children may respond to the music by walking, running, whirling, skipping, galloping, or in many other ways. Let the child choose response to the music.
	7. Play very high and very low tones. Ask the child to show where each tone is by raising or lowering arms. After listening, ask the child where the light, heavy, loud tones were heard.
	8. Do not expect same response of all children.

[36] A. T. Jersild and Sylvia F. Beinstock, *Development of Rhythm in Young Children* (New York: Teachers College, Columbia University, 1937), p. 96.
[37] Ibid., p. 71.

Rhythmic Experiences

Developmental Sequence	Suggestions to the Teacher
	a. Some will respond individually or in small groups—not even all kindergarteners are ready to participate in a large group.
	b. Skipping requires greater skill in muscular control than some of the other activities such as walking or running. Not all fours or even fives can skip. This is another reason for letting a child choose own response rather than asking everyone to skip.

Playing Instruments

Developmental Sequence	Suggestions to the Teacher
The Child:	
1. Manipulates and experiments with instruments; becomes aware of differences in sounds in relation to ways in which the instruments are played; comes to recognize sounds of various instruments.	1. Place instruments so they are available to children. A special music area may be arranged. Provide opportunity for children to experiment freely. Expect "noise" at first. Use instruments both inside and out of doors. Avoid showing child "how to hold instrument." Help child evaluate sound in relation to way tambourine or triangle is held. "Which way sounds better?"
2. Listens to instrument played skillfully by a person or on recording.	Help child discover how to hold an instrument in order to get the best tone.
3. Uses instrument as accompaniment to his or her movements—beats rhythm sticks as he or she marches, but not necessarily in time with his or her steps.	Help child discover tonal qualities of instrument. Which instrument has the highest sound? the lowest? Play the drum with hand, a wooden mallet, a yarn mallet. How does it sound?
4. Listens to music and is able to identify the instrument that makes the appropriate sound.	2. Accept gifts or donations of real instruments, such as drums, string instruments. Make available to children to use experimentally.
5. Plays instrument and responds accurately to tempo of a recording or another instrument.	3. Play music and ask child to listen and to decide which instrument will be appropriate. Play music again and child accompanies with his or her instrument. Let
6. Plays instrument along with a small group of other children.	
7. Is interested in and curious about instruments that adults play.	
8. Learns names of several of the better known instruments, such as the violin or trumpet.	

Playing Instruments

Developmental Sequence	Suggestions to the Teacher
9. Listens and identifies sound of different instruments. Knows when certain instruments are playing in a musical selection.	child choose instrument appropriate for a certain rhythm, such as a rain dance or a Funny Clown, or one that has a certain tone color such as one that sounds like an airplane or the wind. Avoid such statements as, "All drums play," or "All together, play." Listening and responding creatively help the child to develop sensitivity to mood, and good listening habits as well as auditory acuity and discrimination. Such procedure is followed first for individual children and later for the group. The formal rhythm band often requires strict conformity and adherence to the pattern designed by the teacher which may tend to discourage creative listening and responses. Bring real instruments to school for children to see and touch. Invite an adult or a youth to play for the children. Children may visit an orchestra rehearsal. 4. Provide recordings of instrumental music. 5. Tuned bells and the autoharp are effective instruments for exploring music.

Creating

Developmental Sequence	Suggestions to the Teacher
The Child: 1. Chants as he or she swings, piles blocks, or pulls the wagon. This may be a play on words, experimenting with sounds. 2. Experiments with instruments and sounds. 3. Suggests a new word for a song; for example, in the song "Do you know what says, Quack! Quack!?" Child may substitute "bow-wow." or "mew, mew," etc[38] 4. Makes up extra verses for a song.	1. While suggestions here are limited largely to singing, this is not intended to imply that this is the only musical experience which lends itself to the creative approach. Other suggestions were made specifically for rhythmic experiences, p. 452. 2. Create a permissive atmosphere in which the child feels free to chant and sing as he or she works and plays.

[38] Mary J. Nelson and Gladys Tipton, *Music for Early Childhood* (New York: Silver Burdett, 1952), p. 16.

Creating

Developmental Sequence	*Suggestions to the Teacher*
5. Chooses an appropriate instrument and accompanies a song or a recording.	3. Select songs containing words and phrases for which other words may be substituted.
6. Interprets the mood of music in rhythmic movement. Moves expressively.	4. Sing animal song to child. Then ask a question such as "Can you think of another animal which makes a sound? Sing it."
7. Dramatizes a song.	
8. Makes up a song cooperatively and later individually. Sings the words in developing tune.	5. Permit child to listen to song or recording and then select instrument for accompaniment.
9. Creates an original melody or tune.	6. Play recordings characterized by a mood or moods. Let child listen and respond. Properties such as scarves or flags may be helpful in interpreting the mood.
	7. Use songs with words that give clues to movement, or singing games. For example, in the song "This Old Man" children may choose to have the old man come "hopping" or "skipping" home.[39] Another example might be "Community Helpers."[40]
	8. Creating a song may be a group activity. Joe brought a "possum" to the kindergarten. As the group gathered around the piano he asked Miss T., "Do you know a song about a possum?" Miss T.: "No, Joe, I don't, but perhaps we could make up a song about the possum."
	To the group Miss T. said, "Let's see if we can make a song about the possum. What would you want to sing first?"
	Sally: "We could tell his name."
	Miss T.: "Yes, we could, Sing it for us, Sally."
	Sally sang, "Pete the Possum."
	Miss T. repeated Sally's phrase. This procedure was continued until the following song was completed.
	Pete the Possum, in a cage, His tail is long, His nose is sharp.

[39] Ibid., p. 43.
[40] Ibid., p. 19.

Creating

Developmental Sequence	*Suggestions to the Teacher*
	Miss T. played the tune on the piano and recorded the notes. If she had not been able to play the tune she could have sung it several times in order to remember the tune.

As the child progresses through the developmental sequences described for singing, listening, rhythmic experiences, and creating, musical experiences can help him or her to develop in many ways. For certain children music has special advantages. The overactive, aggressive child can be helped to become relaxed and less tense; the shy, timid child can be helped to become involved in group experience. For each child music can:

1. Promote appreciation and enjoyment.
2. Encourage discrimination in the choice of music and other aesthetic experiences.
3. Develop an awareness of and sensitivity to sounds as well as auditory acuity.
4. Develop and extend voice range.
5. Provide experiences in listening.
6. Promote growth in motor control.
7. Develop intellectual and emotional capacities.

MOVEMENT

"Movement in itself is educative and movement is essential to learning in early childhood."[41] Most young children are very active. They are moving, moving, moving. Movement education is closely related to this movement that is so much a part of the young child's life. A child comes to know one's self through one's body movements.[42] Through moving in many ways children develop skills in using their bodies, using and controlling objects, solving problems, gaining knowledge, and acquiring attitudes.

Fundamental activities include walking, running, jumping, galloping, hopping, skipping, sliding, and leaping. These activities are included in both movement education and rhythmic activities, or rhythms. Rhythmic body movement may or may not be accompanied by music. However, when walk-

---

[41] Caroline B. Sinclair, *Movement of the Young Child* (Columbus Ohio: Charles E. Merrill Publishing Co. 1973), p. 10.
[42] Lydia A. Gerhardt, "Movement," in *Curriculum for the Preschool-Primary Child: A Review of Research*, edited by Carol Seefeldt, (Columbus, Ohio: Charles E. Merrill Publishing Co., 1976), p. 257.

ing or when one of the fundamental activities is done "to music" it is usually considered a rhythmic activity. Activities in movement usually precede rhythmic activities. Movement education may be carried on with the entire group, several children, or an individual child. Space is needed both indoors and outdoors.

Movement patterns of children appear at different times in their lives. Some appear in infancy, some later at two, three, or even four years. The child at two can usually walk up the stairs, but he or she may not be hopping until the age of four. Skipping may not be achieved until four and one half or five years.[43] Movement patterns should be appropriate to the child's developmental level. Let the child set the pace.

Much of the spontaneous movement of children includes the fundamental activities of walking, running, jumping, galloping, skipping, sliding, and leap-

[43] Sinclair, op. cit., p. 27.

A   B

Figure 69
Space for movement activities is needed both indoors and outdoors.

ing. In addition, however, the teacher may find the following suggestions helpful.[44] The teacher may ask the child (or children) to:

Walk without touching another child.
Walk and change direction when a signal is given.
Walk as if you are happy, tired.
Walk as if you were in the rain.
Touch your shoulders (and various parts of the body).
Show how many ways you can move your head, arms, legs, and feet.
Touch your knee with your elbow.
Jump over the string.
Jump up high.
Bounce a ball and catch it.
Sit on the floor and bounce a ball.
Move your ball in as many different ways as you can.
Make a circle with the rope.

[44] Barbara Day, *Open Learning in Early Childhood* (New York: Macmillan Publishing Co., 1975), pp. 120–132.

A   B   C

Figure 70
In this movement activity the teacher asked one child to stand in front of another, to stand on one foot, hold out your right hand. Much of children's movement, however, is spontaneous.

Move over the rope in as many ways as you can.
Sit inside the circle.
Toss and catch beanbag with different parts of your body.

Suggested Activities

1. Visit a children's center. Observe children engaged in art activities. Describe the activity and indicate the stage of art development in which several children seem to be.
2. Use one of the recipes, pp. 440–441, and prepare a medium for use by children. Experiment with ways of using the medium. Name the values that you feel the children gained from participating in this activity.
3. Examine one of the scales or studies listed on page 444. Use the information in relation to drawings of several children. How do you feel the scale helped you gain insight into the child's product?
4. Observe a group of young children and note any peer pressures that seem to affect a child's choice of activity or actions. How do you feel such conformity may influence a child's creative activities? What do you feel is the teacher's role in such situations?
5. Visit a center for young children and describe the approach to art or the philosophy of the teacher regarding the art of the young child. What evidence do you see that the philosophy and practices are consistent? What is your philosophy? Discuss your observations with your class.
6. Make a list of art supplies and materials that you might order for your classroom. Compile a list of sources of art supplies. List materials that may be made by the teacher and/or parents.
7. Observe a child's movements and tempo. Accompany child with a percussion instrument, or by clapping hands. Follow the child's tempo.
8. Listen to and evaluate five recordings for use with young children.
9. Learn five songs appropriate for use with young children. Teach them to members of the class and to young children.
10. Reread the suggestions for "creating" in music on pp. 454–456. Select one suggestion and use it with a small group of young children. Do you feel that you accomplished your goals? What changes might you make when you use this activity again?
11. Make a list of instruments appropriate for use with children. Make an instrument to be used by a child.[45]
12. Make a list of ways in which a teacher helps a child or a group of children develop an awareness of sounds in the environment. Did you note additional opportunities that might have been utilized?
13. Formulate some learning objectives of a teacher for using movement education with young children.

---

[45] Day, op. cit., p. 64.

14. Use some of the suggestions for movement on pp. 458–459 with a small group of children. Evaluate.
15. View the film, *Dance With Joy.* Documentary Films, 3217 Trout Gulch Rd., Aptos, Calif., 95003.

Related Readings

Akman, Susan H., and Lynne Sherald. *Woodworking: Processes and Procedures.* College Park: University of Maryland, 1973,

Alexander, C. "The Origin of Creative Power In Children," *Art For The Preprimary Child.* Washington, D.C.: National Art Education Association, 1972.

Allen, Ann Wright, with Daveen Herley. *Art Through Your Child's Eyes.* Southampton, N.Y.: Suffolk County Early Childhood Education Council, 1975.

Andrews, Palmyra. "Music and Motion: The Rhythmic Language of Children," *Young Children,* 32:1 (1976), pp. 14–19.

Aranoff, Frances W. *Music and Children.* New York: Holt, Rinehart and Winston, 1969.

Cherry, Clare. *Creative Art for the Developing Child.* Belmont, Calif.: Fearon, 1972.

Cohen, Elaine P., and Ruth S. Gainer. "Art as Communication with Children," *Child. Educ.,* 53:4 (1977), pp. 199–202.

———. "Does Art Matter in the Education of the Black Ghetto Child?" *Young Children,* 29:3 (1974), pp. 170–181.

Danoff, Judith. "Children's Art: The Creative Process," *Children Today,* 4:4 (1975), pp. 7–10.

Dimondstein, G. *Exploring the Arts with Children.* New York: Macmillan Publishing Co., 1974.

Eisner, E. W. *Educating Artistic Vision.* New York: Macmillan Publishing Co., 1972.

Hattwick, Melvin S. "The Role of Pitch Level and Range in Singing of Preschool, First Grade and Second Grade Children," *Child Develp.,* 4:4 (1933), pp. 281–291.

Herberholz, Barbara. *Early Childhood Art.* Dubuque, Iowa: William C. Brown Publishers, 1974.

Jersild, A. T., and Sylvia F. Beinstock. "The Influence of Training on the Vocal Ability of Three-Year-Old Children," *Child Develop.,* 11:4 (1931), pp. 272–291.

Johnson, Harriet M. "The Art of Block Building," in *The Block Book,* edited by Elisabeth Hirsch. Washington, D.C.: NAEYC, 1974, pp. 9–24.

Kellogg, Rhoda, "Understanding Children's Art" in *Readings in Psychology Today,* 2nd ed. Del Mar, Calif.: CRM Books, 1972.

Moffitt, Mary W. *Woodworking for Children.* 196 Bleecker St., New York: Early Childhood Education Council of New York, 1972.

Nelson, Mary J., and G. Tipton. *Music in Early Childhood.* New York: Silver Burdette Co., 1952.

Nye, Vernice. *Music for Young Children.* New York: William C. Brown Co., 1975.

Pile, Naomi, *Art Experience for Young Children.* New York: Macmillan Publishing Co., 1973.

Seefeldt, Carol. "Art," in *Curriculum for the Preschool—Primary Child,* edited by Carol Seefeldt, Columbus, Ohio: Charles E. Merrill Publishing Co., 1976.

Shelley, Shirley J. "Music," in *Curriculum for the Preschool—Primary Child,* edited by Carol Seefeldt, Columbus, Ohio: Charles E. Merrill Publishing Co., 1976.

Stecher, Miriam B., and H. McElheny, *Music and Movement Improvisation.* Threshold Early Learning Library, Vol. 4. New York: Macmillan Publishing Co., 1972.

Stinson, Susan W. "Movement as Creative Interaction with the Child," *Young Children,* 32:6 (1977), pp. 49–53.

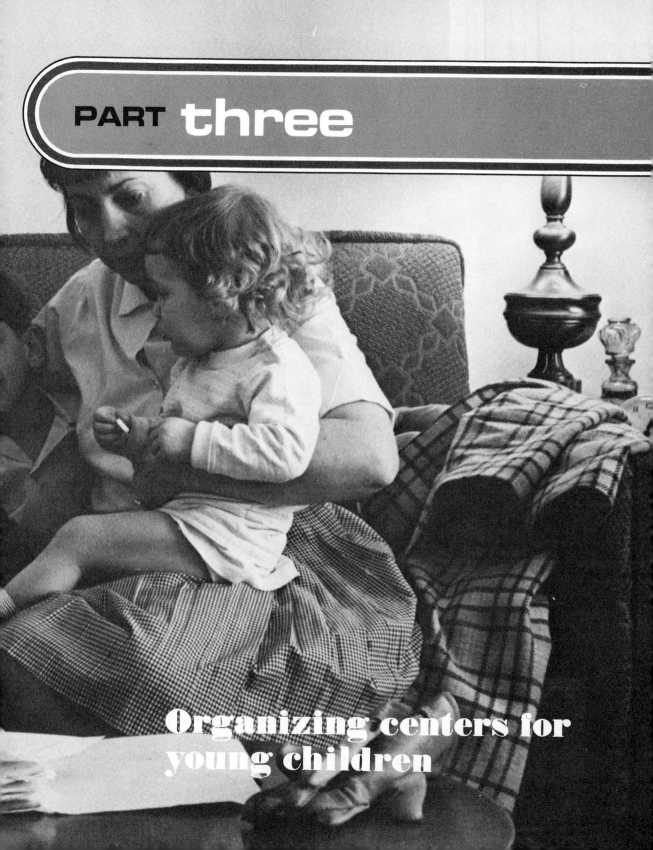

PART three

Organizing centers for young children

chapter 20

Involving parents as partners

In recent years the idea that parents play an important role in the education of their children has come to be accepted. Authors known to Early Childhood Educators and currently supporting this point of view are Bronfenbrenner[1] and Gordon.[2]

[1] U. Bronfenbrenner, "Reality and Research in the Ecology of Human Development," *Proceedings of the American Philosophical Association*, 119 (1975), pp. 433–469.

[2] I. J. Gordon, *On the Continuity of Development*, ACEI Position Paper (Washington, D.C.: ACEI, 1976).

THE CONCEPT OF PARENT INVOLVEMENT

Since the last revision of this text there have been important developments regarding the role of parents in the education of their young children. Perhaps the most important factor was political in nature resulting in a demand, growing out of the civil rights movement, on the part of low-income and minority groups that control of the education of their children be returned to them. This demand resulted from the fact that the public schools had failed to enable children of such groups to succeed in school and at the same time allow time to retain pride in their respective cultural heritage. A second factor was the mounting research evidence pointing to the importance of parent-child interactions in bringing about conditions, the exact variables of which are not yet clearly understood, that are necessary for the stimulation of early cognitive development. Theoretically, at least, such stimulation is necessary if children are to be able to cope with the expectations of the public schools.

So great was the conviction of the importance of the above factors that federally sponsored programs such as Head Start, Follow Through, and the Parent Child Center, mandated parent involvement. The implementation of these mandates varied from complete control, including conducting the instructional program itself, to more or less superficial participation in occasional meetings, invited classroom visits, and field trips. As a further safeguard to be sure parents were involved, half the members of Advisory Councils or Committees had to be parents of the children served. In theory, these groups had considerable power in making decisions regarding staffing, the nature of the program, and influence on administrative and supervisory matters. In practice, these groups often participated only to the extent of approving what those in charge wished them to approve. As time went on, with encouragement from consultative services provided to the programs, poor people were, for the first time, learning to have a part in the destiny of their children.

Although parent involvement certainly is educational in nature for parents, a clear distinction should be made between parent education and parent involvement, as the concept of parent education appears in much of the earlier educational literature. The term *parent education* connotes that the parents are learners being "taught." *Parent involvement* places stress on parents as teachers of their children and having a decision-making role in what should be taught and by whom. Implicit was the argument that children disadvantaged by racial discrimination and poverty have a cumulative deficit of early home and community experiences seemingly necessary for later academic success in the public schools. Hence the need arises for involvement of parents in the early and/or compensatory education of their children. However, there may be an "inherent contradiction between the arguments that have to do with cumulative deficit and those which support ethnic pride and self-determination for ghetto communities."[3] If the goal of later success in public school is to be reached, then parents must acquire the skills and strategies necessary to be the teachers of their young children. Accordingly, parent education and parent involvement cannot be independent of each other. This complex problem calls for innovation and change never before demanded of education.

Both the home and the school or center have important functions to serve in educating the child. Neither can work effectively without the understanding, support, and assistance of the other. Guiding the development of the child is a cooperative endeavor. The parent and the teacher or caregiver need to see whole child, as he or she reacts in life at school and at home in order to provide a complete program. The quality of the teacher-parent relationships during this early period will have an influence upon the child throughout the formative years.

The seeds of the point of view described at the beginning of this chapter had been sowed in earlier educational literature. However, the present concept of involvement, giving the parent a major role, had not evolved until recently.

During the past three decades, recognition of the importance of the changing role of parents in their relationships to the school has been pointed out by many educators. For example, in 1953 Hymes[4] stated,

> Home-school relations have two broad goals:
> To bring about a better understanding, between parents and leaders, of what children are like; and
> To bring about a better understanding, between teachers and parents, of good education.

He further states:[5]

> When these goals are achieved, parents and teachers work together as a united team, and youngsters gain in two ways:
>
> They have a richer, fuller, more nourishing life, in school and out, than otherwise would be open to them; and
>
> They have more consistent guidance in school and out; they stand a better chance of living up to the peak of their powers.

[3] Robert D. Hess, et al., "Parent Involvement in Early Education," in *Day Care: Resources for Decisions*, edited by Edith H. Grotberg (Washington, D.C.: Office of Economic Opportunity, 1971), p. 267.
[4] J. L. Hymes, Jr., *Effective Home-School Relations* (Englewood Clifs, N.J.: Prentice-Hall, 1953), p. 9.
[5] Ibid.

PARENTS AND TEACHERS WORK TOGETHER

Placing emphasis on parents and teachers working together, Washington[6] reports on an effective approach for helping urban children develop positive "I can" concepts. Paramount is a systematic approach designed to help parents improve their effectiveness as builders of self-esteem in their children. Enabling parents to accept responsibility as educators of their children, especially in the affective area, and to realize that success or failure in life for their children may depend on their effectiveness in this role is one of the major goals of the SUCCESS program.

Contact between parents and teacher should be a two-way process, from home to school and from school to home. In schools or centers where parent involvement is not required parents often feel the school should contact them and many times the teacher wishes the parents would invite her or him into the child's home for a friendly visit. Some teachers are hesitant to call the parents' attention to this need for partnership in working with the child, either because the teacher is rather inexperienced or the parent has given a false impression of dominance or lack of interest in discussing the child's development. The teacher may have given parents this false impression by being too impersonal, distant, or hurried. Some parents do not understand that the teacher is interested in the child's home life from the time he or she leaves school until his or her return, because it will assist the teacher in working with the child at school. As late as 1959 the concept that parents could have "correct" educational goals for their children seemed remote as indicated by the following quotation from Brim:

> The educator must know and state his own values, work with parents to do the same with theirs, assist in the achievement of those which are agreed upon, seek democratically to win the parent to his point of view, where they disagree, by rational persuasion, and, finally, withdraw and refuse to help where the parent insists on the pursuit of goals which the educator believes to be evil.[7]

Inadequate communication between school and home pertaining to aims or goals may hinder the continuous progress of the child.[8]

According to Leonard, Vandeman, and Miles, "When school and home enjoy understanding it is comparatively easy for one to approach the other in any individual or group situation that may exist. When teachers and parents discover ways of accomplishing common goals, and when their common activ-

---

[6] K. R. Washington, "SUCCESS: A Parent Effectiveness Approach for Developing Urban Children's Self Concepts," *Young Children*, 32:5 (July, 1977), pp. 5–10.

[7] O. G. Brim, Jr., *Education for Child Rearing* (New York: Russell Sage Foundation, 1959), p. 90.

[8] Grace Langdon and I. W. Stout, *Teacher-Parent Interviews* (Englewood Cliffs, N.J.: Prentice-Hall, 1954).

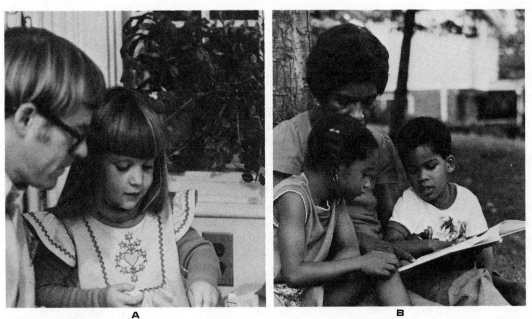

A   B

Figure 71

Parents play an important role in the education of their children.

ities are an essential part of the school, some sort of teacher-parent counseling system is already in operation."[9]

Parents and teachers can offer invaluable assistance to each other in their efforts to understand the child. Too often parents feel the teacher is the person who knows "all about children." The teacher may try to discover more about the child through his or her parents but might not quite know how to do this. Thus, each adult is seeking to know the other, but doesn't seem able to reach the other. Differences in educational, social, and economic levels may cause some parents and teachers to feel insecure in the presence of each other.

What appears to be parental indifference is often in reality insecurity and low self esteem. Thus, reaching and knowing such a parent may become a challenge to the teacher. Providing transportation, arranging meeting times suitable to the parents, avoiding formal meetings, and encouraging participation may be ways to involve such parents. The parents need to know the daily and weekly happenings that involve their child so that they may supplement and extend at home the experiences the child has at school. Most schools use a variety of procedures for the teacher and the parent to work together and to

[9] Edith M. Leonard, Dorothy D. Vandeman, and Lillian E. Miles, *Counseling with Parents in Early Childhood Education* (New York: Macmillan Publishing Co., 1954), p. 2.

keep the parent informed as to the activities planned for the year, as well as changes occurring in the weekly schedule.

In many programs these experiences are maximized when the parent has a part in the actual planning of the program. In others, parents work with the children as aides or volunteers. In some instances parents assume major instructional responsibilities after having served as aides and participated in "on the job" training. Many experimental and pilot projects, described elsewhere, have been developed with the principal goal being to assist parents to serve in the role of teacher of their own children. While the Cooperative preschool movement has flourished for several decades, one of its major goals was to provide preschool experiences for children at a modest cost to parents.

When parents are unfamiliar with the purpose and plan for the activities of the school, they may be suspicious of the total program. Since the parents will feel more comfortable if they know what is expected of them, the teacher may find many ways to keep them informed. Bulletin board displays are placed so as to be easily observed when the parent brings or comes for the child. Notices of meetings, lists of children for various group activities, menus for the day, special notices, displays of children's work, and interesting material for parents are posted and changed frequently so that the parent is challenged to stop, look, and read. Some teachers send short notes home with the children. These notes assist in keeping all parents informed of special events and unusual happenings; the note may even be on some particular item of interest related specifically to their child's activities.

Even though all parents are different, they are alike in their desire to secure the best education for their child. They may also share the fear that their child is not like other children. Many parents are concerned that they are not providing adequately for their child. They need assistance and guidance in understanding what to provide and what not to provide. The wise teacher utilizes these concerns and builds upon the similarity of parents as plans are made for parent meetings and group study. Since the program needs to be concerned about differing social status, it provides an excellent opportunity for parents and children to have social experiences that will make it possible for the children to learn to live and work together with people from different backgrounds.

Nedler[10] explains and directly attacks the problem of why parents do not participate more in parent–teacher endeavors. For some time now it has been known that "parents on the run" as Nedler puts it, simply cannot take part because of the time schedule traditionally used by schools. These parents are working or otherwise detained with family responsibilities at scheduled times. What Nedler's suggestions boil down to is the simple fact that if parents

[10] Shari Nedler, "Working with Parents on the Run," *Childhood Educ.*, 53:3 (January 1977), pp. 128–132.

are to participate in center or school activities schedules must be flexible and personalized enough to make the school or center personnel and facilities at night and during the weekends. This requires a commitment and a major re-scheduling of personnel.

PARENTS AND TEACHERS COMMUNICATE

Regardless of the type and goals of the center or school, its program will be greatly enhanced by maximum parent involvement and participation. The strategies suggested in the following several pages have been useful in many different types of situations in an attempt to improve parent-teacher-child understandings and relationships.

Sheehy states that, "Person'-to-person and day-by-day relationships are important, not only in their immediate results, but they affect the entire school and community. Organizations are important and necessary but, as long as teachers continue to 'speak' to parents and parents to teachers, there will be no gaps to bridge between the school and the community."[11] Teachers and parents communicate in many ways including the following:

Home visits

Too often plans are made for the parents to come to the school for a visit and yet no recognition is given to the need for the teacher to become acquainted with the child in his own home. A family interview, in order to fill out a child's history, is a helpful way to learn the home surroundings. The child becomes better acquainted with the teacher by actually seeing her or him visit in the child's home. The parent is more at ease in familiar surroundings and more apt to verbalize problems or questions. The teacher gains much through actually seeing how the family lives and how they feel about sending the child to school. Insight into feelings between family members may result from such a home visit. Teachers usually find a home visit will be more profitable if (a) the visit is arranged at the convenience of the parents, (b) there is adequate time for both teacher and parent to talk uninterruptedly, and (c) the child is playing nearby where he can be observed, yet not always within hearing distance of the adults' discussion.

Home visits before the child enters school are valuable for the teacher and the parent in becoming acquainted and in giving insight into the background of the child. A friendly social visit will make the child, as well as the parent,

---

[11] Emma D. Sheehy, *The Fives and Sixes Go to School* (New York: Holt, Rinehart and Winston, 1954), p. 356.

more comfortable on the first day at school. The visit will make the child feel important in the eyes of the teacher, and it will help him or her to feel secure as the circle of peers at school is enlarged.

Today, thousands of children have had one, two, or more years of preschool group experience before entering public kindergarten or first grade. In Home Start, Head Start, Parent Child Centers, and similar type programs, much of the instructional program will have been carried out in the home by the staff members as well as by the parents themselves. Wise public school leadership will find ways to continue this close working relationship with parents. Otherwise, there is a real danger of alienating parents to the extent that children accustomed to having their parents as partners in their education may well lose some of the gains made earlier.

School visits

The parent, accompanied by the child, needs to visit before the child enters to become acquainted with the facilities and to encourage the child to anticipate entering the program. These visits also make it possible for the parent to learn about the program and to assist the teacher in orienting the child to her or his first days at school.

Communication between parents and teacher needs to be encouraged when the parent brings the child to school each morning. Some teachers give parents the impression that it is not necessary or desirable for the parent to remain at school. Thus, the parent gradually builds up the feeling that it is not good to linger or to spend a part of a day in the school. When this results, communication has broken down between teacher and parent. The parent should be encouraged to stay long enough to see that the child is engaged in an activity, then leave.

Too often the personnel give the impression that they feel parents are prying into their activities. Not only do the parents have the right, but they also have the responsibility to know what the school is doing for the child and how the school plans to develop its program. Both the teacher and the parent may gain further insight into the child's behavior through a conference held soon after a visit or planned observation. Scheduling the visits so that only one child's parents observe and visit the school on a given day will be more profitable and less disturbing to the children and the activities under the teacher's direction, than if several parents visit on the same day. The teacher needs to (a) develop an understanding of the place for and the importance of a planned visit to the school, (b) plan ahead, setting the actual time and date of the visit, (c) plan the procedures for the visit with both the child and the parent, and (d) provide for free time to discuss the child's activities as the parent observes the child or at an early time shortly after the visit. If a simple observation guide in the form of suggestions for the visit is provided, the parent will feel more comfortable and the first observations may be more profitable. Soon parents will feel less dependent on an extrinsic factor. However, these written suggestions may be profitable at each visit, if they are planned to point out certain phases and aspects of the program or to assist the parents in gaining deeper insight into their child's development as he or she works, plays, and lives in a school situation. Some teachers do not find it desirable to prepare an observation guide; they prefer to make accessible pad and pencil so that the parents may jot down questions or comments to be discussed later in the follow-up conference.

For example, one teacher planned for parent observations to follow a group meeting that was devoted to the specific topic, "The Child's Adjustment at School." Following a discussion of the topic, the teacher talked with the parents about planned observations at school and distributed "guides" pointing out various aspects of adjustment to be observed. A school visit was then scheduled for each parent, to be followed by an individual conference.

Telephone conversations

Frequently a telephone conversation is thought to substitute for a scheduled conference. Like casual visits, these conversations make a definite contribution and have a place in communicating with parents. Minor routine situations, unexpected developments such as illness or a visit to the doctor, or some item which the teacher does not wish to discuss before the child may be discussed on the telephone. Scheduled conferences can be confirmed by the teacher with the parent in a telephone conversation, especially if the parent does not have the opportunity or does not avail herself or himself of the privilege of casual contacts.

Casual visits

Parents communicate much information to the teacher and to other parents as they bring children to school or call for them later. The teachjer can secure many cues as to a child's behavior and parent's attitude through analyzing remarks made in these casual contacts. It is necessary for the teacher to be alert to these cues because they may aid in gaining insight into how to work most profitably with the child during the day. The mother who states "We are running late this morning, we all overslept as we had unexpected relatives arrive late last night," may be giving many hints of how this will affect her child's day at school. These contacts also give the teacher an opportunity to comment to the parent about the child. For example, she or he may say, "Janie seemed tired today. Did she watch television after her bedtime last night?" or, "Jimmy sang alone in music today."

The value of casual contacts should not be underestimated; they make a significant contribution to the parent-teacher relationship by establishing rapport, paving the way and providing a means for scheduling the planned conference at a later date. Through these contacts, the teacher, the parent, and the child share moments of unified interest and learn to talk freely, one with the other.

Planned conferences

Through these frequent, casual contacts, many so-called conferences are held by parents and teacher. However, they should not replace the scheduled conference. Sometimes teachers feel that it is not necessary to hold regularly scheduled conferences if they know the family and can develop an understanding of the child's home background through these informal discussions. Too often the true feelings of the parent, or the teacher, or the child, may not be revealed in a casual visit; the problems needing discussion may be of the nature that the parent and the teacher do not wish those nearby to overhear. In addition, the teacher has not had time to study the child's record and to prepare for the conference, and the time is too limited to discuss problems, plans, purposes, procedures, progress, and follow-up activities. Many more areas can be discussed, recorded information studied, and feelings communicated in a planned conference.

The teacher needs to build an understanding of the need for and the purpose of a regular conference with the parent, whether it be held only once during the year or more often. Each child as an individual needs to be carefully considered and some tentative plans made by the teacher prior to the conference in order to discuss progress with the parents. Types of records are discussed in detail in Chapter 21, "Recording the Development of Children." An individual folder for each child is recommended in which the teacher may insert short notes from time to time. Many teachers keep a written account of a child's reactions, achievements, and problems during the day; these are added to the collection in the folder. By reviewing each child's folder frequently, a teacher can discover children for whom there have accumulated valuable materials and those for whom there is little information. For the latter, the teacher needs to plan for closer observation and recording of information so that a conference about such a child may have more meaning. The teacher may have recorded little about some children because of being absorbed in helping a difficult child or one who is more interesting. Through analyzing the children's records, the teacher can plan to balance her or his time and attention to record activities of all children.

The planned conference should be a two-way affair in which the parent may not only learn of the child's progress, but may also have an opportunity to discuss differences of beliefs and procedures relative to working with the child. In many instances the child may not have made much progress or change. Although the teacher recognizes the child as a growing, maturing individual, there are times when there appears to be little or no growth or change. The parent may not understand that this is satisfactory progress for the child at this time. The teacher needs to interpret what the behavior in the school situation means to the total growth of children.

Many teachers ask how they can actually communicate with a parent in a conference. A teacher needs to:

Recognize that each parent is an individual with personal needs, attitudes, values, and beliefs and accept the parent as a person even though differing with his or her beliefs.

Accept her or his responsibility to plan and prepare for the conference by organizing thoughts and materials prior to the conference.

Arrange for a place for the conference where there will be no interruptions.

Provide uninterrupted time and give the impression of being unhurried and interested in the child and the parent and of being informed as to goals for the progress of the child.

Be warmly accepting of what the parent has to contribute.

Be honest and truthful; keep personal feelings, facial expressions out of the situation and avoid appearing shocked.

Listen and find out why the parent feels or thinks as he or she does.

Encourage the parent to work out possible ways of meeting problems.

Avoid destructive criticism.

Allow time for changed thinking, do not force thinking or advice on parent.

Remember that the conference should be kept strictly confidential and treat a parental or child problem in confidence.

Conclude the conference on a helpful and professional basis, by questioning what suggestions the parent has for follow-through or further work with the child at school, as well as planning with the parent for home activities and for future conferences.

Reassure the parent that the teacher and the parent are partners in planning for and working with the child at all times.

The teacher can communicate by means of such phrases as "Have you noticed how well Susan can walk the planks now?" or "I have been so proud of Harold lately, he is beginning to share the tricycle more readily." The way a teacher phrases staements and the tone of voice used will assist her or him in talking easily and profitably with any parent, and especially with one who may be on the defensive worrying over what problems the teacher has encountered with his or her child.

Since communication between teachers and parents is a two-way process, the following positive suggestions may assist adults in gaining insight into relationships with each other.

Show genuine interest in the child.
Avoid being authoritative or too "teaching."
Avoid arguments, becoming defensive over the way activities are carried through.
Listen for small cues about the child, then ask for clarification of certain points.
Avoid labeling or jumping to conclusions too quickly.
Offer several suggestions as to action rather than just telling what to do.
Attempt to arrive at some conclusions or points to be carried through by all concerned.

OBSERVATION FORM FOR PARENT

A short observation form may be helpful to both the teacher and the parent to use as a guide in a conference after the parent has observed the children in a group situation. A tentative form that chould be useful follows.

AIMS OF THE PARENT OBSERVATION

1. To understand what children are like who are the same age as your child.
2. To know the daily schedule and the why's of various activities.
3. To learn how the teacher guides each child.
4. To attain insights as your child relates to the other children.

As you observe, try to be objective and avoid seeking out your child. Instead observe as many children as you can. Think of this experience as a learning one, stay in the background, write down questions or points as they occur. A planned conference will follow your observation.

POINTS TO OBSERVE

1. Observe the teacher in a variety of activities.
   a. Note how children's questions are answered.
   b. Watch how she or he relates to each child, what is said and done.
   c. How is she or he alert to any and all situations?
   d. How is the group guided smoothly into other activities?
   e. How are difficult situations handled?
2. Would you have handled activities in the same way or what would you have done differently? Why?
3. Observe certain children other than your own.
   Note the following:
   a. How they respond to other children. Examples of sharing, trying to join a group, difficult behavior.
   b. How independent are they in activities?
   c. Are there special abilities shown by certain children in art, music?
   d. Use of language, number of questions.
   e. Length of time the child stays with an activity.

Study groups

A group of parents and teachers may wish to plan a few short discussion groups whereby all may study various aspects of child development or behavior. These groups may meet weekly or monthly, usually in a series consisting of planned meetings. One of the teachers who has been successful with group discussions may wish to begin the planning, leading, and organizing of such a group.

A few parents think that they or their child are the only ones who have a certain problem. Parents often find it very reassuring to discuss common problems. Most study groups have difficulty in finding a suitable meeting time because today's parents are so involved with many outside activities. The success of such a series of discussions comes from finding out ahead of time when the majority who are interested in a given problem can meet. Good leadership is very important. Interesting topics for discussion that will appeal to all attending will avoid turning the discussion into an information type of service. Adults benefit more from study through discussion groups because they have actually participated and voiced opinions, as well as shared experiences.

The planned parent meeting

Many teachers plan meetings regularly to bring parents and teachers together. Some of these parent meetings are planned according to the recommendation of the National Congress of Parents and Teachers; whereas others are initiated only by the program personnel. The purpose of a meeting may be to communicate school policies to parents, to let adults know what the daily program may be or what types of activities or seasonal events are planned, to view a good film, to hear an authority on some phase of child development, or to hold a meeting to get parent input on policy matters.

To hold the continued interest of the parent who previously has had children in school can be a challenge. If meetings become repetitious with little attention paid to the needs of parents, low attendance can be expected. Few fathers can attend parent meetings if they are at inconvenient times. A short social period designed to see that all parents become acquainted will help provide more and better meetings.

Some program personnel may feel it is only necessary to have a meeting of parents at the beginning of the year to "inform the parents" of various policies and another meeting at the end of the school year as a demonstration ceremony "to show the parents" how the child can perform. Such demonstrations may be overstimulating to children and really serve little purpose. Graduation ceremonies for young children may have meaning to adults but hold no place in good programs for young children.

The most successful meetings are ones in which parents help plan and actually participate in the meeting itself. A questionnaire sent home to parents with a list of topics as an "interest finder" may provide helpful information for a parent committee in organizing these meetings. It is important that all the members have an opportunity at the first meeting to list problems according to interests and to plan an agenda of topics. Usually a series of five or six discussion or study meetings will hold the interest better than a large number. Some topics that might lead to continuing group discussion are: Helping Children Learn to Share; How to Prepare the Preschool Child for the Arrival of a New Baby; The Grandparents' Role in the Child's Home; Facing Crises in the Home. The presentation of mental health plays related to one of these topics adds interest and variety.

To provide good group discussion, it may be advisable to utilize additional human or material resources. Advance planning with members to bring in pertinent material or information about a topic, circulating reading material ahead of time, using bulletin board displays prior to the day of the meeting of the study group, are essential activities for the leader's preparation to produce a good flow of discussion from all members.

Parent participation

There are innumerable areas in the school's activities in which the parents can enrich the curriculum. Some parent participation will extend and enrich the school experiences; however, the type and the amount of the participation should be carefully considered so that the amount of the parent activity does not usurp the authority or the leadership of the teacher. Areas in which parent participation is particularly helpful include storytelling, music and art activities, field trips, group parties and picnics, library activities, celebration of special events or holidays, and parent work-parties. Or a parent could be a resource person in a specialized area or activity. As the parents work and talk together with the teacher and the children, they develop a greater interest in and a deeper understanding of the program. In each group of children there will be some parents who have special talents or hobbies and who have the time and facilities to profitably enrich the lives of all the children through use of this talent. Opportunities for all parents to contribute in a variety of activities will build pride in the child's heritage and appreciation of the worth and dignity of all occupations.

In the parent-cooperative school it is expected that each parent will participate at specific times during the week as an assistant teacher. In all the participation of adults in programs for young children, a plan of weekly discussions between the directing teacher and the parents is essential for good management.

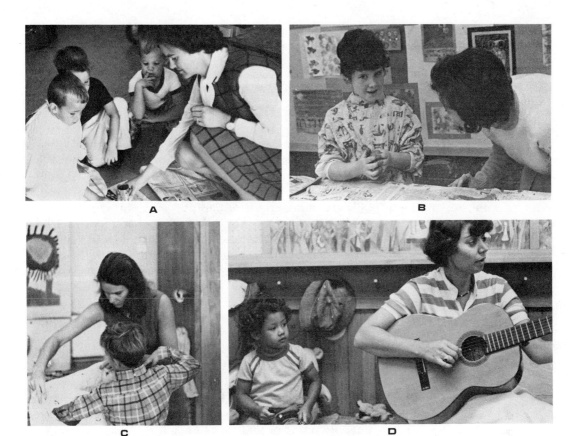

Figure 72
Parent participation can enrich and extend the school's activities.

Parents may feel inferior to their child's teacher. The teacher may need to involve the parents in certain ways in order to know them better and to help them feel more at ease. Learning the skills and abilities of the parents can be a beginning in knowing the parents. A parent who plays a musical instrument or who has a special talent as well as the one who is willing to share in other ways may feel more needed. A broader concept of parent involvement has evolved with Head Start. Parents participate not only as helpers and in parent meetings, but also in decision making that involves certain policies and that concerns the program as related to their own children. Included is the parents' responsibility for carrying out the program both at home and school so that each supplements and supports the other. Additional suggestions may be found in Chapters 7 and 8.

In some regions, non-English speaking parents may need interpretation through a teacher skilled in their language. Also, adult classes in English may have to be arranged. A number of programs for parents that have been successful are described by several supervisors of parent education in certain California schools.[12]

FACILITIES AND MATERIALS FOR PARENTS

A special room for parents at the school where they may spend time looking over books or other materials is important as a parent center for many occasions. In such a room several parents may visit together or a parent conference can be held. Children's art work or other creative achievements can be displayed, or a lending library of materials for parents can be arranged.

Many Directors and Principals have found that rooms used for other purposes, such as storage of obsolete and unused equipment, outdated materials, or just "trash" in general can be easily converted for parent use. In these days of declining enrollments in elementary schools finding space is usually not difficult if the program is housed in either an unused school or in one currently in use for school purposes.

Parents should be given a free hand, within fire and safety requirements, in making the room attractive and suitable for their activities. The addition of newspapers, clipping and filmstrip files, tape recorders and, if possible, the use of a video camera and projector, at least on a scheduled basis, and a radio and a television set will add hominess to such a room. Records and a record player, instructional kits, and any specially developed instructional materials will add significance to, and interest, in the program.

The more the parents are made to feel that the facilities and the program belong to them (as in reality they do) the greater the chances of active participation on their part. One parent should be in charge of scheduling. It is just as important that program personnel get permission to use parent facilities as it is for parents to schedule the use of facilities used by program personnel.

Newsletters

Some programs send out weekly or monthly newsletters to parents; others distribute letters semiannually. As parents and teachers work together on this project, they will find that sharing experiences can be meaningful.

Brochures and bulletins as well as the informal newsletter have an important place in keeping parents informed and assisting them to understand and assume responsibility for extending the child's school experiences so that

[12] Milton Babitz, "Serving Families of the Underprivileged," *Calif. Educ.*, 11:3 (1964), pp. 17–19.

there is no conflict of goal or method between the home and the school. Through these brochures, parents learn about school policies related to school entrance, size of groups, purposes, special services, fees, health provisions, school calendar and plans for parent contacts, participation and visits, as well as of special activities scheduled throughout the year. Printed or mimeographed bulletins assist in interpreting the school program and in building understanding of the purpose and plan for the activities in the school year. Special bulletins can be prepared as new developments indicate a need; for example, during an epidemic a bulletin might give information and policies relating to school attendance or it might serve the purpose of informing the parents that their child had been exposed to a certain disease and indicate procedures to be observed in safeguarding the child and other children.

GUIDE FOR PARENTS IN SELECTING A PROGRAM

A parent's selection of a program for a child under six years of age should be regarded as an important decision in terms of what will contribute most effectively to mental, social, physical, and emotional development. The task is a difficult one as there are no set standards or guarantees as to the qualifications of the program personnel. Here is a list of generally accepted information of use to parents in identifying suitable programs for their children.

PURPOSE

Is the primary purpose to provide a program that fosters the total development of the child?

PROGRAM

Is the primary purpose of the program to provide an organized, continuous experience suited to the maturity level and growth pattern of the children attending?

Is the program so designed that regular continuous attendance is expected of each child?

Does the program provide for continuous uninterrupted growth of the child as he or she progresses to other units within the center and to units outside the center?

Are the records of each child systematically kept and available to the next unit?

Is the period scheduled for operation adequate for such a program?

Does the daily period of operation require additional plans for child care? If so, are these planned to be developmental, and are additional staff and facilities provided for this service?

Are there adequate provisions for the planned educational program? Health program? Nutritional program? Social services?

PERSONNEL

Are the adults in charge professionally competent?

Do teachers meet the certification requirements for specialization in early childhood education?

Are associates, aides, and volunteers utilized?

Is the adult-child ratio adequate so that individual and group experiences are provided for young children under proper guidance?

FACILITIES

Is the center easily accessible?

Is adequate space indoors and outdoors provided?

Are facilities carefully maintained according to best practices for health and sanitation?

Are adequate and appropriate equipment and materials provided?

HEALTH AND SAFETY

Are there adequate provisions for health and safety?

Are food services available, adequately supervised, and sanitary?

Is the food nutritious?

Are health records kept of employees and children?

What plans are made for children who become ill at school or center?

SPECIAL SERVICES

What types of special services are provided?

How are these offered?

Are persons rendering this service fully qualified and certified?

Parents and teachers will find discussions of these questions in Parts II and III of this book.

SUMMARY

The happiest and most successful teacher is the one who regards parents as partners and friends in the program of educating the child. Many feel this goal can best be met by ensuring parents of a larger role in determining and carrying out the educational experiences of their young children. Parents have become active partners with schools and centers in the early education of their children. Instructional materials and strategies designed to be carried out in the home, or begun in the center or school and continued in the home, have become a major influence in early education. Parents working with professionals on advisory committees, or as aides, volunteers, or teachers have become a vital force in Early Childhood Education. These innovations, resulting mainly from research findings indicating parent-child interaction as an essential ingredient of early foundation cognitive development, and the desire of minority group parents to have more control of their children's educational opportunities have placed new and major responsibilities on families, particularly on the parents of low-income families. In turn, the need for further education of the parents themselves has increased. Child Development Centers and schools for young children are becoming true partnership ventures with parents sharing equal responsibilities with staff personnel.

As children enter the traditional public kindergarten and first grade it is important that these responsibilities continue to be shared. Some of the ways to enhance this sharing are home visits, school visits, establishment of parent advisory committees, telephone conversations, casual visits, planned conferences, study groups and parent meetings, parent participation in the classroom, sharing of materials designed for parents, and periodic newsletters and other evaluative materials.

The outcome of early education may well rest primarily on the success or failure of parent involvement in the programs. Every good teacher hopes to help each child with whom she or he works and to challenge the child to learn and to prepare for more complex tasks. These desires are fundamentally the same as those of the parents. The task of the school is one of finding ways through which the drive to reach the goals of both groups may be integrated into a common endeavor.

Suggested Activities

1. Interview a Child Development Center, nursery school, or kindergarten teacher as to the procedure used in making home visits or holding parent conferences. Determine the frequency of such visits, the attitude of the teacher concerning them. From this interview, evaluate your own feelings in regard to the necessity of holding these visits or conferences.
2. Attend a parent meeting held by a Child Development Center, nursery school, or kindergarten. Observe the reactions of parents and note types of questions asked by parents. Determine frequency of meetings and types of usual programs. Evaluate these meetings.
3. Observe the teacher–parent contacts when children are brought to the center, nursery school, or kindergarten or when children are called for at the close of the school session. Note types of information obained through such contacts for further insight into children's actions at school or center.
4. Study the parent bulletin board and parent bookshelf provided in a school for young children and make a report of your findings to the group.
5. Attend a Child Development Center, nursery school, or kindergarten Parent Advisory Council meeting. Determine the degree to which parents are involved in the control of their children's education.
6. Request permission to participate with parents (playing the role of a parent) in the parent program of the school or center in whcih you are a practicum student or stu-

dent teacher. Report to the class on how effective you think the program is and why. List strengths and weaknesses.

Related Readings

Brutten, M., Sylvia Richardson, and C. Mangel. *A Parent's Book About Children with Learning Disabilities.* New York: Harcourt, Brace, Jovanovich, 1973.

Duff, R. Eleanor, Martha C. Heinz, and Charlena Husband. "Toy Lending Library: Additional Mode for Parent-Child-Teacher Interaction. *Young Children* (Spring 1978).

Grams, A. *Parenting: Concept and Process.* Washington, D.C.: ACEI, 1973.

Hartman, Harriet. *Let's Play and Learn.* New York: Human Sciences Press, 1976.

Lane, Mary B. *Education for Parenting.* Washington, D.C.: NAEYC, 1975.

Lazar, J. B., and I. A. Chapman. *Review of the Present Status and Future Needs of Programs to Develop Parenting Skills.* Washington, D.C.: Social Research Group, George Washington University, April 1972.

"Learning From Parents," *Child. Educ.,* 48:3 (1971), entire issue.

Schaefer, E. S. "Parents as Educators: Evidence from Cross-Sectional, Longitudinal, and Intervention Research," *Young Children,* 27:4 (1972), pp. 227–239.

Swick, K. J. "The Parenting Team: Concept-Process-Product. *Dimensions* (February 1978).

———, and R. Eleanor Duff. *The Parent-Teacher Bond: Relating-Responding-Rewarding.* Dubuque, Iowa: Kendall-Hunt Publishing Co., 1978.

"Who's Raising the Kids: the Parent Gap?" *Newsweek* (Sept. 22, 1975), cover story.

Recording the development of children

With the present emphasis on accountability, Management by Objectives, and preplanning in terms of assessed needs, it is imperative that Early Childhood Education personnel be skilled in record keeping, especially in being objective as to what is recorded. The Freedom of Information Act requires that all school records be available to the individual or families on request, unless this right is waived in writing. This makes it desirable that record-keeping be a joint venture, with the parents of each child always being informed or consulted whenever permanent entries are made. Parents should always be a part of deciding what is to be recorded and why.

The best possible time to obtain accurate information, not only concerning a child but also regarding the child's family background, is during the preschool years. Teacher or other personnel and parents feel a closer bond of responsibility for the young child at that time. Never again will the parents express personal feelings, family problems, and other concerns so freely. A careful record, not in scores or numbers alone, but also in accurate, descriptive anecdotes, accounts of actual happenings, and of what is being observed or said will provide the basis later for each child's cumulative school file. Such records have proven of inestimable value to the child's teachers and other school personnel during later school years. All personnel concerned with young children should be skilled in record-keeping and in the ability to share the child's strengths, weaknesses, and needs with parents and other professionals working with the child.

WHAT SHOULD BE RECORDED

Consistent with changing points of view, what is considered as the most important information to know about a child's development has changed drastically during the past decade. Not only has new terminology come into the picture, but new concepts of evaluation have evolved. The use of tests and direct measurement continues, and searches for more meaningful ways of determining behavioral and growth changes are emerging. The search goes on because the traditional IQ and achievement test scores, although valuable, inadequately furnish information needed to justify the cost of intervention or early start programs. As in all phases of business and industry, such concepts as cost analysis and accountability have found their way into the educational world. With early education a high priority area of education, early childhood education has not escaped the demands of lawmakers and parents for accountability. Early attempts using test results have failed to meet the criteria for success needed for continued support of early education programs. After a review of commonly accepted educational rationale for record keeping, the above concepts and their implementation will be treated in more detail later in this chapter.

Many feel that permanent records should not be kept, especially if behavior of a personal nature is recorded. They argue that anyone reading these records later will likely be biased by them and thus actual harm to the child involved might result. Yet no one argues in this manner when physicians record events of a personal nature. The medical profession has long recognized the value of the developmental medical record. Child development specialists, too, know their value. The crux of the matter is that teachers who are truly professional know the importance of the past behavioral development of the children they teach. A child with special problems, even if these are no longer present, may need certain kinds of treatment if the problems are not to recur. Sound curriculum development is always based on the variation present in the needs of each group of children involved. Without a record of what has taken place in the past, the teacher is at a distinct disadvantage. The necessity of accuracy in recording thus becomes evident.

Because development and developmental changes occur so rapidly during the early childhood years, a carefully kept developmental record is essential in planning and providing the best possible activities, learning experiences, and opportunities for the health, safety, and well-being of each child. A teacher or caregiver, knowing that a child walked a little later, or learned to talk somewhat slower than most children, will not have as high expectations in activities involving fine muscular control or language fluency as she or he will have for certain other children. In discussing problems of this type with parents, the teacher probably will learn of the parent's concern and be able to suggest ways in which the parent can be more accepting, thus reducing obstacles to the child's healthy personal or self-development.

INFORMATION FOR PARENTS

The importance of parent-teacher conferences has been recognized and is discussed in Chapter 20. However, the value of a written record of the conference is often overlooked. While teachers find it difficult at times, it is desirable to send to the parents by first-class mail a summary report of periodic parent–teacher conferences. Such letters may, of necessity, omit certain confidential information. Parents find this procedure very helpful and the school copy becomes a valuable part of the child's record.[1] Copies of these letters; health reports including immunization, illnesses, and annual physical examination results; family background file; and the informal type of observations mentioned earlier provide the best possible type of record keeping during the early childhood years. Formal or uniform printed report cards, though often used, probably have little or no place in the preschool program.

The Space Age has already had its impact on early childhood education. There are those who believe that education, particularly reading, should be formalized as early as two or three years of age (see p. 242). Advocates cite the urgency of the times as necessitating immediate and large-scale action in which expediency sometimes takes priority. Only a careful evaluation of each child's abilities and developmental status can provide an adequate basis on which the teacher can judge when children possess a sufficient readiness for specific experiences such as beginning reading. The harmful effects, from a

[1] LaMittice Pearson, "Reaction of Teachers and Parents to the Letter-Summary Method Used for Reporting Parent-Teacher Conferences at the Florida State University Nursery School," unpublished Seminar Study, The Florida State University Institute of Human Development, Tallahassee, 1956.

mental health point of view, of forcing learning experiences too early have long been known. Because readiness is releated to maturation and development rather than chronological age, some children can benefit from certain experiences long before the majority of children of the same age. Guidance, based on observed facts, is as important during the early years as later; thus evaluation based on careful study and records of such evaluation becomes an important responsibility of those guiding young children. Program personnel must now become aware, more than ever before, of the importance of child study as a branch of science and the contributions that have and can be made.

WHY RECORDS ARE NECESSARY

Innovation in program development often brings about changes in procedures, materials used, and teaching strategies employed. Furthermore, all of the above are apt to change from time to time as programmers discover "what is working" or "what is not working." This fact mandates careful recording at all times for more or less continuous decision making.

STUDYING YOUNG CHILDREN

Present-day educational philosophy and practice stress the importance of providing a curriculum, not only in keeping with the goals and purposes of the school, but also in keeping with the ability, growth, and development of the children involved. This implies that the teacher must, at all times, know a great deal about, and understand the motivations of the children taught. This is particularly true of teachers of young children, for important changes occur rapidly at this age. Following the work of Freud, "the present century has witnessed a shift to intensive investigations of early childhood from many theoretical points of view because of a realization of the importance of this period to later development and behavior."[2]

Colleges and universities were quick to see the value of having organized educational programs with young children for research purposes as well as for teacher education purposes. These laboratory and research programs necessitated extensive record keeping, often burdening teachers and students with the task of recording "everything observable."

Today, records are kept for specific purposes. The teacher in a nonresearch school must ask, "What is it that should be known about each child and why?

[2] R. L. Witherspoon, "Studying Young Children," *Nursery School Portfolio*, Leaflet 9 (Washington, D.C.: ACEI, 1961), p. 1.

What should be known about a child's family, neighborhood, health history, personal characteristics, or playmates?" Such questions must be answered and interpreted in terms of the program's purposes and goals. When this procedure is followed, it is likely that no two schools will keep identical records. While records of young children will have much in common, more extensive recording will be required for some children than for others. Although a school may wish to use a standard form for common information about all its children, it must also provide the necessary flexibility in record keeping to enable planning for maximum opportunities for each individual child. Over-standardization of records is probably as undesirable as standard reporting forms in Early Childhood Education programs. In no way should this "be construed as an effort to depreciate the value of good records and reports. In fact, it may necessitate a new look at how and what to record."[3]

Murphy and research collaborators at Sarah Lawrence College presented a detailed study of one child as a sample of normal childhood.[4] This is an excellent example of the difficulty and complexity of the task of assessing and understanding personality development. Study of such materials will enable one to appreciate not only the importance of, but also the care that should be exercised, in gathering and recording information that will be of value in understanding children. A conscientious and continuous effort on the part of the teacher to learn more about each child in the group is essential to a good educational program for young children. Because memory cannot always be relied on to produce accurate recall of important events or the recurrence of significant behavioral incidents, a recording system is necessary. As previously pointed out, such a system must have flexibility to be effective.

HOW TO RECORD

Obviously, everything that happens cannot be recorded. What is recorded, in addition to basic identification information and objective data such as height, weight, health immunizations, and similar materials, will be determined largely by the purpose of the school. Each item recorded should include the date, time, and place, and the name of the person recording. If the program is one of the usual university or college laboratory schools, the information will be organized in keeping with the needs of observing and participating students. The teacher should plan with the students' instructors so that the records will serve a useful purpose in the college classes as well as assist the teacher in an understanding of each child and his or her needs.

If the program serves as a research laboratory, the records will be kept to

---

[3] Ibid.
[4] Lois Barclay Murphy, *Personality in Young Children*, Vol. II (New York: Basic Books, 1956).

satisfy the demands of the particular research being undertaken at the time. Witherspoon indicates that:[5]

> An understanding of approaches used will make the research process more intelligent and provide better results. . . . An experiment may seek only a single, often minute, clue which when fitted into existing or proposed theories may set off a chain reaction of efforts needed in understanding children. A teacher or parent cannot usually be expected to do research, but cooperation with those who are trained to and whose work it is to do research can benefit all concerned.

Summarizing observations of children playing with miniature life toys, Hartley, Frank, and Goldenson have concluded:[6]

> These detailed records have unique value for studying the child at leisure, for checking impressionistic opinions against factual data, and for focusing several minds on a single problem without subjecting the child to intolerable scrutiny.

Many approaches to studying children have been proposed, each demanding different information and different types of records. Witherspoon states the present trend as follows:[7]

> Many students and teachers are finding a problem approach to child study more challenging and profitable than the traditional directed observation, case studies, cumulative records and testing "programs." New insights into individual children and individual parent or teacher motivations will be discovered when a group of teachers undertakes, for example, a study of the development of responsibility in children. When teachers and parents respond to a questionnaire prepared cooperatively and dealing with what they expect of children, they may be surprised to find that they are not in agreement. When children are asked to answer the same questions in relation to the expectations of home and school, more surprises may be expected. Such evidence provides excellent information for individual teacher-parent conferences, parent group discussions, and individual stock-taking by teachers. Getting ready to read, eating patterns, using free time, learning to be friends, what school life is like, leadership and later underachieving, and homework are only a few problems which make interesting "springboards" for studying young children.

The instructional process in the various areas of the curriculum is facilitated by a continuous record of the activities each child engages in. In order to insure a balance among the activities in which each child participates, the teacher keeps a record of his or her choices. A duplicated summary form containing the names of children and activities usually available provides a simple procedure for checking each child's participation. Samples of each child's paintings, crayon drawings, and so on, and teacher-made sketches of the re-

---

[5] Witherspoon, op. cit., p. 3.
[6] Ruth E. Hartley, L. K. Frank, and R. M. Goldenson, *New Play Experiences for Children* (New York: Columbia University Press, 1952), p. 49.
[7] Witherspoon, op. cit., p. 2.

sults of participation in construction activities, along with dates and teacher comments, become a valuable part of the child's cumulative file.

MANAGEMENT BY OBJECTIVES

In the early 1970s, the national Head Start Office mandated that all Head Start programs be implemented by a system of operation known as Management by Objectives. Thus, a behavioral model of methods common to business and industry was adapted to child development programs for young children on a large scale in compensatory, intervention, pilot, and research situations. Many other educational programs are, and have been, based on the same model, which places considerable stress on the prior development of behavioral objectives.This simply means that if the teacher or the research staff is to be able to assess the effectiveness of the program efforts, the teacher must know prior to instruction what the end result of that instruction is expected to be. She or he must be able to observe, or otherwise be able to show, the degree to which each objective has been achieved. For example, if the stated objective is for each child to be able to recognize his or her name in print by the middle of the kindergarten year, the teacher (or test examiner) can arrange situations at midyear that will indicate whether each child recognizes his or her name.

Starting with a set of generalized goals such as ability to classify objects by size, color, and form, the teacher then determines which specific concepts— like big, little, red, blue, round, square, and so on—the child must know in order to achieve the larger goal. Once these specific objectives are spelled out and placed in order of difficulty, teaching strategies and materials are devised to enable the child to experience and thus learn each of the specific concepts necessary to the achievement of the larger goal.

Formative and Summative Evaluation. It is necessary, at any point in time during the above process, to assess where each child is, if instruction is to be meaningful and efficient. As the rate of achievement will vary from child to child, it is essential that daily records be kept. If the objectives have been clearly defined, arranged in a sequence to fit the planned strategies, and available in multiple copies (one for each other), record keeping is greatly simplified. All the teacher has to do is enter the date after each item when it is achieved by each particular child. This is a type of "formative" evaluation and eventually becomes a record of "summative" evaluation. Formative evaluation takes place "while the course or instructional program is in progress, whereas 'summative' evaluation occurs at . . . the end of the instructional program."[8]

[8] Daniel Tanner, *Using Behavioral Objectives in the Classroom* (New York: Macmillan, Publishing Co., 1972), p. 5.

Of course it is impossible to foresee all events and their expected end results. Nevertheless, it is invaluable both from the standpoint of accountability and for planning teaching and learning situations to have an attainable plan for the group and for each individual child. The latter is essential to the success of an individually prescribed instruction program. Fitting expectancies to attained levels of development has long been a goal of education. Careful, accurate, continuous records for each child go a long way toward making this goal attainable.

RECORDING PLANNED OBSERVATIONS

Most authorities agree that planned observation for a specific purpose and a more or less informal type of recording best serve the purposes for which most teachers and caregivers of young children need records. It is desirable to begin records as early as possible: "Young children are honest and frank; they usually express their feelings freely in action and word. Teachers and parents let a golden opportunity pass when they learn to ignore the continuous activities, imaginations, and antics of the children in their presence. They tend to arrive at this conclusion: 'I just don't understand Mary. I guess she never will grow up and get out of my hair.'"[9]

However, although the above is essential for obtaining and maintaining an ongoing global picture of each child's stream of development, such records are insufficient to meet today's accountability standards. Such concepts as cognitive stimulation, intervention, and compensatory education all imply that something is being interjected into the path that the child's development is taking to change its course. School lunch programs have been developed to assure proper nutrition for the growing child. Infant stimulation programs for babies and young children from deprived homes are designed to head off the cumulative learning deficit so commonly found among children from such homes. Remedial reading, for example, strives to help the child make up for missed experiences to enable reading on a level with more fortunate peers. It is no longer sufficient to assume that these and similar programs will produce the desired results or that IQ changes and test scores are the relevant criteria of measurement.

The first rule of good record keeping is to know what it is that should be recorded and why. Short-term and long-term goals defined in attainable and observable objectives enable the teacher "to know" which behaviors and achievements to look for as a result of instructional activities. Take time to stop, look, and listen. Be perceptive of the child's feelings whether they be those of elation or those of fear and insecurity. Once the teacher learns how to

---

[9] Witherspoon, op. cit., p. 2.

be observant and to share in understanding in the child's reactions at all times, it becomes easier "to accept a child for what he is and to include in his record significant events and signs of progress or retardation in his developmental pattern."[10]

A second rule is to recognize the importance of making and recording observations over a period of time. Young children grow and change rapidly and this pattern of change or lack of change should be clearly evident in the record. Many teachers have a pencil and pad handy at all times in order to briefly note situations or events that are expanded into a full account at the close of the day. Anecdotal records and behavior journals provide a convenient method of systematizing records.[11]

Recording of any kind requires objectivity. However, sensitivity to the meaning of what is observed is necessary if a desirable course of action is to be pursued. In the words of Lee and Lee:[12]

> We must try as well as we can to "see" through his [the child's] perceptions—
> first, the situation he is in and, second, what his present actions may accomplish
> for him. We must put aside for the moment the situation as it is and try only to see
> it as he feels it. We must not consider the actions that he really might take in it,
> but rather we must only consider the actions that he, for many reasons, sees him-
> self as able to make.

Many forms, record books, and manuals for recording the behavior of children have been published. Suchman has prepared one of the most extensive guides.[13] A more recent comprehensive guide has been prepared by Lindberg and Swedlow.[14]

The Case Study. Perhaps the most frequently used technique for studying children is the case study, which serves as a means of bringing together in an organized fashion all the information that can be learned about an individual child. Case studies probably serve their purpose best when made for particular children who do not seem to be getting along well academically or socially. The careful collection of accurate information about such a child will usually enable the teacher to evaluate the difficulty. Witherspoon points out that:[15]

[10] Witherspoon, op. cit., p. 2.

[11] For a detailed manual for use of the behavior journal see W. C. Olson, *Child Development,* 2nd ed. (Boston: D. C. Heath, 1959), pp. 467–473.

[12] J. M. Lee and Doris M. Lee, *The Child and His Development* (New York: Appleton-Century-Crofts, 1958), p. 291.

[13] J. Richard Suchman, *Observation and Analysis in Child Development: A Laboratory Manual* (New York: Harcourt, Brace, Jovanovich, 1959).

[14] Lucile Lindberg and Rita Swedlow, *Early Childhood Education: A Guide for Observation and Participation,* Boston: Allyn and Bacon, 1976 (looseleaf).

[15] Witherspoon, op. cit., p. 3.

If the child is to be helped, the teacher must know his unique characteristics and needs and have some knowledge of underlying developmental trends and an understanding of their causes. Because the case study entails a history of what has occurred, it can be very helpful in providing useful insights and at the same time point the way for future development. The case study should not be considered as merely a diagnostic tool but should spell out the direction of events and provide useful suggestions and recommendations for the future.

Most teachers have had adequate training that enables them to experiment with the use of case materials. At first, teachers tend to put emphasis on academic matters, and their case studies tend to be heavily weighted with this type of information. Unfortunately, few school records contain even the most elementary knowledge of the home and family situations from which the children come. Undesirable behavior may be noted without reference to personal or social factors that may be the cause of the behavior described. It is easy for the teacher to interpret findings superficially on the basis of incomplete information and thus confirm earlier suspicions, preconceptions and prejudices. The writing of objective records requires skill and an open mind in order to see the deeper underlying emotional stresses and conflicts. At times it is desirable to call in the school psychologist or other specialist to assist with interpretation. Yet "Despite these shortcomings, the case study approach offers the teacher a challenging opportunity to study objectively certain youngsters and certain problems encountered."[16]

Case studies usually include detailed information organized under such broad categories as developmental history of the child, family characteristics and history, socioeconomic status and community relationships, behavior descriptions, and appraisal and recommendations. A recent manual providing a guide for the preparation of case studies has been prepared by Garrison, Kingston, and Dekle.[17]

The Behavior Journal. Many teachers find the behavior journal, referred to earlier, a convenient and valuable way to keep a continuous developmental record of children. Uses of the behavior journal as summarized by Olson are characteristic of the practical value of other observational techniques. His summary follows:[18]

1. In schools where the report to the parents is of the letter type, the recorded incidents furnish a useful basis for the behavioral aspects of the letter.
2. The journal reveals points of strength and weakness in the public relations program.

[16] Ibid., p. 4.
[17] K. C. Garrison, A. Kingston, and O. T. Dekle, *Students' Workbook for the Psychology of Childhood* (New York: Charles Scribner's Sons, 1967).
[18] Olson, op. cit., p. 471.

3. The recurring problems indicate points at which parent education is needed.
4. The records reveal gaps in curriculum planning.
5. Specific entries provide useful supplementary data for personal, educational, and vocational counseling.
6. The incidents may be used in instruction to illustrate principles of child development.
7. The making of the record stimulates teachers to the consideration of the problems of individual children.
8. The accumulation and persistence of unusual behavior items assists in locating children who require special diagnostic study and treatment.
9. The journal gives the specialist to whom the child is referred additional data for diagnostic purposes.
10. The record points to the incipience and development of special talents.
11. The journal furnishes material for appraisal and research. It may assist in locating significant research issues and in setting the conditions for objective and controlled studies.

Tests. In an educational world where precision and objective measurement are held in high esteem, it is only natural that an effort would be made to apply the same procedures to young children. Consistent with the testing movement in general, early efforts were made to develop tests to measure the intelligence of infants and young children. Typical of these efforts were the *Minnesota Pre-School Scale*,[19] *Cattell Intelligence Scale for Young Children*,[20] *Merrill-Palmer Scale*,[21] and *The California First Year and Pre-School Scales*.[22] The pioneering work of Gesell has provided a wealth of information about the growth and development of children.[23]

Currently, because of the need to measure results of programs for disadvantaged children, many new preschool tests are being developed although long-range values have not yet been established. It is likely that many valuable tests will emerge as a result of the Head Start research program of the Office of Child Development. (Tests being widely used are the *Peabody Vocabulary Test, The Illinois Test of Psycholinguistic Abilities* (ITPA), *The Revised Stanford Binet, the Bayley Scales of Infant Development*, and the *Lexington Developmental Scales*.) Test results used in the context of the purpose for which the test was intended can be invaluable to the teacher in her or his day-to-day planning as well as providing an index of progress over time. However, using

[19] Florence L. Goodenough and M. J. Van Wagenen, *Minnesota Preschool Scales—Forms A and B*, rev. ed. (Minneapolis: Educational Test Bureau, 1940).
[20] Psyche Cattell, *The Measurement of Intelligence of Infants and Young Children* (New York: Psychological Corporation, 1940).
[21] Rachel Stutsman, *Mental Measurement of Preschool Children with a Guide for the Administration of the Merrill-Palmer Scale of Mental Tests* (Yonkers, N.Y.: World Book, 1931).
[22] Nancy Bayley, "On the Growth of Intelligence," *Amer. Psychol.*, *10*:12 (1955), pp. 805–818.
[23] Arnold Gesell and C. S. Amatruda, *Development Diagnosis*, 2nd ed. (New York: Paul B. Hoeber, 1947).

tests to predict later aptitudes can be very hazardous. Preschool tests of intelligence, for example, have been repeatedly shown to be poor predicators of later intelligence test scores.[24] Preschool tests require special training and skills not commonly acquired in testing courses. Tests should not be administered to preschool children unless the examiner is thoroughly familiar with the characteristics of the age of the child being tested if the results are to be valid and useful.

SUMMARY

With the advent of programs for young children based on such concepts as "intervention," "cognitive stimulation," and "compensatory education," as opposed to programs based on more or less fixed inherent and maturational influences, new dimensions have been added to evaluation and record keeping. Of necessity, programs designed to achieve specific goals and desired end results require a new look at the importance of records of children's development. In addition, these programs require careful recording of instructional and teaching strategies employed as well as a continuous assessment of progress. If properly done these records will be an invaluable adjunct to the "child study" type records so long in use. Together such records should help "fit" instructional practices to child needs.

The keeping of developmental records, if they are used later, is one of the most important tasks of the teacher of young children. Adequate records compiled during the early years provide the foundation of, and point the direction for, each child's cumulative school file. They are an invaluable adjunct when reporting to parents whether verbally or in writing. Copies of letters to parents summarizing conferences add valuable understandings to the cumulative file.

Recording skill requires objectivity and a perceptive awareness of the meaning underlying behavior and events. To be of greatest value, records must be kept continuously and maintain flexibility in terms of procedures adopted and the end results desired. Of the many possible study and reporting procedures used today, records of formative and summative evaluation objectively recorded, well-planned observational techniques, purposeful case studies, and concientiously kept behavior journals are among the most promising and challenging. Results of standardized tests when used for the purposes intended provide an invaluable guide to curriculum planning and evaluation. Frequent analyses of the information thus secured and recorded in each child's cumulative file provides one of the most useful means that the teacher has at his or her disposal to assist in understanding and guiding the

[24] Ibid.

growth, development, and behavior of young children. Management by objectives and accountability require careful evaluation based on achieved standards as stated in objectives prior to the educational experience.

Suggested Activities

1. Visit the centers or schools for young children in your community and determine the methods used in each for reporting to parents. Summarize your findings and make recommendations for changes or improvement in these practices.
2. Write to public schools having kindergartens and ask for an explanation of the methods used for reporting pupil progress to parents. Request samples if formal report cards or printed evaluation forms are used. Evaluate your findings in light of the material in this chapter.
3. While visiting schools for young children in your community, ask about the type and number of records kept. Are these records sent to the school when the child enters first grade? Do they become a part of the school's cumulative record for each child?
4. Ask first grade teachers what information they would like to have on each entering child. From these suggestions, formulate a possible record plan for obtaining the necessary information.
5. Discuss the pros and cons of using formal report cards in nursery schools and kindergartens.
6. Review several recent research reports to find out what tests and techniques are currently being used with young children.
7. Find a program that uses a need or problem approach for the basis of records kept. Evaluate this approach. If such a program cannot be easily located, find a research project and determine how the project influences the records kept.

Related Readings

Bayley, Nancy. "On the Growth of Intelligence," *Amer. Psychol., 10*:12 (1955), pp. 805–818.

Bronfenbrenner, U. "Reality and Research in the Ecology of Human Development," *Proceedings of the American Philosophical Association, 119* (1976), pp. 433–469.

Evans, E. D. "Measurement Practices in Early Childhood Education," in *Preschool Education: A Handbook for the Training of Early Childhood Educators*, edited by R. W. Colvin and E. M. Zaffiro. New York: Springer, 1974.

Guilford, J. P. "Intelligence: 1965 Model," *Am. Psychol., 21*:1 (1966), pp. 20–26.

Hayne, W. E. *Advances in Child Development and Behavior*, Vol. II. New York: Academic Press, 1976.

Honig, A. S., and J. R. Lally. "Assessing Teachers' Behavior with Infants in Day Care," in *Infant: Assessment and Intervention:* edited by G. M. Sterritt and B. Friedlander. New York: Brunner/Mazel, 1975a.

Jackson, Nancy E., et al. *Cognitive Development in Young Children*. Monterey, Calif.: Brooks/Cole, 1977.

Johnson, C. C., and J. W. Bommarito. *Tests and Measurements in Child Development: A Handbook.* San Francisco: Jossey-Bass, 1971.

Langdon, Grace, and I. W. Stout. *Teaching in the Primary Grades.* New York: Macmillan Publishing Co., 1964, Ch. 20.

MacCracken, Mary. *Lovely: A Very Special Child.* Philadelphia: J. B. Lippincott, 1976.

Oakland, T., and B. N. Phillips. *Assessing Minority Group Children.* New York: Human Sciences Press, 1973.

Rudolph, Marguerita. *From Hand to Head: A Handbook for Teachers of Young Children.* New York: Schocken Books, 1973.

Tough, Joan. *Listening to Children Talking: A Guide to the Appraisal of Children's Use of Language.* London: Ward Lock, 1976.

chapter 22

Physical facilities, equipment, and materials

In planning for and selecting the physical facilities, equipment, and materials for any age group, consideration must be given to what the children are like, their nature and needs, and how they learn. Recognition must be given to the fact that *children are alike yet different*. Most young children are active and vigorous, curious about the environment, and more apt to learn through concrete rather than through abstract experiences. Therefore, the physical facilities should be functional for the development of children at this maturity level and should be selected to allow for a wide range of abilities and growth patterns. Provisions for the handicapped child must be made as well.

The design of a center should fit the goals for the center. Provision should be made for physical facilities in five general areas: (1) a place for the less mature child to play with blocks or crafts, housekeeping facilities, and manipulative toys; (2) a room or an area for the more mature group which has books, typewriter, audio-visual toys and equipment, science projects, a display space for exhibits, and a tutoring area; (3) an administrative area; (4) a testing center [if needed] and, if observation is a part of the program, an observation booth; and (5) an outdoor area which extends the indoor area and which has rebuildable structures, water and sand areas, and animals for children to feed, and, if small, to hold. Good lighting is necessary whether the center is a new or a remodeled building.

Although physical facilities do not determine the environment, satisfactory facilities greatly assist in developing a challenging and satisfactory learning situation. Either the absence of adequate facilities and materials or the provision of quantities of inappropriate materials may curtail the effectiveness of the learning. Before deciding on the facilities needed, the characteristics, objectives, and purposes of the program should be outlined. The number of children, teachers, aides, parents, and other adults to be accommodated should then be decided.[1]

[1] Minnie P. Berson and William H. Chase, "Planning Preschool Facilities," *Amer. Educ.*, 2:10 (1966), pp. 7–11.

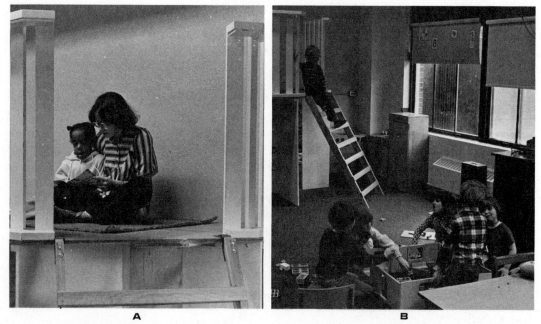

A

B

Figure 73
This "upstairs" provides a quiet space for hearing a story. The ladder calls for climbing.

The ratio between adults and students determines the room arrangement and choice of activities. The planning for and arrangement of facilities should take into account interrelated activities and housekeeping responsibilities so as to make for smooth operation of the child's day of play and work times, transition times, and eating and resting periods.[2]

The adults who play a major role in shaping the preschool child's environment include the teacher, parents, caregiver, doctor, nurse, social worker, secretary, custodian, nutritionist, aide, and the volunteers. When all work as an effectively coordinated team with mutual respect and understanding of children, they become a vital part of the child's learning environment.

"The learning environment is the atmosphere one senses when approaching a school or looking in the door of a classroom."[3] This learning environment, this atmosphere, is important to the attitudes and feelings of children in their first educational adventure. The environment should invite the child to participate in activities and to have experiences through which may be learned the joy of discovering, of exploring, of creating, of experimenting and of observing. This requires many types of materials and equipment in a suitable space; however, the amounts, the variety, and the timing for use should not be such that they overpower the child. The skillful teacher retains some materials and draws upon them throughout the year in order to provide new, richer, and more challenging experiences. The teacher continues the use of many materials over an extended period and adds or takes away others as situations and timing make it advisable.

A room that is "efficiently organized in terms of space, orderliness, and convenience gives the children better opportunity for working effectively and creatively."[4] Suggestions for this type of organization include the following: (1) Equipment and materials requiring close eyework should be in the best light; (2) creative work, block building, and so on, need protection from traffic; (3) space for quiet activities should be provided together, and space for noisy activities should be together and removed from quiet areas; and (4) all equipment and material should be appropriate and in good condition.[5]

Since the room is for the child, it should reflect children's tastes, interests, and activities. Brightness and balance in tone, beauty and hygiene, friendliness and warmth, freedom for movement, places to be alone, arrangements for small cluster groups and for the total group to work, are requisites. The wise

[2] Clara Coble, "Teacher—Planner of the Nursery School," *Space Arrangement Beauty in School* (Washington, D.C.: ACEI, 1958), p. 6.

[3] R. R. Leeper, ed., *Creating a Good Environment for Learning* (1954 Yearbook, ASCD) (Washington, D.C.: ASCD, 1954), p. 3.

[4] Vivienne Hochman, "Kindergarten-Primary Rooms Reflect Interests," *Space Arrangement Beauty in School* (Washington, D.C.: ACEI, 1958), p. 7.

[5] Coble, op. cit., p. 6.

teacher includes the challenge of color in a room that by shape and layout makes provision for exploration, play, and rest, as well as crannies and nooks for quiet thinking and work.

Rooms of simple, free flowing lines, natural materials, and an absence of ostentation are preferred.[6] Converted buildings, including warehouses and fire stations are being used in many programs. Quonset huts, churches, and many types of mobile units serve as a basis for a broader type of service which contacts children and families who were not reached before.

Clean air, adequate lighting, temperature within a satisfactory range for children, a sound level that does not demand competition from external or internal noises, and convenient movable furniture are major specifications for the physical environment.

In planning for space, consideration must be given to the provision for adequate amounts of indoor and outdoor areas according to location, situation, and climate. The proportionate relationship between indoor and outdoor space will differ also in terms of the program to be developed. The location should be accessible to the children and on a site that is drained satisfactorily, is away from distracting noises, and is removed from people who will be annoyed by the children's voices while at play. Adequate and safe parking while vehicles take on and discharge children is essential. The outdoor area needs to be regular in outline so that outdoor play can be supervised satisfactorily. The number of children that should be enrolled depends on the amount of space that can be provided in relation to the number of qualified personnel employed.

The building needs to be adaptable for use, properly insulated against heat and cold, fireproofed and soundproofed, built close to the ground, free from exposed wires, and accessible for delivery of supplies as well as for garbage pick-up and disposal.

Suitable light, both artificial and natural, is required for program development, but it should be used wisely in order to safeguard the child's eyesight. Room arrangements that make satisfactory use of available light are especially important for activities requiring concentration, such as painting and looking at books. Adequate space will make this possible.

Heat and ventilation, sanitary facilities including drinking fountains, lockers, storage for children's wraps and possessions, the walls, the floors, furniture and equipment, dining facilities, space for isolation of a sick child including toilet facilities, storage space for teacher use, space for conferences—all require careful consideration and planning as the provision for space is made.

[6] Minnie P. Berson, *Kindergarten, Your Child's Big Step* (New York: E. P. Dutton, 1959), p. 81.

CRITERIA FOR SELECTION OF FACILITIES, EQUIPMENT, AND MATERIALS

The following questions may be helpful in looking at physical facilities in schools for young children:[7]

1. Is the indoor and outdoor space large enough to permit each child to investigate, explore, and experiment?
2. Does the room arrangement provide for a traffic pattern that permits children to move about with freedom and safety?
3. Is there a sufficient variety of equipment and materials so that some children may play alone, some engage in parallel play and others in groups?
4. Are there materials and equipment for active work and play as well as for quiet work and play?
5. Is each article adaptable to many uses or limited to one? For example, a climbing tower can be used for several purposes, a slide for only one.
6. Is the article so finished and constructed that it will withstand vigorous use by many young children?
7. Must the article be permanently placed or can it be removed when the children have lost interest in it or need stimulation? Is there adequate storage space for such articles when not in use?
8. If adequate equipment and material cannot be supplied, what makeshift arti-

[7] Address by Dr. Hazel Gabbard, reprinted in *Good Schools for Children Under Six in Florida*, (Tallahassee: Florida State University, 1955), pp. 29–30.

Figure 74

A large barrel set lengthwise and firmly in a base affords opportunities for children to climb over and through it. A tree trunk can be used for climbing too. Old equipment, such as cars or boats, stimulates eager minds and bodies.

cle has the teacher provided which will insure a well-rounded program? (If only temporary storage space is possible, what improvised arrangements have been made to help children develop desirable work habits and orderliness?)
9. Does each article of material and equipment have a specific educational objective appropriate to the development and needs of the children?

INDOOR SPACE

The schoolroom should be large enough for children to live and work together without being regimented. The inside work space should be adaptable, flexible, livable, and homelike. The shape and layout are significant. A rectangular room may lend itself more readily to activities than a square one. The room should be on the ground floor and have no hidden areas so that it can be easily supervised. It should also be adjacent to toilet facilities. The entrance should be near the street level. The amount of space should be adequate for the children to move about easily so they may use large muscles; approximately 40 to 60 square feet per child is recommended. If there is no space to grow plants outdoors, opportunities for this activity should be provided indoors.

An area for individual work is needed so that the child may be free from peers and devote full time to special tasks while working with teacher or consultant. This area also can be used for testing of individual children or a small group. The space may also be used for small group or individual activities. This area may be arranged by the use of bookcases and dividers on casters; however, the walls should be transparent or low enough for supervision if there is only one teacher for the center.

Acoustics

Recent information concerning the effect of noise on people both physically and psychologically has pointed to the need for providing satisfactory acoustics in schools for young children. Provision for appropriate communication is difficult when noises from air conditioning and other mechanical equipment, as well as noise of cars and other unwanted sounds, come into the classroom. To eliminate some of the sound, draperies, carpets on floors, and soft materials on walls and ceilings may be added.

Acoustical absorption underfoot appears to be more efficient per dollar invested than materials placed overhead. A carpeted floor is attractive and easy to maintain. It provides a comfortable surface on which the child may work. However, there should be a hard, uncarpeted surface for art work. This area needs to be cleaned daily with water and after any spill during the day. Using carpet of different colors helps to separate the areas of work and provides a pleasing appearance.

Noise from tables and chairs may be reduced by padding with pieces of carpeting on furniture legs. Tablecloths on luncheon tables to reduce clatter, area rugs, a padding on furniture legs, removable pads on surface of tables used for pounding and hammering, and a door or movable screen to keep out kitchen noises are some inexpensive ways to eliminate unnecessary sounds. Some suggested acoustical principles include provision of fewer and movable walls, acoustical flooring, a luminous ceiling, semi-insulation to soften the most fundamental sound reflecting surfaces, satisfactory room arrangements, and isolation of plumbing piping.[8]

Acoustical ceilings ranging from 10 to 11 feet high are desirable to relieve noise and to provide for a feeling of freedom.

Walls

The wall space should be usable and employed to further ongoing activities and not to exhibit the best work of a few children. An abundance of "pinning space" at the eye level of the child is desirable.

The arrangement of windows and doors should allow large spaces for bulletin boards, for attaching things to pull on, and for a small amount of chalkboard. However, portable chalkboards are generally considered preferable to those fastened to the wall because they can be used more functionally. If movable, they may also serve as room dividers or screens. Green chalkboards are more aesthetic and generally considered to be better for the eyes.

The walls may be a type of vinyl porous material, soft pine, or of some material that will deaden the noise and can be used for bulletin space. Walls that are washable, especially to the height of the child, are recommended. Shifting inside walls provide for a wider variety of activities and a greater use of space. According to type, the walls, floor, and ceiling will either subdue or add to the noise and thereby contribute to or detract from the provision for a classroom climate suitable for work and play. Carefully selected colors can add to the light available in the room.

Rooms with walls in a variety of colors provide beauty and challenge as well as add to the feeling of spaciousness. This challenge of color and space is a requisite in the well-planned schoolroom. Upon entering the room, the child, the parent, and the teacher should have a feeling of relaxation as well as challenge; however, the primary colors and challenging situations should be skillfully used so that they do not overstimulate the child. Primary colors, which children like, need to be carefully selected and utilized for toys and equipment to add brightness and to provide accent in an environment of the more subdued tones of the walls and the plain floors.

[8] D. W. Rapp, *Noise in the Nursery School,* Unpublished paper, Human Development Institute, Florida State University, 1966.

Floors

The floors should be sanitary and of a material that can easily be kept clean. Flooring material needs to deaden sound and be suited to hard wear. Because, in schools for young children, much of the child's activity is on the floor, provision for warmth and freedom from drafts is a necessity. No bare concrete flooring should be allowed in the floor space. Popular floor converings include linoleum, a variety of woods, and rubber or plastic tiles.

The dining area may also be the playroom. The floors in this dining space, the tables, and the chairs should be of materials that can be easily cleaned and the space should be adequately ventilated. All food preparation and serving centers should conform to the standards established by the local and state boards of health.

Windows and doors

The exits and windows are an important part of the learning environment. Therefore, their placement and type need careful consideration. The windows should be low enough so that a child can see out. They should be fitted with shades or blinds. Translucent shades or Venetian blinds assist in regulating the light; however, care must be exercised in adjusting Venetian blinds in order to avoid bands of bright light or direct sunlight. An overhanging roof and/or awnings help regulate the glare. All windows should be fitted with guards, screens, or both. The windows in the area used for dining must be screened. If any of the windows look out on a brick wall or unsightly area this space may be covered and used advantageously for classroom displays.

All outside doors should be light in weight so that the children can handle them easily. They should be hung so as to open out of the building. Double doors leading to the playground are desirable. The doorknobs should be low enough to be in easy reach of the child and of the type that he or she can readily turn. No self-locking or swinging doors should be included. Ramps should be availabe for children who need them.

Ventilation, heat, light, and drinking fountains

Draft-free cross ventilation by open windows is desirable. However, climatic conditions in given areas need to be considered. The windows should be easily operated and screened with the screens hooked beyond the child's reach. Humidity should range between 50 percent and 65 percent and the temperature maintained evenly throughout the room at approximately 70°F.[9] The use of radiant heat has become more widespread, even in climates that require little heat. Thermostats and thermometers should be located at the child's eye level or breathing level when seated. These are not for child use, however; therefore, provision should be made to protect them. This will make it possible for them to also be used as a functional part of the curriculum. Electric outlets are needed every 10 to 12 feet. They should be covered and above the reach of the child. The fuse box should be convenient to the teacher but beyond the child's reach.

Although specialists plan the lighting, the teacher should be alert to the need for control of light in terms of changing conditions throughout the day. Plans must be made for light control in order to insure ample quantity of good light evenly distributed over the room. Too bright a light is distracting and frustrating to the child. Paint may be used in making dark areas brighter and in controlling the areas which are too bright. Skylights and transluscent walls help to maintain an effective light situation. Natural light is better for displays of work.

Rest or sleeping facilities

Provision for rest is recognized as important in schools for young children; hence, rest facilities are considered essential. These health and safety facilities are discussed on pp. 381–382, in Chapter 17.

Sanitary facilities

Running water and sinks are essentials in preparing for and cleaning up after activities in the school. The toilet and handwashing facilities should be adjacent to or easily accessible both to the outdoor and the indoor space. One large or two smaller rooms are needed. One for boys and one for girls are provided in some localities; in other localities a large one is used by both groups. Exhaust fans in toilet facilities and an outside window are requisites. The toilet floor should be of ceramic or washable tile. One lavatory and one toilet for every ten children is essential but a ratio of one toilet for five children is preferred. Toilet fixtures with seats varying from 10 to 13 inches from the floor and lavatories 23 to 24 inches from the floor are desirable if four- and five-year-olds are included. The sizes will vary according to the sizes of the chil-

---

[9] In the event that fuel shortages necessitate a lower temperature, children should be dressed warmly.

Figure 75
Movable equipment for climbing can be used indoors on cold and rainy days. Open shelves are needed for storage.

dren who will use them, However, steps can be used for the smaller children to adjust the higher fixtures for their use.

Provision for the fixture of suitable size assists in the development of routines and also promotes a feeling of self-confidence and independence within the child. The lavatory should be placed near the door as a reminder to the child to use it after toileting. The sink in the bathroom and playroom should be large, have automatic tepid water—no hot water—and be equipped with a disposal drain to catch clay, sand, and so on, before draining into the regular disposal unit. Requirements vary from place to place. The local health officials should be contacted for specific requirements.

Lockers and storage space

Well-planned storage space assists the child in learning to accept responsibility for caring for floor equipment. Each child needs a place of his or her own to store wraps and personal belongings. Locker space may take many forms but all types should provide for easy usability by the child. Usually 10 to 15 inches is adequate for depth and 10 to 12 inches for width. The height may total 35 inches with rod or hooks for clothing and include a shelf 7 inches from the top and a rack for shoes 10 inches from the floor. The actual space for hanging coats must be adequate for the child who uses the locker. If the coats and rest pads are stored in the individual lockers, the space should be increased in height and width accordingly. Many nursery schools and kindergartens provide special coat facilities.

The necessary supply cabinets may need to have doors; however, many cupboards and shelves can be built in sections and can be easily moved to

Figure 76
Running water and sinks are essentials in preparing for and cleaning up after activities. Fixtures of suitable size assist in the development of self-confidence and independence.

make work centers or be used as screens. These will need to be equipped with casters, drawers, and trays, as well as open shelves, according to plans for use. Storage space should be provided for large toys, large paper, blocks, and supplies as well as for the smaller articles. All storage space should be well ventilated.

There must be storage space for art materials. Arrangements should be made for both large and standard sized materials. Smaller materials, such as scissors and paints, need separate storage space.

The adults need storage space too. This should include storage space for wraps; space for a lavatory, commode, and possibly a shower; a table or desk; a comfortable chair and something to "stretch out" on. The space should allow for privacy for the adult and also for conferences with child, parent, or fellow workers.

OUTDOOR PLAY SPACE

For a detailed discussion of outdoor play space, see Chapter 18.

EQUIPMENT AND MATERIALS

There should be a close relationship between the equipment and materials provided and the curriculum objectives. The purposes and goals of the program give direction to the use of the equipment and materials. In Chapter 17 (Health and Safety) and Chapter 18 (Play Activities) the selection and use of equipment and materials are presented as they would be used in the development of that phase of the program. Likewise, as each curriculum area is presented, the equipment and materials needed and their use are discussed.

Some of the equipment and materials usually found in facilities for young children are included in the following list. It should be noted that one or more of each type will be found in most schools but not all that are listed may be found in any given school. In addition, many others are available. This is a general list and no item should be included unless it is functional to the program. The amount and quality will vary with the size and type of group and with teachers. The list includes the following:

Art Materials and Supplies. Brushes varying in size and length of handle, easels, clay, crayons, powder paint, finger paint; muslin, oilcloth, paper for finger painting and crayons, newsprint, tagboard; paste and brush, blunt scissors; yarn, sewing basket with varying sizes of thread, and large-eyed needles.

Woodworking. Claw hammers, nails of assorted sizes, files and cards for cleaning files, scraps of soft wood and beaver board, saws, screwdrivers and screws of assorted size, workbench with clamps, yardstick and rulers, hand-drill, monkey wrench, planes, sandpaper, dowel rods, screw eyes, pliers, paint, varnish, shellac, brushes, linseed oil, and paint remover. (See pp. 439–440.)

Science. Aquarium and herbarium with cover (material for making), barometer, thermometer, compass, cage for pets, magnifying glass and access to microscope, horseshoes, glass jars with lids, preserving fluid for specimens, tuning fork, prisms, collection of various types of magnets, iron filings, blotters, seeds, gardening tools, watering cans, weathervane and weather glass, measuring vessels, and spoons.

Musical Instruments. Autoharp, drum, rhythm sticks, songbells, tuned time bells, tom-tom, triangle, tone blocks, xylophone, piano and bench, record player and recordings; also radio and television available for special purposes and for special occasions.

Water Play. A wading pool, hoses, a tube, a table with metal or plastic pans, and a place to wash doll clothes.

Toys. Playhouse toys, water play equipment, puzzles of varying types and difficulty, games, transportation toys of all types, building blocks, and other manipulative construction toys.

Wheel Toys. Wagons, tricycles, "kiddie-kar," wheelbarrow, trucks, tractors, boards equipped with large casters.

Stationary Play Equipment. Jungle gym, climbers of different varieties, slides, swings, bridges, ladders, boards, mazes, gangplanks, pools, sandbox, platforms.

Sandbox. (See "Outdoor Play Space," pp. 402–409.)

Numbers. Dominoes, calendar, measuring cups, containers, measuring spoons, play money, scales, rulers, yardstick, tape measure, peg boards, games, abacus, collection of articles for counting such as beads, buttons, sticks.

Audiovisual Facilities. United States flag, films and filmstrips; record player and recordings; globe, maps, pictures, picture books, costumes, magazines and catalogs, puppets, and access to projectors, screen, and tape recorder.

Animals. See pp. 366–367.

Housekeeping Equipment and Supplies. Suitable and in sufficient quantity— stove and refrigerator may be on casters. If stove not available, a hot plate can be substituted. Equipment for cleaning up "spills" and for child care of room; tissues, paper towels, and roll of brown paper.

Storage. Discussed under physical facilities.

First Aid and Safety. Large Red Cross first-aid kit for emergency, and smaller kit for daily use. Fire extinguisher easily accessible and in good condition at all times.

Miscellaneous Supplies. The teacher will need forms for admitting child, for recording progress and personal data, and for transmitting child's record. The teacher will also need a pencil for china marking, twine, pencils, paste and pastebrushes, boxes for storing, beads and beadlaces, chart rack, large scissors, colored and white tissue, colored construction paper, cleaning tissue, paper towels; roll of 36-inch brown paper, materials for making finger paint and other art media; adhesive and mending tape, scotch tape, masking tape, chalk, erasers, stationery and envelopes, stamps, a marking pad and pencil, erasers, paper clips, large crayons of black and primary colors, pencil sharpener, pen holder and assorted sizes of lettering pens, India ink, felt-tip marking pen, pins (straight and safety), stapler and staples, eyelet punch and eyelets, reinforcements, and rubber bands. The teacher will need access to a primer sized typewriter, typewriter ribbons, paper and carbons, and to a duplicator, carbon, and paper for duplicating.

Sources for securing these supplies and a more detailed list of materials and equipment for an infant, nursery, or kindergarten group, according to age and size of the group, is published by the Association for Childhood Education International.[10] A list of manufacturers and distributors is included. Many of the items may be secured locally.

Furniture

The furniture should be movable, durable, comfortable, attractive, child-sized, storable, and easy to clean. Single-purpose furniture restricts the child and takes up needed play space.

Tables. These should be varied as to height, ranging from 15 to 22 inches high to fit the sizes of the children. Differing shapes provide for a variety of uses.

Chairs. They should be stackable, light enough for children to handle, movable without undue noise. Chairs should be in varied sizes, from 14 to 20 inches high, depending on ages and sizes of children. Check by placing hand, palm down, between front of chair seat and upper part of child's leg; space will not be adequate for adult hand if height is correct. Larger chairs for teacher and other adults are needed.

Display Racks and Bookshelves. Preferably movable on casters—shelves easily accessible to child.

Clock. Large face with arabic numerals, preferably black hands on white face.

Easels. Easily adjustable to child's size (so that elbows are even with bottom of paper), portable with washable surface; include trays to hold cans of paint and provide clips to hold paper.

For equipment to make its contribution to child development, it must be educationally sound. For example, the tone quality of the piano must be good, the books suitably illustrated, and the tools usable (not toy saws and hammer). All equipment and materials have many uses: therefore, no definite plan for exclusive use to develop a single concept or skill is planned. Dangerous swinging objects, apparatus that requires taking turns, and single use equipment restrict a child's ability to create his or her own play or to work creatively in a group.

Parents and children benefit from building or preparing equipment and facilities. For example, pens, cages, and aquariums are essential equipment for

---

[10] *Selecting Educational Equipment and Materials for Home and School* (Washington, D.C.: ACEI, 1976).

Figure 77

Children need places of their own to hang up wraps and store boots and other personal belongings.

a school. They may be purchased; however, there are values to be obtained from building them cooperatively or from sharing one that is brought from a home.

Use and care of equipment

The children need to learn to use and to care for the equipment and materials. Therefore, establishing routines and procedures for use and storing will assist the child and the teacher as they develop such helpful patterns of behavior as:

1. Wearing aprons or coveralls when painting.
2. Returning all tools, scissors, crayons, blocks, toys to designated storage space when not in use. (Cleaning all paint brushes and modeling boards before storing.)
3. Cleaning up all spilled paint, shellac, or varnish immediately. Learning what to use for each. For example, cold water for water paint, turpentine for varnish or paint, and alcohol for shellac.
4. Storing oily rags or cloths with shellac on them in metal containers away from heat or papers.
5. Repairing toys or equipment that need mending immediately. They should not be used until this repair is completed.
6. Cleaning and picking up in the play space after activitiy.
7. Storing hats and coats in a definite place and in an orderly manner.

THE ROLE OF ADULTS

Some activities require an adult to participate, others require an adult to observe, and others may be initiated by the child. An adult must be able to see the children as they use equipment. The placement and arrangement of equipment contribute greatly to its use. Accessibility and easy use in an uncluttered environment is the goal of each teacher. Neatness can be a virtue, but also it can detract from the use of equipment. A certain amount of orderliness is required or the environment will be confusing to the child. The children soon learn the places for things and enjoy using them and replacing them. Frequently, teachers rearrange the equipment; the children will need reorientation to this change unless the teacher and the children together planned and made the change.

Many teachers find it desirable to use a limited amount of movable equipment at one time and add to it as the weeks go by. They and the children plan together for the use, the placing, and the care of this additional material. This type of planning provides for new and challenging experiences with the added equipment and permits the child to have a part in the plans for arrangement. Thus, the classroom truly becomes the children's and the teacher's work-play space.

As opportunities for more complex experiences are offered, other materials and equipment may be needed. As the child uses these materials in work-play activities, he or she makes the equipment or material into whatever the child perceives them to be. Through observation of the child at this work-play, the teacher gains greater insight for further planning of activities, for determining what additional materials will be desirable, and what materials are not suitable for the child at this time.

Regardless of the type and amount of physical facilities, equipment, and materials available and used, the teacher's resourcefulness, vision, initiative, creativity are the most important learning materials in any classroom. It is the use of the space, equipment, and materials that determines the teaching effectiveness. Responsibility and ingenuity are developed through the functional use of buildings, equipment, and materials as teacher and children discover better ways of arranging and using them for a given purpose. Many opportunities for new learnings are provided as teacher and child explore together. The curriculum then challenges and guides the use of materials and resources; it does not limit or curtail the learning activities; neither are materials and resources permitted to limit or to warp the curriculum.

Suggested Activities

1. Observe in a center for young children and describe how the physical environment seems to affect the development of the children, the activities planned, the use of equipment, and provision for individual differences. Note any materials you believe should be added or removed.
2. List and describe the ways in which teachers, parents, and interested community persons can work cooperatively to provide adequate physical facilities for centers for young children. Discuss the relative value of this cooperative effort.
3. Discuss how the environment contributes to the provision for individual differences among young children.
4. Make a list of equipment and supplies essential to the development of a good center for three-, four-, and five-year-olds. Describe how these may be provided. Check local stores and recent catalogs, compare prices and make a purchase order.
5. Draw a diagram of two classrooms and two playgrounds for young children, showing how learning opportunities may be provided in different settings.
6. Examine packaged learning materials. Evaluate these in terms of criteria on pages 214–216.
7. Visit a playground. Note the location of equipment and discuss advantages and disadvantages in terms of the safety of the children and supervision by the teacher and aide.
8. View the following films: *Concept Development in Outdoor Play*. Campus Films, 2 Overhill Road, Scarsdale, N.Y. 10583. Compare and discuss in relation to your observations. *Creating A Playground, Making Things to Learn*, and *Setting Up A Classroom*. Modern Talking Pictures, 2323 New Hyde Park Rd., New Hyde Park, N.Y. 11040.

Related Readings

Butler, Annie L. *Early Childhood Education: Planning and Administering Programs.* New York: Van Nostrand-Reinhold, 1974.
Cherry, Clare. *Nursery School Management Guide.* Belmont, Calif.: Fearon, 1974.
Decker, Celia A., and J. R. Decker. *Planning and Administering Early Childhood Programs.* Columbus, Ohio: Charles E. Merrill Publishing Co., 1976.

Deutsch, M., et al. *Memorandum on Facilities for Early Childhood Education.* New York: Educational Facilities Laboratories, Inc., 1970.

Ford, Bonny E. "The Extended School Day: Privilege, Not Punishment," *Child. Educ., 53*:6 (1977), pp. 297–301.

Jones, Margaret H., "Physical Facilities and Environments," *Early Childhood Education for Exceptional Children.* Reston, Va.: The Council for Exceptional Children, 1977, pp. 182–207.

Kritchevsky, Sybil, and Elizabeth Prescott. *Planning Environments for Young Children—Physical Space,* 2nd ed. Washington, D.C.: NAEYC, 1977.

LaCrosse, E. R. "Thoughts for New Administrators," *Young Children, 32*:6 (1977), pp. 4–13.

Lipson, Rosella. "A Mobile Preschool," *Young Children, 24*:3 (1969), pp. 154–156.

Mitchell, D. "Equipping the Child-Care Center: Some Precautionary Notes," *Selecting Educational Equipment and Materials for School and Home.* Washington, D.C.: ACEI, 1976, pp. 15–17.

Neterer, Elizabeth, et al. "The Developmental Needs of All Children," *Selecting Educational Equipment and Materials for School and Home.* Washington, D.C.: ACEI, 1976, pp. 31–39.

Stevens, J. H., Jr., and Edith W. King. *Administering Early Childhood Education Programs.* Boston: Little, Brown and Co., 1976.

Suter, Antoinette B. "A Playground—Why Not Let the Children Create It?" *Young Children, 32*:3 (1977), pp. 64–69.

Taylor, Anne P., and G. Vlastos. *School Zone: Learning Environments for Children.* New York: Van Nostrand-Reinhold, 1975.

Todd, Vivian Edmiston. *The Years Before School: Guiding Preschool Children,* 3rd ed. New York: Macmillan, Publishing Co., 1977, pp. 113–151.

Tonigan, R., et al. *Child Care and Development Centers, Model Neighborhoods, Albuquerque, New Mexico, or Mr. Architect, This Is How We Want Our Centers to Perform.* Albuquerque, N.M.: University of New Mexcio, Institute for Social Research and Development, 1970.

chapter 23

Providing for children who need uniquely different services

The Exceptional Child—including the gifted, those having learning disabilities, the physically handicapped, the maladjusted, the disadvantaged, or culturally deprived—requires uniquely different services. The preschool years are the most critical for a child's future development. The lack of attention to a child's handicap during the preschool years may lead to deterioration of that child's potential to lead a normal life.

Every child is exceptional in that he or she is unique. Children differ in levels and quality of development. Because of this, equal educational opportunity implies a diversity within a program rather than a similarity, if each child is to reach his or her own maximum potential. Since exceptional children have the same basic needs as other children, except that these needs may be more or less intensive in specific ways, they provide a challenging opportunity for the educational system. Americans have long believed in providing an equal opportunity for all people, yet this idealism has not been translated into practice. Children and adults with special problems or handicapping conditions have been neglected educationally, which has made it difficult for them to participate in the mainstream of activities and opportunities. Education has been slow, in many instances, to provide for those who "don't fit" into the usual educational programs. Recently, an effort has been made to correct this situation. Hence, the term "mainstreaming" has become one of education's popular concepts. While not new, the idea is simply to enable children

Figure 78
It is important that exceptional children find a secure relationship with and acceptance by others in their early years. Here a hard-of-hearing boy explores his world through senses supplementary to auditory and with the assistance of an understanding and professionally trained adult.

with special problems to take part as much as possible under the given conditions in regular programs along with children who do not evidence handicapping behaviors. In many cases, this means spending a part of each day in special rooms or clinics where assistance that cannot be provided by the classroom teacher is available. This necessitates a truly carefully planned or highly personalized approach for each child.

FEDERAL PARTICIPATION

As has been true in many areas of innovation in Early Childhood Education, Head Start took the lead when amendments to the Head Start authorization law in 1972 made it a requirement that all Head Start programs have at least a 10 percent enrollment of children with severe handicapping conditions. The law specifically defined handicapped children as "mentally retarded, hard of hearing, deaf, speech impaired, visually handicapped, seriously emotionally disturbed, crippled, or other health impaired children who by reason thereof require special education and related services."[1] While most Head Start personnel were not equipped either by training or experience to cope with children with severe special needs, experience has shown that when classroom teachers and caregivers receive the support and guidance of professionally trained persons along with continuous and intensive in-service efforts by special agencies, and consultants the results can be most encouraging.

While many laws deal with specific pieces of the total problem of providing education and services to children with specific and different needs, the most far-reaching one is Public Law 94-142 enacted on November 29, 1975, which amended the previous "Education of the Handicapped Act."[2] This law specifically requires the approval of state plans to be made effective in 1977 and thereafter, which guarantees a free public education to all handicapped children between three and eighteen years of age beginning in September 1978. It further requires that such education be provided in settings that include nonhandicapped children, hence, the interest in "mainstreaming." In addition, the law provides that academic and nonacademic services equal those provided other children.

Since there is considerable turmoil in educational circles concerning the implementation of this act, students are urged to contact local schools and appropriate State Department of Education officials for the latest guidelines as to how this program is being operated.

[1] Jenny W. Klein, "Mainstreaming the Preschooler," *Young Children, 30*:5 (July 1975), p. 319.
[2] "Education of Handicapped Children: Assistance to States." *Federal Register* (Washington, D.C.: DHEW, O.E., November 29, 1976.)

PARENT INVOLVEMENT

While most deviant children can benefit from participation in group programs along with so-called normal children, there are always those whose handicap is so severe that special rooms, special equipment, and specially trained teachers are required. There are also those whose handicapping condition is such that service must be provided for them in their homes. In such programs, the personnel must have an acute sensitivity to the rights and needs of parents. It is essential that the parents be made to feel that the responsibility for the child's development always remains with them, not with the program personnel. All involved parties must cultivate an attitude of trust on the part of both the parent and the child if the program is to be successful. Program personnel serve as resources, not only of information and the development of specific skills, but also as aids to the development of a feeling of security and confidence on the part of the parents.[3] (See also Chapter 20.)

PROGRAM DEVELOPMENT

Whenever legislation is put through for programs of considerable magnitude the people it affects run into initial confusion as to the best way to meet its goals and objectives. While special or exceptional child education has been a part of the educational needs of children from the very beginning, well-researched and -developed programs, especially for preschool children, have been few and far between. Yet, the success of such early education programs has been one of the motivating factors for early education for all children.

During the 1970s several carefully designed program development projects have been funded by the Program Development Branch of the U.S. Office of Education Bureau of Education for the Handicapped. These special projects have been helpful in planning programs on a wide scale. It is too early to know what the format of most programs will be, but most will be developed in keeping with the findings of these early Research & Development projects. Many have become renowned for the quality of their work. Some of the well-established major projects are listed in this section.

There are many programs and projects, with and without grants, that have unusual facets for working with children who are uniquely different.[4] Weber lists centers that are established to study certain aspects of education of the

[3] Edith Levitt and Shirley Cohen, "Educating Parents of Children with Special Needs: Approaches and Issues," *Young Children*, *31*:4 (May, 1976), pp. 263–274.

[4] *Program Description, Handicapped Children's Early Education Program* (Program Development Branch, Division of Educational Services, Bureau of Education for the Handicapped, U.S. Office of Education, October 25, 1971).

disadvantaged child.[5] They include (1) A Parent Education Project in Gainesville, Florida; (2) Frank Porter Graham Child Development Center in Chapel Hill, North Carolina; (3) Nurseries in Cross Cultural Education in San Francisco, California; (4) Bank Street Early Childhood Center in New York City; (5) A Piaget Derived Curriculum in Ypsilanti, Michigan; (6) an integrated nursery school in Wayne State University; (7) Parent Participation Nursery Schools and Children's Centers in Berkeley, California; (8) University of Chicago Laboratory Nursery School in Chicago, Illinois; (9) Pre-Kindergarten Demonstration Center in Rochester, New York; and (10) Early Childhood Education Study in Newton, Massachusetts.

MEETING THE NEEDS OF THE EXCEPTIONAL CHILD

Many children with special needs profit greatly from a form of grouping known as "mainstreaming" (being a part of a regular group), for at least some portion of each day.

For some children the extent of being exceptional is such that it is necessary to make special educational provisions for them. As different expectancies are set for children in terms of their capacities, varied teaching procedures, materials, and facilities are provided. These are selected in terms of the level of capacity, the limitations, and the characteristics of the individual child.

It is never too early for the exceptional child to have opportunities to become friends and to play with other children. All children learn from each other how to give and to take, the rules to follow, and to share and to have things shared with them. The physically handicapped, the intellectually handicapped, the maladjusted, and the gifted child need to, and should wish to, be treated in the same manner as other children and be given a chance to share in those tasks they are able to participate in. This is necessary in order to develop the skills and ability to have experiences which are adapted and designed to promote optimum development in relation to the special needs of each child concerned.

The teacher is always the primary factor in the learning situation in any classroom. Recognition of this fact becomes increasingly important when the teacher is expected to meet the demands of one or more children who need something different from or in addition to the planned program for the usual group. Additional qualifications and specialized training are essential for the teacher required to guide the deviations. Because of the specialized demands of working with these children, teachers and leaders in schools for young children find it desirable to establish some criteria to assist in determining how

[5] Evelyn Weber, *Early Childhood Education: Perspectives on Change* (Worthington, Ohio: Charles A. Jones Publishing Co., 1970), pp. 71–95.

Figure 79

It is important that a child's *exception* be found in the early years and that a plan be made for particular educational needs.

(*Courtesy of Head Start.*)

many and which atypical children can be included satisfactorily within the group.

In admitting exceptional children, as with all children, the needs of the child and the school's ability to serve them are the primary factors in determining whether the child can be accepted in a group.

All teachers of young children have the responsibility of identifying the child within the group who needs special assistance and guidance over and beyond what can be provided. Through early identification, diagnosis, and treatment, many deviations can be corrected or adjustments can be made which are difficult if not impossible to make at a later date. Through counsel with the parents, plans can be developed to provide for the special needs of the exceptional child. In the classroom the special differences within the children can be identified and the decision made as to the best school situation for each child's guidance.

According to Olson, "It has become less and less customary to isolate exceptional children, and the tendency is to provide opportunities for work and play among children of all types so they can profit by such association. There is no fixed pattern and there probably should be none at our present state of knowledge. . . . A lush environment has in it both the qualitative and quantitative opportunities for the learning and growth of the least and the most able in any type of activity."[6]

Whenever appropriate, handicapped children should live with, play with, and go to school with "normal" children.[7] The arguments concern whether it is in the best interests for the gifted and for the intellectually handicapped to remain in the regular classroom. The relative values of the provision for the growth of these children within the regular school and within a special school are constantly under study. Research today indicates the acceptance by the normal group of the mentally or physically handicapped child. However, it appears that the mentally retarded child often has difficulty in adjusting to the regular classroom and also in securing acceptance. The physically handicapped usually encounters neither of these problems to a great degree. The demands of the child on the teacher because of the physical handicap will need to be carefully studied and measures provided to relieve the extra demand so that services to the total group are not curtailed.

For an interesting and lucid history of mainstreaming and ingredients that make it work successfully, see Dunlop's article in *Young Children*.[8] The following section examines the different types of the exceptional encountered in children and the provisions made for them.

THE GIFTED CHILD

When the gifted are segregated, their achievements may be spectacular in special areas. However, there appears to be no real evidence that they have gained materially over what they would have acquired in a heterogeneous group working in a rich environment under capable guidance. There is always the problem of what would have occurred if the gifted child had been or had not been accelerated. Any good program for children allows and provides for differences, and the curriculum is developed to meet the needs of the gifted as well as the average and the retarded. The needs of these individuals are identified and planned for in such a way that each child becomes an accepted, contributing member of the group.

All children have gifts. The task of the teacher is to identify and to provide a suitable climate for their growth. As special abilities of children are noticed,

[6] W. C. Olson, *Child Development*, 2nd ed. (Boston: D.C. Heath, 1959), p. 434.
[7] *Report to the President*, op. cit., pp. 199–206.
[8] Kathleen H. Dunlop. "Mainstreaming: Valuing Diversity in Children," *Young Children*, 30:4 (1977), pp. 26–32.

records are made so that they may continue to receive guidance in terms of their special gift, whether the child be intellectually gifted or specially talented. In identifying these children, the teacher does not place total dependence upon her or his own observation and test data but seeks counsel and assistance from other professional sources.

According to Passow, "There are no unique methods for teaching gifted children. In some ways, the apparent differences stem not so much from what the teacher does as from what the gifted child brings to the situation. One's ability to think, understand, create, initiate, relate, and imagine gives a qualitative dimension to the teaching-learning situation which may contrast visibly with the classroom environment of the average student."[9]

It is interesting to note that Harry Passow, cited earlier, was one of the speakers at the first world conference on the gifted held in London, September 8–12, 1975. Earlier goals have not changed for a key speaker, the Secretary of State for Education, stressed the need for early identification and encouragement of giftedness in children.[10]

These gifted children have needs common to all children, including the development of the beginnings of basic concepts in all areas. They need provision for many stimulating and varied opportunities that develop initiative; to have the range and scope of their knowledge increased; to develop the power of working independently; to avoid the danger of becoming "one-sided" or interested in only a limited area; to have the acceptance of their peers even though they have superior ability in one or more areas; to overcome emotional stress in a socially acceptable manner and not to seek refuge in day-dreaming. With these children the teacher places stress on independent thinking and action, and building relationships and concepts as opposed to learning multiple facts. Challenging situations are provided to develop critical thinking.

It is generally agreed that enrichment is the best method of working with intellectually accelerated children. Program personnel will find it helpful to utilize the many available resources—human and physical—to aid and to supplement the instructional process. They do this by implementing plans made in cooperation with parents and sometimes with other community and agency leaders. They know that the child may lose the genuine respect of peers when permitted to "always know the answers," to dictate what needs to be done, to be impatient with slower learners, or to draw attention constantly to self. The teacher may contribute to the antisocial attitude by always holding the child up as an example. Therefore, one must be mindful that the child may become a "mental giant yet be a moral dwarf," and thereby not be capable, as a mature

[9] A. H. Passow, "Enrichment of Education for the Gifted," *Education for the Gifted* (57th Yearbook, Part II, NSSE) (Chicago: University of Chicago Press, 1958), p. 198.
[10] H. Collis (U.K.). "The First World Conference on Gifted Children," *Intern. J. of Early Child.,* 7:2 (1975), pp. 167–168.

person, to make a real contribution to society. A good school for young children will provide adequate challenge for the superior child without "special" consideration and at the same time use these provisions for the enrichment of the educational experiences of the other children.

CHILDREN WITH MENTAL RETARDATION

In working with the child who has difficulty learning, the teacher needs insight into how to help the child discover strengths as well as to assist him or her with liabilities; the teacher needs to accept him or her as a person as well as a child to be taught. It is important that this child's exception be noted in the early years and that a plan be made for his or her particular educational needs.

The degree of retardation is a significant factor in determining the placement of the intellectually handicapped child. If the retarded child is retained in a regular group, progress will be slower than that of the other members of the group; more praise and extrinsic rewards will be needed for successes; tasks will need to be briefer, less complex, and more routine with greater repetition—this repetition may, and should, be in varied situations. Many more and different concrete materials and experiences are required for this child. It will take longer to succeed; more time will be needed to make adjustments socially and emotionally. Serenity, happiness, and acceptance are essential.

Figure 80
In working with the child who has a learning disability the teacher needs insight into how to discover strengths, as well as how to assist in meeting liabilities.

These are secured from the attitudes and feelings of those around the child as well as from the climate of the classroom.

In the life of every parent of a retarded child there comes a time when plans must be made for schooling. "Mental retardation is a very complex problem, and many of these complexities make a difference in how the retarded child is educated."[11] Retarded children have special educational needs in terms of understanding, specially prepared and skilled teachers, and a specially developed curriculum. Because of their difficulty in learning, they need and learn best by special methods. Avery found that benefits from attendance at preschool would seem to indicate that a good preschool is worth a trial even though some people question whether young children of this type suffer by separation from home.[12]

Going to school is a time of many adjustments for all children and it is more complicated for the mentally retarded. Safety, conformity to routines, languages and social readiness, ability in self-help activities, and stability and emotional adaptability need to be considered carefully. It is important to plan for admission of a mentally retarded child and to determine how his or her best interests as well as those of the other children in the group are to be served. Kirk suggests that certain educable children should be placed in a special preschool program at as early an age as possible.[13]

Because it is difficult to predict how well a retarded child will fit into a group, many schools accept these children on a trial basis. The parents will need guidance as to further school plans if the child cannot be retained in the school. Most states have some provision for the child whose retardation is such that he or she cannot be absorbed within a group. Some communities have a school program for the children who are capable of instruction but not with the regular group. Materials on these programs and suggestions for guidance of schools in counseling parents of retarded children may be secured from the National Association for Retarded Children, 2709 Avenue E, Arlington, Texas 76011. Private residential schools have been available for retarded children for many years. A listing of these schools is published annually by the American Association on Mental Deficiency, 5201 Connecticut Avenue. NW, Washington, D.C. 20015.

Early Congressional Acts have given impetus to work with mental retardation and have provided opportunities for assistance to the preschool teacher of the mentally retarded child. Public Law 88-164, the Mental Retardation Facilities and Community Health Centers Construction Act passed by the 88th

---

[11] H. M. Williams, *The Retarded Child Goes to School*, No. 123 (Washington, D.C.: U.S. Dept. of Health, Education, and Welfare, 1960), p. 1.

[12] Charlotte B. Avery, "Social Competence of Pre-School, Acoustically Handicapped Children," *Exceptional Child*, 15 (1948), pp. 71–73, 88.

[13] S. A. Kirk, *Early Education of Mentally Retarded: An Experimental Study* (Urbana, Ill.: University of Illinois Press, 1958), pp. 121–122.

Congress and signed by President Kennedy, October 31, 1963, provided for: (1) research centers, grants for the construction of university affiliated facilities and for the construction of state centers maintained by the state; (2) the construction of community health centers; and (3) the training of teachers of the mentally retarded and other handicapped children as well as for research and demonstration projects in the education of the handicapped child. Public Law 88-156, the Maternal Health and Mental Retardation Amendments of 1963, provides an increase in child health and crippled children's services.[14]

The President's Panel on Mental Retardation in 1962 reported that the symptoms of the mentally retarded child are not always obvious but that early recognition and treatment offer the best prognosis. About 85 percent of the retarded children can benefit from special education. Many children who are considered retarded are later found to be emotionally disturbed rather than having a mental defect existing from birth. To assist in identifying the retarded child, the teacher needs (1) a record of age of development of such skills as creeping, crawling, standing, and talking; (2) an analysis of motor coordination of the child; (3) a record of vocabulary, interest in books, speech habits or impediments, memory span, ability to generalize, perceptual difficulties; (4) a history of physical difficulties, illnesses; and (5) a record of his or her ability to socialize; acceptance and rejection by peers.

When the retarded child is located the teacher works with the parents and with agencies who are skilled in diagnosing such problems. The ratio of pupil to teacher needs to be reduced to provide time for individual guidance; extra space is needed to avoid pushing or crowding and to provide for greater opportunities for creative play.

The above history of concern for the mentally retarded should be updated from time to time. One of the more comprehensive sources of current technical and scientific information on mental retardation is Robinson and Robinson's text.[15]

Identification of the mentally retarded

All personnel in the program should be alert to behavioral cues associated with mental retardation. Here are some of the things to watch for:

> Inability to follow multistep directions.
> Little self-direction in choosing activities.
> Tendency to imitate rather than to create.

[14] *Mental Retardation, Plans and Programs* (Washington, D.C.: Department of Health, Education and Welfare, June 1965).
[15] Nancy B. Robinson and H. B. Robinson. *The Mentally Retarded Child,* 2nd ed., (New York: McGraw-Hill Book Co., 1976).

Poor abstract reasoning ability.
Difficulties in concentrating and learning.
Inability to apply learning from one situation to another, or to anticipate consequences.
Inability to see similarities and differences in objects or situations.
Slower development than other children (walking, talking, and toilet training).
Delayed to poor motor coordination
Poor eye–hand coordination.[16]

LEARNING DISABLED CHILDREN

A relatively new category of uniquely different need children has been labeled "learning disabilities." While there have been many different definitions of this problem, it would appear that there is a growing feeling that the following qualities characterize the child with learning disabilities:

Does not benefit from classroom instruction that aids most children.
Possesses an average or better than average level of intelligence.
There are no evident physical, emotional, or cultural handicaps.

This means that a learning-disabled child is not mentally retarded, is not emotionally disturbed, and is not culturally disadvantaged. All it means is that the child does not respond to the usual classroom instruction. However, given the appropriate instruction for the particular child in question, the learning disability disappears.[17]

Many terms have been used to characterize children with learning problems. Children who are different in terms of learning have been called dullards, underachievers, school failures, minimally brain damaged, dyslexic, and many other pejoratives. Today, it is estimated that there are more than 7 million children in America with this special problem, and many approaches from medical to genetic have been applied to an understanding of it. It stands to reason that since the problem involves the learning process, the point of attack should be at the level of the learning program, and as early as possible. For an interesting, instructive, illuminating, up-to-date, and helpful discussion of learning disabilities, you are heartily encouraged to read Ross's excellent work. Program personnel should suspect some degree of learning disability in children who exhibit any combination of the following characteristics:

Poor visual discrimination: difficulty distinguishing between shapes, letters, and numbers.

---

[16] *Day Care: Serving Children with Special Needs.* (Washington, D.C.: U.S. DHEW, OCD, OE Bureau of Education for the Handicapped, 1972), p. 49.
[17] A. O. Ross. *Learning Disability: The Unrealized Potential* (New York: McGraw-Hill Book Co., 1977).

Poor visual memory: forgetting what is seen and read.

Poor auditory discrimination: inability to distinguish between different sounds or words.

Poor kinesthesia: difficulty distinguishing different objects by feeling.

Poor eye–hand muscle coordination: difficulty making hand do what eyes see.

Poor spatial orientation: difficulty remembering spacial differences.

Poor figure-ground: difficulty selecting one thing from a group.

Perseveration: difficulty shifting from one activity to another.

Hyperactivity: inability to concentrate on a structured activity.

Disinhibition: tendency to be lethargic or hyperactive.

Poor self-image: views herself or himself as anything but normal.[18]

THE PHYSICALLY HANDICAPPED CHILD

Educational services to handicapped children are assisted through federal programs. Services are made available to children who have been identified by state educational agencies as being mentally retarded, visually impaired, deaf, hard of hearing, speech impaired, seriously emotionally disturbed, learning disabled, or otherwise have health impairments to the extent that they can not benefit from the regular educational program. Included in such programs are (1) aid for handicapped in state supported and operated schools, (2) special education and related services, (3) programs to advance creativity in the schools, and (4) vocational education for handicapped children.[19,20]

The orthopedically handicapped child is the least difficult to absorb within a regular group. However, the crippling defect must be minor or special provision must be made for handling the child. Overprotectiveness on the part of the children, teacher, or other adults is one of the problems encountered in working with this type of child. The greatest problem may be the overprotectiveness of the parents. Even though at times it is difficult to enforce, the child must become independent through use of his or her own resources.

The type and degree of the handicap determines the program. Some of these children were born with a handicap; others have acquired it after birth. Some of these handicaps may be fully corrected; however, many children with severe handicaps need to be provided with special kinds of educational services. It is extremely important that handicapped children receive help before starting regular school. If successfully helped at an early age, the problems for the parent as well as for the child are lessened. The opportunities for the child are expanded because of early acceptance of the handicap and participation in a planned educational program to utilize all the child's assets.

[18] *Day Care: Serving Children with Special Needs*, op. cit., p. 53.

[19] *Four Programs for Educational Services to Handicapped Children*. (Washington, D.C.: U.S. DHEW October 1971.), Item 2, Part C, Title II.

[20] *Federal Register*, op. cit., pp. 52404–52407.

Because of the flexibility and work with individuals in programs for young children, an excellent opportunity for such growth is available. Parents of these children increase their ability to help their child by assisting, observing, and working with the teacher. Through conferences, teachers and parents may give each other ideas, that will be helpful in working with the child.

Defective vision

The blind or partially seeing child will need to learn through the other senses; however, he or she must learn to do all things that he or she can do safely and successfully. Children with partial sight need different books, periods of frequent rest for their eyes, and a greater provision for safety. They also need encouragement and a sense of belonging. Often they can excel in games requiring auditory acuity. Many opportunities should be provided for them to develop and use this skill, thereby securing recognition and experiencing success within their peer group.

Children who are having difficulty with vision may rub their eyes frequently or blink when attempting to see objects; they frequently sit in a tense position or make facial expressions indicating intense effort to see. Children exhibiting these characteristics should be referred for testing by competent individuals. In the classroom they should have frequent rest periods and protection from glare or from work requiring close vision.

Impaired hearing

The child with impaired hearing will need help according to the type of hearing impairment. The child who has never heard has a greater problem than one who has lost his or her hearing after acquiring speech. Both of these groups have greater needs than the partially hearing-impaired child. The young child needs his or her hearing tested frequently; often correction can be made if impairment is discovered soon enough. The child with impaired hearing should at all times be seated so as to see the teacher's lips. Careful observation of the child's participation with the group will avoid his or her forming habits of withdrawal because of an inability to hear.

A program for hearing-impaired children was developed at The Florida State University Institute of Human Development in cooperation with personnel from the Department of Education Services for Exceptional Children, and the Speech and Hearing Clinic. Aware of the importance of an early educational start for these children (otherwise the hearing-impaired child will not learn language or achieve social and personal skills possessed by other children of this age), it was decided to place one such child in each of the Insti-

Figure 81
Glasses have opened a new world for these children.

tute's preschool age groups. A teacher with specialized training in the field
devoted half her time to the four children and also served as a consultant to
the regular teachers. One of the major problems faced by atypical children is
the difficulty of achieving group acceptance. How this was accomplished for
one totally hearing-impaired child is described:

> Larry did not enter the group without considerable thought and preparation.
> Since each group of children in the school was to have a hearing-impaired child,
> decisions had to be made as to the group in which each child should be placed.
> This decision fell to the speech and hearing therapist who had worked closely
> with the children and their parents. Armed with the information and insights she
> had gained plus extensive clinical findings, she visited each group to see which
> group of children and teacher might offer the best school environment for each
> child. Larry, age four, who is totally hearing-impaired, was placed in the four-
> year-old group.

The week before Larry was to join the group was a busy one for teacher and children. The teacher felt that the children should have some sense of the world, different from their own, in which Larry lived. They also needed to understand that he had not had the 4½ months of playing together which they had shared so he would be lacking in the degree of social living they had obtained. It was decided that an approach to sounds around them might be an opening wedge in evolving this awareness. The children listened to the sounds around them during sharing period. They talked about what they heard. Stories were read, like "Muffin" the little black dog who got a cinder in his eye and couldn't see, but could hear. When the children's interest was high, the teacher asked the children to tell her what they heard when they put their hands over their ears tightly. In unison they replied, "Nothing."

Then the teacher told them about Larry who couldn't hear yet wanted to come to school. She asked them how they could talk to him if he couldn't hear. Don said, "We could show him," and began to point directions. The children eagerly took up the suggestion and began to communicate with each other by gestures.

Larry entered school, a welcome addition to the group. His welcome was short-lived, however. He was not accustomed to such social acceptance and before long was entering each group like a friendly puppy, knocking down block houses with a wide friendly grin or grabbing a doll from the doll house and running to

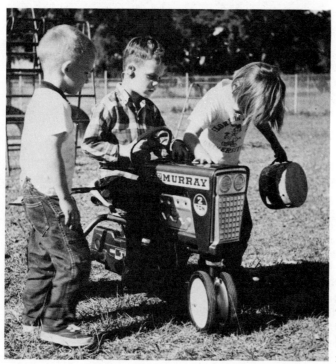

Figure 82
This boy can hear the other children better now that he is wearing a hearing aid. He has become an accepted member of the group.

the far end of the yard. The warm acceptance changed to resentment and isolation for Larry by the group.

A week later at discussion time, while Larry was attending speech class, the teacher asked them what they thought of Larry. "We don't like him," came the reply. "Why?" asked the teacher. "He knocks down our blocks," was a quick response. "Why do you suppose he does that?" she asked them. For a minute there was silence and then Susan said, "Maybe he doesn't know how to play with us. Tom used to knock them down too." The rest of the group agreed. The conversation turned to what they could do to help him. "We could tell him not to knock down our blocks by shaking our heads," Tom suggested. This was tried but Larry thought the children were playing again. The children smiled as they shook their heads. Another discussion brought out the need for a serious face as the negative head shake was given.

Despite these initial difficulties, after four months in nursery school, Larry is an accepted member of the group, with no more than the usual four-year-old setbacks for outbursts of destruction. The warmth of acceptance permeates the group. This warmth was shown one day as Larry entered the door of the nursery school and met Tom coming out. Impulsively Tom threw his arms around Larry and kissed him on the cheek. Larry smiled in happy surprise and both boys went their individual ways.

Each of the hearing-impaired children made a surprisingly good adjustment to the group and, as a result of intensive therapy, attained language facility. It is likely that these children will experience much less retardation during later school years than is common for children with severe or total hearing handicaps. The responsibility of the teacher in charge, in adapting to the needs of these children, is to provide constant language stimulation—sometimes referred to as auditory bombardment."[21] Through the use of a wide variety of art materials, dramatic play, structured music experiences, story sharing, and an assortment of toys, expressive outlets are provided for the frustrations experienced by the child.

Impaired speech

The majority of cases of impaired speech involve faulty articulation. Most of these articulatory speech difficulties occur at an early age. Stuttering and non-fluency rate are other commonly found forms of speech impairment. The teacher needs to distinguish between actual speech impairment and speech difficulties that are a normal part of the child's developmental sequence. The child with impaired speech will need special help apart from the group even

[21] Alicia Hamilton, "A Preschool Program for Children with Limited Hearing," *Young Children*, *21*:5 (1966), p. 267.

though he or she benefits from participating with the regular group. Physical defects such as cleft palate and harelip will need medical attention and correction.

Whatever the speech problem, personnel should identify the children who need help; secure counsel and assistance; provide special help to the child to the degree that training, experience, and teaching load permit; and work with parents and other agencies in providing for the total needs of the child.

A calm, helpful, and accepting manner in a relaxed climate is an effective method of work with children with speech difficulties. The teacher must be careful not to embarrass the child. In a classroom where a free, spontaneous atmosphere prevails, where tension is dispelled with a friendly remark or humorous situation, the speech of many children will improve. However, there are special skills and procedures for which the teacher must have training. If the teacher does not have this competency, she or he may secure assistance from individuals with special training.

The teacher is ever alert to insure that problems of these children are not being developed in the other members of the group. For example, the attention and help on a speech problem with one child may encourage imitation on the part of another child in order to secure the desired attention.

THE MALADJUSTED CHILD

The child who experiences social and emotional conflict situations often has problems of personal and group adjustment. All children have conflicts, but most children develop the ability to resolve these conflicts through socially approved activities and procedures. The release of tensions through dramatics, play experiences, or creative activities has been discussed in previous chapters. A few children need help from adults to release their tensions and to resolve their conflicts. Careful guidance by the teacher may be all that is required. However, if these problems continue and are serious, the teacher and the parents need and should have the help of a specially trained person. The teacher identifies these children and refers them to the proper agencies. The teacher then cooperates in working out a satisfactory solution. In working with children who can be retrained in the group, the teacher will find helpful suggestions in the material in Chapter 5.

THE CULTURALLY DIFFERENT CHILD

Thousands of children each year enter school with severe educational disadvantages. Prior to 1960 the focus of education for the disadvantaged was on programs for dropouts, and remedial work in the slums. By 1960, it had become evident that such programs come too late in the child's life and that pre-primary education programs for culturally different children are essential. (See Chapters 6 and 9.)

Because of cultural and value differences, as well as different child-rearing practices, culturally different children often experience failure when entering the mainstream of child life at the primary school level. Because of this fact, experiences at the preschool level are particularly important for this group. During this period children explore their physical world, become sensitive to the environment, have opportunities for action responses, reproduce and symbolize experiences, and learn to use language to develop and understand concepts. The child who is culturally different from the majority of children may not have had an opportunity to communicate in standard English or to share and have close relationships with others from different backgrounds. The educational program will have to make certain adjustments to accommodate the uniquely different needs of these children. The problems faced by these children are varied and complex.

In planning programs for culturally different children it is helpful to consider what changes and additional provisions are required and how they may be achieved. Recognition of their problems has rapidly led to the establishment of preschool programs inasmuch as the deprivation effects build barriers to later achievement. Such lack of commonly expected early experiences progressively limits children as they attempt to fit into schools with children who have had different care, parental teaching, and value development. Their program must provide a balance between order and freedom in a steady routine, but which permits freedom to explore, to ask questions, and to expect and receive answers from adults. This type of program needs to be continued without interruption. The parents of these children should be actively involved in the program to provide for this continuity in the child's home environment. Because the development of the child's self concept takes place along with the development of language it is important that the program for these children begin at an early age.

Instructional plans are based on the recognition that culturally different children are not dull children. Every effort should be made to include activities and experiences that assure an enriched environment; provision for helping the child master language related to specific situations; opportunities for helping mothers develop the cognitive facilities needed by their children; provision for differentiated instruction; utilization of informal language; and gradual development of a more formal mode of communication.

OTHER CHILDREN NEEDING UNIQUELY DIFFERENT SERVICES

Children of working mothers

Although many women who work place their children in preschool programs, there are many more who do not, either because of short hours, the cost, or for other reasons.[22]

Employment of women is increasing at a rapid rate. A survey made in 1965 revealed that only 5 percent of the children under five years were cared for in day-care centers; the others were cared for by relatives; or were cared for in other homes of nonrelatives. In their concern for the safety of their child, many parents do not place a high priority on educational experiences prior to first grade. Safety and care are essential if the mother, or both the mother and father are to work. In spite of the recent decline in the birthrate, preprimary enrollments in programs for children from three to five years of age have increased from 3.2 million in 1964 to more than 5 million in 1976, or an increase of 91 percent. This increase parallels the increase in women entering the workforce, which was from 18 million in 1950 to 36 million in 1974. Understandably, the need is for full day care and nursery care, and not for the traditional part-time nursery school experience.[23] (See also Chapter 8.)

A program of care involves physical safety and development, nutritional needs, health needs, and educational activities under guidance. The environment is important, but the greatest need is the presence of a warm, loving adult who takes time to listen, is sympathetic and encouraging but also assists the child in selecting activities to help him or her grow and become independent. Some type of parental involvement is necessary; however, it is more difficult to schedule especially if the mother works long hours.[24]

The migrant child

Providing preschool experiences for the children of migrant families presents difficulties because of the pattern of work—moving from place to place as the need for labor arises. In addition, the migrant families have their own values

---

[22] S. Low and Pearl G. Spindler, *Child Care Arrangements of Working Mothers in the United States* (Washington, D.C.: U.S. Department of Health, Education, and Welfare and U.S. Department of Labor, 1967), pp. 3–9.

[23] "House EL/SEC Panel Hears How Population Trends Affect Education," *Educ. Daily* (May 17, 1977), p. 3.

[24] Annie L. Butler, *The Child's Right to Quality Day Care* (Washington, D.C.: ACEI, 1970).

in terms of speech, honesty, and love. They give their children a sense of belonging to the family but not to the larger group.

There are, however, significant developments in migrant education that include aide training, use of consultants, continuous progress plans, demonstration schools, evaluation, health and nutrition, home and family education, interagency involvement, interstate cooperation, instructional packages, migrant centers, mobile units, parent involvement, preschool programs, six-month extended day programs, programs for Spanish speaking children, student and volunteer involvement, teacher education, uniform migrant transfer record forms. There are also plans for computerized services.[25,26] Florida, Idaho, New York, and Oregon have developed educational programs for migrant children. The programs involve the use of teacher aides and volunteer services. Special teacher education projects and in-service education programs have also been developed. Except during school hours, no law protects the children, and facilities vary from community to community.

PROFESSIONAL RESOURCES AND PROGRAMS

While there are numerous local, state, and national professional organizations concerned with children who have uniquely different needs, only one is included here for each specific area of difference. This is intended as a starting point for each area of interest, from which information can be secured about locating other resources at the local, state, and national levels, as well.

Council for Exceptional Children
Reston, Virginia 22070

Association for Childhood Education International (ACEI)
3615 Wisconsin Avenue, NW
Washington, D.C. 20016

Day Care and Child Development Council of America, Inc.
1426 H Street, NW
Washington, D.C. 20005

National Association for the Education of Young Children (NAEYC)
1834 Connecticut Avenue, NW
Washington, D.C. 20009

[25] Sylvia Sunderlin, ed., *Migrant Children: Their Education* (Washington, D.C.: ACEI, 1971), pp. 3–6, 35–61.
[26] H. A. Curtis and J. A. Klock, *Florida Prekindergarten Migrant Compensatory Program: An Evaluation.* Florida State University, Tallahassee, Florida, 1972. (Mimeographed.)

National Association for Retarded Children (NARC)
2709 Avenue E East
Arlington, Texas 76011

Association for Children with Learning Disabilities
2200 Brownsville Road
Pittsburgh, Pennsylvania 15210

National Easter Seal Society
2123 West Ogden Avenue
Chicago, Illinois 60612

Association for Education of the Visually Handicapped
711 14th Street, NW
Washington, D.C. 20005

The American Speech and Hearing Association
9030 Old Georgetown Road
Bethesda, Maryland 20014

National Association for Mental Health
10 Columbus Circle
New York, N.Y. 10019

Write to the following for very useful and easily used screening checklists:

Does Your Child Have Any of the Warning Signs of Possible Abnormalities?
State of Utah, Office of Child Development
250 East Fifth Street South
Salt Lake City, Utah 84111
Learning Disabilities Checklist
The N.Y. Institute of Child Development, Inc.,
36 East 36 Street
New York City, N.Y. 10016

Suggested Activities

1. Observe a group a group of children. List ways the teacher adjusts activities for exceptional children. List activities in which exceptional children participate as regular members of the group. Discuss the value of both types of activities.
2. Read and discuss in class references available in your library that are related to work with children who are uniquely different in their early years.
3. Make a list of special services available for assisting the teacher as she or he works with children who are uniquely different as members of a regular group. Describe

how these are selected, contacted, and used with special children. Indicate how this special assistance is valuable.

4. List guides for the teachers in schools for young children in identifying and working with exceptional children—the gifted, the emotionally disturbed, the mentally retarded, the hearing-impaired, the partially sighted, the speech defective, the physically handicapped, and the culturally deprived.

5. Determine the provisions made for children who are uniquely different in your community.

6. Visit such a center and describe how the program is adjusted to the level of each of the differences observed.

7. Secure from your State Department of Education a copy of the approved state plan for mainstreaming children who require uniquely different educational services. Become familiar with the details of the plan including implementation. Arrange a seminar in order to acquaint all members of your class with the details of how your state provides educational services to its children whose needs differ greatly from those of the majority of children in the group.

Related Readings

Bosco, J. J., and S. S. Robin. *The Hyperactive Child and Stimulant Drugs.* Chicago: The University of Chicago Press, 1977.

French, A. P. *Disturbed Children and Their Families: Innovations in Evaluation and Treatment.* New York: Human Sciences Press, 1977.

Jones, R. L. *Mainstreaming and the Minority Child.* Reston, Va.: The Council for Exceptional Child, 1976.

Jordan, June E., et al. (eds.). *Early Childhood Education for Exceptional Children: A Handbook of Ideas and Exemplary Practices.* Reston, Va.: The Council for Exceptional Child, 1977.

Levin, J. R., and V. L. Allen. *Teaching Exceptional Children.* New York: Academic Press, 1976.

Mainstreaming Training Series—A series of Training Packets for Teachers, Administrators, and Parents. Austin, Tex.: Learning Concepts, 1977.

Meier, J. *Developmental and Learning Disabilities.* College Park: University of Maryland Press, 1976.

Newton, Mariana. *Speech, Hearing, and Language Problems.* Lincoln, Neb.: Professional Educator's Publications, 1977.

Thorum, A. R., et al. *Instructional Materials for the Handicapped: Birth Through Early Childhood.* Salt Lake City, Utah: Olympus Publishing Co., 1976.

Weston, A. J. *Articulation Disorders: Methods of Evaluation and Therapy.* Lincoln, Neb.: Professional Publisher's Publications, 1975.

Yearbook of Special Education, 1977–78. Chicago: Marquis Academic Media, 1977.

Zeitlin, Shirley. *Kindergarten Screening: Early Identification of Potential High Risk Learners.* Springfield, Ill: Charles C Thomas, 1976.

chapter 24

The next step

Preparation for the "next step" from a children's center, a nursery school, a kindergarten, or a children's program of any kind into the first grade requires the help of the adults in the child's preschool life as well as the support of the parent, or parents. The teacher in the school the child will attend will also need the help of the parent or parents and other responsible adults, including the preschool personnel. The child will learn when he or she is ready to learn. All concerned must learn to recognize that each child is different from all other children and will need to be allowed to learn at his or her own pace.

Each child thinks, learns, and acts as an individual and will need help in continuing to be encouraged, to be made to feel secure, and to know that there is a guiding hand available when taking this next big step. Wise preschool personnel know this and prepare the child to look forward to this new experience with both joy and anticipation. As their world expands, each child needs to feel the security of a sound foundation based on satisfactory experiences in accepting responsibility, planning and deciding wisely, completing tasks undertaken, and in meeting failure and success with equal confidence.

The two primary factors in determining the child's adjustment to the new environment are: (1) pattern of individual growth, and (2) background or home experience. Many preschools provide opportunities for children to visit the school they will be attending, to talk to the teacher and children, to become familiar with the facilities, and to see the various fascinating objects and materials they will use in their program the following year. Schools may vary in type and plan of organization, but all will have common elements that will assist the children to continue in their growth and development. The children will feel more secure if the preschool teacher as well as the parent or parents show that they have confidence in the school and that it will be a happy place for children to continue their work.

A conference between the parents and the first-grade teacher has a two-pronged advantage: It helps provide for satisfactory adjustment to the new situation and tends to create parent interest in the school, setting up lines of communication between home and school. Among the topics that can be discussed are transportation plans, the child's previous experiences, health records, and special interests and problems. The thrust of the conference is not concern for the child's future in terms of expectations, but for the "now as it affects the future." Preschool personnel are effective contributors to these discussions and plans. In addition to having worked with the child, they have records of activities the child has taken part in and an assessment of overall progress that will assist the first-grade teacher in guiding the child. Thus, growth will not be interrupted through frustration, repetition, unnecessary overt demands, or fear. The teacher-to-be cannot know how to respond appropriately until she or he had developed the skills necessary for teaching each and every child. However, learning from the adults who have figured in the child's life space will usually be helpful.

The skilled teacher knows that to be successful, the child needs to build on all that has gone before. The child enters school wanting to learn and will not be helped by being pushed or prodded beyond his or her level of maturity. Each child is a functioning human being who is not helped by being subjected to many divided aspects of life. When entering first grade, many children suffer from a variety of conceptual errors. For example, it can be tragic if a child develops a feeling of inadequacy simply because the teacher fails to recognize that certain problems may be a function of a maturation rate that is slower than that of other children in the group. Failure in the beginning of a school career can be disastrous to a person's self-concept.

Preschool personnel should provide certain basic information to the school the child will enter. They know the value of this procedure and should prepare the parents of the children by seeing that each child's record is forwarded to the school personnel of the school to be attended. The next step may be into another group within the same school environment, to another school in the same community, or even to a school in another community.

As the child takes the next step, the preschool personnel, the child, and the parent or parents are confident that the early experience has helped the child to:

1. Look at himself or herself objectively determining own strengths and weaknesses.
2. Be self-directing, making new friends in the broader social and scientific world.
3. Make better decisions after weighing the differing results of choices made.
4. Draw upon a rich matrix of experiences for thinking, feeling, and learning while participating in new and broader activities.
5. Communicate with peers and with adults while learning to live in more complex situations.
6. Express feelings in esthetic experiences.
7. Maintain health and grow physically.
8. Take parents into partnership while participating in larger activities because security has been gained from preschool life as parent, or parents, and teachers have worked cooperatively for the child's maximum development.

Suggested Activities

1. Make a list of activities that may be provided to assist the preschool child become oriented to the new school situations.
2. Plan an interview between parents and teacher in the new school. Collect records that will need to be given to the teacher of the child as he or she takes the next step. List activities of the preschool teacher to assist parents in preparing for the interview.

Related Readings

Della-Piana, G. *How to Talk with Children (and Other People)*. New York: John Wiley and Sons, 1973.

Frazier, A. *Adventuring, Mastering, Associating: New Strategies for Teaching Children*. Washington, D.C.: ASCD, 1976.

Ginnott, H. *Teacher and Child.* New York: Macmillan Publishing Co., 1972.

Glasser, W. *Schools Without Failure.* New York: Harper & Row, 1969.

Lesser, G. *Children and Television: Lessons from Sesame Street.* New York: Random House, 1974.

U.S. Department of Health, Education and Welfare. *Your Child from 6 to 12.* Washington, D.C.: HEW, 1970.

References

See additional references at end of each chapter.

Articles

ACEI Teacher Education Committee. "Standards for Teachers in Early Childhood Education," *Child. Educ.*, 35:2 (1958), pp. 65–66.

Allen, D. W., and P. Wagschal. "New Look in Credentialing," *Clearing House, 44*:3 (1969), pp. 137–140.

Allen, W. C., et al. "Performance Criteria for Education Personnel Development: A State Approach to Standards." *J. Teacher Educ., 20*:2 (1969), pp. 133–135.

Almy, Millie. "Spontaneous Play: An Avenue for Intellectual Development," *Young Children*, 22:5 (1967), pp. 265–277.

Alpenfels, Ethel S. "Foreword—Children at Work," *Child. Educ.*, 37:8 (1961), pp. 364–365.

Alper, Thelma G., H. T. Blane, and Barbara K. Abrams. "Reaction of Middle and Lower Class Children to Finger Paints as a Function of Class Differences in Child-Training Practices," *J. Abnorm. and Soc. Psychol.*, 51:3 (1955), pp. 439–448.

Ames, Louise B. "The Development of the Sense of Time in the Young Child," *J. Genet. Psychol.*, 68:1 (1946), pp. 97–125.

Anderson, J. E. "A Half Century of Learning About Children," *NEA J.*, 42:3 (1953), pp. 139–141.

Avery, Charlotte B. "Social Competence of Pre-School Acoustically Handicapped Children," *Except. Child.*, 15 (1948), pp. 71–73, 28.

Babitz, M. "Serving Families of the Underprivileged," *Calif. Educ.*, 11 (1964).

Bain, Katherine. "Commentary: The Physically Abused Child," *Pediatrics*, 31:6 (1963), pp. 895–897.

Baker, D. "Worlds of Play," *Child. Educ.*, 55:5 (1977), pp. 247–248.

Banks, J. A. "Cultural Pluralism and the Schools," *Educ. Leadership*, 32:3 (1974), pp. 163–166.

Bayley, Nancy. "On the Growth of Intelligence," *Amer. Psychol.*, 10-12 (1955), pp. 805–818.

Bean, C. H. "An Unusual Opportunity to Investigate the Psychology of Language," *J. Genet., Psychol.*, 40:2 (1932), 181–202.

Beit-Hallahad, Benjamin, and A. L. Rabin. "The Kibbutz as a Social Experiment and as a Child Rearing Laboratory," *Amer. Psychol.*, 32-7 (1977), pp. 532–541.

Berkman, D. "The Myth of Educational Technology," *Educ. Record*, 36:4 (1972), pp. 451–460.

Berson, Minnie P., and W. H. Chase. "Planning Preschool Facilities," *Amer. Educ.*, 2:10 (1966), pp. 7–11.

———, and C. E. Sherman. "Divergent Views on Prekindergarten Teacher Education, 34:2 (1976), pp. 143–149.

Beyer, Evelyn. "Montessori in the Space Age?" *NEA J.*, 52:9 (1963), pp. 35–36.

Bliss, Leora B. "Certification of Teachers in Nursery Schools and Day Care Centers," *Child. Educ.*, 34:6 (1958), pp. 275–278.

Brieland, D. "Cultural and Social Change," *Young Children*, 20:4 (1965), pp. 223–229.

Brophy, Alice M. "Children's Centers—Three Decades of Progress," *J. of Nursery Educ.*, 19:3 (1964), pp. 173–181.

Brunner, Catherine. "Deprivation—Its Effects, Its Remedies," *Educ. Leadership*, 23:2 (1965), pp. 103–107.

Burtt, Merilyn. "The Effect of a Man Teacher," *Young Children*, 21:2 (1965), pp. 92–98.

Butler, L. G. "Language Acquisition of Young Children: Major Theories and Sequence," *Elementary English*, 51:8 (1974), pp. 1120–1123.

Caldwell, B. M. "The Rationale of Early Intervention," *Except. Children*, 36:9 (1970), pp. 717–726.

Calvin, A. D., et al. "Studies in Adult Learning Since 1930," *J. Educ. Res.*, 50:4 (1956), pp. 273–285.

REFERENCES

Caras, R. "Time to Join the World," *Early Years, 2*:9 (1972), pp. 36–37.

Carleton, Charles S. "Head Start or False Start," *Am. Educ., 2*:8 (1965), pp. 20–22.

Carlson, Ruth K. "Emergence of Creative Personality," *Child. Educ., 36*:9 (1960), pp. 402–404.

Carnegie Corporation of New York Quart., 9:2 (1961), pp. 3–4.

Carroll, J. B. "Foreign Languages for Children—What Research Says," *Nat. Elem. Prin., 39*:6 (1960), pp. 12–15.

Carroll, Marian. "Academic Achievement and Adjustment of Underage and Overage Third-graders," *J. Ed. Res., 50*:8 (1963), pp. 415–419.

"CDAC Reaches New Milestone: Thousandth Credential," *Dateline CDAC, 3*:2 (May 1977), p. 1.

Chilman, Catherine. "Child-Rearing and Family Relationship Patterns of the Very Poor," *Welfare in Review* (January 1965).

Collis, H. "The First World Conference on Gifted Children," *International J. of Early Childhood, 7*:2 (1975), pp. 167–168.

Costin, Lela B. "Training Nonprofessionals for a Child Welfare Service," *Children 13*:2 (1968), pp. 63–68.

Darwin, C. "Biographical Sketch of an Infant," *Mind, 2* (1877), pp. 285–294.

Day Care: Serving Children With Special Needs. Washington, D.C.: U.S. DHEW, OCD, OE Bureau of Education for the Handicapped (1972), p. 49.

Denemark, G. W., and W. J. Matson. "Why Teach Children a Foreign Language?" *Nat. Elem. Prin., 39*:6 (1960), pp. 6–11.

Deutsch, M. "Facilitating Development in the Pre-School Child: Social and Psychological Perspectives," *Merrill-Palmer Quart., 10*:3 (1964), pp. 249–263.

Dunlop, Kathleen H. "Mainstreaming: Valuing Diversity in Children," *Young Children, 30*:4 (May 1977), pp. 26–32.

Durkin, Dolores. "A Six-Year Study of Children Who Learned to Read at the Age of Four," *Reading Research Quarterly, 10*:1 (1974–1975), pp. 9–61.

Early Childhood Project Newsletter. Denver, Colorado: The Education Commission of the States (April 1977), p. 2. (Published Monthly.)

Education Daily, February 25, 1977.

"Education of Handicapped Children: Assistance to States," *Federal Register* (November 29, 1976), pp. 52404–52407.

"Family Affairs," *Instructor* (September 1977), Special Section.

Fantini, M. D. "Public Schools of Choice and the Plurality of Publics," *Educ. Leadership, 28*:6 (1971), pp. 585–591.

Fauls, Lydia B., and W. D. Smith. "Sex-Role Learning of Five Year Olds," *J. Genet. Psychol., 89*:2 (1956), pp. 105–117.

Feingold, B. F. "Are Today's Kids Different than Yesterday's?" *Instructor,* (September 1977), Special Section.

Fenton, E. "Moral Education: The Research Findings," *Social Educ., 40*:4 (1976), pp. 189–193.

Findley, D., and K. T. Henson. "Teacher Aides: Should They be Certified,?" *Contemporary Educ., 42*:4 (1971), pp. 177–180.

Fisher, M. F. "Language Patterns of Pre-School Children," *J. Exp. Educ., 1*:1 (1932), pp. 70–74.

Fite, Mary D., and A. T. Jersild. "Aggressive Behavior in Young Children and Children's Attitudes Toward Aggression," *Genet. Psychol. Monogr.*, 22:2 (1940), pp. 151–319.

Foshay, A. W. "A Modest Proposal," *Educ. Leadership, 18*:8 (1961), pp. 506–516, 528.

Fraenkel, J. R. "The Kohlberg Bandwagon: Some Reservations," *Social Educ.*, 40:4 (1976), pp. 216–222.

Fritz, Sara. "Only 7 Per Cent of U.S. Families Now Typical," *Extra* (September 1977).

Gates, A. I. and Bond, G. L. "Reading Readiness: A Study of Factors Determining Success and Failure in Beginning Reading," *Teach. Coll. Rec.*, 37:8 (1936), pp. 679–685.

Getzels J. W., and Jackson, P. W. "Giftedness and Creativity," *Newsletter.* Chicago: University of Chicago, November 1960.

Glasser, W. Quoted in "Are Today's Kids Different Than Yesterday's?" *Instructor* (September 1977), Special Section.

Goldschmidt, M. L. "Early Cognitive Development and Preschool Education," *Internat. J. of Early Child. Educ.*, 3:1 (1971), pp. 1–7.

Gorton, H. B., and R. L. Robinson. "For Better Results: A Full Day Kindergarten," *Educ.*, 89:3 (1969), pp. 217–221.

Grant, Gloria W. "Criteria for Cultural Pluralism in the Classroom," *Educ. Leadership*, 32:3 (1974), pp. 190–192.

Guanella, Frances M. "Block Building Activities of Young Children," *Arch. Psychol.*, 26:174 (1934) p. 92. (Cited by D. H. Russell in *Children's Thinking*, Boston: Ginn Co., 1956.)

Hall, G. S. "The Contents of Children's Minds," *Pedag. Sem.*, 1:2 (1891), pp. 139–173.

Halliwell, J. W., and Belle W. Stein. "Achievement of Early and Late School Starters," *Elem. English, 41*:6 (1964), pp. 631–639.

Hammond, Sarah Lou, et al. "Good Days for Children," *Child Educ.*, 36:1 (1959), pp. 4–16.

Hampleman, R. S. "A Study of the Reading Achievement of Early and Late School Starters," *Elem. English, 36*:5 (1959), pp. 331–334.

Harms, E. "The Development of Religious Experience in Children," *Amer. J. Sociol.*, 50:2 (1944), pp. 112–122.

Harrison, M. Lucile. "The Nature and Development of Concepts of Time Among Young Children," *Elem. Sch. J.*, 34:7 (1934), pp. 507–514.

Havighurst, R. J. "Moral Character and Religious Education," *Relig. Educ.*, 51:3 (1956), pp. 163–169.

Headley, Neith. "The Kindergarten Comes of Age," *NEA J.*, 43:3 (1954), pp. 153–154.

Hendrickson, P. R., and E. P. Torrance. "Some Implications for Art Education from the Minnesota Studies of Creative Thinking," *Creativity in Art Education.* Washington, D.C.: NAEA, 1963, pp. 20–25.

Hess, R., and D. Easton. "The Role of the Elementary School in Political Socialization," *The School Review, 70*:3 (1962), pp. 265–275.

Hess, R. D., et al., "Parent Involvement in Early Education," *Day Care: Resources for Decisions,* Grotberg, Edith H., ed., Washington, D.C.: Office of Economic Opportunity, (1971), pp. 265–285.

Hicks, J. A. "The Acquisition of Motor Skill in Young Children: A Study of the Effects of Practice in Throwing at a Moving Target," *Child. Develpm., 1*:2 (1930), pp. 379–392.

REFERENCES

"House EL/SEC Panel Hears How Population Trends Affect Education," *Educ. Daily* (May 17 1977), p. 3.

House, E. R., G. V. Glass, L. D. McClean, and D. F. Walker. "No Simple Answer: Critique of the 'Follow Through' Evaluation," *Educ. Leadership, 35*:6 (1978).

Huey, Frances. "Learning Potential of the Young Child," *Educ. Leadership., 23*:2 (1965), pp. 119–120.

Hymes, J. L., Jr. "Montessori," *Educ. Leadership, 23*:2 (1965), pp. 127–131.

Ilgenfritz, M. P. "Mothers on Their Own—Widows and Divorcees," *Marr. and Fam. Liv., 23*:1 (1961), pp. 38–41.

Jersild, A. T., and Sylvia F. Beinstock. "A Study of the Development of Children's Abilty to Sing," *J. Educ. Psychol., 25*:10 (1939), pp. 481–503.

Johnson, Marguerite W. "The Effect on the Behavior of Variation in the Amount of Play Equipment," *Child Develpm., 6*:1 (1935), pp. 56–68.

Kagan, H. E. "Teaching Values to Our Children," in *Children and Youth in the 1960's.* Washington, D.C.: White House Conference on Children and Youth, 1960, pp. 57–65.

Kaljo, Maija. "Love, Nature and the Recycling Heap," *Early Years, 2*:9 (1972), pp. 38–39.

Kamerman, Shelia B., A. J. Kahn, and Brenda G. McGowan. "Research and Advocacy," *Children Today, 1*:2 (1972), pp. 35–36.

Katz, Lillian G. "Stop, Look and Listen Before You Condition," *ERIC/ECE Newsletter, 5*:6 (1971), pp. 1–2.

———. "Teachers in Preschools: Problems and Prospects," *International J. of Early Childhood, 9*:1 (1977), pp. 111–123.

Keister, B. U. "Reading Skills Acquired by Five-Year-Old Children," *Elem. Sch. J., 41*:8 (1941), pp. 587–596.

"Kindergarten Children Demonstrate Reading Ability for Parents," *CEMREL Newsletter, 6*:2 (Spring 1972), p. 8.

"Kindergarten: Time to Read," *Washington Monitor,* Supplement to *Education U.S.A.* Washington, D.C.: NSPRA, September 29, 1966.

Klaus, R. A., and Susan W. Gray. "Murfreesboro Preschool Program for Culturally Deprived Children," *Child. Educ., 42*:2 (1965), pp. 92–97.

Klein, Jenny W. "Head Start: Intervention for What?" *Educ. Leadership, 29*:1 (1971), pp. 16–19.

———. "Mainstreaming the Preschooler," *Young Children, 30*:5 (July 1975), pp. 317–326.

Kohlberg, L. "Early Intervention, A Cognitive Developmental View," *Child Develpm., 39*:4 (1968), pp. 1013–1062.

Kunz, Jean, and Joan E. Moyer. "Comparison of Economically Disadvantaged and Economically Advantaged Kindergarten Children, *J. of Educ. Res., 62*:9 (1969), pp. 372–395.

Lawrence, Susan. "Panel Takes Up Children as Subjects," *APA Monitor, 8*:2 (1977), p. 2.

Leeper, R. R. "A Time for Reevaluation," *Educ. Leadership, 29*:1 (1971), pp. 3–6.

Lemkau, P. V. "A Psychiatrist's View of Housing," *Proceedings of Housing Conference,* Publication 180. Philadelphia: Pennsylvania State University, College of Home Economics. (Copyrighted Paper.)

Levenson, "Whatever Happened to Early Childhood Education?", *Instructor* (October 1977), pp. 71–72; 134–138.

Levitt, Edith, and Shirley Cohen. "Educating Parents of Children With Special Needs: Approaches and Issues," *Young Children, 31*:4 (May 1976), pp. 263–275.

Loving, A. D. "Intervention for What?" *Educ. Leadership, 29*:1 (1971), p. 7.

McAulay, J. D. "Social Studies in the Primary Grades," *Soc. Educ., 18*:8 (1954), pp. 357–358.

McConkie, G. W., and Marie M. Hughes. "Quality of Classroom Living Related to Size of Kindergarten Group," *Child. Educ., 32*:9 (1956), pp. 428–432.

McCormick, Sandra. "Should You Read Aloud to Your Children?" *Language Arts 54*:2 (1977), pp. 130–143.

Margolin, Edythe. "Critical Factors in Contemporary Childhood Education," *Child. Educ., 45*:8 (1969), p. 503.

Mason, G., and Norma Prater. "Early Reading and Reading Instruction," *Elem. English, 43*:5 (1966), pp. 483–488.

Mauser, A. J. "The Paraprofessional: Panacea or Frankenstein?" *Contemporary Educ., 41*:3 (1970), pp. 139–141.

Mills, W. H., and G. L. McDaniels. "Montessori, Yesterday and Today," *Young Children, 21*:3 (1966), pp. 137–141.

Milner, Esther. "Study of the Relationships Between Reading Readiness in Grade One School Children and Patterns of Parent-Child Interaction," *Child Develpm., 22*:2 (1951), pp. 95–112.

Moore, Shirley, G. "The Effects of Head Start Programs with Different Curricula and Teaching Strategies," *Young Children, 32*:6 (1977), pp. 54–60.

————. "The Effects of Television on the Prosocial Behavior of Young Children," *Young Children, 32*:5 (1977), pp. 60–64.

Morphett, Mabel V., and C. Washburne, "When Should Children Begin to Read?" *Elem. Sch. J., 31*:7 (1931), pp. 496–503.

Moyer, Joan E., and Guillermina Englebrecht. "Multicultural Education: Where Do We Begin?" *Child Educ., 53*:5 (1977), pp. 241–244.

Mukerji, Rose. "Roots in Early Childhood for Continuous Learning," *Young Children, 20*:6 (1965), pp. 342–351.

Murchison, C., and S. Langer. "Tiedemann's Observations on the Development of the Mental Faculties of Children," *J. Genet. Psychol., 34*:2 (1921), pp. 205–230.

Murphy, Lois B. "Multiple Factors in Learning in the Day Care Center," *Child. Educ., 45*:6 (1969), pp. 311–320.

Mutsfield, H. "Science Experiences Afford Opportunity for Experimentation," *Child. Educ., 29*:2 (1952), p. 81.

Nedler, Shari. "Working with Parents on the Run," *Child. Educ., 53*:3 (1977), pp. 128–132.

Newgarten, B. L., and K. Weinstein. "The Changing American Grandparents," in *Marr. and Fam. Liv., 16*:1 (1964).

Noel, Doris I. "A Comparative Study of the Relationship Between the Quality of a Child's Language Usage and the Quality and Types of Language Used in the Home," *J. Educ. Res., 47*:3 (1953), pp. 161–167.

Oakden, E. C., and M. Sturt. "Development of Knowledge of Time in Children," *Brit. J. Psychol., 12*:4 (1922), pp. 309–336.

Ojemann, R., and K. Pritchett. "Piaget and the Role of Guided Experience in Human Development," *Perceptual and Motor Skills, 17* (1963).

Osborn, Keith. "Project Head Start—An Assessment," *Educ. Leadership, 23* (1965), pp. 98–103.

Palmer, E. L. "Television Instruction and the Preschool Child," *International J. of Early Child., 4*:1 (1972), OMEP, Dublin, Ireland: Irish University Press, pp. 11–17.

Park, G. E., and Clara Burri. "Eye Maturation and Reading Difficulties," *J. Educ. Psychol., 34*:9 (1943), pp. 535–546.

Parten, M. B. "Social Participation Among Pre-School Children," *J. Abnorm. Soc. Psychol., 27*:3 (1932), pp. 243–269.

Paulsen, M. G. "Legal Protections Against Child Abuse," *Children, 13*:2 (1966), pp. 43–48.

Pines, Maya. "How Three Year Olds Teach Themselves to Read and Love It," *Harper's Magazine, 226*:1356 (1963), pp. 58–64.

"Project Head Start" *NEA J., 54*:7 (1965), pp. 58–59.

Puglisi, D. J. "Two Approaches to Minority Education," *Educ. Leadership, 32*-3 (1974), pp. 173–175.

Raths, J. D. "A Strategy for Developing Values," *Educ. Leadership, 21*:8 (1964), pp. 509–512.

Ross, Irwin. "Head Start Is a Banner Project," *The PTA Magazine, 60*:7 (1965), pp. 20–23.

Russell, D. "Goals for American Education: The Individual Focus," *Educ. Leadership, 28*:6 (1971), pp. 592–594.

Smith, Mary K. "Measurement of the Size of General English Vocabulary Through the Family," *Child Develpm., 6*:1 (1935), pp. 19–25.

Smith, Mary K. "Measurement of the Size of General English Vocabulary Through the Elementary Grades and High School," *Genet. Psychol. Monogr., 24*:2 (1941), pp. 311–345.

Smith, Nila B. "Early Reading: Viewpoints," *Child. Educ., 42*:4 (1965), pp. 229–241.

"Systematic Observation," *J. of Res. and Develpm. in Educ., 4*:1 (1970), Athens, Georgia: College of Education, University of Georgia.

Taine, H. "On the Acquisition of Language by Children," *Mind, 2* (1877), pp. 252–259.

Torrance, E. P. "Adventuring in Creativity," *Child. Educ., 40*:2 (1963), pp. 79–88.

———. "Conditions for Creative Learning," *Child. Educ., 39*:8 (1963), pp. 367–370.

Wann, K. D. "Children Want to Know," *Child. Educ., 37*:1 (1960), pp. 8–12.

Ward, S. A. "Components of a Child Advocacy Program," *Children Today, 1*:2 (1972), pp. 38–40.

Washington, K. R. "Success: A Parent Effectiveness Approach for Developing Urban Children's Self Concept," *Young Children, 32*:5 (1977), pp. 5–10.

"What Are the Sources of Early Childhood Education," *Young Children, 26*:1 (1970), pp. 48–50.

Witherspoon, R. L. "Teacher, Know Thyself," *Child. Educ., 35*:2 (1958), pp. 56–59.

———. "Studying Young Children," *Nursery School Portfolio,* Leaflet 9. Washington, D.C.: ACEI, (1961).

Wolman, Thelma G. "Preschool Program for Disadvantaged Children—The New Rochelle Story," *Young Children, 21*:2 (1965), pp. 98–111.

Young, F. M. "An Analysis of Certain Variables in a Developmental Study of Language," *Genet. Psychol. Monogr.*, 23:1 (1941), pp. 3–141.

Zirbes, Laura. "What Creative Teaching Means," *Child. Educ.*, 33:2 (1956), pp. 51–54.

Books

ACEI. *Sung Under The Silver Umbrella.* New York: Macmillan, 1962.

Almy, Millie C. *Children's Experiences Prior to First Grade and Success in Beginning Reading.* New York: Teachers College, Columbia University, 1949.

———. *The Early Childhood Educator at Work.* New York: McGraw-Hill, 1975.

Anderson, P. S. *Language Skills in Elementary Education,* 2nd ed. New York: Macmillan, 1972.

Andress, Barbara L., et al. *Music in Early Education.* Reston, Va.: Music Educator's National Conference, 1973.

Arbuthnot, May Hill. *Children and Books,* 3rd ed. Glenview, Ill.: Scott, Foresman, 1964.

———. *Time for Poetry.* Chicago: Scott, Foresman, 1951.

ASCD, *Toward Better Teaching,* 1949 Yearbook (ASCD). Washington, D.C.: ASCD, 1949.

Bailey, Eunice. *Discovering Music With Young Children.* New York: Philosophical Library, 1958.

Beadle, Muriel. *A Child's Mind.* Garden City, New York: Doubleday, 1970.

Beatty, Walcott H., ed. *Improving Educational Assessment & An Inventory of Measures of Affective Behavior.* Washington, D.C.: ASCD, NEA, 1969.

Bengtsson, A. *Environmental Planning for Children's Play.* New York: Praeger, 1970.

Bereiter, C., and S. Englemann. *Teaching Disadvantaged Children in Preschool.* Englewood Cliffs, N.J.: Prentice-Hall, 1966.

Berman, Louise M. *New Priorities in the Curriculum.* Columbus, Ohio: Charles E. Merrill Publishing Co., 1968.

Bernstein, B. A. "A Sociolinguistic Approach to Socialization: With Some Reference to Educability," in F. Williams, ed. *Language and Poverty: Perspectives on a Theme.* Chicago: Markham Publishing Co., 1970.

Berson, Minnie P. *Kindergarten, Your Child's Big Step.* New York: E. P. Dutton, 1959.

Bettelheim, B. *The Uses of Enchantment: The Meaning and Importance of Fairy Tales.* New York: Knopf, 1976.

Beyer, Evelyn, et al., eds. *Montessori in Perspective.* Washington, D.C.: NAEYC, 1971.

The Block Book. Washington, D.C.: NAEYC, 1974.

Bloom, B. S. *Stability and Change in Human Characteristics.* New York: Wiley, 1964.

Blough, G. O., and J. Schwartz. *Elementary School Science and How to Teach It,* 5th ed., New York: Holt, Rinehart and Winston, 1974.

Bowlby, J. *Attachment and Loss,* Vol. I, New York: Basic Books, 1969.

Breckenridge, Marion E., and E. Lee Vincent. *Child Development,* 4th ed. Philadelphia: W. B. Saunders, 1960.

Brim, O. G., Jr. *Education for Child Rearing.* New York: Russell Sage Foundation, 1959.

Bronfenbrenner, U. "Reality and Research in the Ecology of Human Development," *Proceedings of the American Philosophical Association, 119* (1975).

———. *Two Worlds of Childhood, U.S. & U.S.S.R.* New York: Russell Sage Foundation, 1970.

Brown, R. *A First Language.* Cambridge, Mass.: Harvard University Press, 1973.

Bruner, J. S. *Beyond the Information Given.* New York: W. W. Norton, 1973.

———. *On Knowing.* Cambridge, Mass.: Harvard University Press, 1962.

———. *The Process of Education.* Cambridge, Mass.: Harvard University Press, 1961.

———. *Toward A Theory of Instruction.* New York: W. W. Norton, 1968.

———, Allison Jolly, and Kathy Sylva. *Play: Its Role in Development and Evolution.* New York: Basic Books, 1976.

Burns, P. C., Betty L. Broman, and Alberta L. Lowe. *The Language Arts in Childhood Education,* 2nd ed. Chicago: Rand McNally, 1971.

Buros, O. K., ed. *The Seventh Mental Measurements Yearbook,* 2 Vols. Highland Park, N.J.: Gryphon Press, 1972.

Butler, Annie L. *Current Research in Early Childhood Education: A Compilation and Analysis for Program Planners.* Washington, D.C.: EKNE, 1970.

Cantor, Pamela. *Understanding A Child's World.* New York: McGraw-Hill, 1977.

Cattell, P. *The Measurement of Intelligence of Infants and Young Children.* New York: Psychological Corporation, 1940.

Cazden, Courtney B. *Child Language and Education.* New York: Holt, Rinehart and Winston, 1972.

———. "The Neglected Situation in Child Language Research and Education," in F. Williams, *Language and Poverty.* Chicago: Markham Publishing Co., 1970.

Chalupsky, A. B., and G. J. Coles. *Exploring the Impact of Educational Innovation.* Palo Alto: American Institutes for Research, 1976.

Cherry, Clare. *Creative Art for the Developing Child.* Belmont, Calif.: Lear Siegler, Inc., Fearon Publishers, 1972.

Child Abuse—The Problem and Its Management, Vol. I (First of three volumes). U.S. DHEW Publication no., (ORD) 75-30073, Washington, D.C.: U.S. Government Printing Office, 1975.

Children in a Changing World. Washington, D.C.: The Golden Anniversary White House Conference on Children and Youth, 1960.

Chilman, C. S. *Growing Up Poor.* U.S. DHEW, Welfare Administration, Division of Research No. 13. Washington, D.C.: U.S. Government Printing Office.

Chomsky, N. *The Logical Structure of Linguistic Theory.* New York: Plenum, 1975.

Combs, A. W. "A Perceptual View of the Adequate Personality," in *Perceiving, Behaving, Becoming,* 1962 Yearbook. Washington, D.C.: ASCD, 1962, pp. 50–64.

———, Chm. *Perceiving, Behaving, Becoming,* 1962 Yearbook. Washington, D.C. ASCD, 1962.

Comenius, J. A. (Komensky). *The Great Didactic.* 1657.

———. *Orbis Pictus.* 1658.

Commission on the English Curriculum of the National Council of Teachers of English, Dora V. Smith, Ch. *Language Arts for Today's Children.* New York: Appleton-Century-Crofts, 1954.

Compilation of Legislation on Title I Financial Assistance to Local Educational Agen-

cies for The Education of Children of Low Income Families. (Reflecting 1966, 1967, and 1970 Amendments). Washington, D.C.: HEW, July 1971.

Conference Proceedings. Washington, D.C.: Midcentury White House Conference on Children and Youth, 1950.

————. Washington, D.C.: The Golden Anniversary White House Conference on Children and Youth, 1960.

Copeland, R. W. *How Children Learn Mathematics: Teaching Implications of Piaget's Research.* New York: Macmillan, 1970.

Coxford, A., and L. Ellerbuch. "Fractional Numbers," *Mathematics Learning in Early Childhood.* Reston, Va.: National Council of Teachers of Mathematics, 1975.

Crowe, E. G. "A Study of Kindergarten Activities for Language Development," in F. Williams, ed. *Language and Poverty.* Chicago: Markham Publishing Co., 1970.

Curtis, H. A., and J. A. Block. *Florida Pre-kindergarten Migrant Compensatory Program: An Evaluation.* Tallahassee, Fla.: The Florida State University, 1972. (Mimeographed.)

Dansky, J. L., and I. W. Silverman. "Effects of Play on Associative Fluency in Pre-School Children," in J. S. Bruner, et al. *Play—Its Role in Development and Evolution.* New York: Basic Books, 1976.

Databook; The Status of Education Research and Development in the United States. Washington, D.C.: NIE, U.S. DHEW, 1976.

Day, Barbara. *Open Learning in Early Childhood.* New York: Macmillan, 1975.

Deese, J. "Comments and Conclusions," in U. Bellugi and R. Brown, *The Acquisition of Language, Monogr. Soc. Res. Child Develpm.,* 29:1 (1964).

Della-Piana, G. *How to Talk with Children (and Other People).* New York: Wiley, 1973.

Deutsch, M. "Early School Environment: Its Influence on School Adaptation," in *Pre-School Education Today.* Garden City, N.Y.: Doubleday & Co., 1966.

————, and Associates. *The Disadvantaged Child.* New York: Basic Books, 1967.

Dewey, R. E., F. W. Gramlich, and D. Loftsgordon. *Problems of Ethics.* New York: Macmillan, 1961.

Dinkmeyer, D. C. *Child Development: The Emerging Self.* Englewood Cliffs, N.J.: Prentice-Hall, 1965.

Dittman, Laura, ed. *Early Child Care: The New Perspectives.* New York: Atherton Press, 1968.

Doman, G. *How to Teach Your Baby to Read.* New York: Random House, 1964.

Durkin, Dolores. *Teaching Them to Read.* Boston: Allyn and Bacon, 1970.

————. *Teaching Young Children to Read,* 2nd ed. Boston: Allyn and Bacon, 1976.

Educational Programs that Work, 3rd ed. San Francisco, Calif.: Far West Laboratory for Educational Research and Development, 1977.

Educational Research: Limits and Opportunities. Washington, D.C.: U.S. DHEW, NIE, 1977.

Elyot, Sir Thomas. *The Boke Named the Governour,* 1531. London: J. M. Dent, 1907.

Flavell, J. H. *The Developmental Psychology of Jean Piaget.* New York: Van Nostrand, 1964.

Focus on Children and Youth. Washington, D.C.: The Golden Anniversary White House Conference on Children and Youth, 1960.

REFERENCES

Fostering Growth in Perceptual Skills. Darien, Conn.: CCM Threshold Learning, Inc., 1970.

Fraser, Dorothy M. "The Organization of the Elementary School Social Studies Curriculum," *Social Studies in the Elementary School*, 56th Yearbook, Part II (NSSE). Chicago: University of Chicago Press, 1957, pp. 129–162.

Froebel, F. *The Education of Man.* New York: Appleton-Century-Crofts, 1903.

Frost, J. L., ed. *Early Childhood Education Rediscovered.* New York: Holt, Rinehart and Winston, 1968.

Frostig, Marianne. *Frostig Program For The Development of Vision Perception.* Chicago: Follett Publishing Co., 1964.

Gabbard, Hazel F. "Status and Trends in Early Childhood Education," in *Those First School Years*, 39th Yearbook. Washington, D.C.: NEA, pp. 219–239.

Galton, F. *Hereditary Genius*, 1869.

Garrison, K. C. *Growth and Development*, 2nd ed. New York: Longmans, Green, 1959.

———, and Jones, F. R. *The Psychology of Human Development.* Scranton, Pa.: International Textbook Co., 1968.

———, et al. *Student's Workbook for the Psychology of Childhood.* New York: Scribner's, 1967.

Gerhardt, Lydia A. "Movement," in Carol Seefeldt, *Curriculum for the Preschool–Primary Child: A Review of Research.* Columbus, Ohio: Charles E. Merrill Publishing Co., 1976.

Gesell, A. L., and C. S. Amatruda. *Developmental Diagnosis*, 2nd. ed. New York: Paul B. Hoeber, 1947.

———, et al. *The First Five Years of Life.* New York: Harper and Row, 1940.

———, and Frances Ilg. *Child Development.* New York: Harper and Row, 1949.

———, Frances Ilg, and G. E. Bullis. *Vision, Its Development in Infant and Child.* New York: Paul B. Hoeber, 1948.

Gewirtz, J., ed. *Attachment and Dependency.* Washington, D.C.: Winston, 1972.

Gibb, Glenadine, and Alberta M. Castaneda. "Experiences for Young Children," *Mathematics Learning in Early Childhood.* Reston, Va.: National Council of Teachers of Mathematics, 1975, pp. 99–124.

Ginnott, H. *Teacher and Child.* New York: Macmillan, 1972.

Ginzberg, E., ed. *The Nation's Children*, 3 vols. Washington, D.C.: The Golden Anniversary White House Conference on Children and Youth, 1960.

———, ed. *Children and Youth in the 1960's, Survey Papers.* Washington, D.C.: The Golden Anniversary White House Conference on Children and Youth, 1960.

Glasser, W. *Schools Without Failure.* New York: Harper and Row, 1969.

Goertzel, Mildred G., and V. Goertzel. *Cradles of Eminence.* New York: Little, Brown, 1962.

Gollnick, Donna, F. H. Klassen, and J. Yff. *Multicultural Education and Ethnic Studies in the United States: An Analysis and Annotated Bibliography of Selected ERIC Documents.* Washington, D.C.: AACTE and ERIC, 1976.

Goodenough, Florence L. "Anger in Young Children," *Univ. Minn. Inst. Child Welf. Monogr. Series*, No. 9, 1931.

———. "Children's Drawings," in *A Handbook of Child Psychology.* C. A. Murchison, ed. Worcester, Mass: Clark University Press, 1931.

————, and M. J. Van Wagenen, *Minnesota Preschool Scales—Forms A and B*, rev. ed. Minneapolis: Educational Test Bureau, 1940.

Goodlad, J. I., and M. Frances Klein, and Associates, *Behind the Classroom Door.* Worthington, Ohio: Charles A. Jones Publishing, Co., 1970.

Goodykoontz, Bess, et al. "Recent History and Present Status of Education for Young Children," in *Early Childhood Education*, 46th Yearbook, Part II (NSSE). Chicago: The University of Chicago Press, 1947.

Gordon, I. J., ed. *Early Childhood Education*, The 71st Yearbook (NSSE), Part II. Chicago: The University of Chicago Press, 1972.

————. *The Florida Parent Education Early Intervention Projects: A Longitudinal Look.* Champaign-Urbana, Ill.: University of Illinois Publication Office, 1975.

————. *The Infant Experience.* Columbus, Ohio: Charles E. Merrill Publishing Co., 1975.

————, and R. D. Hess. *Parents as Teachers of Young Children: An Evaluative Review of Some Contemporary Concepts and Programs.* Palo Alto, Calif. Stanford University, 1975.

Gray, Susan, et al. *Before First Grade: The Early Training Project.* New York: Teachers College, Columbia University, 1966.

Green, J. A., ed. *Life and Work of Pestalozzi.* London: W. B. Clive, 1913.

Greene, H. A., and W. T. Petty. *Developing Language Skills in the Elementary School,* 5th ed. Boston: Allyn and Bacon, 1963.

Grotberg, Edith H., ed. *Critical Issues in Research Relating to Disadvantaged Children.* Princeton, N.J.: Educational Testing Service, 1969.

————. *Day Care: Resources for Decisions.* Washington, D.C.: OEO, 1971.

Hall, Mary Anne. *Teaching Reading as a Language Experience.* Columbus, Ohio: Charles E. Merrill Publishing Co., 1970.

Hamlin, Ruth, Rose Mukerji, and Margaret Yonemura. *Schools for Young Disadvantaged Children.* New York: Teachers College Press, Teachers College, Columbia University, 1967.

Harris, D. B. *Children's Drawings as Measures of Intellectual Maturity* (A revision and extention of Goodenough Draw-A-Man Test). New York: Harcourt Brace Jovanovich, 1963.

Hartley, Ruth E., and R. M. Goldenson. *The Complete Book of Children's Play.* New York: Crowell, 1957.

————, L. K. Frank, and R. M. Goldenson. *New Play Experiences for Children.* New York: Columbia University Press, 1952.

Hartshorne, H., and M. A. May. *Studies in Deceit.* New York: Macmillan, 1928.

Hartup, W., ed. *The Young Child—Reviews of Research, Vol. II.* Washington, D.C.: NAEYC, 1972.

————, and Nancy Smothergill, eds. *The Young Child—Reviews of Research*, Vol. I. Washington, D.C.: NAEYC, 1970.

Havighurst, R. J. *Developmental Tasks and Education,* 3rd ed. New York: David McKay, 1972.

Hechinger, F. M., ed. *Pre-School Education Today.* Garden City, N.Y.: Doubleday, 1966.

Heinz, Mamie W. *Growing and Learning at the Kindergarten.* Richmond, Va.: John Knox, 1959.

REFERENCES

Hellmuth, J., ed. *Disadvantaged Child: Head Start and Early Intervention.* Seattle, Wash.: Brunner Mazel, Inc., 1968.

———, ed. *Disadvantaged Child*, Vol. I. Seattle, Wash.: Special Child Publications, 1967.

Hendrickson, P. R., and E. P. Torrance. "Some Implications for Art Education from the Minnesota Studies of Creative Thinking," *Creativity in Art Education.* Washington, D.C.: NAEA, 1963, pp. 20–25.

Herrick, V. E., and L. B. Jacobs. *Children and the Language Arts.* Englewood Cliffs, N.J.: Prentice-Hall, 1951.

Herrick, V. W., and Marcella Nerbovig. *Using Experience Charts with Children.* Columbus, Ohio: Charles E. Merrill Publishing Co., 1964.

Herron, R. E., and B. Sutton-Smith. *Child's Play.* New York: Wiley, 1971.

Hess, R. D., and Roberta M. Bear, eds. *Early Education.* Chicago: Aldine Publishing Co., 1968.

———, and Doreen J. Croft, *Teachers of Young Children.* Boston: Houghton Mifflin, 1972.

Hildreth, Gertrude. *Readiness for School Beginners.* Yonkers, N.Y.: World Book, 1950.

Hilgard, E. *Theories of Learning*, 2nd ed. New York: Appleton-Century-Crofts, 1956.

Hirsch, Elisebeth, S. "Block Building—Practical Considerations for the Classroom Teacher," in *The Block Book.* Washington, D.C.: NAEYC, 1974, pp. 89–76.

Hoffman, M. L. "Moral Development," in L. Carmichael, ed. *Manual of Child Psychology.* New York: Wiley, 1970, pp. 251–359.

Hollingshead, A. B., and F. C. Redlich. *Social Class and Mental Illness.* New York: Wiley, 1958.

Huck, Charlotte S. *Children's Literature in the Elementary School*, 3rd ed. New York: Holt, Rinehart and Winston, 1976.

Hunt, J. McVey. *Intelligence and Experience.* New York: Ronald Press, 1961.

Hurd, G. E. *Primary Enrollment.* Washington, D.C.: U.S. DHEW, OE, 1969.

Hutt, Corrine, and Reena Bhavnani. "Predictions from Play," in J. S. Bruner, et al. *Play—Its Role in Development and Evolution.* New York: Basic Books, 1976.

Hymes, J. L. Jr. *Behavior and Misbehavior.* Englewood Cliffs, N.J.: Prentice-Hall, 1955.

———. *Effective Home-School Relations.* Englewood Cliffs, N.J.: Prentice-Hall, 1953.

———. "Teaching Reading to the Under-Six Age: A Child Development Point of View," in *Claremont Reading Conference 34th Yearbook.* Claremont, Calif.: Clarmont Graduate School, 1970, pp. 79–83.

Jahoda, M. Current Concepts of Positive Mental Health. New York: Basic Books, 1958.

Jarolimek, J. *Social Studies in Elementary Education.* 5th ed. New York: Macmillan, 1977.

Jefferson, Blanche. *Teaching Art to Children.* Boston: Allyn and Bacon, 1959.

Jenkins, Gladys G., Helen Schacter, and W. W. Bauer. *These Are Your Children*, 2nd ed. Chicago: Scott, Foresman, 1953.

Jersild, A. T. *Child Psychology*, 6th ed., Englewood Cliffs, N.J.: Prentice-Hall, 1968.

———. *When Teachers Face Themselves.* New York: Teachers College, Columbia University, 1955.

————, and Sylvia Beinstock. *Development of Rhythm in Young Children.* New York: Teachers College, Columbia University, 1937.

————, and Francis B. Holmes. "Children's Fears," *Child Develpm. Monogr.,* No. 20, 1935.

————, and F. V. Markey. "Conflicts Between Preschool Children," *Child Develpm. Monogr.,* 21, 1935.

Johnson, O. G., and J. W. Bommarito. *Tests and Measurement in Child Development: A Handbook.* San Francisco: Jossey-Bass, Inc., 1971.

Joint Committee on Health Problems in Education of the NEA and AMA. *Why Health Education?* Chicago: AMA, 1965.

Jones, Mary Alice. *Guiding Children in Christian Growth.* Nashville, Tenn.: Abingdon Press, 1949.

Jowett, B., trans. *Dialogues of Plato,* 2 vols. New York: Random House, 1937.

Kagan, H. E. "Teaching Values to Our Children," *Children and Youth in the 1960's.* Washington, D.C.: White House Conference on Children and Youth, 1960, pp. 57–65.

Kagan, J., and H. Moss. *Birth to Maturity.* New York: Wiley, 1962.

Kahl, J. A. *The American Class Structure.* New York: Holt, Rinehart and Winston, 1959.

Kelley, E. C. "The Fully Functioning Self," *Perceiving, Behaving, Becoming,* 1962 Yearbook. Washington, D.C.: ASCD, 1962, pp. 9–20.

Kellog, Rhoda. *What Children Scribble And Why.* San Francisco: San Francisco Golden Gate Nursery, 1955.

Kennedy, W. A. *Child Psychology.* Englewood Cliffs, N.J.: Prentice-Hall, 1971.

Kirk, S. A. *Early Education of Mentally Retarded: An Experimental Study.* Urbana, Ill.: University of Illinois Press, 1958.

Kohl, Herbert R. *The Open Classroom.* New York: A New York Review Book distributed by Random House, 1969.

Kohn, S. *The Early Learning Center* (Profiles of Significant Schools). New York: Educational Facilities Laboratories, Inc., 1970.

Kolberg, L. "Development of Moral Character and Ideology," in *Review of Child Development Research,* Vol. I. New York: Russell Sage Foundation, 1964, pp. 383–431.

Lacey, Joy M. *Social Studies Concepts of Children in the First Three Grades.* New York: Teachers College, Columbia University, 1932.

Lambert, Hazel M. *Early Childhood Education.* Boston: Allyn and Bacon, 1960.

Lambert, W. E., and O. Klineberg. *Children's Views of Foreign Peoples.* New York: Appleton-Century-Crofts, 1967.

Landreth, Catherine. *The Psychology of Early Childhood.* New York: Alfred A. Knopf, 1958.

Langdon, Grace, and I. W. Stout. *Teacher–Parent Interviews.* Englewood Cliffs, N.J.: Prentice-Hall, 1954.

Language Arts for To-day's Children. National Council of Teachers of English. New York: Appleton-Century-Crofts, 1954.

Lavatelli, Celia S. *Piaget's Theory Applied to an Early Childhood Curriculum.* Boston: American Science and Engineering, Inc., 1970.

REFERENCES

Lay, Margaret V., and J. C. Dopyers. *Becoming A Teacher of Young Children.* Lexington, Mass.: D.C. Heath, 1977.

Lease, Ruth G., and Geraldine B. Siks. *Creative Dramatics in Home, School, and Community.* New York: Harper and Row, 1952.

Lee, J. M., and Dorris M. Lee. *The Child and His Development.* New York: Appleton-Century-Crofts, 1952.

Leeper, R. R., ed. *Creating a Good Environment for Learning,* 1954 Yearbook (ASCD). Washington, D.C.: ASCD, 1954.

Leonard, Edith M., et al. *Counseling with Parents in Early Childhood Education.* New York: Macmillan Publishing Co., 1954.

Lesser, G. *Children and Television: Lessons from Sesame Street.* New York: Random House, 1974.

Lindberg, Lucile, and Rita Swedlow. *Early Childhood Education: A Guide for Observation and Participation.* Boston: Allyn and Bacon, 1976 (Tear Sheets).

Locke, John. *An Essay Concerning Human Understanding,* Bk. 2, 1689.

Low, S., and Pearl G. Spindler, *Child Care Arrangements of Working Mothers in the United States.* Washington, D.C.: HEW and Department of Labor, Children's Bureau, 1968.

Lowenfeld, V., and W. L. Brittain, 5th ed. *Creative and Mental Growth.* New York: Macmillan, 1970.

McCarthy, Dorothea. "Language Development in Children," *Manual of Child Psychology,* ed. L. Carmichael, 2nd ed. New York: Wiley, 1954, pp. 492–630.

MacDonald, J. "The Open School: Curriculum Concepts," in *Open Education* Georgianna Engstrom, ed. Washington, D.C.: NAEYC.

McFee, June King. *Preparation for Art,* 2nd ed. San Francisco: Wadsworth, 1970.

Mager, R. F. *Preparing Instructional Objectives.* Palo Alto, Calif.: Fearon Publishers, 1962.

Malone, Margaret. *Congressional Research Service, A Summary of Selected Proposals Related to Child Care.* Washington, D.C.: Library of Congress, June 24, 1971.

Margolin, Edythe. *Sociocultural Elements in Early Childhood Education.* New York: Macmillan, 1974.

Marks, J. L., et al. *Teaching Arithmetic for Understanding.* New York: McGraw-Hill, 1958.

Mascho, G. "Familiarity with Measurement," *Mathematics Learning in Early Childhood.* Reston, Va.: National Council of Teachers of Mathematics, 1975.

Matterson, E. M. *Play and Playthings for the Preschool Child.* Baltimore, Md.: Penguin Books, 1967.

Mead, M., and M. Wolfenstein. *Childhood in Contemporary Cultures.* Chicago: University of Chicago Press, 1955.

Merry, Frieda K., and R. V. Merry. *The First Two Decades of Life,* 2nd ed. New York: Harper and Row, 1958.

Miel, Alice, and Peggy Brogan. *More Than Social Studies.* Englewood Cliffs, N.J.: Prentice-Hall, 1957.

Millar, Susanna. *The Psychology of Play.* New York: Jason Aronson, 1974.

Mills, Belen C., ed. *Understanding the Young Child and His Curriculum.* New York: Macmillan, 1972.

Monroe, Marion. *Growing into Reading.* Chicago: Scott, Foresman, 1951.

Monroe, W. S., ed. *Comenius' School of Infancy.* Boston: D. C. Heath, 1908.

Montessori, Maria. *The Montessori Method.* New York: Frederick A. Stokes, 1912.

Moss, Bernice R., W. H. Southworth, and J. L. Reichert, eds. *Health Education,* 5th ed. Washington, D.C.: NEA, 1961.

Munro, T. "Children's Art Abilities: Studies at the Cleveland Museum of Art," E. W. Eisner and D. W. Ecker, *Readings in Art Education.* Waltham, Mass.: Blaisdell Publishing Co., 1966, pp. 163–180.

Murphy, Lois Barclay. *Personality in Young Children,* Vol. II. New York: Basic Books, 1956.

––––––. *Social Behavior and Child Personality: An Exploratory Study of Some Roots of Sympathy.* New York: Columbia University Press, 1937.

Mussen, Paul H., ed. *Carmichael's Manual of Child Psychology,* Vol's I & II, 3rd ed. New York: Wiley, 1970.

––––––, J. J. Conger, and J. Kagen. *Readings in Child Development and Personality.* New York: Harper and Row, 1970.

Mycock, Mary A. "Vertical Grouping" in V. R. Rogers, *Teaching in the British Primary School.* New York: Macmillan, 1970.

National Education Association and AASA, Educational Policies Commission. *Moral and Spiritual Values in Public Schools.* Washington, D.C.: NEA & AASA, 1951.

Navarra, J. G. *The Development of Scientific Concepts in a Young Child.* New York: Teachers College, Columbia University, 1955.

Nelson, Mary J., and Gladys Tipton. *Music for Early Childhood.* New York: Silver Burdett, 1952.

Nimnicht, G., Oralee McAfee, and J. Meier. *The New Nursery School.* New York: General Learning Corporation, Early Learning Division, 1969.

Nye, R. E., and Vernice T. Nye. *Music in the Elementary School,* 3rd ed. Englewood Cliffs, N.J.: Prentice-Hall, 1970.

Nye, Vernice. *Music for Young Children.* New York: William C. Brown Co., 1975.

Ojeman, R. *A Teaching Program On Human Behavior and Mental Health.* Iowa City: State University of Iowa, 1960.

––––––. "Social Studies in Light of Knowledge about Children," in *Social Studies in the Elementary School,* 56th Yearbook, Part II (NSSE). Chicago: University of Chicago Press, 1957, pp. 76–119.

Oleron, P. (trans. by R. P. Lorion). *Language and Mental Development.* Hillsdale, N. J.: Lawrence Erlbaum Associates, 1977.

Olson, W. C. *Child Development,* 2nd ed. Boston: D.C. Heath, 1959.

Orem, R. C. *A Montessori Handbook.* New York: Capricorn Books, 1966.

Osborn, D. K., and Janie D. Osborn. *Discipline and Classroom Management.* Athens, Ga.: Education Associates, 1977, p. 34.

Passow, A. H. "Enrichment of Education for the Gifted," *Education for the Gifted,* 57th Yearbook, Part II (NSSE). Chicago: University of Chicago Press, 1958, pp. 198–221.

Penfield, W., and L. Roberts. *Speech and Brain Mechanisms.* Princeton, N.J.: Princeton University Press, 1959.

Pestalozzi, J. H. *How Gertrude Teaches Her Children,* 1898.

Phillips, J. L. *The Origins of Intellect.* San Francisco: W. H. Freeman & Co., 1969.

REFERENCES

Piaget, J. *The Child and Reality.* (trans. by A. Rosin). New York: Grossman Publishers, a Division of Viking Press, 1974.

———. *Language and Thought of the Child.* New York: Humanities Press, 1951.

———. The Origins of Intelligence in Children. New York: International Universities Press, 1952.

———. *Play, Dreams, and Imitation in Childhood.* (trans. by Gattengo and Hodgson). New York: W. W. Norton, 1962.

Pitcher, Evelyn Goodenough, et al. *Helping Children Learn.* Columbus, Ohio: Charles E. Merrill Books, 1966.

Prescott, D. A. *The Child in the Educative Process.* New York: McGraw-Hill, 1957.

Preyer, W. *Die Seele des Kindes,* 2 vols., 1888.

Profiles of Children, White House Conference on Children, 1970. Washington, D.C.: U.S. Government Printing Office, 1970.

Rambusch, Nancy McCormick. *Learning How to Learn—An American Approach to Montessori.* Baltimore, Md.: Helicon Press, 1962.

Rapport, Virginia, and Mary N. S. W. Parker. *Learning Centers—Children on Their Own.* Washington, D.C.: ACEI, 1970.

Rasey, Marie, and J. W. Menge. *What We Learn from Children.* New York: Harper and Row, 1956.

Raths, L. E., M. Harmin, and, S. B. Simon. *Values and Teaching: Working With Values in the Classroom.* Columbus, Ohio: Charles E. Merrill Books, 1966.

Read, Katherine H. *The Nursery School.* Philadelphia: W. B. Saunders, 1960.

Report to the President, White House Conference on Children, 1970. Washington, D.C.: U.S. Government Printing Office, 1970.

Richardson, Sybil K., and Faith W. Smitter. "The Learner," in *Learning and the Teacher,* 1959 Yearbook (ASCD). Washington, D.C.: NEA, 1959, pp. 27–36.

Robison, Helen F. *Exploring Teaching in Early Childhood Education.* Boston: Allyn and Bacon, 1977.

———. *Project Child: Evolution of A Curriculum to Heighten Intellectual and Language Development.* New York: Teachers College, Columbia University Press, 1969.

Robinson, Edith, M. Mahaffey, and D. Nelson. "Measurement," *Mathematics Learning in Early Childhood.* Reston, Va.: National Council of Teachers of Mathematics, 1975.

Robinson, Nancy B., and H. B. Robinson. *The Mentally Retarded Child.* 2nd ed. New York: McGraw-Hill Book Co., 1976.

Ross, A. O. *Learning Disability, the Unrealized Potential.* New York: McGraw-Hill, 1977.

Rogers, V. R. *Teaching in the British Primary School.* New York: Macmillan, 1970.

Rousseau, Jean-Jacques. *Emile,* trans. Barbara Foxley. London: J. M. Dent, 1911.

Ruderman, Florence. *Child Care and Working Mothers.* New York: Child Welfare League of America, Inc., 1968.

Rusk, R. R. *The Doctrines of Great Educators.* London: Macmillan, 1926.

Sawyer, Ruth. *The Way of the Story Teller.* New York: Viking Press, 1962.

Schramm, L. J., and E. B. Parker. *Television in the Lives of Our Children.* Stanford, Calif.: Stanford University Press, 1961.

Schultz, Beth. "Ecology for the Child," *Environmental Education in the Elementary School.* Washington, D.C.: NSTA, 1972, pp. 14–15.

Schultz, Beth. "Your Town: A Biotic Community with People," *Environmental Education in the Elementary School.* Washington, D.C.: NSTA, 1972, pp. 33–35.

Schulz, Lillian. "The Caterpillar," in ACEI, *Sung Under the Green Umbrella.* New York: Macmillan, Inc., 1962.

Sears, Pauline S., and Edith M. Dowley. In N. L. Gage, ed. "Research on Teaching in the Nursery School," in *Handbook of Research on Teaching.* Chicago: Rand McNally, 1963, Chap. 15.

Sears, R., E. Maccoby, and H. Levin. *Patterns of Child Rearing.* Evanston, Ill.: Row, Peterson, 1957.

Seefeldt, Carol. *Curriculum for the Preschool–Primary Child: A Review of Research.* Columbus, Ohio: Charles E. Merrill Publishing Co., 1976.

Sheehy, Emma E. *The Fives and Sixes Go to School.* New York: Holt, Rinehart and Winston, 1954.

Siks, Geraldine, B. *Creative Dramatics, An Art for Children.* New York: Harper and Row, 1958.

Sinclair, Caroline B. *Movement of the Young Child.* Columbus, Ohio: Charles E. Merrill Publishing Co., 1973.

Skinner, B. F. *Walden Two.* New York: Macmillan, 1948.

Smart, Mollie S., and Smart, R. C. *Children—Development and Relationships.* 2nd ed. New York: Macmillan, 1972.

Smith, Dora V. "Developmental Language Patterns of Children," in H. Newman, *Effective Language Arts Practices in the Elementary School: Selected Readings.* New York: Wiley, 1972.

————. "Growth in Language Power as Related to Child Development," *Teaching Language in the Elementary School*, 43rd Yearbook, Part II (NSSE). Chicago: University of Chicago Press, 1944, pp. 52–97.

Smith, L. M., and Pat M. Keith. *Anatomy of Education Innovation: An Organizational Analysis of the Elementary School.* New York: Wiley, 1971.

Smith, R. B. *Music in the Child's Education.* New York: Ronald Press, 1970.

Socolov, Judith, General Ed. *Early Childhood Education Project.* New York: The Modern Language Association of America, 1971.

Spodek, B. "Introduction," in *Open Education.* Washington, D.C.: NAEYC, 1970.

Squire, J. M., ed. *A New Look at Progressive Education, 1972 Yearbook.* Washington, D.C.: ASCD, 1972.

Stagner, R. *Psychology of Personality*, 2nd ed. New York: McGraw-Hill Book Co., 1948.

Stahl, Dona K., and Patricia Murphy Anzalone. *Individualized Teaching in the Elementary School* West Nyack, N.Y.: Parker Publishing Co., 1970.

Stant, Margaret A. *The Young Child: His Activities and Materials.* Englewood Cliffs, N.J.: Prentice-Hall, 1972.

The States Report on Children and Youth. Washington, D.C.: The Golden Anniversary White House Conference on Children and Youth, 1960.

Statistical Abstracts of the United States. Washington, D.C.: U.S. Bureau of the Census. U.S. Government Printing Office, 1962, 1964, 1966, 1970, 1976.

Stendler, Celia B. *Children of Brasstown*. Urbana, Ill.: University of Illinois Press, 1949.

———, and W. Martin. *Intergroup Education in Kindergarten-Primary Grades*. New York: Macmillan, 1953.

Stone, L. J., and J. Church. *Childhood and Adolescence*, 2nd ed. New York: Random House, 1968.

Stutsman, Rachel. *Mental Measurement of Preschool Children With A Guide for the Administration of the Merrill-Palmer Scale of Mental Tests*. Yonkers, N.Y.: World Book, 1931.

Suchman, J. R. *Observation and Analysis in Child Development: A Laboratory Manual*. New York: Harcourt Brace Jovanovich, 1959.

Swenson, Esther J. *Teaching Mathematics to Children*, 2nd ed. New York: Macmillan, 1973.

Tanner, D. *Using Behavioral Objectives in the Classroom*. New York: Macmillan, 1972.

Thompson, G. G. *Child Psychology: Growth Trends in Psychological Adjustment*. Boston: Houghton Mifflin, 1952.

Thorndike, E. L., et al. *Adult Learning*. New York: Macmillan, 1928.

Thorum, A. R., et al. *Instructional Materials for the Handicapped: Birth Through Early Childhood*. Salt Lake City: Olympus Publishing Co., 1976.

Todd, Vivian E., and Heffernan, Helen. *The Years Before School*, 3rd ed. New York: Macmillan, 1977.

Torrance, E. *Guiding Creative Talent*. New York: Ronald Press, 1960.

Tough, Joan. *Listening to Children Talking: A Guide to the Appraisal of Children's Use of Language*. London: Ward Lock, 1976.

Trafton, P. "The Curriculum," *Mathematics Learning in Early Childhood*. Reston, Va.: National Council of Teachers of Mathematics, 1975, p. 39.

Trager, Helen G., and Marian R. Yarrow. *They Learn What They Live: Prejudice in Young Children*. New York: Harper and Row, 1952.

Tryon, Caroline, and J. W. Lilienthal. "Development Tasks: The Concept and Its Importance," *Fostering Mental Health in Our Schools*, 1950 Yearbook. Washington, D.C.: ASCD, 1950.

U.S. Bureau of the Census, *Statistical Abstracts of the United States*. Washington, D.C.: U.S. Government Printing Office, 1962, 1964, 1966.

U.S. Office of Education, Biennial Survey of Education in the U.S. *Statistics of State School Systems, 1949–50*. Washington, D.C.: U.S. Government Printing Office, 1952, Chap. IV.

Van Alstyne, Dorothy. *Play Behavior and Choice of Play Materials of Preschool Children*. Chicago: University of Chicago Press, 1932.

von Marenholz-Bülow, Baroness B. *Reminiscences of Frederick Froebel*, 1877.

Vygotsky, L. S. "Play and Its Role in the Mental Development of the Child," in J. S. Bruner, et al. *Play—Its Role in Development and Evolution*, New York: Basic Books, 1976.

Wadsworth, B. J. *Piaget's Theory of Cognitive Development*. New York: David McKay, 1971.

Wann, K. D., Miriam S. Darn, and Elizabeth A. Liddle. *Fostering Intellectual Develop-

ment in Young Children. New York: Teachers College, Columbia University, 1962.

Watson, R. I. *Psychology of the Child.* New York: Wiley, 1959.

Weber, Evelyn. *Early Childhood Education: Perspectives on Change.* Worthington, Ohio: Charles A. Jones Publishing Co., 1970.

Weikart, D. P., et al. *The Cognitively Oriented Curriculum.* Washington, D.C.: NAEYC (ERIC & NAEYC Publication), 1971.

Willcockson, Mary, ed. *Social Education of Young Children.* Washington, D.C.: National Council for the Social Studies, 1950.

Williams, F., ed. *Language and Poverty.* Chicago: Markham Publishing Company, 1970.

Wills, Clarice D., and Lucile Lindberg. *Kindergarten for Today's Children.* Chicago: Follett, 1967.

———, and W. H. Stegeman. *Living in the Kindergarten.* Chicago: Follett, 1956.

Yamamoto, Kaoru, ed. *The Child and His Image.* Boston: Houghton-Mifflin, 1972.

Zaporozhets, A. V. "The Development of Perception in the Preschool Child," in *European Research in Cognitive Development, Monogr. Soc. Res. Child Develpm., 30*:2 (1965), pp. 83–101.

Pamphlets, Bulletins, and Other Published Materials

Almy, Millie. "New Views on Intellectual Development in Early Childhood Education," *Intellectual Development, Another Look.* Washington, D.C.: ASCD, 1964, pp. 12–25.

AASA. *Open Space Schools.* Washington, D.C.: AASA, 1971.

American Council on Education. *The Function of the Public Schools in Dealing with Religion.* A Report on the Exploratory Study made for the American Council on Education by the Committee on Religion and Education, 1953.

Anderson, J. E. "Principles of Child Development," *Early Education.* Washington, D.C.: NEA, 1956, pp. 14–21.

Austin, Mary C. "Current Reading Practices," *Teaching Young Children to Read* (U.S. Office of Education). Washington, D.C.: U.S. Government Printing Office, 1964, pp. 16–20.

Baker, Katherine Read, "Extending the Indoors Outside," *Housing for Early Childhood Education.* Washington, D.C.: ACEI, pp. 59–66.

Becker, W. C., D. R. Thomas, and D. Carnine. *Reducing Behavior Problems: An Operant Conditioning Guide for Teachers.* Urbana, Ill.: ERIC Clearing House, University of Illinois, 1969.

Berman, Louise M. *Toward New Programs for Young Children.* College Park, Md.: University of Maryland, 1970.

Better Health for Florida's Children (Bull. 4E) Tallahassee: Florida State Department of Education, 1957.

Biber, Barbara. *Young Deprived Children and Their Educational Needs.* Washington, D.C.: ACEI, 1967.

————, et al. *Promoting Cognitive Growth: A Developmental-Interaction Point of View.* Washington, D.C., 1971.

A Bibliography of Books for Children. Washington, D.C.: ACEI, 1977.

Burgess, Evangeline. *Values in Early Childhood Education.* Washington, D.C.: NEA, 1965.

Butler, Annie L. *The Child's Right to Quality Day Care.* Washington, D.C.: ACEI, 1970.

CEMREL Newsletter. St. Louis, Mo.: CEMREL, 10646, St. Charles Rd. 63074.

Child Care Data and Materials. Committee on Finance, U.S. Senate, June 16, 1971.

"Child Care and Guidance." *A Suggested Post High School Curriculum.* Washington, D.C.: U.S. DHEW, OE., 1967.

Chilman, Catherine. "Child Rearing and Family Relationship Patterns of the Very Poor," *Welfare in Review.* Washington, D.C.: U.S. DHEW, January, 1965.

Class, E. *Licensing of Child Care Facilities by State Welfare Departments.* Washington, D.C.: U.S. DHEW, Social Rehabilitation Service, Children's Bureau, 1968.

Coble, Clara. "Teacher-Planner of the Nursery School," *Space Arrangement Beauty in School.* Washington, D.C.: ACEI, 1958, pp. 4–6.

Cohen, M. D., ed. *That All Children May Learn We Must Learn.* (Reprinted). Washington, D.C.: ACEI, 1970.

Combs, A. W. "Personality Theory and Its Implications for Curriculum Development," in *Learning More About Learning.* Washington, D.C.: ASCD, 1959, pp. 5–20.

Council of Chief State School Officers. *Responsibilities of State Department of Education for Nursery School and Kindergarten, A Policy Statement.* Washington, D.C.: NEA, 1961.

Creating with Materials for Work and Play, Leaflet 5. Washington, D.C.: ACEI, 1957.

Crosby, Muriel. "Identifying Oral Language Relationships," *Children and Oral Language.* Washington, D.C.: ASCD, 1964, pp. 3–9.

Curriculum Is What Happens. Washington, D.C.: NAEYC, 1970.

Cutts, W. G. *Teaching Young Children to Read* (U.S. Office of Education). Washington, D.C.: U.S. Government Printing Office, 1964.

Darney, Elizabeth Doak. *What Does the Nursery Teacher Teach?* Washington, D.C.: NAEYC, 1965.

Davis, Edith A. *The Development of Linguistic Skill in Twins, Singletons With Siblings, and Only Children From Age Five To Ten Years,* Institute Child Welf. Monogr. Series No. 14. Minneapolis: University of Minnesota Press, 1937.

Davis, Mary Dabney. *Nursery Schools, Their Development and Current Practices in the United States* (Bull. No. 9, U.S. Office of Education). Washington, D.C.: U.S. Government Printing Office, 1932.

Davis, R. B. *The Changing Curriculum: Mathematics.* Washington, D.C.: ASCD, 1967.

Dawson, Mildred. *Learning to Listen,* Language Arts Notes, No. 3. Yonkers-on-Hudson, N.Y.: World Book Company.

Day Care Licensing: Policies and Practices: A State Survey, July 1975. Report Number 72. Denver, Colorado: The Education Commission of the States, 1975.

Day, D. E., and D. W. Allen. "Organization for Individual Work," *Learning Centers: Children on Their Own.* Washington, D.C.: ACEI, 1970, pp. 26–37.

Dunfee, Maxine. *Elementary Social Studies: A Guide to Current Research.* Washington, D.C.: ASCD, 1970.

"Early Childhood Development: Alternatives for Program Implementation in the States." Denver: Education Commission of the States, 1971.

Early Childhood Programs: A State Survey 1974–75, Report no. 65. Denver, Colorado: The Education Commission of the States, 1975.

Evans, Eleanor. "Vents for Children's Feelings," *Discipline.* Washington, D.C.: ACEI, 1957, pp. 25–31.

Experiencing the Language Arts, Bull. No. 34. Tallahassee: Florida State Department of Education, 1948.

Four Programs for Educational Services to Handicapped Children. Washington, D.C.: U.S. DHEW. OE., 1971 (Item 2, Part C. Title II).

Frazier, A. *Adventuring, Mastering, Associating: New Strategies for Teaching Children.* Washington, D.C.: ASCD, 1976.

Friedburg, M. P. *Playgrounds of City Children*, Washington, D.C.: ACEI, 1969.

Good and Inexpensive Books for Children. Washington, D.C.: ACEI, 1972.

Goodlad, J. I., M. Frances Klein, and Associates. *Behind the Classroom Door.* Worthington, Ohio: Charles A. Jones Publishing Co., 1970.

Grams, A. *Parenting: Concept and Process.* Washington, D.C.: ACEI, 1973.

A Guide: Early Childhood Education in Florida Schools. Bulletin, 76. Tallahassee: Florida State Department of Education, 1969.

A Guide for Organizing and Developing A Kindergarten Program in Florida Bull. No. 53A, rev. Tallahassee, Fla.: Florida State Department of Education, 1955.

Hochman, Vivienne. "Kindergarten-Primary Rooms Reflect Interests," *Space Arrangement Beauty in School.* Washington, D.C.: ACEI, 1958.

The Home Start Demonstration Program: An Overview. Washington, D.C.: DHEW, OCD, 1973.

Hoppock, Anne A. *All Children Have Gifts.* Washington, D.C.: ACEI, 1958.

Horowitz, Sandra B. *From Theory to Practice: A Personal Dairy of A Teacher of Young Children.* College Park, Md.: University of Maryland, 1971.

Howard, A. E. *Characteristics of Early Childhood Teacher Education.* Washington, D.C.: ACEI, 1967.

Hymes, J. "They Act Their Age," *Discipline.* Washington, D.C.: ACEI, 1957, pp. 18–25.

Implementation of Planned Variations in Head Start, 1969–70. Washington, D.C.: Institute of Child Study, University of Maryland, and OCD, DHEW, 1970.

Implementing Mathematics Programs in California, A Guide K-8. Menlo Park, Calif., 1965.

Intellectual Development: Another Look. Washington, D.C.: ASCD, NEA, 1964.

Interim Policy Guide for the 4-C Program Pilot Phase. Washington, D.C.: OCD, HEW, 1969.

An Invitation to Help Head Start Developmental Programs. Washington, D.C.: Project Head Start, OEO, 1967.

Jacobs, L. B. "Enjoying Poetry with Children," *Literature with Children.* Washington, D.C.: ACEI, 1972, pp. 32–35.

Jefferson, Ruth E. "Bulletin Boards for Young Children," *Involvement Bulletin Boards.* Washington, D.C.: ACEI, 1970, pp. 57–63.

———. "Indoor Facilities," *Housing for Early Childhood Education.* Washington, D.C.: ACEI, 1968, pp. 41–52.

REFERENCES

Kritchevsky, Sybil, and Elizabeth Prescott. *Planning Environments for Young Children—Physical Space*. Washington, D.C.: NAEYC, 1969.

Krogman, W. M. "Physical Growth as a Factor in the Behavioral Development of the Child," *New Dimensions in Learning*. Washington, D.C.: ASCD, 1963, pp. 8–23.

Lane, Mary B. *Educating for Parenting*. Washington, D.C. NAEYC, 1975.

Lantz, Beatrice. *Easel Age Scale*. Los Angeles: California Test Bureau, 1955.

Leiserson, Marion Lawrence. *Creating "Loving" Environment for Children*. College Park: University of Maryland, 1971.

Loban, W. *The Language of Elementary School Children*. Champaign, Ill.: NCTE, 1963.

Malone, Margaret. *Summary of Selected Proposals Related to Child Care*. Washington, D.C.: Library of Congress, Congressional Research Service, Education and Welfare, June, 1971.

A Manual of Certification Requirements for School Personnel in the United States, 1970 ed. Washington, D.C.: National Commission on Teacher Education and Professional Standards, NEA, 1970.

McAfee, Oralie. "To Make or Buy?" *Selecting Educational Equipment and Materials for Home and School*. Washington, D.C.: ACEI, 1976. pp. 25–27.

McKee, P., and J. E. Brzeinski. *The Effectiveness of Teaching Reading in Kindergarten*. Denver, Colorado: Denver Public Schools and the Colorado State Department of Education, 1966.

Mental Retardation, Plans and Programs. Washington, D.C.: U.S. DHEW, OE, June, 1965.

A National Survey of the Impact of Head Start Centers on Community Institutions. Washington, D.C.: Prepared for the Office of Child Development, U.S. DHEW by Kirschner Associates, Inc., 1970.

Perez, O. E. *Spanish in Florida Elementary Schools*. Tallahassee: Florida State Department of Education, 1960.

Plan of Action for Children 1953–55. Washington, D.C.: ACEI, 1953.

Preliminary Report of Ad Hoc Joint Committee On the Preparation of Nursery and Kindergarten Teachers. Washington, D.C.; National Commission on Teacher Education and Professional Standards, NEA, 1969.

Prelude to School, An Evaluation of An Inner-City Program. Report No. 3. Washington, D.C.: U.S. DHEW, Dept. of Health, 1968.

Preparation Standards for Teachers in Early Childhood Education. Washington, D.C.: ACEI, 1967.

Prereading, Bulletin 246. Rockville, Md.: Montgomery County Public Schools, 1974.

Prescott, Elizabeth. *A Pilot Study of Day-Care Centers and Their Clientele*. Washington, D.C.: U.S. Government Printing Office, 1965.

Program Description, Handicapped Children's Early Education Program. U.S. DHEW, OE., Bureau of Education for the Handicapped, Program Development Branch, Division of Educational Services, 1971.

Project Head Start. *Head Start—A Community Action Program*. Washington, D.C.: U.S. Government Printing Office, 1968.

Project Head Start. *Project Head Start, Health Services—A Guide for Project Directors and Health Personnel*. Washington, D.C.: U.S. Government Printing Office, 1969.

Project Head Start Statistical Fact Sheet Fiscal Year 1971. Washington, D.C.: OEO, HEW, 1971.

Rampton, C. L., ed. *Early Childhood Development: Alternatives for the Program Implementation in the States.* Denver, Colorado: Education Commission of the States, 1971.

"Report of the Program Committee," SRCD Biennial Meeting, New Orleans, March 17–20, 1977. Topeka Kansas: Box 829, The Menninger Foundation, *SRCD Newsletter* (Summer), 1977.

Research Relating to Children. ERIC Clearing House on Early Childhood Education. Washington, D.C.: Superintendent of Documents. U.S. Government Printing Office, Current.

Robbins, E. L. "Language Development Research," *Interpreting Language Arts Research for the Teacher.* Washington, D.C.: ASCD, 1970, pp. 3–12.

Roche, Ruth L. *The Child and Science—Wondering, Exploring, Growing.* Washington, D.C.: ACEI, 1977, p. 2.

Shoemaker, Rowena. *All in Play.* New York: Play Schools Association, Inc., 1958.

Smith, Madorah E. "An Investigation of the Development of the Sentence and the Extent of Vocabulary in Young Children," *Univ. Iowa Studies Child Welf.*, 3:5 (1926).

Smith, Nila B. "Trends in Beginning Reading Since 1900," in *Teaching Young Children to Read* (U.S. Office of Education). Washington, D.C.: U.S. Government Printing Office, 1964, pp. 5–15.

State Agencies Administering Services Under Title V, Parts 1 and 2, and Title IV, Part B of the Social Security Act. Washington, D.C.: U.S. DHEW, Social and Rehabilitative Services, Children's Bureau, 1969.

Stone, Jeanette Galambos. *Play and Playgrounds.* Washington, D.C.: NAEYC, 1970.

Strickland, Ruth G. *The Contribution of Structural Linguistics to the Teaching of Reading, Writing, and Grammar in the Elementary School.* Bloomington: School of Education, Indiana University, 1963.

———. *The Language of Elementary School Children: Its Relationship to the Language of Reading Textbooks and the Quality of Reading of Selected Children.* Bloomington: School of Education, Indiana University, 1962.

Study of Selected Children in Head Start Planned Variations 1969–1970, 3 Case Studies of Children. Washington, D.C.: University of Maryland and OCD, HEW, October 1970.

Sunderlin, Sylvia, ed. *Aides to Teachers and Children.* Washington, D.C.: ACEI, 1967.

———. *Equipment and Supplies Tested and Approved for Preschool Home School.* Washington, D.C.: ACEI, 1967.

———. *Migrant Children: Their Education.* Washington, D.C.: ACEI, 1971.

Tanner, Daniel. *Using Behavioral Objectives in the Classroom.* New York: Macmillan, Inc., 1972.

Teaching The Disadvantaged Young Child. Washington, D.C.: NAEYC, 1966.

Templin, Mildred C. *Certain Language Skills in Children,* Institute of Child Welf. Monogr. Series XXVI. Minneapolis: University of Minnesota Press, 1957.

United States Department of Health, Education and Welfare. *Your Child from 6 to 12.* Washington, D.C.: HEW, 1970.

REFERENCES

Using Title XX to Serve Children and Youth. New York: Child Welfare League of America, 1975.

Weikart, D. P. *The Cognitively Oriented Curriculum.* Washington, D.C.: NAEYC, 1971.

Williams, H. M. *The Retarded Child Goes to School,* U.S. Dept. of Health, Education and Welfare, Pamphlet No. 123, Washington, D.C., 1960.

Witherspoon, R. L. "Studying Young Children," *Nursery School Portfolio,* Leaflet No. 9. Washington, D.C.: ACEI, 1961.

Unpublished Materials

Blough, G. O. "Content and Process in Kindergarten," Address, New England Kindergarten Conference, November 1966.

Brown, B. "Long-Term Gains from Early Intervention: An Overview of Current Research." Paper presented at the 1977 Annual Meeting of the American Association for the Advancement of Science, Denver, Colorado, February 23, 1977.

Evans, Elizabeth A. Project Dir., "Project CARE." Tallahassee, Fla.: Leon Co. Schools —Kate Sullivan School, 1977 (Unpublished Project Abstract).

Forbes, Marcia Boyer. "Parental Selection of Schools for Pre-School Children." Unpublished Master's Thesis, Florida State University, 1960.

Gabbard, Dr. Hazel. Address, reproduced in *Good Schools for Children Under Six in Florida,* Florida State University, Tallahassee, 1955, pp. 29–32.

Godshall, Tricia. *Discover Cooking with Preschoolers.* Coral Gables, Fla.: Project Florida Head Start, University of Miami, no date (Mimeographed).

Goldsmith, Nancy. "Sample Schedule." Distributed by the Regional Head Start Training Office. College Park, Md.: University of Maryland, 1970 (Mimeographed).

Guinagh, J., and I. J. Gordon. "School Performance as a Function of Early Stimulation." (Final Report, Grant No. NIH-HEW-OCD-90-C-638) Institute for the Development of Human Resources, University of Florida, 1976.

Housing Starts, 1977. September news reports on TV citing the Federal Home Loan Bank and the U.S. Dept. of Commerce as sources.

Lacayo, Maria. "Organizing a foreign Language Program in a County." Address, National Convention of the American Association of Spanish and Portuguese, Chicago, December 30, 1961.

McKee, P., and J. E. Brezeinski. "The Effectiveness of Teaching Reading in the Kindergarten," *Cooperative Research Project No. 5-0371,* The Denver Public Schools and The Colorado State Department of Educ., Denver, 1966 (Mimeographed).

Nelson, Susan Blourock. *Mainstreaming.* Report in Partial Fulfillment of Master of Education Degree. College Park, Md.: University of Maryland, 1977.

Pearson, LaMattice. "Reaction of Teachers and Parents to the Letter-Summary Method Used for Reporting Parent-Teacher Conferences at the Florida State University Nursery School." Unpublished Seminar Study, The Florida State University Institute of Human Development, Tallahassee, 1956.

The Preparation and Status of Preschool Teachers. Oslo, Norway: OMEP, July 1966 (Mimeographed).

REFERENCES

Rapp, Don. "Noise in the Nursery School," an unpublished paper, Human Development Institute, Florida State University, 1966.

Rhodes, Frances. *A Study of the Effects of Various Types of Rest Periods in a Morning Kindergarten on the Behavior Characteristics of Five Year Olds.* Unpublished Graduate Paper, Florida State University, Tallahassee, 1954.

Seitz, Victoria, Nancy Apfel, and Carol Efron. "Long-Term Effects of Early Intervention: A Longitudinal Investigation." Paper presented at the 1977 Annual Meeting of the American Association for the Advancement of Science, Denver, Colorado, February 23, 1977.

Shull, C. N. "A Study of Children's Vocal Literature Written by Selected Distinguished Composers." Unpublished Dissertation, Florida State University, Tallahassee, June 1961.

Some Suggestions for the Development of Sensory and Language Skills at the Kindergarten and Primary Level. Rockville, Md.: Montgomery County Public Schools, 1970 (Mimeographed).

Wakefield, Carolyn S. *Evaluation of Packaged Materials for Young Children.* Unpublished Graduate Paper, University of Maryland, College Park, 1971.

Author index

Subject index

Developmental Characteristics

Social Development

AGES 3-4	AGES 5-7

1 Family

Parents provide sex role models

Parental attitudes are primary source of child's self-esteem and sense of security

Adult direction important for child's physical safety

Child learns family expectations with regard to control of aggression, achievement, degree of independence

Able to express caring behavior toward others

Interested in and able to do small chores around the home

Learning to take direction and follow rules

Energetic to the point of adult exhaustion

Tests limits set by others

Beginning of strong feelings for family and home

Parents communicate expectancies for sex roles which may or may not be typical

Child faces many new demands upon entering school; e.g., the ability to function independently is severely tested

2 Peers

Friendships short in duration

Parallel play is common, with the beginnings of cooperative play; boys and girls play together

Beginning of concern for others' feelings; aware of attitudes of peers

Enjoys new people and experiences

Aware of racial differences

Imaginary playmates are not uncommon

Beginnings of empathy; sees others' point of view

Peer criticism for deviation from expected sex roles is particularly severe for boys

Peer criticism for physical, intellectual, and socio-cultural differences begins

Beginnings of conformity to peers regarding language, dress, etc.

Two or three best friends, which change frequently

Play groups are small and of short duration

Quarrels frequent but short lived

Peers become increasingly important, but adults remain primary source of guidelines and support

Beginning of sex cleavage, less boy-girl interaction

Peer group influence important

Shares and takes turns

Participates in organized games requiring coordinated efforts

3 School

Preschool experiences facilitate social development

Positive preschool experiences can exert influence upon cognitive development

Teacher affection and approval are important for achievement, positive peer interaction, and self esteem

Devoted to the teacher

Successful school experience is critical in establishing positive attitudes toward learning and later educational experience

Open to perceiving school and learning as an exciting experience; eager to participate

Children aware of and influenced by teachers' social attitudes and values communicated through behavior

Physical Development

AGES 3-4	AGES 5-7

Increasing skill in large muscle coordination—girls ahead of boys

Opportunities and independence for physical activity and exploration important

Increase in speed, coordination, and motor skills

High physical energy level

Dresses and undresses self

Walks up and down stairs—alternating feet each step

Girls ahead of boys in physical development and physical achievement

Small muscle and eye-hand coordination developing

Increasingly skillful in handling tools and materials

Physical skills are beginning to be important in influencing status among peers and in developing a positive self-concept

Is able to draw a recognizable human figure

Continued high energy level

Masters physical skills necessary for game playing

Ready for beginning reading